PERSONAL CONTROL IN ACTION

COGNITIVE AND MOTIVATIONAL MECHANISMS

THE PLENUM SERIES IN SOCIAL/CLINICAL PSYCHOLOGY

Series Editor: C. R. Snyder

University of Kansas
Lawrence, Kansas

Current Volumes in the Series:

ADVANCED PERSONALITY
Edited by David F. Barone, Michel Hersen, and Vincent B. Van Hasselt

AGGRESSION
Biological, Developmental, and Social Perspectives
Edited by Seymour Feshbach and Jolanta Zagrodzka

AVERSIVE INTERPERSONAL BEHAVIORS
Edited by Robin M. Kowalski

COERCION AND AGGRESSIVE COMMUNITY TREATMENT
A New Frontier in Mental Health Law
Edited by Deborah L. Dennis and John Monahan

PATHOLOGICAL SELF-CRITICISM
Assessment and Treatment
Raymond M. Bergner

PERSONAL CONTROL IN ACTION
Cognitive and Motivational Mechanisms
Edited by Miroslaw Kofta, Gifford Weary, and Grzegorz Sedek

THE PSYCHOLOGY OF VANDALISM
Arnold P. Goldstein

SELF-EFFICACY, ADAPTATION, AND ADJUSTMENT
Theory, Research, and Application
Edited by James E. Maddux

SOCIAL COGNITIVE PSYCHOLOGY
History and Current Domains
David F. Barone, James E. Maddux, and C. R. Snyder

SOURCEBOOK OF SOCIAL SUPPORT AND PERSONALITY
Edited by Gregory R. Pierce, Brian Lakey, Irwin G. Sarason, and Barbara R. Sarason

---

A Continuation Order Plan is available for this series. A continuation order will bring delivery of each new volume immediately upon publication. Volumes are billed only upon actual shipment. For further information please contact the publisher.

PERSONAL CONTROL IN ACTION

COGNITIVE AND MOTIVATIONAL MECHANISMS

EDITED BY

MIROSLAW KOFTA

University of Warsaw
Warsaw, Poland

GIFFORD WEARY

The Ohio State University
Columbus, Ohio

AND

GRZEGORZ SEDEK

University of Warsaw
Warsaw, Poland

PLENUM PRESS • NEW YORK AND LONDON

Library of Congress Cataloging-in-Publication Data

Personal control in action : cognitive and motivational mechanisms /
edited by Miroslaw Kofta, Gifford Weary, and Grzegorz Sedek.
p. cm. -- (The Plenum series in social/clinical psychology)
Includes bibliographical references and index.
ISBN 0-306-45720-2
1. Self-control. 2. Self-management (Psychology) I. Kofta,
Mirosław. II. Weary, Gifford, 1951- . III. Sedek, Grzegorz.
IV. Series.
BF632.P46 1998
153.8--dc21 98-21501
CIP

ISBN 0-306-45720-2

A Division of Plenum Publishing Corporation
233 Spring Street, New York, N.Y. 10013

http://www.plenum.com

10 9 8 7 6 5 4 3 2 1

Printed in the United States of America

CONTRIBUTORS

JÜRGEN BECKMANN, Institute for Sports Science, University of Potsdam, 14469 Potsdam, Germany

JACK W. BREHM, Department of Psychology, University of Kansas, Lawrence, Kansas 66045

DAPHNE BLUNT BUGENTAL, Department of Psychology, University of California, Santa Barbara, California 93106

BEVERLY H. BRUMMETT, Department of Psychiatry and Behavioral Sciences, Duke University Medical Center, Durham, North Carolina 27710

JOSEPH CIARROCHI, School of Psychology, University of New South Wales, Sydney 2052, Australia

DARIUSZ DOLINSKI, Department of Psychology, University of Opole, Oleska 48, 45-951 Opole, Poland.

SEYMOUR EPSTEIN, Department of Psychology, University of Massachusetts, Amherst, Massachusetts 01003

JOSEPH P. FORGAS, School of Psychology, University of New South Wales, Sydney 2052, Australia

JEFF GREENBERG, Department of Psychology, University of Arizona, Tucson, Arizona 85721

ROBERT JOHNSON, School of Psychology, University of New South Wales, Sydney 2052, Australia

LAURA A. KING, Department of Psychology, Southern Methodist University, Dallas, Texas 75275-0442

MIROSLAW KOFTA, Faculty of Psychology, University of Warsaw, 00-183 Warsaw, Poland

MARIA LEWICKA, Faculty of Psychology, University of Warsaw, 00-183 Warsaw, Poland

JEFFREY CLAYTON LEWIS, Department of Psychology, Petzer College, Claremont, California 91711

KEITH D. MARKMAN, Department of Psychology, Marywood University, Scranton, Pennsylvania 18059

JESSICA MARKUS, Department of Psychology, University of Miami, 5665 Ponce de Leon Blvd., Coral Gables, Florida 33124

DANIEL N. McINTOSH, Department of Psychology, University of Denver, Denver, Colorado 80208

HENRY MONTGOMERY, Department of Psychology, Stockholm University, S-10691 Stockholm, Sweden

ANDRZEJ NOWAK, Faculty of Psychology, University of Warsaw, Stawki 5/7, 00-183 Warsaw, Poland

TOM PYSZCZYNSKI, Department of Psychology, University of Colorado, Colorado Springs, Colorado 80933-7150

MICHAEL ROSENBAUM, Department of Psychology, Tel Aviv University, Tel Aviv 69978, Israel

GRZEGORZ SEDEK, Faculty of Psychology, University of Warsaw, 00-183 Warsaw, Poland

WOLFGANG SCHÖNPFLUG, Studiengang Psychologie, Freie Universität Berlin, Habelschwerdter Allee 45, D-14 195 Berlin-Dahlem, Germany

SHELDON SOLOMON, Department of Psychology, Skidmore College, Saratoga Springs, New York 12866

JENNIFER STRAUSS, Department of Psychology, University of Miami, 5665 Ponce de Leon Blvd., Coral Gables, Florida 33124

ROBIN R. VALLACHER, Department of Psychology, Florida Atlantic University, Boca Raton, Florida 33431

GIFFORD WEARY, Department of Psychology, Ohio State University, Columbus, Ohio 43210

REX A. WRIGHT, Department of Psychology, University of Alabama at Birmingham, Birmingham, Alabama 35294

PREFACE

Human beings are agents: They may exert influence over their own fate. They initiate their actions, experience a considerable degree of freedom and control in their mundane activities, and respond adversely to external constraints to their agency; they are able to monitor and modify their motivation, affective states, and behavior.

Since the sixties, the notion of person-as-agent has become increasingly accepted in scientific psychology. Nowadays, personal control is a standard topic in research on personality, motivation, and social behavior. The most popular approach identifies personal control with a feeling or judgment: To have control means to perceive the self as a source of causation. Within this perspective, such consciously accessible contents like perceived freedom and self-determination, feelings and expectations of control, or perceived self-efficacy and competence emerge as natural targets of research (see e.g., Alloy, Clements, & Koenig, 1993; Bandura, 1977; DeCharms, 1968; Deci & Ryan, 1985; Harvey, 1976; Rotter, 1966; Thompson, 1993; Wortman, 1975).

It is certainly true that people develop subjective construals of themselves as agents and that these construals play an important role in adaptation. However, a deeper understanding of human agency may require a nonphenomenological perspective centering on mechanisms of executive agency. Not only is it important to know how people feel about themselves as controlling agents, it seems equally important to understand the processes behind the development, exercise, and maintenance of personal control, and the psychological processes mediating the human response to control threatening situations. This approach has, in fact, a quite old tradition and is evident in a number of the seminal works on psychological reactance, learned helplessness, delay of gratification, and adaptation to urban stress (see e.g., Brehm 1966; Glass & Singer 1972; Mischel 1966; Seligman 1975; Wortman & Brehm, 1975). More recently, the rapidly expanding research areas of control motivation (e.g., Burger, 1992; Fiske & Depret, 1996; Miller, 1980; Pittmann & D'Agostino, 1985, Weary, Marsh, Gleicher, & Edwards, 1993) and action control (e.g., Cantor & Zirkel, 1989; Carver & Scheier, 1981; Kuhl & Beckmann, 1985; Gollwitzer & Bargh, 1996; Vallacher & Wegner, 1987) provide various new insights into the nature of control processes.

The chapters in this volume continue these more recent traditions. In this book, we address personal control in action in both meanings of this phrase. Control processes play, we believe, a critical role in the development of human action. Therefore, issues concerning the interplay of mind and action, and the role of internal control in action initiation and management, occupy a prominent place in this book

However, the phrase "personal control in action" refers also to control in the making, that is to say, to the very nature of self-regulation. How does the person-as-agent operate to exercise and defend control? Which cognitive, affective, and motivational mechanisms participate in successful or unsuccessful control attempts? These and related questions are addressed in the various chapters in this book.

It is important to point out that personal control is not a specialized, separate topic within personality and social psychology; rather, it seems to be an important aspect or dimension of various phenomena studied. Many researchers and theorists consider human behavior to be the result of an "internal dialogue" between two specialized psychological systems or modes of operation. One system often is thought to engage predominantly cognitive, low-energy operations; the other system is thought to engage predominantly high-energy motivational processes with a clear affective component. Typically, the former is seen as a source of controlling influences, whereas the latter is seen as a source of processes to be controlled. Of importance, states of the high-energy system may influence the way cognitive control operates (e.g., affect intensity may be implicated in a switch in the cognitive strategies used for affect management). We believe that researchers relying on this "dual-system perspective" may fruitfully contribute to understanding personal control as a process, regardless of whether they work on personality structure and functioning, interpersonal behavior, affect and motivation, cognitive processing, or psychophysiology.

This book presents new and, we hope, exciting developments in research on personal control and self-regulation. Specific interests of the authors differ: They range from momentary controlling activity, such as management of energy expenditure during task performance or the mental control of intrusive thoughts, to life-span control phenomena, such as life dreams or the strategic control of the terror associated with awareness of one's mortality.

Further, they differ in whether they examine the personal control processes at the level of an individual, as most psychologists do, or at the level of interpersonal relationships. Finally, they differ in whether they focus primarily on self-control (the processes modifying one's own responses) or on environmental control (the processes modifying some parameters of external events like task outcomes or behavior of other people).

It is fascinating to observe that, despite all these differences, important communalities emerge across different research areas. These communalities seem to define a shared discourse space for the psychology of control: Among other things, they indicate "hot topics" currently under debate and the type of language suggested for their examination.

The first such topic is the ontological status of the agent. Some authors approach personal control as a conscious and effortful process involving a considerable degree of deliberation. For them, an intention to modify something in the environment or in oneself is clearly experienced by the person. However, other authors tend to look at control processes in terms of an unintentional, fast, automatized procedure, one frequently acting below the level of conscious awareness. However, these two perspectives on control should not be seen as mutually exclusive: In actuality, they may refer to different levels of the same self-regulatory activity. A deeper understanding of the functional relationships between these modes of operation remains one of the major challenges for the psychology of personal control.

Another overarching theme is the relationship between mental activity and action control. Several authors suggest that personal control of action is achieved by means of internal mental dynamics. That is, a constructive process goes on in the mind that generates an inner frame of reference for behavior in the form of judgments, goals, plans, problem solutions, preferences, decisions, and action commitments. Due to this self-generated, productive process, the person is mentally prepared to move from thought to action, maintaining an action orientation and succeeding in goal attainment despite internal distractions and an unsupportive environment

At a more concrete level, this mental activity may have variety of manifestations such as the generation of alternative action identifications and choice of a particular identification as a major frame, mental control through suppression of unwanted thoughts or intentions, augmentation of desired action tendencies, generation of counterfactuals (hypothetical alternative scenarios of events), generation and tests of solution hypotheses in the course of problem-solving, and finally, bolstering during a predecisional phase the value of a to-be-chosen alternative and deemphasizing the value of alternatives to be rejected. These various processes engage mental capacity and effortful processing to varying degrees.

The relationship between constructive mental dynamics and action is, of course, reciprocal. It is not only that mind controls action, but also that action controls mind. And it does so in a variety of ways. First and foremost, action may provide critical information regarding the quality and utility of the individual's mental frames (e.g., hypotheses, judgments, goals, plans). As a result, it may reduce the frequency and duration of unrealistic thoughts. Further, people may intervene in the external environment to change it; such interventions may provide support for one of the mental frames more than for others and may set the stage for effective action. Thus, the notion of mind–action reciprocity emerges in this book as one of the major principles of self-regulation.

As several authors suggest, an important aspect of control processes is a preferential reliance on specific types of information-processing strategies. For instance, control concerns may induce a confirmatory set in hypothesis evaluation and may be associated with a shift from heuristic to systematic processing or, in the domain of affect control, from substantive to motivated processing. The type of strategy preferred may change depending on such factors as the particular action phase, the type of process to be controlled, or the degree of control deprivation. The idea that control efforts might be intimately associated with a preference for some class of cognitive rules in processing information or information-processing style emerges as one of the major topics addressed in this book and as one of the leading topics for future research.

In addition to several new insights into the nature of self-regulation, new modes of control are suggested in this book. According to the traditional view, control processes aim at decreasing the variability of human behavior: They tend to reduce the "degrees of freedom" for our experience and action through eliminating alternative mental frames, committing people to only one line of behavior out of several possible, keeping emotions within the limits, and so on. However, in several chapters it is suggested that different, "nonrepressive" modes of control may also play a considerable role in self-regulation. These modes of control are directed toward strengthening positive involvement in current activity (instead of mental suppression), opening individuals to immediate experience in its totality, initiating an intrinsically motivated behavior set on developing new skills and competencies, and so on. By and large, these modes of control result in enrichment of our mental, emotional, and behavioral repertoires.

Finally, among important issues under debate in this book is the motivation to control. Classical conceptions in personality and social psychology frequently refer to (differently labeled) a need for control, a basic drive that makes us initiate actions, influence environments, generate predictions as to the course of events, and so on (e.g., Bandura, 1977; DeCharms, 1968; Kelley, 1967; White,1959). Even if the existence of such a drive as a psychological reality is granted, one may nevertheless identify several circumstances in which personal control is relinquished or transferred to someone else. One such circumstance has already been mentioned: Suspending direct control may sometimes result from the transition to a different, nonrepressive mode of control. Among other important factors suggested in this book are the perceived difficulty of the task relative to one's own ability, self-defensive motives (control relinquishment or its transfer to others my help maintain positive self-esteem), and previous experience (e.g., control deprivation). Finally, in social organizations based on a division of labor, "delegating" control to other people might be necessitated by the demands of systemic rationality. Thorough discussion of this issue in our book suggests the importance of a distinction between strategic withdrawal from direct action in the service of control attainment (which is, in fact, a change of means rather than ends) and "real" control relinquishment enforced by low perceived ability, self-defensive motives, or the experience of helplessness.

Another important and related issue is that of the human response to threatened control. Whereas one of the widespread views in the literature emphasizes people's tendency to defend and restore threatened control, the other view focuses on such consequences of control deprivation as increased behavior passivity and cognitive or emotional disruption. These two traditions, in a modern "cognitivistic dressing," are represented in several chapters dealing with threats to power in interpersonal settings, helplessness phenomena, and depression. Interestingly, some authors suggest that these approaches to understanding reactions to threatened control are not necessarily incompatible: They may refer to phenomena that develop simultaneously at different levels of processing and manifest overtly in different cognitive contexts, e.g., on tasks differing in mental load.

This brief review of the major themes represented in the various chapters of this book is far from exhaustive. Rather, our intention is to address common issues under debate, new dimensions for the analysis of personal control, topics that provoke interest and (sometimes) disagreement, and—last but not least—open questions for the future.

Before concluding, let us offer a few words about the organization of the book. Our book is composed of three parts. The first part deals with the person as a source of control, and focuses on higher-order structures of control and self-regulation (including human mind, personality and the self, basic motivational orientations, and major classes of control strategies). The second part is more analytical: Several mechanisms of executive agency are addressed from a variety of theoretical perspectives; in particular, the roles of cognitive, affective, and motivational processes in self-regulation are under debate. The third and final part addresses the major theme of human responses to situations involving actual or perceived threats to personal control, ranging from attempts at control restoration to disengagement and helplessness. The motivational or cognitive mechanisms of these phenomena are thoroughly discussed.

Finally, we wish to express our sincere thanks to many people. Foremost, we must thank the contributors of this volume without whose commitment and hard work this book would not have been possible. With editors and fellow contributors in six different countries, their patience with sometimes shifting and difficult schedules and with various electronic and mail delivery service delays was greatly appreciated and critical. Second, we would like to extend our thanks to our publisher, Plenum Press, to Eliot Werner, Senior Editor at Plenum, and to the series editor, C. R. Snyder. Their support for this undertaking has been constant and invaluable.

Miroslaw Kofta
Gifford Weary
Grzegorz Sedek

ACKNOWLEDGMENTS

The editorial work of Miroslaw Kofta and Grzegorz Sedek was supported by grant 1/H01F/079/08 from the Polish Committee for Scientific Research.

REFERENCES

Alloy, L. B., Clements, C. M., & Koenig, L. J. (1993). Models of perceived control. In G. Weary, F. Gleicher, & K. L. Marsh (Eds.), *Control motivation and social cognition* (pp. 33–73). New York: Springer.

Bandura, A. (1977). Self-efficacy: Toward a unifying theory of behavioral change. *Psychological Review, 84,* 191–215.

Brehm, J. W. (1966). *A theory of psychological reactance.* New York: Academic Press.

Burger, J. M. (1992). *Desire for control: Personality, social, and clinical perspectives.* New York: Plenum.

Cantor, N., & Zirkel, S. (1989). Personality, cognition, and purposive behavior. In L. A. Pervin (Ed.), *Handbook of personality: Theory and research* (pp. 135–164). New York: Guilford.

Carver, C. S., & Scheier, M. F. (1981). *Attention and self-regulation: A control theory approach to human behavior.* New York: Springer.

DeCharms, R. (1968). *Personal causation: The internal affective determinants of behavior.* New York: Academic Press.

Deci, E. L., & Ryan, R. M. (1985). *Intrinsic motivation and self-determination in human behavior.* New York: Plenum.
Fiske, S. T., & Depret, E. (1996). Control, interdependence, and power: Understanding social cognition in its social context. *European Review of Social Psychology* (Vol. 7, pp. 31–61). Chichester: Wiley.
Glass, D. C., & Singer, J. E. (1972). *Urban stress.* New York: Academic Press.
Gollwitzer, P. M., & Bargh, J. A. (Eds.), *The psychology of action: Linking cognition and motivation to behavior* (pp. 424–453). New York: Guilford.
Harvey, J. H. (1976). Attribution of freedom. In J. H. Harvey, W. I. Ickes, & R. F. Kidd (Eds.), *New directions in attribution research* (Vol. 1). Hillsdale, NJ: Erlbaum.
Kelley, H. H. (1967). Attribution theory in social psychology. In D. Levine (Ed.), *Nebraska symposium on motivation* (Vol. 15, pp. 192–240). Lincoln: University of Nebraska Press.
Kuhl, J., & Beckmann, J. (Eds.)(1985). *Action control: From cognition to behavior.* Berlin: Springer.
Mischel, W. (1966). Theory and research on the antecedents of self-imposed delay of reward. In B. A. Maher (Ed.), *Progress in experimental personality research* (Vol. 3, pp. 85–132). New York: Academic Press.
Miller, S. M. (1980). Why having control reduces stress: If I can stop the roller coaster, I don't want to get off. In J. Garber & M. E. P. Seligman (Eds.), *Human helplessness: Theory and applications* (pp. 71–95). New York: Academic Press.
Pittmann, T. S., & D'Agostino, P. R. (1985). Motivation and cognition: Control deprivation and the nature of subsequent information processing. In G. Weary & J. Harvey (Eds.), *Attribution: Basic issues and applications* (pp. 117–141). New York: Academic Press.
Rotter, J. B. (1966). Generalized expectancies for internal versus external control of reinforcement. *Psychological Monographs, 80* (1, Whole No. 69).
Seligman, M. E. P. (1975). *Helplessness: On depression, development, and death.* San Francisco: Freeman.
Thompson, S. C. (1993). Naturally occurring perceptions of control: A model of bounded flexibility. In G. Weary, F. Gleicher, & K. L. Marsh (Eds.), *Control motivation and social cognition* (pp. 74–93). New York: Springer.
Vallacher, R. R., & Wegner, D. M. (1987). What do people think they're doing? Action identification and human behavior. *Psychological Review, 94,* 3–15.
Weary, G., Marsh, K. L., Gleicher, F., & Edwards, J. A. (1993). Depression, control motivation, and the processing of information about others. In G. Weary, F. Gleicher, & K. L. Marsh (Eds.), *Control motivation and social cognition* (pp. 255–287). New York: Springer.
White, R. W. (1959). Motivation reconsidered: The concept of competence. *Psychological Review, 66,* 297–333.
Wortman, C. B. (1975). Some determinants of perceived control. *Journal of Personality and Social Psychology, 31,* 282–294.
Wortman, C. B., & Brehm, J. W. (1975). Responses to uncontrollable outcomes: An integration of reactance theory and the learned helplessness model. In L. Berkowitz (Ed.), *Advances in experimental social psychology* (Vol. 8, pp. 277–336). New York: Academic Press.

CONTENTS

Chapter 4

Chapter 5

II: AFFECTIVE AND COGNITIVE MECHANISMS OF EXECUTIVE AGENCY 129

III: THREATENED PERSONAL CONTROL: MOBILIZATION VERSUS DEMOBILIZATION 315

Chapter 15

Chapter 16

PART I

THE PERSON AS AN AGENT OF CONTROL

The chapters in this first part focus on self-regulation at a molar, system level of analysis. The focus is on how the self-system accommodates to external demands, coordinates actions, and as a unit functions to meet internal demands and conflicts, represent and coordinate internal and external realities, and obtain desired and avoid undesired outcomes. Each chapter, however, involves a consideration of different systems involved in effective self-regulation. More specifically, we find a focus on the various and sometimes opposing, sometimes complementary, mental, motivational, or response systems that humans engage in the pursuit of effective control over their lives.

Epstein's cognitive-experiential self-theory specifies two major systems by which people adapt to their environments, the rational and the experiential. The rational system contains conscious beliefs about the self and the world, is driven by logic and reason, and operates in a relatively controlled (effortful and intentional) fashion. The experiential system contains implicit beliefs about the self and the world that are generalizations derived from emotionally significant experiences. In contrast to the rational system, the experiential system is driven by affect and operates in a relatively automatic, effortless fashion. In his chapter, Epstein examines the typical causes of a lack of personal control from the viewpoint of his influential cognitive-experiential self-theory. His main thesis is that through understanding the complex interactions of these two conceptual systems (e.g., inability of the rational system to override the basic needs and motives of the experiential system, the biasing influence of the experiential on the rational, dissociations of the experiential system), we can gain insight into how people obtain increasing control over their lives.

Vallacher, Nowak, Markus, and Strauss also pursue, albeit from a very different perspective than the one offered by Epstein, the notion of two major modes of social thought. In particular, these authors identify one mode as that which is dynamic, often turbulent, and close to William James's notion of "stream of consciousness." The other mode emphasizes the higher-order, structural elements of thought that give coherence and stability to our representations of the world and form the basis for effective action. Certainly, much of contemporary social psychological theory and research has focused on this latter kind of mental process. Vallacher et al., however, argue persuasively that mental dynamism and structure are two complementary forms of thought that together provide the basis for cognitive and behavioral accommodation in everyday life. In their chapter, they discuss how the moment-to-moment flow of cognitive contents gives rise to higher-order structures that permit stable and coherent understandings of the self and the world. These structures, in turn, then influence the dynamics of thought. Far from leaving their social thinker lost in thought, Vallacher et al. use this dynamical framework to examine mind and action coordination and reciprocity. They suggest that the mental states generating action differ in their relative dynamism and that such differences are associated with differences in motivational and action tendencies. When there is a breakdown in mind–action coordination, self-consciousness results and self-corrective tendencies are initiated. In the end, their analysis represents a forceful argument and method for consideration of the temporal dimension of human thought and behavior and the critical role of such in action control.

According to Rosenbaum, the ultimate goal of self-control is to overcome self-generated impediments. In his chapter, Rosenbaum focuses not on two mental systems, but on two response strategies involved in self-control processes: the opening and closing strategies. Whereas the former entails an acceptance of one's affective reactions to immediate experience, the latter involves a cognitive transformation or control of such reactions. Rosenbaum analyzes the cognitive processes involved in the decision to control or not to control responses to experience. He argues that individuals must first make decisions about when and why they want to exert control. They then must decide whether to direct their control efforts toward openness to or closure from their experiences. Finally, they must decide if they have the requisite skills to enact the desired self-control strategy. The essential points of Rosenbaum's analysis are, first, that acceptance of experience and giving up of control are important ingredients of successful self-control and, second, that a balance between opening and closing responses is essential for effective adjustment.

Pyszczynski, Greenberg, and Solomon offer their own unique and provocative take on self-regulation. They argue that rather than responding just to the immediate demands of the situation and to current levels of internal stimulation, individuals can be oriented toward abstract conceptions, values, and standards of self. In this way, individuals can create an abstract and unique self and one that has personal value. This conception of self then serves as a vehicle for the regulation of behavior; however, it also provides a magical means of controlling that which is entirely beyond individuals' control—their own death. Briefly, Pyszczynski, Greenberg, and Solomon argue that self-esteem and faith in cultural worldviews shield individuals from the terror that awareness of their own mortality can produce and that they do so largely by offering a symbolic transcendence of death to those who meet personal and cultural standards of value. From this perspective, then, the exercise of control is rooted, in part, in a need to manage the potential for terror that results from people's awareness of the inevitability of their death They also note, however, that people seek control for reasons of mastery, or the development and expansion of their competencies. For these authors, effective self-regulation and, in fact, human existence depends on a delicate balance of these two opposing motive systems of terror management and self-expansion.

Finally, King also notes that the experience of mastery, of control over one's life, and the perception that one has impact on the world are critical to the experience of subjective well-being. She argues further that effective pursuit of daily goals is a part of this process, particularly when they are embedded within a consideration of their relationship to a broader life plan or dream. In essence, King argues that the strongest evidence of self-as-agent lies in the realization of one's life dreams and that the formulation and pursuit of daily goals that are relevant to the life dream result in greater attainment of both proximal and distal goals. The evidence reviewed in this chapter provides a strong case for how distal goals or life dreams can serve as a source of agency and meaning. What happens when a life goal proves unattainable? King suggests that to reinstate a sense of personal agency, individuals must reconstruct a personal future and reinvest in a new life dream. This chapter should go a long way to make explicit the too often implicit relationship between goal commitment, importance, progress, and disengagement to the everyday experience of agency.

CHAPTER 1

PERSONAL CONTROL FROM THE PERSPECTIVE OF COGNITIVE-EXPERIENTIAL SELF-THEORY

SEYMOUR EPSTEIN

A not unreasonable definition of personal control is the ability of a person to carry out his or her intentions. If I am in control of a situation, I can influence the outcome to come out as I intend. If I am in control of myself I can make myself behave as I intend. Under what circumstances do I not have control? There are several such conditions. First, I may not have the ability to influence the outcome as I wish. I may desire to play the violin magnificently, or to have a devastating tennis serve, but lack the ability to do so. To improve my control I would have to improve my skill.

A second reason why people lack control is that, despite having the ability to exert control, they are unable to overcome underlying motives of which they are aware. Many people would like to lose weight by maintaining a diet, but although they know how not to eat, the allure of tempting food is more than they can resist. Such problems encompass a wide range of situations, from minor self-discipline issues, such as a failure to carry out New Year's resolutions, to seriously pathological conditions, such as

SEYMOUR EPSTEIN • Department of Psychology, University of Massachusetts, Amherst, Massachusetts 01003. E-mail: sepstein@psych.umass.edu

Personal Control in Action, edited by Kofta et al., Plenum Press, New York, 1998.

drug abuse and compulsive gambling. In these situations, although people are able to identify their maladaptive motives, they are unable to control them.

A third reason why people lack control is that their conscious reasoning is influenced by their preconscious, automatic information processing. In such situations, people believe they are behaving as they intend. However, they generally intend to behave rationally, and it is this intention that is subverted by their automatic processing.

A fourth reason why people lack control is that their behavior is determined by sensitivities and compulsions. These are rigid ways of reacting that were learned under conditions of high arousal and that people have great difficulty changing.

A fifth reason why people lack control is that their behavior is influenced by unconscious, dissociated, or repressed mental content or motives. Such situations produce the most dramatic examples of out-of-control, ego-alien behavior, such as that of a "model boy" who stabs an attractive babysitter 70 times and later says he acted as if in a trance.

In this article, I discuss the various kinds of lack of control from the perspective of cognitive-experiential self-theory (CEST). The lack of control associated with inability is the simplest to understand, because in such situations people are behaving rationally. They are doing the best they can, and they know that to do better they have to improve their ability. Nevertheless, as will be shown, the perspective of CEST is helpful because it draws attention to the different roles of intuitive-experiential and analytical-rational information processing in acquiring skill.

CEST has more to say about the other kinds of problems, in which people have the requisite skills but are unable to apply them despite their conscious desire to do so. Such a condition suggests that there is a source of information processing that operates by different principles from people's conscious, rational thinking. Freud's greatest contribution was that he proposed just such a mode of information processing, one that operated at an unconscious level according to what he referred to as the "primary process," that differed from a conscious, rational system that operated by what he referred to as the "secondary process." Freud was right in emphasizing the importance of an unconscious mode of information processing for understanding human irrationality, but he was seriously in error about the manner in which he believed it operated.

COGNITIVE-EXPERIENTIAL SELF-THEORY

Cognitive-experiential self-theory (CEST) is a global theory of personality that is similar to psychoanalysis in many respects, such as emphasizing the importance of unconscious information processing and psychodynamics, but also differs in some fundamental ways, the most important of which is that it has a very different conception of the unconscious.

Basic Principles

It is assumed in CEST that there are two major conceptual systems, rational and experiential, by which people adapt to their environments. It is evident that people have conscious beliefs about themselves and the world, and how to get along in it. Together, these views, which reside in the rational system, constitute a person's explicit theory of reality. What is less evident, and is uniquely assumed in CEST, is that people also have a corresponding implicit theory of reality in their experiential system. The constructs in the rational system are referred to, in CEST, as beliefs, and those in the experiential system as schemata, or, alternatively, as implicit beliefs. The schemata, which are the building blocks of the implicit theory of reality, consist primarily of generalizations derived from emotionally significant experiences.

There are two fundamental kinds of schemata, descriptive and motivational. Descriptive schemata are generalizations about what the self and world are like. Examples include, "Authority figures are dangerous," and, "I am a cooperative person." Examples of motivational schemata are, "The way to deal with authority figures is to placate them," and "If I work hard, I can succeed in whatever I attempt." Note that motivational schemata simply describe means–end, or if–then, relations, and are not sufficient, in themselves, to promote action. Action in the experiential system is produced by anticipated affect. Believing that hard work will result in success will motivate hard work in the experiential system only if the person desires success in that system, which is determined by the affect acquired from previously relevant experience.

In contrast, motivation in the rational system is based on conscious beliefs and inferences about the reasonable way to behave to achieve certain ends. The desired ends, or goals, in the rational system may be derived from reflection on emotionally significant past experience, but they are also derived from other sources, such as having been convinced by others that certain goals are worth pursuing. Since the rational system is better able to delay gratification than the experiential system, it is more apt to take into account long-term considerations, such as the belief that studying hard is desirable, even if unpleasant. Motivation in the experiential system, on the other hand, is more apt to be concerned with immediate consequences. Given the different orientations concerning time and affect between the two systems, it follows that motivation in the two systems will sometimes conflict with each other.

It is important to recognize that, according to CEST, the schemata in the experiential system are not isolated constructs, but are organized into an overall adaptive system. The schemata thus affect and are affected by the other constructs in the system. Evidence attesting to an overall organized experiential system is provided by the integrated behavior of animals lacking a rational system, and by the susceptibility of the experiential system in both human and nonhuman animals to total disorganization following an emotionally significant unassimilable experience. Such reactions are observed in the experimental neuroses in animals (Pavlov, 1941), and in acute schizophrenic disorganization in humans (Epstein, 1979; Perry, 1976). Disorganization of a system necessarily implies, of course, a prior state of organization.

As demonstrated by research in cognitive dissonance (Festinger, 1957), people have a need to correct inconsistencies in their rational systems. According to CEST, dissonance in the rational system is far less disruptive than dissonance in the experiential system. Thus, it is common for people to maintain all kinds of inconsistencies in their rational system without it generating any kind of distress until they are made aware of an inconsistency. Following such awareness, people usually are motivated to establish coherence, but they do not exhibit overwhelming distress or a tendency to disorganize.

An implicit theory of reality has two major divisions, a world theory and a self-theory, and connecting propositions. (Nonhuman animals also construct a model of reality, but it does not include a self-theory.) A theory of reality is not developed for its own sake, but, rather to make life as livable, meaning as emotionally satisfying, as possible. Thus, a fundamental assumption in CEST is that the experiential conceptual system is emotionally driven.

Attributes of the Experiential System

Table 1 provides a summary of the comparative features of the experiential and rational systems. The experiential system has a very long evolutionary history and operates in a similar manner in nonhuman and human animals. Because of their more highly developed brains, it operates in more complex ways in humans. Moreover, in animals it affects only their behavior. In humans, it affects their conscious thoughts as well as their behavior. At its lower levels of operation, the experiential system is a crude system that automatically, rapidly, effortlessly, and efficiently processes information. At its higher reaches, and in interaction with the rational system, it is a source of intuitive wisdom and creativity. Although it represents events primarily concretely and imagistically, the experiential

TABLE 1 Comparison of the Experiential and Rational Systems

Experiential system	Rational system
1. Holistic	1. Analytic
2. Automatic, effortless	2. Intentional, effortful
3. Affective: Pleasure–pain oriented (what feels good)	3. Logical: Reason oriented (what is sensible)
4. Associationistic connections	4. Logical connections
5. Behavior mediated by "vibes" from past events	5. Behavior mediated by conscious appraisal of events
6. Encodes reality in concrete images, metaphors, & narratives	6. Encodes reality in abstract symbols, words, & numbers
7. More rapid processing: Oriented toward immediate action	7. Slower processing: Oriented toward delayed action
8. Slower and more resistant to change: Changes with repetitive or intense experience	8. Changes more rapidly and easily: Changes with strength of argument and new evidence
9. More crudely differentiated: Broad generalization gradient; stereotypical thinking	9. More highly differentiated
10. More crudely integrated: Dissociative, emotional complexes; context-specific processing	10. More highly integrated: Context-general principles
11. Experienced passively and preconsciously: We are seized by our emotions	11. Experienced actively and consciously: We are in control of our thoughts
12. Self-evidently valid: "Experiencing is believing"	12. Requires justification via logic & evidence

Note. Adapted with permission from "Cognitive-experiential self-theory: An integrative theory of personality" by S. Epstein. In R. C. Curtis (Ed.), *The relational self: Theoretical convergences in psychoanalysis and social psychology*. New York: The Guilford Press. Copyright 1992.

system is capable of abstraction through generalization and the use of prototypes, metaphors, and narratives.

The rational system, in contrast, is a deliberative, effortful, abstract system that operates primarily in the medium of language, and has a very brief evolutionary history. It is capable of high levels of abstraction and long-term delay of gratification. However, it is a relatively inefficient system for responding to everyday events, and its long term adaptability remains to be demonstrated, as it has the potential for great destructiveness through technological advances unmatched by wisdom relating to human relationships.

Sequence of Events from Perception to Action

As previously noted, the operation of the experiential system is intimately associated with the experience of affect, including "vibes," which refer to subtle, vague feelings, such as relatively low levels of agitation, disquietude, and annoyance, of which people are often only dimly aware or completely unaware. When a person responds to an emotionally significant event, the sequence of reactions is assumed to be as follows: The experiential system automatically searches its memory for related events and their emotional accompaniments. The recalled feelings, including vibes, influence the course of further processing and reactions, which, in nonhuman animals, are actions and, in humans, conscious and unconscious thoughts as well as actions. If the activated feelings are pleasant, they motivate thoughts and actions anticipated to reproduce the previous outcomes and associated feelings. If the feelings are unpleasant, they motivate thoughts and actions anticipated to avoid the previous outcomes and feelings.

Psychodynamics

All behavior is assumed, in CEST, to be the product of the joint operation of the two systems. It is assumed that their relative contributions vary along a continuum from complete dominance by one system to complete dominance by the other, and that they are influenced by a number of parameters, including individual differences in style of thinking and situational variables, such as the degree to which a situation is identified as requiring formal analysis. As the experiential system is intimately associated with experience and affect, an increasing degree of experience concerning an event, particularly if it is emotionally involving, tends to shift the relative influence of the two systems in the direction of increasing dominance of the experiential system.

The Interaction of Basic Needs

Most theories of personality posit a single fundamental need, or motive. For Freud (1900/1953), it was the pleasure principle, i.e., the need to maximize pleasure and minimize pain; for Rogers (1959), Lecky (1961), and other phenomenologists, it was the need to maintain a stable, coherent conceptual system; for Bowlby (1988), Fairbairn (1954), and other object-relations theorists, it was the need for relatedness; and for Adler (1954), Allport (1961), and Kohut (1971), it was the need to enhance self-esteem or, relatedly, to overcome feelings of inferiority. According to CEST, these motives are equally important, and behavior is determined by their combined influence.

The question may be raised as to the relation of the need for control to the four basic needs proposed by CEST. Is it superordinate, subordinate, or equal to the others? The need for control is considered, in CEST, to be less basic than the others, as it can be derived from them. It is subordinate to the need to maximize pleasure and minimize pain because a major reason for control is to maximize the achievement of pleasure and to minimize the experience of pain. It is subordinate to the need to maintain a stable, coherent, realistic conceptual system because another important purpose of control is to make the world predictable. It is subordinate to the need for self-esteem because control is often exerted in order to protect or enhance self-esteem. It is subordinate to the need for relatedness because one of the important purposes of control is to maintain and establish relationships. Thus, given the four basic needs, it follows that people will be motivated to establish control over events, and therefore control is less fundamental than the four basic needs postulated by CEST. Nevertheless, it is an extremely important motive in its own right, and it clearly plays a critical role in fulfilling the other needs.

Several interesting consequences follow from the assumption that there are four basic needs that influence behavior simultaneously. One consequence, as already noted, is that behavior often represents a compromise among two or more basic needs. A second consequence is that the needs serve as checks and balances against each other. When one need is fulfilled at the expense of the others, the frustration of the other needs increases, and, accordingly, the need to fulfill them increases, which normally moderates the influence of the first need, keeping it within adaptive limits. An important source of maladaptive behavior is when a particular need becomes so compelling that it is satisfied in extreme ways, including ones that severely frustrate the fulfillment of other needs, thereby bypassing their adaptive checks-and-balances function. A third, related principle is that good adjustment is fostered by the fulfillment of the four basic needs in a harmonious manner, and poor adjustment by fulfilling them in a conflictual manner.

The four needs provide a useful framework for understanding some otherwise anomalous behavior. For example, it has been suggested by some that the widespread view that realistic thinking is an important criterion of adjustment is incorrect because research has demonstrated that well-adjusted people characteristically maintain positive illusions (see review in Taylor & Brown, 1988). This paradox is readily resolved once it is recognized that self-evaluation is influenced by both the need to maintain a realistic, coherent conceptual system and the need for self-enhancement. The interaction of these two needs fosters a compromise in the form of most people favoring a modest degree of self-enhancement. Thus, the observation that well-adjusted people have modest positive illusions does not indicate that reality awareness is an inadequate criterion of adjustment, but only that it is not the only criterion.

By postulating a basic need other than the pleasure principle, namely, the need to maintain a stable, coherent conceptual system, CEST is able to account for a phenomenon that has been extremely troublesome for psychoanalysis. In the most widely accepted version of his theory, Freud assumed that the pleasure principle is the most fundamental need. However, he later was compelled to revise his theory when he learned about the dreams of traumatized soldiers. Rather than representing wish fulfillment solutions, the dreams recapitulated the trauma in all its terrifying intensity. These dreams, as well as observations of compulsively repetitious behavior in everyday life, led Freud (1920/1959) to introduce the concepts of the repetition compulsion and the death instinct, which he believed were no less fundamental than the pleasure principle. His speculations in his new theory were so fanciful that most of his adherents preferred his old theory, despite its limitations.

Explanations of the traumatic neurosis and the repetition compulsion follow simply and directly from basic assumptions in CEST. The nature of a trauma is that a person has an experience of such emotional significance that it cannot be ignored, and so discrepant with fundamental schemata in his or her conceptual experiential system that it cannot be assimilated. The compulsive repetition in memory, which people experience as highly distressing and uncontrollable, is the result of attempts to assimilate emotionally significant material that is unassimilable in the extant experiential conceptual system (for elaboration of this view, see Epstein, 1991a; for similar views by others that were influenced by CEST, see Janoff-Bulman, 1992, and McCann & Pearlman, 1990; see also Horowitz, 1976).

Wegner and his associates, in a series of laboratory studies (e.g., Wegner & Schneider, 1989), have demonstrated that the more people attempt not to think about a white bear, the more they think about it. Of course, the problem in the real world is that unwanted thoughts are generated by unassimilable schemata, not by the admonition by an experimenter not to think about thoughts that he or she has given participants not to think about. Thus, the condition for establishing control, unlike in the laboratory situation, is not distraction, as has been found in laboratory studies, but in assimilating previously unassimilable schemata. This is not to deny that attempting to directly suppress unwanted compulsive thoughts (e.g., not thinking about a white bear) may be a self-defeating process, but rather to indicate that such attempts are not the root of the problem but are, at most, a relatively minor complication.

The Interaction of the Two Processing Modes

Like psychoanalysis, CEST is a psychodynamic theory that posits two modes of information processing that function according to different principles. Also, like psychoanalysis, CEST assumes that the unaware level influences the conscious level. This assumption is well supported by priming studies (e.g., Bargh, 1989; Chaiken & Maheswaren, 1994; Edwards, 1990; Epstein, 1994; Epstein, Lipson, Holstein, & Huh, 1992; Epstein, Donovan, & Denes-Raj, in press; Higgins, 1989; Pacini, Epstein, & Barrows, 1996), in which it has been demonstrated that priming the automatic level of information processing influences processing at the conscious level. Like psychoanalysis, there is an emphasis in CEST on the interaction of needs, both within and across modes of processing. However, unlike psychoanalysis, which emphasizes the pleasure principle as the single, most important need, as previously noted, CEST assumes three other needs are equally important.

As in psychoanalytic theory, CEST assumes there is a ubiquitous influence of thinking outside of awareness on conscious thinking and behavior. In most situations, according to CEST, the automatic processing of the experiential system is dominant over the rational system because it is less effortful and more efficient. Moreover, because it is often associated with the experience of affect, it is apt to be experienced as more compelling than is dispassionate logical thinking. Finally, because the influence is outside of awareness, the rational system fails to control processing in the experiential system because the person does not know there is anything to be controlled. For example, people usually regard the experience of their emotions as uncontrollable because they do not consciously choose to have their emotions, but, rather, are "seized" by them, sometimes against their conscious desire. They are aware that they can control acting on their emotions, but this is not the same as controlling the onset of the emotion. They do not realize that they can influence their experience of emotions by controlling the automatic thoughts that precede them. The advantage of insight, in such situations, is that it permits the person to identify the source of the problem that has to be solved, thereby putting the person into an improved position for establishing control.

By recognizing the ubiquitous influence of the experiential on the rational system, CEST does not diminish the importance of the unconscious in human behavior relative to psychoanalysis, but emphasizes a different source of unconscious influence. It also has different implications for establishing control over unconscious influences on conscious thought and behavior. Psychoanalysis places great emphasis on the importance of insight, in its own right, whereas CEST regards insight as useful in controlling maladaptive behavioral tendencies once they are aroused, but only as a first step in the more fundamental task of correcting the maladaptive schemata in the experiential system that are the source of the maladaptive tendencies.

Repression and Dissociation

One important source of lack of control is repression. According to psychoanalysis, repression occurs when a person has unconscious thoughts or impulses that, if consciously accepted, would generate high levels of anxiety. The result is that the unacceptable mental content is forcefully kept in a state of inaccessibility by the expenditure of psychic energy. The repressed material, with a presumed energy of its own, strives for expression, thereby generating conflict with the forces of repression. The result is tension and displacement, manifested in the form of symptoms, dream content, and the psychopathology of everyday life. The task of psychoanalysis is to eliminate the more troublesome repressions. By making the unconscious conscious, the person is able to bring his or her intelligence to bear on solving problems in living. Thus, psychoanalysis places great faith in rational thinking.

According to CEST, material is dissociated when it cannot be assimilated. There are two kinds of dissociation: that between the experiential and rational systems, which corresponds to the psychoanalytic concept of repression, and dissociation within the experiential system itself. If dissociated material is activated to the extent that the dissociation within the experiential system cannot be maintained, the breakthrough of the unassimilable material can threaten the stability of the entire experiential conceptual system. The striving for expression of the dissociated material is not because it has an energy of its own that seeks expression, as proposed by Freud, but because there is a fundamental motive to assimilate representations of emotionally significant experience into a unified, coherent conceptual system. Material that can be neither ignored nor assimilated keeps intruding into consciousness in abortive attempts at assimilation. This process continues until assimilation (if ever) is accomplished. The process is essentially adaptive, since it promotes assimilation and therefore the construction of a coherent model of the world that is consistent with experience.

The main sources of maladjustment from the perspective of CEST are disharmony, including dissociation, within the experiential system, a failure in need fulfillment, and sensitivities and compulsions (to be discussed later), not a discrepancy between conscious and unconscious thinking. From this perspective, insight is not fundamental, although it can be useful for identifying problems in the experiential system that have to be solved. The task of therapy is to correct maladaptive schemata and promote coherence in the experiential system, which includes replacing conflictual with harmonious need fulfillment. To the extent that insight is helpful in this endeavor, it is therapeutic. If it is not, it may simply succeed in making a neurotic without insight into one with insight.

Other Sources of Information about CEST

It is beyond the scope of this chapter to describe CEST in greater detail. More complete information is available elsewhere (for reviews of the overall theory, see Epstein 1973, 1980, 1991b, 1991c, 1993c; 1994; for in-depth discussions of particular aspects of the theory see Epstein, 1976, 1983, 1984, 1985, 1987, 1990, 1991a, 1991b, 1993a, 1993b; Epstein & Erskine, 1983; Epstein & Katz, 1992; Epstein & Meier, 1989; Epstein, Lipson, Holstein, & Huh, 1992.)

IMPLICATIONS OF COGNITIVE-EXPERIENTIAL SELF-THEORY FOR PERSONAL CONTROL

Lack of Control as a Result of Limitations in Ability

According to CEST, learning directly from experience in the experiential system involves a very different process from learning from books and lectures in the rational system. It follows that knowledge of what one has to do to perform well at an intellectual level is often insufficient for performing well. It also follows that people can learn to do things naturally by processing information at the experiential level, yet be at a loss to understand what happened intellectually. An interesting example is provided by an experiment by Piaget (1973), in which he wished to illustrate the difference between what he referred to as the cognitive unconscious and the affective unconscious. Young children were given the task of getting a tetherball into a box by releasing the string at the proper moment. With practice, they eventually succeeded. However, when asked to explain how they did it, they incorrectly said they released the string when the ball was pointing directly at the target. When older children were given the same task, they correctly reported that they released the string well before the ball was pointed at the target. The younger children had acquired the skill as well as the older children, but were unable to translate their tacit knowledge in the experiential system into explicit knowledge in the rational system.

It is evident in the case of motor skills, as in the example of the tetherball, that certain kinds of learning have to occur at the experiential level and that intellectual understanding is not enough. This is not meant to deny that intellectual knowledge can be helpful under certain circumstances. For example, it would be useful to someone first attempting the tetherball task to be informed when to release the string. Practice would still be necessary, but the amount of practice could be reduced by the intellectual knowledge. However, under other circumstances, intellectual knowledge could actually impede the process of acquiring control over a motor act (Gallwey, 1974) and of making appropriate judgments (Wilson & Schooler, 1991).

It is not surprising that control over certain processes that involve motor dexterity is in the province of the experiential system and requires repetitive experience. CEST has little new to offer concerning such situations. Everyone knows that learning to play the piano requires a great deal of practice and cannot be accomplished by reading a manual on piano playing. It is less obvious that the same is true of other kinds of behavior that involve relations within the self and between the self and others. Here it is particularly helpful to have a theory that distinguishes between experiential and rational knowledge.

The value of distinguishing between the operation of experiential and rational processing was well illustrated in a course I taught on coping with stress. Students kept daily records on special forms of their most stressful events of the day and of how they responded to them. They were also taught the principles of CEST. A very common reaction was for the students to become disillusioned when they discovered that their feelings and behavior did not change immediately when they identified the maladaptive, automatic thoughts they had preceding certain kinds of events. They eventually learned that intellectual understanding was not enough, and that they had to practice their new ways of interpreting events before the interpretations became automatic (embedded in the experiential system) and significantly affected their feelings. Knowledge of two systems was useful to them in arriving at such an understanding, which encouraged them to continue with the procedure rather than give up prematurely.

Lack of Control Because of the Difficulty in Overriding Motives in the Experiential System

In this section I discuss the difficulty of overcoming motives in the experiential system. In the first part, I consider conflicts between the two systems in general terms, and in the second part, I focus on the four basic needs.

Lack of Control Associated with Everyday Conflicts between the Experiential and Conceptual Systems

Let us begin with an everyday example of a young man who is motivated to study in his rational system, but does not have a corresponding desire in his experiential system. The latter system would have him riding his bicycle or socializing with friends. The result is that he has to "force" himself to study. What can such a statement possibly mean? Since he is one person, what aspect in him is forcing what other aspect in him to do something it does not want to do? In the language of CEST, the rational system is imposing its will on a reluctant experiential system. Contrast his situation with one in which a student derives pleasure from studying because he finds the material intrinsically interesting. In this situation, the motivation to study exists not only in the rational system, but also in the experiential system, as evidenced by the positive affect. The example indicates that there are two different ways in which a person can be motivated that have vastly different consequences. When the motivation exists only in the rational system, the individual acts out of a sense of duty or obligation and derives no pleasure from the activity. In contrast, when the motivation exists at the experiential level, the individual acts enthusiastically. Ironically, in the former case, the person has the feeling that he or she is exercising control or willpower, whereas in the latter case the individual has the feeling that he or she is acting naturally, without having to exercise control. The situation is ironic because the person who feels he or she is using control is actually under less control, since the control is more likely to ultimately fail. This is because motivation in the experiential system can be very insistent and, therefore, in the long run, ultimately override the forced control of the rational system or, by causing the individual to pay a price in other ways, such as through stress-induced illness, may prevent maintenance of the control. The lesson in this is that control in the rational system is most effectively exercised when it is consistent with motivation in the experiential system. It follows that, whenever possible, it is to a person's advantage to enlist the support of the experiential system by making whatever control is exercised intrinsically rewarding.

What is the nature of the two systems that causes them to frequently conflict with each other? A perusal of Table 1 reveals that there are many ways in which the systems process information differently that can cause them to promote different behavior. Three differences are particularly important, namely, that the experiential system has a short-term focus, that it is intimately associated with affect, and that the outcome of experiential processing is experienced as self-evidently valid. In contrast, the rational system's interests are long term, its processing is relatively affect free, and the validity of its outcomes has to be established by logic and evidence. Because long-term interests often differ from short-term interests, because what is considered reasonable often differs from what is pleasurable, and because beliefs derived from experience often differ from beliefs derived from logic and evidence, it is inevitable for conflict to occur between the two systems. The wonder of it is not so much that conflict arises, but that it does not arise more often. For most of the people most of the time, their two systems operate in well-orchestrated synchrony.

The question may be raised as to whether the orchestration of the synchrony between the two systems requires a metacontrol system that can understand and communicate with both systems. According to CEST, no such assumption is necessary, as the synchrony can be produced by the interaction between the two systems and by the ability of the rational system to understand the experiential system. The rational system has the capacity to function as a metacontrol system, since it is capable of understanding, communicating with, and directing the operation of both the experiential system and itself. Through understanding how the experiential system operates, the rational system can both learn from the experiential system and train it. Through these means people can obtain increasing control over their lives (Epstein, 1993c).

Lack of Control Related to the Four Basic Needs

As the experiential system has evolved over millions of years, the basic needs associated with it are highly insistent. Examples of the difficulty people have in controlling the need to maximize pleasure and avoid pain include their inability to remain on a diet and to resist drugs once they have experienced their desirable affective consequences, whether it be the acquisition of pleasure or the avoidance of anxiety. In such situations people know (in their rational system) what they have to do if they wish to succeed in dieting or in giving up drugs, but are unable to override the motivation in their experiential system.

The situation is more subtle when the need to maintain the stability and coherence of the conceptual system is involved; people are normally unaware of this need. As a result, they are at a loss to understand what is happening to them when they experience distressing intrusive thoughts following traumatic events. Because of their inability to control such thoughts, they often are concerned that they are losing their minds. They do not realize that the essence of a traumatic event is that it invalidates basic beliefs in the experiential system (such as that the world is a reasonably safe place in which to live) and that the automatic occurrence of intrusive thoughts represents attempts by the experiential system to assimilate material that cannot be assimilated into their current conceptual system. In order for the assimilation to occur, the way must be prepared for it by accommodation of the experiential system. For example, the person might have to accept, at a deeply compelling experiential level, that despite the world being far more capricious and dangerous than it was previously considered to be, it is under most circumstances reasonably predictable, controllable, and safe. Until such accommodation takes place, thoughts about the traumatic event will keep intruding into consciousness, prompting an examination of the implications of the trauma (Epstein, 1991a; Horowitz,

1976; Janoff-Bulman, 1992; McCann & Pearlman, 1990). Similar reactions, but of reduced intensity, can be observed in responses to everyday minor challenges to the validity of schemata in the experiential system.

When people have emotionally significant experiences that are difficult for them to assimilate, such as when they believe they have been betrayed by someone whom they trusted, they are often distressed at their inability to control the intrusive thoughts that automatically follow. Such reactions are particularly likely when the validity of a basic belief is implicated. For example, the rejected lover whose belief about relatedness in the form of trustworthiness of significant others is invalidated is obsessed with thoughts of the loved one and with the reasons for the rejection. Similarly, the person whose self-esteem has been seriously threatened by a significant failure has difficulty getting the troublesome incident out of his or her mind. It is noteworthy that the reactions in both cases are adaptive in the sense that they ensure that people will not ignore situations that are of great emotional significance for them, but rather will consider them in every manner possible until appropriate accommodation occurs within the experiential system. Such accommodation consists of fully accepting that such experiences can occur and making one's peace with them in one manner or another. This may include interpreting an irrevocable outcome from a past or anticipated event from a new perspective, or taking action to correct a situation or prevent a reoccurrence when such behavior is feasible. The process is maladaptive only when it involves obsessive repetition in the absence of progress toward constructive accommodation of the schemata in the experiential system (Epstein, 1991a).

Up to this point, I have discussed the difficulty of suppressing basic needs, which become increasingly insistent over time as they are increasingly frustrated. But what if, with great diligence, people do succeed in suppressing the fulfillment of a basic need? The result is that they may become duty driven rather than passion driven and may pay a price in terms of boredom, a lack of positive affect, depression, stress, and the physiological accompaniments of such states. It is noteworthy, in this respect, that Horney (1950) discusses a "false self" as central to neurosis. A person with a false self has an intellectually imposed conceptual and motivational system that is out of touch with the person's "true" self. The true self is spontaneous and a source of enthusiasm as well as adaptive negative emotions. The task of therapy, according to Horney, is to reestablish contact with, and fulfill the needs of, the true self, thereby allowing the person to become a more natural, enthusiastic, and fulfilled person.

CEST is in agreement with Horney that alienation from the true self, which corresponds to the experiential self in CEST, can be a source of serious problems in living. However, CEST also recognizes that the experiential self has as serious limitations as the rational self. According to CEST, effective adjustment requires an appropriate balance between the two systems, with the irrational excesses of the heart moderated by the reasoning of the mind, and the cold logic of the rational mind invigorated and humanized by the involvement of the heart. Expressed in terms of control, insufficient control of the experiential system by the rational system can be as maladaptive as excessive control.

Lack of Control Associated with the Biasing Influence of Experiential on Rational Processing

People like to think of themselves as rational. If asked why they behaved as they did when it can be established that their behavior was determined predominantly by their experiential processing, they often report that their behavior was rationally determined. For example, we found that when estimating the behavior of others in certain situations, people reported that others would behave predominantly according to the principles of the experiential system, but when they estimated their own behavior, they incorrectly stated that they would behave according to the principles of the rational system (Kirkpatrick & Epstein, 1992). In other research, it has been demonstrated that priming the experiential system influences subsequent responses in the rational system. If particular words or images are primed outside of awareness, they influence the conscious thoughts that follow (e.g., Bargh, 1989; Higgins, 1989; see review in Fiske & Taylor, 1991). If processing in terms of the mode of operation of the experiential principle is primed, it influences subsequent responses when people attempt to respond in the mode of the rational system. That is, people continue to respond according to the principles of experiential processing while believing they are responding by the principles of the rational system (Chaiken & Maheswaren, 1994; Epstein, Lipson, Holstein, & Huh, 1992; Epstein, Donovan, & Denes-Raj, in press).

The pervasive influence of experiential on rational processing has important implications for the ability of people to rationally control their behavior. It suggests that the only way to be truly rational is to be in touch with one's experiential processing so that one can compensate for it. The alternative is to be unconsciously controlled by one's automatic experiential processing.

Lack of Control Associated with Sensitivities and Compulsions

Most schemata in the experiential system are applied with reasonable flexibility with respect to situational demands and are open to modification with new experiences. Neither of these conditions holds true for sensitivities and compulsions. Sensitivities refer to rigid, experientially derived, descriptive schemata that certain kinds of situations or events are dangerous. An example of a sensitivity is a person reacting to constructive criticism as if it were a devastating attack on his or her integrity. Compulsions refer to rigid, experientially derived motivational schemata that certain kinds of behavior are effective ways of reducing threat. Sensitivities and compulsions are resistant to modification because they were learned under conditions of high emotional arousal, and have, over time, become nuclei of cognitive-affective-behavioral networks.

Compulsions, as defined in CEST, differ from their more traditional meaning in abnormal psychology in one important respect. When used to describe abnormal behavior, they refer to narrowly defined classes of pathological behavior. An example is a hand-washing compulsion, in which a person feels compelled to wash his or her hands more than a hundred times a day. In CEST, the meaning of the term is expanded to include more complex patterns of behavior that, although maladaptive, are not abnormal in the usual sense of the word, because they are relatively common, often corresponding to the most salient, inflexible characteristics of individuals.

The hallmark of a sensitivity is that whenever certain stimuli or situations arise, the individual reacts excessively emotionally. The hallmarks of a compulsion are as follows: (1) The person acts in the same rigid way in certain kinds of situations, such as always having to be dominant or always having to be ingratiating; (2) the person experiences distress whenever he or she is unable to behave in the manner associated with the compulsion; and (3) the compulsion becomes exaggerated when the person is threatened, particularly when the threat involves a relevant sensitivity. To the extent that people are controlled by their sensitivities and compulsions they obviously lack rational control of their behavior. Although everyone is controlled by their automatic experiential processing to some extent, the degree of such influence is considerably greater in the case of sensitivities and compulsions.

From the viewpoint of CEST, and contrary to the view in psychoanalysis, sensitivities and compulsions are more important sources of maladjustment than repression. Repression simply adds a complication by making the sources of sensitivities and compulsions unavailable to awareness. Accordingly, in many cases, removing repressions (making the unconscious conscious) is not enough to correct maladaptive behavior, because the initial sensitivities and compulsions remain. This is not to deny that repression is an important source of lack of control and maladjustment in its own right.

Lack of Control Associated with Dissociation

Dissociated schemata involve a loss of control in two major ways, depending on whether the dissociation is between the experiential and rational systems or entirely within the experiential system. Schemata in the experiential system that are dissociated from the rational system (corresponding to the Freudian concept of repression) tend to remain dormant until activated by relevant cues. When dissociations are activated, depending on the degree of activation, they are apt to be expressed either in displaced form, representing compromises between the experiential and rational systems, or as ego-alien behavior that is consistent with the dissociated schema and inconsistent with a person's usual behavior. In the former case, people are unlikely to be aware that their unconsciously influenced behavior is not completely under their conscious control. In the latter case, they are more likely to be aware that their behavior is "out of control," at least at a later time, if not at the moment they are engaged in it. Because of the inaccessibility of schemata dissociated from the rational system, control of the resulting displaced behavior and symptoms is particularly difficult in the absence of identification of the repressed schemata. Identification, however, by itself is often insufficient for acquiring control, as the basic sensitivity remains to be corrected.

Another way that dissociation between the experiential and rational systems contributes to a loss of control is that it produces regions of thought that have to be actively avoided in order to keep from experiencing increased anxiety. Thus, the person's freedom of thought, and therefore of control, is restricted. This also applies to dissociations within the experiential system, which are considered next.

Dissociations within the experiential system have particularly destructive potential. Depending on the strength and breadth of the dissociated material, a failure in dissociation can seriously disrupt the functioning of the experiential system, and in extreme cases produce total disorganization of a person's experiential conceptual system, as can be observed in acute schizophrenic reactions. In such cases, the person is rendered experientially nonfunctional, which involves a complete loss of control.

The question may be raised as to the effect of disorganization of the experiential system on the integrity of the rational system. The answer is that it is not possible for the rational system to function properly when there is serious disruption in the experiential system. The systems are interactive and, as processing in the experiential system influences processing in the rational system, distortions in the experiential system are reflected in distortions in the rational system. In some conditions, as in paranoid schizophrenia, the process of rational inference may be preserved, but the major premises from which the rational processing proceeds are severely distorted, as in delusions of grandeur and of persecution. In such conditions, coherence of the experiential and rational conceptual systems is maintained, but at the sacrifice of reality awareness.

A yet more extreme condition occurs when there is total disorganization of the experiential conceptual system. In such cases the distortions and fragmentation in the experiential system must grossly affect the person's capacity for rational reasoning. A similar conclusion can be derived from the consideration that from an evolutionary perspective the rational system, as a higher order system, is dependent on the more fundamental experiential system. If the latter is nonfunctional, the former has no solid basis on which to operate, and is also nonfunctional. This may operate, in part, through emotions. Emotions indicate what is significant to an individual at the experiential level, and therefore exert an important influence on the direction of attention and on decision making. It follows that if emotions were absent or nonfunctional, which they would be with a total collapse of the experiential system, people would be unable to adaptively direct their attention and make decisions, which would make it impossible for them to function rationally. In conclusion, loss of control at the experiential level implies loss of control at the rational level.

Remedial Procedures for Establishing Control

It is beyond the scope of this chapter to provide a detailed description of therapeutic procedures for achieving personal control. It will have to suffice to note that CEST provides a framework for integrating a variety of therapies, including insight approaches, cognitive approaches, behavioral approaches, and experiential approaches (e.g., Gestalt therapy and psychosynthesis).

According to CEST there are basically three fundamental approaches to therapy. First, the rational system can be used to correct the experiential system, as in disputing maladaptive thoughts in the manner of cognitive therapy (e.g., Beck, 1976; Ellis, 1973). Second, the experiential system can be provided with corrective experiences from which it can directly learn. Examples of this include homework assignments in which adaptive behaviors are practiced in real-life situations, and the experience of corrective relationships with significant others in real life or in therapy. Third, the rational system can communicate with the experiential system in its own medium, through the use of imagery, fantasy, and metaphor (Epstein, 1993c; Singer & Pope, 1978). With the aid of this procedure, the rational system can influence the experiential system, as in the use of guided imagery. Equally important, the rational system can learn from the experiential system. Through attending to the productions of the experiential system in fantasy and imagery, problems that are inaccessible by direct verbal report can be accessed, and clues about their resolution obtained (Epstein, 1991a).

ACKNOWLEDGMENTS

Preparation of this article and the research reported in it were supported by National Institute of Mental Health Research Grant MH01293 to Seymour Epstein.

I wish to express my appreciation to Alice Epstein for her constructive comments on an earlier version of this chapter.

REFERENCES

Adler, A. (1954). *Understanding human nature*. New York: Fawcett.

Allport, G. W. (1961). Pattern and growth in personality. New York: Holt, Rinehart & Winston.

Bargh, J. A. (1989). Conditional automaticity: Varieties of automatic influence in social perception and cognition. In J. S. Uleman & J. A. Bargh (Eds.), *Unintended thought* (pp. 3–51). New York: Guilford Press.

Beck, A. T. (1976). *Cognitive therapy and the emotional disorders*. New York: International Universities Press.

Bowlby, J. (1988). A secure base. New York: Basic Books.

Chaiken, S., & Maheswaren, D. (1994). Heuristic processing can bias systematic processing: Effects of source credibility, argument ambiguity, and task importance on attitude judgment. *Journal of Personality and Social Psychology, 66*, 460–473.

Edwards, K. (1990). The interplay of affect and cognition in attitude formation and change. *Journal of Personality and Social Psychology, 59*, 202–216.

Ellis, A. (1973). *Humanistic psychotherapy*. New York: Macmillan.

Epstein, S. (1973). The self-concept revisited, or a theory of a theory. *American Psychologist, 28*, 404–416.

Epstein, S. (1976). Anxiety, arousal and the self-concept. In I. G. Sarason & C. D. Spielberger (Eds.), *Stress and anxiety* (pp. 183–224). Washington, DC: Hemisphere.

Epstein, S. (1979). Natural healing processes of the mind: I. Acute schizophrenic disorganization. *Schizophrenia Bulletin, 5*, 313–320.

Epstein, S. (1980). The self-concept: A review and the proposal of an integrated theory of personality. In E. Staub (Ed.), *Personality: Basic issues and current research* (pp. 82–132). Englewood Cliffs, NJ: Prentice-Hall.

Epstein, S. (1983). The unconscious, the preconscious and the self-concept. In J. Suls & A. Greenwald (Eds.), *Psychological perspectives on the self* (Vol. 2, pp. 219–247). Hillsdale, NJ: Erlbaum.

Epstein, S. (1984). Controversial issues in emotion theory. In P. Shaver (Ed.), *Annual review of research in personality and social psychology* (pp. 64–87). Beverly Hills, CA: Sage.

Epstein, S. (1985). The implications of cognitive-experiential self-theory for research in social psychology and personality. *Journal for the Theory of Social Behaviour, 15*, 283–310.

Epstein, S. (1987). Implications of cognitive self-theory for psychopathology and psychotherapy. In N. Cheshire & H. Thomae (Eds.), *Self, symptoms and psychotherapy* (pp. 43–58). New York: Wiley.

Epstein, S. (1990). Cognitive-experiential self-theory. In L. Pervin (Ed.), *Handbook of personality: Theory and research* (pp. 165–192). New York: Guilford Press.

Epstein, S. (1991a). The self-concept, the traumatic neurosis, and the structure of personality. In D. Ozer, J. M. Healy, Jr., & A. J. Stewart (Eds.), *Perspectives in personality* (Vol. 3A, pp. 63–98). London: Jessica Kingsley.

Epstein, S. (1991b). Cognitive-experiential self-theory: Implications for developmental psychology. In M. Gunnar & L. A. Sroufe (Eds.), *Minnesota symposia on child psychology: Self-processes and development* (Vol. 23, pp. 79–123). Hillsdale, NJ: Erlbaum.

Epstein, S. (1991c). Cognitive-experiential self-theory: An integrative theory of personality. In R. Curtis (Ed.), *The relational self: Convergences in psychoanalysis and social psychology* (pp. 111–137). New York: Guilford Press.

Epstein, S. (1993a). Bereavement from the perspective of cognitive-experiential self-theory. In M. S. Stroebe, W. Stroebe, & R. O. Hansson (Eds.), *Handbook of bereavement: Theory, research, and intervention* (pp. 112–125). New York: Cambridge University Press.

Epstein, S. (1993b). Emotion and self-theory. In M. Lewis & J. Haviland (Eds.), *Handbook of emotions* (pp. 313–326). New York: Guilford Press.

Epstein, S. (1993c). Implications of cognitive-experiential self-theory for personality and developmental psychology. In D. Funder, R. Parke, C. Tomlinson-Keasey, & K. Widamen (Eds.), *Studying lives through time: Personality and development* (pp. 399–438). Washington, DC: American Psychological Association.

Epstein, S. (1994). Integration of the cognitive and the psychodynamic unconscious. *American Psychologist, 49,* 709–724.

Epstein, S., & Erskine, N. (1983). The development of personal theories of reality. In D. Magnusson & V. Allen (Eds.), *Human development: An interactional perspective* (pp. 133–147). New York: Academic Press.

Epstein, S., & Katz, L. (1992). Coping ability, stress, productive load, and symptoms. *Journal of Personality and Social Psychology, 62,* 813–825.

Epstein, S., & Meier, P. (1989). Constructive thinking: A broad coping variable with specific components. *Journal of Personality and Social Psychology, 57,* 332–350.

Epstein, S., Lipson, A., Holstein, C., & Huh, E. (1992). Irrational reactions to negative outcomes: Evidence for two conceptual systems. *Journal of Personality and Social Psychology, 62,* 328–339.

Epstein, S., Donovan, S., & Denes-Raj, V. (in press). The missing link in the paradox of the Linda conjunction problem: Beyond knowing and thinking of the conjunction rule, the intrinsic appeal of heuristic processing. *Personality and Social Psychology Bulletin.*

Fairbairn, W. R. D. (1954). *An object relations theory of the personality.* New York: Basic Books.

Festinger, L. (1957). A theory of cognitive dissonance. Palo Alto, CA: Stanford University Press.

Fiske, S.T., & Taylor, S. E. (1991). *Social cognition* (2nd ed.). New York: McGraw Hill.

Freud, S. (1953). The interpretation of dreams. In J. Strachey (Ed. & Trans.), *The standard edition of the complete psychological works of Sigmund Freud* (Vols. 4 and 5). London: Hogarth. (Original work published 1900.)

Freud, S. (1959). *Beyond the pleasure principle.* New York: Norton. (Original work published 1920.)

Gallwey, W. T. (1974). *The inner game of tennis.* New York: Random House.

Higgins, E. T. (1989). Knowledge accessibility and activation: Subjectivity and suffering from unconscious sources. In J. S. Uleman & J. A. Bargh (Eds.), *Unintended thought* (pp. 75–123). New York: Guilford Press.

Horney, K. (1950). *Neurosis and human growth.* New York: Norton.

Horowitz, R. J. (1976). *Stress response syndromes.* Northvale, NJ: Jason Aronson.

Janoff-Bulman, R. (1992). *Shattered assumptions.* New York: Free Press.

Kirkpatrick, L. A., & Epstein, S. (1992). Cognitive-experiential self-theory and subjective probability: Further evidence for two conceptual systems. *Journal of Personality and Social Psychology, 63,* 534–544.

Kohut, H. (1971). *The analysis of the self.* New York: International Universities Press.

Lecky, P. (1961). *Self-consistency: A theory of personality.* Hamden, CT: Shoe String Press.

McCann, I. L., & Pearlman, L. A. (1990). *Psychological trauma and the adult survivor: Theory, therapy, and transformation.* New York: Brunner/Mazel.

Pacini, R., Epstein, S., & Barrows, P. (1996). Lessons in intuitive reasoning from the ratio-bias phenomenon: Principles of operation of the intuitive system and their interaction with rational reasoning. Unpublished manuscript.

Pavlov, I. P. (1941). *Conditioned reflexes and psychiatry* (W. H. Gantt, Trans.). New York: International Universities Press.

Piaget, J. (1973). The affective unconscious and the cognitive unconscious. *Journal of the American Psychoanalytic Association, 21,* 249–261.

Perry, J. W. (1976). *Roots of renewal in myth and madness.* San Francisco: Jossey-Bass.

Rogers, C. R. (1959). A theory of therapy, personality, and interpersonal relationships, as developed in the client-centered framework. In S. Koch (Ed.), *Psychology: A study of a science* (Vol. 3 pp. 184–256). New York: McGraw-Hill.

Singer, J. L., & Pope, K. S. (1978). *The power of human imagination.* New York: Plenum.

Taylor, S. E., & Brown, J. D. (1988). Illusion and well-being: A social psychological perspective on mental health. *Psychological Bulletin, 103,* 193–210.

Wegner, D. M., & Schneider, D. J. (1989). Mental control: The war of the ghosts in the machine. In J. S. Uleman, & J. A, Bargh (Eds.), *Unintended thought.* New York: Guilford Press.

Wilson, T. D., & Schooler, J. W. (1991). Thinking too much: Introspection can reduce the quality of preferences and decisions. *Journal of Personality and Social Psychology, 60,* 181–192.

CHAPTER 2

DYNAMICS IN THE COORDINATION OF MIND AND ACTION

ROBIN R. VALLACHER, ANDRZEJ NOWAK, JESSICA MARKUS, AND JENNIFER STRAUSS

Social psychology is of two minds when it comes to the mind. One perspective recognizes the potential for fluidity and turbulence in mental process, with the elements of thought popping in and out of consciousness in a seemingly whimsical fashion. This, of course, is the view of mind that James (1950/1890) had in mind when he coined the term "stream of consciousness" to characterize phenomenal experience. It is hard to deny the dynamic nature of human thought conveyed by this metaphor. In the most mundane of settings and in the absence of external instigation, the flow of cognitive elements seems to have a life of its own, producing an uninterrupted sequence of images, feelings, memories, and concerns, to which we often feel like mere spectators. Since James's time, there have been admirable attempts to capture the nature of the elements populating the stream of thought, typically through speak-a-loud or thought-listing protocols (e.g., Klinger, Barta, & Maxeiner, 1980; Pennebaker, 1988; Pope & Singer, 1978;

ROBIN R. VALLACHER • Department of Psychology, Florida Atlantic University, Boca Raton, Florida 33431. ANDRZEJ NOWAK • Faculty of Psychology, University of Warsaw Stawki 5/7, 00-183 Warsaw, Poland. JESSICA MARKUS and JENNIFER STRAUSS • Department of Psychology, University of Miami, 5665 Ponce de Leon Blvd., Coral Gables, Florida 33124.

Personal Control in Action, edited by Kofta et al., Plenum Press, New York, 1998.

Singer, 1988; Singer & Bonnano, 1990). Such work has revealed, for instance, how fantasies, current concerns, and fragments of repressed memories seem to pop spontaneously into consciousness with little or no priming from environmental cues and often with no obvious connection to ongoing behavior.

Ironically, the very ubiquitousness of dynamism in thought renders it a poor candidate for generating scientific theories on the nature of social thinking. Theories, after all, are based on regularities and patterns associated with invariant features, not on nonrepeating sequences of idiosyncratic elements. The stream of consciousness may be a true reflection of phenomenal experience, but its turbulent nature seems antithetical to fundamental properties that transcend particular individuals and their unique experiences. Confounding the problem is the apparent independence of moment-to-moment thinking from overt behavior, a state of affairs that suggests that the stream of consciousness is epiphenomenal and thus largely irrelevant to social psychology's overarching concern with overt behavior. This is where the other perspective on mind enters the picture. To discern regularities and invariant properties in social thinking, it is common for theorists and researchers to ignore the turbulent undercurrent of phenomenal experience and focus instead on those elements of thought that admit to stability and structure. Within social psychology especially, the emphasis is typically on higher order units of thought, such as trait ascriptions, schemata, stereotypes, and global evaluations, that presumably lend stability and coherence to phenomenal experience (see Fiske, 1995; Fiske & Taylor, 1991; Higgins & Bargh, 1987; Markus & Zajonc, 1985; Wegner & Vallacher, 1977). The turbulent flow of lower-level elements is not denied in this perspective on mind, but it is effectively rendered irrelevant to understanding and prediction in social psychology.

We suggest that this implicit theoretical split between the turbulent mind and the stable mind is unnecessary. To the contrary, we argue that dynamism and structure are complementary aspects of mind that together provide the basis for cognitive and behavioral accommodation in our daily lives. The general notion is that the flow of cognitive elements gives rise to higher-order structures and that these structures in turn influence the dynamics of moment-to-moment thought. This reciprocal causal relationship between lower-level and higher-level units of thought, meanwhile, is constrained and shaped by overt behavior. We begin by considering the relation between mental dynamism and structure, with emphasis given to two means by which higher order integrative frames emerge from the flow of basic cognitive elements. We then describe a recently developed paradigm for capturing and characterizing the invariant properties of moment-to-moment changes in thought content and the emergence of higher-order structure. This paradigm, which is based on recent work on nonlinear dynamical systems in the natural sciences, is then used to explore the reciprocal feedback between mind and action and the implications of this connection for the mental control of behavior. In a concluding section, we argue for the viability of reframing models of human action in dynamical terms and provide some suggestions on how this might be accomplished.

MENTAL DYNAMISM AND INTEGRATION

When social psychologists explore the dynamics of social judgment, they typically focus on changes in evaluation, attribution, and the like as a result of outside factors impinging on the person, such as new information or social influence. Because such changes are driven by external factors, we may refer to them as *extrinsic dynamics*. Although social judgment is clearly responsive to new information and external influence, there is reason to believe that judgment may display meaningful temporal variation due to the workings of the cognitive-affective system, even in the absence of external factors. We refer to such internally generated change as *intrinsic dynamics*. Whereas extrinsic dynamics are informative about the evaluative structure of incoming information, intrinsic dynamics provide a window into the workings of the cognitive-affective system producing judgment—and hence into basic properties of the stream of consciousness.

The potential for intrinsic dynamics in social judgment reflects the fact that all the elements pertaining to a target are rarely activated at the same time. Instead, because of the limitations of working memory, only subsets of elements can be active concurrently. It is the successive activation of such subsets that gives rise to temporal variation in social judgment. Because each activated subset of elements represents a unique configuration that can be characterized in terms of a summary evaluation (see Anderson, 1981; Asch, 1946; Kim & Rosenberg, 1980; Wegner & Vallacher, 1977), temporal variation in judgment carries with it the potential for temporal variation in global evaluation.

Static versus Dynamic Integration

Despite the potential for shifting evaluations inherent in the stream of consciousness, there is a press to achieve an integrated judgment that can provide a stable frame of reference for action. Our theoretical framework proposes that the way in which the press for judgmental integration and stability is satisfied depends on the subjective importance of the judgment. In particular, variation in importance plays a critical role in determining whether judgment will display diminishing temporal variation and attain *static integration* or instead display sustained temporal variation and attain what we call *dynamic integration*.

Consider first the judgment scenario when the judgment is relatively unimportant to the judge. This occurs, for example, when the consequences of the judgment are nil or when the target lacks personal relevance for the judge. Under such conditions, different subsets of elements become activated over time, each associated with a particular valence. The greater the variability in the respective valences associated with the succession of subset configurations, the more pronounced the moment-to-moment variation in evaluation. Without a strong investment in the judgment, each judgmental state is relinquished upon activation of the succeeding subset of elements. Eventually, however, judgment begins to stabilize as the various states become integrated via some combinatorial rule, such as the algebraic weighting of information (e.g., Anderson, 1981). In phenomenological terms, the judge may be said to find a compromise that effectively balances the pros and cons associated with the target, perhaps by simply averaging the most salient pieces of information. This state of mind can be said to reflect static integration.

Consider now the judgment scenario when the judgment is highly important for the judge. This occurs, for example, when the consequences of judgment are significant or when the target holds personal relevance for the judge. In this case, we propose that each activated subset of elements may give rise to a provisional higher order frame or schema and an associated valence. With diverse or inconsistent information, a single frame may not be sufficient to provide integration. Elements that cannot be integrated into a provisional frame become especially salient (see Hastie, 1980) and set the stage for the emergence of a new, integrative frame. With successive activation of diverse subsets of cognitive and affective elements, then, a set of interpretative frames or gestalten are generated from the stream of thought, each supplanting the lower-level elements that gave rise to it. In effect, judgment becomes detached from the lower-level information concerning the target, reflecting instead a set of higher-order cognitive units.

If the emergent higher-order frames are evaluatively consistent or otherwise easy to integrate, they become progressively integrated into yet higher order frames, eventually leading to a stable, integrated judgment. Judgment, then, is generated in a manner similar to that purported to occur for less important judgments (e.g., simple averaging of the valences associated with each frame). On the other hand, if the higher-order frames have mutually conflicting valences or are otherwise irreconcilable, it may be impossible to maintain such frames in mind at the same time, particularly if there is overlap in their respective elements. These frames will then alternate in prepotence, each frame in turn providing distinct integration for the respective lower-level elements and hence producing a different judgment. Because higher order units of cognition are not easily relinquished in favor of other units at the same level (see Vallacher, 1993), the oscillation among the emergent frames is likely to be sustained over time. In effect, the judge cannot settle on a single interpretative frame, just as someone viewing a Necker cube continuously alternates between conflicting figure–ground interpretations.

Ironically, then, under conditions of conflicting information, the more important the judgment, the less likely it is that stable integration will be attained. The state of mind here can be said to reflect *dynamic integration*, as opposed to the static integration of inconsistent information attained when judgmental concerns are less salient. In this sense, the conflict between competing judgments is resolved through the allocation of time to each integrative frame and its associated judgment. Of course, at some point even conflicting frames can give rise to static integration. Judgments provide the basis for decisions and courses of action, and in the face of such pressures for integration, vacillation among conflicting frames must cease. Under these conditions, we propose that integration is achieved by the ascendance of one interpretative frame at the expense of the other (or others). Rather than reflecting a compromise between evaluative states, judgment becomes linked to the most prepotent higher order frame.[1]

The notion that dynamic integration promotes the ascendance of one higher order frame at the expense of others is consistent with research by Latané and Nowak (1994) showing that whereas attitudes on unimportant issues are distributed normally, attitudes on personally important issues tend to be bimodal, with the midpoint of the scale being psychologically unavailable. This suggests that the task of integration for important judgments involves choosing between conflicting interpretations rather than finding an intermediate position representing the weighting of irreconcilable perspectives. This possibility is also consistent with depictions of successful dissonance reduction and of thought-induced polarization of attitudes (Tesser, 1978). It is noteworthy that in both of these models, the respective effects are observed only when the judgment is important by some criterion. Thus, research on the preconditions for dissonance has established that the inconsistent action must be freely chosen and associated with significant consequences (see Wicklund & Brehm, 1976). In the polarization paradigm, on the other hand, research has revealed that the object or topic being evaluated must be schematic (i.e., personally important) in order for extremification to occur (e.g., Liberman & Chaiken, 1991; Tesser & Leone, 1977).

Assessment of Dynamism

It is difficult to document empirically the scenario we have described. Assessment of people's thoughts and judgments regarding a person, event, or topic typically relies on self-report methodology. Beyond the well-documented issues concerning the validity of self-report (social desirability, limits to introspective access, etc.), this assessment strategy cannot hope to capture the fine-grained dynamics purported to be at work in action understanding. The turnover in thought that people experience during periods of instability likely operates on very short time scales, perhaps those involving milliseconds. Even if the validity of self-reports were beyond reproach, it is simply impossible to obtain self-reports of cognitive process with anything approaching that degree of temporal resolution.

A possible solution to this problem is provided by a paradigm recently developed to capture the moment-to-moment fluctuations in judgment of social stimuli (Vallacher & Nowak, 1994b). This approach centers on a computer mouse used to control a cursor on a computer screen. Two symbols are presented on the screen: a small circle positioned in the middle of the screen and an arrow showing the position of the cursor. The circle is said to represent a particular target of judgment, and the arrow is said to represent the subject. Subjects read a description of the target person, or of an event involving themselves and the target person, and then are asked to think about and evaluate the target person. As they do so, they adjust the arrow in relation to the target circle by moving the mouse so as to express their moment-to-moment feelings of the target over a 2-min period.

Instructions for the task trade on the idea that evaluation is an implicit approach–avoid response (see Hovland, Janis, & Kelley, 1953). The experimenter informs subjects that if they feel positive about the target, they should move the arrow toward the circle by moving the mouse. By the same token, if subjects feel negative about the target, they should move the arrow away from the target. Subjects' placement of the cursor in relation to the target circle, in other words, represents their global evaluation at each point in time; the closer the cursor is placed to the circle, the more positive the evaluation. If their feelings about the target change, meanwhile, they are instructed to move the arrow toward or away from the target to express these changes. Subjects are free to adjust their position relative to the target as often and as much as is necessary to reflect their feelings about the target as they continue to think about him or her. Movement of the cursor, then, signals instability in global evaluation; the more movement in a given period of time, the greater the instability in judgment.

A 20-s practice session is typically provided, during which subjects move the mouse and observe the corresponding movement on the screen. The screen then clears, a description of the target person appears, and subjects begin the 2-min mouse procedure. The location of the arrow is assessed 10 times per second for a total of 1,200 potential data points. The program preserves the Cartesian coordinates of each data point, although for purposes of our research thus far, only the absolute distance (in pixels) from the target has been considered. This distance provides a measure of subjects' moment-to-moment feelings about the target. Changes in this distance, in turn, reveal the volatility in subjects' feelings. Special emphasis is given to the variance in distance in a given time period, to the speed (pixels per .1 s) and acceleration (change in speed) of mouse movements, and to the time at rest (number of seconds without movement), since these measures provide intuitive and direct assessments of the turnover in subjects' feelings. The greater the variance in distance, the greater the range in evaluation; the greater the speed, the more rapid the turnover; the greater the acceleration, the more unstable the rate of turnover; and the greater the time at rest, the greater the stability in evaluation.

Research utilizing the mouse paradigm suggests that this approach provides a window into the dynamic nature of social thinking (Vallacher & Nowak, 1994b, 1997; Vallacher, Nowak, & Kaufman, 1994). A pair of studies by Vallacher et al. (1994), for instance, exposed the differential dynamics underlying evaluatively consistent (univalent) and inconsistent (mixed valence) representations in social judgment. Subjects read descriptions intended to generate positive, negative, or ambivalent feelings about someone they knew. They then performed the mouse procedure and completed self-report questions with respect to the target person. Each dynamic measure (variance in distance, etc.) was calculated separately for the first 40 s and the last 40 s of the mouse period. This allowed us to assess changes over time in the dynamics of judgment.

Because evaluatively consistent representations (whether positive or negative) are highly integrated, we expected that whatever temporal variation existed during the initial phases of judgment would dissipate over time, giving way to a stable judgment of the target (regardless of its personal importance). Evaluatively diverse representations are unintegrated, however, so we expected that personally important judgments based on them would show relatively high temporal variation and would not stabilize over time. These expectations were supported. Static integration was observed for the univalent targets: Subjects judging a positive target showed moderate initial volatility (speed, acceleration) and then stabilized at a point close to the target, whereas subjects judging a negative target showed somewhat higher initial volatility and then stabilized at a point farther from the target. Subjects judging mixed valence targets, however, showed yet higher volatility that persisted throughout the judgment period with no signs of stabilization. These subjects, in other words, did not form a stable evaluation during the judgment period, but rather moved between different judgmental states that presumably could not be easily integrated. Rather than demonstrating static integration, then, subjects in the mixed valence condition provided evidence of dynamic integration.

Although instability of this kind can be an unpleasant experience, particularly if extended for long periods of time, it may be a necessary precondition for cognitive growth. Moment-to-moment variation in feelings about a social stimulus (e.g., a new acquaintance, a political figure, an unusual event) represents a condition in which the cognitive system is not ready to settle down on a stable equilibrium but rather samples different evaluative states. If the various states can be integrated, or if one of the states becomes locked in by some environmental influence (e.g., social feedback, new information), movement between different evaluative states sets the stage for the evolution of a representation that provides coherent and stable understanding.

THE COORDINATION OF MIND AND ACTION

In principle, mental dynamics could exist in isolation, divorced from real-world contexts and constraints. In practice, however, autonomous thought is a very rare occurrence. When people think and form judgments, it is usually for reasons that are grounded in very real concerns about how to behave in specific contexts and with respect to particular individuals. The same is true for overt behavior. Apart from such things as reflexes, personal mannerisms, motor habits, and overlearned behavioral sequences (e.g., driving a car, typing, answering a phone), the things people do seem to be associated with higher order thought processes. Thus, people plan their actions, monitor their performances, and reflect on their consequences and implications (see Frese & Sabini, 1986; Gollwitzer, 1996; Vallacher & Wegner, 1985). Mind and action, in other words, are linked to each other in a reciprocal fashion, with judgments providing a basis for action and action providing information regarding the quality and utility of one's judgments. In this section, we develop the nature of the feedback between mind and action. We focus first on how mind is implicated in action, with special consideration given to the genesis of action plans and goals. We then examine the influence of action on mental process, with emphasis on the corrective influence that action provides. With the features of the mind–action system in hand, we discuss the factors that promote versus hinder effective calibration between mind and action.

The Mental Representation of Action

It is possible to act without thinking. Reflexes have this nature, of course, and on occasion we engage in more sustained behavior on the basis of impulses that seem to have little if any deliberation and thoughtfulness associated with them. When social psychologists speak of action, however, they typically have in mind behavior that is in the service of goals or reflective of values and personal concerns (see Gollwitzer & Bargh, 1996). The emphasis on goal-directedness in action implies rather directly the need for deliberation, planning, and other conscious mental processes. To be sure, plans and goals in a given circumstance may be activated through nonconscious channels such as subliminal priming (Bargh & Barndollar, 1996), but the implementation and monitoring of the action with respect to plans and goals require at least some degree of conscious mental control. Our model of mental dynamics certainly allows for the generation of higher order thought capable of directing action. If anything, in fact, the mental system we have described is capable of producing a surplus of thoughts with implications for action, since there is no limit in principle to the number of ways in which basic elements of thought can be organized into conceptual frames. How is it, then, that people manage to act with a single purpose much of the time despite the potential for multiple higher order frames?

In broad form, insight into this question is provided by principles of action identification theory (see Vallacher, 1993; Vallacher & Wegner, 1985, 1987). This theory holds that any action can be identified in many different ways and that these act identities can be arranged in a cognitive hierarchy, from those representing basic action components (low level) to those representing comprehensive and often abstract goals, consequences, and self-evaluative implications (high level). The act of "writing a chapter," for instance, can be identified by the writer in basic terms such as "formatting the manuscript" and "choosing words," in somewhat higher-level terms such as "organizing the points" and "choosing examples," and in yet higher-level terms such as "meeting a deadline (more or less)," "contributing to a potentially important book," and "describing one's theory and research." The notion of identification level has rather immediate implications for the mental control of action. Undertaking an action with a relatively high level identity for the act in mind is tantamount to having a goal or plan for the action and thus is consistent with theories that emphasize goal-directedness and purposefulness (e.g., Carver & Scheier, 1981; Emmons, 1996; Gollwitzer, 1996). Any action, of course, can be represented in terms of larger goals and plans as long as one does not have to perform it. But in the conduct of action itself, a sustained high level orientation is typically limited to acts that can be performed relatively effortlessly and automatically, with lower-level control (concern with details and immediate situational constraints) assuming prepotence for actions that are difficult or novel or that have been disrupted in some way.

Despite the utility of low level identification in many instances, it does not seem to be a personally satisfactory way of thinking about one's behavior (see Vallacher & Wegner, 1985, 1987; Wegner & Vallacher, 1986). People seem to prefer instead to think about their action in more comprehensive, meaning-laden terms, even when such higher-level identities provide insufficient guides to action performance. In talking with someone, for example, one normally thinks about one's action as "exchanging information," "impressing someone," "having a good time," and so forth, rather than as "uttering words" or "moving one's lips" (Vallacher et al., 1992). In effect, people maintain their actions with respect to lower-level identities only when they have to because of difficulty or disruption. When a more comprehensive identity for an action is available, that identity provides an avenue of emergence from the low level state. So although lower-level control may help to achieve one's higher-level objectives, it is also possible for the original plan to become derailed instead, with action taking off in a new direction that is at odds with what one had in mind at the outset.

There is considerable evidence for this process of action emergence (see Vallacher, 1993, for a recent review). Several studies have shown that when people are induced to think about what they are doing in relatively low-level terms, they become acutely sensitive to the context surrounding the act and embrace whatever cues to higher-level identification the context provides. Subjects who were asked to think about the details of their participation in a recent social interaction, for example, became very accepting of feedback suggesting that they had demonstrated either cooperative or competitive personality tendencies in their behavior (Wegner et al., 1986). The subjects apparently were eager to appreciate the higher-level meaning of their specific acts and so became especially vulnerable to whatever high-level cues were provided, even if these had questionable connection to the lower-level details. Low level identification, in other words, is a relatively unstable state that sets the stage for the integration of basic elements into higher order frames that provide coherence and stability in the mental system and a basis for goal-directed action in the action system.

Intrinsic Dynamics of Action Emergence

Research on action emergence to date has provided the high-level organizing themes with which subjects can integrate their lower-level identities in service of comprehensive understanding. This is entirely reasonable, since salient cues to higher-level meaning are common in everyday contexts. But one can envision circumstances in which such cues are lacking or perhaps mutually contradictory, and thus require people to generate their own higher-level meaning for what they are doing or have done. In talking with a new acquaintance, for instance, it is sometimes hard to tell whether one is coming across as charming or flippant, constructive or critical, interesting or self-absorbed. All one knows for sure is that one is saying words, making gestures, maintaining eye contact, and the like. In such instances, people are left to their own devices to generate higher-level meaning for their behavior. In view of the many ways in which a set of lower-level identities can be reidentified in high-level terms (Vallacher & Wegner, 1985, 1987), we suggest that the emergence process in this case will be characterized by the generation of several potential higher-level identities for the act in question. To the extent that these high-level identities compete for prepotence, people will demonstrate dynamic as opposed to static integration in their mental representation of their behavior. Because of the press toward a single frame for action, however, this oscillation should be fairly short-lived, with one of the identities, or perhaps some integration of one or more of them, assuming prepotence.

Insight into this form of emergence is provided in a recent study using the mouse paradigm (Vallacher, Nowak, & Markus, 1996). We asked subjects to think about their behavior in a recent social interaction with an opposite-sex person. Half the subjects were induced to think about their behavior in low-level, mechanistic terms (e.g., "spoke rapidly") and half were induced to think about their behavior in high-level, comprehensive terms (e.g., "offered support," "gave criticism"). In both cases, subjects generated five act identities and entered them into the computer. All subjects were then asked to think about how they felt about having performed the behavior they had just identified. They then used the mouse task to express these feelings for a 2-min period. They moved the cursor toward the circle—representing themselves—if they felt good about the behavior and away from the circle if they felt bad about the behavior.

Half the subjects began the mouse task immediately after generating the act identities (no delay), and half thought about their behavior for 1 min before beginning the mouse task (delay). We predicted that low and high level subjects would display different trajectories of self-evaluation and that the delay manipulation would enable us to capture different portions of these trajectories. Because high-level subjects begin the judgment process with a set of provisional higher-order frames for their behavior, they should show pronounced temporal variation at the outset, reflecting the valences associated with these frames. Low-level subjects, on the other hand, must generate higher-level identities before they can oscillate among them in service of integration. In the no-delay condition, then, high-level subjects should demonstrate greater temporal variation in their judgment at the beginning of the mouse task than should low-level subjects. This difference should begin to diminish by the end of the 2-min period as high-level subjects move toward integration and low-level subjects begin to generate high-level identities. In the delay condition, meanwhile, high-level subjects are likely to have achieved a fair degree of integration before beginning the mouse task, whereas low-level subjects are likely to have begun generating and oscillating among provisional higher-level identities by this time. High-level subjects should therefore demonstrate *less* temporal variation in their judgment than should low level subjects, and this difference might increase from the beginning to the end of the mouse task.

To test these predictions, we computed the variance in subjects' positioning of the cursor vis à vis the target circle (measured in pixels), both early (initial 40 s) and late (final 40 s) in the mouse task. This measure reflects the degree of variability in subjects' feelings about their behavior and hence indicates the extent to which they are considering different higher-level perspectives. The results involving this measure provide encouraging support for the hypotheses. High-level subjects displayed the greatest temporal variation in evaluation in the no-delay condition and the least temporal variation in the delay condition, whereas the opposite pattern was observed for low level subjects (see Figure 1).

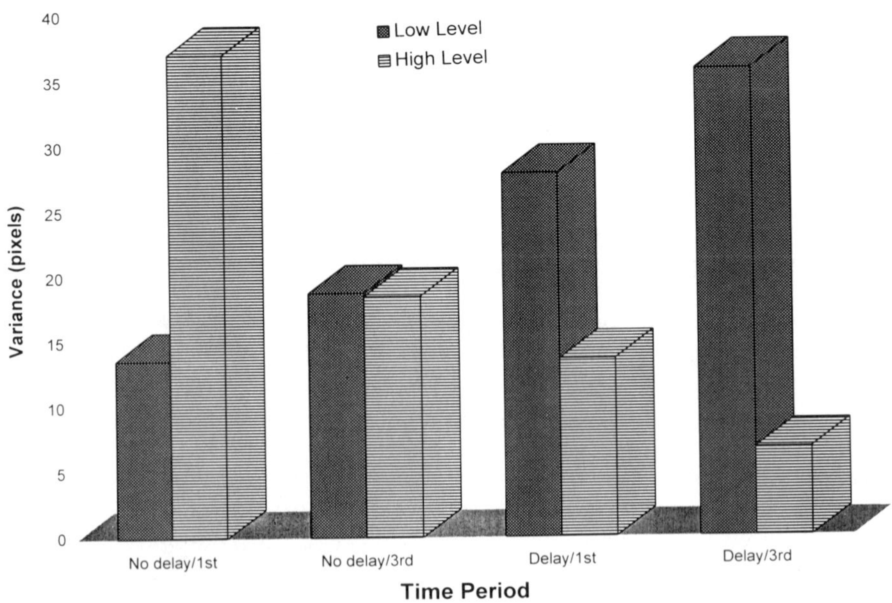

FIGURE 1 Dynamism in evaluation by identification level and time.

As an additional test of the hypotheses, we asked a group of students to rate the self-evaluation implicit in each of the five identities generated by subjects. We then computed the variance in these ratings and correlated this measure with the measure of variance in mouse movements. As predicted, results revealed that the greater the evaluative variance in the identities generated by high-level subjects, the greater the variance in their mouse movements in the initial period of the mouse task in the no-delay condition.

The results of this study suggest that subjects for whom low level cognitive elements are prepotent lag behind subjects for whom higher level integrative frames are prepotent. Presumably, high-level subjects begin by considering their higher order frames, oscillating among them to achieve integration, whereas low-level subjects have to generate such frames from more basic cognitive elements before they can begin the process of integration. This interpretation assumes, of course, that the judgment is personally important—a reasonable assumption in light of the self-relevance of subjects' task, but one that warrants explicit examination in future work.

Dynamics and the Control of Action

The transition from moment-to-moment volatility to a single action plan as one achieves integration is interesting to consider in light of Gollwitzer's (1996) work on action phases. In common with other perspectives on action (e.g., Atkinson & Birch, 1970; Jones & Gerard, 1967; Klinger, 1986; Reither & Staudel, 1986), Gollwitzer points out that not all mental states are equally conducive to goal-directed action. In particular, a distinction is made between predecisional and postdecisional mind-sets (e.g., Beckman & Gollwitzer, 1987; Heckhausen & Gollwitzer, 1987). In the predecisional stage, people are said to have a deliberative state of mind, in which they consider possible action goals that are salient and in which they process information relevant to each of these goals. Thus, the actor entertains, often in fairly rapid succession, the positive and negative implications associated with different courses of action or with different goals for the same action. In deciding how to approach an upcoming interaction, for example, the person might think about the pros and cons associated with such diverse interaction goals as showing sensitivity, offering criticism, and demonstrating wit.

The person's mind set changes dramatically after he or she has chosen a course of action and decided on a goal for the action. In this postdecisional stage, the person is said to become oriented toward implementing the chosen goal. The vacillation between good and bad features of the action possibilities associated with the predecisional phase thus gives way to an unquestioned commitment to the goal and a focus on its performance-relevant features. It is important to note that, in contrast to dissonance theory, this selectivity in information processing and thought is not in the service of justifying the chosen goal by emphasizing only its positive features. Rather, the goal is accepted as a given, with subsequent thought devoted to how best to achieve the goal. Once the person has decided to show sensitivity in an interaction, for instance, his or her thoughts no longer center on the likely benefits (or possible drawbacks) of having this goal, but rather are given over to the best way of achieving the goal.

The distinction between deliberative and implementational mind-sets corresponds nicely to the distinct patterns of mental dynamics demonstrated in the Vallacher et al. (1996) study. Thus, considering possible actions and goals can be seen as generating and evaluating various higher-level identities, while developing and maintaining an unequivocal commitment to a single goal can be seen as the achievement of static integration in the service of action. In the former state, the mind is likely to demonstrate evaluative volatility, as the person considers the positive and negative implications of various goals (high-level identities). In light of the preconditions for dynamic integration, one might expect this mind-set to be sustained for a notable period of time if the action's lower-level identities all point to consequential but mutually inconsistent higher-level identities. In the postdecisional stage, on the other hand, the person's mental state is likely to demonstrate little evaluative variability over time because he or she has locked in on a particular high-level orientation. Of course, the sampling of high level states purportedly demonstrated by subjects in our research was retrospective rather than predecisional. However, given the potential for erasure of high-level identities through low-level inductions (cf. Vallacher, 1993), the volatility we demonstrated for low level subjects is consistent in principle with the deliberative mind-set observed for subjects in Gollwitzer's research who have yet to commit to a single goal.[2]

This view of mental control suggests, almost by definition, that action is more likely to take place when the person's mind-set is implementational (the postdecisional stage) as opposed to deliberative (the predecisional stage). In terms of action identification dynamics, we would expect the expression of overt behavior to be unlikely when the person is demonstrating heightened volatility reflecting the generation and consideration of different higher-level identities for the action in question. Once the person locks onto a high-level identity that provides integration for the lower-level identities, however, the likelihood of overt behavior should increase dramatically.[3] This does not mean, however, that people always inhibit behavior during periods of heightened mental dynamism. People clearly act on occasion without the benefit of an unequivocal behavior orientation (Jones & Gerard, 1967), and sometimes with little if any regard for the consequences of their behavior. Indeed, psychologists and laypeople alike commonly sort behavior into two distinct types, one corresponding to goal-directed action, the other to unplanned and impulsive behavior. Strictly speaking, of course, even impulsive behavior is in the service of goals, in the sense that the person undertakes the act with some (low-level) identity for the act in mind (Vallacher & Wegner, 1985). Impulsive behavior, though, tends to be inconsistent with other behavior and erratic with respect to goals, suggesting that the underlying mental state generating the behavior is similarly inconsistent and erratic, displaying substantial variation on a relatively short time scale. Goal-directed action, in contrast, tends to be integrated and can be maintained over long periods of time, reflecting an integrated mental state that dampens moment-to-moment volatility in thought process.

The Active Control of Mind

Action may well require a mind to guide it, but the reverse is equally true—perhaps more so. Without the reality checks provided by the outcomes of one's action, the mind can go horribly wrong. As long as one does not have to carry out a plan, for instance, it is easy to maintain belief in its value, no matter how unreasonable it might be. Thus, a person might conclude that he or she can win an argument with a lawyer or master calculus or carpentry within a week, but unless the person attempts these acts there is no basis for revising the original estimates or refining their means of implementation to accommodate reality. In the absence of overt behavior, the mental system has the potential for becoming caught up in a self-reinforcing feedback loop in which a host of increasingly out-of-touch thoughts go unchallenged and hence uncorrected.

The importance of reciprocal feedback between mind and action follows from the logic of action identification theory. A key principle of the theory is that people prefer to think about their behavior in high-level terms, moving to lower-levels only when necessary to execute a difficult or unfamiliar action or to deal with disruption (cf. Vallacher & Wegner, 1987). In the absence of action execution, then, people's minds would quickly become populated with high-level identities for every act imaginable. Given the tremendous potential people have for abstraction, an unchecked press for superordinate understanding is a breeding ground for fantasy and the attribution of exaggerated importance to every conceivable act. And in light of the wide range of high-level identities available for any action, a lack of reality constraints would likely promote idiosyncrasy in thought regarding possible courses of conduct. In effect, each person would be a self-contained system of fanciful thoughts with little coordination with other such systems or with the environment they all inhabit.

Of course, people do engage in action and thus avoid the Twilight Zone feel of the above scenario. Some people are less inclined to test their act identities through action than others, however. The avoidance of reality checks seems especially likely for people whose act identities revolve around fear of failure and other dimensions of negative mental content. Depressed people, for example, are notorious for not expending effort in situations where such effort could well make a difference (e.g., Abramson, Metalsky, & Alloy, 1989; Seligman, 1976). In like manner, shyness can promote avoidance of social situations and intimate contact for fear of embarrassment and rejection (cf. Zimbardo, 1977). Yet other dimensions of individual difference (e.g., pessimism, low self-esteem, external locus of control) can be considered in this manner. In each case, there is a breakdown in the feedback between mind and action, such that the person's system of thoughts is not brought into alignment with the world of likely effects and consequences. Given the self-reinforcing nature of a detached mental system, one would expect the distortion of one's capacities and traits to become magnified over time (although evidence on this point apparently is not forthcoming at present). By the same token, however, the corrective potential of action suggests that the cycle of dysfunctional thought in some circumstances can be broken by encouraging the person to engage in concrete action and providing him or her with cues to emergent understanding (provided, of course, the person is capable of successfully performing the action). In short, although humans may not be able to control their own thought process directly through force of will (see Ansfield & Wegner, 1996), they may be able to do so through overt behavior.

PROBLEMS IN MIND–ACTION COORDINATION

It is fair to say that the lay (and scientific) fascination with psychology is attributable in large part to problems in the feedback system between mind and action we have described. People routinely fail to do what they intend, after all, and often fail to profit from their mistakes in subsequent planning and behavior. To a certain extent, of course, such lapses in mental calibration can be traced to the performer's lack of skill or experience with respect to the action in question. If failures in action signified only a lack of preparation or ability, however, the interest in psychology would center primarily on issues of learning and skill development, with the study of personality and social psychology occupying a subsidiary role. Fortunately for our field, people commonly make mistakes in spite of having the requisite skill, experience, and even motivation to perform the action effectively (e.g., Bandura, 1986; Baumeister & Showers, 1986; Norman, 1981; Reason & Mycielska, 1982). Yet, we have argued that mind and action define a dynamical system with self-correction tendencies working in both directions. How does one square this view of the mind and action with everyday observations of noteworthy lapses in the mental control of action?

Sources of Faulty Calibration

Despite the general tendency toward mind–action calibration, it is clear that people's mental dynamics are not always in perfect resonance with their overt behavior. This is apparent, for example, when one attempts almost any action for the first time, or a particularly complex action for the hundredth time. Even actions that are relatively easy and familiar, however, can misfire by virtue of inappropriate mental plans, strategies, and concerns. In terms of the present perspective, this means that people are sometimes led to monitor and control what they are doing with respect to a level in the identification hierarchy that is inappropriate for the coordinated discharge of the action. Simply put, faulty calibration occurs when the person's prepotent conscious representation of the action is either too high or too low in level for effective discharge of the action's components (see Vallacher & Wegner, 1985, 1987, 1989; Vallacher, Wegner, & Somoza, 1989; Wegner & Vallacher, 1986).

The mismatch between mental representation and action can occur because the available identities for an act are constrained by the context in which the action occurs. Most of the contexts defining everyday life are stacked in favor of relatively high-level identities, in that there are usually salient cues to an action's causal effects, socially labeled meanings, and potential for self-evaluation. When a person is offered a reward or threatened with punishment for a particular act, for instance, it may prove impossible for him or her not to define what he or she is doing in these terms. In like manner, situations involving competition, audience evaluation, or other pressures to do well may keep the person mindful of high-level identities of a self-evaluative nature (e.g., "demonstrating my skill," "trying to win," "impressing others") at the expense of the action's more molecular representations. If the action at stake is personally difficult and thus best monitored and controlled with respect to relatively low level identities, the context-induced high-level identities will lack sufficient detail and coordination of components to conduct the action effectively.

Apart from the research on action identification per se (e.g., Vallacher et al., 1989), evidence in support of this reasoning is provided by research demonstrating that performance of a complex or unfamiliar action is adversely affected by factors that charge the action with significance. Performance on a complex task has been shown to suffer, for example, when salient rewards are made contingent on the task (e.g., Condry, 1977; McGraw, 1978; Schwartz, 1982), when the task is performed in the presence of an evaluative audience (e.g., Cottrell, 1972; Innes & Young, 1975; Paulus, Shannon, Wilson, & Boone, 1972), or when the task is performed under conditions emphasizing competition (e.g., Baumeister, 1984; Sanders, Baron, & Moore, 1978; Seta, Paulus, & Risner, 1977). Each of these factors imparts a fairly high-level representation to the task (earning a reward, impressing an audience, demonstrating one's skill), so it is not surprising that they impair performance when the task is difficult or unfamiliar and hence best discharged with respect to more molecular representations. In effect, the basic action elements are discharged without the degree of conscious control necessary to assure their moment-to-moment coordination.

By the same token, some contexts can induce a level of action control that is too *low* for effective calibration. This state of affairs is likely to occur when the situation contains distractions, obstacles, or other sources of disruption that serve to render the details of one's action prepotent (Vallacher & Wegner, 1989; Vallacher et al., 1989; Wegner, Vallacher, Macomber, Wood, & Arps, 1984). A jammed keyboard or a bandaged finger, for instance, can reduce "preparing a chapter" to a series of discrete keystrokes. Low-level identities tend to come to mind as well when one is doing something in a novel setting lacking familiar cues to higher-level meaning. In yet other contexts, a person may simply be asked to monitor the details of his or her behavior as it is being enacted and in this way experience a lower level of identification than would normally be the case (e.g., Wegner et al., 1986, Experiment 2; Wegner et al., 1984, Experiment 1). If the action is personally easy for the person and thus best performed with respect to relatively high-level identities, the prepotence of lower-level identities resulting from disruption, novelty, or instruction can undermine the quality of the person's performance. In support of this argument, research has shown that performance can be disrupted when attention is drawn to the overlearned details of an action (e.g., Kimble & Perlmuter, 1970; Langer & Imber, 1979; Marten & Landers, 1972; Vallacher et al., 1989). The more overlearned the action is, the greater the performance impairment engendered by a conscious concern with how to perform the act (Kimble & Perlmuter, 1970). A proficient piano player, for instance, can become completely derailed in the middle of a familiar piece if he or she looks at the music and tries to think about how to play a section. In effect, consciousness is trying to micromanage a problem that is best left to lower-level echelons to work out among themselves.

In a broader sense, this line of reasoning suggests that the secret to effective performance is knowing when to let go of the action, allowing the lower-level elements to run off without further conscious intervention. After all, such lowly animals as cockroaches and pigeons function quite well without any reliable trace of conscious consideration and control of their behavior at any level. Of course, these species are not exactly known for the complexity of their behavior or their ability to inhibit behavior in the service of some larger goal. Assuming consciousness emerges, both phylogenetically and ontogenetically, as a means of maintaining complex, time-consuming actions in a coordinated structure pending their discharge, it is perfectly understandable that consciousness is often an integral part of human action. But consciousness can be overdone, functioning to subvert as well as facilitate effective action. In general, a person should be conscious of his or her action only enough to keep the undischarged components of the action in an organized queue. Actions that can be discharged directly—simple movements, for example—are probably better left alone. The same can be said of an overlearned act. Sometimes the best way to control an action, it seems, is not to control it at all.

Mind, Action, and Emotion

Perhaps the most basic and widely accepted division of psychological processes is the tripartite distinction between action, cognition, and emotion. To this point, we have focused on the reciprocal links between two of these—cognition and action—with little or no mention of emotion. This is not to suggest that emotion is irrelevant to mental control, or even that it is subsumed by more basic processes of cognition and action. Quite the contrary, we suggest that emotion plays a key role in calibrating the mind–action system. It does so by providing the hedonic basis for achieving and maintaining coordination between thought and behavior.

Emotion serves this function by signaling when mind and action are not well calibrated. In general terms, this contention is consistent with theories suggesting that negative emotion commonly results from the interruption of goal-directed action (cf. Berkowitz, 1988; Carver & Scheier, 1990; Mandler, 1975; Simon, 1967). Interruption can take many forms, of course, from environmental obstacles to the interference of other people. Our perspective suggests another important type of interruption: nonoptimal identification of one's action. Thus, attempting to control one's action at either too low or too high a level can disrupt the successful implementation and coordination of elements composing an action. Interruption is said to promote arousal, which in turn is said to engage epistemic concerns regarding the source of the arousal, presumably in service of choosing an appropriate course of action (see Mandler, 1975). In like manner, we suggest that a breakdown in mind–action coordination can promote heightened arousal that alerts the performer to possible reasons for the breakdown. Indeed, this is another way of describing the corrective influence of action on mind discussed above. In essence, the ineffective performer examines his or her mental content with respect to the action, with an eye toward finding another way to think about what he or she is doing. Arousal stemming from faulty calibration, then, becomes manifest phenomenologically as a special form of self-scrutiny.

In this light, it is interesting to note the emphasis on self-focused attention in various models of task performance. There seems to be consensus among researchers that focusing attention on oneself is associated with heightened arousal (e.g., Wegner & Giuliano, 1980) and that it tends to impair performance. There is little consensus, however, regarding the means by which self-focused attention produces this effect. In some models, to be self-conscious is to be aware of the potential self-evaluative implications of what one is doing (e.g., Hull & Levy, 1979; Wicklund & Frey, 1980). Defined in this general way, self-focused attention is considered by many to impair performance by reducing attention to task-relevant features (e.g., Cottrell, 1972; Henchy & Glass, 1968; Morris & Liebert, 1969; Sarason, 1972; Wine, 1971). Test anxiety, for instance, is said to occur when the test taker is preoccupied with self-evaluative thoughts (e.g., "I'm going to fail," "I'll be embarrassed") to the relative exclusion of attention to the subtleties of the task at hand (Sarason, 1972; Wine, 1971). In other formulations (e.g., Kimble & Perlmuter, 1970; Langer, 1978), meanwhile, self-consciousness refers to heightened awareness of the processes or mechanics underlying the execution of behavior (e.g., the discrete physical movements involved or the coordination of such movements). Several models of performance embrace this definition of self-focused attention, arguing that a conscious concern with the process of performance essentially disintegrates the action, robbing it of its fluidity and rhythm (e.g., Baumeister, 1984; Langer & Imber, 1979; Marten & Landers, 1972).

These contrasting views of self-consciousness map directly onto action identification level, the key variable in our account of the mind-action system. Thus, the self-evaluative implications of behavior constitute a special class of relatively high level action identification, whereas the mechanics of behavior reflect considerably lower levels of action identification. In terms of mind–action dynamics, neither orientation is inherently linked to self-consciousness; rather, each can give rise to such a state depending on the personal difficulty of the action. Specifically, the experience of self-consciousness arises whenever one's conscious level of action control is either too high or too low, given the action's personal difficulty. When performing a simple act or a complex one that has become fairly automated, people will feel self-conscious to the extent that they are conscious of the molecular features of the action. For a difficult act that is best performed with such features in mind, however, self-consciousness is associated instead with sensitivity to the act's larger meanings and effects.

Evidence for this perspective on self-consciousness and its role in performance is provided in a study of speech fluency by Vallacher et al. (1989). Subjects were asked to deliver a prepared speech to either an easy-to-persuade audience or a difficult-to-persuade audience. Half the subjects were induced to think about the action in high-level terms (e.g., "try to persuade the audience"), whereas the remainder were induced to focus on the lower-level details of delivering the speech (e.g., their voice quality). As predicted, subjects made fewer speech errors when their level of action identification was calibrated with the difficulty of the act—that is, when the task was personally easy and identified at high level and when the task was personally difficult and identified at low level. Subjects also rated themselves with respect to their performance and feelings while delivering the speech. Results showed that ratings of self-consciousness (as well as anxiety, tension, etc.) paralleled the pattern obtained for speech fluency: It was greatest when the easy task was identified in low-level terms and the difficult task was identified in high-level terms.

The idea that self-consciousness is the phenomenological signal of a breakdown in mind–action coordination helps tie together several diverse lines of research. To begin with, it clarifies why self-consciousness is sometimes identified theoretically as a concern with self-evaluative implications of one's behavior, and sometimes as dysfunctional attention to action details. Beyond that, this analysis captures the generally aversive nature commonly accorded to self-focused attention (cf. Duval & Wicklund, 1972). In a related vein, Csikszentmihalyi (1990) has observed that when people experience a congruence between their capabilities and the demands of the task—a state he refers to as "flow"—they report a loss of self-awareness. Wicklund's (1986) notion of "dynamic orientation" captures this same insight. This description of phenomenal experience is clearly consistent with the idea that self-consciousness dissipates when mind and action achieve effective calibration. Finally, if the function of arousal is to alert the person that his or her action plan has gone awry (e.g., Mandler, 1975), this reasoning is consistent with research showing that heightened arousal is a critical precondition for self-focused attention (Wegner & Giuliano, 1980).

Intrinsic Motivation

The arousal and negative emotion associated with faulty calibration diminish as people bring their conscious representation of what they are doing into line with the action's difficulty. This does not mean, however, that a person's affective state goes flat when mind–action calibration is achieved. It seems instead that a special kind of positive affect is experienced by people when there is a perfect match between the demands of a task and their mental and behavioral readiness to perform the task. As noted above, this experience of flow (Csikszentmihalyi, 1978, 1990) or dynamic orientation (Wicklund, 1986) is characterized by a loss of self-consciousness and a total absorption in the activity. Cast in more pedestrian terms, the joy of task involvement during the flow experience is said to represent the ideal state midway between boredom and anxiety.

This perspective on action enjoyment is not particularly consistent with models that emphasize expectancies, incentive value, rewards, and the like, but it does resonate well with our model of mind–action coordination. In this view, the driving force for behavior is not the desire to attain stimuli with *a priori* reward value, but rather the desire to achieve effective mental control of action (see Vallacher, 1993). Research has shown, for example, that a concern with achieving competence can work independently of, or even override, a concern with tangible rewards. Thus, monkeys, children, and adult humans will willingly work at tasks that offer nothing beyond the completion of the task itself (Harlow, 1950; Hunt, 1965; White, 1959). Variations on this general theme have long been central to discussions of intrinsic motivation (e.g., Deci, 1975; Harlow, 1950; Hunt, 1965; Piaget, 1957). It is interesting in this regard that when performance quality is included as a dependent measure in this line of research, it is typically responsive to the various experimental manipulations in the same way that the attitudinal and behavioral measures of task interest are (e.g., Greene & Lepper, 1974; Kruglanski, Friedman, & Zeevi, 1971; Lepper, Greene, & Nisbett, 1973; McGraw & Cullers, 1974; Ross, 1975).

The mind–action coordination perspective is also consistent with an emerging consensus concerning the effects of material rewards on intrinsic motivation. Money, prizes, and the like appear to have their detrimental effect on enjoyment when they are promised for simply engaging in the activity. When rewards are made contingent on the quality of performance, they often have the effect of maintaining or even enhancing the enjoyment of performing the action (Boggiano & Ruble, 1979; Enzle & Ross, 1978; Harackiewicz, Abrahams, & Wageman, 1987; Pittman & Heller, 1987). In this case, rewards signify competence at the activity—the very thing that, from the present perspective, is the basis for action enjoyment.

We wish to emphasize, though, that there are limits to the enjoyment-enhancing value of competence feedback. People can be led to believe they have done well on tasks for which they have no other basis for evaluation, such as those commonly employed in research on intrinsic motivation. In everyday life, however, there are clearly other bases for determining the effectiveness of one's attempt at action control, and these may work at cross-purposes with rewards that purportedly signal competence. Indeed, the likelihood that rewards can come to signify effective mental control and thereby enhance action enjoyment is constrained by the nature of the action in question. For an action to be effectively performed, and hence enjoyed, it must be represented at a level of consciousness that matches the difficulty of performing the action. As noted earlier, because salient reward contingencies foster high-level representation of what one is doing (e.g., "earning a reward"), they are likely to impair the performance of complex actions that require conscious monitoring of lower level components. If the act is personally easy, however, the presence of a reward contingency may *enhance* the enjoyment of the act.

Evidence in support of this contention is provided in a recent experiment by Rudich and Vallacher (1995). We asked college students to solve a set of anagrams that were either relatively easy or relatively difficult for students. Half the subjects were instructed to concentrate on the details of solving the anagrams, whereas the others were instructed to focus on one of two higher level identities—"demonstrating ability" or "earning $3.00." Pilot research had confirmed that the focus-on-details set sensitizes subjects to the molecular aspects of solving anagrams (e.g., "looking for patterns") and that the two high level sets render these high level identities prepotent (i.e., "demonstrating anagram skill" vs. "getting a reward"). We looked at subjects' performance on the anagrams as well as their expressed enjoyment and desire to solve anagrams again. By both sets of measures, results provided evidence for mental calibration reasoning. When working on the difficult anagrams, subjects in the low-level condition performed better and indicated greater enjoyment and enthusiasm for the task. When working on the easy anagrams, on the other hand, the best performance and highest enjoyment was observed among subjects who identified their behavior as earning money, and to a lesser extent, as demonstrating ability.

The potential for intrinsic desire to perform an action provides the affective counterpart to anxious self-scrutiny in helping to forge and maintain a working relationship between mind and action. Although the nature of mental calibration is such that mental representations tend to become effectively coordinated with action over time, this tendency may be a fragile one, overpowered on occasion by the cues to action meaning or detail provided in the context surrounding an action's performance. Emotion is nature's way of signaling distress when this occurs, and sets into motion self-corrective tendencies. When calibration is regained, or achieved for the first time, affect again comes into the picture, this time providing a phenomenal state that signals all is well with the coordination scheme that has developed between mind and action. Simply put, when mind and action are working together harmoniously, it feels good.

SUMMARY AND CONCLUSIONS

Mental Dynamics in Action

An explicit consideration of dynamics provides a new perspective on the link between mind and action. This perspective suggests that the mental states generating action can be characterized in terms of their relative dynamism, and that such differences in dynamism are associated with differences in motivational propensities and action tendencies. Some states are characterized by heightened volatility, with oscillation between evaluatively diverse representations occurring over short intervals of time. This happens when the person has only low-level identities for what he or she has done, is doing, or contemplates doing, and samples possible higher-level identities for the act in question. Because the concern here is with achieving an unambiguous action orientation, the expression of action itself tends to be inhibited. If action does occur, it tends to be impulsive and erratic, reflecting the unstable succession of different representations (goals, concerns, etc.) that can vanish as quickly as they arise.

Things are quite different for mental states characterized by relatively little dynamism. The person in such a state presumably has a more or less stable cognitive structure for his or her behavior. In reflecting on past action, the person is sensitive to an evaluatively consistent set of consequences or self-evaluative implications; in thinking about ongoing or future action, the person is committed to a single goal or anticipated outcome. Because of the integration, stability, and consistency of action understanding in this state, there is less equivocation in the expression of action. Assuming integration takes the form of a desired goal, the person's motivation in this state centers on implementation, with mental deliberation devoted to how best to achieve one's aims. Because behavior in this state is goal-directed and reflects a stable cognitive structure, it captures what many commentators feel to be the essence of human action.

Mind and Action as a Dynamical System

In a broader sense, the present perspective suggests that mind and action form a dynamical system (cf. Nowak & Lewenstein, 1994), in which mind influences the course of action and action shapes states of mind. The most important property of dynamical systems is their ability to evolve in time, such that the state of the system at one time determines the state of the system at the next moment in time. The nature of the feedback loops between the system's elements are critical in determining the system's dynamics. In the mind–action system, the most important link in the feedback loop is the process of action identification. Hence, changes in this link can dramatically transform the dynamics of the mind–action system.

The movement from low to high level, first of all, dampens the volatility of the system and orients the action toward a clear goal or set of goals. The downside here is that the system can break down when confronted with difficulties or disruptions association with lower-level acts. The movement from high to low level, meanwhile, increases the volatility and irregularity of the action. These changes are due to two factors. First, there is less guidance by higher level identities for the stabilization of action. Lacking such guidance, the action is likely to be influenced by random external events that introduce new elements to the actor's attention. Second, a movement to low level creates the potential for establishing a direct feedback loop between a low-level element and the system as a whole. In physical systems where the global behavior is coupled to the state of low-level elements, irregular and chaotic behavior is often observed. Low-level identification may create a feedback loop of this nature, so that an unimportant feature of an action sequence may come to control the action as a whole. A concern with an irrelevant low-level element of playing tennis (e.g., whether the logo on the racket is facing upward), for instance, can have a ripple effect throughout the entire identity structure for playing tennis, disrupting the regularity and coordination of the act, ultimately interfering with achieving one's original goal (e.g., winning the match).

In view of the centrality of action identification to the mind–action system, we can envision a host of other ways in which the properties of one's act identities can dictate the flow of action. The positivity versus negativity of people's high level identities, for example, can influence the likelihood of acting on the basis of the identities. As suggested earlier, negative mental content holds potential for disrupting the feeback between mind and action, with mind developing as an autonomous system divorced from real-world consequences. Positive high-level identities, in contrast, may better promote a well-coordinated mind–action system, with continual refinement in one's thinking and progressive mastery in one's action. The general point to keep in mind, however, is that action identification is not a single event, but rather a process in which prepotent identification at one point in time influences the future course of action and its identification. The most appropriate perspective on the control of action, in short, is one that gives explicit consideration to the dynamics of mind and action.

Viewing mind and action as a dynamical system suggests a new way of classifying the basic types of human action, one that follows from a well-documented taxonomy in the study of nonlinear dynamical systems (see Schuster, 1984). The usual tack in social psychology for building taxonomies is to focus on the content of people's behavior. This approach has generated important insights into the basic themes underlying superficially different behaviors. Thus, although every act is unique with respect to the specifics of its enactment, virtually everything a person does can be seen in service of such goals and concerns as achievement, affiliation, cooperation, competition, egotism, altruism, self-enhancement, self-consistency, self-assessment, and the like. As a complement to the focus on content, the dynamical approach to identifying invariant features of action focuses on the dimension of time. In particular, we suggest that the myriad of actions performed by people may sort themselves into three basic forms, each defined in terms of a particular type of temporal trajectory or attractor.

The most familiar temporal pattern is convergence on a single goal or state of affairs. This pattern, referred to as a fixed-point attractor in dynamical systems theory, represents the default action pattern in social psychology. Goal-directed behavior is commonly understood in these terms (e.g., Carver & Scheier, 1990; Gollwitzer, 1996), as is behavior in the service of reducing guilt or other unpleasant affective states (e.g., Cialdini & Kenrick, 1976; Higgins, 1996; Wicklund & Frey, 1980). The dynamism associated with fixed-point behavior is typically confined to the consideration of possible options for accomplishing one's goals and thus dissipates quickly as lower level strategies are developed. Not all behavior, however, is so unequivocally tied to a single end state. Everyday experience suggests instead that any given act can be identified with respect to multiple effects and consequences, some of which have contradictory implications for behavior (Vallacher & Wegner, 1985). Actions of this type may demonstrate periodicity in their enactment, akin to periodic attractors in dynamical systems. Thus, in line with our notion of dynamic integration, a person's behavior toward certain people (e.g., an intimate partner) may alternate between two extremes, such as affection and hostility, and this pattern rather than either of the endpoints may provide the best characterization of what he or she does. There is a press for static integration, of course, but such fixed-point stability may be hard to achieve for certain actors, targets, or behavioral dimensions (cf. Miller, 1944).

The final temporal pattern looks like random behavior, with the person displaying unpredictable changes in his or her action toward the same person, or in the same context, for no apparent reason. Although truly random behavior is always a possibility, it is tempting to view such a temporal pattern in terms of deterministic chaos (see, e.g., Vallacher & Nowak, 1997). Indeed, one of the most exciting and provocative ideas to emerge from the work on nonlinear dynamical systems in recent years centers on the potential for behavior that varies unpredictably over time, yet in accordance with deterministic rules. The chaotic nature of such behavior reflects the nonlinear interactions among the forces at work (see Nowak &

Lewenstein, 1994). This is somewhat analogous to the idea of statistical interactions in social psychology (Carver, 1997), where the effect of one variable depends on the level of the other variables at that time. In a complex system, of course, there are often numerous variables and hence the potential for interactions can easily exceed the "2 by 2" scheme that dominates our theorizing and experimental designs. It is also the case that the interactions themselves interact with the time dimension, producing a highly complex temporal trajectory as the action unfolds.

The potential for chaotic trajectories in action provides an intriguing way to rethink issues of determinism and prediction in human thought and behavior (Vallacher & Nowak, 1994a). It is easy to equate failure in prediction with failure to identify relevant causal forces and mechanisms. Indeed, this equation provides the very foundation for experimental social psychology. If a hypothesis is not confirmed in a study, the obvious conclusion to draw is that the phenomenon under investigation was not responsive to the factors that were manipulated. In the natural sciences, however, even a small number of variables interacting in real time can produce a pattern of changes that defies simple description, let alone prediction. The variables may be truly causal, yet the interactions among them can be tricky enough to disguise their influences, particularly if the nature of the interactions changes with each iteration of the process over time. Conceivably, then, the failure to reject the null hypothesis in an experiment can be misinterpreted as signifying a failure to identify causal mechanisms.[4]

The complex interplay of forces giving rise to chaotic trajectories in action can be just as opaque to the actor as to an observer. After all, even simple isolated causes that are apparent to an observer (or to an experimental psychologist) can be lost on an actor, leaving him or her to invent reasons for what he or she did (see Nisbett & Wilson, 1977). As the web of determining factors becomes increasingly interconnected in nonlinear fashion, then, it should come as no surprise that people fail to see the causal underpinnings of their thought and behavior, investing themselves instead with a sense of self-determination and free will—or alternatively, with a sense of being at the whim of random forces they cannot hope to understand, let alone control. From this perspective, people's sense of free will is, ironically, a testament to their connection to the multiplicity of forces and mechanisms defining the natural world.

NOTES

1. It is interesting to consider this form of integration in light of theory and research documenting people's tendency to avoid or reject conflicting information. When there are two

(or more) conflicting frames for organizing information, the consistency versus inconsistency of any element of information will depend on which of these frames is currently prepotent—an element that is highly consistent with respect to one frame may well be inconsistent with the other frame. Because the prepotence of these frames changes over time, the degree of conflict associated with each element necessarily shows temporal dependency as well. This means that no information is likely to be permanently suppressed in a system characterized by dynamic integration.

2. Gollwitzer and his colleagues identify two other mind sets, corresponding to the actual conduct of action and the completion of the action (e.g., Beckmann & Gollwitzer, 1987). In terms of the present analysis, we would expect the "actional" mind set to be associated with relatively low level identification (assuming the act requires at least some attention to detail) and the "postactional" mind set to be associated with reemergence to relatively high level identification. In both cases, evaluative volatility should be nominal, although this has yet to be demonstrated in our research program.
3. To demonstrate this mapping of mental dynamics onto behavior, of course, it would be necessary to have subjects think about an action they have an opportunity to perform subsequently, rather than asking them to reflect on a past action, as in the Vallacher et al. (1996) study.
4. This does not mean that experimental research is misleading or worthless, of course. To the contrary, the experimental approach to social psychological phenomena has been quite successful in identifying meaningful interactions among well-defined variables of particular theoretical interest. We do argue, however, that to understand a phenomenon in all its complexity requires the adaptation of methods and analytical tools originally developed for the investigation of nonlinear dynamical systems. Elsewhere we have provided guidelines and specific recommendations concerning this approach (Nowak, Lewenstein, & Vallacher, 1994; Vallacher & Nowak, 1997) and we have assembled theorists and researchers with expertise in dynamical analyses and their application to topics in social psychology (Vallacher & Nowak, 1994c).

Acknowledgments

The preparation of this chapter was supported in part by Grant SBR 95-11657 from the National Science Foundation.

REFERENCES

Abramson, L. Y., Metalsky, G. I., & Alloy, L. B. (1989). Hopelessness depression: A theory-based subtype of depression. *Psychological Review, 96*, 358–372.

Anderson, N. H. (1981). *Foundations of information integration theory*. New York: Academic Press.

Ansfield, M. E., & Wegner, D. M. (1996). The feeling of doing. In P. M. Gollwitzer & J. A. Bargh (Eds.), *The psychology of action: Linking cognition and motivation to behavior* (pp. 482–506). New York: Guilford.

Asch, S. E. (1946). Forming impressions of personality. *Journal of Abnormal and Social Psychology, 41*, 258–290.

Atkinson, J. W., & Birch, D. (1970). *The dynamics of action*. New York: Wiley.

Bandura, A. (1986). *Social foundations of thought and action*. Englewood Cliffs, NJ: Prentice-Hall.

Bargh, J. A., & Barndollar, K. (1996). Automaticity in action: The unconscious as repository of chronic goals and motives. In P. M. Gollwitzer & J. A. Bargh (Eds.), *The psychology of action: Linking cognition and motivation to behavior* (pp. 457–481). New York: Guilford.

Baumeister, R. F. (1984). Choking under pressure: Self-consciousness and paradoxical effects of incentives on skillful performance. *Journal of Personality and Social Psychology, 46*, 610–620.

Baumeister, R. F., & Showers, C. J. (1986). A review of paradoxical performance effects: Choking under pressure in sports and mental tests. *European Journal of Social Psychology, 16*, 361–383.

Beckmann, J., & Gollwitzer, P. M. (1987). Deliberative versus implemental states of mind: The issue of impartiality in predecisional and postdecisional information processing. *Social Cognition, 5*, 259–279.

Berkowitz, L. (1988). Frustrations, appraisals, and aversively stimulated aggression. *Aggressive Behavior, 14*, 3–12.

Boggiano, A. K., & Ruble, D. N. (1979). Competence and the overjustification effect: A developmental study. *Journal of Personality and Social Psychology, 37*, 1462–1468.

Carver, C. S. (1997). Dynamical social psychology: Chaos and catastrophe for all. *Psychological Inquiry, 8*, 110–119.

Carver, C. S., & Scheier, M. F. (1981). *Attention and self-regulation: A control-theory approach to human behavior.* New York: Springer-Verlag.

Carver, C. S., & Scheier, M. F. (1990). Principles of self-regulation: Action and emotion. In E. T. Higgins & R. M. Sorrentino (Eds.), *Handbook of motivation and cognition* (Vol. 2, pp. 3–52). New York: Guilford.

Cialdini, R. B., & Kenrick, D. T. (1976). Altruism as hedonism: A social developmental perspective on the relationship of negative mood state and helping. *Journal of Personality and Social Psychology, 34*, 907–914.

Condry, J. (1977). Enemies of exploration: Self-initiated versus other-initiated learning. *Journal of Personality and Social Psychology, 35*, 459–477.

Cottrell, N. B. (1972). Social facilitation. In C. G. McClintock (Ed.), *Experimental social psychology* (pp. 185–236). New York: Holt, Rinehart & Winston.

Csikszentmihalyi, M. (1978). Intrinsic rewards and emergent motivation. In M. R. Lepper & D. Greene (Eds.), *The hidden costs of reward.* Hillsdale, NJ: Erlbaum.

Csikszentmihalyi, M. (1990). *Flow: The psychology of optimal experience.* New York: Harper & Row.

Deci, E. L. (1975). *Intrinsic motivation.* New York: Plenum.

Duval, S., & Wicklund, R. A. (1972). *A theory of objective self-awareness.* New York: Academic Press.

Emmons, R. A. (1996). Striving and feeling: Personal goals and subjective well-being. In P. M. Gollwitzer & J. A. Bargh (Eds.), *The psychology of action: Linking motivation and cognition to behavior* (pp. 313–337). New York: Guilford Press.

Enzle, M. E., & Ross, J. M. (1978). Increasing and decreasing intrinsic interest with contingent rewards: A test of cognitive evaluation theory. *Journal of Experimental Social Psychology, 14*, 588–597.

Fiske, S. T. (1995). Social cognition. In A. Tesser (Ed.), *Advanced social psychology* (pp. 149–193). New York: McGraw-Hill.

Fiske, S. T., & Taylor, S. E. (1991). *Social cognition* (2nd ed.). New York: McGraw-Hill.

Frese, M., & Sabini, J. (Eds.) (1986). *Goal-directed behavior: The concept of action in psychology.* Hillsdale, NJ: Erlbaum.

Gollwitzer, P. M. (1996). The volitional benefits of planning. In P. M. Gollwitzer & J. A. Bargh (Eds.), *The psychology of action: Linking motivation and cognition to behavior* (pp. 287–312). New York: Guilford Press.

Gollwitzer, P. M., & Bargh, J. A. (Eds.) (1996). *The psychology of action: Linking cognition and motivation to behavior.* New York: Guilford.

Greene, D., & Lepper, M. R. (1974). Effects of extrinsic rewards on children's subsequent intrinsic interest. *Child Development, 45,* 1141–1145.

Harackiewicz, J., Abrahams, S., & Wageman, R. (1987). Performance evaluation and intrinsic motivation: The effects of evaluative focus, rewards, and achievement orientation. *Journal of Personality and Social Psychology, 53,* 1015–1023.

Harlow, H. F. (1950). Learning and satiation of response in intrinsically motivated complex puzzle performance by monkeys. *Journal of Comparative and Physiological Psychology, 43,* 289–294.

Hastie, R. (1980). Schematic principles in human memory. In E. T. Higgins, C. P. Herman, & M. P. Zanna (Eds.), *Person memory: The cognitive basis of social perception.* Hillsdale, NJ: Erlbaum.

Heckhausen, H., & Gollwitzer, P. M. (1987). Thought contents and cognitive functioning in motivational versus volitional states of mind. *Motivation and Emotion, 11,* 101–120.

Henchy, T., & Glass, D. (1968). Evaluation apprehension and the social facilitation of dominant and subordinate responses. *Journal of Personality and Social Psychology, 10,* 446–454.

Higgins, E. T. (1996). Ideals, oughts, and regulatory focus: Affect and motivation from distinct pains and pleasures. In P. M. Gollwitzer & J. A. Bargh (Eds.), *The psychology of action: Linking cognition and motivation to behavior* (pp. 91–114). New York: Guilford.

Higgins, E. T., & Bargh, J. A. (1987). Social cognition and social perception. In M. R. Rosenzweig & L. W. Porter (Eds.), *Annual review of psychology* (Vol. 38, pp. 369–425). Palo Alto, CA: Annual Reviews.

Hovland, C., Janis, I., & Kelley, H. H. (1953). *Communication and persuasion.* New Haven, CT: Yale University Press.

Hull, J. G., & Levy, A. S. (1979). The organizational functions of the self: An alternative to the Duval and Wicklund model of self-awareness. *Journal of Personality and Social Psychology, 37,* 756–768.

Hunt, J. M. (1965). Intrinsic motivation and its role in psychological development. In D. Levine (Ed.), *Nebraska symposium on motivation* (Vol. 13). Lincoln: University of Nebraska Press.

Innes, J. M., & Young, R. R. (1975). The effect of presence of an audience, evaluation apprehension, and objective self-awareness on learning. *Journal of Experimental Social Psychology, 11,* 35–42.

James, W. (1950). *The principles of psychology.* New York: Dover. (Original work published 1890).

Jones, E. E., & Gerard, H. B. (1967). *Foundations of social psychology.* New York: Wiley.

Kim, M. P., & Rosenberg, S. (1980). Comparison of two structural models of implicit personality theory. *Journal of Personality and Social Psychology, 38,* 375–389.

Kimble, G. A., & Perlmuter, L. C. (1970). The problem of volition. *Psychological Review, 77,* 361–384.

Klinger, E. (1986). Missing links in action theory. In M. Frese & J. Sabini (Eds.), *Goal-directed behavior: The concept of action in psychology.* Hillsdale, NJ: Erlbaum.

Klinger, E., Barta, S. G., & Maxeiner, M. E. (1980). Motivational correlates of thought content frequency and commitment. *Journal of Personality and Social Psychology, 39,* 1222–1237.

Kruglanski, A. W., Friedman, I., & Zeevi, G. (1971). The effects of extrinsic incentive on some qualitative aspects of performance. *Journal of Personality, 39,* 606–617.

Langer, E. J. (1978). Rethinking the role of thought in social interaction. In J. H. Harvey, W. Ickes, & R. F. Kidd (Eds.), *New directions in attribution research* (Vol. 2, pp. 35–58). Hillsdale, NJ: Erlbaum.

Langer, E. J., & Imber, L. G. (1979). When practice makes imperfect: Debilitating effects of overlearning. *Journal of Personality and Social Psychology, 37*, 2014–2024.

Latané, B., & Nowak, A. (1994). Attitudes as catastrophes: From dimensions to categories with increasing involvement. In R. R. Vallacher & A. Nowak (Eds.), *Dynamical systems in social psychology* (pp. 219–249). San Diego: Academic Press.

Lepper, M. R., Greene, D., & Nisbett, R. E. (1973). Undermining children's intrinsic interest with extrinsic reward: A test of the overjustification hypothesis. *Journal of Personality and Social Psychology, 28*, 129–137.

Liberman, A., & Chaiken, S. (1991). Value conflict and thought-induced attitude change. *Journal of Experimental Social Psychology, 27*, 203–216.

Mandler, G. (1975). *Mind and emotion*. New York: Wiley.

Markus, H., & Zajonc, R. B. (1985). The cognitive perspective in social psychology. In G. Lindzey & E. Aronson (Eds.), *The handbook of social psychology* (3rd ed., Vol. 1, pp. 137–230). New York: Random House.

Marten, R., & Landers, D. M. (1972). Evaluation potential as a determinant of coaction effects. *Journal of Experimental Social Psychology, 8*, 347–359.

McGraw, K. O. (1978). The detrimental effects of reward on performance: A literature review and a prediction model. In M. R. Lepper & D. Greene (Eds.), *The hidden costs of reward* (pp. 33–60). Hillsdale, NJ: Erlbaum.

McGraw, K. O., & Cullers, J. C. (1974). The distracting effect of material reward: An alternative explanation for the superior performance of reward groups in probability learning. *Journal of Experimental Child Psychology, 18*, 149–158.

Miller, N. E. (1944). Experimental studies of conflict. In J. M. Hunt (ed.), *Personality and the behavior disorders*. New York: Ronald.

Morris, L. W., & Liebert, R. M. (1969). Effects of anxiety on timed and untimed intelligence tests. *Journal of Consulting and Clinical Psychology, 33*, 240–244.

Nisbett, R. E., & Wilson, T. D. (1977). Telling more than we can know: Verbal reports on mental processes. *Psychological Review, 84*, 231–259.

Norman, D. A. (1981). Categorization of action slips. *Psychological Review, 88*, 1–15.

Nowak, A., & Lewenstein, M. (1994). Dynamical systems: A tool for social psychology? In R. R. Vallacher & A. Nowak (Eds.), *Dynamical systems in social psychology* (pp. 17–53). San Diego: Academic Press.

Nowak, A., Lewenstein, M., & Vallacher, R. R. (1994). Toward a dynamical social psychology. In R. R. Vallacher & A. Nowak (Eds.), *Dynamical systems in social psychology* (pp. 279–293). San Diego: Academic Press.

Paulus, P. B., Shannon, V. C., Wilson, D. L., & Boone, T. D. (1972). The effects of operator presence on gymnastic performance in a field situation. *Psychonomic Science, 29*, 88–90.

Pennebaker, J. W. (1988). *Opening up: The healing power of confiding in others*. New York: William Morrow & Company, Inc.

Piaget, J. (1957). *Play, dreams, and imitation in childhood*. New York: Norton.

Pittman, T. S., & Heller, J. F. (1987). Social motivation. *Annual review of psychology, 38*, 461–489.

Pope, K. S., & Singer, J. L. (Eds.) (1978). *The stream of consciousness: Scientific investigations into the flow of human experience*. New York: Plenum.

Reason, J., & Mycielska, K. (1982). *Absent-minded? The psychology of mental lapses and everyday errors*. Englewood Cliffs, NJ: Prentice-Hall.

Reither, F., & Staudel, T. (1986). Thinking and action. In M. Frese & J. Sabini (Eds.), *Goal-directed behavior: The concept of action in psychology*. Hillsdale, NJ: Erlbaum.

Ross, M. (1975). Salience of reward and intrinsic motivation. *Journal of Personality and Social Psychology, 32*, 245–254.

Rudich, E., & Vallacher, R. R. (1995). The identification and enjoyment of action. Unpublished research data.

Sanders, G. S., Baron, R. S., & Moore, D. L. (1978). Distraction and social comparison as mediators of social facilitation. *Journal of Experimental Social Psychology, 14*, 291–303.

Sarason, I. G. (1972). Experimental approaches to test anxiety: Attention and the uses of information. In C. D. Spielberger (Ed.), *Anxiety: Current trends in theory and research* (Vol. 2, pp. 383–403).

Schuster, H. G. (1984). *Deterministic chaos.* Vienna: Physik Verlag.

Schwartz, B. (1982). Reinforcement-induced behavioral stereotypy: How not to teach people to discover rules. *Journal of Experimental Psychology: General, 111*, 23–59.

Seligman, M. E. P. (1976). *Learned helplessness and depression in animals and humans.* Morristown, NJ: General Learning Press.

Seta, J. J., Paulus, P. B., & Risner, H. T. (1977). The effects of group composition and evaluation on task performance. *Bulletin of the Psychonomic Society, 9*, 115–117.

Simon, H. A. (1967). Motivational and emotional controls of cognition. *Psychological Review, 74*, 29–39.

Singer, J. L. (1988). Sampling ongoing consciousness and emotional experience: Implications for health. In M. J. Horowitz (Ed.), *Psychodynamics and cognition* (pp. 297–346). Chicago: University of Chicago Press.

Singer, J. L., & Bonnano, G. A. (1990). Personality and private experience: Individual variations in consciousness and in attention to subjective phenomena. In L. A. Pervin (Ed.), *Handbook of personality: Theory and research* (pp. 419–444). New York: Guilford Press.

Tesser, A. (1978). Self-generated attitude change. In L. Berkowitz (Ed.), *Advances in experimental social psychology* (Vol. 11, pp. 85–117). New York: Academic Press.

Tesser, A., & Leone, C. (1977). Cognitive schemas and thought as determinants of attitude change. *Journal of Experimental Social Psychology, 13*, 340–356.

Vallacher, R. R. (1993). Mental calibration: Forging a working relationship between mind and action. In D. M. Wegner & J. W. Pennebaker (Eds.), *Handbook of mental control* (pp. 443–472). Englewood Cliffs, NJ: Prentice-Hall.

Vallacher, R. R., & Nowak, A. (1994a). The chaos in social psychology. In R. R. Vallacher & A. Nowak (Eds.), *Dynamical systems in social psychology* (pp. 1–16). San Diego: Academic Press.

Vallacher, R. R., & Nowak, A. (1994b). The stream of social judgment. In R. R. Vallacher & A. Nowak (Eds.), *Dynamical systems in social psychology* (pp. 251–277). San Diego: Academic Press.

Vallacher, R. R., & Nowak, A. (Eds.) (1994c). *Dynamical systems in social psychology.* San Diego: Academic Press.

Vallacher, R. R., & Nowak, A. (1997). The emergence of dynamical social psychology. *Psychological Inquiry, 8*, 73–99.

Vallacher, R. R., Nowak, A., & Kaufman, J. (1994). Intrinsic dynamics of social judgment. *Journal of Personality and Social Psychology, 94*, 20–34.

Vallacher, R. R., Nowak, A., & Markus, J. (1996). Self-evaluation in action: Intrinsic dynamics of the emergence process. Manuscript in preparation.

Vallacher, R. R., & Wegner, D. M. (1985). *A theory of action identification.* Hillsdale, NJ: Erlbaum.

Vallacher, R. R., & Wegner, D. M. (1987). What do people think they're doing? Action identification and human behavior. *Psychological Review, 94*, 3–15.

Vallacher, R. R., & Wegner, D. M. (1989). Levels of personal agency: Individual variation in action identification. *Journal of Personality and Social Psychology, 57*, 660–671.

Vallacher, R. R., Wegner, D. M., McMahan, S. C., Cotter, J., & Larsen, K. A. (1992). On winning friends and influencing people: Action identification and self-presentation success. *Social Cognition, 10*, 335–355.

Vallacher, R. R., Wegner, D. M., & Somoza, M. P. (1989). That's easy for you to say: Action identification and speech fluency. *Journal of Personality and Social Psychology, 56,* 199–208.

Wegner, D. M., & Giuliano, T. (1980). Arousal-induced attention to self. *Journal of Personality and Social Psychology, 38,* 719–726.

Wegner, D. M., & Vallacher, R. R. (1977). *Implicit psychology: An introduction to social cognition.* New York: Oxford University Press.

Wegner, D. M., & Vallacher, R. R. (1986). Action identification. In R. M. Sorrentino & E. T. Higgins (Eds.), *Handbook of motivation and cognition* (pp. 550–582). New York: Guilford.

Wegner, D. M., & Vallacher, R. R. (1987). The trouble with action. *Social Cognition, 5,* 179–190.

Wegner, D. M., Vallacher, R. R., Kiersted, G., & Dizadji, D. (1986). Action identification in the emergence of social behavior. *Social Cognition, 4,* 18–38.

Wegner, D. M., Vallacher, R. R., Macomber, G., Wood, R., & Arps, K. (1984). The emergence of action. *Journal of Personality and Social Psychology, 46,* 269–279.

Wicklund, R. A. (1986). Orientation to the environment versus preoccupation with human potential. In R. M. Sorrentino & E. T. Higgins (Eds.), *Handbook of motivation and cognition* (Vol. 1, pp. 64–95). New York: Guilford.

Wicklund, R. A., & Brehm, J. W. (1976). *Perspectives on cognitive dissonance.* Hillsdale, NJ: Erlbaum.

Wicklund, R. A., & Frey, D. (1980). Self-awareness theory: When the self makes a difference. In D. M. Wegner & R. R. Vallacher (Eds.), *The self in social psychology* (pp. 31–54). New York: Oxford University Press.

Wine, J. D. (1971). Test anxiety and the direction of attention. *Psychological Bulletin, 76,* 92–104.

Zimbardo, P. G. (1977). *Shyness: What it is and what you can do about it.* Reading, MA: Addison-Wesley.

CHAPTER 3

OPENING VERSUS CLOSING STRATEGIES IN CONTROLLING ONE'S RESPONSES TO EXPERIENCE

MICHAEL ROSENBAUM

INTRODUCTION

A 60-year-old woman living in Tel Aviv suffered from fear of flying. When asked what she was afraid of she said that she was afraid of the commotion that would occur on the plane in case she would faint. She was also afraid that emergency medical treatment would not be available on the plane when she would need it. She knew that her fear was not rational because only once in her life had she fainted and all the medical tests indicated that she was in very good health. She was able to fly only on short flights (up to four hours) but avoided longer flights. She asked for therapy because she wanted to fly from Tel Aviv to California to see her newly born grandchild who resided in San Francisco.

She told the therapist that on short flights she was able to control her fears by using various cognitive and behavioral methods. For example, she would fly only in the first class section because there was more "fresh air" and fewer passengers. She was able to reason away her fears by con-

MICHAEL ROSENBAUM • Department of Psychology, Tel Aviv University, Tel Aviv 69978, Israel. E-mail: miker@freud.tau.ac.il

Personal Control in Action, edited by Kofta et al., Plenum Press, New York, 1998.

vincing herself that she could cope with short flights because there she is less likely to run short of breath. Furthermore, on short flights she was able to distract herself by reading a book, taking a nap, or by suppressing her thoughts. These types of responses to the fear experience (i.e., cognitive distraction and reframing) belong to what will be called here "the cognitive-closing system of self-controlling responses" (Rosenbaum, in press). The client was able to activate them on short flights but not on longer flights that she has been avoiding altogether. In therapy I used self-exposure techniques with this client (Marks, 1978) that are based on what will be called here "the opening system of self-controlling responses" (Rosenbaum, in press). Instead of trying to control her fear by putting a cognitive barrier between herself and the fear, she was asked to embrace the fear. Essentially, I trained my client to focus her attention on experiencing her fear: how it "feels" and how it increases and decreases over time. She was asked to experience the fear as fully as possible without trying to distract herself or run away from it via cognitive means. These type of behaviors enabled my client to genuinely accept her fear and experience it "as it is" without judging or controlling it.

The present chapter focuses on how people control their responses to their immediate experiences whether they are unpleasant (pain, sadness, frustration, anxiety) or pleasant (happiness, hearing music). It will be proposed that there are two systems of responses to experience: an opening and a closing system. The opening system enables individuals to approach their experience as it is, without preconceived ideas and with as much attention to the present stimuli as possible. On the other hand, the closing system helps people to distance themselves from their immediate experiences by either trying to avoid them or by cognitively transforming them. It should be noted that whereas one's immediate experiential reactions can not be self-controlled, opening or closing responses to experience can be (but do not have to be) under volitional control. For example, the urge to smoke can not be *directly* controlled by the smoker but his or her reaction to the urge can be controlled. After a short description of what is meant by "experience," I will describe the cognitive processes that lead individuals to decide whether to control or not to control their responses to experience. Following that I will propose a self-control model that takes into account both opening and closing responses to experiences as well as individual differences in self-control skills. Finally, the implications of the proposed self-control model to coping with stress and to psychotherapy will be elucidated.

THE NATURE OF EXPERIENCE

Experiencing is "...a way of knowing that is immediate, embodied, holistic, and contextual" (Bohart, 1993, p. 52). Experience is a complex state that has perceptual-sensory, action-motoric, and visceral components. It is the *immediate* reaction of the individual to the context in which he or she operates. Feelings and moods are a prime example of experiencing. An important characteristic of an experience is that it is continuously changing in concert with bodily and contextual fluctuations. Although not always perceived so by the individual every experience is a new experience. A person does never step twice to the same river, because the river as well as the person are continuously changing. People define experiences as being "new" or "old" on the basis of their ability to detect differences between one experience and another. Furthermore, experiences are neither "bad" nor "good." The definitions of goodness or badness, as well as novel or old, are part of one's cognitive responses to experience that can be controlled by the individual.

The dictionary offers a number of definitions of the term "experience." Basically, a distinction can be made between *immediate* experience and *accumulated* experience. Immediate experience refers to a particular event or events that a person actually participates in, is in contact with, and is perceived by her (e.g., "experiencing a chill"). Accumulation of such events over time leads the person to have knowledge, skill, or understanding of a specific area (e.g., a person has experience as a teacher). Individuals' behavior may be a reflection of their immediate experience and/or a reflection of their accumulated experiences. That distinction is not always clear in the psychological literature. When humanistic psychologists (e.g., Mahrer, 1989; Perls, Hefferline, & Goodman, 1951; Rogers, 1980) write about "experience" they refer to what one dictionary of psychology (Harriman, 1947) defines as experience: "a conscious response to stimuli devoid of interferences, expectations, and other distortions," namely, to one's immediate experience. On the other hand, when S. Epstein (1994; this volume), for example, discusses "experiential thinking," he refers to intuitive thinking that is based on the person's accumulated experience (in contrast to thinking that is based on rational rules). In the present chapter the term experience refers to one's immediate experience.

The self-control of one's responses to experiences consists of three main parts. First, individuals must decide when and for what purpose they want to control their responses to experience. Second, once they have commenced the self-control process they must decide whether their self-control efforts should be directed toward openness to or closure from experience. As will be demonstrated the decision to be closed or open to experience will depend to a large extent on whether individuals are primarily motivated to control their emotional states or to achieve their behavioral goal (task- versus state-oriented motivation). Third, the whole self-control process cannot be carried out unless people have the appropriate self-control skills in their behavioral repertoire. Each aspect of the self-control process will be discussed below.

ON THE DECISION TO SELF-CONTROL ONE'S RESPONSES TO EXPERIENCE

Since I believe that one cannot control one's immediate experiences, all self-control processes refer to the control of one's responses to experience. The impulse to eat a freshly baked apple strudel cannot be controlled directly, the impulse will be there whatever is done, but one can control one's reactions to this impulse. The question is then what one wants to control and for what purpose. In general, it can be said that the aim of self-control behavior is to overcome any of a wide range of self-generated impediments to a desired target behavior (F. Kanfer & Gaelick-Buys, 1991). In the example given above, the target behavior might be "not eating the cake" because it is in line with one's long-range goal of losing weight. The function of self-control behavior in this case is *reformative*—changing current behavior, even if it causes stress in the short run, in order to avoid future stresses and problems (Rosenbaum, 1988, 1990b). In another case, a person is working on writing a long overdue paper and he is disturbed by thoughts about resolving an urgent personal problem. Self-control efforts in this case are directed at minimizing the interference of the intrusive thoughts on one's work on the paper. This type of self-control has been labeled *redressive* or corrective self-control (Rosenbaum, 1988, 1990b). The redressive function of self-control is most obvious in cases when individuals want to reduce the interfering effects of affective experiences (e.g., anxiety, depressive mood) on the smooth execution of a target behavior. However, there are cases in which the goal of self-control efforts are directed at the person's wish to be open to the momentary experience with no attempt to change or avoid it. For example, an anorexic adolescent who automatically reacts to any self-felt hunger for food by suppressing any thoughts about food and by denying any hunger related sensations (often viewed as "overcontrol") may be encouraged by her therapist to fully experience and enhance her suppressed hunger sensations. In this case the goal of self-control would be to enhance the feeling of hunger, to be fully engrossed in it and eventually to "give in" to it and eat. It should be noted that anorexic persons tend to avoid not only the feeling of hunger but also other emotional experiences (Foreyt & McGavin, 1988). As King (1996) has noted, "loss of control" and spontaneity are also controlled processes. I have called this function of self-control *experiential* self-control (Rosenbaum, 1993). The behaviors that are aimed at achieving the reformative and the redressive goals of the self-control process are part of the cognitive-closing system of responses, whereas behaviors associated with the experiential goals of self-control are part of the opening system of responses (Rosenbaum, in press). Table 1 summarizes the three functions of self-control behavior.

TABLE 1 The Three Functions of Self-Control

	Types of self-control		
	Redressive	Reformative	Experiential
Goals:	• Keep current behavior on target. • Reduce the interfering effects of internal experiences on performance. • Achieve homeostasis.	• Change current habits. • Interfere with current behavior and replace it with a new and well defined behavior. • Create heterostasis.	• Facilitate the generation of new behaviors. • Reduce interferences to current emotional and other experiences. • Create heterostasis. • Enrich personality repertoires.
Required skills:	• Emotion and thought regulation (e.g., thought suppression, distraction, cognitive reframing).	• Planning • Delay of immediate gratifications. • Problem-solving. • Emotion and thought regulation.	• Absorption in the momentary experience. • Letting go of analytical thinking. • Focus on sensations and feelings. • Create images. • Tolerate new experiences.

How do people decide whether to use self-control or not? In a previous paper (Rosenbaum, 1990a) I have suggested that individuals go through a number of stages before they finally decide to control their behavior. These decisional processes have been labeled "process regulating cognitions" (PRC; Rosenbaum, 1988, 1990a). The chain of events that leads individuals to consider controlling their behavior starts with the apprehension that experiential reactions interfere with the ability to attain a desired goal. For example, a student may become aware of the fact that her anxiety interferes with her ability to answer questions on a test. This awareness is followed by a shift in attention toward her anxiety reactions, and she starts self-monitoring and self-evaluating her anxiety. In the self-evaluation phase of the self-control process, individuals engage in what Lazarus and Folkman (1984) have labeled "primary and secondary appraisals." In primary appraisal, the person evaluates whether the disruptions are desirable or undesirable. If the person concludes that there is nothing at stake for her in the disruption, she will ignore it and no self-control behavior will ensue. However, if the person feels that the disruption is real and it is a serious obstacle on her way to achieve a certain goal, she engages in secondary appraisal. Namely, she appraises whether there is a way to minimize the adverse effects of the disruption and if she can do it. Bandura (1977, 1982) has referred to the former as outcome expectancies and to the latter as self-efficacy expectancies. Bandura considers these two types of expectancies as the basic motivating force behind self-control behavior. Individuals who believe that events are caused by their own actions and that these actions are modifiable (i.e., they do not reflect some global personal deficiency) are likely to pursue their attempts at self-control. In the example given above, the student who appraises her anxiety as a major barrier to success on the test (primary appraisal) may then evaluate whether something can be done to alleviate her anxiety and whether she is capable of performing it (secondary appraisal). If the answers to these questions are affirmative, she is likely to try to self-control her test anxiety. Her success in controlling her anxiety would be determined to a large part by her having the necessary repertoire of self-control skills.

However, before engaging in specific self-control behaviors individuals determine for themselves whether they are going to be "open" or "closed" to their experiences. For example, should they direct their self-control efforts toward a nonevaluative acceptance of their test anxiety or try to change it through various cognitive transformation methods. What are the psychological conditions that call for either self-directed openness or self-directed closure?

TASK- VERSUS STATE-ORIENTED MOTIVATION IN SELF-CONTROL PROCESSES

In every self-control process there are two kinds of goals that have to be achieved: the execution of the aspired target behavior and the mental control of internal responses (feelings and thoughts) that interfere with the smooth execution of the target behavior. On the one hand, individuals have to self-motivate themselves to keep attention and effort on the task (task orientation) when immediate external reinforcers are not available, and on the other hand, they have to control the internal states that interfere with smooth execution of the task (state orientation) (R. Kanfer, 1996; Kuhl, 1985). For example, a person who decides to reduce her body weight sets for herself a series of proximal behavioral goals aimed to accomplish a more distal goal of weight reduction. However, on the way to accomplishing these behavioral goals she is likely to face numerous experiential impediments such as dysphoric mood and the interfering thoughts ("why do I need all this suffering?"). The person has to allocate attention and efforts to the task (changing her eating behavior) as well as to controlling her internal states that detract her from the task at hand.

In fact, people who attempt to self-control their behavior are faced with two motivational forces within themselves. On the one hand, they are motivated to accomplish a self-determined target behavior, and on the other hand, they are motivated to mentally control the unpleasant psychological reactions that hinder any significant behavioral changes. Mental control of aversive psychological reactions is often characterized by attempts to suppress and avoid these reactions. Unfortunately, in many instances, the more people try to control their thoughts and feelings, the stronger these thoughts and feelings become. For example, when people try not to think about a particular stimulus, they are most often unsuccessful; they find themselves thinking about the very stimulus they are trying to avoid (Wegner, 1994). Furthermore, when the motivation to reduce unpleasant feelings and dysphoric moods surpasses the motivation to accomplish a desired behavioral target, people may fail at self-controlling their behavior. People who aspire to control their eating behavior, but are highly motivated to avoid any bad feelings, are likely to fail in their dietary goals. Similarly, students who are more motivated to avoid any anxious feelings than to complete their course work may decide not to take a final examination even if they have studied for it.

It may sound paradoxical, but one of the major reasons for failures in self-control is the striving for *absolute* control over one's internal responses. When one adopts the belief that "I *must* have complete control over my anxiety before I will do something that might be anxiety arousing," then one is likely not to be able to self-control his or her anxiety. In fact, the biggest hurdle in the treatment of people who suffer from problems such as phobias, substance abuse, and eating disorders, is their lack of *acceptance* of the fact that they could never be in full control of their moods, thoughts, and behavior. By "acceptance" I mean present-centered openness to emotional and other experiences, and not resignation and passive tolerance of unpleasant experiences (Hayes et al., 1994). As is emphasized in different parts of the present exposition, openness to experience and "giving-up control," are important ingredients for success in self-control.

Most of the present day models of self-control focus on the self-motivational aspects of the self-control process. According to these models people motivate themselves by setting goals or standards that they would like to accomplish. Their desire to reduce the gap between their actual behavior and their behavioral standards is the prime motivating force for self-control (Carver & Scheier, 1996). Thus, Bandura (1996) noted that the three most important factors in the self-control process are "perceived self-efficacy to fulfill given standards, affective self-reactions to substandard performance, and readjustment of personal standards in light of the progress being made" (Bandura, 1996, p. 30). Underlying these processes are "goal-approaching" motivational forces. However, as I have indicated in this section, during one's attempts to self-control one's behavior, one may be faced with unpleasant experiences that one would like to avoid or to suppress (i.e., "to control"). When the motivation to avoid or to control these experiential reactions is stronger than the motivation to reach a desired target behavior then self-control efforts are likely to fail. On the other hand, when people are highly motivated to reach a behavioral goal and they are willing to accept certain unpleasant experiences (such as feeling tense, low mood, physical pain) that interfere with the smooth execution of a desired behavior, their success at self-control could benefit from attempts to control these experiences via "closing responses." For example, a heavy smoker who desires to quit smoking but is not willing to face the emotional tension that might be involved in self-controlling her smoking behavior would benefit by being first trained to be open and accepting of her affective experiences (i.e., experiential self-control training) and only later by specific methods on how to quit smoking (i.e., reformative self-control training). On the other hand, smokers who are genuinely accepting and open to their feelings may require mostly reformative self-control techniques (i.e., planning, setting goals, stimulus control, etc.) that most programs on smoking cessation emphasize.

The balance between task control motivation and state control motivation changes according to the problem to be treated and the stage of task acquisition. For example, in treating people who avoid specific stimuli because they are afraid of being overwhelmed by negative emotions when confronting these stimuli, the state control motivation (i.e., controlling one's fear) is usually much higher than the task control motivation (i.e., to confront the situations that have been avoided). In such cases, treatment directed at enhancing experiential self-control enables individuals to be open and accepting of their emotional reactions. It helps to reduce the state control motivation and increase task control motivation (i.e., exposure to fear-arousing situations). Yet, in other cases where the prime motivation is to acquire a new skill, task control motivation is likely to be stronger than state control motivation. For example, learning to drive on the left-hand side of the road instead of the right-hand side of the road requires reformative self-control (planning and problem-solving behavior) to control the task and redressive self-control for emotional control of the anxious feelings that arise during the performance of the new task.

The balance between task and state control motivation may also vary according to the various stages of the self-control process. At earlier stages of tasks that require behavioral changes such as dieting and smoking cessation, task control motivation may be considerably higher than state control motivation. At these early stages salient changes reinforce the individual in their task control efforts. Later on when changes are not as salient as before, individuals become disenchanted and frustrated with the process and the motivation to "feel good" rather than to "suffer" becomes stronger and may eventually lead to the abandonment of self-control efforts altogether. Furthermore, redressive self-control methods (suppression of unpleasant experience and cognitive reframing methods) may be effective at the earlier stages of overcoming negative affective states, but later on when individuals realize that they could not be in absolute control over their emotional reactions, learning to be genuinely open and accepting of their internal responses helps them to keep on task by reducing state control motivation.

To summarize, to keep the self-control process on course the task control motivation must be stronger than the state control motivation. The control of the psychological state of the person is mostly achieved through the employment of closing responses (redressive self-control methods such as cognitive transformation, distraction, etc.). However, when people are more strongly motivated to control their psychological states than to attain their behavioral goals, self-control efforts may fail. To surmount the adverse effects of excessive state control motivation, individuals must let go of mental control and be genuinely open to their present experience through the use of experiential self-control skills. The nature of these and other self-control skills will be discussed in the next section.

A SKILL PERSPECTIVE ON SELF-CONTROL

As has already been stated, because the nature of the self-control process is such that it calls for changing one's behavior against various environmental pulls, most models of self-control focus on the self-motivational aspect of the self-control process (Bandura, 1977; Carver & Scheier, 1990, 1996; Heckhausen & Schulz, 1995; Rothbaum, Weisz, and Snyder, 1982). Furthermore, research in self-control has focused more on situational variables than on individual differences and personality related variables. Without denying the importance of self-motivational factors and situational variables, it is also important to note that people differ in the extent to which they are capable of self-controlling their own behavior. Moreover, these capabilities can be learned and they are acquired through life like any other cognitive or social skill. Furthermore, as has been already discussed, people do apply their self-control skills only after they decide that a specific situation requires the use of self-control skills.

When treating clients with self-control related problems it is important to first ascertain whether or not the clients have the necessary self-control skills. If they are deficient in these skills they would benefit from a self-control training program. However, if they have the skills but fail to apply them to their problems, then therapeutic efforts should be directed at changing the cognitions and the motivation underlying the decision to self-control one's problematic behavior. Hence, a measure for assessing self-control skills is most useful in planning therapy. In addition, the selection of people for jobs that require a relatively high level of self-control skills could also benefit from an instrument that assesses self-control skills.

The assessment of self-control skills has to rely mostly on self-report. Although it is possible to test individuals on a series of behavioral tasks requiring self-control in order to evaluate their self-control skills, such an assessment procedure would be too costly and cumbersome. Furthermore, since self-control occurs mainly "in the head," one cannot be completely sure whether behavior on self-control-related tasks is indeed an indication of the use of cognitive self-control skills. Consequently, like in the assessment of other psychological traits, self-report with all its inherent flaws is still the most efficient way to assess self-control skills. Of course, the predictive validity of a self-report measure of self-control skills has to be established under conditions in which individual differences in self-control skills are expected to play a significant role.

Each of the three functions of self-control (i.e., the redressive, the reformative, and the experiential) requires somewhat different self-control skills (see Table 1). Whereas redressive self-control requires skills that are often associated with emotion and thought control, reformative self-control calls for planning and problem-solving behavior. Experiential self-control calls for a completely different set of skills, such as being accepting of one's experiences, being absorbed in, and open to, one's immediate experiences, and adopting a nonjudgmental stance toward one's affective and somatic experiences. The redressive and reformative functions of self-control are part of the closing response system because they help the individual to make sense of her experience in terms of existing constructs and plans and thus tend to close the individual from experiencing things "as they are." On the other hand, the skills associated with experiential self-control assist the individual to be as open as possible to his or her immediate experience, and thus these types of behavior are part of the opening system.

In the next sections I will discuss the assessment of individual differences in self-directed cognitive closure skills and opening-to-experience skills. Since openness to experience is not usually associated with the self-control process, more space will be devoted to experiential self-control than to redressive and reformative self-control skills.

INDIVIDUAL DIFFERENCES IN SELF-CONTROLLED COGNITIVE CLOSING SKILLS

Most theoretical models on stress and coping suggest that the most effective methods of coping with stress is via cognitive closure, i.e., making sense of stressful events that befall the person in unpredictable and uncontrollable ways. This can be seen, for example, in Kobasa's (1979) concept of "hardiness," which, according to its author, moderates the stress-illness relationship. In this conception, hardy people cope well with stress because they judge their activities as being valuable and important ("commitment"), controllable, and challenging (Orr & Westman, 1990). The evaluation and judgment of the experience are the hallmark of the closing response system. To the same category also belongs Antonovsky's (1990) "sense of coherence," a personality disposition to construe stressful experiences as comprehensible, manageable, and meaningful. Closure to experience can also be discerned in Seligman's distinction between persons with an "optimistic" explanatory style, who cope well with stress, and those with a "pessimistic" explanatory style, who cope less well (Seligman, 1990). The very possession of an explanatory style implies the evaluation of current experience on the basis of habitual ways of information processing that characterize a closing approach to experience. Scales were developed on the basis of these models to assess individual differences in the use of the respective cognitive transformational strategies.

Working within this general conceptual framework I have developed a scale that measures individual differences in self-control skills (the Self-Control Schedule, SCS; Rosenbaum, 1980b). My starting point was Meichenbaum's stress inoculation program in which he trains and instructs individuals in the use of different skills and behaviors to self-control their behavior in such a way that they could cope effectively with stressful events (Meichenbaum, 1985). The major components of the stress inoculation program are (1) self-monitoring of maladaptive thoughts, images, feelings, and behaviors (required for the initiation of the self-control process); (2) problem-solving skills (required mostly for reformative self-control); and (3) emotion regulation and other self-control skills (required mostly for redressive self-control). Meichenbaum (1977) found that persons who have acquired these skills develop a sense of "learned resourcefulness," i.e., the belief that they can effectively deal with manageable levels of stress. Consequently, I have labeled the personal repertoire of self-control skills that individuals have acquired through their life as learned resourcefulness (Rosenbaum, 1983, 1990b), and I derived items for the SCS that describe the skills learned in a stress inoculation program (for example, positive self-talk and problem-solving strategies).

More specifically, the SCS covers the following content area: (1) use of cognitions and self-instructions to cope with emotional and physiological responses, (2) application of problem-solving strategies (e.g., planning, problem definition, evaluating alternatives, and anticipation of consequences), (3) ability to delay immediate gratification, and (4) a general belief in one's ability to self-regulate internal events. These are not subscales of the SCS; they are just the content areas that were used to construct the scale. In a factor analysis performed on the SCS by Gruber and Wildman (1987), the following three factors emerged: (1) problem-focused coping (which corresponds to skills needed for reformative self-control), (2) mood and pain control (which corresponds to skills related to redressive self-control), and (3) externality (e.g., "I need outside help to get rid of some of my bad habits"), which negatively corresponds to one's general belief in one's ability to self-control. Rude (1989), in a more recent factor analysis of the SCS, found a major factor, which she has labeled "thought management," that accounted for nearly half of the total variance. This factor corresponds closely to the first content area of the SCS that is mentioned above and what I have later called "redressive self-control." The other four factors found in her study were labeled helplessness, systematic and planful approach, external control of habits, and impulsivity. The latter three factors correspond closely to "reformative self-control." Sugiwaka and Agari (1993, 1995) developed a Japanese version of the SCS that consists of 20 items drawn from the original SCS and three well-identified factors (redressive and reformative self-control as well as confidence in one's self-control abilities).

In previous publications (Rosenbaum, 1988, 1990b; in press) I have summarized most of the evidence on the validity of the SCS as a measure of learned resourcefulness (namely, of redressive and reformative self-control). There is strong evidence that highly resourceful subjects (i.e., those who score high on the SCS), in comparison to less resourceful subjects (scoring low on the SCS), cope more effectively with physical and mental stressors (Derry, Chovaz, McLachlan, & Cummings, 1993; Rosenbaum, 1980a; Rosenbaum & Palmon, 1984; Weisenberg, Wolf, Mittwoch, & Mikulincer, 1990), adhere more closely to health-promoting behavior (Carey, Carey, Carnrike, & Meisler, 1988; Katz & Singh, 1986; Leon & Rosenthal, 1984; Rosenbaum & Ben-Ari Smira, 1986), and respond better to cognitive and self-management therapies (Simmons, Lustman, Wetzel, & Murphy, 1985). In a more recent study (Najman, 1995) it has been found that highly resourceful subjects in comparison to less resourceful subjects perceived more self-control behavior in another person who faces a stressor. The findings of this study indicate that people who score high on the SCS are not only more skilled in self-control but also have a general "self-control set" that influences their perceptions of the behavior of other people.

In sum, there is ample evidence that people who are skilled in controlling their internal states via the use of cognitive self-control methods are quite effective in coping with stress and in leading a healthy style of life. Research has demonstrated that people who reframe their stressful experiences in terms of meaningful and manageable events, who explain their misfortunes in terms least damaging to their self-esteem, and who develop optimistic expectations for future events are those who adjust best to the vagaries of life. According to the present conceptualization these people respond to their immediate experiences by cognitively closing themselves from their experiences "as they are."

OPENING TO EXPERIENCE: THE OTHER SIDE OF THE COIN

Opening to experience consists of two major elements: a nonevaluative acceptance of one's experiential reactions with no attempt to deny or cognitively transform them and the ability to be fully absorbed in the immediate experience if so desired. In the humanistic/experiential approaches to therapy, *acceptance* of one's present experiences plays a central role in a healthy psychological life (Greenberg, 1994; Perls et al., 1951; Rogers, 1980). In particular, the emphasis is on acceptance of feelings as they are experienced in the immediate present. Acceptance is contrasted with avoidance and suppression of feelings. Whereas most current cognitive theories on coping with stress suggest that effective coping consists of reframing the way one interprets one's emotional reactions (in fact, encourages avoidance of one's feelings), the humanistic/experiential models suggest that the key for effective coping is to be fully aware and accepting of one's affective responses. "Change occurs when one becomes what one is, not when one tries to become what one is not" (Greenberg, 1994, p. 56). Clearly, then, there are two seemingly conflicting views of what constitutes an effective way of coping with stress. The first view encourages one to become aware and accepting of one's affective reactions with no attempt to cognitively appraise them ("opening system of responses"), whereas the second view suggests that one should engage in cognitive reappraisal of the stress and consequently one's feelings will change (the "closing system of responses"). The conception advanced in the present chapter is that effective adjustment to stress requires *both* the ability to be open and accepting of one's affective reactions the ability to cognitively transform them.

In contrast to the humanistic/experiential theories, I believe that a person needs the *experiential self-control skills*, described in Table 1, in order to learn to genuinely accept his or her feelings. Acceptance does not occur automatically under the "right" interpersonal conditions (i.e., warmth, empathy, and unconditional positive regard) as has been suggested by the humanistic theories (e.g., Rogers, 1980), but it requires certain specific learnable abilities. In fact, openness and acceptance of one's own emotional reactions, especially negative emotions such as anxiety and frustration, may be most important to one's well-being in particular at times when one is lacking social support.

The second component of openness to experience is the ability to be fully engrossed in the immediate experience. It is the capability to respond to one's experience with maximal congruence with it, without any attempt to judge or to evaluate it, whether on the basis of logical rules or existent personal constructs, and without comparison to past experiences or anticipation of the future. It is the enhancement and expansion of present experiences. For example, being absorbed in music, in a book, or in relaxation calls for this element of openness to experience. The ability to enjoy potentially pleasant experiences requires "letting go" of evaluative processes and "giving in" to the present experience. People who are prone to depression often lack this ability.

Although openness to experience appears to be at the opposite pole from closure from experience, both represent the hallmark of effective coping and adjustment. Both are the two sides of the same coin.

INDIVIDUAL DIFFERENCES IN SELF-CONTROLLED OPENING TO EXPERIENCE

As has been discussed throughout this chapter, people differ in the extent to which they have acquired self-controlled closing skills (i.e., redressive and reformative self-control) and in the extent to which they are skilled in opening skills (i.e., experiential self-control). Whereas the stress and coping literature is rich with training programs directed at helping people to cope with stress via cognitive closure techniques, there is a dearth of training programs that focus on opening skills with one notable exception: hypnotizability training.

Lynn, Rhue, and Weekes (1990), in an extensive review of the hypnotic literature, cogently argue that the performance of hypnotic responses requires "a formidable degree of mental control" (p. 171), and in my terms they require an extensive repertoire of experiential self-control skills. Lynn et al. (1990) describe how the hypnotic context promotes perceptions of involuntariness by inhibiting self-reflection and opening to experience: "In Diamonds' (1989) terms, 'letting go' begins with a conscious choice and involves an attempt to 'experience what (s)he is experiencing. Underlying this apparent passivity is an active decision to be open-to experience oneself as the experiencer or recipient of suggested effects…"(p. 173). There is an initial decision to enter the hypnotic state, behavior is goal directed, and the person is active in producing images and sensations, and in focusing attention on the immediate experience. Spanos, Lush, and Gwynn (1989) have shown how these behaviors assist the person to become fully absorbed in the hypnotic experience.

In addition, training in techniques such as relaxation (Smith, 1988), mindfulness (Marlatt, 1994; Kabat-Zinn, 1990), and a variety of "acceptance" skills (Linehan, 1994) is in fact training in the experiential self-control skills that facilitate opening to experience. For example, in relaxation exercises, clients learn how to let go of analytical processes and to focus on current experiences. Smith (1988) suggested three processes that are basic to all relaxation techniques: "*focussing*, the ability to identify, to differentiate, maintain attention on, and return attention to simple stimuli for an extended period; *passivity*, the ability to stop unnecessary goal directed and analytic activity; and *receptivity*, the ability to tolerate and accept experiences that may be uncertain, unfamiliar, or paradoxical" (p. 312). All three behaviors—focusing, passivity, and receptivity—are part of the experiential self-control repertoire.

On the basis of these programs and on the assumption that people who are capable of opening responses when they wish to make them have a rich repertoire of experiential self-control, we have developed the Experiential Self-Control Scale (E-SCS; Hefer, 1991; Rosenbaum, in press) to assess individual differences in experiential self-control. The scale is in the early stages of development and will probably undergo a number of modifications. At this stage, the E-SCS consists of 29 items, each describing a common everyday experience in which experiential self-control is likely to be called for. Most of the items refer to personal and interpersonal activities that we assume the average individual would like to fully experience, such as being at a party, having a love relationship, listening to music, reading a book, watching a movie, or taking a bath. Subjects are asked to indicate the extent to which they "allow themselves" to be fully involved in these experiences.

The internal reliability of the scale is $\alpha = .83$. Factor analysis yielded four factors: a. enjoyment of pleasant activities ("At a party with friends who know how to have fun, I allow myself to be carried along"); b. emotional expressiveness ("When I get really good news, I get so carried away by excitement that I practically sing for joy"); c. readiness to give up analytical thinking ("I very much enjoy losing my head whenever possible"); and d. focusing on the momentary experience ("Listening to music I like makes me forget my surroundings"). As expected, the E-SCS positively correlated with the Tellegen Absorption Scale (TAS; Tellegen & Atkinson, 1974), which was found to be highly correlated to hynotizability and associated with the Openness scale of the Revised Neurotic Extroversion Openness Personality Inventory (NEO-PI; Costa & McCrae, 1992; Roche & McConkey, 1990). It was not found to be correlated with Spielberger's Trait Anxiety Scale (Spielberger, Gorsuch, & Lushene, 1970) or with the Social Desirability Scale (Crowne & Marlowe, 1960). Furthermore, the E-SCS was consistently found to be orthogonal to our measure of learned resourcefulness, the SCS. It clearly assesses a different dimension of self-control than redressive and reformative self-control.

Nevertheless, both the SCS and the E-SCS were positively correlated with Burger and Cooper's (1979) Desirability of Control Scale and with King and Emmons's (1990) Emotional Expression Questionnaire and negatively related to their Ambivalence Over Emotional Expressiveness Questionnaire (AEQ). In other words, individuals who have a tendency to use self-control behavior, whether it is redressive, reformative, or experiential, are likely to express a general desire for control, be emotionally expressive, and be less ambivalent about overt emotional expression than those less inclined to self-control.

As could be expected, individuals who scored high on the E-SCS were able to get into a deeper state of relaxation (according to various physiological indices) than those who scored low on the E-SCS (Amrami, 1996). During the writing of this chapter, we are in the midst of a series of experiments in which we are investigating the relationship between opening responses to a variety of new experiences such as listening to a strange sounding piece of music or watching unusual movie clips, and scores on the E-SCS and SCS. Furthermore, in these experiments we are also testing the hypothesis that participants who do not try to cognitively evaluate the various stimuli presented to them will be more experientially involved in the experimental task and will enjoy it more in comparison to participants who try to make sense of the presentations. A recent study by Cameron Wild, Kuiken and Schopflocher (1995) has demonstrated that absorption and openness as personality traits are positively associated with experiential involvement in a work of art.

Preliminary data on the E-SCS are encouraging, though further experimental studies are required to better establish its validity as a measure of experiential self-control.

THE JOINT EFFECTS OF CLOSING AND OPENING RESPONSES ON PSYCHOLOGICAL WELL-BEING

For the promotion of physical and mental health individuals must strike a balance between openness to experience and closure from experience. This is the central proposition of the present essay. In terms of self-control skills, well-being comes, on the one hand, from the ability to accept and to be fully engaged in the momentary experience and, on the other hand, from the ability to cognitively reframe and restructure one's experiences in light of one's existing conceptual system.

To test this proposition we employed the E-SCS as a measure for opening to experience skills and the SCS as a measure for cognitive closing skills and their joint effects on coping with stress and subjective well-being. For example, in a master's thesis that was done under the supervision of the author, Agam (1995) studied the coping behavior of 49 end-stage renal disease patients in renal dialysis. The patients completed the SCS, the E-SCS, and a self-efficacy measure asking them to assess their expected ability to effectively cope with their renal disease. When separately analyzed, neither the E-SCS nor the SCS scores were correlated with self-efficacy. However, a multiple regression analysis showed that, along with the patients' age and gender, the SCS and E-SCS did *jointly* predict the patients' self-efficacy expectancies. Participants who were low on both learned resourcefulness (SCS; closing skills) and experiential self-control (E-SCS; opening skills) had the lowest self-efficacy expectancies, while those who were high on both expressed the strongest convictions that they could cope effectively with their renal disease. Those who could be open to their experiences while cognitively controlling them (that is, able to apply a closing approach when needed) had the greatest confidence in their ability to cope with their disease. In addition, it has been found in this study that participants high on both the SCS and the E-SCS reported the highest perceived quality of life, while subjects low on both reported the lowest.

King and Emmons (1990) reported that conflict over emotional expressiveness (as assessed by the AEQ) is related to measures of physical and psychological well-being. The conflict may be an outcome of the individual's efforts to control his or her emotions (Emmons, King, & Sheldon, 1992), or of the fear of losing control once emotions are openly expressed. If the latter is the cause, then people who have the cognitive-closing and experiential-opening self-control skills to manage their emotional responses can be expected to be less ambivalent about expressing their emotions. The results of a study that was run in our laboratory (Yoschpe, 1995) lend support to the latter hypothesis: Participants' scores on the SCS and E-SCS were negatively related to their scores on the AEQ and positively related to their scores on King and Emmons' (1990) Emotional Expressiveness Questionnaire. Since the SCS and the E-SCS do not correlate with one another, each of these scales shares a unique variance with the AEQ. In addition, the study found that ambivalence about emotional expressiveness mediated the effects of cognitive-closing self-control skills (SCS) and experiential-opening self-control skills (E-SCS) on participants' subjective well-being.

In our laboratory we are currently working on a new measure that simultaneously assesses both opening and closing responses to a variety of positive and negative experiences. We hope that this new scale will enable us to test in a more accurate way the proposition that both opening and closing responses contribute to effective coping and to psychological well-being.

OPENNESS AND CLOSURE AS BASIC PERSONALITY TRAITS

The centrality of the opening and closing response systems to human functioning is also illustrated in the five-factor model of personality. The five-factor model of personality provides a well-defined framework for organizing personality scales and constructs (Church, 1994; McCrae, 1989). It has been claimed that the "big five" dimensions, singly or in combination, will be found in virtually all personality instruments (McCrae & John, 1992).

Two of the five personality factors are conceptually related to the SCS and the E-SCS; the Conscientiousness (C) and the Openness to Experience (O) factors. The C factor refers to self-control as an "active process of planning, organizing, and carrying out tasks" (Costa & McCrae, 1992, p. 16; see also Digman, 1990). It consists of six facets, three of which are very similar to the SCS—sense of competence, self-discipline, and deliberation (the tendency to think before acting)—and three that describe more the endorsement of traditional norms and moral standards: orderliness, dutifulness, and achievement striving. Overall, the C factor, similar to the SCS, appears to reflect a personal inclination toward cognitive-closing responses. Indeed, the C scale of the NEO-PI was found to be positively correlated with the SCS (Marshall, Wortman, Vickers, Kusulas, & Hervig, 1994). Furthermore, like the SCS it was found to be associated with adherence to a medication regimen (Christensen & Smith, 1995), to physical fitness (Hogan, 1989), and to better health habits (Booth-Kewley & Vickers, 1994). The O scale of the NEO-PI consists of six facets that are rather loosely related (McCrae 1993–94): active imagination, aesthetic sensitivity (the ability to be deeply engrossed in music, poetry, and other works of art), attentiveness to inner feelings, preference for variety, intellectual curiosity, and independence of judgment. The first three facets measure aspects similar to those measured by the E-SCS. At this point in time, a research project is underway in our laboratory to assess among other things, if scores on these two scales are correlated.

Marshall et al. (1994) noted that C and the O factors of the five-factor model of personality have received relatively little attention in the health and coping–relevant personality research. Moreover, the prevailing tendency to separately investigate the association of each of these personality factors with health and coping–related variables rather than studying their joint effects may not be fruitful.

It is interesting to note that Bergman et al. (1993) report that in the Swedish adoption / twin study the Openness and Conscientiousness traits show moderately high heritability and little evidence of shared rearing environment effects. These findings are consistent with those of Tellegen et al. (1988), who found similar levels of heritability for scales measuring the related traits of Absorption (openness) and Control (closure).

There might also be a physiological angle to these two traits. Nadel (1992) has proposed the existence of two memory-learning systems (the "locale" and the "taxon" systems) that appear to account for the kind of behaviors that have been classified within the opening and closing systems. The locale learning system is based on one trial (immediate) learning and on storing the unique properties of an event *without categorizing it on the basis of previous learning*. Locale learning is characterized by flexibility and by the generation of spontaneous behavior. On the other hand, taxon learning is based on previous learning and on processes that involve judgmental and categorization processes. Locale learning appears to be the basis for opening responses to experience, whereas taxon learning provides the basis for cognitive-closing responses.

In contrast, in the present chapter I have depicted opening and closing self-control skills as learned skills. Yet like any other skills, some people achieve higher levels of skill proficiency than others regardless of their training history, probably because of inherited individual differences. Whether openness to experience and closing from experience are traits or skills, they constitute an essential part of human functioning.

CONCLUSIONS AND IMPLICATIONS

The opening and closing response systems represent the dialectic nature of human beings' interaction with their social and physical environment. On the one hand, people strive toward stability, predictability, equilibrium, homeostasis, and self-organization. Cognitive-closing reactions help achieve that stability by enabling individuals to interpret their primary experience in accord with their previously established conceptual system. On the other hand, since the environment is in perpetual flux, there is no such thing as permanent stability (Lewis, 1995), and the person is forever driven toward change and development. In a major way, change and development are the products of disequilibrium, heterostasis, and instability. The opening response system enables the genuine acceptance of these changes (experiences) and thus enhances the development of new behaviors. In fact, new behaviors appear spontaneously precisely when people do not expend mental effort to evaluate and judge their experiences (R. Epstein, 1991). It is the intricate interplay between openness to and cognitive closure from the ever-changing experiences that characterizes human beings' adjustment and adaptation to the vagaries of life. As has been explicated in this chapter, opening and closing responses to one's momentary experiences can be self-controlled. The term "learned resourcefulness" that has been used as a label for cognitive-closing self-control skills (Rosenbaum, 1983) should now be extended also to include experiential-opening self-control skills.

Cognitive psychotherapies have tended to emphasize the use of the cognitive-closing response system as a strategy to overcome the obstructive effects of undesirable experiential reactions such as anxiety and depression (Beck, 1976; Ellis, 1973). Clients are taught to cognitively restructure their experiences in a more functional way and develop new and more adaptive personal theories. On the other hand, there are some behavioral procedures that rely heavily on the opening response system, for example, techniques that focus on exposure to new experiences in the treatment of phobic behavior. The phobic clients who are encouraged to face anxiety-provoking situations are asked to accept their anxiety as it is without trying to "explain it away" (Marks, 1978). In humanistic/existential and Gestalt therapies (Rogers, 1980; Perls et al., 1951), openness to experience and acceptance of feelings are the most central concepts.

In recent years there is a tendency among some cognitive therapies to add to their therapeutic methods techniques that are based on the opening response system. Most notable in this trend is the work of Linehan (e.g., Linehan & Schmidt, 1995) on dialectic behavior therapy. This treatment integrates emphasis on change, typical of cognitive therapy interventions, and emphasis on openness and acceptance typical of Rogerian therapy (Linehan & Schmidt, 1995). Recent research supports the view that the addition of "opening" techniques such as relaxation, hypnosis, and mindfulness training (Kabat-Zinn, 1990) to the standard procedures of cognitive therapy substantially enhances treatment outcome (Kirsch, Montgomery, & Sapirstein, 1995; Linehan, 1994; Marlatt, 1994; Teasdale, Segal, Williams, 1995). The self-control model described in the present chapter that is based on both the cognitive-closing and the opening response systems provides the basis for integration between cognitive-behavioral and humanistic/existential therapies.

REFERENCES

Agam, S. (1995). The impact of learned resourcefulness and experiential self-control on adjustment of dialysis patients. Unpublished master's thesis. Tel Aviv: Tel Aviv University.

Amrami, E. (1996). The impact of two repertoires of self-control (learned resourcefulness and experiential self-control) and type of relaxation instructions (directive vs. nondirective) upon the relaxation response. Unpublished master's thesis. Tel Aviv: Department of Psychology, Tel Aviv University.

Antonovsky, A. (1990). Pathways leading to successful coping and health. In M. Rosenbaum (Ed.), *Learned resourcefulness: On coping skills, self-control and adaptive behavior* (pp. 31–63). New York: Springer.

Bandura, A. (1977). Self-efficacy: Toward a unifying theory of behavior change. *Psychological Review, 84*, 191–215.

Bandura, A. (1996). Failures in self-regulation: Energy depletion or selective disengagement? *Psychological Inquiry, 7*, 20–24.

Beck, A. T. (1976). *Cognitive therapy and the emotional disorders*. New York: International University Press.

Bergman, C. S., Chipuer, H. M., Plomin, R., Pedersen, N. L., McClearn, G. E., Nesselroade, J. R., Costa, P. T., & McCrae, R. (1993). Genetic and environmental effects on Openness to Experience, Agreeableness, and Conscientiousness—an adoption/twin study. *Journal of Personality, 61*, 159–179.

Bohart, C. A. (1993). Experiencing: The basis of psychotherapy. *Journal of Psychotherapy Integration, 3*, 51–67.

Booth-Kewley, S., & Vickers, R. R. (1994). Association between major domains of personality and health behavior. *Journal of Personality, 62*, 282–298.

Burger, J. M., & Cooper, H. M. (1979). The desirability of control. *Motivation and Emotion, 3*, 381–393.

Cameron Wild, T., Kuiken, D., & Schopflocher, D. (1995). The role of absorption in experiential involvement. *Journal of Personality and Social Psychology, 69*, 569–579.

Carey, M. P., Carey, K. B., Carnrike, C. L. M., & Meisler, A. W. (1988, November). Learned resourcefulness, drinking, and smoking. Paper presented at the annual meeting of the Association for the Advancement of Behavior Therapy, New York, NY.

Carver, C. S., & Scheier, M. F. (1990). Origins and functions of positive and negative affect: A control-process view. *Psychological Review, 97*, 19–35.

Carver, C. S., & Scheier, M. F. (1996). Self-regulation and its failures. *Psychological Inquiry, 7*, 32–40.

Christensen, A. J., & Smith, T. W. (1995). Personality and patient adherence: Correlates of the five-factors model in renal dialysis. *Journal of Behavioral Medicine, 18*, 305–313.

Church, A. T. (1994). Relating the Tellegen and five-factor models of personality structure. *Journal of Personality and Social Psychology, 67*, 898–909.

Costa, P. T., & McCrae, R. R. (1992). *Revised NEO Personality Inventory (NEO-PI-R) and NEO Five-Factor Inventory (NEO-FFI) professional manual*. Odessa, FL: Psychological Assessment Resource.

Crowne, D. P., & Marlowe, D. A. (1960). A new scale of social desirability independent of psychopathology. *Journal of Consulting Psychology, 66*, 547–555.

Derry, P. A., Chovaz, C. J., McLachlan, R. S., & Cummings, A. (1993). Learned resourcefulness and psychosocial adjustment following temporal lobectomy in epilepsy. *Journal of Social and Clinical Psychology, 12*, 454–470.

Diamond, M. J. (1989). The cognitive skills model: An emerging paradigm for investigating hypnotic phenomena. In N. P. Spanos & J. Chaves (Eds.), *Hypnosis: The cognitive-behavioral perspective* (pp. 380–399). New York: Prometheus Books.

Digman, J. M. (1990). Personality structure: Emergence of the five-factor model. *Annual Review of Psychology, 41*, 417–440.

Ellis, A. (1973). *Humanistic psychotherapy: The rational-emotive approach*. New York: McGraw-Hill.

Emmons, R. A., King, L. A., & Sheldon, K. (1992). Goal conflict and the self-regulation of action. In D. M. Wegner & J. W. Pennebaker (Eds.), *Handbook of mental control* (pp. 528–551). Englewood Cliffs, NJ: Prentice-Hall.

Epstein, R. (1991). Skinner, creativity, and the problems of spontaneous behavior. *Psychological Sciences, 2*, 362–370.

Epstein, S. (1994). Integration of the cognitive and the psychodynamic unconscious . *American Psychologist, 49*, 709–724.

Foreyt, J. P., & McGavin, J. K. (1988). Anorexia nervosa and bulimia. In E. J. Mash & L. G. Terdal (Eds.), *Behavioral assessment of childhood disorders* (2nd ed., pp. 776–808). New York: Guilford Press.

Greenberg, L. (1994). Acceptance in experiential therapy. In S. C. Hayes, N. S. Jacobson, V. M. Follette, & M. J. Dougher, (Eds.), *Acceptance and change: Content and context in psychotherapy* (pp. 53–67). Reno, NV: Context Press.

Gruber, V. A., & Wildman, B. G. (1987). The impact of dysmenorrhea on daily activities. *Behavior Research and Therapy, 25,* 123–128.

Harriman, P. L. (1947). *Dictionary of psychology.* New York: The Wisdom Library.

Hayes, S. C., Jacobson, N. S., Follette, V. M., & Dougher, M. J. (Eds.) (1994). *Acceptance and change: Content and context in psychotherapy.* Reno, NV: Context Press.

Heckhausen, J., & Schulz, R. (1995). A life-span theory of control. *Psychology Review, 102,* 284–304.

Hefer, C. (1991). Releasive self-control. Unpublished master's thesis. Tel-Aviv: Department of Psychology, Tel-Aviv University.

Hogan, J. (1989). Personality correlates of physical fitness. *Journal of Personality and Social Psychology, 56,* 284–288.

Kabat-Zinn, J. (1990). *Full catastrophe living.* New York: Delacorte.

Kanfer, F. H., & Gaelick-Buys, L. (1991). Self-management methods. In F. H. Kanfer, & A. P. Goldstein (Eds.), *Helping people change: A textbook of methods* (pp. 305–360). New York: Pergamon.

Kanfer, R. (1996). Self-regulatory and other no-ability determinants of skill acquisition. In P. M. Gollwitzer & J. A. Bargh (Eds.), *The psychology of action: Linking cognition and motivation to behavior* (pp. 404–423). New York: Guilford.

Katz, R. C., & Singh, N. (1986). A comparison of current smokers and self-cured quitters on Rosenbaum's Self-Control Schedule. *Addictive Behaviors, 11,* 63–65.

King, L. (1996). Who is regulating what and why? Motivational context of self-regulation. *Psychological Inquiry, 7,* 57–60.

King. L., & Emmons, R. A. (1990). Conflict over emotional expression: Psychological and physical correlates. *Journal of Personality and Social Psychology, 58,* 864–877.

Kirsch, I., Montgomery, G., & Sapirstein, G. (1995). Hypnosis as an adjunct to cognitive-behavioral psychotherapy: A meta-analysis. *Journal of Consulting and Clinical Psychology, 53,* 214–220.

Kobasa, S. C. (1979). Stressful life events, personality, and health: An inquiry into hardiness. *Journal of Personality and Social Psychology, 37,* 1–11.

Kuhl, J. (1985). Volitional mediators of cognition-behavior consistency: Self-regulatory processes and action versus state orientation. In J. Kuhl & J. Beckman (Eds.), *Action control: From cognition to behavior* (pp. 101–128). New York: Springer-Verlag.

Lazarus, R. S., & Folkman, S. (1984). *Stress, appraisals, and coping.* New York: Springer.

Leon, G. R., & Rosenthal, B. S., (1984). Prognostic indicators of success or relapse in weight reduction. *International Journal of Eating Disorders, 3,* 15–24.

Lewis, M. D. (1995). Cognition-emotion feedback and the self-organization of developmental paths. *Human Development, 38,* 71–102.

Linehan, M. M. (1994). Acceptance and change: The central dialectic in psychotherapy. In S. C. Hayes, N. S. Jacobson, V. M. Follette, & M. J. Dougher (Eds.), *Acceptance and change: Content and context in psychotherapy* (pp. 73–86). Reno, NV: Context Press.

Linehan, M. M., & Schmidt, H. (1995). The dialectics of effective treatment of borderline personality disorder. In W. O'Donohue & L. Krasner, *Theories of behavior therapy: Exploring behavior change* (pp. 553–584). Washington, DC: American Psychological Association.

Lynn, S. J., Rhue, J. W., & Weekes, J. R. (1990). Hypnotic involuntariness: A social cognitive analysis. *Psychological Review, 97,* 169–184.

Mahrer, A. R. (1989). *Experiential psychotherapy: Basic practice.* Ottawa: University of Ottawa Press.

Marks, I. M. (1978). *Living with fear.* New York: McGraw-Hill.

Marlatt, G. C. (1994). Addiction, mindfulness, and acceptance. In S. C. Hayes, N. S. Jacobson, V. M. Follette, & M. J. Dougher (Eds.), *Acceptance and change: Content and context in psychotherapy* (pp. 175–197). Reno, NV: Context Press.

Marshall, G. N., Wortman, C. B., Vickers, R. R., Kusulas, J. W., & Hervig, L. K. (1995). The five-factor model of personality as a framework for personality-health research. *Journal of Personality and Social Psychology, 67*, 278–286.

McCrae, R. R. (1989). Why I advocate the five-factor model: Joint factor analysis of the NEO-PI with other instruments. In D. M. Buss & N. Cantor (Eds.), *Personality psychology: Recent trends and emerging directions* (pp. 237–245). New York: Springer-Verlag.

McCrae, R. R. (1993–94). Openness to experience as a basic dimension of personality. *Imagination, Cognition and Personality, 13*, 39–55.

McCrae, R. R., & John, O. P. (1992). An introduction to the five-factor model and its applications. *Journal of Personality, 60*, 175–215.

Meichenbaum, D. (1977). *Cognitive-behavior modification: An integrative approach*. New York: Plenum.

Meichenbaum, D. (1985). *Stress inoculation training*. New York: Pergamon Press.

Nadel, L. (1992). Multiple memory systems: What and why. *Journal of Cognitive Neuroscience, 4*, 179–188.

Najman, C. R. (1995). Learned resourcefulness, cognitive schema, and schema relevant information processing. Unpublished master's thesis. Department of Psychology, Tel Aviv University.

Orr, E., & Westman, M. (1990). Does hardiness moderate stress, and how?: A review. In M. Rosenbaum (Ed.), *Learned resourcefulness: On coping skills, self-control and adaptive behavior* (pp. 64–94). New York: Springer.

Perls, F., Hefferline, R. F., & Goodman, P. (1951). *Gestalt therapy*. New York: Dell Publishing.

Roche, S. M., & McConkey, K. M. (1990). Absorption: Nature, assessment, and correlates. *Journal of Personality and Social Psychology, 59*, 91–101.

Rogers, C. R. (1980). *A way of being*. Boston: Houghton Mifflin.

Rosenbaum, M. (1980a). Individual differences in self-control behaviors and tolerance of painful stimulation. *Journal of Abnormal Psychology, 89*, 581–590.

Rosenbaum, M. (1980b). A schedule for assessing self-control behaviors: Preliminary findings. *Behavior Therapy, 11*, 109–121.

Rosenbaum, M. (1983). Learned resourcefulness as a behavioral repertoire for the self-regulation of internal events: Issues and speculations. In M. Rosenbaum, C. M. Franks, & Y. Jaffe (Eds.), *Perspectives on behavior therapy in the eighties* (pp. 54–73). New York: Springer.

Rosenbaum, M. (1988). Learned resourcefulness, stress, and self-regulation, In S. Fisher & J. Reason (Eds.), *Handbook of life stress, cognition and health* (pp. 483–496). Chichester, UK: John Wiley & Son.

Rosenbaum, M. (1990a). A model for research on self-regulation: Reducing the schism between behaviorism and general psychology. In G. H. Eifert & I. M. Evans (Eds.), *Unifying behavior therapy: Contribution of Paradigmatic Behaviorism* (pp. 126–149). New York: Springer.

Rosenbaum, M. (1990b). The role of learned resourcefulness in self-control of health behavior. In M. Rosenbaum (Ed.), *Learned resourcefulness: On coping skills, self-control and adaptive behavior* (pp. 3–30). New York: Springer.

Rosenbaum, M. (1993). The three functions of self-control behavior: Redressive, reformative and experiential. *Work & Stress, 7*, 33–46.

Rosenbaum, M. (in press). The self-regulation of experience: Openness and construction. In P. Dewe, T. Cox, & A. M. Leiter (Eds.), *Coping and health in organizations*. London: Taylor & Francis.

Rosenbaum, M., & Ben-Ari Smira (1986). Cognitive and personality factors in the delay of immediate gratification of hemodialysis patients. *Journal of Personality and Social Psychology, 51,* 357–364.

Rosenbaum, M., & Palmon, N. (1984). Helplessness and resourcefulness in coping with epilepsy. *Journal of Consulting and Clinical Psychology, 52,* 244–253.

Rothbaum, F. M., Weisz, J. R., & Snyder, S. S. (1982). Changing the world and changing the self: A two-process model of perceived control. *Journal of Personality and Social Psychology, 42,* 5–37.

Rude, S. S. (1989). Dimensions of self-control in a sample of depressed women. *Cognitive Therapy and Research, 13,* 363–375.

Seligman, M. E. P. (1990). *Learned optimism.* New York: Pocket Books.

Simmons, A. D., Lustman, P. J., Wetzel, R. D., & Murphy, G. E. (1985). Predicting response to cognitive therapy : The role of learned resourcefulness. *Cognitive Therapy & Research, 9,* 79–90.

Smith, J. C. (1988). Steps toward a cognitive-behavioral model of relaxation. *Biofeedback and Self-Regulation, 13,* 307–329.

Spanos, N. P., Lush, N. I., & Gwynn, M. I. (1989). Cognitive skill-training enhancement of hypnotizability generalization effects and trance logic reasoning. *Journal of Personality and Social Psychology, 56,* 795–804.

Spielberger, C. D., Gorsuch , R. L., & Lushene, R. E. (1970). *Manual for the State-Trait Anxiety Inventory.* Palo Alto, CA: Consulting Psychologists Press.

Sugiwaka, H., & Agari, I. (1993). Two kinds of self-control as effective stress-management techniques: Combination of redressive and reformative functions. Presented at the International Congress of Health Psychology, Tokyo, Japan.

Sugiwaka, H., & Agari, I. (1995). The effects of controllability and predictability as situational factors on two types of self-control. Presented at the World Congress of Behavioral and Cognitive Therapies, Copenhagen, Denmark.

Teasdale, J. D., Segal, Z., & Williams, M. J. (1995). How does cognitive therapy prevent relapse and why should attentional control (mindfulness) training help? *Behavior Research and Therapy, 33,* 25–39.

Tellegen, A., & Atkinson, G. (1974). Openness to absorbing and self-altering experiences ("absorption"), a trait related to hypnotic susceptibility. *Journal of Abnormal Psychology, 83,* 268–277.

Tellegen, A., Lykken, D. T., Bouchard, T. J., Wilcox, K. J., Segal, N. L., & Rich, S. (1988). Personality similarity in twins reared apart and together. *Journal of Personality and Social Psychology, 54,* 1031–1039.

Wegner, D. M. (1994). Ironic processes of mental control. *Psychological Review, 101,* 34–52.

Weisenberg, M., Wolf, Y., Mittwoch, T., & Mikulincer, M. (1990). Learned resourcefulness and perceived control of pain: A preliminary examination of construct validity. *Journal of Research in Personality, 24,* 101–110.

Yoschpe, O. (1995). The impact of learned resourcefulness and experiential self-control on subjective well-being via their impact on ambivalence about emotional expression. Unpublished master's thesis. Tel Aviv: Department of Psychology, Tel Aviv University.

CHAPTER 4

A TERROR MANAGEMENT PERSPECTIVE ON THE PSYCHOLOGY OF CONTROL

CONTROLLING THE UNCONTROLLABLE

TOM PYSZCZYNSKI, JEFF GREENBERG, AND SHELDON SOLOMON

INTRODUCTION

Although humans share many features with other animals, the system through which they control their behavior is radically different from that found in any other species. Rather than relying entirely on genetically endowed, fixed response patterns and simple learned responses to environmental stimuli, humans exert a measure of control over their *own* behavior through a complex system of meanings and values that evolved over the millennia to provide a measure of flexibility and adaptability in human affairs that far surpasses that found in any other life-forms. Although the human system of self-regulation is constructed upon the simpler systems by which the behavior of other species is regulated, only humans use a linguistically based concept of *self* as the focal point for cognitive, behavioral,

TOM PYSZCZYNSKI • Department of Psychology, University of Colorado, Colorado Springs, Colorado 80933-7150. E-mail: tpyszczy@brain.uccs.edu JEFF GREENBERG • Department of Psychology, University of Arizona Tuscon, Arizona 85721. SHELDON SOLOMON • Department of Psychology, Skidmore College, Saratoga Springs, New York 12866.

Personal Control in Action, edited by Kofta et al., Plenum Press, New York, 1998.

and affective control—which is effected and affected by focusing attention on this symbolic self. Because a substantial proportion of human activity is driven by this abstract linguistic self, we transcend the purely physical realm in which all other species reside and enter a different plane of subjective existence.

The purpose of this chapter is to explore the implications of our species' use of an abstract conception of self to regulate behavior for understanding the psychology of control. Toward this end, we will propose that (1) an abstract linguistic concept of self evolved to provide a more flexible form of behavioral control, enabling our species to adapt to and prosper in widely varying and rapidly changing environments; (2) people seek to perceive themselves as in control of their lives, and consequently attempt to exert control in whatever domains in which they have invested their egos, to enhance their self-esteem because self-esteem provides an illusion of magical power over the ultimate realities of life and death—matters over which we in fact have little or no control; (3) the pursuit of mastery or the enhancement of individual capacities is rooted in an intrinsic self-expansion motivational system that produces positive affect when one's capacities are maximally engaged by an activity; (4) this self-expansion system also provides the impetus for the creative integration of external influences with preexisting internal psychological structures, thus providing the potential for the self-creation of a semiautonomous self; and, (5) the dialectical operation of the defensive and expansive motive systems gives rise to a basic human paradox: Whereas creative integrative activity requires successful control of deeply rooted fears, successful control of deeply rooted fears is typically achieved through slavish conformity to cultural dictates and values; consequently, human existence entails a precarious balance between the control of existential terror and the free expression of individual creativity.

A CYBERNETIC MODEL OF SELF-CONTROL

We begin our discussion of the unique system through which humans regulate their behavior with a brief overview of a model of the cybernetic system of control through which all self-regulatory systems operate. Although a variety of models of this process have been proposed over the past 30 years or so (cf. Miller, Gallanter, & Pribram, 1960; Powers, 1978), we will focus on Carver and Scheier's (1981; Carver, 1979) cybernetic model of self-regulation, because it provides the clearest explication of a role for the abstract conception of self in the process of behavioral control.

From this perspective, systems can be said to be self-regulating to the extent that the behavior of the system is adjusted to meet the changing demands of the environment. This is accomplished by the integration of a *comparator* process, which compares the current state of the system with an internally or externally supplied standard, and an *operate* process, through which action of some sort is taken to reduce any discrepancies between current state and standard that are detected by the comparator process. The operation of a system of this sort implies no need for consciousness, volition, or free will. Indeed, Carver and Scheier use the example of a mechanical thermostat, which compares current temperature with an externally supplied standard and then engages either a heating or air-conditioning mechanism to reduce detected discrepancies, as a simple example of just such a system. Clearly, there is no need to impute consciousness to such a mechanism, but it is just as clear that such a mechanism does indeed exert some measure of control over its own functioning.

Regardless of whether one is trying to explain the changing of potassium levels across a cell's membrane, the actions of a predator hunting its prey, or the purposeful behavior of a student pursuing a medical degree, this concept of a negative feedback loop can be used as the model upon which all self-regulating systems are based. From simple reflex actions to complex planned behavior sequences, self-regulation is achieved by comparing current state with relevant standards and then adjusting behavior to bring current state in line with these standards. All systems in all living things—including humans—are thought to self-regulate by means of this same basic blueprint. How then does this square with our claim that the system through which human behavior is controlled is *radically* different from that found in any other species?

The Nature of Self

Although humans share with all other living things the basic negative feedback loop as the mechanism for adjusting behavior to achieve their goals, the flexibility of this process is increased exponentially by the sophisticated cognitive abilities that have evolved in us over the eons, and the potential for awareness and abstraction to which these abilities give rise. As a great deal of theory and research suggests (for reviews, see Greenberg, Pyszczynski, & Solomon, 1986; Pyszczynski, Greenberg, & Solomon, 1997), much human behavior is oriented toward the pursuit of a particular abstract conception of who one is, in service of the goal of maintaining a positive self-image. A large body of theory and research also suggests that the self-regulatory activities of the human individual are greatly intensified when attention is directed toward this abstract conception of self (cf. Scheier & Carver, 1988). As Duval and Wicklund (1972) initially proposed, focusing attention on the self sets in motion a self-evaluative process by which one's current perception of self is compared with whatever standard for that dimension is currently salient, and, if a discrepancy is detected, behavior is engaged to bring the current state in line with that standard. A large body of research has supported this analysis of the role of self-focused attention in human self-regulatory behavior (for reviews, see Gibbons, 1990; Pyszczynski, Greenberg, Hamilton, & Becker, 1991; Scheier & Carver, 1988). This abstract conception of self provides guidelines for human action, makes the willful pursuit of long-term goals possible, and, in general, gives human behavior coherence over space and time. Rather than responding only to the immediate demands of the environment and current levels of internal stimulation, the individual can be oriented toward abstract conceptions, values, and standards of self.

Furthermore, as Rank (1932/1989), Deci and Ryan (1991), and many others have argued, the individual is able to creatively abstract elements from a wide range of socializing influences and carve out his or her own unique identity or conception of who he or she is and desires to be. Thus, within the limits set by one's genetic endowment and experience, each individual has the potential to create himself or herself by imaginatively combining diverse elements from the panoply of socializing influences to which he or she is exposed, and integrating these influences with previously assimilated and accommodated past experiences. This capacity to regulate our own behavior toward the pursuit of abstract standards and conceptions that we ourselves have creatively integrated from a diverse array of external inputs gives human behavior its free, self-determined flavor.

This is not to say that human behavior is free or undetermined in any absolute sense. Like all other species, human action is determined by a complex set of psychological processes through which internal regulatory systems take in information from the environment and transform that information into specific responses to maximize positive outcomes and minimize negative outcomes. What is different among humans is that many of the outcomes that humans seek entail meeting abstract standards of value that are (to varying degrees) creatively derived by each individual from humanly created cultural conceptions of reality.

From the standpoint of Carver and Scheier's model, this abstract conception of self is tied to increasingly concrete subgoals, and this hierarchical organization of subgoals links the individual's abstract concept of an ideal self to more specific identities, goals through which these identities can be satisfied, strategies through which these goals can be reached, actions through which these strategies can be put in motion, and increasingly concrete behavior segments, and, ultimately, changes in body chemistry through which these actions are performed. In other words, this hierarchical organization of standards and means of meeting these standards enables the individual to transform abstract identity goals into concrete action. It is this capacity to link abstract linguistic representations of an idealized version of self to concrete action that gives human behavior both its coherence and its flexibility. And it is the capacity to form an abstract conception of self that makes this coherence and flexibility possible.

This abstract conception of self is what William James referred to as the "me," or the self as known. It is the internal representation of who one is that self-theorists for the past century have referred to as the self-concept, self-schema, or self-representation. It is the individual's own conception of who he or she is, an internal *representation* of that person, rather than the person itself. In contrast, James's concept of the "I," or self as knower or agent, can be thought of as the individual's entire hierarchical system of standards and behavioral options for meeting these standards. The stream of consciousness that James also sometimes referred to as the "I" can be thought of as an emergent property of this hierarchical system of self-control. In this sense, the "I" uses the "me" as a vehicle for the control and regulation of it's own behavior.

A DUAL MOTIVE APPROACH TO THE PURSUIT OF MASTERY AND CONTROL

Over the past 20 years or so, a variety of contemporary theorists and researchers have argued that, beyond the specific goals that the individual may be motivated to achieve, such as acquiring food, career advancement, or social support, the exercise of control can, in and of itself, be rewarding, and a loss or lack of control can be severely detrimental (e.g., Glass & Singer, 1972; Langer & Rodin, 1976; Seligman, 1975). It has been argued that a sense of control over one's world is an essential ingredient to good mental health, and that a lack of such perceived control can be a precursor to depression, anxiety, suicide, physical illness, and even death. In the following sections, we consider this notion of a control motive from the perspective of terror management theory, and present a model of the psychology of control that makes a critical distinction between the exercise of control in the realm of the controllable and the exercise of control in the realm of the uncontrollable. The implications of this model will then be considered.

The Role of Anxiety in the Exercise of Self-Regulation and Control

The cybernetic model of self-control conceptualizes control as being achieved by engaging in behavior to reduce discrepancies between current and desired states. In other words, the exercise of self-control is essentially a negatively reinforced behavior pattern, in which behavior is engaged to reduce detected negative self-standard discrepancies. Although Carver and Scheier (1981, 1990) explicitly eschew any role for negative affect in the instigation of such discrepancy-reducing behavior, the operation of a negative feedback loop is nonetheless a process of negative reinforcement, because the reinforcement here entails the elimination of a current environmental state. Note that Skinner's (1938) analysis of negative reinforcement also viewed subjectively experienced affect as playing an unimportant role in this process.[1]

Up to this point, the model of control that we have been discussing provides no special status for the *perception* of control. Self-regulating systems operate to reduce discrepancies between current states and salient reference values, and although the pursuit of minimal discrepancies between current states and standards propels the execution of instrumental actions to achieve particular end states, the attainment of control over important outcomes is not in and of itself a goal that is sought. However, Carver and Scheier pointed out that the attainment of control over internal and external events can be a standard or reference value within the system that the system then operates to meet. In other words, at a higher level of abstraction, the individual can monitor the relationship between his or her behavior and outcomes, and work hard to insure that a high level of contingency between behavior and outcomes is maintained. Carver and Scheier (1990) argued that it is at this secondary level of control that affect is aroused and that this affect plays a crucial role in disengagement from unattainable goals.

In other words, the attainment of control can be a value in and of itself, and individuals can achieve a sense of personal value by maintaining the perception that they are in control. Note that the psychologically active, self-esteem-providing ingredient here is the *perception* of control rather than the actual *attainment* or exercise of control. Carver and Scheier have suggested that the pursuit of a sense of personal value may be the superordinate goal in the hierarchy of standards through which humans regulate their behavior. This perception of personal value or self-esteem may be what ties together the diverse goals, roles, attributes, and competencies that people pursue throughout their lives. But why do people need to perceive themselves as valuable?

The Birth of Terror

An unfortunate by-product of the complex intellectual abilities that make this flexible and efficient form of self-regulation possible is the awareness of the finitude of human existence. Because of our intelligence, we are aware that death is inevitable and can come at any time for any number of reasons. Terror management theory (Greenberg et al., 1986;

Greenberg, Solomon, & Pyszczynski, 1997; Pyszczynski et al., 1997; Solomon, Greenberg, & Pyszczynski, 1991a) posits that this awareness of the inevitability of death in an animal instinctively programmed for self-preservation creates the potential for paralyzing terror. The evolving human species used the same sophisticated intellectual abilities that gave rise to the problem of terror to provide a partial solution to this problem, through the creation of cultural worldviews, or benign conceptions of reality, that give human life meaning, stability, permanence, value, and perhaps most importantly, some means of transcending death. Cultural worldviews manage the potential for terror by promising either *literal immortality*, the belief that life continues indefinitely after one's physical death (e.g., heaven, nirvana), or *symbolic immortality*, the feeling that one is part of something larger, more powerful, and longer-lasting than oneself, such as the family, nation, or corporation. As the awareness of the inevitability of death arose in the human species, the potential for terror it created put a press on evolving cultural conceptions of reality such that any worldview that was to be widely accepted, and thus survive, needed to provide some means of controlling this terror.

In other words, the existence of a self, and all of the cognitive capacities that this implies, creates some unique problems for the human species, most importantly, awareness of the inevitability of death. The human species "solved" the problem of death through the creation of (1) culture, a shared theory of reality that gives life meaning and creates the potential for individuals to have value, and (2) self-esteem, which is achieved by living up to the standards of value that one's culture prescribes. People are motivated to pursue self-esteem and faith in their cultural worldviews because of the vital role that these two structures play in controlling deeply rooted fears concerning human vulnerability and mortality.

Although self-esteem and faith in one's cultural worldview do not bear on the inevitability of death in any logical way, these psychological structures shield the individual from the abject terror that awareness of their inevitable fate can produce. These structures serve their function by (1) separating humans from the rest of the material world and (2) offering the possibility of literal or symbolic death transcendence, or both, to those who meet the cultural standards of value (for discussion of various modes of death transcendence offered by cultures throughout the world, see Becker, 1973; Lifton, 1983; Rank, 1936/1978; Yalom, 1980). This symbolic "magical" means of controlling uncontrollable outcomes contrasts sharply with more rationally based control strategies that might actually delay the occurrence of the dreaded event (e.g., maintaining a low-fat diet, exercise, quitting smoking, etc.). Whereas the symbolic terror management control strategies address the implicit knowledge of the inevitability of death, the more rational direct control strategies merely convince one that this inevitability can be temporarily forestalled. Thus from the perspective of terror management theory, people live most of their lives in a humanly created world of death-denying symbols, with much of their behavior oriented toward maintaining a consistent and benevolent conception of reality and a positive conception of themselves to protect themselves from the deeply rooted anxiety inherent in the human condition.

A broad range of evidence is consistent with this perspective (for a recent review, see Greenberg et al., 1997). Research has shown that increasing self-esteem or faith in the cultural worldview makes one less prone to subjectively experienced anxiety, physiological arousal, or death-denying defensive distortions (e.g., Greenberg, Pyszczynski, et al., 1993; Greenberg, Solomon, et al., 1992). In addition, over 50 separate studies conducted in five different countries have shown that reminding people of their mortality increases their need for the protection provided by their cultural worldviews and thus leads to more positive reactions to entities that support their worldviews and more negative reactions to entities that threaten their worldviews. Specifically, mortality salience has been shown to lead to (1) enhanced positive evaluations of those who support the worldview and enhanced negative evaluations of those who challenge it (e.g., Greenberg, Pyszczynski, et al., 1990; Greenberg, Pyszczynski, Solomon, Simon, & Breus, 1994), (2) harsher evaluations of moral transgressors (e.g., Florian & Mikulincer, 1994; Ocshmann & Reichelt, 1994; Rosenblatt, Greenberg, Solomon, Pyszczynski, & Lyons, 1989), (3) increased preference for those who share one's religious beliefs over those with divergent beliefs (Greenberg, Pyszczynski, et al., 1990), (4) increased in-group bias in the minimal group situation if group assignment is believed to be based on some meaningful criterion (Harmon-Jones, Greenberg, Solomon, & Simon, 1995), and (5) decreased aggression toward those who support the worldview and increased aggression toward those who threaten it (McGregor, Lieberman, et al., in press). Mortality salience has also been shown to lead to (6) increased tendencies to behave in accord with the standards of the cultural worldview (e.g., Greenberg, Simon, Pyszczynski, Solomon, & Chatel, 1992), (7) greater stress and difficulty behaving in ways that violate such standards (Greenberg, Porteus, Simon, Solomon, & Pyszczynski, 1995), (8) increased optimal distinctiveness strivings (Simon, Greenberg, Clement, Pyszczynski, Arndt., & Solomon, 1997), (9) increased perceptions of social consensus for socially important attitudes among those who hold minority positions (Pyszczynski, Wicklund, et al., 1996), (10) increased value placed on prosocial behavior (Pyszczynski, Schimel, et al., in preparation), and (11) increased avoidance of self-focused attention (Arndt, Greenberg, Solomon, & Pyszczynski, in press). We have also found that mortality salience effects are unique to thoughts of death (Greenberg, Simon, et al., 1995), are minimal among individuals with high levels of self-esteem (Harmon-Jones, Simon, et al., 1997) and stronger among mildly depressed subjects (Simon, et al., 1996), and occur only when death is highly accessible but not in conscious awareness (Arndt et al., 1997; Greenberg, Pyszczynski, et al., 1994). The overall picture that is emerging is that self-esteem and faith in the cultural worldview function to protect us from deeply rooted, largely unconscious fears concerning death and vulnerability, and that a significant portion of human behavior occurs at least in part in the service of terror management concerns.

Terror management theory thus posits that from very early on in our history as a species, humans used their advanced intellectual abilities to manage basic fears concerning life and death. From very early on in the development of culture, belief systems were selected for that provided means of protecting us from that which we fear. And from very early on in the history of our species use of an abstract linguistic conception of self as a vehicle for the control of its behavior, these abstract conceptions were used to provide a magical means to control that which is actually completely beyond our control. We are proposing then, that part of the reason that people strive for control over the various events in their lives *is the feeling of personal value that such control provides, and that this sense of personal value functions to provide a more global, magical sense of control over that which we, in fact, have no control.*

Direct and Symbolic Means of Control

The terror management analysis suggests that people often seek comfortable views of self and the world rather than accurate ones; in contrast, other theorists have argued that people strive for an accurate understanding of the world. In fact, this tension between the needs for accurate and comforting conceptions of reality has been the grist for a great deal of debate among theorists of social motivation: Do people seek accurate, consistent, or pleasing conceptions of themselves and the world in which they live (e.g., Swann, 1987; Taylor & Brown, 1988). This is related to the question of whether people actively strive to change the external reality of the environment in which they behave, or work to alter their internal perceptions and beliefs so as to find an optimal accommodation to the realities of the universe—the distinction between primary and secondary control. We agree with Rothbaum, Weisz, and Snyder's (1982) very sensible suggestion that people seek both. Some individuals and some cultures lean more toward one strategy than the other, and some situations call more for one than the other, but by and large, both of these control orientations are necessary for successful adaptation to the realities of the human condition.

Terror management theory makes a similar distinction between *direct* and *symbolic* means of self-preservation. We argue that the instinctive desire for self-preservation functions as *a* (not necessarily *the*) master motive from which a great many other human needs and desires are ultimately derived (for a more thorough presentation of this argument, see Pyszczynski et al., 1997). From an evolutionary perspective, an instinctive desire for continued existence must have arisen very early in the history of life because of its very obvious value for furthering the survival of the individual, and thus the perpetuation of that individual's genes into future generations. This very primitive attraction to life can be thought of as a prime directive toward which many of the biological systems of the body are oriented. By maintaining appropriate balance within internal systems controlling levels of oxygen, sugar, and so on, these systems all ultimately function to keep the organism alive. Similarly, by creating desires for food, water, warmth, etc., these systems motivate instrumental behavior that serves the same function. Thus direct means of self-preservation function to maintain life itself, and motivate behavior that keeps the organism alive.

Symbolic means of self-preservation, on the other hand, manage the potential for abject terror that is created by the human awareness of the inevitability and unpredictable nature of death. Rather than functioning to keep the biological systems of the body operating in a smooth and effective manner, these purely psychological motives function to control the havoc that awareness of the realities of the human condition create for our species. These are the abstract conceptions of self and world that we refer to as the dual components of the human cultural anxiety-buffer, which function to make it possible for humans to face life with something approaching equanimity.

Terror management theory posits that people deal with the problem of death by employing two distinct modes of defense: *direct*, rational, threat-focused defenses, which function to reduce the individual's perception of his or her vulnerability to life-threatening conditions, and thus push the problem of death into the vague and distant future; and *symbolic*, cultural defenses, which embed the individual as a valuable part of an eternal conception of reality that is bigger, stronger, and more enduring than any individual. Although both modes of defense help the individual cope with the problem of human vulnerability and mortality, they do so in very different ways, and have very different implications for the psychology of control. Research has shown that whereas direct threat-focused defenses are put into motion immediately after a threatening event, while the threatening material is still in conscious focal attention, symbolic terror management defenses emerge only after a delay and distraction, when the threatening material is highly accessible but outside of current focal attention (e.g., Arndt et al., 1997; Greenberg et al., 1993, 1996). For example, in one recent study (Greenberg et al., 1996), we found that whereas immediately after a mortality salience induction subjects denied their vulnerability to an early death but did not show exaggerated responses to others who challenged their cultural worldviews, after a delay and distraction they did not deny their vulnerability to an early death but did show exaggerated responses to those who challenged their worldviews.

Controlling the Uncontrollable

Terror management theory posits that people control the uncontrollable by living their lives within the context of a humanly created cultural conception of reality that enables them to deny or at least temporally escape confrontation with the inevitable. By investing in a cultural worldview, we are able to carry on with our lives with minimal anxiety, *as if* life can and will go on forever. We are able to escape—at least temporarily—the tremendous burden that awareness of our inevitable fate would otherwise produce. Of course, investing in a cultural cosmology and living the cultural drama do not really alter the laws by which the universe operates. Presumably there is an external reality that exists independently of our conception of it. This is precisely why Alfred Adler argued that *all* human conceptions of reality are "convenient fictions," and why Ernest Becker referred to culture and character as "vital lies." Our conceptions of ourselves and the world in which we live serve the vital human function of enabling us to navigate the vicissitudes of life with minimal anxiety. Although an accurate conception of reality that comes as close as possible to a one-to-one correspondence with actual physical reality certainly would have many advantages, and is no doubt highly sought after in some circumstances (cf. Kruglanski, 1980; Pyszczynski & Greenberg, 1987; Swann, 1984), there are clearly many other forces operating on our quest to understand our world that lead us to embrace comforting but inaccurate conceptions.

The terror management analysis of the need for self-esteem implies that, under most circumstances, people will be highly motivated to believe that they have control, even when in fact their behaviors bear little or no relation to the outcomes they receive. Demonstrations of a robust illusion of control in work by Langer (1975) and Wortman (1975) document this strong desire for control; Alloy and Abramson's (1979) demonstration that depressed people, who often appear to have lost their desire for self-esteem, seem to lose this illusion of control is also consistent with our analysis. The foregoing analysis also suggests that one source of individual differences in the desire or need for control (see Burger, 1992) may be the extent to which the individual has been socialized to consider being in control as a necessary precursor to personal worth.

The view of perceived control as a pathway to self-esteem also implies that either a loss of control in a domain in which one previously had control, or the absence of control in a domain in which one has set control as a standard of personal value, should be aversive, produce anxiety, and lead to compensatory behaviors aimed at restoring the security provided by a positive self-image. Consistent with this analysis, Glass and Singer (1972) have shown that individuals find uncontrollable outcomes to be especially aversive, stressful, and anxiety provoking. Conversely, our analysis implies that the loss or absence of control in a domain in which control is unexpected or difficult, or in which one has not set the perception of control as a standard of personal worth, should not be particularly upsetting. Consistent with this reasoning, Solomon, Holmes, and McCaul (1980) demonstrated that subjects expecting to receive a series of painful electric shocks were less aroused (physiologically and self-reported affect) when they had no control over the shocks than another group of subjects for whom control of the shocks was possible but difficult to exert. Indeed, people sometimes find a lack of control pleasant or desirable when such an absence of control is an explicit choice, as in the case of alcohol and drug intoxication, group activities, amusement park rides, etc.

The literature on self-serving attributions is also consistent with the idea that people want to perceive themselves as in control of what happens to them only to the extent that such control has positive implications for their self-esteem. Literally hundreds of studies have shown a ubiquitous tendency to deny responsibility for failure and other negative outcomes (for a review, see Zuckerman, 1979). By denying responsibility, the individual essentially denies that he or she had any control of the outcome. Such after-the-fact denial of control is especially likely to occur when the outcome is high in ego relevance. Interestingly, when people fear failure on an ego-involving task, they sometimes will actively take steps to reduce their control over such outcomes so as to make it easier for them to later deny responsibility for the feared failure (e.g., Berglas & Jones, 1978). For example, people may consume alcohol or drugs, choose to hear distracting music, or seek various other self-handicaps to absolve themselves from responsibility. More generally, as Fromm (1941/1969) and more recently, Baumeister (1991) have argued, there may be a wide variety of activities that people enjoy in part because they provide an escape from the burden of responsibility that the freedom of individuality and being in control entails.

To the extent that the perception of control serves a defensive terror management function, it follows that loss of control in an area where control is expected would lead to efforts to restore that control, or compensatory efforts to reexert one's control in other domains. Research stemming from Brehm's (1966) reactance theory shows that threats to freedom increase one's desire to reassert that freedom only to the extent that the individual expected freedom in that domain in the first place (see Brehm & Brehm, 1980; Wortman & Brehm, 1975). More recently, Brehm, Wright, and colleagues (e.g., Brehm, Wright, Solomon, Silka, & Greenberg, 1983) have shown that the motivation to obtain or avoid an outcome increases as the difficulty of achieving this goal increases. Pittman and colleagues (e.g., Pittman & Pittman, 1980) have demonstrated compensatory increases in control motivation by showing increased epistemic activity in response to losses of control in domains unrelated to the loss of control.

In sum, to the extent that a perception of self as in control of important outcomes is central to one's perception of oneself as valuable, then losses of perceived control should have effects similar to any other type of threat to self-esteem, and should instigate direct and compensatory efforts to cope with such threats. It seems clear, then, that at least part of the motivation to perceive oneself as in control is rooted in the implications of such perceptions of control for one's feelings of personal value. And as we have argued above, this sense of personal value provides a magical means of controlling that which is completely beyond our control—the fact that we will someday die and that our death could come at any time in any number of none-too-pleasant ways.

How Does It Work?

What is it about perceiving oneself as valuable that provides a sense of control over the uncontrollable? Terror management theory posits that self-esteem acquires its anxiety-buffering properties early in life as a result of the contingencies between safety and personal value that we learn through our interactions with parents and primary caregivers. From early on, we come to associate safety, comfort, need fulfillment, and life itself with the love and approval provided by our parents. As our capacities for control over our behavior increase, our parents gradually increase their demands for what sorts of behavior on our part qualify for this love and protection. Fairly soon, we learn that good behavior—that is, behavior that meets the parentally transmitted cultural standards of value—is associated with high levels of love and protection and that bad behavior—that is, behavior that violates the parentally transmitted cultural standards of value—is associated with a reduction or absence of parental love and protection. This primitive contingency between personal value and safety is then reinforced throughout life through a myriad of cultural teachings in which the virtuous are rewarded and the evil are punished, ultimately culminating in an unconscious assumption that the world is a just place where good things happen to good people and bad things happen to bad people (Lerner, Miller, & Holmes, 1976). Thus we learn that by being valuable members of a meaningful universe, we can be spared that which we fear.

We are suggesting, then, that self-esteem and a conception of the universe as a just and meaningful place work together to provide protection from deeply rooted fears. Because of their need for this protection, people are highly motivated to maintain faith in both their personal value and the validity of their cultural worldviews. By striving to be a valuable contributor to a meaningful universe, the individual escapes the uncontrollable existential realities of life and death and lives his or her life on an abstract plane in which some measure of security can be attained by successfully living the cultural drama. Although this commitment to the cultural drama in no way alters the harsh reality that death is inevitable, it provides protection from the abject terror that this reality would otherwise produce. Living the cultural drama thus provides a form of secondary control (Rothbaum et al., 1982) in which, rather than controlling the reality of the outcome, the individual controls his or her emotional reaction to the inevitability of the outcome.

From this perspective, the active pursuit of personal value within the context of the cultural worldview is actually a means to exert a form of secondary control over one's fear of outcomes over which no primary control is possible. Thus many of the goals that people *are* able to exert control over, such as interpersonal relationships, career advancement, and achievements of many types, are actually ultimately rooted in a desire to control that which they cannot control. By exercising control over potentially controllable events within the context of the cultural drama, we demonstrate our value, and thus erect a shield against the terror of the uncontrollable. From this perspective, the exercise of control is ultimately rooted in a need to manage the potential for terror that results from our awareness of the inevitability of death, the ultimate aversive outcome.

The Rewards of Mastery

The view that control-seeking behavior is a means of proving our value that ultimately functions to protect us from deeply rooted fear explains part of the motive for control. But there are also other important reasons people seek control. Although the system through which behavior is regulated is essentially a negative feedback loop that operates according to the principle of negative reinforcement by reducing discrepancies between current states and salient reference values, there are also emergent properties of this process that provide positive incentives for the expansion of the individual's capacities to control his or her environment. Many theorists have argued that the maximum engagement of one's capacities produces a sense of exhilaration, invigoration, positive affect, or flow, that can become a much sought after end in and of itself (e.g., Csikszentimihalyi, 1975; Deci & Ryan, 1991; Maslow, 1955; White, 1959). As we have argued elsewhere (Greenberg, Pyszczynski, & Solomon, 1995; Pyszczynski, Solomon, Greenberg, & Steward-Fouts, 1995), this positively reinforcing sense of exhilaration may be a by-product of the process of integrating existing internal knowledge, structures, and schemata with new externally provided information (cf. Deci & Ryan, 1991), which thus produces an incentive for growth and self-expansion. In other words, the positive affect produced by the integrative activity that occurs when one's capacities are maximally engaged by an activity may provide the impetus for intrinsically motivated action and the expansion of one's capacities. [2]

This suggests that the pursuit of mastery may be partially an intrinsically motivated form of behavior that entails a higher-order use of the more basic negative feedback loop through which most behavior is regulated. Although many of the component actions involved in the pursuit of mastery no doubt entail the reduction of discrepancies between current and desired states, the ultimate source of motivation behind the pursuit of mastery may be the positive affect or exhilaration that the pursuit (rather than the attainment) of mastery provides. Following Rank (1932/1989), Maslow (1955), White (1959), Deci and Ryan (1991), and others, we suggest that this self-expansive growth motivation is fundamentally different from the discrepancy-reducing system through which most human (and nonhuman) action is controlled (for a more thorough discussion of this distinction, see Greenberg, Pyszczynski, & Solomon, 1995).

Whereas the terror management system is oriented toward the maintenance of the death-denying symbols of culture and self, the growth-expansion system is oriented toward the development of competencies, independent of what value awareness and labeling of such competencies might imply for the individual. Whereas the terror management system is oriented toward the aggrandizement of the individual's representation of self, the growth-expansion system is oriented toward the development of abilities and knowledge, independent of what these entities imply for an individual's sense of personal value. Whereas growth and expansion probably occur best when the individual is in a state of subjective self-awareness, the pursuit of self-esteem and validation of one's beliefs and values is set in motion by a state of objective self-awareness (cf. Plant & Ryan, 1985; Duval & Wicklund, 1972). Whereas the terror management system functions to minimize anxiety and negative affect, and thus operates according to the principles of negative reinforcement (or in Higgins's [1987] terms, a negative outcome focus), the growth-expansion system functions to maximize positive affect, and thus operates according to the principles of positive reinforcement (or what Higgins refers to as a positive outcome focus).

The positive affect that results from the integrative activity that occurs when one's capacities are maximally engaged provides an additional motivational impetus for the pursuit of control. People seek the sense of exhilaration that accompanies expanding their skills and understandings.

In this case, however, it is the *process* of expanding skills and understandings that produces the exhilaration rather than the *product*, or end state, of having attained a new skill or understanding. Whereas the process of skill or knowledge enhancement produces exhilaration, which provides positive reinforcement for such integrative activity, the product of having new skills or knowledge produces the perception of control, which enhances self-esteem, and ultimately functions to provide protection against existential fear. Thus the desire to perceive oneself as in control is an anxiety-buffering derivative of the terror management system that operates according to the principle of negative reinforcement, whereas the exhilaration-induced allure of the process of expanding one's capacities is an intrinsically motivating emergent property of integrating new information with existing structures that functions according to the principle of positive reinforcement.

Although we view the two systems as conceptually distinct and as unique motivational forces in the life of the individual, they usually work together to control behavior. We are not suggesting that some people or behaviors are exclusively growth oriented and others are purely terror driven. Both systems exert a simultaneous influence, of varying degrees, on the ongoing behavior of the individual across a wide range of settings and situations. Both systems are necessary for successful adaptation to the realities of life. Overemphasis on one or the other system either in individual psychological functioning or in theoretical analyses of human behavior is likely to prove maladaptive in the long run.

The Self-Creation of Self

> ...we have good reason for assuming *that this creativity begins with the individual himself—that is, with the self-making of the personality into the artist* .... The creative artistic personality is thus the first work of the productive individual, and it remains fundamentally his chief work, since all his other works are partly the repeated expression of this primal creation .... (Rank, 1932/1968, p. 28, emphasis in original)

The intrinsically motivating feeling of positive affect that accompanies integrative activity also provides the motivational impetus for the creative construction of a unique self and individualized version of the cultural worldview. As we suggested earlier, the self-expansive motivational system leads people to creatively abstract elements of new experiences and integrate them with existing internal structures. This ongoing integrative activity is what makes each individual unique. In this sense, individuals can be thought of, in part, as the unique products of their own creative integrative activity. Indeed, Rank (1932/1989) argued that one's own personality should be viewed as the individual's ultimate act of creativity.

Over the years, many theorists have argued that pursuing one's own creatively integrated standards provides a firmer basis for psychological stability than pursuing external or introjected standards (e.g., Maslow, 1955; Rogers, 1961). More recently, Deci and Ryan (1995) have argued that true self-esteem can be acquired only by regulating one's behavior toward thoroughly integrated self-determined standards, and that pursuit of external or introjected standards leads to a much less stable false sense of self-worth. From this perspective, behavior is free and self-determined to the extent that it is guided by well integrated standards rather than external forces or introjected standards that are taken into the individual with minimal processing. Deci and Ryan argue that because of the human integrative capacity, people can indeed have genuine control over their lives, and that when they pursue external, introjected, or incompletely integrated standards, they feel less free and more driven by forces beyond their control.

In a related vein, Kuhl and Beckmann (1995) have recently argued that performing behaviors that have no personal meaning produces a state of alienation that puts one out of touch with one's true desires and preferences and leads to apathy and an inability to later act on one's true preferences. Consistent with this reasoning, they have shown in several studies that performing alienating activities leads to a lack of initiative taking when options to do what one truly enjoys come available.

Of course, in some instances, very limited integrative processing is enacted on the social and cultural inputs to which the individual is exposed. Deci and Ryan (1991) refer to such unprocessed adoption of external influences as introjection of a false self. We suggest that fear is the primary force that stands in the way of creative integration and self-construction. When the individual is not adequately protected from basic underlying fears, he or she will be attracted to the easy answers provided by the social and cultural mainstream, and be unable to risk changes in internal structure that might get in the way of the security provided by allegiance to the mainstream. Of course, countercultural belief systems can also sometimes provide the security of social consensus on a smaller, more intimate scale. Countercultural movements may be appealing because they offer something of a compromise between the cultural mainstream and the lonely isolation of the true deviant, in that they may provide at least somewhat more anxiety-assuaging validation of creative integration on the part of the individual than that provided by the mainstream.

The distinction between true and false selves generally fits well with our analysis of defensive terror management and expansive growth motivation. Whereas a false self is a product of terror-driven conformity to the dictates of culture with little processing or creative integration, an authentic self is the product of intrinsically motivated growth motivation, and requires that basic terror management concerns be effectively addressed before such successful integrative activity can be undertaken. However, we differ from Deci and Ryan in one important way. Whereas they would argue that the false self is unnecessary and even detrimental to mental health, we, in contrast, believe that a culturally constructed conception of self as living up to standards of value is essential for anxiety control and psychological equanimity. From our perspective, successful adaptation to life requires a balance between defensive and growth-oriented motivational systems. Although we agree that the more a person can experience life from the basis of a well-integrated authentic self, the better off that person is likely to be, we believe that the ability to maximize such experiences is predicated on having a stable sense of the meaningfulness of life and the value of oneself.

All of this suggests that regulating one's behavior toward well-integrated, self-determined standards may provide a fundamentally different type of emotional security than that provided by the pursuit of merely introjected cultural values. Whereas the pursuit of culturally sanctioned values provides a sense of personal value that protects against basic existential fear, the pursuit of creatively integrated self-determined standards may provide a more stable type of autonomy that ultimately becomes self-perpetuating in that it provides the freedom from anxiety that enables the self-expansive capacities to function smoothly and more thoroughly integrate new experience with existing structures. Because the sense of value conferred by conforming to social standards ultimately depends on the social validation that only others can provide, the individual must remain constantly vigilant regarding the reactions of others and thus must remain in a constant state of defensive readiness. Part of the benefit of self-determined behavior may lie in the fact that pursuing one's own creative vision of self is much less dependent on social validation from others.

One could also ask, however, if fully integrating cultural values into oneself makes one truly more independent—or more fully and happily enslaved by cultural dictates? Our analysis in no way denies the important influence of social, cultural, and biological forces in the genesis of the self. Clearly, the raw materials for the self-creation of a semiautonomous self all come from the external environment and one's genetic endowment. Given the need to control deeply rooted anxiety, there are probably limits to how far from the cultural mainstream a person can go in his or her self-creation of a unique and semiautonomous self. These limitations notwithstanding, we suggest that the integrative self-expansive system has the capacity to transform these varying inputs in unique and creative ways so that a new and unique individual can emerge as a hybrid creation of these various influences.

Unfortunately, the foregoing analysis raises a cruel paradox: In order for the individual to be sufficiently free of anxiety for successful creative integration to be undertaken, he or she must first successfully manage the terror inherent in being an animal driven to stay alive but aware of the inevitability of his or her own mortality. However, in order to manage this terror, the individual must align himself or herself with cultural values and pledge at least some degree of allegiance to the cultural mainstream. The human condition seems to entail an ongoing dialectic opposition of these competing motives for terror management and creative self-expansion of one's capacities.

Interestingly, Otto Rank (1932/1989) grappled with these issues in his classic *Art and Artist*, and came to very similar conclusions about the difficulty of pursuing a truly creative individualized version of self. Whereas application of one's creative capacities toward the creation of a new version of self has the benefits of providing maximum freedom and self-determination, it often comes at the cost of social ostracism and vulnerability to great anxiety. In other words, although the creative individual may be free, he or she is also likely to be tortured and miserable because of his or her break with social conventions. Without the social validation that comes with conformity, the creative individual may be haunted by doubts about the value of his or her accomplishments and the very significance of his or her existence. Although it is hard to know whether truly creative people have been more or less miserable than the rest of us, or to characterize all creative types in one way, clearly many of the artists lauded in contemporary Western culture experienced more than their share of misery and torment; witness Beethoven, Bizet, Doestoyevsky, Michelangelo, Schubert, Van Gogh, or more recently Charlie Parker, John Coltrane, John Lennon, and Kurt Cobain. Perhaps because of their break with the cultural mainstream, the creative person simply has to cope on a grander scale with the terror we all try to control and the joy we try to maximize in each of our own unique journeys through life.

SUMMARY AND CONCLUSION

In sum, we are positing that the cognitive capacities of the human species gave rise to a unique system for the control of behavior that, although based on the systems existing in other species, provides greater flexibility, adaptability, and potential for freedom and self-determination. Only humans use a linguistically based abstract conception of self as a central focus for the regulation of their own behavior. The desire to exert control is ultimately rooted in two very distinct motivational systems. The desire to *perceive* oneself as in control is a means to establish a sense of personal value that ultimately functions to provide protection against deeply rooted existential fear. A great deal of control and mastery seeking behavior is thus aimed at proving one's unique value as an individual in the service of exerting a magical means of control over the uncontrollable realities of life and death. However, the integrative activity that results from maximum engagement of one's capacities in an activity can give rise to a feeling of exhilaration or positive affect that functions as an incentive for further engagement in the development of skills and understandings. The operation of this intrinsically motivated system that integrates new information with existing psychological structures gives humans the potential to creatively combine varying ideas and values to construct a unique, semiautonomous self that plays a central role in self-regulation. Although these negative and positive reinforcement functions of control and mastery derive from distinct motivational systems, they typically work together to provide the impetus for control-seeking behavior. Unfortunately for those seeking easy answers to the complexities of the human dilemma, the dialectical operation of these two distinct motivational systems gives rise to the paradox of having to effectively control one's core anxieties in order for the self-expansion system to operate most effectively, while at the same time needing to conform to mainstream values that typically run counter to creative self-expansion in order to achieve the level of terror management necessary for maximum creative functioning.

NOTES

1. We differ from Carver and Scheier in that we have argued that discrepancies may or may not engender consciously experienced negative affect, depending on the level of abstraction at which the discrepancy is conceptualized by the individual. The more abstractly the discrepancy is construed, the more aware the individual is of the breadth of the implications of the discrepancy for higher-order psychological needs for meaning and value, and thus, the more affect is aroused. We have further argued, however, that it is the potential for affect that is inherent in the hierarchical connection between low-level concrete standards and higher-level abstract standards that provides the impetus for discrepancy-reducing behavior, whether or not this affect is actually experienced (see Pyszczynski & Greenberg, 1992, and Pyszczynski, Greenberg, Solomon, & Hamilton, 1990, for detailed elaboration of this position).
2. Viewing self-expansive motivation as an emergent product of the process through which new information is integrated with existing structures is quite different from viewing it as a basic biological need that fuels exploration and the pursuit of competence. Self-expansive motivation does not entail a "need" for competence, control, or exploration. Although such behavior is rewarding by virtue of the exhilaration it often produces, people can and often do function quite well without such active pursuit of growth and enrichment. Self-expansive motivation lacks the driven sense of urgency that accompanies needs or drives. In Maslow's (1955) terms, the self-expansive side of control motivation functions as a "being need," and the defensive terror management side of control motivation functions as a "deficiency need."

REFERENCES

Alloy, L., & Abramson, L. (1979). Judgment of contingency in depressed and non-depressed students: Sadder but wiser? *Journal of Experimental Psychology: General, 108*, 441–485.

Arndt, J., Greenberg, J., Solomon, S., Pyszczynski, T., & Simon, L. (1997). Suppression, accessibility of death-related thoughts, and worldview defense: Exploring the psychodynamics of terror management. *Journal of Personality and Social Psychology, 73*, 5–18.

Arndt, J., Greenberg, J., Solomon, S., Pyszczynski, T., & Simon, L. (in press). Terror management and self-awareness: Evidence that mortality salience provokes avoidance of the self-focused state. *Personality and Social Psychology Bulletin*.

Baumeister, R. F. (1982). A self-presentational view of social phenomena. *Psychological Bulletin, 91*, 3–26.

Baumeister, R. F. (1991). *Escaping the self: Alcoholism, spirituality, masochism, and other flights from the burden of selfhood*. New York: Basic Books.

Becker, E. (1973). *The denial of death*. New York: Free Press.

Berglas, S., & Jones, E. E. (1978). Drug choice as a self-handicapping strategy in response to non-contingent success. *Journal of Personality and Social Psychology, 36*, 405–417.

Brehm, J. W. (1966). *A theory of psychological reactance*. New York: Academic Press.

Brehm, J. W., Wright, R. A., Solomon, S., Silka, K., & Greenberg, J. (1983). Perceived difficulty, energization and the magnitude of good valence. *Journal of Experimental Social Psychology, 19*, 21–48.

Brehm, S. S., & Brehm, J. W. (1980). *Psychological reactance*. New York: Academic Press.

Burger, J. M. (1992). *Desire for control: Personality, social, and clinical perspectives*. New York: Plenum.

Carver, C. S. (1979). A cybernetic model of self-attention processes. *Journal of Personality and Social Psychology, 37*, 1251–1281.

Carver, C. S., & Scheier, M. F. (1981). *Attention and self-regulation: A control theory approach to human behavior*. New York: Springer-Verlag.

Carver, C. S., & Scheier, M. F. (1990). Origins and functions of positive and negative affect: A control theory view. *Psychological Review, 97*, 19–35.

Csikszentmihalyi, M. (1975). *Beyond boredom and anxiety*. San Francisco: Jossey-Bass.

Deci, E., & Ryan, R. (1991). A motivational approach to self: Integration in personality. In R. Dienstbier (Ed.), *Nebraska symposium on motivation: Perspectives on motivation*. Lincoln, NE: University of Nebraska Press.

Deci, E., & Ryan, R. (1995). Human autonomy: The basis for true self-esteem. In M. H. Kernis (Ed.), *Efficacy, agency, and self-esteem*. New York: Plenum.

Duval, S., & Wicklund, R. (1972). *A theory of objective self-awareness*. New York: Academic Press.

Florian, V., & Mikulincer, M. (1994). Fear of personal death and the judgment of social transgressions: An expansion of terror management theory. Unpublished manuscript. Ramat Gan, Israel: Bar-Ilan University.

Fromm, E. (1969). *Escape from freedom*. New York: Avon. (Original work published in 1941.)

Gibbons, F. X. (1990). Self-attention and behavior: A review. In M. P. Zanna (Ed.), *Advances in experimental social psychology* (Vol. 23, pp. 249–303). New York: Academic Press.

Glass, D., & Singer, J. (1972). *Urban stress*. New York: Academic Press.

Greenberg, J. Porteus, J., Simon, L., Solomon, S. & Pyszczynski, T. (1995) Evidence of a terror management function of cultural icons: The effects of mortality salience on the inappropriate use of cultural symbols, *Personality and Social Psychology Bulletin, 21*, 1221–1228.

Greenberg, J., Pyszczynski, T., & Solomon, S. (1986). The causes and consequences of the need for self-esteem: A terror management theory. In R. F. Baumeister (Ed.), *Public self and private self*. New York: Springer Verlag.

Greenberg, J., Pyszczynski, T., & Solomon, S. (1995). Toward a dual motive depth psychology of self and social behavior. In M. Kernis (Ed.), *Self, efficacy, and agency*. New York: Plenum.

Greenberg, J., Pyszczynski, T., Solomon, S., Pinel, E., Simon, L., & Jordan, K. (1993). Effects of self-esteem on vulnerability-denying defensive distortions: Further evidence of an anxiety-buffering function of self-esteem. *Journal of Experimental Social Psychology, 29*, 229–251.

Greenberg, J., Pyszczynski, T., Solomon, S., Rosenblatt, A., Veeder, M., Kirkland, S., & Lyon, D. (1990). Evidence for terror management theory II: The effects of mortality salience reactions to those who threaten or bolster the cultural worldview. *Journal of Personality and Social Psychology, 58*, 308–318.

Greenberg, J., Pyszczynski, T., Solomon, S., Simon, L., & Breus, M. (1994). Role of consciousness and accessibility of death-related thoughts in mortality salience effects. *Journal of Personality and Social Psychology, 67*, 627–637.

Greenberg, J., Simon, L., Pyszczynski, T., Solomon, S., & Chatel, D. (1992). Terror management and tolerance: Does mortality salience always intensify negative reactions to others who threaten one's worldview? *Journal of Personality and Social Psychology, 63*, 212–220.

Greenberg, J., Simon, L., Arndt, J., Pyszczynski, T., & Solomon, S. (1996). Direct and symbolic means of defending against the fear of death: Immediate vs. delayed reactions. Unpublished manuscript. Tucson, Arizona: University of Arizona.

Greenberg, J., Simon, L., Harmon-Jones, E., Solomon, S., Pyszczynski, T., & Lyon, D. (1995). Testing alternative explanations for mortality salience effects: Terror management, value accessibility, or worrisome thoughts? *European Journal of Social Psychology, 25*, 417–433.

Greenberg, J., Solomon, S., Pyszczynski, T., Rosenblatt, A., Burling, J., Lyon, D., & Simon, L. (1992). Assessing the terror management analysis of self-esteem: Converging evidence of an anxiety-buffering function. *Journal of Personality and Social Psychology, 63*, 913–922.

Greenberg, J. Solomon, S., & Pyszczynski, T. (1997). Terror management theory of self-esteem and cultural worldviews: Empirical assessments and conceptual refinements. In M. Zanna (ed.), *Advances in experimental social psychology* (Vol. 29, pp. 61–139). San Diego, CA: Academic Press.

Harmon-Jones, E., Greenberg, J., Solomon, S., & Simon, L. (1996). The effects of mortality salience on intergroup bias between minimal groups. *European Journal of Social Psychology, 26*, 677–681.

Harmon-Jones, E., Simon, L., Greenberg, J., Pyszczynski, T., Solomon, S., & McGregor, H. (1997). Terror management theory and self-esteem: Evidence that increased self-esteem reduces mortality salience effects. *Journal of Personality and Social Psychology, 72*, 24–36.

Higgins, E. T. (1987). Self-discrepancy: A theory relating self and affect. *Psychological Review, 94*, 319–340.

Kruglanski, A. W. (1980). Lay epistemology process and contents. *Psychological Review, 87*, 70–87.

Kuhl, J., & Beckman, J. (1995). Alienation: Ignoring one's preferences. In J. Kuhl & J. Beckman (Eds.), *Volition and personality: Action versus state orientation*. Seattle, WA: Hogrefe & Huber.

Langer, E. J. (1975). The illusion of control. *Journal of Personality and Social Psychology, 32*, 311–328.

Langer, E. J., & Rodin, J. (1976). The effects of choice and enhanced personal responsibility for the aged: A field experiment. *Journal of Personality and Social Psychology, 34*, 191–198.

Lazarus, R. S. (1966). *Psychological stress and the coping process.* New York: McGraw Hill.
Lerner, M. J., Miller, D. T., & Holmes, J. G. (1976). Deserving and the emergence of forms of justice. In L. Berkowitz (Ed.), *Advances in experimental social psychology* (Vol. 9, pp. 133–162). New York: Academic Press.
Lifton, R. J. (1983). *The broken connection: On death and the continuity of life.* New York: Basic Books.
Maslow, A. (1955). Deficiency motivation and growth motivation. In M. R. Jones (Ed.), *Nebraska symposium on motivation.* Lincoln: University of Nebraska Press.
McGregor, H., Lieberman, J., Greenberg, J., Solomon, S., Arndt, J., Simon, L., & Pyszczynski, T. (in press). Terror management and aggression: Evidence that mortality salience motivates aggression against worldview threatening individuals. *Journal of Personality and Social Psychology.*
Miller, G. A., Galanter, E., & Pribram, K. H. (1960). *Plans and the structure of behavior.* New York: Holt, Rinehart & Winston.
Ochsmann, R., & Reichelt, K. (1994). Evaluation of moral and immoral behavior: Evidence for terror management theory. Unpublished manuscript, Universitat Mainz , Mainz, Germany.
Pittman, N. L., & Pittman, T. S. (1980). Deprivation of control and the attribution process. *Journal of Personality and Social Psychology, 39,* 377–389.
Plant, R. W., & Ryan, R. M. (1985). Intrinsic motivation and the effects of self-consciousness, self-awareness, and ego-involvement: An investigation of internally controlling styles. *Journal of Personality, 53,* 435–449.
Powers, W. T. (1978). Quantitative analysis of purposive systems—Some spadework at the foundations of scientific psychology. *Psychological Review, 85,* 417–435.
Pyszczynski, T., & Greenberg, J. (1987). Self-regulatory perserveration and the depressive self-focusing style: A self-awareness theory of the development and maintenance of reactive depression. *Psychological Bulletin, 102,* 1–17.
Pyszczynski, T., Greenberg, J., Solomon, S., & Hamilton, J. (1990). A terror management analysis of self-awareness and anxiety: The hierarchy of terror. *Anxiety Research, 2,* 177–195.
Pyszczynski, T., Greenberg, J., Hamilton, J., & Becker, S. (1991). Self-focused attention and well-being. In C. R. Snyder & D. Forsyth (Eds.), *Handbook of social and clinical psychology: The health perspective.* New York: Pergammon.
Pyszczynski, T., & Greenberg, J. (1992). *Hanging on and letting go: Understanding the onset, progression, and remission of depression.* New York: Springer-Verlag.
Pyszczynski, T., Solomon, S., Greenberg, J., & Stewart-Fouts, M. (1995). The liberating and constraining aspects of self: Why the freed bird finds a new cage. In A. Oosternwegel, & R. A. Wicklund (Eds.), *The self in European and North American culture: Development and processes.* Dordrecht, The Netherlands: Kluwer.
Pyszczynski, T., Wicklund, R. A., Floresku, S., Gauch, G., Koch, H., Greenberg, J., & Solomon, S. (1996). Whistling in the dark: Exaggerated consensus estimates in response to incidental reminders of mortality. *Psychological Science, 7,* 332–336.
Pyszczynski, T., Greenberg, J., & Solomon, S. (1997). Why do we need what we need? A terror management perspective on the roots of human motivation. *Psychological Inquiry, 8,* 1–20.
Pyszczynski, T., Schimel, J., Greenberg, J., & Solomon, S. (in preparation). Mortality salience and the value of prosocial behavior. University of Colorado, Colorado Springs, CO.
Rank, O. (1978). *Truth and reality.* New York: W. W. Norton. (Original work published 1936.)
Rank, O. (1989) *Art and artist: Creative urge and personality development.* New York: W. W. Norton. (Original work published 1932.)
Rogers, C. (1961). *On becoming a person.* Boston: Houghton Mifflin.

Rosenblatt, A., Greenberg, J., Solomon, S., Pyszczynski, T., & Lyons, D. (1989). Evidence for terror management theory I: The effects of mortality salience on reactions to those who violate or uphold cultural values. *Journal of Personality and Social Psychology, 57,* 681–690.

Rothbaum, F., Weisz, J. R., & Snyder, S. S. (1982). Changing the world and changing the self: A two-process model of perceived control. *Journal of Personality and Social Psychology, 42,* 5–37.

Scheier, M. F., & Carver, C. S. (1988). A model of behavioral self-regulation: Translating intention into action. In L. Berkowitz (Ed.), *Advances in experimental social psychology* (Vol. 21, pp. 303–326). New York: Academic Press.

Seligman, M. E. P. (1975). *Helplessness.* San Francisco, CA: W. H. Freeman.

Simon, L., Harmon-Jones, E., Greenberg, J., Solomon, S., & Pyszczynski, T. (1996). Mild depression, mortality salience, and defense of the worldview: Evidence of intensified terror management in the mildly depressed. *Personality and Social Psychology Bulletin, 22,* 81–90.

Simon, L., Greenberg, J., Arndt., J., Pyszczynski, T., Clement, R., & Solomon, S. (1997). Perceival consensus, uniqueness, and optimal distinctiveness striving: Compensatory responses to inclusion and distinctiveness following mortality salience. *Personality and Social Psychology Bulletin, 23,* 1055–1066

Skinner, B. F. (1938). *The behavior of organisms.* New York: Appleton-Century-Crofts.

Solomon, S., Holmes, D., & McCaul, K. D. (1980). Behavioral control over aversive events: Does control that requires effort reduce anxiety and physiological arousal. *Journal of Personality and Social Psychology, 39,* 729–736.

Solomon, S., Greenberg, G., & Pyszczynski, T. (1991a). Terror management theory of self esteem. In C. R. Snyder & D. Forsyth (Eds.), *Handbook of social and clinical psychology: The health perspective.* New York: Pergamon.

Solomon, S., Greenberg, J., & Pyszczynski, T. (1991b). A terror management theory of social behavior: The psychological functions of self-esteem and cultural worldviews. In M. P. Zanna (Ed.), *Advances in experimental social psychology.* San Diego: Academic Press.

Swann, W. B. (1984). Quest for accuracy in person perception: A matter of pragmatics. *Psychological Review, 91,* 457–477.

Swann, W. B. (1987). Identity negotiation: Where two roads meet. *Journal of Personality and Social Psychology, 53,* 1038–1051.

Taylor, S. E., & Brown, J. D. (1988). Illusion and well-being: A social psychological perspective on mental health. *Psychological Bulletin, 103,* 193–210.

Weiner, B., Frieze, I., Kukla, A., Reed, L., Rest, B., & Rosenbaum, R. (1971). *Perceiving the causes of success and failure.* Morristown, NJ: General Learning Press.

White, R. (1959). Motivation reconsidered: The concept of competence. *Psychological Review, 66,* 297–334.

Wortman, C. B. (1975). Some determinants of perceived control. *Journal of Personality and Social Psychology, 31,* 282–294.

Wortman, C. B., & Brehm, J. W. (1975). Responses to uncontrollable outcomes: An integration of reactance theory and the learned helplessness model. In L. Berkowitz (Ed.), *Advances in experimental social psychology* (Vol. 8). New York: Academic Press.

Yalom, I. (1980). *Existential psychotherapy.* New York: Basic Books.

Zuckerman, M. (1979). Attribution of success and failure visited, or: The motivational bias is alive and well in attribution theory. *Journal of Personality, 47,* 245–287.

CHAPTER 5

PERSONAL GOALS AND PERSONAL AGENCY

LINKING EVERYDAY GOALS TO FUTURE IMAGES OF THE SELF

LAURA A. KING

INTRODUCTION

Goal perspectives on personality emphasize the everydayness of human life: the daily "to do" lists that drive everyday behavior and experience (Pervin, 1989). In studies on personalized goals, individuals are asked to list the goals they are typically trying to accomplish in their everyday behaviors (e.g., Emmons, 1989). Daily goals can range in their significance from "to grow my nails" or "to eat less fat" at one end, to "to fight racism and misogyny wherever I see them" or "to bring God's kingdom to Earth" at the other. Given the tendency of some of these goals to draw upon the most mundane aspects of life, we might well question the role of daily goals in the grander process of realizing one's destiny. How can potentially "trivial pursuits" factor into our understanding of human agency? This chapter will address this issue in three ways. First, I will explore the ways research on daily goals can inform our understanding of the every-

LAURA A. KING • Department of Psychology, Southern Methodist University, Dallas, Texas 75275-0442. E-mail: lking@mail.smu.edu

Personal Control in Action, edited by Kofta et al., Plenum Press, New York, 1998.

day self-as-agent by incorporating consideration of more distal life plans. The role of long-range life plans has been largely ignored, as research has focused instead on highly contextualized daily goals. In this chapter, I'll highlight the ways that distal goals or life dreams can serve as a source of agency and meaning. In reviewing some recent research in this area, I will demonstrate the connections that exist between everyday goals and the enactment of a broader life plan. From this perspective, daily goals can be seen as the building blocks of destiny, the incremental steps toward fulfilling one's life dreams.

Second, I will suggest ways that considering proximal and distal goals in the context of major life change might improve our understanding of the ways individuals reinstate agency via rewriting the life dream. Major life changes, by definition, impinge upon an individual's life goals. In response to such changes, one task facing the individual is to reinvest in some life dream from which to gain a sense of meaning. Finally, I will consider the ways that mundane goals provide implicit information about the "creation of agency in everyday life" (Harlow & Cantor, 1995). Idiographic goals reveal much about the aspects of life over which individuals feel a sense of control and through which they are able to express agency.

The experience of mastery, of control over outcomes in one's life, and the perception that one has impact on the world are vital to the experience of subjective well-being (Bandura, 1982; Deci & Ryan, 1995). Effective goal pursuit is clearly part of this process. Yet, the mundane goals that drive everyday behavior do not sufficiently explain motivational influences on behavior, experience, and well-being. In order to contribute to the experience of meaning in life, these goals must be placed in the context of a larger, overarching purpose (Baumeister, 1991). Murray (1938) referred to this hierarchical structure of goals as "subsidiation," recognizing the importance of instrumental links between lower- and higher-level life concerns. Control theory (e.g., Carver & Scheier, 1981) emphasizes the embeddedness of daily goals in a motivational hierarchy. This hierarchy is characterized on the bottom by concrete behaviors and plans and at the top by more abstract, global motives (Emmons & King, 1989, 1992; Emmons & McAdams, 1991). A control perspective would suggest that lower-level daily goals that serve higher levels of the hierarchy ought to be appraised as more important by the individual. Moreover, success or failure at such goals should play a greater role in the psychological and physical functioning of the organism.

THE ROLE OF DISTAL GOALS IN SUBJECTIVE WELL-BEING

Research on idiographic goals has tended to focus on the importance of having valued daily pursuits to experience and subjective well-being.

This research has typically taken a "bottom-up" approach to the experience of agency—examining the ways that the minute goals of daily life provide opportunities for agency. Although the role of more superordinate constructs (e.g., the self or broad motives) in this relation has been acknowledged, the dynamic relations between higher- and lower-level goals has not been fully explored. For instance, although it is clear that beliefs about the self influence goal choice (e.g., Markus, 1983), the goal-directed quality of the higher levels of functioning remains implicit. Goal choice is determined not only by traits, abilities, and beliefs, but also by actual long-term life goals. Typically, in describing the higher levels of the control hierarchy of motivation, researchers have tended to resort to very broad constructs or constructs that are unavailable to awareness (e.g., Aronoff & Wilson, 1985; Emmons & McAdams, 1991). Intuitively, it seems clear that the experience of agency has no better manifestation than in the realization of one's life dream. Yet, the importance of long range (conscious) life plans has not been a major focus of research.

Fortunately, personality psychologists have a wealth of conceptualizations of high level, abstract, superordinate goals. Long-range life aspirations have been conceptualized by Tomkins (e.g., 1992) as "commitment scripts," by Allport (1961) as "propriate strivings," and by Adler (1927) as "fictional finalisms." All of these constructs include an investment in some imagined future that promises a "happily ever after." Similarly, McAdams' s"generativity script" (see McAdams & de St. Aubin, 1992) includes the plan or outline specifying how one might leave one's mark on the world. The concept of the imagined future has been captured more generally in the construct of "possible self." Possible selves are representations of the self in the past and the future (Markus & Nurius, 1986; Markus & Ruvolo, 1989). Possible selves serve as incentives in goal directed activity and provide a context for one's present self-evaluations. The content of possible selves and the number of possible selves an individual generates have been linked to important variables such as delinquency, task performance, and well-being (Oyserman & Markus, 1990; Ruvolo & Markus, 1992; Ryff 1991). Importantly, possible selves include both positive "hoped for" possible selves and negative "dreaded" possible selves. Thus, they allow for an examination not only of working toward a valued end but also of avoiding a dreaded outcome.

While research has tended to indicate that having a varied and flexible repertoire of possible selves is related to well-being (Markus & Nurius, 1986), little research has addressed the importance of having a particular valued future or life dream toward which to strive. Highly complex plans and goals for the future have been demonstrated to relate to personality development (McAdams, Ruetzel, & Foley, 1986), but the relations of life plans to subjective well-being remain ambiguous. Indeed, to some extent the literature provides a caution to those who invest in the future—as "outcome focus" in goal pursuit has been seen as potentially problematic (e.g., Harlow & Cantor, 1995).

In order to examine the relation of distal goals to subjective well-being, we conducted a study collecting narratives about hoped for and dreaded possible selves (King & Stemmerich, 1996). Eighty college students generated narratives in response to instructions to imagine that everything in their lives had worked out as well as they possibly could, that they had succeeded at achieving all of their goals (cf. Markus & Ruvolo, 1989). In addition, these subjects generated narratives about their dreaded future selves—their lives in the future if they had worked hard but failed to achieve their goals. After writing each narrative, subjects completed questionnaire measures of the salience of their hoped for and dreaded selves. Items included the ease with which they could imagine the scenario, the clarity of the possible self in their mind, how much their current behavior would aid in the scenario coming true, the commitment they felt to making sure the scenario does (or doesn't) come true, and how much they think of this scenario when they are working hard at a task. Subjects also completed measures of life satisfaction, sense of coherence (Antonovsky, 1988), and optimism (Scheier & Carver, 1985). Results indicated that the hoped for future self tended to be more salient than the worst-possible self. In addition, the salience of the hoped for possible self was significantly positively correlated with life satisfaction, sense of coherence, and optimism (King & Stemmerich, 1996).

These hoped for and dreaded self narratives were also content analyzed for themes related to intrinsic versus extrinsic motivation (Deci & Ryan, 1995). Intrinsic motivation is defined as motives emerging from the individuals "integrated sense of self" (Deci & Ryan, 1994). Extrinsic motivation is defined as motivation that is controlled by external consequences. Kasser and Ryan (1993) found that individuals who valued material wealth (an extrinsic value) over other more intrinsic values tended to show lower adjustment (Kasser & Ryan, 1993, Studies 1 and 2), less social productivity, and more behavioral disorders (Kasser & Ryan, 1993, Study 3).

In this study, then, we were interested in examining the ramifications of the content of distal goals to well-being. In the content analytic strategy we employed, intrinsically motivated themes were self-acceptance, competence, personal growth, generativity, and intimate relationships (Sheldon & Kasser, 1995). Examples of instances coded for intrinsic themes in the best possible self narratives include, "I am more self confident," "I will have made a real difference in the world," "I will fight racism so that my children will live in a better world," and "I have a wonderful, supportive marriage." Extrinsic content scoring included themes of money or other financial gain, fame and glory, material possessions (e.g., houses, cars), and physical appearance (Sheldon & Kasser, 1995). Examples of instances of these topics include, "I have lots of money," "I am world-renowned for my work and am paid millions to endorse products I don't use," "I have two cars and three houses, one in Europe," and "I remain thin throughout my life" (King & Stemmerich, 1996). Previous research has supported the notion that seeking extrinsic ends (such as money) is related to lowered well-being (Kasser & Ryan, 1993, 1996), while pursuit of more intrinsically motivated ends has been found to relate to self-actualization. In our sample, using an open-ended narrative methodology, intrinsic content was positively associated with life satisfaction, but no relations emerged between extrinsic content and subjective well-being. In hierarchical regression analyses, controlling for content, the salience of best- and worst-possible future selves did contribute significantly to the prediction of subjective well-being. Hoped-for-possible-self salience positively predicted subjective well-being (standardized beta = .33) and worst-possible-self salience negatively predicted subjective well-being (standardized beta = –.28). The sense that the imagined, hoped for future was keenly present in one's current mental life was a positive predictor of subjective well-being, regardless of the nature of that future distal goal.

Our results largely fail to replicate the findings of Kasser and Ryan (1993), failing to indict the "darker side of the American Dream." One reason for this difference may lie in differing approaches to measuring well-being, as well as life goals. Kasser and Ryan used "self-actualization" as an outcome measure in their study, rather than simply subjective well-being, or meaning in life. In addition, Kasser and Ryan forced people to consciously weigh their valuing of money over other aspects of life. In our study, subjects were free to describe any and all aspects of the goals toward which they were striving. Indeed, it may be that the American Dream is less dark than gray—that individuals strive toward materialistic ends as well as more intrinsic ends simultaneously.

Because these results are correlational, no causal conclusions can be drawn. Indeed, it seems reasonable that individuals who are satisfied with their lives might be better able to generate and focus on long-term goals. In addition, one's current emotional state might be thought of as a gauge of success in one's goal pursuits. Happy people might be more likely to see themselves as actively pursuing their life dreams because they feel so good. This circularity may not be merely a conundrum of the correlational researcher but rather a reflection of reality. It may be that progress toward one's valued goals does feed into the self, allowing the individual to gain in competence and esteem, and therefore to embark on more difficult and more encompassing life goals (cf. Harlow & Cantor, 1995).

THE HIERARCHICAL RELATIONS OF PROXIMAL AND DISTAL GOALS

Given that having an ultimate life dream is related to the experience of life as happy and meaningful, we might then ask what the implications are of the vertical relations between mundane daily goals and these more ultimate life dreams. At least two important areas deserve some attention: first, the implications of these relations for the experience of life satisfaction and meaning and, second, the implications of these relations for goal attainment.

Generally, research has treated proximal and distal goals as "either-or" propositions. For instance, subjects have been assigned distal or proximal goals (e.g., Manderlink & Harakiewicz, 1984). In such studies, proximal goals have been linked to feelings of success and self-efficacy (Bandura & Schunk, 1981; Morgan, 1985). Distal goals have been related to heightened intrinsic motivation (Manderlink & Harakiewicz, 1984). Correlational research has also addressed the tendency of individuals to frame their goals in an abstract, long-term way or in more concrete immediate terms (e.g., Vallacher & Wegner, 1989). Emmons (1992) found that individuals who had a preponderance of concrete personal strivings were likely to feel more positive affect but also to have physical symptoms, while those who were focused on more abstract personal strivings were likely to experience more psychological distress but fewer physical symptoms.

In reality, individuals possess both abstract, long-term, distal goals and more concrete, immediate, proximal goals. Extrapolating from the research mentioned thus far, it seems that, ideally, an individual would enjoy the feelings of success and efficacy associated with the achievement of proximal goals while experiencing the intrinsic motivation, deeper satisfaction and meaning associated with working toward a larger life plan. In such a situation, the individual might possess attainable short-term goals that are linked instrumentally to the accomplishment of some more long-range life plan. More proximal goals may allow an individual to remain actively engaged in a broader, more complex life plan (see Vallacher & Wegner, 1989).

Little research has addressed the vertical relations that may exist between daily life goals and ultimate life programs and the implications of these relations for subjective well-being. Sheldon and Kasser (1995) explored the relations among personal strivings and more distal goals. They found that instrumental correspondence between lower-level goals and broader, enduring goals was positively related to well-being, provided that those enduring life goals were intrinsic in nature. Importantly, having proximal goals in the service of distal goals allows individuals to benefit from progress in the proximal goal while also experiencing a sense of purpose in life provided by the more abstract life plan. It is also possible to examine the implications of striving to avoid dreaded possible futures. For instance, a person's dreaded possible self may include having a boring, unrewarding job, and the daily goals of that person,"to work hard in school so I can have really exciting career that interests me." Thus, an individual may have a lower-level goal in service of a more ultimate goal and devoted to avoiding a dreaded future.

A recent study (King, Richards, & Stemmerich, 1998) addressed these very issues. Eighty-three college students enrolled in upper-level courses were asked to generate the personal strivings that typically drive their everyday behavior (Emmons, 1989). In addition, these subjects listed their ultimate life goals ("those things you would like to accomplish with your life in the future") and worst fears. Daily goals were content analyzed for relevance to the accomplishment of the life goals or the avoidance of the worst fears. Examples of personal strivings and life goals that were judged as relevant included, "to get A's in my classes" and "to get accepted into a clinical graduate program" and "to be understanding of others" and "to marry a wonderful man and have a warm, understanding relationship" (King, Richards, & Stemmerich, 1998). Examples of strivings and worst fears that were judged as relevant included "to be a good friend to others" and "to die alone" and "to work hard in school" and "to never get a good job." Each striving was given a total relevance to ultimate goal score and a total relevance to worst-fear score. Summing over goals provided an overall score for each subject.

Initial analyses addressed the relations between these relevance scores and the appraisals that subjects gave their daily strivings. Subjects had rated their personal strivings on the dimensions of importance, ambivalence, difficulty, progress, and conflict. First, these goal appraisal dimensions were standardized within subject to remove the influence of individual differences in goal appraisals. Thus these analyses are based on approximately 1,030 strivings generated in this sample. Correlations were computed among the striving appraisal dimensions and relevance scores for ultimate goals and worst fears. Personal strivings relevant to ultimate life goals were appraised as more important ($r = .17, p < .001$) but also more difficult ($r = .11, p < .05$). Personal strivings that were linked to worst fears were also rated more important ($r = .14, p < .001$) and more difficult ($r = .07$, $p < .05$; King, Richards, & Stemmerich, 1998).

Finally, in order to examine the interaction of relevance of personal strivings to worst fears and ultimate goals on personal-striving appraisal, a 2 (relevant vs. not relevant to realizing ultimate goal) × 2 (relevant vs. not relevant to avoiding worst fear) multivariate analysis of variance (MA-

NOVA) was performed on all of the striving appraisal dimensions. The MANOVA revealed a significant interaction, $F_{(4,\ 1020)} = 4.48$, $p < .001$. Univariate *F*s were significant for ambivalence ratings, $F_{(1,\ 1023)} = 4.21$, as well as importance, $F_{(1,\ 1023)} = 13.21$ (both *p*s < .01). Subjects were most ambivalent over strivings that were linked to either fears or ultimate goals but not both. Subjects rated strivings that were linked to both best- and worst-possible outcomes as most important to them.

Next, analyses examined the relations among the relevance scores and subjective well-being measures. It had been predicted that individuals whose daily goals were relevant to the accomplishment of some overarching life plan would experience heightened subjective well-being. Additionally, those individuals whose daily goals were devoted to avoiding some dreaded outcome were expected to show greater distress. In a hierarchical regression equation predicting subjective well-being, appraisal dimensions of importance, ambivalence, progress, conflict, and difficulty were entered on the first step, and total personal-striving relevance scores for ultimate goals and worst fears were entered on the second. Personal-striving appraisal dimensions contributed significantly to the prediction of subjective well-being, on the first step. Progress ratings were positively related to well-being and ambivalence was negatively related to well-being (standardized betas = .26 and −.19, respectively, both *p*s < .01). Entered on the second step, ultimate goal and worst-fear relevance scores contributed significantly to the prediction of subjective well-being (standardized betas = .27 and −.33, respectively, both *p*s < .01). In support of predictions, having daily goals that were instrumental to the accomplishment of one's ultimate life goals was positively related to subjective well-being, and having daily goals that focus on avoiding one's worst fears was negatively related to subjective well-being.

A robust conclusion that has emerged from daily goal research is that individuals who are working on attainable, moderately difficult, and important goals are better off psychologically than those who are working on more long-term difficult, endeavors (e.g., Emmons, 1992). The results of this study on daily goals, ultimate life goals, and worst fears indicate that attainable short-term goals are particularly beneficial to the individual if they are attached to some long-term life plan. Proximal everyday personal strivings provide a feeling of satisfaction to the extent that they provide a bridge to long-term life aspirations. These results indicate at least one reason why working toward important goals is beneficial to the person's experience of self-as-agent—these goals are likely to be subordinate to some overarching life plan. Success at such goals is more than simply a check mark on a "to do" list. These goals engage individuals because they are informed by more enduring lifelong projects. Success brings one closer to the fruition of a life dream, if only in a small way. Additionally, these results help to explain why people remain engaged in difficult daily goals. Although working toward difficult daily goals may be less likely to produce momentary positive affect, difficult goals may be goals that have relevance to accomplishing one's ultimate life dream.

IMPLICATIONS OF DAILY GOAL STRIVING FOR THE EXPERIENCE OF AGENCY: ENACTING A LIFE DREAM

One implication of this discussion of daily goals in the context of a life dream is that individuals who generate daily goals that are relevant to a life dream ought to be more successful at attaining that life dream. Effectively seeking a high-level goal may require the enactment of lower-level daily goals. In keeping with the "bottom-up" character of most goal research, studies have focused on the attainment of lower-level goals as a function of the relation of these goals to higher-level, or at least broader, life concerns. For instance, Yetim (1993) found that individuals are more likely to report progress in goals that are linked to imagined representations of the self. In a study in which subjects rated progress on their daily goals over a three-month period, subjects rated themselves as more successful at goals that were related to their ultimate life plans (King, 1994). Research on visualization and goal setting also provides some support for the hypotheses discussed here. The degree to which individuals visualize their future lives and goals influences behavior and performance. Simply verbalizing a hypothetical success or failure before beginning a task predicts performance in the expected direction (e.g., Sherman et al., 1981). Research in the area of sport supports the notion that visualization may enhance performance (Kato & Markus, 1993; Markus & Ruvolo, 1989; Ruvolo & Markus, 1992).

Still, the question remains, does having current daily goals that further one's life dream allow the individual to strive effectively toward that dream? This issue was addressed in a study of 83 first-year college students who were all enrolled in the premed curriculum at Southern Methodist University (King & Williams, 1996). All of these students stated at the beginning of their college careers that they intended to become doctors and were actively engaged in striving toward that life dream. Premed students present an ideal sample for exploring these issues, since these are individuals who are embarking on a life plan that is truly in its infancy. For many of these students, becoming a doctor is a long-standing life dream. In addition, the premed curriculum is set up so that they enroll in a number of quite difficult courses "up front." Thus, the first year of college represents a time in which this life dream is sorely tested. The premed students who enrolled in the study completed narratives about their hoped for and dreaded possible future selves, as well as daily personal-striving lists. A sample of a hoped-for-self generated by a subject in this study demonstrates the level of elaboration of this ultimate goal that many of these subjects shared:

> If everything in my life has gone as well as it possibly could have, the future would be great, and I would be extremely busy. If I do become a doctor I will more than likely spend almost every hour working with people. I like to help people, especially if it is unknown what is wrong with them. I can see myself 'married to my work.' The future would just be busy because that's the way I would want it. If I did get married, my husband would rarely see me—except on the long vacation I'd take each year. Even though I'd stay busy, I would definitely need some time to myself. I would like to make a lot of money, but that is not the reason I would have become a doctor.

Daily personal strivings were content analyzed for relevance to best- and worst-possible selves. Each subject was given a score for the number of daily strivings they possessed that related to their ultimate life dream. At the end of the first year, subjects' academic information was provided by the university registrar. First-year college grade point average was predicted by the relevance of daily personal strivings to the life dream of becoming a doctor, controlling for Scholastic Aptitude Test (SAT) scores (partial $r = .30$, $p < .03$). In addition, whether subjects had to change majors was predicted by the relevance of daily goals to best-possible selves (point biserial $r = -.41$, with change coded as "1" and no change coded as "0"), although it was not significantly related to worst-fear relevance ($r = -.18$). The relation of the relevance of personal strivings to life dream and changing majors persisted, controlling for SAT scores as well as high school grade point average ($r = -.40$; King & Williams, 1996).

These results provide compelling evidence that, regardless of ability, individuals who spontaneously formulated daily goals that were relevant to their ultimate life dream actually were more effective at working toward that dream.

One explanation for this success may be that the generation of daily goals reveals implicit information about level of the commitment and control and ability beliefs of the person (a possibility that will be considered later). That is to say, individuals who feel high levels of commitment and control will be more likely to generate such goals. Thus the experience of agency leads to goal generation. On the other hand, it may be that setting and successfully pursuing these daily goals provides the individual with a sense of control and leads to greater commitment. In any case, whether daily goals are seen as by-products of agency or expressions of agency, these mundane goals seem to function as a link between the person's daily life and his or her ultimate life goals—a means by which individuals may enact their life dreams.

Another reason we might expect individuals whose daily goals work toward some valued end to experience success at their goal pursuits is because such goals should play a vital role in the person's emotional life (see Emmons, 1991). The individuals response to success or failure at a daily goal is likely to depend on the relation of the daily goal to the superordinate life goals of the individual. Daily events that are relevant to the life dream should be responded to with more intensity than less relevant events. Events that impinge on the mundane goals that act as stepping stones to a life dream should be responded to with greater intensity than other events. This contingency between affect and events would indicate efficient feedback in the motivational system (Carver & Scheier, 1981). That is to say that progress at daily goals that are linked to higher levels of the motivational system ought to be more intimately tied to the person's emotional life, as emotions act as a gauge in active goal pursuit (e.g., King & Emmons, 1991). Thus, the individual ought to be able to monitor progress on these goals with greater precision, and tailor their efforts accordingly. Such a system of feedback might well lead to heightened goal success.

In order to examine the impact of seeking one's life dream via daily goals on daily thought and mood, 53 of the premed students also participated in a 21-day mood study in which they completed daily mood forms twice a day. Mood reports included ratings of positive and negative mood adjectives, as well as questions about the events contributing to subjects' positive and negative moods and their most memorable events of each day. Mood reports were content analyzed for relevance to personal strivings. The likelihood of a striving being mentioned in daily reports was correlated with the striving's relevance to the subject's best- and worst-possible selves. For instance, the frequency with which a striving occurred in daily thought was significantly correlated with its relevance to the dream of becoming a doctor ($r = .26, p < .01$) as well as its relevance to subjects' dreaded worst-possible self ($r = .22, p < .01$). Additionally, subjects were more likely to mention life dream–relevant events as contributing to their negative moods ($r = .20, p < .01$) and to mention worst-fear-relevant events as contributing to positive moods ($r = .25, p <$ 01). Aside from supporting the notion that daily mood is intertwined with progress on goals related to one's life dream, these results also illustrate the types of emotional responses that characterized the lives of these subjects. Apparently, relief at not failing (i.e., not realizing one's worst-possible self) is a predominant "positive" emotional reaction, and disappointment at failing to achieve one's goals predominates one's negative emotional life for individuals engaged in a challenging life dream. These conclusions resonate with the life strategy identified as "defensive pessimism" (Norem & Illingworth, 1993). These results also jibe with previous research demonstrating that important but difficult goals have been associated with the experience of negative emotions (Zirkel & Cantor, 1990). Because this sample is known *a priori* to be striving toward a very difficult end, it is unclear if these results generalize to life dream pursuit per se.

Expanding on these previous results, however, the premed study illustrates why these goals may prove to be problematic. These goals tend to be associated with avoiding the worst-case scenario, a difficult proposition in any case (e.g., Wegner & Erber, 1992).

These results also add support to the anecdotal evidence provided by the narratives generated by these subjects. A typical "worst possible self" was the following:

> If everything does not work as well as I plan, I would be highly disappointed. All the sacrifices, commitment to study would be in vain. I have practically given up all of the fun from life and my sacrifices would have no purpose. I would have to start all over. I would not have faith in myself for a while. I would begin to hate myself. I would be ashamed to encounter my parents and friends. (collected in King & Williams, 1996)

In the premed study, the number of daily goals subjects devoted to attaining their life dream was negatively correlated with daily positive affect (partial $r = -.39$, $p < .01$) and marginally correlated with daily negative affect (partial $r = .27$, $p < .10$), controlling for academic performance. These subjects demonstrated their willingness to sacrifice present happiness for a future life dream. This commitment colored their present emotional life to a large degree.

REWRITING THE LIFE DREAM AND PERSONAL GROWTH

Investment in attainable proximal goals that serve broader, enduring life aspirations has been hypothesized to give life meaning, to predict well-being, and to facilitate behavior regulation, leading to heightened goal progress. Investing in the future is a risky business, however. Although delay of gratification may be a hallmark of self-regulation, putting off positive experiences in the present in favor of hoped for larger rewards in the future may not always be adaptive (cf. Baumeister, & Heatherton 1996; King 1996). As fictions, life dreams are subject to revision. What happens when a hoped for future self is irrevocably lost because of failure or circumstance? One way to look at loss or change is to consider how the loss impacts a person's future self horizon, focusing on the ways life changes implicate identity and require a revision of one's life dream. Major life change or smaller losses in one's life may be construed as lost possible selves. Lost possible selves may be defined as representations of the self in the future that were once imbued with the promise of positive affect but that are now unattainable.

Klinger (e.g., 1975, 1977) has presented an impressive examination of disengagement from unattainable goals. He suggested that failure to disengage from unattainable goals is linked to depressive symptoms. Although this distress is considered a normal part of the process of letting go of valued goals, Klinger (1977) suggested that reduced daily goal functioning and increased psychological distress may result from expending daily thought and emotion toward unfulfilled goals. Kuhl and Helle (1986) experimentally demonstrated that individuals who failed to disengage from unattainable goals tended to show depressive symptoms and limited opportunities for new goals.

While on the one hand the superior affective feedback provided for future-relevant daily goals might allow individuals to attend to failure and actively change their goals, theory and research on lost incentives does not suggest that this will be the case. Research on constructs that tap "unfinished business" (e.g., regrets, interrupted goals, etc.) indicate that lost possible selves may be likely to become the subject of great rumination. The Zeigarnik effect (1938) is a classic example of the power of interrupted goals on thought and behavior. In addition, Wegner's (e.g., Wegner & Erber, 1992) work on the ironic influence of thought suppression suggests that actively trying not to think about these lost possibilities may have the exact opposite effect. Regrets can be particularly painful when the individual has come close to achieving the goal and realizes that he or she controlled the situation (cf. Gilovich, 1995). Generating daily goals in the service of an ultimate life dream is an implicit manifestation of one's belief that one has control over this outcome. In addition, these goals represent the level of effort the individual is willing to make in the service of a broader life goal. Not surprisingly, among those individuals in the premed study who eventually were forced to change majors, a high emotional toll was clearly taken. For subjects who did have to change majors ($n = 34$), the extent to which daily goals served the achievement of the life dream was strongly related to depression at the end of the study ($r = .67, p < .01$; $r = .15$, n.s. for those not changing majors).

Despite the tantalizing attraction of lost futures, there is a great deal of evidence that people can and do cope effectively with losses that dramatically change their future selves. Examinations of individuals in a variety of severely negative circumstances suggests that even in the worst situations imaginable individuals are able to "cheat chaos" by "not only surviving but also thoroughly enjoying their lives" (Csikszentmihalyi, 1990, p. 193; cf. Antonovsky, 1988; Frankl, 1984). Studies by Massimini in Milan (cited in Csikszentmihalyi, 1990) found that paraplegics identified their accident as one of the most negative and one of the most positive things ever to happen to them. One of the benefits of this loss was a new clarity of purpose and valuable reordering of priorities.

An interesting case in point is provided by parents who have had a child with Down's syndrome. Firestein (1989) noted that as individuals go about building a family, wishful images arise spontaneously. It might be expected that parents with a child with Down's would be likely to be tormented by such wishful images. Yet, Van Riper, Ryff, and Pridham (1992) found evidence of adaptive functioning and resilience among these parents. Indeed, Carr (1988), in a longitudinal study spanning 22 years, found many positive sentiments at late follow-ups.

In an ongoing study of parents of children with Down's syndrome ($N = 51$; Ligon, 1996), we've asked parents to construct retrospective accounts of their hopes and dreams for the child before they were informed that the child had Down's syndrome. Participants also completed questionnaire measures of life satisfaction, meaning in life, distress, and defensiveness and constructed a narrative about their current hopes and dreams for their child now. From these data, we've developed a coding strategy for "lost selves" and possible selves that reliably discriminates among defensive individuals, realistically happy individuals, and distressed individuals (Ligon, 1996). From the "lost-future" perspective, satisfied, nondefensive individuals tended to write narratives characterized by self-deprecation (e.g., "I hardly knew what to expect," "I was probably pretty naive," "I suppose I was just like anyone else"), objectivity, and admission of loss. Subjects scoring high in defensiveness tended to minimize the loss (e.g., "my life has not been changed by my child's Down's syndrome, except in very tiny ways"), and those who score high on measures of distress had very specific lost life dreams (e.g., "I always imagined that my son would take over the family business"). With regard to current future selves, subjects scoring low in defensiveness and high in measures of satisfaction and meaning in life tended to score highly on dimensions of awareness of limitations, realism, and admission of difference from a "norm." Thus, successfully rewriting one's future seems to involve truly relinquishing the lost "happily ever after" and investing in a new life dream—commensurate with the one that has been lost—a bittersweet investment. The process of reinstating agency may be characterized as a process of reconstructing and reinvesting in a future toward which to strive.

Central to the issue of rewriting one's life dream is Block's (1982) discussion of Piaget's developmental processes of assimilation and accommodation in personality development. In assimilation, the individual avoids any meaningful change of orientation and manages to simply assimilate a new experience into his or her existing framework. In accommodation, the individual is forced to adopt a more complex frame of reference in adapting to the world. Through accommodation, experience results in increased differentiation and integration of personality. Helson and her colleagues (e.g., 1992; Helson & Roberts, 1994; Helson & Wink, 1992) have demonstrated that "difficult times" may be a catalyst for personality growth. For example, women who had a higher degree of "life stimulation" (e.g., a woman pursuing a career in the late 1950s or early 1960s, or experiences of disruption such as divorce or career failure) tended to show a greater degree of ego development over 31 years. Similarly, Bursik (1991) found that women who had gone through divorce and experienced it as disequilibrating but who had successfully coped experienced an increase in ego development. Difficult life circumstances may be seen as an accommodative challenge, as opportunities to grow.

An important aspect of dealing with significant irrevocable life change is the accommodative process of reconstructing a personal future, shifting one's possible-self horizon. In our work with groups who have experienced major life changes (e.g., parents of children with Down Syndrome, women who've divorced after more than 15 years of marriage), two processes clearly emerge: first, the confrontation of loss and, second, the rebuiliding of a viable future, a reasonable source of hope. For this new possible self to be sufficient for life to have meaning, it must be as elaborate and emotionally engaging as the life dream it is replacing. The importance of successfully completing this task is indicated in research on hopelessness, optimism, meaning in life, and physical and mental health (e.g., Antonovsky, 1988; Scheier & Carver, 1985, 1993).

These assertions are supported to some extent by the program of research on confronting traumatic experiences by Pennebaker and his colleagues (e.g., Pennebaker, Colder, & Sharp, 1990). This research indicates that individuals who confront a traumatic experience by writing about it are likely to show enhanced immune and improved psychological and physical well-being (Pennebaker, 1993). The utility of writing about traumatic experiences in adjustment to life change and trauma has been demonstrated in a wide variety of contexts and samples. Importantly, recently Pennebaker (1993) has found that specific aspects of writing are associated with health gains. Individuals who freely express negative emotions and those who grow in their feelings of insight and positive emotion about the traumatic experience tend to benefit most from the experience of writing. Moreover, individuals who improve on measures of functioning also tended to increase in the "storied" quality of their writing. Thus, constructing a meaningful story, with a beginning, middle, *and end,* has been linked to health and well-being. This evidence lends powerful support to the notion that in order to effectively cope with a loss or change in one's future self, one must not only confront what is lost but reach some sort of resolution about it (see Miner & King, 1996).

One issue that warrants mention is the potentially stabilizing effects of daily goals during changes in one's ultimate life goals. Proximal goals may serve to buffer the loss of a treasured future by allowing the individual to maintain a sense of agency through life change. It may be possible for the individual to change longer-term enduring goals that drive daily goals without necessarily radically changing the content of daily goals themselves. Thus, an individual who finds that he or she will never become a world class athlete may persist in the personal strivings—"to strive to be the best at all I do"—even as the ultimate vision of the self in the future involves being a great gymnastics coach, rather than an Olympic gymnast. A mother in our sample of parents of children with Down's syndrome listed the following daily goals: "to help all of my children realize their potential; to ensure that my children have 'easy lives'; to be a good wife." These daily goals could function as a source of agency, regardless of the specific circumstances of the future story toward which they might be focused.

THE IMPLICIT AGENCY OF DAILY LIFE

To some extent, the information that mundane goals have to offer about the everyday experience of agency remains implicit in goal research. Certainly, this research indicates that having valued goals and experiencing progress in goal pursuit are vital to the experience of subjective well-being. Goal commitment, importance, progress, and the absence of ambivalence and conflict among and within goals have all been linked to psychological well-being (e.g., Emmons, 1989; Omodei & Wearing, 1990) and physical well-being as well (Emmons & King, 1988). Processes that underlie the formation of daily goals, the content of those goals, and the enactment of goals can tell us a great deal about the struggle for mastery, self-enhancement, and personal growth. Harlow and Cantor (1995) have described how the strategies that people use to achieve their life tasks constitute the creation of agency in daily life. More remains to be said, however, about the implicit agent—who generates and acts upon daily goals. Setting a goal at all reveals that an individual experiences at least some sense of control over outcomes in a particular area. The breadth of the goal may reveal the extent to which the individual perceives himself or herself as impactful in that area. To the extent that individuals embark on difficult goals they demonstrate the capacity to forego positive affective payoffs in the present for later, more highly valued, rewards. Thus, the ability to remain engaged in difficult daily goals is a sign of self-regulation. Furthermore, research on personalized goals reveals that actively pursuing personally important goals, i.e., the daily experience of self-as-agent, has implications for spontaneous thought and guides emotional reactions (Emmons, 1991), lending structure to experience (Cantor et al., 1991). Daily thought and mood are colored by our daily goal pursuits—pursuits that impinge on the content of thought and quality of mood. The relations of concrete goals to more abstract hopes and dreams suggest an implicit belief in the controllability of one's destiny. Daily goals may be seen as evidence of control beliefs, mastery, competence, and efficacy, just as they are source of these experiences as well.

Consideration of seemingly mundane, everyday goals has provided researchers a view of the minutia of human experience. The hum of daily life is captured in these snapshots of intention. At the same time, everyday goals reveal much about the assumptions that drive daily behaviors—the outcomes that are viewed as controllable and those that are seen as valuable and worthy of investment. Placed in the broader context of the life dreams toward which individuals strive, daily goals provide information about the ways we invest in the future and how this investment is manifested in daily experience. Research reviewed in this chapter suggests that daily goals that serve our life dreams are more likely to be valued by us, although they are also likely to be difficult goals as well. Daily goals that serve our life dreams (or that avoid our most dreaded futures) are also more likely to appear in daily thoughts and to be relevant to everyday behaviors. Finally, events that are relevant to our life dreams are more likely to be seen as impinging on daily mood. In a sample of individuals seeking a very difficult life goal (i.e., becoming a doctor), negative mood was more likely to be related to negative events in the area of a life dream. Furthermore, positive events relevant to avoiding a worst fear were more likely to impinge on positive mood. Daily goals provide a bridge from everyday experience to a hoped for future. Examining low-level goals allows us to track the self-as-agent in his or her everyday existence. Placing these goals in a broader motivational context allows us to see their role in the larger drama of human life.

ACKNOWLEDGMENTS

The studies described in this chapter, as well as the preparation of the chapter itself, were supported by NIMH/FIRST Award 54142-02 to Laura A. King, Ph.D.

REFERENCES

Adler, A. (1927). *The practice and theory of individual psychology.* New York: Harcourt Brace Jovanovich.

Allport, G. W. (1961). *Pattern and growth in personality.* New York: Holt, Rinehart and Winston.

Antonovsky, A. (1988). *Unraveling the mystery of health.* San Francisco: Jossey-Bass.

Aronoff, J., & Wilson, J. P. (1985). *Personality in the social process.* Hillsdale, NJ: Erlbaum.

Bandura, A. (1982). The self and mechanisms of agency. In J. Suls (Ed.), *Psychological perspectives on the self* (pp. 3–39). Hillsdale, NJ: Erlbaum.

Bandura, A., & Schunk, D. H. (1981). Cultivating competence, self-efficacy, and intrinsic interest through proximal self-motivation. *Journal of Personality and Social Psychology, 41*, 586–598.

Baumeister, R. F. (1991). *Meanings of life*. New York: Guilford.

Baumeister, R. F., & Heatherton, T. F. (1996). Self-regulation failure: An overview. *Psychological Inquiry, 7*, 1–15.

Block, J. (1982). Assimilation, accomodation, and the dynamics of personality development. *Child Development, 53*, 281–295.

Bursik, K. (1991). Adaptation to divorce and ego development in adult women. *Journal of Personality and Social Psychology, 60*, 300–306.

Cantor, N., Norem, J., Langston, C., Zirkel, S., Fleeson, W., & Cook-Flanagan, C. (1991). Life tasks and daily life experience. *Journal of Personality, 59*, 425–451.

Carr, J. (1988). Six weeks to twenty-one years old: A longitudinal study of children with Down's syndrome and their families. *Journal of Child Psychology, 29*, 407–431.

Carver, C. S., & Scheier, M. F. (1981). *Attention and self-regulation: A control theory approach to human behavior.* New York: Springer-Verlag.

Csikszentmihalyi, M. (1990). *Flow*. New York: Harper & Row.

Deci, E. L., & Ryan, R. M. (1991). A motivational approach to the self: Integration in personality . In R. Dienstbier (Ed.), *Nebraska symposium on motivation* (Vol. 38, pp. 237–288). Lincoln, NE: University of Nebraska Press.

Deci, E. L., & Ryan, R. M. (1995). Human autonomy: The basis for true self-esteem. In M. H. Kernis (Ed.), *Efficacy, agency, and self-esteem* (pp. 31–50). New York: Plenum.

Emmons, R. A. (1989). The personal striving approach to personality. In L. A. Pervin (Ed.), *Goal concepts in personality and social psychology* (pp. 87–126). Hillsdale, NJ: Erlbaum.

Emmons, R. A. (1991). Personality strivings, daily life events, and psychological and physical well-being. *Journal of Personality, 59*, 453–472.

Emmons, R. A. (1992). Abstract versus concrete goals: Personal striving level, physical illness and psychological well-being. *Journal of Personality and Social Psychology, 62*, 292–300.

Emmons, R. A., & King, L. A. (1988). Conflict among personal strivings: Immediate and long-term implications for psychological and physical well-being. *Journal of Personality and Social Psychology, 48*, 1040–1048.

Emmons, R. A., & King, L. A. (1989). On the personalization of motivation. In R. Wyer & T. Srull (Eds.), *Advances in Social Cognition*. Hillsdale, NJ: Erlbaum.

Emmons, R. A., & King, L. A. (1992). Thematic analysis, personal goals and thought sampling. In C. Smith (Ed.), *Thematic content analysis for motivation and personality research* (pp. 73–86). New York: Cambridge University Press.

Emmons, R. A., & McAdams, D. P. (1991). Personal strivings and motive dispositions: Exploring the links. *Personality and Social Psychology Bulletin, 17*, 648–654.

Firestein, S. K. (1989). Special features of grief reactions with reproductive catastrophe. *Grief and Care, 3*, 37–45.

Frankl, V. E. (1984). *Man's search for meaning*. New York: Simon & Schuster.

Gilovich T. (1995). The experience of regret: What, when, why. *Psychological Review, 102*, 379–395.

Harlow, R. E., & Cantor, N. (1995). Overcoming lack of self-assurance in an achievement domain: Creating agency in daily life. In M. H. Kernis (Ed.), *Efficacy, agency, and self-esteem* (pp. 171–191). New York: Plenum.

Helson, R. (1992). Women's difficult times and the rewriting of the life story. *Psychology of Women Quarterly, 16*, 331–347.

Helson, R., & Roberts, B. (1994). Ego development and personality change in adulthood. *Journal of Personality and Social Psychology, 66*, 911–920.

Helson, R., & Wink, P. (1992). Two conceptions of maturity examined in findings of a longitudinal study. *Journal of Personality and Social Psychology, 53*, 531–541.

Kasser, T., & Ryan, R. M. (1993). A dark side of the American dream: Correlates of financial success as a central life aspiration. *Journal of Personality and Social Psychology, 65*, 410–424.

Kasser, T., & Ryan, R. M. (1996). Further examining the American Dream. *Personality and Social Psychology Bulletin, 22*, 63–73.

Kato, K., & Markus, H. R. (1993). The role of possible selves in memory. *Psychologia, 36*, 73–83.

King, L. A. (1994). Personal strivings and ultimate life goals: Linking the present with the future. Paper presented in a symposium entitled, "Goal units in personality: Development and change of personal goals." C. Langston, Chair, 102nd Annual Convention of the American Psychological Association, Los Angeles, California, August, 1994.

King, L. A. (1996). Who is regulating what and why? The motivational context of self-regulation. *Psychological Inquiry, 7*, 57–61.

King, L. A., & Emmons, R. A. (1991). Psychological, physical and interpersonal correlates of emotional expressiveness, conflict and control. *European Journal of Personality, 5*, 131–150.

King, L. A., Richards, J. H., & Stemmerich, E. D. (1998). Daily goals, life goals, and worst fears: Means, ends, and subjective well-being. *Journal of Personality*, in press.

King, L. A., & Stemmerich, E. D. (1996). Salience and content of possible selves: Does it matter what we strive towards? Manuscript submitted for publication. Southern Methodist University, Dallas, Texas.

King, L. A., & Williams, T. (1996). Enacting the life story: Daily goals, life dreams, and well-being. Unpublished manscript. Southern Methodist University, Texas.

Klinger, E. (1975). Consequences of commitment to and disengagement from incentives. *Psychological Review, 82*, 223–231.

Klinger, E. (1977). *Meaning and void: Inner experience and the incentives in people's lives*. Minneapolis: University of Minnesota Press.

Kuhl, J., & Helle, P. (1986). Motivational and volitional determinants of depression: The degenerated-intention hypothesis. *Journal of Abnormal Psychology, 95*, 247–251.

Ligon, G. (1996). Rewriting the future: The case of parents of children with Down Syndrome. Unpublished data. Southern Methodist University, Texas.

Manderlink, G. & Harakiewicz, J. M. (1984). Proximal versus distal goal setting and intrinsic motivation. *Journal of Personality and Social Psychology, 47*, 918–928.

Markus, H. (1983). Self-knowledge: An expanded view. *Journal of Personality, 51*, 543–565.

Markus, H., & Nurius, P. (1986). Possible selves. *American Psychologist, 41*, 954–969.

Markus, H., & Ruvolo, A. (1989). Possible selves: Personalized representations of goals. In L. A. Pervin (Ed.), *Goal concepts in personality and social psychology* (pp. 211–242). Hillsdale, NJ: Erlbaum.

McAdams, D. P., & de St. Aubin, E. (1992). A theory of generativity and its assessment through self-report, behavioral acts, and narrative themes in autobiography. *Journal of Personality and Social Psychology, 62*, 1003–1015.

McAdams, D. P., Ruetzel, K., & Foley, J. M. (1986). Complexity and generativity at mid-life: Relations among social motives, ego development and adults' plans for the future. *Journal of Personality and Social Psychology, 50*, 800–807.

Miner, K. N., & King, L. A. (1996). Writing about traumatic events and recovery: Implications for psychological and physical well-being. Paper presented at the American Psychological Association Convention, Toronto, Canada, August, 1996.

Morgan, M. (1985). Self monitoring of attained subgoals in private study. *Journal of Educational Psychology, 77*, 623–630.
Murray, H. A. (1938). *Explorations in personality*. New York: Oxford University Press.
Norem, J. K., & Illingworth, K. S. (1993). Strategy-dependent effects of reflecting on self and tasks: Some implications of optimism and defensive pessimism. *Journal of Personality and Social Psychology, 65*, 822–835.
Omodei, M. M., & Wearing, A. J. (1990). Need satisfaction and involvement in personal projects: Toward an integrative model of subjective well-being. *Journal of Personality and Social Psychology, 59*, 762–769.
Oyserman, D., & Markus, H. R. (1990). Possible selves and delinquency. *Journal of Personality and Social Psychology, 59*, 112–125.
Pennebaker, J. W. (1989). Confessions, inhibition, and disease. In L. Berkowitz (Ed.), *Advances in experimental social psychology* (Vol. 22, pp. 211–244). New York: Academic Press.
Pennebaker, J. W. (1993). Putting stress into words: Health, linguistic, and therapeutic implications. *Behavior Research and Therapy*, 31, 539–548.
Pennebaker, J. W., Colder, M., & Sharp, L. K. (1990). Accelerating the coping process. *Journal of Personality and Social Psychology, 58*, 528–537.
Pervin, L. A. (Ed.). (1989). *Goal concepts in personality and social psychology*. Hillsdale, NJ: Erlbaum.
Ruvolo, A. P., & Markus, H. R. (1992). Possible selves and performance: The power of self-relevant imagery.Self-knowledge: Content, structure, and function [special issue]. *Social Cognition, 10*, 95–124,
Ryff, C. D. (1991). Possible selves in adulthood and old age: A tale of shifting horizons. *Psychology and Aging, 2*, 286–295.
Scheier, M., & Carver, C. S. (1985). Optimism, coping and health: Assessment and implications of generalized outcome expectancies. *Health Psychology, 4*, 219–247.
Scheier, M., & Carver, C. S. (1993). On the power of positive thinking: The benefits of being optimistic. *Current Directions in Psychological Science, 2*, 26–30.
Sheldon, K. M., & Kasser, T. (1995). Coherence and congruence: Two aspects of personality integration. *Journal of Personality and Social Psychology, 57*, 1069–1081.
Sherman, S. J., Skov, R. B., Hervitz, E. G., & Stock, C. B. (1981). The effects of explaining hypothetical future events: From possibility to actuality and beyond. *Journal of Experimental Social Psychology, 17*, 142–158
Tomkins, S. S. (1992). Script theory. In R. A. Zucker, A. I. Rabin, J. Aronoff, & S. J. Frank (Eds.), *Personality structure in the life course* (pp. 152–217). New York: Springer.
Vallacher, R. R., & Wegner, D. M. (1989). Levels of personal agency: Individual variation in action identification. *Journal of Personality and Social Psychology, 57*, 660–671.
Van Riper, M., Ryff, C., & Pridham, K. (1989). Parental and family well-being in families of children with Down syndrome. *Research in Nursing and Health, 15*, 227–235.
Wegner, D. M., & Erber, R. (1992). The hyperaccessibility of suppressed thoughts. *Journal of Personality and Social Psychology, 63*, 903–912.
Yetim, U. (1993). Life satisfaction: A study based on the organization of persons projects. *Social Indicators Research, 29*, 277–289.
Zeigarnik, B. (1938). On finished and unfinished tasks. In W. D. Ellis (Ed.), *A source book of gestalt psychology* (pp. 300–314). New York: Harcourt, Brace, & World.
Zirkel, S. & Cantor, N. (1990). Personal construal of life tasks: Those who struggle for independence. *Journal of Personality and Social Psychology, 58*, 172–185.

PART II

AFFECTIVE AND COGNITIVE MECHANISMS OF EXECUTIVE AGENCY

Whereas the chapters of Part I examined various control functions at the level of the self-system, the chapters in Part II focus more on control at a lower level of analysis. They concentrate on different subsystems (e.g., affective, cognitive, physiological) or subsets of subsystems involved in self-regulation. However, all emphasize the role played by the various subsystems in meeting everyday challenges to effective control over the environment.

Brehm and Brummet's chapter, for example, analyzes the factors that control affectively neutral and emotional behaviors. Of these, the most critical is goal importance. According to Brehm and Brummet, routine goal-directed behaviors require guidance primarily from the cognitive system. That is, in the course of mundane, routine daily activities, an individual must decide which goals to pursue, how best to do so, and when the level of goal attainment is satisfactory, not worth the effort expenditure, impossible, and so on. All of these activities require cognitive assessments. In the case of important outcomes, the authors argue that the emotional system also plays a major role in behavior control. Important outcomes engender emotional reactions that, in turn, urge the person to take appropriate instrumental activity. To the degree that any factors interfere with, restrain, or act against the function of the engendered emotion, its intensity will rise to a level necessary to overcome such deterrents. Brehm and Brummet note, however, that maximum control over behavior is maintained by minimizing the intensity of emotion. In a review of the research findings from their own and others' laboratories, Brehm and Brummet make a good case for their argument that emotions function like motivational states in that they function to control the intensity and direction of behavior. One of the more intriguing points made in this chapter is that far from being disruptive of rational behavior, emotions often encourage it.

Interestingly, Forgas, Johnson, and Ciarrochi also take issue with the widespread notion that affect disrupts rational thought processes. Like Brehm and Brummet, they contend that emotions and mood states often resemble motivational states in their influence on cognition and behavior. Their major focus, however, is on mild affective states that typically do not intrude into consciousness. They note that control over such affective states, although often not seen as such, is at the very heart of personal control.

In their chapter, Forgas and his colleagues present a detailed and elegant theory of mood management, one that focuses on the various situational, task, and individual difference factors that facilitate or hinder effective emotional self-regulation. They argue that the major goal of the mood management system is affective equilibrium and that mild affective states give rise to one of two subtle and often subconscious cognitive strategies designed to maintain or change the current state. These two strategies are substantive and motivated information processing, and they result in affect infusion (the impact of mood on cognition in a mood-congruent direction) and affect control (targeted cognitive activity in the service of mood management), respectively. According to Forgas, Johnson, and Ciarrochi, people have the ability to calibrate and correct their mood states by relying on the complementary operation of affect infusion and control.

Wright's chapter concerns a different focus of self-regulatory activity: cardiovascular (CV) responsivity in the face of behavioral challenges. The importance of this particular physiological outcome for Wright lies in its intimate relation to task engagement or effort expenditure in pursuit of control over various outcomes. One of the primary determinants of such control and CV reactivity in response to challenges is the individual's perceived ability level. Traditional approaches to the relation between CV responsivity and perceived ability assert that in circumstances where the goal is to gain some positive outcome through action, CV responsivity increases as perceived ability increases; however, in circumstances where the goal is to avoid some undesirable outcome, CV responsivity decreases as ability increases. Wright argues that the traditional view is inadequate on a number of grounds. Building upon Brehm's theory of motivational intensity, he presents instead an integrative analysis that specifies the various determinants of momentary effort expenditure. In particular, he examines how task difficulty, as well as the need state, incentive value, and the expectancy of goal attainment given successful instrumental behavior all influence the perceived ability–CV responsivity relation. A review of Wright's and others' research on these and related factors reveals promising initial support for his integrative analysis. He concludes with a discussion of practical and theoretical implications of his new ability perspective.

In her consideration of the pragmatic bases of action, Lewicka concentrates on a cognitive bias that she feels can explain apparent departures from rationality in hypothesis testing, causal reasoning, judgments of covariation, control judgments, and judgments under uncertainty—namely, the confirmation bias. The particular form of this bias with which her analysis is concerned is the confirmatory strategy of hypothesis testing whereby the truth of a hypothesis is ascertained by checking only positive and not negative instances. According to Lewicka, this bias results from an overemphasis on sufficient rather than on necessary conditions of events, or too much attention being paid to errors of commission (false positives) compared to errors of omission (false negatives). Far from being an irrational process, Lewicka considers the confirmation bias to be a reasonable strategy of hypothesis testing chosen for the sake of cognitive simplicity and ease and for its adaptive value. Very simply, she argues that the confirmation bias ensures the individual will attain gains or benefits without undue exposure to uncertainty and risk. It also facilitates the individual's commitment to goal-oriented action strategies.

Beckmann's chapter also focuses on various cognitive strategies that facilitate or hinder goal-oriented action. The primary targets under consideration in his chapter are mechanisms of attentional control. Beckmann takes on the imposing task of analyzing the manner in which the cognitive system via these mechanisms controls the access of internal and external inputs to consciousness and thereby facilitates or hinders the enactment of action control strategies. He proposes a hierarchy of attention controllers, or gatekeepers, that function to mediate changes in thought content. Some of these gatekeepers operate at an unconscious level, passing along information to the next controller if the informational input exceeds a requisite threshold level. What determines this threshold level? The answer to this question forms one of the major aspects of Beckmann's theory of intrusive thought. In part, the answer concerns the contents of current and competing thought. If the content of competing thought is not strong enough to exceed the threshold, then automatic attentional inhibition results. There also are two auxiliary functions of the controllers that can be engaged to control the contents of conscious thought, both of which involve volition on the part of the individual. This chapter, in its consideration of the cognitive, affective, and motivational supports for effective goal-directed behavior, has important implications for theories of action control. It also touches on many of the underlying themes addressed by the authors of other chapters in this section.

In another examination of the role of the cognitive system in action control, Montgomery points out that theories of decision making generally have failed to acknowledge or deal systematically with the relationship between decisions and actions. He argues that decisions, in essence, are commitments to act and that predecisional processes are oriented toward facilitating resultant action. In his chapter, Montgomery presents his theory of human decision processes. He suggests that when faced with alternative courses of action, individuals often evaluate the attractiveness of the attributes associated with each alternative and attempt to structure or restructure the attribute information in such a way that a single solution becomes the self-evident choice. He refers to this process as a search for dominance structure (SDS). Research relevant to an evaluation of Montgomery's SDS theory is presented. Montgomery concludes with an examination of the ways in which the various phases of the decision-making processes are related to and support action. In so doing, he reminds us that thinking is for doing.

Whereas the other chapters in this section all focus on interactions within and among the person's cognitive, affective, and physiological systems in the self-regulation of behavior, in the final chapter Schönpflug argues that ecologically valid theories of action control must also consider the role of external resource systems. Those who want to achieve outcomes beyond their personal limitations must rely on external resources, such as tools or other people, to obtain desired outcomes. However, theoretical consideration of such extended control systems requires attention to a number of issues. Schönpflug notes that one such issue is the distinction between external resources as agents of control or as objects of control. The importance of this distinction lies in its implications for the individual's perceived level of personal control. The former may well result in feelings of a loss of control, whereas the latter may result in feelings of enhanced control. Through presentation of a series of intriguing studies designed to examine several implications of his model of extended control, Schönpflug makes clear the complexity of the regulation of human activity and brings home the importance of his central point—namely, that theories of control must include a consideration not only of the individual's intentions, goals, internal conflicts, and skills but also of the potentially great impact of the broader social and technical environment.

CHAPTER 6

THE EMOTIONAL CONTROL OF BEHAVIOR

JACK W. BREHM AND BEVERLY H. BRUMMETT

While preparing a lecture for your class two weeks hence, you are distracted by a fly buzzing around your head and you look around for some way to get rid of the fly even though this interrupts your train of thought regarding the lecture. In contrast, if you are desperately trying to meet a deadline for a grant proposal that is due the next day, the fly is hardly noticed. However, if what is buzzing around your head is not a fly but rather a wasp, and you know from past experience that you are allergic to being stung, you interrupt your train of thought on the grant proposal in order to do something about the wasp. Your focus of attention is controlled by whatever is most important to you, and even if you are trying to deal with two or more possible events at the same time, your focus of attention at any moment tends to be on one or the other, not on both. Furthermore, even though the fly is nothing compared to the lecture, and even though the chance of being stung by the wasp is extremely slight, one's focus of attention is greatly influenced by the momentary importance of events. But what is the process whereby important events influence behavior?

Let's return to the example and ask ourselves what else must be going on in the person in our example. If we were to interview the person pre-

JACK W. BREHM • Department of Psychology, University of Kansas, Lawrence, Kansas 66045. E-mail: jbrehm@kuhub.cc.ukans.edu BEVERLY H. BRUMMETT • Department of Psychiatry and Behavioral Sciences, Duke University Medical Center, Durham, North Carolina 27710.

Personal Control in Action, edited by Kofta et al., Plenum Press, New York, 1998.

paring the lecture, we would presumably hear that the person was mildly interested in finishing the lecture and felt annoyed by the fly and felt frightened by the wasp. In contrast, the person preparing the grant application would presumably report being really eager to get the application done, felt nothing about the fly ("What fly?"), and felt very frightened by the wasp. What is the role of these affective responses?

It is obvious, and has long been the subject of attention of psychologists, that affective states influence behavior. For example, some of Thorndike's (1911) early work focused on rewards and punishments as factors that could increase or decrease the likelihood that a behavior would be repeated. Other investigators (e.g., Young, 1961) have focused on affect-producing stimuli as instigators of behavior, as exemplified by the behavior induction power of certain odors or sights that relate to edibility. Similarly, while researchers have frequently viewed emotions as special, complex instances of affective states, they have also frequently noted the prominent motivational character of some emotions, such as anger or fear; at least some emotions appear to energize and direct behavior, two functions frequently cited as properties of motivational states. What we will argue in the following pages is that emotions in general have the characteristics of motivational states: their function is to control the intensity and direction of behavior.

A theory concerning the emotional control of behavior (Brehm, 1992) is presented in the following paragraphs. The theory assumes there is at least one additional and relatively independent source of intended behavior, namely, a system in which energy is generally available and requires only the guidance of a cognitive system in order to produce behavior. In the latter kind of system, an understanding of how intended, or goal-directed, behavior occurs is a problem of how the cognitive system guides and maintains behavior in relationship to goals; energization and the absolute intensity of activity are considered as secondary or uninteresting aspects of the process (Atkinson and Birch, 1970). However, in the more general action orientation approach (Heckhausen, 1991), it is plausible to assume that cognitive and emotional processes may mutually influence the course of behavior. This interplay between cognitive and emotional processes is assumed for the following theoretical presentation; it has apparent implications for an understanding of action control.

THE THEORY

The theoretical considerations most pertinent to the present argument are captured in five assumptions, with their accompanying explanations.

1. Emotions have the character of motivational states; they have the function of urging an adaptive response to an actual or potential outcome of greater than average importance. As indicated in our opening example, it is possible for a person to carry out a task, such as preparing a lecture two weeks in advance, without a great deal of feeling. The task is one that must be done, but there is no unusual importance to having it done two weeks early, and if the topic is not one of great concern to either the lecturer or the audience, no unusual effort need be made in its preparation. It is only when some additional event intrudes, like a fly buzzing around one's head or the recollection that someone special will be sitting in on the lecture being prepared, that some affect occurs, in this case a feeling of annoyance or of concern, and that affective state urges one to eliminate the annoyance or concern.
2. The magnitude of the urge produced by an emotion is directly proportional to the intensity of the emotion—i.e., to the magnitude of feeling. This assumption means only that the intensity of feeling is the motivational state, and this fact should be reflected in psychological and physiological measures associated with that state.
3. The upper limit to the intensity of an emotion is a direct function of the personal importance of the actual or potential outcome that is the occasion for the emotion. Whatever event or potential event that may occur to a person has some meaning to him or her in terms of the values that the person holds. Events connected with nothing but inconsequential values should not be capable of causing emotional responses. Events of great consequence to the person—those that have a great influence on the person's well-being—are capable of creating emotions of very high intensity, and will do so if other conditions hold. Those other conditions are specified in the fourth and fifth assumptions.
4. The intensity of an emotion is a nonmonotonic function of the magnitude of deterrents to its function: When deterrents are small, intensity will be low; when deterrents are moderate, intensity will be moderate; and when deterrents are so great that they outweigh the importance of the potential or actual outcome, intensity will be low. This proposition is portrayed in Figure 1. The underlying assumption is that maximal control over behavior is maintained by minimizing the intensity of emotion; intensity should rise only to the level necessary to overcome deterrents. However, the meaning of this proposition depends on one's understanding of deterrent. A deterrent is any factor that interferes with, restrains, or acts against the function of an emotion. While the research described in the next section will do much to clarify

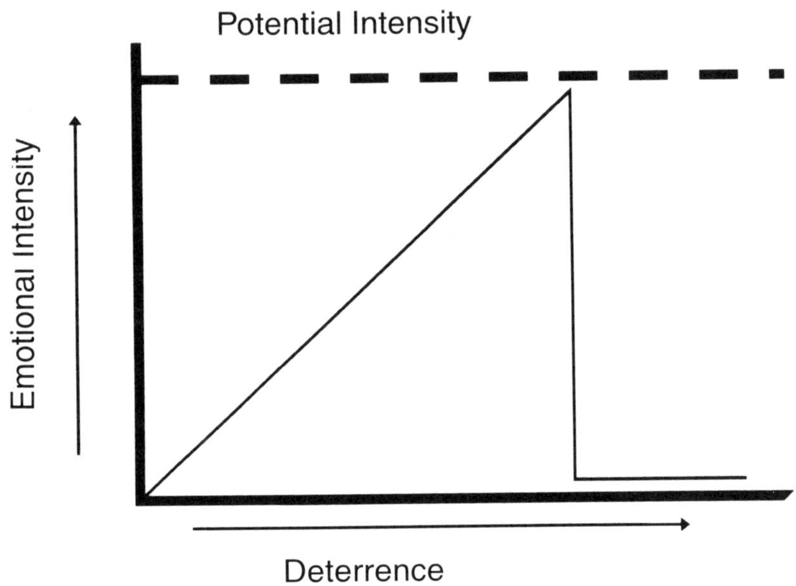

FIGURE 1 The theoretical effect of deterrents on the intensity of emotion.

the meaning of deterrence, a brief example here may also be helpful. Consider a person whose home has just been robbed, which is a good and important reason for feeling anger. Such anger is directed toward correction of the injustice, including recovery of lost items, repair of any damage to property, and perhaps some punishment to the robber to provide retribution. Deterrents, then, are factors that interfere with anger's providing these various functions. For example, a bad telephone connection when one was trying to report the robbery would be a deterrent to the functions of anger; so too would be the potential distraction of learning that a good friend was in the hospital with appendicitis; and so would attempts by a friend to improve one's mood by making jokes or advising that the matter was of no great importance. In short, deterrents include the sheer difficulty of carrying out whatever the emotion urges one to do, as well as any other factors that would draw attention from the emotion or its causes, and factors that would potentially cause conflicting emotions (urges) or behaviors.

5. When the magnitude of deterrents is unclear, the intensity of an emotion is a direct function of outcome importance. Because

many of the major emotions, such as fear, anger, or empathy, occur from situational crises—i.e., conditions that have occurred suddenly and unexpectedly—subjective assessment of relevant deterrents may not be possible. This assumption states that the overriding principle in the operation of the emotional system is dealing with the crisis rather than maintaining intensity at the minimum necessary to overcome deterrents. The underlying assumption here is that when the existence of deterrents is unclear, the emotion will hold sway over one's behavior in direct proportion to the importance of the event that gives rise to it.

EVIDENCE

Research dating from the early 1980s (e.g., Brehm, Wright, Solomon, Silka, & Greenberg, 1983) has provided compelling evidence that both physiological arousal and affective processes are implicated in motivational states. The bulk of this research (see, e.g., Wright & Brehm, 1989; Wright, 1996, for reviews) has demonstrated that the anticipatory condition of humans just prior to the initiation of instrumental behavior is one of heightened cardiovascular arousal and goal attractiveness. If experimentally produced differences in goal attractiveness can be assumed to reflect differences in affective intensity, then the first systematic evidence that motivational states and emotions are similar or identical comes from this work on the intensity of motivation. Let us, then, first look at an example of this motivational research.

The Intensity of Motivation

Where the traditional study of motivation has stressed the role of internal states such as needs and external conditions such as goals in the determination of motivational arousal, more recent work has focused attention on the role of instrumental behavior as a determinant of motivational arousal. The major reason for motivational arousal—the energizing process that takes place through the cardiovascular system—is to facilitate the expenditure of effort, either physical or mental. At the time our own work started (Brehm et al., 1983), we also believed that the energizing process would be accompanied by psychological processes such as judgments about the magnitude of needs or the attractiveness of goals. Much of the early research was designed to show only the psychological aspects of energization, and it did so by measuring goal attractiveness as a function of the difficulty of anticipated instrumental behavior. This early work demonstrated quite clearly that goal attractiveness increases as the difficulty of instrumental behavior increases, up to a point. Beyond that point, which is where the amount of effort required outweighs the desirability of the goal, or where the difficulty is beyond the person's capacity, goal attractiveness decreases. The assumption that these changes in goal attractiveness were directly related to motivational arousal received additional important support from subsequent work by Wright and his coworkers. We will briefly describe two of these studies.

An experiment by Wright, Contrada, and Patane (1986) was designed to provide evidence on cardiovascular arousal using a procedure and design that was typical of earlier studies that had shown goal attractiveness effects. Participants were first told that a list of nonsense trigrams would be projected onto a screen in front of them. Next they were told that they would win a prize (a pen) if they memorized the list within 2 min. Depending on group assignment, participants then learned that 2 trigrams (described as a very easy task for most people), 6 trigrams (described as a very difficult, yet possible, task for most people), or 20 trigrams (described as an impossible task for most people) would be presented. Measures of goal attractiveness and cardiovascular arousal were then taken while participants anticipated commencement of the memorization task. The predicted quadratic effect was reliable for both systolic blood pressure (SBP) and goal attractiveness, with SBP and attraction being higher for the difficult task than for the easy or nearly impossible task.

A second research example, and one that is particularly instructive, was carried out by Wright, Heaton, and Bushman (described in Wright & Brehm, 1989). This experiment is one of a few that has tested our assumption 5, namely, that when the magnitude of deterrents is unknown, intensity of emotion will be proportional to the importance of the outcome. In this experiment, some participants learned they could gain a valuable record album while others learned they could gain an inexpensive pen. Within each of these goal-value conditions, some participants were led to expect an easy memorization task while others were led to believe their memorization task could be any of five, which ranged from very easy to very difficult. Measures taken while participants anticipated task performance indicated that those who confronted ambiguity about task difficulty, compared to those who expected an easy task, had higher systolic blood pressure and saw their goal as more attractive. Among participants who confronted the ambiguous degree of difficulty, but not for those who knew the degree of difficulty, systolic blood pressure was higher for the more valuable incentive. And for those in the high incentive condition, but not for those in the low, the goal was rated as more attractive in the ambiguous than in the known difficulty condition. These data are consistent with the assumption that when deterrents are unspecified, the intensity of emotion is a direct function of the importance of the event (e.g., goal) that gives rise to the emotion.

Active Emotions

Many investigators of emotion acknowledge that some emotions can be characterized as "active," while others appear to be "passive." Active emotions urge action, while passive emotions frequently appear to have no associated overt behavior. Examples of the former are fear and anger; of the latter, sadness and pride (Lazarus, 1991). An obvious candidate to fit a theory that asserts that emotions function like motivational states would be an active emotion. The following brief review of experimental research designed to test the theory begins with active emotions.

Anger

As mentioned earlier, a number of possible deterrents could affect the intensity of anger. Any stimuli that threaten to distract the individual from attention to the cause of anger, any reasons for feeling good rather than angry, and any difficulty in carrying out aggression urged by the anger, including inhibitions from internal or external sources, would all serve as deterrents. A study by Dill (1997) examined the hypothesis that humor stimuli, cartoons, would act as deterrents to anger.

The participants, college students of both sexes, were individually shown on a computer an ostensible account by a college student about being victimized by a graduate teaching assistant for a required lecture course. The account described a number of ways in which the student felt mistreated. Participants were encouraged by written instructions to identify with the student's problem. When the participant indicated that the last page of the account had been read, a cartoon was superimposed over the last page. After the cartoon had been inspected and the caption read, a questionnaire asked participants to indicate their current feelings on a number of emotion dimensions, including, of course, anger.

The participants were randomly assigned to see either no cartoon or one of four different cartoons that had been rated as differentially funny by other undergraduate participants. Those who saw no cartoon provided an estimate of how much anger was produced by simply reading the account. This estimate should be approximately the highest level of anger that could be produced by a deterrent because the deterrents can make it easy or difficult to be angry but they should not add to the importance of the reasons for anger. The mean reported anger in this no-cartoon condition was 4.39 (0 = not at all, 10 = extremely).

The question of interest, of course, is whether or not participants would report feeling more angry, the funnier the cartoon that they saw. Their anger reports revealed just that—a linear trend ($F(1, 68) = 4.1$, $p = .05$), and no other effects. Mean anger varied from 2.4 at the lowest humor level to 4.2 at the highest humor level. Theoretically, if the dominant affective response is anger at the moment that the humorous stimulus is introduced, then what should be affected is anger, not friendly or kind feelings. Linear effects were obtained for some items that are closely related to anger: offended, furious, mean, and hostile. An opposing linear effect was obtained for the positive item good-natured. Not significantly affected were friendly, kind, irritated, sympathetic, mad, tender, agreeable, cooperative, and understanding. The effect appears to have been fairly well centered on anger. No evidence for a quadratic effect was obtained in this study.

Evidence for a quadratic effect was found in a study by Brummett (1996), and in this study anger was instigated directly rather than through vicarious experience, memory, or imagination. She led male undergraduates to believe that her marketing study was sponsored jointly by the department of psychology and the business school, and consequently, each participant would be asked at the end of the session to evaluate the study and the researcher, and she told each she hoped they would give very high ratings on these questions. Participants therefore knew from the beginning that they could damage the experimenter by giving low ratings on the evaluation questionnaire.

In the remaining procedure, the experimenter blamed the participant for a procedural error actually caused by the experimenter, accused the participant of wasting time because of the procedural error, and said that even though the length of time for his participation would run over the scheduled half hour, the participant would not receive additional credit for participation because the delay was his own fault. Thus each participant was mistreated by the experimenter in three different ways.

After this treatment, the participant filled out a short questionnaire about his prior experience with marketing research and his interest in majoring in business. Attached to this questionnaire was a gift certificate from a local sporting goods store. Written instructions explained that the certificate was donated to the business school and it was for the participant to keep and do with as he pleased. (It should be noted that the gift certificate did not come from the experimenter.) Participants received either a \$1, \$2, \$3, or \$5 certificate. In order to assess the maximum amount of anger that participants might experience just from the insulting treatment and the possibility of aggressing against the experimenter at the end of the session, a fifth group went through exactly the same procedure except that they received no gift certificate nor was there any mention of gift certifi-

TABLE 1 Reported Anger and Measured Aggression as a Function of Deterrents

	Deterrents				
Measure	Control	$1	$2	$3	$5
Anger	3.06	1.09	2.86	2.42	1.29
Aggression	1.94	1.00	1.64	1.75	0.79

cates. Following this form, participants were asked to indicate on scales running from zero to ten their current feelings on a number of affect dimensions including, of course, anger. Finally, the participant filled out the evaluation form for the study and researcher. The measure of aggression was how low the experimenter was rated on competence (1 = Not at all; 5 = Very).

Receiving an unexpected gift certificate should be a reason for not feeling anger—a deterrent. Thus, as the amount of the gift certificate increased, the intensity of anger should have increased at least up to the point where the certificate was more important than the reasons for anger, in which case anger should be replaced by happiness. The results for reported anger, however, failed to yield clear support for these expectations because there were two outliers in the $1 condition. While elimination of these two cases does in fact result in a reliable quadratic effect in support of the theoretical prediction, Brummett also reasoned that participants who perceived the gift certificate as unnoteworthy would not respond in accordance with the theory whatever condition they were in. Accordingly, she analyzed the anger data with participants (8) omitted if they rated the gift certificate as very low in attractiveness (0 or 1 on an 11-point scale).

First, it should be noted that the level of anger in the control condition was rather low. That was presumably because there was no reason for participants to become more angry than was necessary to carry out aggressive ratings on the final questionnaire. Given this somewhat low ceiling on anger in the deterrent conditions, the demonstration of the predicted effects seems problematic. Nevertheless, the resulting means for anger in Table 1 provide strong support for the theoretical predictions. The quadratic trend is significant at better than the 1% level, and the increase in anger from the $1 condition to the $2 is significant at the 2% level. The decrease in anger from the $3 condition to the $5 was not reliable, but that from the $2 condition to the $5 was significant at the 2% level. Also consistent with predictions, there was a quadratic effect ($p < .04$) on rated competence of (aggression against) the experimenter, with competence being lowest in the $2 and $3 conditions (reverse scored in Table 1). A significant quadratic effect was also obtained on mad, disgusted, and, in the opposite direction, good mood. No quadratic effects were obtained on the other affective measures: happy, frustrated, energetic, glad, bad mood, irritated, pleased, content, surprised, fearful, grouchy, nervous, incensed, helpless, sad, hopeful, cheery, and tense. Again, the affective responses seem relatively specific.

Brummett's results, along with the previously reported study by Dill (1997), provide fairly strong support for the hypothesis that anger increases as deterrents to anger increase, and Brummett's results support the prediction of a nonmonotonic effect of deterrents on anger. They further suggest that anger may be understood, at least in part, as a motivational state.

Sympathy

Sympathy appears to occur when an observed person receives an undeserved negative outcome, and at least at times, it seems to be an active emotion because it urges one to help the victim. Perhaps more generally, sympathy is identified with empathy, and the latter is sometimes conceptualized (e.g., Batson & Shaw, 1991) as an emotion that gives rise to altruistic motivation. In the work to be reported here, no distinction is made between sympathy and altruistic motivation, and sympathy is understood as a measure of desire to help.

Billings and Brehm (1996) carried out two small experiments, each designed to examine the effect of deterrents on sympathy. In both, the immediate reason for sympathy was a person who appeared to have a hip injury that forced her to use crutches to walk. Specifically, she carried one leg folded up against the other so that it seemed to be useless. To insure that this negative outcome was seen as undeserved, in both studies the experimental session commenced with the experimenter's asking the confederate if she had sprained her ankle, to which she replied that she had a birth defect.

The first of the two studies was an after-only design in which the deterrent to sympathy was manipulated by training the confederate to behave in regard to one aspect of the procedure in a mildly, moderately, or strongly rude way. Female participants were scheduled one at a time, and upon arrival were shown into a small research room, where the experimenter explained that the study concerned how people form opinions about another person they have just met. It was further explained that a second participant would be taking part and the two of them would have a short, structured interaction, and each would be asked to fill out a questionnaire about the other person. The experimenter then left to see if the other (the confederate) had arrived, and she reentered with the confederate, who was walking with crutches. After the exchange between the experimenter and the confederate to establish the cause and character of the disability, the experimenter asked for a volunteer to conduct an interview of the other, at which point the confederate volunteered.

Both the confederate and participant were given copies of the structured interview, which contained many questions about campus activities, and which they were supposed to complete within 10 min. During the actual 5 min that were allowed for the interview, the mild, moderate, and strong deterrents were effected by the confederate's interrupting answers that the participant attempted to give 3, 5, or 10 times, respectively. The experimenter stopped the interview and explained that the two of them would fill out questionnaires about each other in separate rooms in order to insure their candor, and the experimenter then gave a questionnaire to each and led the confederate out. The questionnaire was designed to measure the participant's impression of the confederate on a variety of dimensions, both positive and negative, and included a measure of sympathy.

The theoretical prediction, of course, is that as deterrents increase, sympathy should increase, and if deterrents become strong enough, sympathy should decrease, resulting in a quadratic effect. The analysis of sympathy ratings showed that while the simple effects between mild (M = 2.8), moderate (M = 4.6), and strong (M = 3.1) deterrents were not significant, the quadratic effect was significant at the 5% level. It should also be noted that the confederate was ignorant of the theory and hypothesis, and in confirmation of her constant behavior across conditions, no differences were found on ratings of attractive, socially skilled, smooth, enjoyable, friendliness, or liking. However, on the negative evaluative items—anger, irritation, and disliking—there was a reliable ($p = .05$) linear effect indicating a more negative evaluation the greater the deterrence. This evidence is consistent with the manipulation of deterrence. There were also differences on how friendly the subject felt toward the confederate, a dimension close to sympathy: mild (M = 5.00), moderate (M = 5.25), and strong (M = 3.10), yielding significant quadratic and linear *F*s. Once more, the affective responses are relatively specific and support the predicted effects of deterrents on sympathy. But one cannot rule out the possibility that the confederate somehow directly elicited more sympathy in the moderate deterrent condition compared to the mild and strong conditions.

Billings and Brehm (1996) therefore carried out a second study designed in part to keep the confederate blind to the manipulation of deterrents and in part to examine the effect of a different kind of deterrent. The design was a before-after with three levels of deterrents. A different female student served as confederate, but her training was similar to that for the first study, and she arrived on crutches and explained to the experimenter that her disability was from a birth defect. As before, she conducted a brief structured interview of the female participant and for all of them, she interrupted responses to questions five times, which should have enhanced initial sympathy. Roles were then reversed for the two, and the participant interviewed the confederate for a few minutes. The experimenter then took the participant to another room, thereby separating the two, ostensibly so they could candidly fill out questionnaires about each other. The participant then went through the following steps: she rated the confederate on a number of dimensions, including sympathy; she filled out a four item questionnaire, the answers to which would supposedly be given to the other person; she wrote a short autobiographical statement, also to be given to the other person; she received the other person's four-item rating of her and autobiographical statement; and based on the new information about the other, she rated the confederate a second time on a number of dimensions including sympathy. The ratings the participant received served as the deterrent to sympathy; the items were friendly, intelligent, mature, and interesting, and the ratings were either moderately positive (mild deterrence), minimally positive (moderate deterrence), or slightly negative (strong deterrence).

The change in sympathy ratings from after the initial structured interview to after the reception of the other's ratings is the dependent effect of theoretical interest. However, in this second study, the participant was confronted with evaluations of herself that should have been more impactful as deterrents to sympathy than the interruptions of answers used in the first study. To the extent that she received low ratings from the confederate, we could expect that she would feel less positive toward the confederate and would consequently give her lower ratings on the final evaluation. It was therefore impossible to predict the absolute changes in sympathy that might occur. Consequently, the appropriate measure of change in sympathy is a comparison with change in other evaluative items. Thus, to the extent that the ratings on friendly, mature, intelligent, and interesting act as a deterrent to sympathy for the confederate, change in sympathy should be positive relative to change in the other evaluative ratings. In other words, sympathy should increase with the magnitude of deterrence in comparison to changes in evaluation on other dimensions. If the magnitude of deterrence is sufficiently high, sympathy should decrease relative to other evaluative measures.

Correlations among the change measures indicated that the various evaluative items related positively to each other (with negative items reverse scored) except for the item feeling friendly. A composite of these evaluative items was therefore used as the baseline against which to assess change in sympathy.

Table 2 shows the mean changes in the composite evaluation and sympathy as a function of the deterrent level. As expected, there was a sharp decrease in evaluation of the confederate as a function of increased deterrence (receiving lower ratings). Nevertheless, sympathy tended to

TABLE 2 Changes in Composite Rating and Sympathy as a Function of Ratings Received by Participants

	Ratings received		
Measure	Moderate	Low	Very low
Composite rating	1.14	.29	−1.90
Sympathy	−.83	−.50	.29

increase with increasing deterrents, though this linear trend is not reliable. In keeping with our expectations, there was a difference in linear trends between sympathy and the composite ratings ($p < .05$). Quite clearly, sympathy, relative to other impressions, increases as deterrence increases. There was no evidence in this second study for a quadratic effect.

Taken together, these two studies on sympathy for a disabled person demonstrate that the intensity of sympathy increases as deterrents to sympathy (reasons for not feeling sympathetic) increase. The first study also produced evidence supporting the additional, plausible hypothesis that relatively high degrees of deterrence can decrease sympathy. An implication of these results, like those reported on anger, is that active emotions function like motivational states.

Passive Emotions

That active emotions function, at least in part, like motivational states should not be too surprising. Their label suggests that they have implications for overt behavioral responses and, of course, differ in that respect from "passive" emotions. The latter produce no overt behavior, unless, as Frijda (1986) says, "doing nothing" can be considered a behavior. Yet the theory on which the present chapter is based assumes that all emotions function like motivational states—they urge one to accomplish some end. Hence, even if we do not know what that end is (e.g., solving a psychological problem by mental processes), we can examine the effect of deterrents on the intensity of the emotion. Finding that passive emotions respond to deterrents just as active emotions do would provide presumptive evidence that passive emotions have the character of motivational states. To this end, we will describe first some research on sadness and then two experiments on happiness.

Sadness

One reason that sadness may plausibly be considered a passive emotion is that frequently the event that gives rise to it is an irrevocable loss of a loved one or friend or valued object or pet, so that no action can be taken in regard to prevention or modification of the event. For the same reason, creating sadness by an experimental event presents a problem for the investigator of emotion. As a consequence, the investigation of emotion has tended to use recalled, imagined, or vicarious experience, and the present research is no exception. A study and replication (Brehm, Brummett, & Harvey, 1998) will be reported in which male college student participants read an account purportedly written by a person similar to themselves, but which was expressly designed to make the reader feel sad.[1] The author recounted how he had recently been dumped by his girlfriend after they had been together for several years.

Participants, run individually, were led to believe the purpose of the research was to see how people feel about a wide variety of items ranging from consumer items to personal stories and TV scripts. Ostensibly because there were so many items, each participant was asked to respond to only two of them, selected at random. The participant was then left in an experimental room with materials and written instructions on how to proceed. The participant was requested to read the story and consider the plight of the author, to then open a second envelope and follow the instructions inside, and finally to open a third envelope and fill out the questionnaire it contained. The second envelope contained the deterrent to sadness. The instructions said that the gift certificate attached was donated to the research project, and the gift certificate was to be kept by the participant and used in whatever way he wanted. Participants received either a \$1, \$2, or \$3 gift certificate to a local sporting goods store, and they were asked to take a moment to consider what they might do with it. The instructions for the questionnaire simply noted that the questionnaire was specifically designed to obtain their responses to the two items they saw, that their responses were anonymous and they should be as honest as possible in answering the questions. The first question asked participants to indicate the extent to which they felt sad on an 11-point scale running from 0 (not at all) to 10 (extremely). Participants also reported the extent to which they felt guilty, fearful, full of pep, happy, tense, angry, content, hopeless, disgusted, surprised, good mood, bad mood, and how attractive they thought the gift certificate.

The results we will report here are the combination of a study and a replication. While the first study was carried out by three experimenters, two female and one male, with male participants, the second was carried out by a single, different, male experimenter, again with male participants. Because the only effect due to replications was a main effect on bad mood, the results are combined for the sake of simplicity in presentation.

It was hypothesized that sadness would increase with increased amount of the gift certificate, though it was possible that the largest gift certificate would result in reduced sadness and a quadratic effect. The mean sadness reports in the \$1, \$2, and \$3 conditions were 3.89, 5.63, and 2.67, producing a marginal simple effect between \$1 and \$2 ($t(35) = 1.61$, $p = .12$), a reliable simple effect between \$2 and \$3 ($t(35) = 2.73$, $p = .01$), and a reliable quadratic effect across the three deterrents to sadness ($t(35) = 2.55$, $p < .02$). The only other effects obtained were marginal quadratic effects on good mood ($p = .06$) and bad mood ($p = .09$), and the expected linear effect on rated gift certificate attractiveness ($p = .05$). The pattern for bad mood paralleled that for sadness, while the quadratic for good mood is due primarily to a relatively high level in the \$3 gift certificate condition. As would be expected theoretically, there is a tendency for good mood to supplant sadness for those who receive the \$3 gift certificate. More generally, the affective consequences are quite specific to the initial dominant state and the character of the deterrent.

In a third study, using female participants, the same story but rewritten for females, and in which only \$1 and \$2 gift certificates were given to participants, the increase in sadness as a function of the deterrent was supported more strongly. The \$2 certificate produced much more sadness (M = 6.43) than did the \$1 certificate (M = 3.19), $p < .01$.

Even though these data appear to give reasonable support to the theory and the assumption that passive emotions, like active ones, function like motivational states, caution is warranted because sadness was created vicariously. One could have more confidence that the theory works for passive emotions if the reason for the emotion could be created in the experimental setting. Two additional studies have been carried out on the passive emotion of happiness, one of which involved a more direct instigation than the reading of a story.

Happiness

It may be somewhat controversial to call happiness "passive." People do sometimes jump for joy and otherwise celebrate their good fortune. But Lazarus (1991) has carefully analyzed the major emotions and has failed to find a clear behavioral implication of happiness. Furthermore, happiness, like sadness, is frequently created by an event that has already occurred and over which the individual has no more control. So we assume that happiness can be passive.

In the first of two studies, D'Anello (1997) presented all participants (both males and females) with an initial event designed to make them feel happy. Specifically, the participant was met by the experimenter on the sixth floor of the building holding the psychology department, and then taken down the stairs to the fifth floor for the ostensible research project for which the participant had volunteered. Halfway down the stairs they were met by a young lady coming up who greeted the experimenter and said, "You know I am really happy, my sister had a baby, I got my first niece, and I am celebrating, please take these Snickers." She then handed a Snickers candy bar to the participant and one to the experimenter, and the experimenter then expressed her own happiness and congratulated the confederate on her good news.

The participant was then shown to a small experimental room where the study was described as consumer research. Written instructions asked the participant to select one of four sealed envelopes placed on the table; two of the four were said to contain a gift certificate like the one shown on the instruction sheet, that the gift certificates had been donated by a company interested in supporting research, and if they selected an envelope with a certificate, it was theirs to keep. After selecting an envelope and looking inside, the participants were instructed to fill out a questionnaire that asked how they felt on a number of affective dimensions, including happiness. The gift certificate attached to the instruction sheet was for $1, $2, $3, or $4. However, none of the envelopes contained a gift certificate, so the deterrent to happiness was losing the lottery, and the higher the value of the gift certificate, the greater should have been the deterrent to happiness. Also included in the design was a condition in which participants experienced the happiness induction and then responded to the measure of affects without any reference to a lottery or gift certificates.

The by now familiar expected effect is an increase in happiness as the magnitude of the deterrent increases, with a possible decrease at the highest level of deterrent. As with the prior research, the "no deterrent" condition should indicate the maximum level of happiness that a deterrent could create. These theoretical expectations are clearly supported by the mean happiness scores: control = 7.1; $1 = 3.9; $2 = 5.8; $3 = 5.9; and $4 = 4.1. The increase between $1 and $2 and the decrease between $3 and $4 are reliable at better than the 2% level; the quadratic effect is significant at beyond the 1% level.

The questionnaire included measures on a number of potentially related affective states: good mood yielded a reliable quadratic trend like that of happiness, while frustration, sadness, and disappointment yielded significant quadratic trends opposite to that of happiness. Not showing quadratic effects were fear, tense, angry, disgusted, hopeless, bad mood, and surprised, on the negative side, and full of pep and content, on the positive side. Once again, the affective responses to the deterrents were fairly specific, but there were some negative responses as well. The character of the negative responses, frustration, disappointment, and sadness, suggests they occurred in direct response to the deterrent, the failure to win the lottery.

Not content with this demonstration regarding a relatively trivial cause for happiness, D'Anello (1997) carried out a second study in which the deterrent to happiness was a threat to health. Male and female college students were first asked, supposedly as part of a health psychology study on well-being, to imagine a situation that would make them feel very, very happy, and then they were asked to describe the situation in a paragraph. Second, as part of the same study, they were asked to take a saliva test that purportedly indicated the possibility they would get a disease of the pancreas. Participants were told that if their saliva turned a test strip green (and it always did), it meant that there was either 0%, 2%, 30%, 80%, or 100% chance of getting the disease. Finally, participants were asked to fill out a questionnaire assessing their psychological well-being. This questionnaire contained a number of emotion items, including happiness.

The initial analysis of happiness ratings revealed not only the predicted quadratic effect, but also an interaction between deterrent level, experimenter, and sex of participant. Further analysis demonstrated that only female participants clearly conformed to the theoretical expectations, as seen in the means for each level of deterrence: 0% = 7.6; 2% = 3.3; 30% = 5.6; 80% = 4.1; 100% = 2.7. Excluding the 0%, or control, condition, the quadratic effect was reliable ($p = .02$); the increase in happiness from the 2% to the 30% conditions also was reliable ($p = .03$), as was the decrease from the 30% to the 100% condition ($p = .01$). The males differed from the females mainly in that their happiness level was higher in the 2% condition. No quadratic effects appeared on any of the other measures of positive affect: optimism, relieved, joy, content, energetic, satisfaction, and good mood.

Three measures of negative affects, frustration, worried, and fearful, showed quadratic effects opposite to those of happy for the combined sample of males and females. However, when looked at separately by sex of participant, only worried and distressed yielded quadratic effects, and then only among female participants. On each of these measures, the males in the 2% condition were lower than the females. Apparently, the male participants were not particularly threatened by a 2% chance of getting the liver disease. Measures of negative affect that showed no quadratic effects were sadness, pessimism, anxiety, tense, hopeless, angry, bad mood, and surprise. Once more, the affective responses tended to be rather specific, particularly in regard to the deterred state of happiness, and there were negative responses centered around the deterrent threat to health.

In general, the female participants provided good support for the theory and the assumption that happiness functions like a motivational state. Although the state of happiness in this second study was selected by the participant and could have been active rather than passive, inspection of the episodes reported by participants suggests that approximately 75% of them described a passive form of happiness.

Summary of Evidence

Anger, an active emotion, has been shown to increase with increases in deterrents in the form of humor and of gift certificates and to vary nonmonotonically with increased size of gift certificates. Sympathy, another active emotion, has been shown to relate positively to deterrents in the form of rudeness and of low ratings of the participant by the target person, and to vary nonmonotonically with rudeness. Sadness, a passive emotion, was shown to increase and to vary nonmonotonically with increased value of gift certificates. Happiness, a second passive emotion, was found to increase as deterrents in the form of lottery loss or health threat increased, and to vary nonmonotonically with both lottery loss and health threats, though these effects of health threat were obtained only among female participants. The evidence so far suggests that emotions, even those that are normally considered passive, work like motivational states. Their intensity is a joint function of the importance of the causal event and the magnitude of deterrents acting against the emotion.

THE INTERPLAY BETWEEN COGNITIVE AND EMOTIONAL CONTROL OF BEHAVIOR

The theoretical basis for the preceding discussion and review of evidence assumes that humans in their waking state normally have energy available and can therefore carry out goal-directed activity if there is some process for determining direction of behavior. Which goals are pursued and by what means are determined by cognitive processes, including evaluation of both means and ends.

The implications we see in such a process are, first, that the goals involved are not very important to the individual—certainly they are not above average importance. Second, the affective tone of goal pursuit is neutral or of very low intensity—there is a lack of passion. Third, and perhaps most significantly, the individual's focus of attention remains on the goal and relevant instrumental behavior only so long as potential outcomes of greater significance do not occur to the person, or, sheer salience of other goals or activities does not occur. In sum, we speculate that motivated behavior that utilizes normal energy levels occurs with goals of low to average importance, is relatively passionless, and is easily sidetracked when more important or salient goals or activities occur to the individual.

Clear empirical support for our speculative analysis appears to be unavailable. What is needed is an experimental study in which goal-directed behavior is examined as a function of the importance of the goal, crossed by a manipulation of focus of attention to either the goal or to the necessary instrumental behavior. We would expect that focusing attention on the relevant goal or instrumental behavior would increase goal-directed activity for relatively unimportant goals, but not for important goals. Goal-directed activity always should be relatively high for important goals.

While the crucial study outlined above seems not yet to have been done, there is important evidence for half of the above analysis, namely, the effect of focusing attention on activity that is instrumental for attaining a goal of relatively low importance. The school of thought first made prominent by Ach (1910, as reported in Heckhausen, 1991), focusing on volition, and the elaboration of that point of view by Heckhausen and Kuhl (1985) and Heckhausen and Gollwitzer (1987), emphasizing implementational mind-sets, deals, we believe, with the problem of routine behavior, namely, that the goals of routine behavior are not sufficiently important to insure goal attainment. Most cogently, Gollwitzer (1996) reported studies demonstrating that goal attainment is facilitated by planning instrumental behaviors, thus lessening the impact of distractions, increasing recognition of appropriate behaviors when opportunities arose, and fostering positivity toward the goal and the impression of feasibility.

Interestingly, Gollwitzer (1996) speculated that the facilitating effects for goal attainment of planning and other aspects of implemental mind-sets may be automatic when goals are very important. This coincides with our own speculation about the effect of goal importance, though we posit explicitly that what is different is that outcomes, including goals, of above average importance produce emotions. In the case of goals, the typical emotion is desire, and great desire should automatically produce attention to pertinent instrumental behaviors as well as keeping the person's mind on the goal.

In contrast to an earlier view by academic psychology that emotions are disruptive of rational behavior, the present thesis is that emotions result from the actual or potential occurrence of important outcomes and they urge one to carry out appropriate instrumental behaviors. In other words, the emotion provides the impetus for planning how to attain the desired end state; consequently, explicit instructions for an implemental set or planning would not necessarily enhance goal-directed behavior or goal attainment. However, the truth of this assertion can be determined only by further research.

The idea that emotions are disruptive refers, of course, to the notion that emotions disrupt rational behavior. Our analysis suggests that this disruption is inevitable and adaptive. When behavior is controlled by goals of relatively low importance, and the behavior is guided by rational processes, the occurrence of an outcome that is highly important should take control of behavior. While, to an observer, the disruption of rational behavior relevant to the unimportant goal may seem irrational, to the actor, the orientation to a new, highly important outcome may be essential. For example, the scientist who cannot keep her mind on the paper she is writing because her baby keeps crying is responding to an urge (compassion) to attend to the more important goal. It is difficult to gainsay the writer's assignment of importance to the two possible outcomes—the publication of the paper and the welfare of her baby. Looked at in this way, important outcomes produce emotions that urge one to take adaptive action, that is, action consonant with one's values, as reflected in the importances of the possible goals.

In a similar vein, when an outcome or potential outcome has created a dominant emotion that interrupts routine goal-directed behavior, attempts to restore the routine behavior through implemental sets can increase the intensity of the interfering emotion. For example, a student who is preparing for a course examination might learn that a good friend had died, thus creating sadness and grief. Reminders of the upcoming examination and what the student needed to do to be successful on the exam might only increase the intensity of her sadness, rather than producing renewed effort to prepare for the exam. The death of the friend is more important to the student than is success on the examination, and the intensification of sadness provides protection against concern for the exam.

It should not be assumed, however, that just because an outcome is important, it will produce only adaptive tendencies. For example, Oettingen (1996) studied the weight reduction behavior and success of overweight people who joined a weight reduction program. It seems safe to assume that if people were overweight and voluntarily joined the program, the goal of weight reduction was relatively high in importance. What Oettingen found was that people who have positive fantasies about weight reduction are distracted and possibly experience substitute satisfaction, thereby hindering goal attainment. At the same time, positive fantasies intermittently contrasted with thoughts about required routine behavior enhanced goal attainment. Oettingen also found that positive expectations (optimism) coupled with alternating thoughts about fantasy and reality result in high levels of motivation, while negative expectations undermine the effect of these contrasting cognitions and result in low levels of motivation. Some of these effects may be understood in terms of deterrents to the desire to lose weight, but the whole picture is clearly more complicated.

SUMMARY

We have pointed out that important outcomes give rise to emotions, which in turn urge goal directed behavior. The strength of the emotional feeling and consequent urge are a nonmonotonic function of the magnitude of deterrents—potential resisting, inhibiting, or counter-forces. As those forces increase from zero, the intensity of emotion increases and continues to increase until it has reached its limit, which is set by the importance of the event or thought that gives rise to it. If the magnitude of deterrents passes that limit, the intensity of that emotion will drop to a low level, though, of course, a different emotion may occur in its place (see, for example, Epstein, 1984).

This view of the interplay between the factors that control affectively neutral and emotional behavior depends primarily on the importance to the person of possible goals or outcomes. Those that are of no greater than average importance not only allow but in a sense require guidance from the cognitive system. A person must make judgments about which outcomes to seek or avoid, which should come first and which later, and by what means they should be pursued or avoided. Such judgments will be based on the importances of the outcomes, the costs or rewards of instrumental activities, and so forth. In contrast, relatively important outcomes compel attention and have the capability to create an affective state that urges and guides a person's response. But an emotional response is not simply automatic.

The perception of importance will usually involve at least some minimal judgment having to do with potential harm or benefit to the self or to one's values. To the extent that there are multiple outcomes to consider, comparative judgments must be made even if outcomes are above average importance. And, of course, where outcomes or potential outcomes are of greater than average importance, what affective state results is determined by appraisal of potentially relevant factors. At a minimum, according to the view presented here, the presence and magnitude of deterrents to the function of the appropriate affective state would normally be included in the appraisal.

NOTE

1. The original story was composed by Joy Weeks. We are indebted to C. Daniel Batson for making the story available for our use. A second story that was used in this research failed to be a reliable producer of sadness, and the data from that story are omitted here.

ACKNOWLEDGMENTS

Support for the development of the theory and for some of the research reported here was provided by a Senior Research Award to Jack W. Brehm from the Alexander von Humboldt Foundation. Beverly H. Brummett is currently on a postdoctoral fellowship at the Duke University Medical Center.

REFERENCES

Atkinson, J. W., & Birch, D. A. (1970). *A dynamic theory of action*. New York: Wiley.

Batson, C. D., & Shaw, L. L. (1991). Evidence for altruism: Toward a pluralism of prosocial motives. *Psychological Inquiry, 2*, 107–122.

Billings, L. & Brehm, J. W. (1996). Determinants of sympathy for the disabled. Unpublished manuscript, University of Kansas, Lawrence.

Brehm, J. W. (1992). The intensity of emotion. Unpublished manuscript, University of Kansas, Lawrence.

Brehm, J. W., Brummett, B. H., & Harvey, L. (1998). Paradoxical sadness. Manuscript under review.

Brehm, J. W., Wright, R. A., Solomon, S., Silka, L., & Greenberg, J. (1983). Perceived difficulty, energization, and the magnitude of goal valence. *Journal of Experimental Social Psychology, 19*, 21–48.

Brummett, B. H. (1996). The intensity of anger. Ph.D. dissertation, University of Kansas, Lawrence.

D'Anello, S. C. (1997). Paradoxical effects of losing money and experiencing a health threat on happiness intensity. Unpublished Ph.D. dissertation, University of Kansas, Lawrence.

Dill, J. (1997). Paradoxical anger: Investigations into the emotional and physiological predictions of Brehm's theory of emotional intensity. Unpublished Ph.D. dissertation, University of Missouri, Columbia.

Epstein, S. (1984). Controversial issues in emotion theory. In P. Shaver (Ed.), *Review of personality and social psychology: Emotions, relationships, and health* (pp. 64–88). Beverly Hills, CA: Sage.

Frijda, N. H. (1986). *The emotions*. Cambridge, England: Cambridge University Press.

Gollwitzer, P. M. (1996). The volitional benefits of planning. In P. M. Gollwitzer & J. A. Bargh (Eds.), *The psychology of action: Linking cognition and motivation to behavior* (pp. 287–312). New York: Guilford.

Heckhausen, H. (1991). *Motivation and action*. New York: Springer-Verlag.

Heckhausen, H., & Gollwitzer, P. M. (1987). Thought contents and cognitive functioning in motivational versus volitional states of mind. *Motivation and Emotion, 11*, 101–120.

Heckhausen, H., & Kuhl, J. (1985). From wishes to action: The deadends and shortcuts on the long way to action. In M. Frese & J. Sabini (Eds.), *Goal-directed behavior: Psychological theory and research on action* (pp. 134–160). Hillsdale, NJ: Erlbaum.

Lazarus, R. S. (1991). *Emotion and adaptation*. New York: Oxford University Press.

Oettingen, G. (1996). Positive fantasy and motivation. In P. M. Gollwitzer & J. A. Bargh (Eds.), *The psychology of action* (pp. 287–312). New York: Guilford.

Thorndike, E. L. (1911). *Animal intelligence*. New York: Macmillan.

Wright, R. A. (1996). Brehm's theory of motivation as a model of effort and cardiovascular response. In P. M. Gollwitzer & J. A. Bargh (Eds.), *The psychology of action: Linking cognition and motivation to behavior* (pp. 424–453). New York: Guilford.

Wright, R. A., & Brehm, J. W. (1989). Energization and goal attractiveness. In L. Pervin (Ed.), *Goal concepts in personality and social psychology* (pp. 169–210). Hillsdale, NJ: Erlbaum.

Wright, R. A., Contrada, R. J., & Patane, M. J. (1986). Task difficulty, cardiovascular response, and the magnitude of goal valence. *Journal of Personality and Social Psychology, 51*, 837–843.

Young, P. T. (1961). *Motivation and emotion*. New York: Wiley.

CHAPTER 7

MOOD MANAGEMENT

THE ROLE OF PROCESSING STRATEGIES IN AFFECT CONTROL AND AFFECT INFUSION

JOSEPH P. FORGAS, ROBERT JOHNSON AND JOSEPH CIARROCHI

INTRODUCTION

The dual nature of the human mind, comprising a combination of rational and emotional characteristics, has been a source of fascination to philosophers and laymen since time immemorial (Hilgard, 1980). How does affect influence a person's cognitive processes, and how does cognition impact on affective states? Although this question lies at the heart of understanding personal control, it has only been the focus of determined scientific study for the past few decades or so. Yet popular interest in affect control has never been higher. Bookshops are filled with popular psychology titles offering us advice on how to improve our self-worth by thinking positively, get a better sex life by emotional empowerment, or make a fortune by feeling good about ourselves. These books sell because people want to believe that they can influence their own feelings, thoughts, and desires. Just what is the role of affect and mood in influencing our thoughts and be-

JOSEPH P. FORGAS, ROBERT JOHNSON, AND JOSEPH CIARROCHI • School of Psychology, University of New South Wales, Sydney 2052, Australia. E-mail: jp.forgas@unsw.edu.au; internet: http://www.psy.unsw.edu.au/staff/jforgas.htm

Personal Control in Action, edited by Kofta et al., Plenum Press, New York, 1998.

haviors? What are the circumstances that lead to an accentuation or an attenuation of a prevailing mood state? And just how effective are various cognitive strategies in influencing our affective states? This chapter will review some of the available evidence for spontaneous affect infusion into social judgments and behaviors, and will also consider the complementary role of controlled, motivated processing in producing affect control. A general theory of mood management based on our recent Affect Infusion Model (Forgas, 1995a) will be outlined.

Traditionally, affect infusion (when affect influences cognition in a mood-congruent direction) and affect control (when targeted cognitive activity is employed to control or change affect) have been thought of as distinct, separate processes that have little in common with each other. This chapter will argue that the processes of affect infusion and affect control represent two sides of a single, integrated mood management system. Whether a prevailing affective state leads to affect infusion or affect control often depends on subtle contextual differences that may selectively trigger one of two different information processing strategies: elaborate, substantive processing (the major vehicle for affect infusion), or directed, motivated processing (the mechanism for affect control). Extrapolating from the recently proposed Affect Infusion Model (Forgas, 1995a), we will propose here that affect infusion in the course of substantive processing, and affect control during motivated processing function as two complementary cognitive strategies that jointly constitute a self-correcting, automatic mood management system.

The second point we will argue here is that affect control encompasses a far more subtle, wide-ranging and heterogenous set of strategies than has been traditionally recognized to date. Affect control is not limited to the kind of conscious, effortful cognitive strategies typically employed by people to cope with a specific aversive emotional state. Rather, we will argue that managing our affective states is a continuous, subtle, and frequently subconscious process in which people selectively search for and use information in ways that help them to calibrate their prevailing moods, and typically do so without any conscious awareness of these strategies. We will use the term *mood management* to describe this ongoing process, to encompass both affect infusion and affect control mechanisms. We will also review specific evidence demonstrating the operation of mood management strategies in the second half of the chapter. First, however, we need to consider some of the background of contemporary theorizing about the links between affect and cognition in psychology.

The Historical Position of Affect in Psychology

The nature of the relationship among basic mental faculties such as thinking, feeling, and conation remains one of the most fundamental and enduring issues in psychology. Although the tripartite division of the human mind into cognition, affect, and conation originated in philosophy, it has become deeply entrenched in empirical psychology throughout the 20th century (Hilgard, 1980). The necessarily close interdependence between affect and cognition, feeling and thinking, has traditionally been taken for granted by philosophers (Descartes, 1649/1961; James, 1890). In contrast, most empirical research in psychology this century has proceeded on the implicit assumption that cognition, emotion, and behavior can be studied in isolation, as completely separate, independent faculties (Hilgard, 1980). Of the two paradigms that have dominated the psychology discipline so far, neither behaviorism nor the more recent cognitivist orientation have accorded much importance to the study of affect. Within the radical behaviorist tradition, the study of affect as an intrapsychic phenomenon has been, by definition, of no interest. Traditional cognitive theories viewed affect, if considered at all, as merely a source of intrusion or interruption of "normal," that is, affectless thinking and ideation. This view, that affect in a sense subverts or degrades rational thinking, is still very common and has motivated much research on processes of affect control. It is now increasingly recognized, however, that the ideal of affectless, or "cold," cognition may be a meaningless abstraction (Neisser, 1982). It is far more realistic to assume that cognition is always affectively loaded, and thus, that affective states exert a subtle but important influence on the way people deal with their social world (Bower, 1991; Clore & Parrott, 1991; Damasio, 1994; Mayer, Gaschke, Braverman, & Evans, 1992).

Contemporary Approaches to Affect

In contrast with the historical neglect, during the past decade or so interest in affective phenomena has been on the increase in psychology. Unfortunately, research on affect continues to be hampered by serious unresolved conceptual issues, such as the lack of clear and widely accepted definitions and the absence of a reliable taxonomy of affective phenomena. There continues to be little general agreement about how best to define terms such as affect, feelings, emotions, and mood (Fiedler & Forgas, 1988; Forgas, 1991a, 1991b; Frijda, 1986). For the purpose of the present discussion, *affect* will be used as a broad, generic label to refer to both moods and emotions (Mayer, 1986; Petty, Gleicher, & Baker, 1991). *Moods*, in turn, can be defined as "low-intensity, diffuse and relatively enduring affective states without a salient antecedent cause and therefore little cognitive content (e.g. feeling good or feeling bad)," whereas *emotions* "are more intense, short-lived and usually have a definite cause and clear cognitive content" (e.g., anger or fear; Forgas, 1992a, p. 230). Traditionally there has been far more interest in the study of emotions rather than moods. However, recent research suggests that moods, even though less intense, may often have a potentially more enduring, subtle, and insidious influence on people's thinking and behaviors than do distinct and intense emotions (Forgas, 1992a, 1993a, 1993b; Mayer, 1986; Mayer et al., 1992; Sedikides, 1992a). Most of the following discussion will focus on subtle and subconscious mood management processes, rather than the conscious, intentional strategies people use to deal with salient and intense emotional states.

Another unresolved conceptual issue concerns the relationship between affect and cognition. Should affect be treated as part of the cognitive representational system or should it be seen as an entirely separate mental faculty (Fiedler & Forgas, 1988; Hilgard, 1980; Salovey & Mayer, 1990)? Zajonc (1980) argued for a separate-systems view, suggesting that affect often precedes and is distinct from cognitive processes. Such a view is also implicit in recent affect-as-information theorizing that seems to assign independent informational values to affective states (Schwarz & Clore, 1983). On the other hand, treating affect as part of an integrated cognitive representational system has yielded major new insights into how feelings interact with our thinking and judgments (Bower, 1981; Mayer et al., 1992; Sedikides, 1995). Ultimately, the validity of the separatist position may depend on how broadly one defines the domain of cognition (Lazarus, 1984). The status of the relationship between affect and cognition, at present at least, remains theoretically unresolved. However, for the purposes of the present discussion we believe that it is useful to consider affective phenomena as part of, and interacting with, a general inclusive cognitive representational system. This view is also supported not only by neuropsychological evidence (Damasio, 1994) but also by numerous studies demonstrating subtle affect infusion processes into cognition, and complementary evidence showing that motivated cognitive activity is one of the primary avenues for achieving affect control (Weary, Marsh, & McCormick, 1994; Wegner & Erber, 1993). However, the relationship between thinking as a means of controlling feelings is by no means simple or straightforward, as the next section will indicate.

Cognition and Affect Control

The basic idea that mental control can be effectively applied to affective phenomena has been increasingly in the forefront in recent clinical and social cognitive theorising (Forgas, 1990, 1995a; Ottaviani & Beck, 1988; Pennebaker, 1989; Roemer & Borkovec, 1993; Weary, Marsh, & McCormick, 1994; Wenzlaff, 1993). Several specific strategies for affect change have been proposed, such as information control, decision control, cognitive control, retrospective control, and secondary control (Fiske & Taylor, 1984; Wegner & Pennebaker, 1993). All of these control strategies involve directed, conscious cognitive processes. In cognitive control, for example, a patient undergoing a painful medical procedure may focus on the benefits that will be achieved through the procedure rather than on the pain they are currently experiencing. A prerequisite for successful affect control is the motivation to change, and empirical evidence indicates that increased cognitive processing of information is apparent by persons temporarily deprived of control (Pittman & D'Agostino, 1989; Weary et al., 1994) and by those who are dispositionally high in control motivation (Burger & Hemans, 1988). Indeed, some theorists suggest that the need to perceive the world as an organized and controlled place is an almost universal human characteristic (Heider, 1958; Kelley, 1955). It certainly seems that a sense or belief in personal control over life events is necessary for psychological health (Wegner & Pennebaker, 1993).

The traditional view that affective states disrupt and interfere with reasoned, rational thinking has been based on various observations. Extreme states of stress can clearly have detrimental cognitive consequences, and even milder affective states can adversely influence decision-making processes (Janis & Mann, 1977). On the other hand, certain moderate affective states can also produce beneficial cognitive consequences, such as enhancing the performance of well-rehearsed tasks (Zajonc, 1965), and may even improve decision-making (Janis & Mann, 1977). In fact, some interesting neuropsychological evidence suggests that persons who lack the usual emotional responses due to damage to their ventromedial prefontal cortex, although of normal intelligence, frequently manifest suboptimal decision-making ability in their social and personal lives (Damasio, 1994). These results suggest that emotional responses, and some kind of "emotional memory" in particular, is not only not disruptive but may also play an adaptive role in facilitating rational decision-making in complex situations (Salovey, Hsee, & Mayer, 1993). Thus, the critical issue for mental control is not simply how undesirable affective states can be limited or eliminated. Rather, appropriate affective responses can be an essential and highly informative component of adaptive social behaviour (Damasio, 1994; Frijda, 1988).

This complex interdependence between affect and cognition is nicely illustrated by several recent research paradigms. For example, studies of worrying (Roemer & Borkovec, 1993) show that it is "mostly thinking,...conceptual, verbal-linguistic process" (p. 223) that is triggered by an attempt to control aversive expected events. Paradoxically, worry itself often becomes uncontrollable and a source of anxiety. Thus, as "an example of mental control, worry appears to be in some ways successful, and in other ways not" (p. 226). Although worrying may help to suppress some of the somatic experiences associated with anxiety through distraction, it also tends to inhibit the development of effective strategies for dealing with the anticipated aversive event, and may itself become a new source of uncontrollable negative affective reactions. In a similar vein, others have also concluded that "the mental control of depression is a tricky enterprise" (Wenzlaff, 1993, p. 251). Efforts by depressed individuals to suppress negative thoughts are often ineffectual, and may backfire by "creating a link between the unwanted thoughts and the depressive mood, thereby helping to assure the continuance of both" (p. 254). Such a conclusion is also supported by the results of Nolen-Hoeksema (1987), who suggests that the ruminative, reflective cognitive style often adopted by depressed women can exacerbate rather than improve their problems. It appears then that attempts to use active, cognitive strategies to confront and deal with negative affective states is by no means always successful, and may even be counterproductive. It seems far more promising to think of affect and cognition as essentially interactive, interdependent mental faculties; rather than emphasizing cause–effect relationships in achieving mental control, we might do better by concentrating on the homeostatic processes that help to regulate and maintain an affective equilibrium over time. This is the approach taken in the mood management model to be proposed here.

Affect Control and Mood Management

Our interest here, then, is not in the kinds of targeted, conscious mental control strategies designed to deal with intense, problematic affective states. Rather, this chapter will focus on the subtle interaction between cognitive activity, and the relatively mild affective states and moods that typically do not intrude into consciousness, yet can have a significant influence on our thinking and behaviors. More to the point, even such weak mood states can and do elicit automatic and often subconscious cognitive strategies designed to prolong (mood maintenance) or extinguish (mood repair) the prevailing affective state (Clark & Isen, 1982; Forgas, 1992a). In other words, affect control need not be limited to conscious cognitive strategies designed to deal with salient and problematic emotional states. Rather, mood management can be understood here as the sum total of the built-in automatic mood regulation mechanisms employed by persons to deal with low-intensity affective states in the course of their everyday lives.

From this perspective, mood management is not an extraordinary, conscious event, but is part and parcel of the routine, automatic cognitive strategies people employ in their daily lives to calibrate, maintain, or suppress various low-intensity and often subconscious mood states. Such automatic mood management mechanisms have not until very recently received the broader attention that they deserve (Wegner & Pennebaker,

1993). One of the objectives of this chapter is to offer a clearer understanding of the conditions likely to facilitate or hinder effective mood management strategies based on our recent multiprocess Affect Infusion Model (Forgas, 1995a). Affect infusion—the gradual coloring of cognition by a prevailing affective state—is now a well-established phenomenon, and may often be the trigger that initiates mood management. We shall next consider the mechanisms that allow the continuous infusion of even mild affective states in our thinking, judgments, and, ultimately, behaviors before looking at the complementary process of mood management, that of affect control.

AFFECT INFUSION

Experiences of positive or negative affect accompany us throughout our daily lives. Most of the time these underlying mood states are not intense or salient enough to command conscious attention. Yet there is growing evidence suggesting that transient mood states nevertheless do have a significant influence on both the content of cognition (what people think) as well as the process of cognition (how people think) (Bower, 1981; Forgas, 1992a, 1995a; Schwarz & Clore, 1988). In this section we will review the evidence and describe a model dealing with the impact of moods on cognition, the Affect Infusion Model (AIM). A later section will look at the complementary process of how cognition impacts on affect.

For the purposes of this discussion, *affect infusion* may be defined as the process whereby affectively loaded information exerts an influence on, and becomes incorporated into, a person's cognitive processes, entering into their constructive deliberations and eventually coloring the outcome in a mood-congruent direction (Forgas, 1995a). Processing novel social information usually requires high-level inferential cognitive processes. The classic work of Asch (1946), Heider (1958), and Kelly (1955) established that even the simplest kinds of judgments of brief lists of adjectives are subject to such highly constructive biases. Social information processors can only create a meaningful pattern or Gestalt by the constructive use of their preexisting thoughts, memories, and associations to create a cognitive representation of the social world. Under certain conditions, the prevailing affective state of a person can become part of the constructive informational base used when interpreting information, producing a judgment, or planning a behavior (Fiedler, 1991).

There is now clear evidence suggesting that affect infusion is most likely to occur in the course of such *constructive processing* that involves the substantial transformation rather than mere reproduction of existing cognitive representations. In other words, affect "will influence cognitive processes to the extent that the cognitive task involves the active generation of new information as opposed to the passive conservation of information given" (Fiedler, 1990, pp. 2–3). Research has also shown, however, that affect infusion is not an invariable phenomenon. Frequently, the affective state of a person has no influence on the content of cognition, and may even have an inconsistent, mood-incongruent influence (Erber & Erber, 1994; Sedikides, 1994). How can we explain these apparently contradictory findings?

The Affect Infusion Model (AIM)

The recently proposed Affect Infusion Model (AIM) (Forgas, 1995a) argues that the nature and extent of affect infusion into cognition fundamentally depends on what kind of cognitive strategy is adopted by a person in response to contextual requirements. The model identifies four distinct processing strategies, each characterized by different affect infusion potentials. Two of these processing strategies, (1) the *direct access* of preexisting information, and (2) *motivated processing* in service of a preexisting goal, represent highly predetermined and directed information search patterns that require little generative, constructive processing, limiting the scope of affect infusion effects. In contrast, when a cognitive task requires a degree of open, elaborate, constructive processing, people may adopt either (3) a *heuristic*, simplified or a (4) a *substantive*, elaborate processing strategy to compute a new outcome. These are high-infusion strategies that involve some degree of constructive thinking (Fiedler, 1990; 1991; Forgas, 1992a), that allow affect to either indirectly, through primed associations (Forgas & Bower, 1988) or directly (Schwarz & Clore, 1988) infuse the outcome. A complete description of the AIM and the evidence supporting it is presented by Forgas (1995a), so it will not be reviewed in detail here. The major relevance of the AIM here is that it seeks to provide a framework within which instances of affect infusion (when affect leads to a congruent cognitive outcome), as well as instances of affect control—based on motivated processing—can be specified. Together, these two complementary processes—affect-infusion (e.g., during substantive processing) and affect-control (e.g, during motivated processing)—may be considered as part of a single mood management system.

According to the AIM, most affect infusion occurs when people employ *substantive processing*. This involves selecting, learning, and interpreting novel information, and relating this information to preexisting knowledge structures. Substantive processing is more likely when the task is complex or atypical, there is adequate cognitive capacity, and there are no specific motivational goals to predetermine the outcome. Most cognitive models implicitly assume that such elaborate information processing is the norm. In contrast, the AIM suggests that substantive processing is adopted only when simpler and less effortful strategies prove unequal to the task. Affect infusion during substantive processing is best understood in terms of memory principles that can account for the role of affect in the selection, learning, interpretation, and assimilation of novel information into a preexisting knowledge base (Bower, 1981, 1991). The more elaborate the processing strategy used, the more likely that affect infusion may influence the outcome (Fiedler, 1991; Forgas, 1992b; 1993a,b).

In contrast, the *motivated processing strategy* occurs when processing is guided by a specific goal, leading people to employ highly selective, motivated information search and integration strategies designed to produce a preferred outcome. As a result, little open, constructive processing occurs, reducing the likelihood of affect infusion. Motivated processing is the prime technique for achieving mood repair, as suggested by several recent studies (Clark & Isen, 1982; Erber & Erber, 1994; Forgas, 1990; Forgas & Fiedler, 1996; Wegner & Erber, 1993). Motivated processing as defined here involves more than just a motivation to be accurate (cf. Kunda, 1990); it assumes that a specific goal (such as mood-control) dominates and guides information search strategies. We shall have more to say about this strategy when discussing mood-control in a following section.

Distinguishing between these four processing strategies has considerable benefits for our understanding of the delicate interplay between affect and cognition, and affect-infusion and affect-control in particular. Since different processing strategies do imply different mood effects on cognition (see Figure 1), affect control can now been seen as specifically linked to a particular processing strategy—motivated processing—and not to others. Affect infusion in turn is most likely to occur in the course of substantive processing. The model predicts that constructive processing (substantive processing in particular) is the prerequisite for affect infusion to occur, while mood-control should be limited to conditions conducive to motivated processing.

Mechanisms of Affect Infusion

In terms of the model, affect infusion occurs because moods can either indirectly (through primed associations) or directly (through misattribution) infuse constructive processing. Affect-priming (Bower, 1991; Forgas & Bower, 1988) is more likely when substantive processing is adopted, while affect-as-information (Schwarz & Clore, 1988) should be limited to conditions when heuristic processing is used.

The *affect-as-information* model suggests that "individuals may . . . ask themselves: 'How do I feel about it?' [and] in doing so, they may mistake feelings due to a preexisting state" as informative about the current

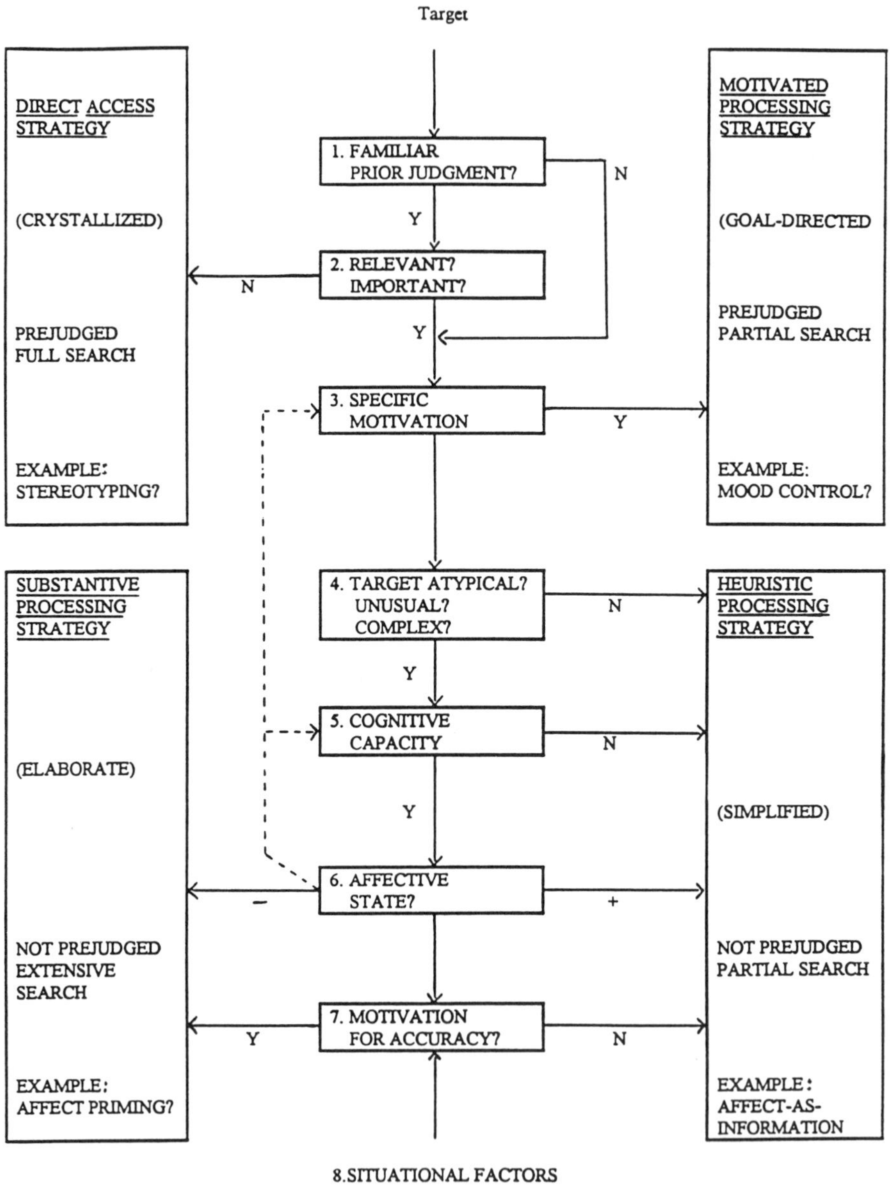

FIGURE 1 Outline of the multiprocess Affect Infusion Model (AIM): affect infusion in social judgments depends on which of four alternative processing strategies is adopted in response to target, judge and situational features; direct access and motivated processing are low infusion strategies with little mood congruence in judgments, while heuristic and substantive processing are high infusion strategies with marked mood congruence in judgments (after Forgas, 1995a).

situation (Schwarz, 1990, p. 529). Supporting evidence for this comes from studies reporting mood congruence in certain evaluative judgments (Clore & Parrott, 1991). However, many of these results can be equally well explained by alternative, affect-priming models. Further, the affect-as-information model also lacks parsimony, as it deals with mood effects at the retrieval-judgmental stage only. The kind of simple, heuristic processing implied by the affect-as-information approach is most likely when processing resources are limited, prior knowledge and evaluations are not available, and the task is unfamiliar, nonspecific and, most important, of little personal relevance (Figure 1). There is no evidence that this model plays any role in mood management strategies.

In contrast, the *affect-priming* principle suggests that affect can indirectly infuse cognitive processes by facilitating access to related cognitive categories (Bower, 1981; Isen, 1984). According to this view, affective states have a "specific node or unit in memory that . . . is also linked with propositions describing events from one's life during which that emotion was aroused.. . . Activation of an emotion node also spreads activation throughout the memory structures to which it is connected" (Bower, 1981, p. 135). In terms of the model, affect can influence selective attention to mood-congruent details, and the selective learning and encoding of such information (Bower, 1981; Forgas & Bower, 1987; Forgas,1992b). Affect can also selectively influence retrieval processes, as affectively congruent information (mood-congruent recall) or information encountered in a matching affective state (mood-state-dependent retrieval) are more likely to be retrieved than are other details (Bower, 1991; Forgas & Bower, 1988; Mayer, Gayle, Meehan, & Harman, 1990). Affect can also prime the kind of associations elicited by a stimulus and thus influence its subsequent interpretation (Forgas & Bower, 1987).

There is now strong evidence supporting this model. Despite some initial difficulties (Blaney, 1986), many studies using rich and elaborate encoding, and retrieval cues have reliably demonstrated the predicted mood-priming effects (cf. Bower, 1991; Forgas, 1990, 1991b, 1992b; Forgas & Bower, 1987, 1988; Mayer et al., 1992; Salovey, O'Leary, Stretton, Fishkin, & Drake, 1991). The prediction of mood-congruence in conditions that are conducive to substantive processing has also been supported in numerous studies looking at selective attention, learning, retrieval, and associative processes (cf. Bower 1991; Forgas, 1991b, 1992b; Forgas & Bower, 1987, 1988; Mayer et al., 1992; Petty et al., 1991; Salovey et al., 1991). In particular, counterintuitive evidence indicating that the degree of affect infusion increases the longer, more elaborate, and more constructive the processing strategy adopted by a person specifically supports the affect-priming account (e.g., Forgas, 1992b, 1993b, 1995b).

WHAT DETERMINES PROCESSING STRATEGY?

According to the AIM, choice of processing strategy (and thus, subsequent affect-infusion or affect-control outcomes) should depend on three sets of factors: features of (1) the task, (2) the person, and (3) the situation, respectively (cf. Forgas, 1992a; 1995a). Task features include familiarity, typicality, and complexity; person features include subjective relevance, specific motivation, cognitive capacity, motivation to be accurate, affective state, and individual difference variables; situational factors include features such as degree of critical scrutiny expected, accuracy expectations, etc. The schematic links between these predictor variables are shown in Figure 1. Several testable principles may be derived from this model. For example, cognitive tasks that are familiar should be processed using a direct access strategy, unless further processing is recruited by other variables (Srull, 1983; 1984). A strong prior motivation should also lead to directed and truncated information search strategies and the absence of affect infusion. Such a pattern was found in several recent experiments looking at mood effects on motivated partner choices (Forgas, 1991b,c) and intergroup decisions (Forgas & Fiedler, 1996). Motivated processing is also the mechanism that can reverse the usual mood-congruent pattern, as judges selectively process mood-incongruent information (Erber & Erber, 1994; Sedikides, 1994), an issue we will return to later.

In the absence of familiarity or specific motivation, atypical, unusual or complex tasks should recruit substantive processing, and typical or simple targets should recruit heuristic processing. This pattern was supported in several recent studies, showing greater affect infusion linked to the more substantive processing of complex or atypical targets (Forgas, 1992b; 1993a,b). The model also predicts that all things being equal, personally relevant tasks are more likely to be processed using the motivated strategy (if a prior objective exists), as found in some recent experiments (Forgas, 1989, 1991b). Finally, pragmatic situational demands (e.g., expected publicity or scrutiny, expectations of accuracy) also impact on processing choices, triggering substantive rather than heuristic or direct access processing (Wegner & Erber, 1993).

AFFECT AND PROCESSING CHOICES

According to the AIM, affect itself plays a critical, dual role in regulating processing strategies, influencing both the processing choices judges make (*how* people think) and the kind of information they subsequently consider (*what* they think). Three kinds of explanations for the processing consequences of affect have been proposed. In terms of *capacity explanations*, affect itself may impair attention and cognitive-processing capacity both in negative (Ellis & Ashbrook, 1988) and in positive moods (Stroessner & Mackie,1992). In terms of *functionalist* explanations, affective states "exist for the sake of signaling states of the world that have to be responded to" (Frijda, 1988, p. 354). Positive affect also seems to generate more loose, creative, and heuristic processing strategies (Fiedler, 1988; Hertel & Fiedler, 1994; Isen, 1987), whereas negative affect recruits more careful and substantive processing styles (Forgas, 1992b; Forgas & Bower, 1987; Ottaviani & Beck, 1988; Schwarz, 1990; Weary, Marsh, Gleicher, & Edwards, 1993). Good mood, in a sense, informs us that the situation is favorable and that little processing effort is required. Bad moods, in turn, signal incipient danger and recruit more vigilant, systematic processing strategies (Schwarz,1990; Weary et al., 1994). Finally, in terms of *motivational* explanations, affect may also be the source of a specific motivation, recruiting controlled, motivated processing in the service of mood maintenance (in positive moods) or mood repair (in negative moods) and thus reducing the likelihood of affect infusion occurring (Clark & Isen, 1982; Erber & Erber, 1994; Forgas, 1991c).

What determines processing strategy and subsequent affect infusion when mood and task characteristics seem to call for different processing styles? For example, what happens when a happy person (inclined to process heuristically) is asked to perform a complex social judgment that requires substantive processing? Empirical evidence now suggests that in such instances, affect typically plays a secondary role in determining processing choices (Forgas, 1995a). In several studies, it has been found that happy subjects will adopt substantive rather than heuristic processing as demanded by a complex or an atypical target, allowing positive mood to infuse the judgment as a result of affect-priming effects (Forgas, 1992b, 1993b,1994). It seems, then, that the various processing and informational consequences of moods can be best understood in conjunction with contextual influences that regulate processing choices. The AIM provides an integrative framework within which these complex, and often complementary influences can be explained. How can we apply this multiprocess framework to an understanding of issues of personal control, and everyday, automatic mood management strategies in particular?

THE PROCESS OF MOOD MANAGEMENT

Within the AIM framework, the ongoing task of mood management can be understood as people routinely and automatically switching between two complementary information processing strategies: substantive processing that results in affect infusion, and motivated processing that results in affect control outcomes, respectively. The mood management model proposed here is thus a refinement and development of the relevant aspects of the earlier and more general Affect Infusion Model (Forgas, 1995a). A schematic summary of the mood management hypothesis is presented in Figure 2. As this figure shows, the choice of either a substantive (affect infusion) or motivated (affect control) processing strategy is determined by a combination of input variables. Most of the variables that feed into the mood management system are personal rather than situational. So far, we know that motivated rather than substantive processing is more likely when (1) the task is of direct personal relevance (Forgas, 1991c), (2) people experience self-directed attention (Berkowitz, 1993), (3) they score high on individual differences measures that indicate motivated tendencies (Forgas, 1996a), and (4) they experience aversive affect (Weary et al., 1994). Situational variables may also impact on processing choices (Wegner & Erber, 1993); however, by their very nature, the kind of motivational goals derived from situations tend to recruit a high level of awareness, and thus fall outside the scope of the kind of automatic, self-correcting mood management system we are primarily interested here.

A critical feature of this mood management model is that it incorporates a feedback loop between the valenced outcome of the existing processing strategy, and processing choices. As a consequence, the model provides for the possibility of automatic and continuous changes in processing style as a function of the prevailing mood state, a link that is now strongly supported by empirical evidence (Clark & Isen, 1982; Forgas, 1995a; Sedikides, 1994). In practical terms, this means that if as a result of an existing substantive processing strategy and ongoing affect infusion processes the level of negativity in a person's thinking—and mood—reach a threshold level, an automatic correction may take place that consists of a switch to motivated processing and subsequent preference for mood-incongruent materials. Such a pattern has recently been demonstrated both in experimental studies (Forgas, 1991c; Sedikides, 1994) and in research with mildly depressed persons as well (Weary et al., 1993). In the next section we will briefly survey some of the evidence illustrating affect infusion processes in the course of substantive processing.

The Evidence for Affect Infusion

Numerous studies have found that a person's affective state is likely to infuse cognitive processes in circumstances that, according to the AIM, should trigger constructive, substantive processing strategies. In a particularly challenging early test of the affect infusion hypothesis, even basic interpretations of observed social interactions were significantly distorted in a mood-consistent direction (Forgas, Bower, & Krantz, 1984). Other re-

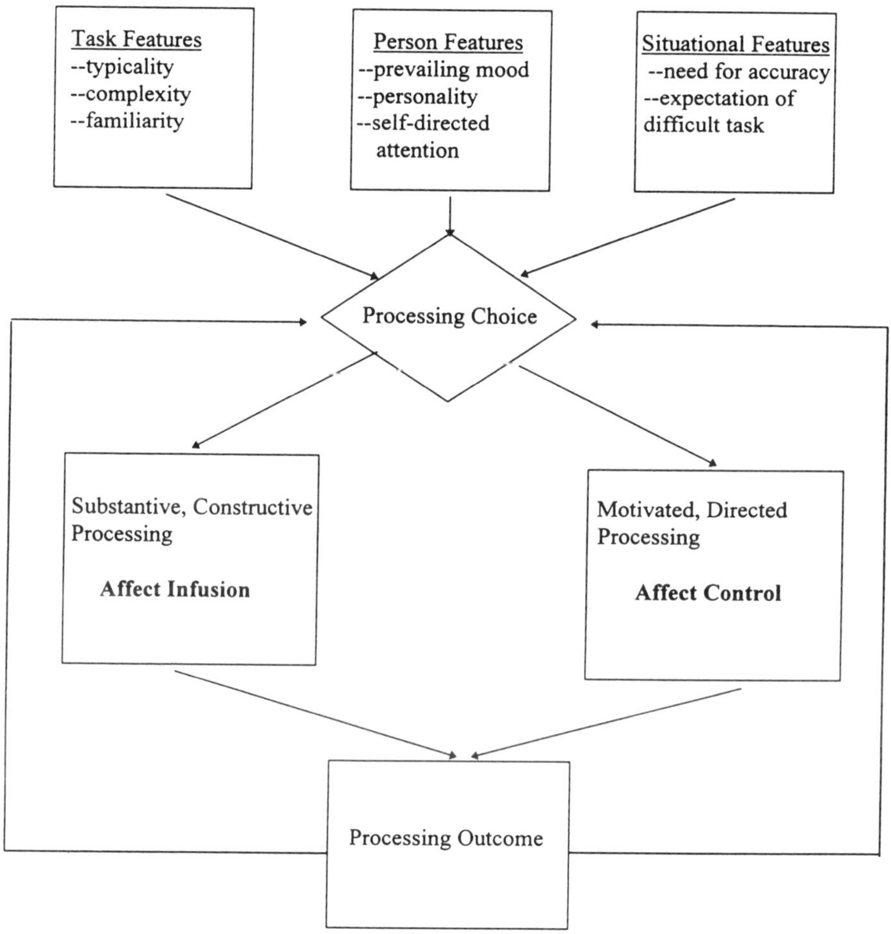

FIGURE 2 The mood management model, showing the predicted relationship between affect infusion (during substantive processing) and affect control (during motivated processing), and the variables influencing processing choices.

searchers used a more realistic personnel selection task and found an almost identical pattern of affect infusion in interviewers' reactions to job applicants (Baron, 1987). Affect infusion may also distort highly important personal judgments, such as perceptions of health and illness (Croyle & Uretzky, 1987; Salovey & Birnbaum, 1989). As implied by the AIM, "negative mood can affect subjective appraisals of health by increasing the accessibility of illness-related memories" (Croyle & Uretzky, 1987, p. 239).

Affect infusion has also been demonstrated with children: those in a good mood after watching a happy videotape recalled significantly more positive information and made more positive judgments than those in a negative mood (Forgas, Burnham, & Trimboli, 1988). Even nonvalenced cognitive tasks, such as identifying and attributing the causes for various outcomes, can be subject to affect infusion effects in conditions of substantive processing (Forgas, Bower, & Moylan, 1990). Sad people may thus be more likely to credit success to external causes, and blame failure on internal causes, a pattern with potentially significant clinical implications. Affect can also infuse the way people deal with persuasive messages under conditions of substantive processing (that is, high elaboration likelihood) (Petty et al., 1991). For example, subjects who feel happy after viewing a videotape are more likely to have positive attitudes to a persuasive message, but only if they score high on need for cognition (that is, habitually use substantive rather than heuristic processing) (Wegener, Petty, & Klein, 1994).

Affect infusion has been demonstrated not only in the laboratory but also in many real-life situations. In one of the largest unobtrusive field studies on this topic, involving almost a thousand subjects (Forgas & Moylan, 1987), in a "street survey," we approached people who were just leaving movie theaters having seen happy or sad films and asked them to make a number of judgments about topical issues, political figures, and their life satisfaction. On all questions, happy subjects made significantly more positive and lenient judgments than did sad subjects. Significant affect infusion was also found with stereotype judgments, "consistent with the affect-priming explanation" (Haddock, Zanna, & Esses, 1994, p. 203).

Affect infusion into self-related cognition may be particularly significant, as such tasks often recruit substantive processing strategies (Forgas et al., 1984). Such self–other differences were also found in people's social comparison strategies (Wheeler & Miyake, 1992). Research on depressed cognition has also yielded comparable results, showing that depressed individuals are more likely to be critical when thinking about themselves than others (Ottaviani & Beck, 1988). The impact of depressed mood on cognition seems particularly marked for individuals (often women) who have a tendency to adopt a more elaborate, ruminative, substantive processing style (Nolen-Hoeksema, 1993). In a study specifically testing the AIM, Sedikides (1995) found that peripheral self-conceptions that required the most elaborate, substantive processing were in fact most influenced by affect infusion, as predicted by the AIM. Specific evidence for the role of processing strategies in affect infusion also comes from the direct analysis of processing latency and memory data, summarized below.

Affect Infusion and Processing Latencies

A growing number of studies produced specific evidence for the process mediation of affect infusion effects. In one such study, happy, control, or sad moods were induced by bogus feedback about performance, followed by impression formation judgments and a recall task about persons presented on a computer screen (Forgas & Bower, 1987). The experiment found significant mood-congruence; it also found that subjects took longer to process and encode mood-congruent information into a presumably more extensive, activated associative base, but were faster to produce mood-congruent judgments consistent with the AIM.

One of the more important and counterintuitive predictions of the AIM is that the longer and more extensively a person needs to substantively process a task, the more likely that affect infusion will occur. This prediction was supported in several recent studies, in which the time required for processing was manipulated and recorded through varying the complexity and typicality of targets to be judged, using people (Forgas, 1992b), relationships (Forgas, 1993a, 1995b; Forgas & Moylan, 1991; Forgas, Levinger & Moylan, 1994), and conflict episodes (Forgas, 1994) as stimuli. One set of experiments found greater affect infusion in memory and judgments about atypical rather than typical people (Forgas, 1992b), and these greater mood effects were consistently linked to more prolongued processing latencies.

Another series of studies demonstrated greater affect infusion into judgments about unusual, mismatched rather than well-matched couples, due to the more substantive, elaborate processing recruited by such targets (Forgas, 1993a; 1995b; Forgas & Moylan, 1991). Indeed, when several features of the target couples were simultaneously manipulated to create various degrees of "match" between them, we found that the size of mood effects on judgments was proportional to the degree of mismatch between the partners, and the length of processing required to produce a reaction (Forgas, 1995b; see Figure 3). Interestingly, these affect infusion effects also occur in highly complex and personally relevant cognitive tasks, such as perceptions of one's real-life initimate relationships (Forgas et al., 1994), and people's explanations for their more or less serious interpersonal conflicts (Forgas, 1994). Once again, these mood effects were most marked for serious, involving conflicts that required longer, more extensive processing, rather than for simple, superficial conflicts, as suggested by the AIM (Forgas, 1994; see Figure 4).

Affect Infusion and Social Behavior

Affect infusion impacts not only on cognitive and judgmental processes but also on social behaviors that are the result of cognitive processing. Several recent studies showed such a behavioral mood effect. In one project, happy or sad subjects engaged in two different kinds of negotiation tasks: an informal, interpersonal bargaining and a formal, intergroup

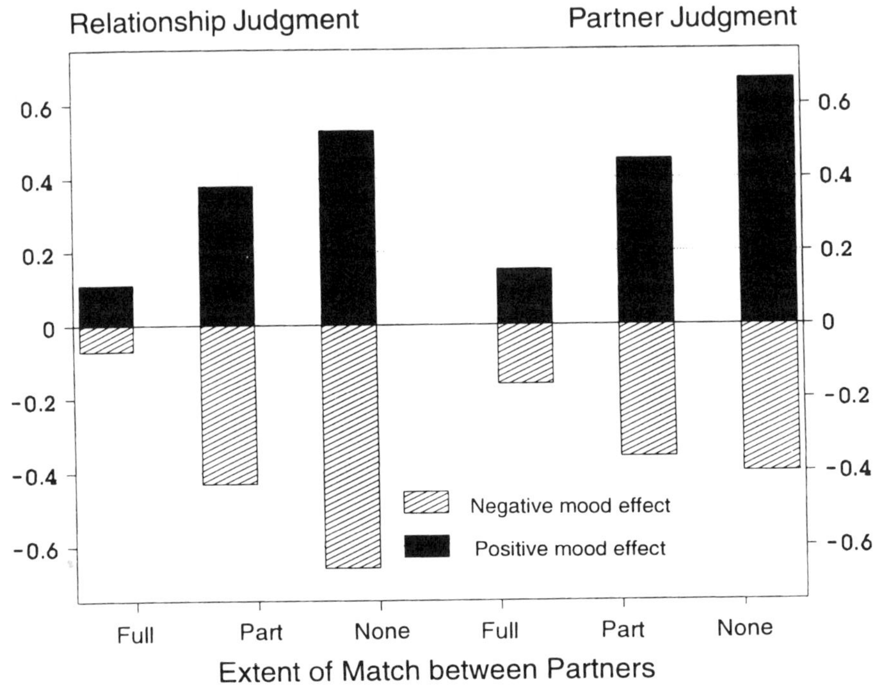

FIGURE 3 Mood effects on the perception of well-matched, partially matched and badly-matched couples: the size of the mood effect is proportional to the degree of mismatch between the couples (After Forgas, 1995b).

negotiation (Forgas, 1996a). People induced to feel happy planned to be more cooperative and less competitive, set themselves higher expectations, and did in fact use significantly more cooperative, integrative bargaining strategies in both encounters. Sad persons in contrast were more pessimistic about the chances for cooperation, planned and actually used more competitive strategies, and did in fact achieve significantly worse outcomes. The results indicate that in a social context that is likely to promote substantive processing (i.e., a complex, well-structured negotiation task) mood infuses not only social cognition and judgment; it also infuses important social behaviors.

Mood may also infuse the way people generate and respond to complex verbal messages, such as requests (Forgas, 1996b). Sad persons were found to prefer significantly more polite, indirect requests consistent with their more pessimistic assessment of the likelihood of giving offense by being too direct. In contrast, when it came to responding to requests, sad persons were particularly sensitive to how a request is phrased. Dysphoric

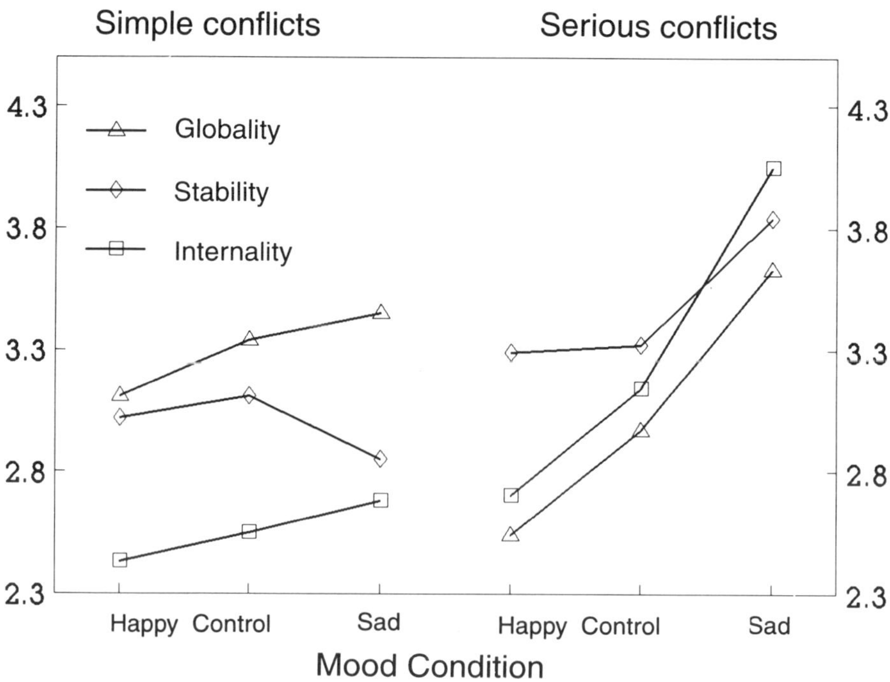

FIGURE 4 Mood effects on explanations about simple and serious relationship conflicts: mood has a greater impact on judgments about serious, complex conflicts requiring longer, more substantive processing (After Forgas, 1994).

subjects tended to comply more with polite requests, but refused impolite requests more than did happy subjects, while happy persons remained more impervious to different request formulations. These mood-induced differences were greatest in circumstances when more extensive, substantive processing was required in a more problematic situation, as suggested by the AIM.

Affect Infusion and Personal Control

The cumulative evidence for mood effects on cognition and behavior reviewed here indicates that affect infusion may represent a serious threat to our ability to maintain and manage a balanced affective state and, ultimately, personal control. However, automatic affect infusion processes may also facilitate personal control, depending on the specific circumstances. For example, a number of studies have now shown that affect infusion can have a beneficial influence on the cognitive processes involved in the evaluation of perceived pain (Johnson, 1994; Johnson & Spence,1994, 1996a, 1996b; Johnson, Spence, Champion, & Ziegler, 1994). In one study (Johnson & Spence, 1996a), subjects were children who were experiencing acute postoperative pain in a hospital. They were assigned to positive, negative, and neutral mood conditions such that their perceived level of pain was matched across groups. Their mood was manipulated through the presentation of happy, sad, or control videotapes on a bedside monitor. Subsequent self-evaluation of their pain showed that subjects in a positive mood perceived their pain to be significantly less than did subjects in a negative mood.

In this instance, then, automatic affect infusion processes served to aid in the achievement of personal control by apparently reducing the perceived aversiveness of pain. In contrast, children in the negative mood condition evaluated their pain as having increased over the same period. Such a symmetric mood effect suggests that mood-primed material became associated with the pain evaluation response. Results also showed some mood congruency in the recall of pain-related words (Johnson & Spence,1994, 1996b), suggesting that these mood effects were due to changes in cognitive processing, and not simply mood-induced changes in physiologically determined pain thresholds.

These studies suggest an interesting, and so far little understood role for affect infusion in the service of personal control. It appears that some aversive states and experiences may be interpreted as less noxious simply because of the affect infusion effects of a prevailing positive mood. The possibility of using good mood as a possible prophylactic against aversive experiences may have important clinical implications. These experimental findings are also broadly consistent with extensive epidemiological evidence showing that happiness, positive affect, and good mood are generally associated with better psychological and health outcomes (Argyle, 1987). Of course, the influence of temporary mood changes on coping with experiences such as pain is likely to be moderated by chronic affective states, especially in clinical populations. We shall discuss the links between state and trait aspects of affectivity in a subsequent section.

Taken together, these results may have important implications for our understanding of everyday mood management strategies. We have argued here that low-level fluctuating moods have a continuous, and often imperceptible, influence on the way we think about, remember, and evaluate complex social information. Such affect infusion processes seem most marked when a person needs to engage in constructive, substantive information processing in response to a problematic task. Several of the experiments described here confirm that the longer and more constructively we need to think about a task, the more likely that affect infusion will have a mood-congruent impact on the outcome. Specifically, mood has been shown to have a significantly greater distorting effect on tasks that are rare, unusual, atypical or complex. Affect infusion is only one side of the mood management equation, however. We shall next turn to the complementary process of affect control during motivated processing.

AFFECT CONTROL: THE MOTIVATED PROCESSING STRATEGY

Affect infusion—the mood-congruent impact of affect on cognition—represents one important aspect of the delicate interrelationship between affect and cognition. While affect can and does impact on our cognitive processes, often in ways that we barely realize, the opposite can also occur: targeted, motivated cognitive activity can influence and control our affective states. This reverse process, affect control, occurs in conditions when a motivated processing strategy is adopted in terms of the AIM. This strategy, *motivated processing*, is most likely to be employed by a person when there are strong and specific motivational pressures for a particular cognitive outcome to be achieved. The defining feature of motivated processing is that people engage in highly selective, guided, and targeted information search and integration strategies designed to achieve a preexisting motivational objective. Motivated processing is not only a low affect infusion strategy but also is the major vehicle for balancing affect infusion and achieving mood-incongruent outcomes, often in the service of personal control.

Emotions that are characterized by extensive cognitive associations and clearcut appraisal qualities often directly trigger motivated processing (Wegner & Pennebaker, 1993). In contrast, the motivational consequences of moods tend to be more subtle, interactive, and indirect. Nevertheless, motivated processing may often be used to achieve mood maintenance as well as mood repair (Clark & Isen, 1982; Erber & Erber, 1994). In terms of the mood management model proposed here, motivated processing should be adopted after a prevailing affective state reaches a threshold level due to ongoing affect infusion processes, occasioning a change in processing style (Sedikides, 1994). It appears that merely directing a person's attention to his or her affective state seems also sufficient to trigger deliberate, motivated strategies, and this can have the paradoxical effect of not only reducing affect infusion but also of producing mood-incongruent outcomes (Berkowitz, 1993). In several recent studies, we were able to document the step-by-step targeted information search and processing strategies elicited by a combination of sad mood and a personally relevant task in subjects who were thus becoming motivated to achieve a mood repair through achieving a rewarding outcome in their affiliative choices (Forgas, 1989, 1991c).

It is important to note that motivated processing, as understood here, does not simply refer to a generic motivation to be careful and accurate (cf. Kunda, 1990). Rather, it assumes that a specific, preexisting goal guides a person's information search and processing strategies. Recent studies have demonstrated motivated processing in the service of such goals as mood repair and mood maintenance, self-evaluation maintenance, ego enhancement, achievement motivation, and affiliation (Berkowitz, 1993; Erber & Erber, 1994; Forgas, 1991c; Forgas et al., 1990; Tesser, 1986). In fact, most of these goals relate to personal control, and affect control in particular.

Despite growing interest in motivated processing (Forgas, 1992a; Janis & Mann, 1977; Kunda, 1990; Martin, 1986), the precise processing consequences of this strategy have received insufficient attention, as most studies of social cognition use artificial and relatively uninvolving tasks. Nevertheless, several studies have now shown that affect infusion effects disappear under conditions that are conducive to motivated processing, such as a high self-relevance or a high level of awareness about the primed material, when attention is directed to the mood state, in tasks requiring deliberate processing, or when subjects compensate for unbalanced information by "resetting" the input array (Berkowitz, Troccoli, & Monteith, 1994; 1993; Erber & Erber, 1994; Martin, 1986).

The Evidence for Affect Control and Motivated Processing

As we saw previously, affect itself can be crucial in triggering motivated processing. Several studies suggest that people will engage in targeted information search and retrieval to alleviate dysphoria, consistent with the view that "people are active mood regulators who are sensitive to situational demands" (Erber & Erber, 1994, p. 6). Such motivated processing in the service of affect control in an attribution task was demonstrated by Baumgardner and Arkin (1988), who reported that sad subjects were more inclined to selectively attribute their failures to external causes and their successes to internal causes in an apparent attempt to control an aversive state.

Motivated affect control may also be involved in the way people go about choosing interaction partners for various activities, a common and important judgmental task in everyday life. Schachter (1959) was among the first to show that anxious or frightened people prefer the company of others, and particularly of those in a predicament similar to theirs, in an apparent effort to control negative affect by seeking social comparisons about an impending noxious event. Other studies also found that people tend to be motivated to select and interact with partners who are in a matching rather than different mood (Locke & Horowitz, 1990). Such goal-oriented partner choices are consistent with a motivated affect-control strategy (Clark & Isen, 1982) that, according to the AIM, should constrain affect congruence in judgments and lead to effective affect control.

To gain further insight into motivated affect control processes, in a recent series of experiments we asked happy or sad subjects to perform a complex cognitive task—select a partner—either for themselves (personally relevant task) or for another person (personally irrelevant task). As expected, the combination of sad mood and high personal relevance led to a highly motivated processing strategy: These subjects selectively looked for and found a rewarding companion, whereas subjects in other conditions chose task-competent partners (Forgas, 1989). Sad subjects also later recalled more diagnostic information about potentially rewarding rather than competent partners (Forgas, 1991c, Experiment 1).

In subsequent experiments, information about potential partners was provided on a series of information cards (Forgas, 1991c, Experiment 2), and on a computer file, allowing us to precisely record and analyze subjects' step-by-step information search and decision strategies, as well as the processing latencies associated with each information unit examined (Forgas, 1991c, Experiment 3). Once again, sad subjects making a personal choice selectively searched for and selected rewarding partners (Figure 5) were faster in reaching for diagnostic information that served their affect control objective, but they studied these motivationally relevant details at greater length and more frequently than other information, and remembered them better later on. As predicted by the AIM, we found no evidence for affect infusion in any of these tasks. Rather, instead of focusing on affect-congruent information, information processors preferentially looked for and used rewarding information most relevant to servicing their motivational objective (in this instance, affect control).

Sometimes the objective of controlling one's own affect can lead to the more negative evaluations of, and even discrimination against, others. Evidence for such a motivated pattern was obtained in recent experiments by Forgas and Fiedler (1996). These studies were designed to investigate the role of mood states in influencing intergroup discrimination; specifically, happy and sad subjects were asked to make reward allocation decisions to ingroup and outgroup members, using the minimal group paradigm designed by Tajfel (e.g., Tajfel & Forgas, 1981). In this task, rewards are allocated to people based on nothing more than information about their ingroup or outgroup status, an almost "pure" test of intergroup bias. We found that in conditions when group membership was of little personal relevance to subjects, happy persons tended to process information more quickly and superficially, relying more on the heuristic group membership information. As a result, happy subjects discriminated more against the outgroup than did sad subjects (Figure 6).

FIGURE 5 The effects of mood and personal relevance on motivated interpersonal choices: Sad people performing a personally relevant choice selectively preferred potentially socially rewarding partners, while in all other conditions task competent partners were preferred (higher values indicate preference for more task competent rather than rewarding partners). (After Forgas, 1991c.)

The pattern was reversed, however, when group membership was made personally salient. Under these conditions, motivated processing was observed. This time, sad subjects, to whom group membership was now personally relevant, engaged in significantly more intergroup discrimination than did happy subjects. Sad subjects now assigned more rewards to members of their ingroup than the outgroup, and tried to maximize intergroup differences even when this could only be achieved at the cost of reduced ingroup rewards (Figure 6). In other words, negative mood led to an apparent attempt to bolster one's self-esteem and mood by engaging in motivated thinking designed to maximize differences between ingroup and outgroup members. This study provides an interesting illustration of how processing strategies can be readily switched by people in reaction to fairly minor changes in the nature of the task, resulting in completely different outcomes. The results of these experiments also show how motivated processing in the service of affect control can be an impor-

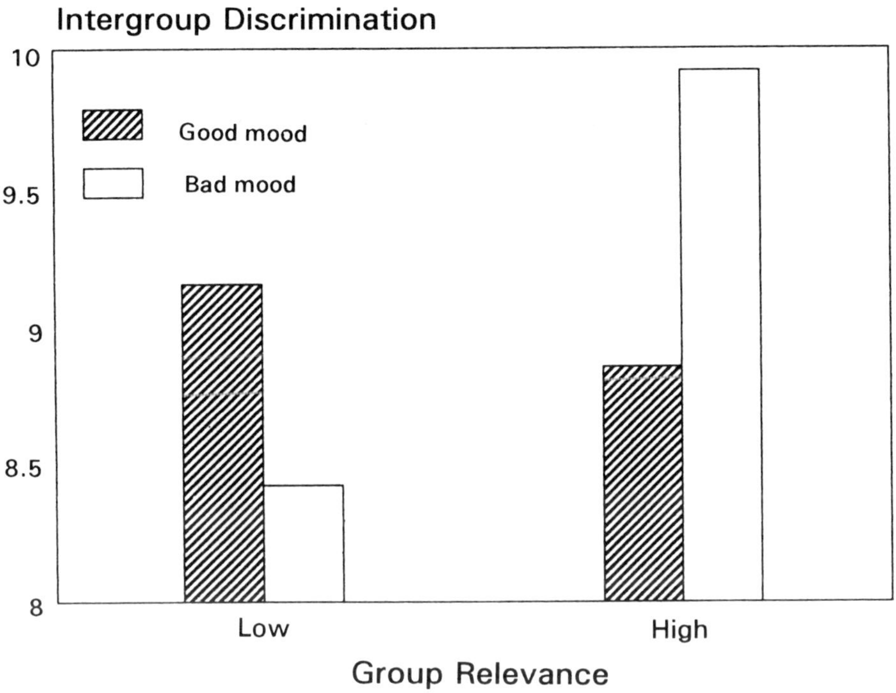

FIGURE 6 The effects of mood and personal relevance on intergroup discrimination: when the personal relevance of the group is low, happy subjects show greater ingroup favoritism; when group relevance is high, sad subjects engage in motivated processing and show greater ingroup favoritism. (After Forgas & Fiedler, 1996.)

tant source of prejudice and discrimination in circumstances when elevating the status of one's own group is a plausible source of positive affect.

There is also considerable evidence for motivated processing in the service of affect control from other studies (Weary et al., 1993). For example, Weary et al. (1994) found that depressed subjects selectively preferred others perceived as potentially most useful to them. In another recent study, Erber and Erber (1994) reported that "when subjects were motivated to change their sad mood . . . they tended to recall mood incongruent, that is positively valenced material" (p. 86), as part of a motivated affect control strategy when the situation demanded it. In another series of ingenuous experiments, Berkowitz (1993; Berkowitz et al., 1994) found that judgments were "affectively congruent when the subjects' attention was directed away from themselves, presumably because of the relatively automatic influence of the affective state, but displayed an affective incongruence . . . after the subjects had attended to their feelings" (Berkowitz et al., 1994, p. 2). It appears that self-directed attention alone was sufficient to induce a controlled, motivated affect control strategy in these subjects.

The operation of automatic, mood-management strategies, and the apparent switch from affect infusion to affect control are particularly nicely illustrated in a recent study by Sedikides (1994). In this experiment, subjects received a guided imagery mood induction; subsequently, they were asked to generate open-ended self-descriptions. Initial responses showed a clear mood congruent pattern consistent with the operation of affect infusion mechanisms. Remarkably, with the passage of time, later self-descriptions changed and now showed significant mood incongruent pattern. This result suggests that subjects came to adopt a motivated affect control strategy to "repair" their sad mood, but only after the initial negative mood effects due to affect infusion generated a sufficiently aversive state. This pattern is entirely consistent with the kind of feedback-loop proposed here as part of an automatic mood management system (Figure 2). Clearly, future studies need to explore the mechanisms involved in switching from affect infusion to affect control in realistic processing tasks. We are currently involved in running several experiments in which, following mood induction, subjects are asked to generate either self-relevant or not self-relevant information; the valence of their responses will be analyzed over time to detect if and when a switch from affect infusion to affect control is likely to occur. Preliminary results suggest that the processing switch observed by Sedikides can be replicated, and that trait variables (such as anxiety scores) are significantly related to the speed and efficacy of a person's mood management strategies.

Other researchers have also demonstrated motivated processing in the service of affect control. For example, Tesser's (1988) self-evaluation maintenance (SEM) model suggests that affect also plays a major role in inducing SEM behaviors. Ego-threatening comparisons tend to be associated with negative affect and arousal, and ego-enhancing reflection processes are linked to positive affect and arousal (Tesser, Millar, & Moore, 1988). The motivated character of these processes is supported by studies showing that people with higher levels of unattributed arousal display more marked patterns of motivated SEM behaviors (Tesser, Pilkington, & McIntosh, 1989). Interestingly, SEM is used under the same kinds of conditions that are predicted to lead to motivated processing according to the AIM, with personal relevance and closeness to the partner as critical triggering conditions.

In addition to self-relevance and self-directed attention, group interaction can also be a trigger to elicit motivated processing. When discussing issues in a group, the information and opinions provided by others often create normative pressures, highlighting socially desirable values (Brown, 1965), and generating pressures toward a consensus outcome. Surprisingly, the possibility that group interaction can significantly impact on social information-processing strategies and outcomes has received relatively little attention in the recent social cognition literature predominantly focused on individual cognition (e.g., Forgas, 1983). In one recent study, we asked people induced into a happy, sad, or neutral affective state to make judgments about nine types of people (e.g., doctors, farmers, Jews, Catholics, etc.). They were asked to do this first as individuals, and the procedure was repeated two weeks later in a group setting. This time, they were asked to discuss the information about each person type, and try to arrive at a consensus decision, using a procedure adapted from group polarization research. Individual judgments showed a strong pattern of affect infusion, as happy subjects made significantly more positive judgments than did sad subjects. Subsequent group interaction, however, had a surprisingly asymmetric effect: having discussed the task with others further increased the influence of positive mood on judgments, but significantly reduced the impact of negative moods. This result is consistent with sad subjects selectively adopting a motivated processing strategy directed at controlling negativity in judgments, as a result of relevant social norms and values becoming more salient in the course of group interaction (Brown, 1965).

Extensive research on depressed affect has also focused attention on the critical role of automatic mood regulation mechanisms in everyday life. Depressed people often perceive that they have little control over events. Indeed, a major difference between depressed and nondepressed persons is the tendency of the former to attribute events to uncontrollable causes (Anderson & Riger, 1991). Depressed people also often feel a sense of uncertainty and doubt about their ability to understand or predict events and control their own world (Weary, Elbin, & Hill, 1987; Weary, Jordan, & Hill, 1985).

There is some evidence to suggest, however, that in the mildly depressed person the feelings of uncertainty and lack of control may result in an automatically increased information search and the more careful and vigilant processing of social information (Weary et al., 1985). Indeed, depressed people have been found to have more complex schemata relevant to the interpretation of social behaviors (Marsh & Weary, 1989). They often show greater interest in certain types of social comparison (Weary et al., 1987), make more use of available social information (McCaul, 1983), and generate more inferences about others (Gleicher & Weary, 1991). Their general style of impression formation has been found to be effortful and systematic compared to nondepressed persons (Edwards and Weary, 1993). In the absence of more detailed information about processing latencies and outcomes in these studies, it is difficult to know to what extent depressed people are using targeted, motivated processing strategies in attempting to cope with their dysphoria. There is little doubt, however, that the increases in information-processing effort demonstrated by Weary and her colleagues represent one example of attempted mood management by depressed persons in their quest for personal control.

In any case, the adaptive shift to more effortful cognitive processes to control an aversive affective state may be limited to those suffering from less severe, or temporary, states of depression (Marsh & Weary, 1994). By definition, such strategies have failed to achieve their purpose in those suffering from enduring and serious episodes of depression. The role of affect, and aversive mood in particular, in triggering motivated processing strategies as part of an automatic mood management system is now receiving growing attention (Erber & Erber, 1994; Forgas, 1992a; Weary et al., 1993). The results reviewed here establish that motivated processing is indeed a low-infusion process, liable to eliminate mood congruence and often capable of producing mood-incongruent outcomes, as predicted by the AIM.

Motivated Processing to Control Positive Affect

Most research so far considered shows that motivated processing can be triggered to control negative, aversive affective states. There are also situations, however, in which excessively positive mood states may have equally deleterious effects, calling for motivated thinking to tone down euphoria (Parrott, 1993). For example, when people expect to undertake a complex, demanding task (such as meeting a stranger for the first time), they may prefer to enter this situation in a calm, low-key affective state. The role of the surrounding social situation in the regulation of both good and bad moods was first emphasized by Goffman (1974), and this point was recently reiterated by Wegner and Erber (1993). In an interesting study illustrating the engagement of motivated processing to control positive mood, these authors used music to induce good or bad mood in subjects, who expected either to interact with a stranger or to spend some time alone. They then had an opportunity to select between depressing, neutral, or cheerful newspaper articles to read. Results showed that people who expected to be alone preferred mood-consistent articles. However, subjects who expected a demanding interaction with a stranger preferred to read articles that were the opposite in affective tone to their own mood, as if trying to tone down their prevailing mood. These results nicely illustrate that situational factors can play a dominant role in selectively triggering affect infusion or affect control strategies.

Overall, we have seen in this section that when information processing is influenced and guided by a strong, preexisting motivation—such as affect control—then little open and constructive processing occurs, limiting the scope for affect infusion. Affect itself, and negative affect in particular, may often have such motivational consequences. Indeed, we believe that the pattern of fluctuating positive and negative mood states most of us experience in the course of our daily lives may best be understood as the product of two complementary information-processing strategies designed to achieve affect control (in the course of motivated processing), or allowing affect infusion (in the course of substantive processing). Of course, there are important individual differences between people in their tendency to rely on these mechanisms, as we shall see below.

INDIVIDUAL DIFFERENCES IN MOOD MANAGEMENT

Individual differences between people appear to be one of the critical factors determining a person's ability to successfully engage in effective mood management strategies. In this section we will briefly survey some of the available evidence for the role of individual difference variables in mediating mood management (affect infusion and affect control) strategies. This issue has received some attention in recent years, and the still ill-defined concept of "emotional intelligence" has been advanced to refer to differences between people in how they deal with emotions (Mayer & Salovey, 1988; Salovey & Mayer, 1990). Several attempts have been made to develop and operationalize various facets of emotional awareness and communication (King & Emmons, 1990; Lane & Schwartz, 1987), although, as Salovey et al. (1993) conclude, "the field of emotional self-regulation represents fertile, albeit largely unexplored territory" (p. 273).

Unfortunately, evidence for the role of individual difference variables in affect infusion or affect control processes is still relatively scarce. Interestingly, there may well be some gender-based differences in preferred processing strategies that mediate affect infusion effects. It appears that the more ruminative, substantive processing style adopted by women rather than men when in a depressed mood significantly enhances affect infusion and tends to prolong and exacerbate depression (Nolen-Hoeksema, 1993). Several experimental studies also provide suggestive evidence for the role of individual differences in mediating affect infusion processes. We have already mentioned the study by Haddock et al. (1994), that showed a significant affect infusion effect into stereotyping and intergroup judgments. These effects were significantly greater for individuals high in affect intensity who used more elaborate processing strategies. It appears that "high /affect intensity Ss/ may have a more elaborate network of information connected to their mood states, thus leading to heightened mood-judgment effects" (p. 203).

A somewhat similar link between individual differences in cognitive style and affect infusion was reported by Wegener et al. (1994), who found that after a mood induction using videotapes, happy subjects overestimated positive outcomes and had more positive attitudes to a persuasive message, but only if they had high scores on a need for cognition measure—that is, they were most inclined to process information in a constructive, generative way.

On the other hand, affect infusion tends to be reduced for people who score high on individual difference measures that would lead them to treat an issue in a motivated, predetermined manner. Several lines of evidence seem to support this proposition. In an intriguing study, Rhodewalt, Strube, and Wysocki (1988) found that there were significant affect infusion effects on perceptions of control by people who had a Type B personality profile. Surprisingly, affect infusion effects were reduced for individuals who manifested a Type A personality. As we know that Type A persons are characterized by a high level of concern with control, as well as feelings of time pressure, urgency, and tension, it seems likely that these individuals processed information in a more targeted, motivated manner that eliminated affect infusion effects.

Evidence consistent with this prediction also comes from an interesting recent series of experiments by Smith and Petty (1995), who found that negative mood led to mood-congruence in low self-esteem (SE) subjects, but resulted in mood-incongruence in high self-esteem individuals, consistent with their more motivated processing strategies in the service of mood regulation. After a sad mood induction, high SE subjects generated more positive than negative stories in response to TAT items and recalled more positive memories from their school days, while low SE persons showed a mood-congruent response. In fact, the more sad high SE people felt, the more positive their autobiographical memories.

In a recent series of studies (Forgas 1996a), we explored the effects of temporary good or bad mood on people's planned, and actual, bargaining strategies in a negotiating encounter. This study also examined the role of two individual difference variables in mediating mood effects on negotiation: need for approval (social desirability; Crowne & Marlowe, 1964), and macchiavellism (Christie, 1968). Results showed that affect infusion effects were weaker for subjects who scored high on these measures, and thus approached the bargaining task from a preexisting motivated perspective, such as the motivation to be successful manipulators (high macchiavellians), or the motivation to obtain approval (high social desirability scores) (Figure 7). These results suggest that affect-infusion is constrained when people are inclined to use targeted, motivated processing rather than open, substantive processing in assessing a situation (Forgas, 1991c; Sedikides, 1994).

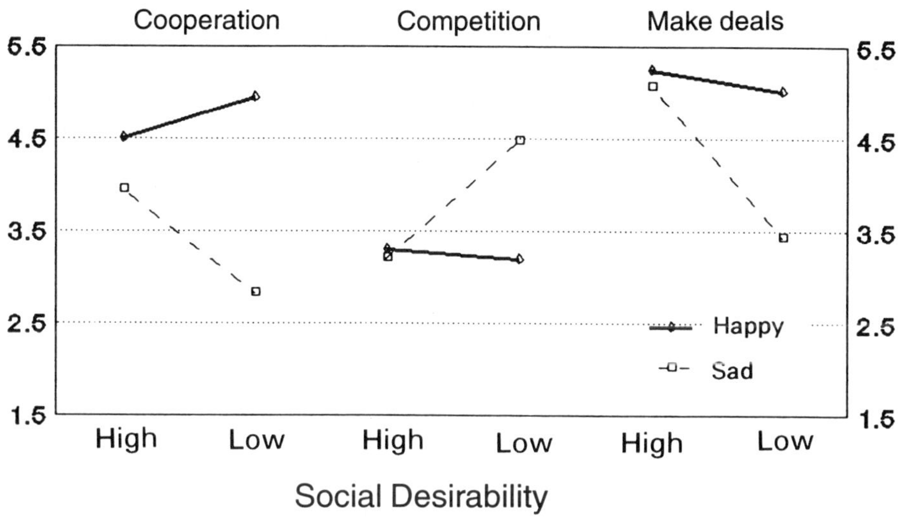

FIGURE 7 The role of individual differences in mediating affect infusion into social behaviors: People scoring high on individual differences measures predictive of a motivated approach to interpersonal tasks, such as social desirability, are less influenced by mood than are low scorers (after Forgas, 1996a).

Anxiety is another trait that seems to play a significant role in mediating mood management strategies. This is not particularly surprising, since trait anxiety and self-esteem are significantly negatively correlated (Scheier, Carver, & Bridges, 1994). It appears that aversive mood leads high trait-anxious people to shift attention toward threatening information. In contrast, low trait-anxious people shift attention away from threatening information (Broadbent & Broadbent, 1988; MacLeod, 1990). In one illustration of this effect, MacLeod and Mathews (1988) found that trait anxiety had no impact on attention to threat when subjects felt relaxed (several weeks before an important exam). However, when subjects felt tense (one week before the exam), high trait anxious subjects showed an attentional bias toward threat-related materials, and low trait-anxious subjects showed a bias away from the same materials. A similar pattern was also reported by Broadbent and Broadbent (1988) and by MacLeod (1990). These results show that high trait anxiety, just like high levels of depression, can have a paradoxical effect on cognitive strategies: instead of engaging in motivated processing designed to alleviate an aversive affective state, there may be a dysfunctional tendency by high trait-anxious people to focus on affect-enhancing information.

Such a pattern was confirmed by Ciarrochi (1996) in a recent series of studies looking at the role of trait anxiety in mediating aversive mood effects on social judgments. White undergraduates in an aversive or control condition read information about a threatening, radical black group and then made judgments and recalled information about the group. There were significant interactions between trait anxiety and aversive mood. Interestingly, aversive mood decreased the negativity of judgments among high trait anxious subjects. In contrast, negative mood appeared to infuse the judgments of low trait anxious people. It appears that in this case aversive mood led high trait-anxious people to engage in motivated processing, and as a result, trait anxiety did not infuse these judgments. This pattern was also confirmed in a more recent experiment (Moylan & Ciarrochi, 1996), in which happy and sad students who scored high or low on neuroticism were asked to make performance appraisal judgments about university professors. Highly neurotic individuals showed a significant mood-incongruent bias: in other words, the more negative their mood, the more positive the judgments they made. This result again suggests that negative affect selectively led high neurotic people to switch to motivated processing and thus to correct their familiar negative tendencies, while low neurotics showed no such effect.

SUMMARY AND CONCLUSIONS

This chapter argued that automatic and often subconscious mood management strategies represent an important and so far rather neglected aspect of personal control processes. We suggested that mood management is fundamentally comprised of two closely linked cognitive processing strategies. Affect infusion—the impact of mood on cognition in a mood-congruent direction—largely occurs in circumstances that are conducive to the adoption of constructive, substantive processing strategies. Affect control—the imposition of targeted cognitive control on affect—is the complementary strategy, when motivated processing is adopted in the service of some preexisting personal goal. Although there has been some past evidence for both affect infusion and affect control processes, few attempts have been made to combine these essentially complementary processing strategies into something like an automatic, self-correcting mood management model as proposed here.

The principle underlying the mood management hypothesis is based on the AIM (Forgas, 1995a), and its core assumption is that people may engage several alternative processing strategies when performing a cognitive task. This notion of process specificity in cognitive outcomes is now increasingly accepted in the recent social cognition theorizing (Fiedler, 1991; Kruglanski, 1989; Petty et al., 1991). In terms of the AIM, the choice between alternative processing strategies is determined by a combination of judge, target, and situational characteristics, that can ultimately be summarized in the form of a series of testable predictions (Figure 1). Despite the overall promise of such an integrated mood management model, much work remains to be done in exploring the role of specific situational, personal, and task characteristics in processing choices.

What we attempted to do here is to outline the basic characteristics of such an integrated mood management model, and to review a range of empirical studies that illustrate the occurrence of affect infusion in conditions of substantive processing, and affect control in conditions of motivated processing. Evidence for affect infusion, in particular, included a variety of interesting, if counterintuitive, findings now confirmed in several experiments. It appears that more extensive and substantive processing recruited by unusual, complex, or otherwise problematic tasks will paradoxically increase rather than decrease affect infusion effects, as such strategies offer greater scope for affectively valenced information to be incorporated into constructive cognitive processes. An analysis of processing times and judgmental latencies in several of these experiments establishes affect-priming as the major mechanism of affect infusion in the course of substantive processing (Forgas & Bower, 1987; Forgas, 1992a,c; 1993b; 1994).

Generally, this evidence suggests that there is a pervasive tendency for moods to infuse our thoughts and judgments under conditions when substantive processing strategies are adopted. Such affect infusion in the way information is selected, retrieved, and interpreted plays an important role in many real-life decisions and judgments in organizations, in consumer choices, in clinical practice, and in health-related judgments (Baron, 1987; Forgas & Moylan, 1987; Sedikides, 1992b). We may conclude, then, that affect infusion has a potentially significant impact on personal control, as it can amplify existing moods and also influence a wide range of cognitive and judgmental processes, including perceptions and judgments about the self, and about one's critically important personal relationships (Forgas, 1994; Sedikides, 1992a). The personal control implications of affect infusion may be particularly serious, since we now know that these infusion effects are most likely to occur when the information base is complex and elaborate, selective and constructive processing is required, and the evidence is capable of supporting alternative interpretations. These are conditions that are likely to characterize many of our most important and personally relevant choices and decisions (Fiedler, 1990, 1991; Forgas, 1992).

According to the mood management hypothesis, however, a normally functioning mood management system should be able to automatically detect and correct excessive affect infusion effects by switching from a substantive to a motivated processing strategy. Such a feedback loop between outcomes and processing choices is an integral part of the model (Figure 2). A wide range of studies also illustrate the operation of affect control involving motivated processing strategies. Numerous experiments have now demonstrated that, with normal subjects at least, excessive negativity in memory, feelings, associations, and judgments typically leads to a change in processing style toward a more motivated mood repair strategy that specifically targets positive or personally rewarding information (Forgas, 1991c; Forgas & Fiedler, 1996; Sedikides, 1994). Aversive affect is not the only trigger for motivated processing, however. We have seen that people are also more likely to adopt motivated processing strategies in reaction to quite subtle shifts in such variables as the personal relevance of the task, or a change toward more self-focused attention (Berkowitz, 1993; Forgas, 1991c). Only the first hesitant steps have been taken so far to understand the precise processing mechanisms that motivated thinking entails. It seems that motivated processing is characterized by a high degree of information selectivity, faster access to motivationally relevant rather than irrelevant contents, longer processing latencies associated with such targeted details, and the overall faster completion of motivated tasks thanks to the more directed and restricted information search strategies employed (Forgas, 1991c).

Clearly motivated processing is a major avenue for achieving personal control, as it is through this processing style that we are able to influence our feelings, thoughts, and desires. A fair bit of attention has been devoted to the study of conscious, highly aware processing strategies designed to cope with various aversive experiences. Our suggestion here is that such motivated thinking often occurs automatically, without conscious awareness as part of a self-correcting mood management system.

The role of individual difference variables in mediating personal control processes in general and mood management strategies in particular is also increasingly recognized in the literature (Mayer & Salovey, 1988; Salovey & Mayer, 1990). In this chapter, we have surveyed some of the evidence for the role of individual differences in mood management. Two basic principles can be discerned here. People scoring high on individual difference measures that are indicative of a motivated, predetermined approach to a particular cognitive task (such as social desirability, macchiavellism, Type A personality, etc.) generally show reduced affect infusion effects compared to low scorers. These results are consistent with our prediction that motivated processing precludes affect infusion. However, high scores on measures that tap into the general syndrome of negative affectivity (such as trait anxiety, neuroticism, and clinical depression) tend to show a different reaction: high scorers on these measures seem to be more aware of their own negative tendencies, and appear to adopt moti-

vated processing to control and reduce the negativity of their judgments of others (Ciarrochi, 1996; McLeod, 1990).

As this chapter suggests, much has been achieved in exploring the subtle interplay among personal control, processing strategies, and affect regulation. We argued here that in addition to the highly salient, conscious aspects of personal control, people also have the ability to manage and correct their own mood states, relying on the complementary operation of affect infusion and affect control processes to achieve this. We hope that the proposed mood management model, and the evidence presented here supporting its operation will stimulate further interest in this important and still rather neglected area of research.

Acknowledgments

Support from the Australian Research Council and the Alexander von Humboldt Foundation, Germany, is gratefully acknowledged.

REFERENCES

Anderson, C. A., & Riger, A. L. (1991). A controllability attribution model: Dimensional and situational interactions in the prediction of depression and loneliness. *Social Cognition, 9*, 149–181.

Argyle, M. (1987) *The psychology of happiness.* London: Methuen.

Asch, S. E. (1946). Forming impressions of personality. *Journal of Abnormal and Social Psychology, 41*, 258–290.

Baron, R. (1987). Interviewers' moods and reactions to job applicants: The influence of affective states on applied social judgments. *Journal of Applied Social Psychology, 16*, 911–926.

Baumgardner, A. H. & Arkin, R. M. (1988). Affective state mediates causal attributions for success and failure. *Motivation and Emotion, 12*, 99–111.

Berkowitz, L. (1993). Towards a general theory of anger and emotional aggression. In T. K. Srull & R. S. Wyer (Eds.), *Advances in social cognition* (Vol. 6, pp. l-46). Hillsdale, NJ: Erlbaum.

Berkowitz, L., Jo, E., Troccoli, B. T., & Monteith, M. (1994). *Attention-activated regulation of feeling effects.* Unpublished manuscript, University of Wisconsin, Madison.

Blaney, P. H. (1986). Affect and memory: A review. *Psychological Bulletin, 99*, 229–246.

Bower, G. H. (1981). Mood and memory. *American Psychologist, 36*, 129–148.

Bower, G. H. (1991). Mood congruity of social judgments. In J. P. Forgas (Ed.), *Emotion and social judgments* (pp. 31–53). Elmsford, NY: Pergamon Press.

Broadbent, D., & Broadbent, M. (1988). Anxiety and attentional bias: State and trait. *Cognition and Emotion,* 2, 165–183.

Brown, R. (1965). *Social psychology.* San Francisco: Freeman.

Burger, J. M., & Hemans, L. T. (1988). Desire for control and the use of attribution processes. *Journal of Personality, 56*, 531–546.

Christie, R. (1968). The Machiavellism scale. Unpublished, Columbia University, New York.

Ciarrochi, J. (1996). The effect of trait anxiety in mediating state anxiety effects on social judgments about outgroups. Unpublished, University of New South Wales, Sydney, Australia.

Clark M. S., & Isen, A. M. (1982). Towards understanding the relationship between feeling states and social behavior. In A. H. Hastorf & A. M. Isen (Eds.), *Cognitive social psychology* (pp. 73–108). Amsterdam: Elsevier/North-Holland.

Clore, G. L., & Parrott, G. (1991). Moods and their vicissitudes: Thoughts and feelings as information. In J. P. Forgas (Ed.), *Emotion and social judgments* (pp. 109–123). Elmsford, NY: Pergamon Press.

Crowne, D., & Marlowe, D. (1964). *The approval motive*. New York: Wiley.

Croyle, R. T. & Uretsky, M. B. (1987). Effects of mood on self-appraisal of health status. *Health Psychology, 6*, 239–253.

Damasio, A. R. (1994). *Descartes' error*. New York: Grosste/Putnam.

Descartes, R. (1961). *Passions of the soul: Essential work of Descartes* (L. Blair, Trans.). New York: Bantam Books. (Original work published 1649.)

Edwards, J. A., & Weary, G. (1993). Depression and the impression-formation continuum: Piecemeal processing despite the availability of category information. *Journal of Personality and Social Psychology, 64*, 636–645.

Ellis, H. C., & Ashbrook, T. W. (1988). Resource allocation model of the effects of depressed mood state on memory. In K. Fielder & J. P. Forgas (Eds.), *Affect, cognition and social behavior* (pp. 25–43). Göttingen, Germany: Hogrefe.

Erber, R., & Erber, M. W. (1994). Beyond mood and social judgment: Mood incongruent recall and mood regulation. *European Journal of Social Psychology, 24*, 79–88.

Fiedler, K. (1988). Emotional mood, cognitive style, and behaviour regulation. In K. Fiedler & J. Forgas (Eds.), *Affect, cognition and social behavior* (pp. 100–119). Göttingen, Germany: Hogrefe.

Fiedler, K. (1990). Mood-dependent selectivity in social cognition. In W. Stroebe & M. Hewstone (Eds.), *European review of social psychology* (Vol. 1, pp. 1–32). New York: Wiley.

Fiedler, K. (1991). On the task the measures and the mood in research on affect and social cognition. In J. P. Forgas (Ed.), *Emotion and social judgments* (pp. 83–104). Elmsford, NY: Pergamon Press.

Fiedler, K., & Forgas, J. P. (Eds.). (1988). *Affect cognition and social behavior.* Göttingen, Germany: Hogrefe.

Fiske, S. T., & Taylor, S. E. (1984). *Social cognition.* New York: Random House.

Forgas, J. P. (1983). What is social about social cognition? *British Journal of Social Psychology, 22*, 129–144.

Forgas, J. P. (1989). Mood effects on decision-making strategies. *Australian Journal of Psychology, 41*, 192–214.

Forgas J. P. (1990). Affective influences on individual and group judgments. *European Journal of Social Psychology, 20*, 441–453.

Forgas, J. P. (1991a). Affect and cognition in close relationships. In G. Fletcher & E. Fincham (Eds.), *Cogniton in close relationships* (pp. 151–174). Hillsdale, NJ: Erlbaum.

Forgas, J. P. (Ed). (1991b). *Emotion and social judgments*. Elmsford, NY: Pergamon Press.

Forgas, J. P. (199lc). Mood effects on partner choice: Role of affect in social decisions. *Journal of Personality and Social Psychology, 61*, 708–720.

Forgas, J. P. (1992a). Affect in social judgments and decisions: A multi-process model. In M. Zanna (Ed.), *Advances in experimental social psychology* (Vol. 25, pp. 227–275). San Diego, CA: Academic Press.

Forgas, J. P. (1992b). On bad mood and peculiar people: Affect and person typicality in impression formation. *Journal of Personality and Social Psychology, 62*, 863–875.

Forgas, J. P. (1993a). Affect, appraisal and action: Towards a multi-process framework In R. S. Wyer & T. K. Srull (Eds.), *Advances in social cognition* (Vol. 6, pp. 89–108). Hillsdale, NJ: Erlbaum.

Forgas J. P. (1993b). On making sense of odd couples: Mood efforts on the part of mismatched relationships. *Personality and Social PsychologyBulletin, 19,* 59–71.

Forgas, J.R (1994). Sad and guilty? Affective influences on the explanation of conflict episodes. *Journal of Personal ity and Social Psychology, 66,* 56–68.

Forgas, J. P. (1995a). Mood and judgment: The affect infusion model (AIM). *Psychological Bulletin, 117,* 39–66.

Forgas, J. P. (1995b). Strange couples: Mood effects on judgments and memory about prototypical and atypical targets. *Personality and Social Psychology Bulletin, 21,* 747–765.

Forgas, J. P. (1996a). On feeling good and getting your way: Mood effects on negotiating strategies and outcomes. Manuscript, University of New South Wales, Sydney, Australia.

Forgas, J. P. (1996b). On being sad and polite: The effects of mood on the production and interpretation of requests. Manuscript, University of New South Wales, Sydney, Australia.

Forgas, J. P. & Bower, G. H. (1987). Mood efforts on person perception judgments. *Journal of Personality and Social Psychology, 53,* 53–60.

Forgas, J. P., & Bower, G. H. (1988). Affect in social judgments. *Australian Journal of Psychology, 40,* 125–145.

Forgas, J. P., & Fiedler, K. (1996). Us and them: Mood effects on intergroup discrimination. *Journal of Personality and Social Psychology, 70,* 39–70.

Forgas, J. P., & Moylan, S. J. (1987). After the movies: The effects of transient mood states on social judgments. *Personality and Social Psychology Bulletin, 13,* 478–489.

Forgas, J. P., & Moylan, S. J. (1991). Affective influences on stereotype judgements. *Cognition and Emotion, 5(5/6),* 379–395.

Forgas, J. P., Bower, G. H., & Krantz, S. (1984). The influence of mood on perceptions of social interactions. *Journal of Experimental Social Psychology, 20,* 497–513.

Forgas, J. P. Bower, G. H., & Moylan, S. J. (1990). Praise or blame? Affective influences on attributions for achievement. *Journal of Personality and Social Psychology, 59,* 809–818.

Forgas, J. P., Burnham, D., & Trimboli, C. (1988). Mood, memory, and social judgment in children. *Journal of Personality and Social Psychology, 54,* 697–703.

Forgas, J. P., Levinger, G., & Moylan, S. J. (1994). Feeling good and feeling close: Affective influences on the perception of intimate relationships. *Personal Relationships, 1,* 165–184.

Frijda, N. H. (1986). *The emotions.* Cambridge, Eng.: Cambridge University Press

Frijda, N. (1988). The laws of emotion. *American Psychologist, 43,* 349–358.

Gleicher, F., & Weary, G. (1991). The effect of depression on the quantity and quality of social inference. *Journal of Personality and Social Psychology, 62,* 105–114.

Goffman, E. (1974). *Frame analysis.* Harmondsworth, England: Penguin.

Griffitt, W. (1970). Environmental effects on interpersonal behavior: Ambient effective temperature and attraction. *Journal of Personality and Social Psychology, 15,* 240–244.

Haddock, G., Zanna, M. P., & Esses, V. M. (1994). Mood and the expression of intergroup attitudes: The moderating role of affect intensity. *European Journal of Social Psychology, 24,* 189–206.

Heider, F. (1958). The *psychology of interpersonal relations.* New York: Wiley.

Hertel, G., & Fiedler, K. (1994). Affective and cognitive influences in a social dilemma game. *European Journal of Social Psychology, 24,* 131–146.

Hilgard, E. R. (1980). The trilogy of mind Cognition. affection. and conation. *Journal of the History of the Behavioral Sciences,* 16, 107–117.

Isen, A. (1984). Towards understanding the role of affect in cognition. In R. S. Wyer & T. K. Srull (Eds.), *Handbook of social cognition* (Vol. 3, pp. 179–236). Hillsdale, NJ: Erlbaum.

Isen, A. (1987). Positive affect cognitive processes and social behaviour. In L. Berkowitz (Ed.), *Advances in experimental social psychology* (Vol. 20, pp. 203–253). San Diego, CA: Academic Press.

James W. (1890). *Principles of psychology.* New York: Holt.

Janis, I. L., & Mann, L. (1977). *Decision making: A psychological analysis of conflict, choice and commitment.* New York: Free Press.

Johnson, R. (1994). Pain and cognition: Information processing biases associated with acute pain and chronic pain in children. Unpublished doctoral dissertation, University of Sydney, Sydney, Australia.

Johnson, R., & Spence, S. H. (1994). Pain, affect, and cognition in children: 2. Recall bias associated with pain. In G. F. Gebhart, D. L. Hammond, & T. S. Jensen (Eds.), *Progress in pain research and management: Vol. 2. Proceedings of the 7th World Congress on Pain* (pp. 877–884). Seattle: IASP Press.

Johnson, R., & Spence, S. H. (1996a). Pain, affect and cognition in children: Recall bias associated with pain and affective state. Manuscript submitted for publication.

Johnson, R., & Spence, S. H. (1996b). Pain and cognition in children: Information processing biases associated with acute and chronic pain. Manuscript submitted for publication .

Johnson, R., Spence, S. H., Champion, G. D., & Ziegler, J. B. (1994). Pain, affect and cognition in children: 1. The influence of affective state on pain in children. In G. F. Gebhart, D. L. Hammond, & T. S. Jensen (Eds.), *Progress in pain research and management: Vol. 2. Proceedings of the 7th World Congress on Pain* (pp. 869–875). Seattle: IASP Press.

Kelly G. A. (1955). *The psychology of personal constructs.* New York: Norton.

King, L. A., & Emmons, R. A. (1990). Conflict over emotional expression: Psychological and physical correlates. *Journal of Personality and Social Psychology, 58,* 864–877.

Kruglanski, A. W. (1989). *Lay epidemics and human knowledge: Cognitive and motivational bases.* New York: Plenum.

Kunda, Z. (1990). The case for motivated reasoning. *Psychological Bulletin, 108,* 331–350.

Lane, R. D., & Schwartz, G. E. (1987). Levels of emotional awareness: A cognitive-developmental measure of emotion. *Journal of Personality Assessment, 55,* 124–134.

Lazarus, R. S. (1984). On the primacy of cognition. *American Psychologist, 39,* 124–129.

Locke, K. D., & Horowitz, L. M. (1990). Satisfaction in interpersonal interactions as a function of similarity in level of dysphoria. *Journal of Personality and Social Psychology, 58,* 823–831.

MacLeod, C. (1990). Mood disorders and cognition. In M. W. Eysenck (Ed.), *Cognitive psychology: An international review.* Chichester, Eng.: Wiley.

MacLeod, C., & Mathews, A. (1988). Anxiety and the allocation of attention to threat. *Quarterly Journal of Experimental Psychology, 38A,* 659–670.

Mann, L. (1992). Stress affect and risk taking. In J. F. Yates (Ed.), *Risk-taking behavior* (pp. 202–230). New York: Wiley.

Marsh, K. L., & Weary, G. (1989). Depression and attributional complexity. *Personality and Social Psychology Bulletin, 15,* 325–336.

Marsh, K. L., & Weary, G. (1994). Severity of depression and responsiveness to attributional information. *Journal of Social and Clinical Psychology, 13,* 15–32.

Martin, L. L. (1986). Set/reset: Use and disuse of concepts in impression formation. *Journal of Personality and Social Psychology, 51,* 493–504.

Mayer, J. D. (1986). How mood influences cognition. In N. E. Sharkey (Ed.) *Advances in cognitive science* (Vol. 1, pp. 290–314). Chichester, Eng.: Ellis Horwood.

Mayer, J. D., & Salovey, P. (1988). Personality moderates the interaction of mood and cognition. In K. Fiedler & J. P. Forgas (Eds.), *Affect, cognition and social behavior* (pp. 87–99). Göttingen, Germany: Hogrefe.

Mayer, J. D., Gaschke, Y. N., Braverman, D. L., & Evans T. W. (1992). Mood congruent judgment is a general effect. *Journal of Personality and Social Psychology, 63,* 119–132.
Mayer, J. D., Gayle, M., Meehan, M. E., & Harman, A. K. (1990). Toward a better specification of the mood-congruency effect in recall. *Journal of Experimental Social Psychology, 26,* 465–480.
McCaul, K. D. (1983). Observer attributions of depressed students. *Personality and Social Psychology Bulletin, 9,* 74–82.
Moylan, S., & Ciarrochi, J. (1996). The role of neuroticism in mediating mood effects on appraisal judgments. Manuscript, University of New South Wales, Sydney, Australia.
Neisser, U. (1982). Memory: What are the important questions? In U. Neisser (Ed.), *Memory observed* (pp. 3–12). San Francisco: Freeman.
Nolen-Hoeksema, S. (1987). Sex differences in unipolar depression: Evidence and theory. *Psychological Bulletin, 101,* 259–282.
Nolen-Hoeksema, S. (1993). Sex differences in control of depression. In D. M. Wegner & J. W. Pennebaker (Eds.), *Handbook of mental control* (pp. 306–324). Englewood Cliffs, NJ: Prentice Hall.
Ottaviani, R., & Beck, A. T. (1988). Cognitive theory of depression. In K. Fiedler & J. P. Forgas (Eds.), *Affect, cognition and social behavior* (pp. 209–218). Göttingen, Germany: Hogrefe.
Parrott, W. G. (1993). Beyond hedonism: Motives for inhibiting good moods and for maintaining bad moods. In D. M. Wegner & J. W. Pennebaker (Eds.), *Handbook of mental control* (pp. 278–305). Englewood Cliffs, NJ: Prentice-Hall.
Pennebaker, J. W. (1989). Confession, inhibition, and disease. In L. Berkowitz (Ed.), *Advances in experimental and social psychology* (pp. 211–244). New York: Academic Press.
Petty, R. E., Gleicher, F., & Baker, S. (1991). Multiple roles for affect in persuasion. In J. P. Forgas (Ed.), *Emotion and social judgments* (pp. 181–200). Elmsford, NY: Pergamon Press.
Pittman, T. S., & D'Agostino, P. R. (1989). Motivation and cognition: Control deprivation and the nature of subsequent information processing. *Journal of Experimental Social Psychology, 25,* 465–480.
Rhodewalt, F., Strube, M. J., & Wysocki, J. (1988). The Type A behaviour pattern, induced mood, and the illusion of control. *European Journal of Personality, 2,* 231–237.
Roemer, L., & Borkovec, T. D. (1993). Worry: Unwanted cognitive activity that controls unwanted somatic experience. In D. M. Wegner & J. W. Pennebaker (Eds.), *Handbook of mental control* (pp. 220–238). Englewood Cliffs, NJ: Prentice-Hall.
Salovey, P., & Birnbaum, D. (1989). Influence of mood on health-related cognitions. *Journal of Personality and Social Psychology, 57,* 539–551.
Salovey, P., & Mayer, J. D. (1990). Emotional intelligence. *Imagination, Cognition and Personality, 9,* 185–211.
Salovey, P., Hsee, C. K., & Mayer, J. D. (1993). Emotional intelligence and the self-regulation of affect. In D. M. Wegner & J. W. Pennebaker (Eds.), *Handbook of mental control* (pp. 258–277). Englewood Cliffs, NJ: Prentice-Hall.
Salovey, P., O'Leary, A., Stretton, M., Fishkin, S., & Drake, C. A. (1991). Influence of mood on judgments about health and illness. In J. P. Forgas (Ed.), *Emotion and social judgments* (pp. 241–262). Elmsford, NY: Pergamon Press.
Schachter, S. (1959). *The psychology of affiliation.* Stanford, CA: Stanford University Press.
Scheier, M. F., Carver, C. S., & Bridges, M. W. (1994). Distinguishing optimism from neurotocism (and trait anxiety, self-mastery, and self-esteem): A reevaluation of the life orientation test. *Journal of Personality and Social Psychology, 67(6),* 1063–1078.
Schwarz, N. (1990). Feelings as information: Informational and motivational functions of affective states. In E. T. Higgins & R. Sorrentino (Eds.), *Handbook of motivation and cognition: Foundations of social behavior* (Vol. 2, pp. 527–561). New York: Guilford Press.

Schwarz, N., & Clore, G. L. (1983). Mood, misattribution and judgments of well-being: Informative and directive functions of affective states. *Journal of Personality and Social Psychology, 45*, 513–523.

Schwarz, N. & Clore, G. L. (1988). How do I feel about it? The informative function of affective states. In K. Fiedler & J. P. Forgas (Eds.), *Affect, cognition and social behavior* (pp. 44–62). Göttingen, Germany: Hogrefe.

Sedikides, C. (1992a). Changes in the valence of self as a function of mood. *Review of Personality and Social Psychology, 14*, 271–311.

Sedikides C. (1992b). Mood as a determinant of attentional focus. *Cognition and Emotion, 6*, 129–148.

Sedikides, C. (1994). Incongruent effects of sad mood on self-conception valence: Its a matter of time. *European Journal of Social Psychology, 4*, 161–172.

Sedikides, C. (1995). Central and peripheral self-conceptions are differentially influenced by mood: Tests of the differential sensitivity hypothesis. *Journal of Personality and Social Psychology, 69(4)*, 759–777.

Smith, S., & Petty, R. (1995). Personality moderators of mood congruency on cognition: The role of self-esteem and negative mood regulation. *Journal of Personality and Social Psychology, 68*, 1092–1107.

Srull, T. K. (1983). Affect and memory: The impact of affective reactions in advertising on the representation of product information in memory. In R. Bagozzi & A. Tybout (Eds.), *Advances in consumer research* (Vol. 10, pp. 244–263). Ann Arbor, MI: Association for Consumer Research.

Srull, T. K. (1984). The effects of subjective affective states on memory and judgment. In T. Kinnear (Ed.), *Advances in consumer research* (Vol. 11, pp. 530–533). Provo, UT: Association for Consumer Research.

Stroessner, S. J., & Mackie, D. M. (1992). The impact of induced affect on the perception of variability in social groups. *Personality and Social Psychology Bulletin, 18*, 546–554.

Tajfel, H., & Forgas, J. P. (1981). Social categorisation: Cognitions, values and groups. In: J. P. Forgas (Ed.), *Social cognition*. London: Academic Press.

Tesser, A. (1986). Some effects of self-evaluation maintenance on cognition and action. In R. M. Sorrentino & E. T. Higgins (Eds.), *The handbook of motivation and cognition: Foundations of social behavior* (pp. 435–464). New York: Guilford Press.

Tesser, A. (1988). Toward a self-evaluation maintenance model of social behavior. In L. Berkowitz (Ed.), *Advances in experimental social psychology* (Vol. 21, pp. 181–227). San Diego, CA: Academic Press.

Tesser, A., Millar, M., & Moore, J. (1988). Some affective consequences of social comparison and reflection processes: The pain and pleasure of being close. *Journal of Personality and Social Psychology, 54*, 49–61.

Tesser, A., Pilkington, C., & McIntosh, W. (1989). Self-evaluation maintenance and the mediational role of emotion: The perception of friends and strangers. *Journal of Personality and Social Psychology, 57*, 442–456.

Weary, G., Jordan, J. S., & Hill, M. G. (1985). The attributional norm of internality and depressive sensitivity to social information. *Journal of Personality and Social Psychology, 49*, 1283–1293.

Weary, G., Elbin, S., & Hill, M. G. (1987). Attribution and social comparison processes in depression. *Journal of Personality and Social Psychology, 52*, 605–610.

Weary, G., Marsh, K. L., Gleicher, E., & Edwards, J. A. (1993). Social-cognitive consequences of depression. In G. Weary, E. Gleicher, & K. L. Marsh (Eds.), *Control motivation and social cognition* (pp. 121–142). New York: Springer.

Weary, G., Marsh, K. L., & McCormick, L. (1994). Depression and social comparison motives. *European Journal of Social Psychology, 24*, 117–130.

Wegner, D. M., & Erber, R. (1993). Social foundations of mental control. In D. M. Wegner & J. W. Pennebaker (Eds.), *Handbook of mental control* (pp. 36–56). Englewood Cliffs, NJ: Prentice-Hall.

Wegner, D. M., & Pennebaker, J. W. (1993). Changing our minds: An introduction to mental control. In D. M. Wegner & J. W. Pennebaker (Eds.), *Handbook of mental control* (pp. 1–12). Englewood Cliffs, NJ: Prentice-Hall.

Wegener, D. I., Petty, R. E., & Klein, D. J. (1994). Effects of mood on high elaboration attitude change: The mediating role of likelihood judgments. *European Journal of Social Psychology, 24*, 25–44.

Wenzlaff, R. M. (1993). The mental control of depression: Psychological obstacles to emotional well-being. In D. M. Wegner & J. W. Pennebaker (Eds.), *Handbook of mental control* (pp. 239–257). Englewood Cliffs, NJ: Prentice-Hall.

Wheeler, L., & Miyake, L. (1992). Social comparison in everyday life. *Journal of Personality and Social Psychology, 62*, 760–774.

Zajonc, R. (1965). Social facilitation. *Science, 149*, 269–274.

Zajonc, R. B. (1980). Feeling and thinking: Preferences need no inferences. *American Psychologist, 35*, 151–175.

CHAPTER 8

ABILITY PERCEPTION AND CARDIOVASCULAR RESPONSE TO BEHAVIORAL CHALLENGE

REX A. WRIGHT

CONTROL, PERCEIVED ABILITY, AND CARDIOVASCULAR RESPONSE

To suggest that a person has control over an outcome is to suggest that the person can affect the outcome—that is, impact its presence, quality, or the like—through action (e.g., see Skinner, 1996). There are various determinants of perceived control, including the appraised character of activity that must be carried out to alter an outcome (easy versus difficult), the appraised effectiveness of that activity in accomplishing its purpose, and the appraised ability (or efficacy, Bandura, 1986) of the performer to do what must be done. In this chapter, I focus on the latter determinant of perceived control and consider its relation to cardiovascular (CV) responsivity (i.e., CV elevation above baseline).

Measures of CV responsiveness are among the most common physiological outcomes assessed in psychology, and have been taken to reflect states ranging from empathy (Eisenberg et al., 1989) to stress (Baum, Grunberg, & Singer, 1982). Moreover, they have long been thought to be

---

REX A. WRIGHT • Department of Psychology, University of Alabama at Birmingham, Birmingham, Alabama 35294. E-mail: rwright@uab.edu

Personal Control in Action, edited by Kofta et al., Plenum Press, New York, 1998.

associated with perceptions of ability. In the past few years, my students and I have come to conclude that there is a perceived-ability/CV-response relation, but that it is markedly different from what traditionally has been believed. This conclusion is based in large part on an integrative analysis of effort and CV response that has guided our work for some time now (e.g., Wright, 1996). Although the analysis was not developed with ability perceptions in mind, it is one into which the role of those perceptions can easily be incorporated. The conclusion also is based on a set of ability studies we have carried out and our interpretation of data from some other ability investigations. My main goals in this chapter are to outline the integrative analysis, distinguish its ability perspective from traditional ability views, and review supportive evidence that we and others have obtained. Once I have accomplished these aims, I will consider some findings that appear to support traditional ability views, discuss two additional perspectives regarding the perceived-ability/CV-response relation, and point out several insights that might be gained by thinking in the present, integrative, terms.

PERCEIVED-ABILITY/RESPONSIVITY RELATION: TRADITIONAL CONCEPTIONS

For a person to exert control over an outcome, he or she has to *do* something. What has to be done can be as simple as whispering a command, or as complex as debugging a powerful computer program. But for a link to be established between person and outcome, some action must be carried out. A different way of putting this is to say that, to exert control, a person must *meet a behavioral challenge*. Traditionally, psychologists have held primarily two beliefs concerning the relation between individuals' perception of ability and their CV response to behavioral challenges. These are (1) that CV responsivity *increases* steadily as perceived ability increases and (2) that CV responsivity *decreases* steadily as perceived ability increases. The first belief generally has been held in regard to appetitive circumstances, in which individuals can gain an attractive outcome or set of attractive outcomes by doing well, and has been predicated on a pair of suppositions: (1) that responsivity is directly proportional to effort, or task engagement (Kahneman, 1973; Obrist, 1976, 1981), and (2) that engagement is directly proportional to perceived competence in a particular performance domain (Bandura, 1982; Locke & Latham, 1990). Because effort should be greater in those who feel relatively capable than in those who feel relatively incapable, CV responsivity also should be greater in those who feel relatively capable than in those who feel relatively incapable (Gellatly & Meyer, 1992; Matthews, Davis, Stoney, Owens & Caggiula, 1991).

The second belief generally has been held in regard to aversive circumstances, in which individuals are faced with possible harm or loss if they do poorly, and founded on two suppositions as well. Supposition one, in this case, is that responsivity increases with perceived threat (Cox, 1978; Lazarus, 1966, 1968). Supposition two is that perceived threat is inversely proportional to the perceived ability to cope (Bandura, 1983, 1991; Williams, 1995). Because individuals who feel less able to cope should experience more threat than individuals who feel more able to cope, they also should manifest larger physiological responses than individuals who feel more able to cope (Bandura, O'Leary, Taylor, Gauthier, & Gossard, 1987; Bandura, Reese, & Adams, 1982).

THE INTEGRATIVE PERSPECTIVE

A very different relation between ability perceptions and CV responsiveness is implied by the integrative analysis that has guided research in my laboratory in recent years. The analysis takes as its starting point one of the suppositions above, that CV responsivity is intimately linked to effort. More specifically, based on arguments and data presented by Obrist (1976, 1981; see also Light, 1981), it assumes that sympathetic nervous system (SNS) influence on the heart and vasculature increases with task engagement (what Obrist termed "active coping"). The analysis then uses a theory of motivational intensity by Brehm (e.g., Brehm & Self, 1989) to predict when CV engagement effects will be more and less pronounced.

MOTIVATIONAL INTENSITY THEORY

Brehm's intensity theory is concerned with the determinants of momentary effort, or the amount of effort that is expended at a particular point in time. The theory has been described in detail elsewhere (Brehm & Self, 1989; Wright, 1996; Wright & Brehm, 1989); consequently, I will present it here only in summary form.

1. Momentary effort does not vary directly as a function of variables associated with the importance of satisfying a motive (i.e., of attaining or avoiding an outcome or set of outcomes), as most motivation theories suggest (see Heckhausen, 1989/1991). Rather, it varies as a function of what can, will, and must be done in the service of motive satisfaction.
2. So long as motive satisfaction is viewed as possible and worthwhile, momentary effort should be proportional to instrumental task difficulty, that is, to the difficulty of activity required cur-

rently to satisfy a motive. The theory distinguishes between the amount of work that must be carried out in total and the amount of work that must be carried out at a particular point in time. Even a substantial challenge (moving 100 bricks) would be expected to elicit little momentary effort if individuals spread the work across time (e.g., move the load one brick at a time).

3. Where a motive is perceived to be impossible to satisfy or excessively difficult to satisfy, given its significance (magnitude), effort should be low. In the former case, energy expenditure is, by definition, understood to be futile. In the latter case, subjective cost (in terms of effort) outweighs subjective benefit.
4. The upper limit of what individuals would be *willing* to do to satisfy a motive—termed the level of potential motivation—should be a (multiplicative) function of at least three factors: (1) the need to attain or avoid the outcome or outcomes driving behavior, (2) the quality of the outcome or outcomes driving behavior, and (3) the subjective expectancy of motive satisfaction once necessary instrumental behavior has been successfully executed. The first two factors generally are referred to as "need state" and "incentive value," respectively. The third factor has been discussed most frequently by contemporary writers as the "outcome expectancy" (see Maddux, 1995), although discussions in terms of the "outcome-consequence expectancy" (Heckhausen, 1989/1991), and the "instrumentality of behavior" (Vroom, 1964) are not uncommon. For ease in presentation, I will use the first expression in referring to the factor here.

In considering intensity theory, it may be useful to think of an outcome or set of outcomes driving behavior as a commodity that may be purchased at a price, and effort as the currency that may be expended to make the purchase. How much individuals would be willing to expend in a given circumstance should depend on their need for the commodity, the value of the commodity, and the likelihood that payment will result in the commodity being secured. But how much individuals *will* expend should depend on the price of the commodity. If the price is low, little currency will be expended regardless of individuals' upper price limit. As price increases, so should currency expended up to the point that price either exceeds the bound of what individuals are willing to "pay" or exceeds what individuals are capable of paying. The graphs in Figure 1 illustrate the proposed relation between difficulty (price) and effort (payment) at two levels of potential motivation (upper price limit). Graph A depicts the case in which the upper bound, or price limit, is relatively low; graph B depicts the case in which the upper bound is relatively high.

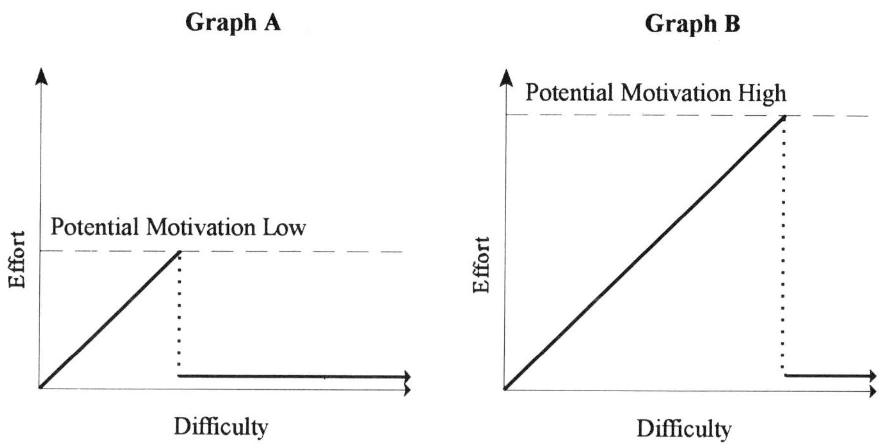

FIGURE 1 Effort–difficulty relation where potential motivation is relatively low and relatively high.

One implication of the graphs is that moderately difficult challenges should tend to evoke greater effort than easy and extremely difficult challenges. This is because effort should be greater where success is (viewed as) difficult, but possible and worthwhile, than where success is (viewed as) easy, "too difficult," or impossible. Taking into account Obrist's engagement (active coping) hypothesis, the suggestion is that sympathetically mediated CV effects should generally be more pronounced under moderate challenge conditions than under easy and extreme challenge conditions. Another implication is that effort and associated CV effects should be determined not only by the difficulty of a challenge, but also by the potential motivation to meet that challenge. So long as a possible challenge is viewed as worthwhile to meet, effort and CV responsivity should be proportional to challenge difficulty, i.e., high if the challenge is substantial and low if the challenge is mild. However, if the difficulty of meeting the challenge surpasses potential motivation, effort and CV responsivity should be low.[1]

Role of Ability Perceptions

Ability perceptions may be incorporated into Brehm's theory by making a straightforward assumption: Those with low perceived ability with respect to a given challenge will view that challenge as more difficult than will those with high perceived ability with respect to the challenge (Ford & Brehm, 1987). In other words, holding constant actual task characteristics (e.g., the nature of a math problem), appraisals of demand should be greater in those who feel incapable in the relevant performance realm (mathematics) than in those who feel capable in the relevant performance realm. This suggestion has considerable intuitive appeal. Moreover, it has been argued (or taken as a given) by various writers over the past 25 years (Bandura, 1986; Kukla, 1972; Locke & Latham, 1994; Meyer, 1987; Pecchinenda & Smith, 1996; Schönpflug, 1983; Smith & Pope, 1992), and can be conceptualized in the same commodity/currency terms that may be used to clarify the basic intensity model. In commodity/currency terms, low- and high-ability individuals have available the same number of currency (effort) units with which to "pay." However, low-ability individuals view their units as having less value, or purchase power, than high-ability individuals do. Because low-ability units are relatively devalued, it takes more of them to meet a given commodity price (i.e., demand level) than it takes high-ability units to meet the commodity price.

If the perceived-ability/difficulty assumption above is safe, then it is a simple matter to map engagement functions separately for low- and high-ability individuals onto the Figure 1 graphs. One merely moves the engagement line (holding slope constant) to a relatively high point on the Y axis for low-ability individuals and to a relatively low point on the axis for high-ability individuals. The idealized depictions in Figure 1, in fact, show engagement where perceived capacity to perform (perceived purchase power) is maximal.

Like the Figure 1 graphs, the modified engagement graphs (see Figure 2) have important implications, in this case concerning the theoretical relation between ability perceptions and CV responsiveness. One implica-

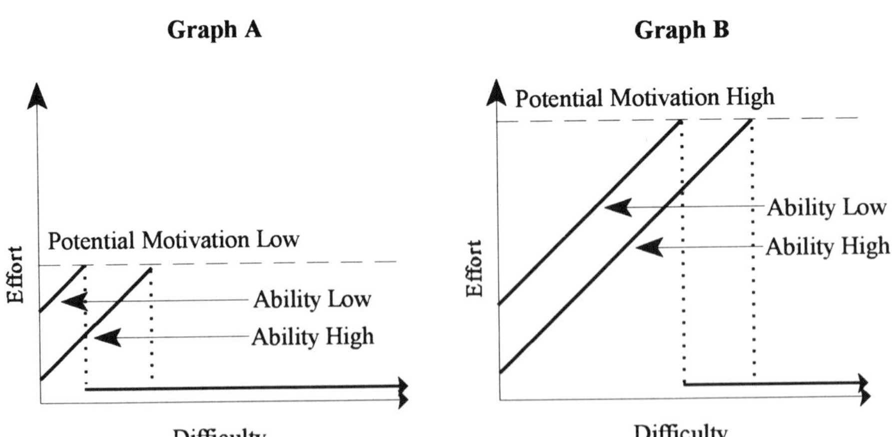

FIGURE 2 Effort–difficulty relation at two levels of potential motivation for individuals with low- and high perceived ability.

tion is that so long as both low- and high-ability individuals view a challenge as possible and worthwhile to meet, sympathetically mediated CV responses should be greater for the former group than for the latter group because the former group should try harder. A second implication is that low-ability individuals should disengage more readily—that is, disengage at a lower level of (objective) demand—than high-ability individuals and, hence, should sometimes show less sympathetic responsiveness than high-ability individuals when presented with a difficult challenge. A third implication is that even those with high perceived ability should disengage if the difficulty of a challenge is great enough. At and beyond this degree of challenge, sympathetic CV responses should be minimal irrespective of the perceived capacity to perform. Finally, a fourth implication is that potential motivation should moderate the relation between ability percepts and sympathetic responsivity to a possible challenge. Because potential motivation should determine the difficulty level at which each ability group disengages, it should determine where responsivity will be (1) greater for low- than high-ability individuals (both groups engaged), (2) lower for low- than high-ability individuals (low-ability individuals disengaged, high-ability individuals engaged), and (3) low for both groups (low- and high-ability individuals disengaged).

I should note that there is no obvious reason to expect low- and high-ability groups to differ systematically in their *potential* motivation to satisfy general motives (to obtain a meal, to have social contact, to earn a particular salary, etc.), although the groups may sometimes differ in potential motivation when the relevant ability conception is associated with a self-definition, or identity (Gollwitzer, Wicklund, & Hilton, 1982; Wicklund & Braun, 1987; Wicklund & Gollwitzer, 1982). Regarding the latter, one might expect that—all things being equal—individuals who believe they are capable in a particular realm (say, music or carpentry) would be more likely to adopt an identity associated with the realm ("musician" or "carpenter") than individuals who think they are not capable in the realm (Hackett & Betz, 1995). To the extent that the capable are relatively more likely to adopt the associated identity, they also should be relatively more likely to be willing to invest energy necessary to meet challenges instrumental to being "complete" with respect to the identity (i.e., to being accomplished in the realm, Gendolla, 1995). I also should emphasize that the ability effects depicted in Figure 2 are presumably performance domain specific (Bandura, 1986; Ewart, 1995; Ford & Brehm, 1987; Maddux, 1995). That is, the figure reflects ability/effort relations only where an ability conception pertains to a current behavioral challenge. Where an ability conception (e.g., regarding mathematics) does not pertain to a current challenge (e.g., to swim 100 meters), the ability conception should not predict engagement.

Differences between the integrative view and the traditional conceptions with regard to the perceived-ability/CV-response relation are plain. Whereas the traditional analyses suggest that the relation should be positive in approach circumstances and negative in avoidance circumstances, the integrative view suggests the relation should be the same in both, at least insofar as CV responses are mediated by effort. Further, whereas the traditional analyses suggest that the relation will be monotonic within each circumstance, the integrative view suggests that the relation will vary dramatically, depending on the difficulty of a challenge, and will be moderated by factors that affect the potential motivation to perform.

NONPHYSIOLOGICAL SUPPORT

Empirical support for the integrative view with respect to the perceived-ability/CV-response relation comes in part from studies that have not included physiological measures, but suggest that low- and high-ability individuals tend to expend different amounts of energy on easy and difficult tasks. One example is a study by Kukla (1974), which classified participants in terms of resultant achievement motivation and construed that individual difference variable in terms of perceived ability. Individuals varying in resultant achievement motivation (ability) were given mental arithmetic problems to perform, with instructions that the problems were easy or moderately difficult. Kukla expected, and found, better performance where the task was described as easy among low need-achievement participants, but better performance where the task was described as moderately difficult among high need-achievement participants. Another example is a study by Sigall and Gould (1977), which manipulated participants' self-esteem (and, thus, possibly their general sense of ability) by providing them with false personality feedback and then gave the participants the opportunity to perform practice problems in preparation for a work session with an experimenter described as easy to please or hard to please. Low self-esteem participants were found to practice more for the easy than hard experimenter, whereas high self-esteem participants were found to practice more for the hard- than easy experimenter (see also Meyer & Hallerman, 1977; Wright, Caldwell, Evans, & Riter, 1991).

PHYSIOLOGICAL SUPPORT

More direct support for the integrative view comes from a series of physiological ability studies my students and I have conducted. The series is part of a broader research program concerned with predicting effort and CV responsivity in individuals confronted with challenges and has involved the assessment of three CV parameters: heart rate (HR), systolic blood pressure (SBP), and diastolic blood pressure (DBP). "Heart rate," of course, refers to the pace at which the heart pumps. "Systolic blood pressure" and "diastolic blood pressure" both refer to pressure exerted on blood vessel walls following a heartbeat. The difference between them is that SBP reflects pressure exerted at the peak of the pulse, whereas DBP reflects pressure exerted in the trough between pulses. Put differently, SBP is the highest pressure on vessel walls following a beat, whereas DBP is the lowest pressure on vessel walls following a beat. It is beyond the scope of this presentation to discuss in detail the determinants of the individual CV parameters. However, it is important to note that the parameters are not considered interchangeable indices of SNS activity. Generally speaking, HR and SBP are thought to be more sensitive to SNS activation than DBP, with SBP being especially sensitive in this regard. Thus, we generally have expected those measures to be more likely than DBP to reflect the predicted engagement pattern. Readers interested in detailed descriptions of HR and blood pressure determinants are referred to excellent discussions by Berntson, Cacioppo, and Quigley (1991, 1993), Hassett and Danforth (1982), Obrist (1981), and Papillo and Shapiro (1990); those interested in more detail about our specific reasoning are referred to Wright (1996).

I will review the ability studies below. But before doing so, I should present a synopsis of evidence pertaining to nonability aspects of the integrative analysis. The synopsis places the ability studies in context; moreover, it addresses a supposition that underlies one of the traditional perceived-ability/CV-response beliefs.

Synopsis of Non-ability Evidence

I pointed out earlier that the integrative analysis has a least two implications that are unrelated to ability perceptions. One is that moderate challenges should tend to evoke more pronounced sympathetically mediated CV responses than mild and extreme challenges (expected simple difficulty effect). The other is that potential motivation should moderate sympathetic CV responses to a possible challenge (expected interactional effect). So long as a possible challenge is viewed as worthwhile to meet, effort and responsivity should correspond to the challenge's difficulty; however, if the challenge is perceived to be too difficult, given its associated benefit, effort and responsivity should be minimal regardless of the magnitude of the challenge.

The first nonability implication is supported by a host of investigations that have examined CV responses as a function of task demand.

Among the earliest studies to show the expected simple difficulty effect were experiments by Elliott (1969, Experiment 2) and Obrist et al. (1978). Elliott found a nonlinear relation between the difficulty of a tone discrimination task that participants performed for money and the participants' HR response over trials, with the greatest HR response occurring where the task was moderately difficult. Obrist et al. found similar effects in individuals told they could avoid electric shock by performing a (key release) reaction time (RT) task. For some (mild challenge), the requirement was to attain a relatively slow RT standard; for others (extreme challenge), the requirement was to attain a very fast RT standard; and for still others (moderate challenge), the requirement was to improve response time on successive trials. Results indicated greater CV responsivity—this time for SBP as well as HR (the Elliott experiment examined only HR)—where the challenge was moderate than where it was mild or where it was extreme.

Subsequent difficulty studies have replicated the Elliott and Obrist et al. CV patterns repeatedly, using a range of experimental tasks and incentives (Light & Obrist, 1980, 1983; Steptoe, Moses, Mathews, & Edwards, 1990; Van Schijndel, DeMey, & Näring, 1984; for relevant reviews, see Brehm & Self, 1989; Manuck, Morrison, Bellack, & Polefrone, 1985). For example, Smith, Baldwin, and Christenson (1990) found nonmonotonic effects on measures of blood pressure (SBP and DBP) and HR responsivity in individuals presented the opportunity to earn a monetary incentive by attaining a low, moderate, or high standard on a social influence (persuasion) task. Similarly, Wright, Brehm, Crutcher, Evans, and Jones (1990) found nonmonotonic effects for SBP and HR responsiveness in a procedure that provided participants the chance to avoid a noxious noise by succeeding on an easy, moderately difficult, or extremely difficult (nonsense trigram) memory task. It is notable that the predicted difficulty effect has been documented not only while participants were engaged, but also while they *anticipated* performance (e.g., see Smith et al., 1990). Data indicating that difficulty effects are anticipatory comport with the view that physiological adjustments of this type serve to prepare individuals for action (Obrist, 1981). The data also limit concerns that observed adjustments may reflect group differences in somatic activity, rather than group differences in engagement (Obrist, Webb, Sutterer, & Howard, 1970).

The second nonability implication is supported primarily by a group of studies that have crossed difficulty manipulations with manipulations of variables that should affect potential motivation, including need (Storey, Wright, & Williams, 1996; Wright, Shaw, & Jones, 1990 Experiment 2), incentive value (Wright, Dill, Geen, & Anderson, in press; Wright, Shaw, & Jones, 1990, Experiment 1; Wright et al., 1995), and the expectancy of motive satisfaction once behavior has been completed (Murray, Wright, & Williams, 1993; Wright & Gregorich, 1989; Wright, Williams, & Dill, 1992;

see also Manuck et al., 1978). Cardiovascular (most commonly SBP and HR) results consistently have borne out the expected interactional effect, both during and just prior to performance. An illustration of the interactional pattern is seen in an experiment (Wright et al., 1992) that presented participants with trials of an easy or moderately difficult digit-recognition task and led them to believe a good performance (90% success rate) would ensure a high (19/20) or low (1/19) chance of avoiding an aversive noise at the end of the work period. As expected, SBP and HR responses assessed while participants worked were greater under moderately difficult than easy conditions when the probabilistic link between success and noise avoidance was strong (i.e., when the outcome expectancy was high), but were low in both difficulty conditions when that link was weak.

Studies pertaining to the nonability implications of the integrative analysis are important in their own right, but especially notable in the present context for at least two reasons. First, they show that there is considerable support for the integrative view independent of any ability research that might be conducted. Because fundamental propositions are well documented, ability studies do not bear the burden of demonstrating entirely new effects, but rather the less weighty responsibility of elaborating on established findings. Second, they provide data directly relevant to a supposition that underlies one of the traditional perceived-ability/CV-response beliefs: that responsivity in aversive contexts varies with perceived threat. This supposition implies that there should have been linear effects in studies that manipulated the difficulty of avoidance behavior, because subjective threat should increase with avoidant demand. The supposition also implies that there should have been two main effects in the Wright et al. (1992) study and studies similar to it (see, for example, Manuck et al., 1978; Murray et al, 1993). Just as subjective threat should be positively related to demand, it also should be negatively related to the probability that success will result in avoidance. Thus, the suggestion is that CV responsiveness should have been higher where difficulty was high than where difficulty was low, and higher where probability was low than where probability was high. Given that a simple perceived-threat/CV-response relation was not observed in these studies, there is reason to question why one should be assumed in other aversive circumstances.

Our Ability Studies

My students and I have carried out six ability studies thus far. Three simply examined ability effects at different difficulty levels and provided data relevant to the first two ability implications described earlier: (1) that sympathetic CV responses should tend to be greater for low- than high-ability individuals where demand is modest and (2) that sympathetic responses should sometimes be greater for high- than low-ability individuals where demand is high. Two studies are somewhat more elaborate and investigated an application of the integrative perspective with respect to ability. Although these address a special issue, as a pair, they also provide data relevant to the first two ability implications, as well as data relevant to the implication that sympathetic responses should be low for both ability groups if demand is high enough. The last ability study differs from the others in that it does not address any of the main ability implications; rather, it addresses the presumed performance domain specificity of CV ability effects.

Our ability studies constitute critical tests of the integrative analysis' predictive validity in the ability realm. Furthermore, some have yet to appear in print. Therefore, I describe the studies in relatively great detail. Readers should note that the variously mentioned statistical effects are reliable at or beyond the 95% confidence level unless otherwise indicated.

Ability Effects at Different Levels of Demand

In the first of the studies to examine ability effects at different demand levels (Wright & Dill, 1993), participants were encouraged to do their best on a brief letter-scanning task and then were provided feedback indicating that they had performed well (87th percentile of previous performances) or poorly (12th percentile of previous performances) in comparison to other students. Given that participants presumably had tried reasonably hard in the initial scanning period, those who received favorable feedback should have inferred that they had relatively high scanning ability, whereas those who received unfavorable feedback should have inferred that they had low scanning ability. And this, in fact, was indicated by subjective ability ratings obtained on a postfeedback questionnaire. Shortly after receiving the feedback and completing the questionnaire, participants were presented with a second scanning task—similar, but not identical, to the first—and told they could earn a prize by attaining a high (85th percentile of previous performances) or low (15th percentile of previous performances) performance standard.

Analysis of SBP responses assessed immediately prior to and during the second performance period revealed the expected feedback × standard interaction. Responses for high-ability participants were greater under high than low standard conditions; by contrast, those for low-ability participants were slightly (not reliably) reduced under high as compared to low standard conditions. Furthermore, whereas responses were slightly greater for low- than high-ability participants when the standard was low, they were lower for low- than high-ability participants when the standard was high. Analysis of DBP responses yielded the same interaction, and means in the same crossover pattern. The only difference in terms of simple effects was that the low–high comparison for high-ability participants fell just short of significance ($p < .06$).

Encouraged by this study's findings, we (Wright, Wadley, Pharr, & Butler, 1994) decided to extend it by examining anticipatory responses evoked (1) in an avoidance context and (2) by natural ability appraisals. High- and low-ability groups were formed by administering in a screening session a questionnaire that included an item that asked respondents to rate their math ability (0–10) and then inviting to participate in the study proper only those individuals with relatively high- and low-ability ratings (values of 7–10 and 0–3, respectively). The original intent was to assess responses under conditions where the groups believed they could avoid a noise by solving math problems described as easy or difficult. However, pilot testing revealed that even the low-ability participants were prepared to attempt the more difficult problems; consequently, we added a third difficulty level at which the problems were depicted as even more challenging (so difficult that only 1 in 100 students are successful). The resulting design was a 2 (low-ability, high-ability) × 3 (low demand, high demand, extreme demand) factorial.

As predicted, the relation between avoidant task demand and anticipatory SBP responsivity was found to differ between the ability groups (ability × demand interaction, $p < .05$, see Figure 3). High-ability participants tended to evince greater systolic responsiveness as demand increased (linear trend, $p < .10$); by contrast, low-ability participants evinced more pronounced systolic responses in the high demand condition than in the low- and extreme demand conditions (quadratic trend, $p < .05$). Comparisons within the demand conditions indicated that low-ability participants had higher systolic responsivity than high-ability participants where demand was high. Low-ability participants had slightly higher systolic responsivity than high-ability participants where demand was low, and slightly lower systolic responsivity than high-ability participants where demand was extreme, but those differences were not significant.

The third investigation of this type (Wright & Dismukes, 1995) also examined ability effects in an avoidance context, but did so experimentally and when behavior was ongoing instead of imminent. As in the first ability study, participants first performed a scanning task and received feedback that they had done well or poorly in comparison to others. They then were exposed to a 1-s sample of (110 dB-A) noxious noise and were told they could avoid extended exposure to the noise by attaining a low (easy) or high (difficult) performance standard on a second task similar to the first. Ability was found to interact with standard to determine SBP, DBP, and HR responses in the second work period (Table 1). In this case,

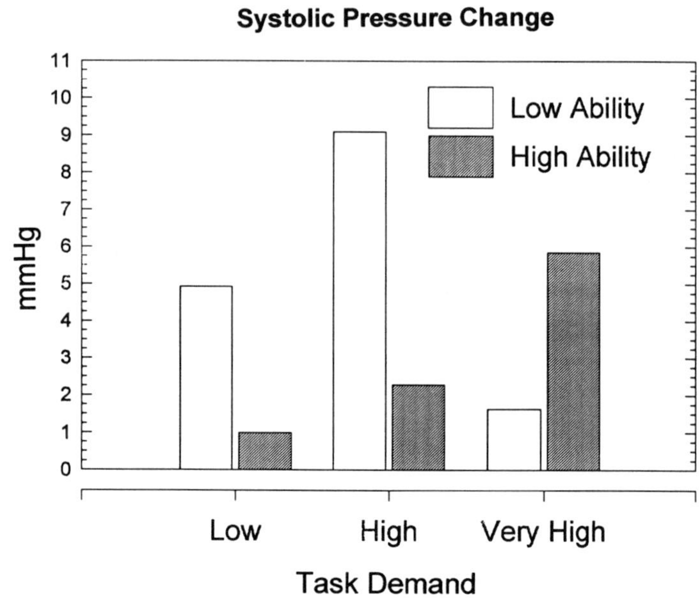

FIGURE 3 Systolic response as a function of perceived ability and task demand. Adapted from Wright et al. (1994).

for reasons that are unclear, the expected crossover pattern was strongest for HR. Heart rate responses were more pronounced in the difficult than easy condition for high-ability participants, but less pronounced in the difficult than easy condition for low-ability participants. Moreover, they tended to be greater for low- than high-ability participants when the standard was easy ($p < .06$), but were lower for low- than high-ability participants when the standard was difficult. Patterns for systolic and diastolic responsivity were similar, although individual cell comparisons for those parameters were less consistently reliable.

Application of the Ability Reasoning

The studies that applied the integrative perspective with respect to ability examined the possibility that the perspective might shed light on reported sex differences in CV response to challenge (Polefrone & Manuck, 1987; Saab, 1989; Stoney, Davis, & Matthews, 1987). The most common sex effect is greater SBP elevations in men than women. However, some investigators have found a reverse CV response pattern and others have obtained CV sex effects that were task specific (Brown & Smith, 1992; Collins & Frankenhauser, 1978; Liberson & Liberson, 1975;

TABLE 1 Blood Pressure and Heart Rate Elevations as a Function of Perceived Ability and Task Demand

	Low ability		High ability	
	Easy	Difficult	Easy	Difficult
Systolic pressure	11.2	7.7	10.6	12.7
Diastolic pressure	12.3	5.0	9.9	10.0
Heart rate	11.0	4.5	5.8	12.7

Note: Adapted from Wright and Dismukes (1995). Copyright by the Society for Psychophysiological Research. Adapted by permission.

Light et al., 1993; Smith, Limon, Gallo, & Ngu, 1996). Questions of where, how, and why the sexes sometimes differ in CV response are of academic interest, but also of practical import because chronically high levels of CV response are suspected to contribute to the development of CV disease, for which men are at increased risk (Blascovich & Katkin, 1993; Turner, 1994).

A popular conjecture has been that women's and men's CV response to a challenge may depend on the *gender relevance* of that challenge (Frankenhauser, 1983; Lash, Eisler, & Schulman, 1990; Lash, Eisler, & Southard, 1995; Lash, Gillespie, Eisler, & Southard, 1991; Matthews et al., 1991; Stoney, Matthews, McDonald, & Johnson, 1988). Specifically, it has been suggested that women may show greater CV elevations in response to "feminine" challenges, whereas men may show greater CV elevations in response to "masculine" challenges. If a challenge is gender neutral, CV responses presumably will be equivalent for the sexes. Research scientists exploring this possibility have not been entirely clear or consistent in conceptualizing gender relevance, nor have they been in complete agreement concerning the mechanism that may mediate gender relevance effects. On the other hand, investigatory operations commonly have identified feminine tasks as those in regard to which women feel especially competent and masculine tasks as those in regard to which men feel especially competent (e.g., Matthews et al., 1991). Moreover, a common supposition has been that relevance effects are mediated by effort, that is, that women will show greater responsivity on feminine tasks because they try harder on them than men do, and that men will show greater responsivity on masculine tasks because they try harder on them than women do (Matthews et al., 1991; Smith et al., 1996).

Although the gender relevance analysis of sex effects seems reasonable and has been examined in numerous investigations, it has received surprisingly little empirical support (Davis & Matthews, 1996; Matthews et al., 1991), perhaps in part because it assumes that effort and associated CV responses are proportional to perceived ability in a performance realm. The integrative reasoning, of course, intimates something different.

It suggests that when those of a certain sex feel especially capable with respect to a task (challenge), they may try harder and manifest greater responsivity than those of the other sex only at relatively high levels of task demand. At lower demand levels—where individuals in both sex groups view success as possible and worthwhile—the relation between sex, on the one hand, and effort and responsivity, on the other, may be reversed. Furthermore, if demand is high enough, there should be no sex difference in CV response because neither women nor men should exert much effort. These implications can be visualized by replacing the "low-ability" and "high-ability" labels in Figure 2 with "less-capable sex" and "more-capable sex" labels.

The first study to examine potential interactional effects of sex, gender relevance, and demand—and thus the integrative perspective with regard to these issues—was by Janie Murray (1994). Murray initially presented participants instructions indicating that a certain memory task was something on which women (feminine conditions) or men (masculine conditions) consistently excel. Differential ability was reflected not only in the text of the instructions, but also in scores described as average for each sex. In the feminine conditions, women were depicted as having an average performance score of 84 (out of a possible 100), and men were depicted as having an average score of 43. In the masculine conditions, the scores for women and men were reversed. Later, Murray took CV measures while the participants performed with the opportunity to avoid a noise by attaining a low (score of 30) or high (score of 90) performance standard. Murray's prediction was that sex would combine with task type and standard to determine CV responsivity, with elevations forming a double-crossover pattern across levels of task type. Where the task depiction was feminine, women were expected to show less responsiveness than men under low standard conditions, but more responsiveness than men under high standard conditions; where the task depiction was masculine, women were expected to show more responsiveness than men under low standard conditions, but less responsiveness than men under high standard conditions.

Analysis of SBP change scores assessed during the work period revealed the expected three-way interaction (Figure 4). Where depiction was feminine, women evinced less responsivity than men under low standard conditions, but slightly (not reliably) more responsivity than men under high standard conditions. Where depiction was masculine, women manifested greater responsiveness than men under low standard conditions, but slightly less responsiveness than men under high standard conditions. Comparisons within sex indicated that responses for women tended to be greater under high than low standard conditions where depiction was feminine ($p < .08$), but were lower under high than low standard condi-

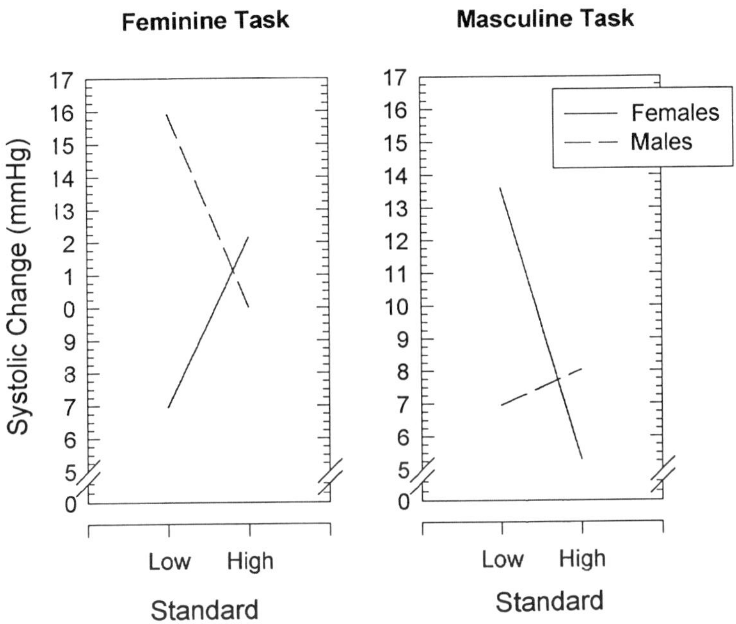

FIGURE 4 Systolic response for females and males under low or high standard conditions where the task was identified as masculine or feminine. Adapted from Murray (1994). Copyright 1994 by J. B. Murray. Adapted by permission of the author.

tions where depiction was masculine. Responses for men were less pronounced under high as compared to low standard conditions where depiction was feminine, but did not differ as a function of standard where depiction was masculine.

The other study to examine the integrative view was by Parker Storey (1996). It was carried out in part to provide further data relevant to predictions regarding responses under high standard conditions and hopefully strengthen the high standard sex differences obtained by Murray. Additional purposes were to extend the Murray investigation by examining responses induced (1) by an attractive incentive and (2) under conditions where the performance standard was extreme.[2] As before, the expectation was that sex would combine with task type and standard to determine CV engagement effects. However, in this case, the prediction was for a pair of three-versus-one patterns, rather than two crossover patterns. Where task depiction was feminine, engagement effects were expected to be greater for women than men under high standard conditions, but low for both sexes under extreme standard conditions. Where task depiction was masculine, engagement effects were expected to be greater for men than women under high standard conditions, but, again, low for both sexes under extreme standard conditions. Predictions assumed that the extreme standard would be viewed as excessively difficult by women and men.

Procedures were highly similar to those used by Murray. Major changes were threefold. First, participants worked to earn one of several prizes on display (rather than to avoid noise). Second, mean scores for the more and less capable sexes were depicted as 64 and 23, respectively (instead of 84 and 43, respectively). Third, the required performance score in the high standard condition was 75 (instead of 90) and that in an extreme standard condition was 95. It should be noted that even though this study's high standard was lower than the high standard used by Murray, the discrepancy between it and the norm for the more capable sex (64, a difference of 11) was somewhat greater than the corresponding discrepancy in the Murray study (a difference of 6). The discrepancy was expanded to make the high standard somewhat more challenging and possibly strengthen sex differences in the high standard conditions. It also should be noted that, even though the extreme standard in this study was close to the high standard used previously, the discrepancy between it and the norm for the more capable sex was substantially greater than the discrepancy between the previous high standard and more capable sex norm. The design was a 2 (female, male) × 2 (feminine, masculine) × 2 (high standard, extreme standard) factorial.

Once again, analysis of the SBP data confirmed expectations (Figure 5). An *a priori* contrast comparing systolic responses of feminine/high-standard women and masculine/high-standard men with systolic responses of other participants proved highly reliable, and yielded a nonreliable residual sum of squares, indicating no (significant) remaining variation among the groups. Follow-up contrasts indicated that systolic responses were greater for feminine/high-standard women than for all other feminine task participants, and greater for masculine/high-standard men than for all other masculine task participants. The individual female-to-male comparison under high standard conditions was reliable where the task depiction was masculine, but not where the task depiction was feminine. As expected, neither of the individual female-to-male comparisons was reliable under extreme standard conditions.[3]

Domain Specificity of Ability Effects

Presumably, perceived ability effects are domain specific, that is, peculiar to tasks and situations. If a given ability conception is related to a current challenge, then that conception should predict effort and associated CV responses; if an ability conception is unrelated to a current chal-

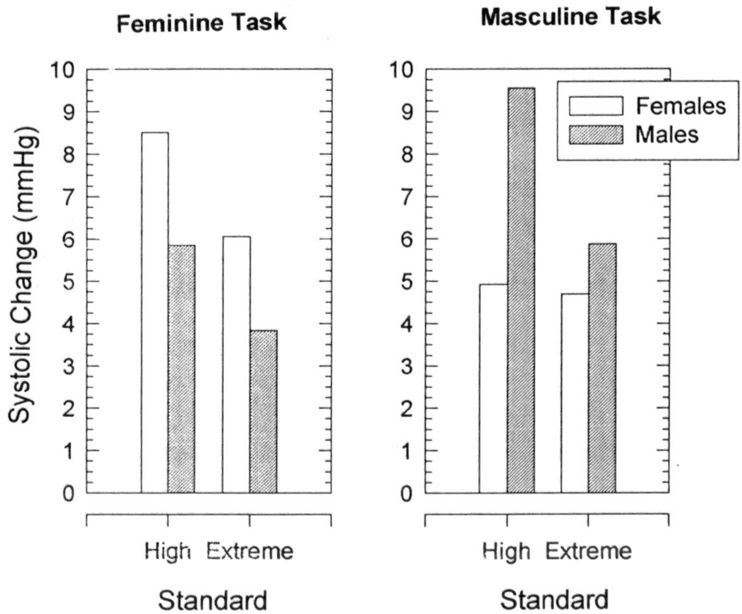

FIGURE 5 Systolic response for women and men under high or extreme standard conditions where the task was identified as masculine or feminine. Adapted from Storey (1996). Copyright 1996 by P. L. Storey. Adapted by permission of the author.

lenge, the conception should not be predictive with respect to these outcomes. This presumption was examined in a study by Debra Carrier (1996).

Participants first listened to a series of tones with instructions to press a computer keypad ("mouse") button as quickly as possible after each tone. Later, participants received performance feedback indicating that they had high or low ability with regard to that type of task, and then performed a second task that was similar or dissimilar to the first, with the opportunity to earn a prize by exceeding a moderate standard (50th percentile of previous scores). The similar task was the same as the first task, except work lasted longer and tones were presented at shorter intervals. The dissimilar task was a discrimination task that required participants to listen to tone pairs and indicate (by pressing mouse keys) which tone in each pair had the highest pitch. Dissimilar task participants were told that scores would be based on both the speed and the accuracy of responses. Assessments of pressure and HR were made in both task periods. Chief predictions were fourfold: (1) Experimental groups should not differ in sympathetic CV response during the first task period; (2) those in the low-ability/similar-task condition should show enhanced sympathetic responsiveness in the second task period as compared to the first because success in the second period should appear relatively difficult, but possible; (3) those in the high-ability/similar-task condition should show a similar or reduced sympathetic response during the second task period as compared to the first because success in the second period should appear relatively easy; (4) ability feedback should be unrelated to sympathetic responses in the second period among those assigned the dissimilar task because the feedback should not generalize to the different performance realm.

Participants' SBP and DBP responses accorded with the main predictions (see Figure 6 for means). As expected, groups manifested equivalent responsivity in the first task period. Also as expected, low-ability participants presented with a similar second task showed increased responsiveness from the first to the second task period, whereas their high-ability counterparts did not. Finally, ability feedback had no impact on responses of those presented with a dissimilar second task.

Overall analyses on the SBP and DBP measures produced task type × period interactions. For both parameters, the interaction reflected two effects: (1) greater responsiveness in the second than first period for the similar task groups, but less responsiveness in the second than first period for the dissimilar task groups and (2) greater responsiveness for the similar task groups than for the dissimilar task groups in the second task period, but no difference in responsiveness between these groups in the first task period. The triple interaction was not reliable for either variable (closest $p = .105$) However, follow-up comparisons indicated that the two-way interactions mainly reflect differences between the low-ability/similar-task group and the two dissimilar task groups. Whereas low-ability/similar-task participants showed greater responsiveness in the second period than in the first, high-ability/similar-task participants did not ($Fs < 1.0$). Furthermore, whereas the low-ability/similar-task group manifested greater responsiveness in the second period than did the two dissimilar task groups, the high-ability/similar-task group did not (closest $p < .08$). Analysis of the HR data revealed only a period effect, reflecting somewhat faster rates in the second period ($M = 83.57$) than in the first ($M=80.25$).

Summary

To sum up, we have, to date, carried out six ability studies. Three evaluated CV responses at different levels of demand. Two others did essentially the same thing, but in a context where ability perceptions were bound up with participants' gender identity. The remaining study addressed the presumed domain specificity of ability findings. Although in-

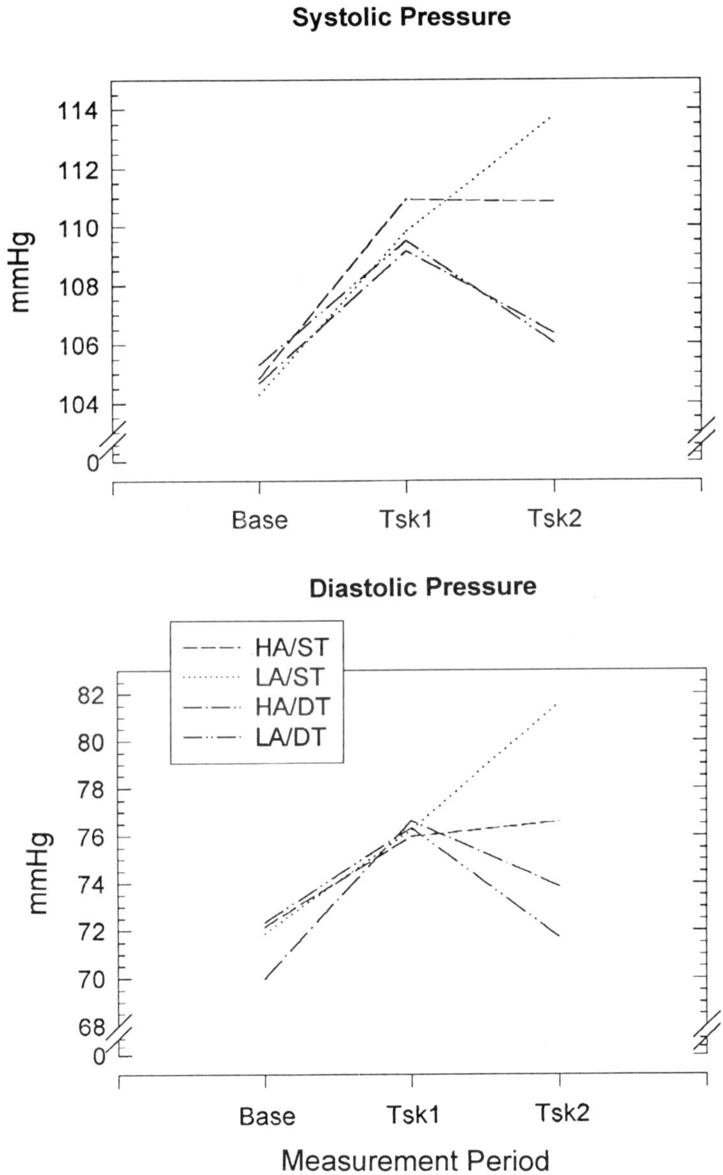

FIGURE 6 Systolic and diastolic responses in the two task periods and at baseline for the four experimental groups. HA/ST = high-ability/similar-task; LA/ST = low-ability/similar-task; HA/DT = high-ability/different-task; LA/DT = low-ability/different-task. Values in the two task periods are covariance adjusted with respect to baseline. From Carrier (1996).

dividual cell comparisons have not always been reliable, overall response patterns have consistently been congruent with predictions. Ability has been studied both as an experimental variable and as a quasi-experimental variable. In no instance where demand was manipulated did ability produce a main effect on responsivity; instead, it produced different effects at different demand levels. None of our studies provide data relevant to the implication that potential motivation should moderate the relation between ability percepts and CV response to challenge. On the other hand, given the number of nonability studies that have shown interactional effects between potential motivation and demand (see previous synopsis), there is good reason to believe this effect can be demonstrated in the future.

SUPPORT FOR TRADITIONAL VIEWS

Collectively, the preceding sets of evidence make a good case for the integrative perspective with respect to the perceived-ability/CV-response relation. At the same time, they cast considerable doubt on the traditional conceptions described earlier. The most challenging data with regard to the traditional views come from the physiological ability studies. In contrast to what the views intimate, the perceived-ability/CV-response relation was not found to vary between approach and avoidance paradigms. And within those paradigms, the relation was not monotonic, but rather variable, depending on the level of demand.

Still, it is not as though the traditional conceptions have no empirical base. To the contrary, there are at least three sets of findings that appear to support the conceptions. In the subsections below I review and evaluate these sets.

Buffering Effects of Control

One set of supportive findings comes from studies concerned broadly with the purported stress-buffering effects of perceived control. Countless investigations, including classics dating back to the first half of this century (Mower & Viek, 1948), have produced data suggesting that people sometimes do "better" with respect to some outcomes under conditions of high as compared to low control (Geer, Davidson, & Gatchel, 1970; Glass, Reim, & Singer, 1971; Overmier & Seligman, 1967; Staub, Tursky, & Schwartz, 1971; Weiss, 1971; for overviews, see Averill, 1973; Burger, 1989; Miller, 1980; Thompson, 1981; and Skinner, 1996). The data frequently are interpreted as documenting the traditional position concerning ability effects in aversive contexts (e.g., O'Leary & Brown, 1995). But they in fact should be considered cautiously in this regard. For one thing, most control studies have examined outcomes that are not physiological, much less cardiovascular. This is crucial because physiological correlates of the outcomes examined (reports of pain, distress, anxiety, etc.) are largely unknown (see, e.g., Fowles, 1982). In addition, those studies that have included CV measures have not always established that "no-control" participants viewed themselves as having *no* control or, in general, taken into account control difficulty as a potential moderator of the outcome(s) being studied (cf. Manuck et al., 1978). Hence, it is possible that many control/no-control comparisons have, in reality, been easy-control/difficult-control comparisons and yielded effects that comport with those in the preceding sections.

SELF-EFFICACY AND PHOBIC FEAR

Another set of supportive findings comes from familiar studies by Bandura and his colleagues that have employed a phobic fear model to investigate self-efficacy effects on stress responses (Bandura, Reese, & Adams, 1982; Bandura, Taylor, Williams, Mefford, & Barchas, 1985; Wiedenfeld et al., 1990). Typically, participants first indicate how confident they are that they can perform various phobia-relevant tasks, and then have physiological measures taken just before and during a period in which they are asked to perform tasks in regard to which their confidence (efficacy) is weak, moderate, and strong. Effects have not been entirely consistent, either among measures or between measurement periods. But overall patterns suggest an inverse relation between efficacy perceptions and physiological responsiveness so long as the tasks participants are asked to perform are within the range of what the participants are willing to attempt. Initial assessments usually are followed by efficacy training and a reevaluation of physiological responses to the challenges that originally were stressful; results typically indicate reduced responding after training.

Like findings from the stress/control studies, findings from the Bandura studies are widely interpreted to document the traditional view with respect to the effect of ability perceptions on CV responsiveness in aversive circumstances. However, particularly in light of the evidence discussed in this chapter, an interpretation in terms of the current integrative analysis seems at least as plausible. That is, prior to efficacy training, participants presumably find it harder to perform tasks of lower efficacy than tasks of higher efficacy, in the same way that they presumably would find it harder to perform math problems that were difficult for them than math problems that were easy for them. Thus, it would be expected that effort and associated CV responses would be negatively related to task efficacy so long as success on the more difficult (less efficacious) tasks appeared possible and worthwhile. After efficacy training, participants presumably find it relatively easy to perform the tasks that previously were hard; thus, effort and CV responsiveness should be relatively low.

In theory, interactional ability effects like the ones we have obtained could be produced in the phobic fear context by examining ability (efficacy) effects at different levels of objective demand. For example, participants more and less phobic with respect to some animal (e.g., a spider) might be assigned different tasks involving the animal, with the opportunity to win a highly attractive prize if they do well. The tasks could be easy ("view a picture of the spider"), difficult ("put a gloved hand on the spider's cage"), and extremely difficult ("allow the spider to crawl over your arm"). Assuming that success was viewed as possible and worthwhile by more phobic participants in the easy and difficult conditions, and possible and worthwhile by less phobic participants in all conditions, CV predictions would be straightforward. Responsivity should increase directly with difficulty for less phobic participants, but be nonmonotonically related to difficulty (i.e., greatest where difficulty was high) for more phobic participants. Furthermore, responsiveness should be greater for the more phobic group than for the less phobic group where difficulty was low and high, but greater for the less phobic group than for the more phobic group where difficulty was extreme.

Self-Efficacy and Motivation

The third set of supportive findings comes from some studies that seem to show a direct correspondence between ability perceptions and motivation, and thus seem to support the traditional position regarding CV ability effects in appetitive situations. One case in point is a recent investigation by Shepperd, Arkin, Strathman, and Baker (1994, Study 1) in which self-reports of competence were found to correlate positively with self-reports of effort. Participants selected from a list of 50 common student activities (e.g., playing a musical instrument, meeting new people) the 10 activities that were most important to them, and then rated (1) how much effort they typically expend when performing the activities and (2) their ability in regard to the activities. Results indicated higher effort on activities in regard to which participants felt relatively more capable.

The main problem with the Shepperd et al. study, from an interpretational standpoint, is that participants were provided no information pertaining to task demand (cf. Meyer & Hallerman, 1977); indeed, the activities under review appear to have been more akin to performance *categories* than to specific behavioral challenges. As I noted earlier, those who feel especially capable in a behavioral realm (e.g., music) should be especially likely to adopt an identity associated with the realm ("musician"). And capable individuals who do adopt an associated identity should be especially willing to invest energy in tasks that facilitate accomplishment in the realm (Gendolla, 1995), many of which are likely to be difficult. So it could be that the Shepperd et al. findings reflect participants' recognition that they typically tackle more difficult challenges, and thus typically expend more energy, when performing activities that are relatively more central to their self-conceptions.

Other cases in point are investigations by Locke, Cervone, and others in which self-efficacy has been found to predict, in a linear fashion, task performance and/or persistence (Cervone, 1989; Cervone & Peake, 1986; Jacobs, Prentice-Dunn, & Rogers, 1984; Locke, Frederick, Lee, & Bobko, 1984; Peake & Cervone, 1989; for reviews, see Bandura, 1989; Schunk, 1995). A general question associated with these studies concerns the relation between the motivational outcomes investigated and *momentary* effort. Individuals could persist indefinitely in performing a task that required little energy. And people can accomplish a lot (i.e., perform well) by investing themselves modestly over an extended period. Thus, evidence of an especially good and/or extended performance does not necessarily imply especially high behavioral intensity and CV responsiveness.[4]

Putting this issue aside, though, there is a critical difference between the procedures typically used in these studies and the procedures used in our ability studies. Whereas participants in our studies are required to meet a specific performance standard to attain or avoid an outcome, participants in the performance/persistence studies generally are allowed to work as hard as they please. This difference is important because in circumstances where a challenge is not specific, or "fixed" (Brehm & Self, 1989; Wright et al., 1995), individuals presumably set their own performance standard, based on an assessment of the benefits and costs of performing at all levels that are possible for them, and then expend that amount of energy that is necessary to meet the set standard. Cost, in terms of effort, should be lower for high-ability individuals than for low-ability individuals. Therefore, it follows that the former group should tend to set higher performance goals than the latter group (Locke & Kristof, 1996; Locke & Latham, 1994), which should tend to result in their performing better and persisting longer than the latter group.

The preceding observations suggest that effects in the performance/persistence studies may not reflect generally greater striving among high- as compared to low-ability individuals, but rather the impact of efficacy perceptions on *goal setting* where a challenge is unfixed. In addition, they intimate that ability-related differences in goal setting in unfixed circumstances may not be accompanied by corresponding differences in effort and CV responsiveness because *modest goals should appear just as difficult to the subjectively incapable as hard goals appear to the subjectively capable*. Where ability perceptions are held constant, we can assume a connection between goal setting and effort. But where ability perceptions are not held constant, we cannot.

As a matter of record, I should note that some performance/persistence studies have included conditions in which a target goal was assigned (e.g., Locke et al., 1984), which could make the preceding analysis of their results appear untenable. However, technically speaking, what makes a challenge fixed or unfixed is not the presence or absence of a suggested goal, but rather the challenge's behavior-outcome contingencies. If contingencies are such that individuals can secure or prevent an outcome or set of outcomes only if they attain a certain standard, the challenge is fixed; if contingencies are such that individuals can secure or prevent different outcomes by attaining different standards, the challenge is unfixed. Commonly, in studies where target goals are provided, participants benefit (e.g., gain money or social approval) to the extent that they *approach* the targets. This allows participants a range of performance standard options, each of which is associated with a different cost and benefit.

OTHER PERSPECTIVES

Although the traditional ability views described at the beginning of this chapter have, historically, been the dominant perspectives in psychology regarding the perceived-ability/CV-response relation, it is not the case that they are the only perspectives other than the integrative view. One additional perspective of note is a view that might be deduced from Heider's (1958) logic regarding the attribution of effort and ability to a performer. Heider proposed that there should be an inverse relation between effort and ability inferences, because people with low ability have to exert more effort to succeed than do people with high ability. Assuming an effort/CV-response connection, this could be taken to suggest that CV responses should decrease as perceived ability increases, irrespective of the valence of the outcome driving behavior.

An additional perspective of even greater note is a view that derives from Blascovich's recent biopsychosocial (BPS) model of arousal regulation (e.g., Blascovich, 1992; Blascovich & Tomaka, 1996; Tomaka, Blascovich, Kelsey, & Leitten, 1993). Briefly, the BPS model proposes that autonomic responses in motivated performance situations are determined in part by the relation between performers' primary and secondary appraisals of those situations. Primary appraisal refers to the degree of demand, uncertainty, and/or danger; secondary appraisal refers to the degree of resources that may be brought to bear. If resources exceed demand, then the overall appraisal becomes one of challenge. On the other hand, if demand exceeds resources, then the overall appraisal becomes one of threat. Central hypotheses are (1) that challenge appraisals induce relatively pure sympathetic-adrenomedullary (SAM) activity, resulting in substantial increases in cardiac performance (e.g., in HR) accompanied by a decline in vascular resistance (resistance to flow in the vascular system, a decline of which would indicate a predominance of vasodilation), and (2) that threat appraisals induce pituitary-adrenocortical (PAC) activity as well as SAM activity, resulting in modest cardiac performance increases accompanied by no decrease in vascular resistance.

The BPS model would seem to imply that ability perceptions should impact CV responses only insofar as they determine overall appraisals of threat and challenge. If group differences in ability perceptions are large enough to yield different challenge/threat appraisals, they should alter the CV response pattern. However, if the differences are not so large as to yield different challenge/threat appraisals, they should not alter the pattern. Further implications are related to the fact that DBP is determined chiefly by vascular resistance (e.g., see Papillo & Shapiro, 1990). Since DBP is directly related to resistance, it should be at least as likely to show ability effects as SBP and HR. Moreover, where ability perceptions do impact overall challenge/threat appraisals and thus the CV response pattern, the association between those perceptions and DBP should be different from the association between those perceptions and HR. Whereas the association between ability perceptions and HR should be positive, the association between ability perceptions and DBP should be negative (because resistance should be lower where ability perceptions are higher). The correspondence between ability perceptions and SBP in such a situation is hard to predict, because SBP is determined by both vascular resistance and the force with which the heart pumps (an aspect of cardiac performance).

Like the traditional ability views, the Heiderian ability perspective plainly has difficulty accounting for the findings presented in the first part of this chapter, the main challenge being the evidence that CV ability effects are not monotonic. Despite its greater physiological sophistication and intellectual richness, the BPS perspective also would seem to have difficulty with the findings. One challenge for the BPS view is the evidence that ability perceptions are inversely related to CV responses where both high- and low ability groups view themselves as having sufficient ability to succeed. As noted above, the BPS model implies that ability perceptions should not be associated with CV responses in such circumstances. Additional challenges are (1) the evidence that, in general, ability effects are more likely to be manifested in terms of SBP than in terms of DBP and (2) the evidence that the perceived-ability/response relation for DBP is not opposite to that for HR and SBP where high-ability groups view success as possible, but low-ability groups do not. Regarding the latter, ability effects have not been obtained on all CV measures in all studies, but when ability effects have been obtained on different measures, those effects generally have corresponded with one another (e.g., see Wright & Dismukes, 1993).

To be fair, a careful evaluation of the BPS perspective with regard to ability perceptions would require direct assessments of such CV outcomes as vascular resistance, contractility, and cardiac output. Future studies involving such assessments could provide greater support for that view.

SOME POSSIBLE INSIGHTS

Naturally, there is no way of knowing whether future research will solidify, dilute, or utterly unravel the existing support for the integrative ability perspective. Nevertheless, it is not too early to begin considering what insights might be gained by thinking in these ability terms. One such insight—that pertaining to the CV sex effects—has already been discussed. Whereas up until now the best guess has been that the effects are largely a function of the character (gender relevance) of tasks, the implication of the integrative perspective is that they may be due to task character in combination with task demand.

Related insights pertain to CV race (Black/White) effects (Anderson et al., 1989; Falkner & Kushner, 1989; James, Hartnett, & Kalsbeck, 1983) and the finding that there is only a limited correspondence between people's CV response to one task and their CV response to others (Kamarck, 1992). Regarding the race effects, studies have produced various outcomes, including greater responsiveness among Whites than Blacks, the reverse of that, and no difference between the races. An obvious possibility, considering our sex analysis, is that the variability is partially due to social experiences Blacks and Whites have that lead them to feel competent in different behavioral realms. If the races do differ in felt competence with respect to some activity, the "racial relevance" of the activity should combine with the activity's difficulty to determine the two groups' effort and CV response. Regarding the correspondence finding, a modest relation would be expected where study participants felt differentially capable with respect to the tasks they were asked to perform. As Carrier's "domain specificity" study illustrates, ability effects obtained with one task should generalize only to other tasks in regard to which performers feel comparably capable.

A rather sobering insight pertains to treatments designed to reduce CV elevations in people for whom they represent a health risk (Jacob & Chesney, 1986). The traditional ability view with respect to aversive circumstances implies that the elevations might be reduced through procedures that foster efficacy perceptions (Bandura, 1991; Ewart, 1995). That is, if therapists can instill a sense of competence in their clients, they should decrease clients' threat appraisals and physiological stress levels. But if the integrative perspective is correct, efficacy-oriented strategies may not always be effective; indeed, they could sometimes *enhance* CV responses by encouraging effort in the face of challenges that are very difficult, or even impossible, to meet. Possibilities of this type give one pause and should serve as a reminder of how important it is for those of us in the research community to be cautious in making claims about what we "know."

NOTES

1. I do not discuss it here, but it is worth noting that Brehm's formulation also posits a correspondence between engagement and subjective *feelings* of motivation, with greater engagement being associated with more intense feelings. Interested readers are referred to Brehm and Self (1989), Brehm, Wright, Solomon, Silka, and Greenberg (1983), and Wright and Brehm (1989).
2. Another original purpose of this study was to conceptually replicate low standard effects obtained by Murray. However, preliminary analyses of subjective data revealed irregularities that called seriously into question the effectiveness of operations in the low standard conditions. One irregularity was on a manipulation check that asked how well the typical male would be likely to do. Contrary to expectation, ratings for masculine men did not differ from those of feminine men ($t = .28$). Other irregularities were on a measure of self-perceived ability. Again, ratings for masculine and feminine men did not differ ($t < 1.0$). Moreover, (1) values were higher for men than for women at both levels of task type and (2) values for women were lower than those for women in the other standard conditions. Still further irregularities were on the manipulation check that asked participants how well they would have to perform to earn the incentive. Ratings were lower where the task was masculine than where the task was feminine; moreover, because of unexpectedly high Feminine values, the low to high comparison was more powerful under masculine conditions ($p < .001$) than under feminine conditions ($p = .05$).

   Reasons for the foregoing irregularities are not clear. Nevertheless, the irregularities are critical in that they suggest that low standard participants did not view the situation in the intended manner and, thus, render virtually uninterpretable the low standard CV effects. Because they have little potential for furthering understanding of CV ability or sex effects, the low standard data are not presented here. These data are included in the original research report (Storey, 1996) and indicate no differences as a function of sex or task type. It should be noted that subjective data in all other conditions of this study, and in all conditions of the Murray study, were generally compatible with expectations.
3. I should note that this study excluded CV change scores that exceeded cell means by more than two standard deviations (Clark et al., 1987), whereas the Murray study did not. A reanalysis of the Murray data, excluding the extreme change scores, is reported by Wright, Murray, Storey, and Williams (1997). Effects from the reanalysis were essentially redundant to those obtained originally.
4. The same question is associated with at least some of the nonphysiological ability studies referred to earlier, which is one reason why the data from those studies are less compelling than the data from the physiological ability studies.

REFERENCES

Anderson, N. B., Lane, J. D., Taguchi, F., Williams, R. B., & Houseworth, S. J. (1989). Race, parental history of hypertension, and patterns of cardiovascular reactivity in women. *Psychophysiology, 26,* 39–47.

Averill, J. R. (1973). Personal control over aversive stimuli and its relationship to stress. *Psychological Bulletin, 80,* 286–303.

Bandura, A. (1982). Self-efficacy mechanism in human agency. *American Psychologist, 37,* 122–147.

Bandura, A. (1983). Self-efficacy determinants of anticipated fears and calamities. *Journal of Personality and Social Psychology, 45,* 464–469.

Bandura, A. (1986). *The social foundations of thought and action: A social cognitive theory.* Englewood Cliffs, NJ: Prentice-Hall.

Bandura, A. (1989). Self-regulation of motivation and action through internal standards and goal systems. In L. A. Pervin (Ed.), *Goal concepts in personality and social psychology* (pp. 19–85). Hillsdale, NJ: Erlbaum.

Bandura, A. (1991). Self-efficacy conception of anxiety. In R. Schwarzer & R. A. Wicklund (Eds.), *Anxiety and self-focused attention* (pp. 89–110). Chur, Switzerland: Harwood.

Bandura, A., Reese, L., & Adams, N. E. (1982). Microanalysis of action and fear arousal as a function of differential levels of perceived efficacy. *Journal of Personality and Social Psychology, 43,* 5–21.

Bandura, A., Taylor, C. B., Williams, S. L., Mefford, I. N., & Barchas, J. D. (1985). Catecholamine secretion as a function of perceived coping self-efficacy. *Journal of Consulting and Clinical Psychology, 53,* 406–414.

Bandura, A., O'Leary, A., Taylor, C. B., Gauthier, J., & Gossard, D. (1987). Perceived self-efficacy and pain control: Opioid and nonopioid mechanisms. *Journal of Personality and Social Psychology, 53,* 563–571.

Baum, A., Grunberg, N. E., & Singer, J. E. (1982). The use of psychological and neuroendocrinological measurements in the study of stress. *Health Psychology, 1,* 217–236.

Berntson, G. G., Cacioppo, J. T., & Quigley, K. S. (1991). Autonomic determinism: The modes of autonomic control, the doctrine of autonomic space, and the laws of autonomic constraint. *Psychological Review, 98,* 459–487.

Berntson, G. G., Cacioppo, J. T., & Quigley, K. S. (1993). Cardiac psychophysiology and autonomic space in humans: Empirical perspectives and conceptual implications. *Psychological Bulletin, 114,* 296–322.

Blascovich, J. (1992). A biopsychosocial approach to arousal regulation. *Journal of Social and Clinical Psychology, 11,* 213–237.

Blascovich, J., & Katkin, E. S. (1993). *Cardiovascular reactivity to psychological stress and disease.* Washington, DC: American Psychological Association.

Blascovich, J., & Tomaka, J. (1996). The biopsychosocial model of arousal regulation. In M. P. Zanna (Ed.), *Advances in Experimental Social Psychology, 28,* 1–52.

Brehm, J. W., & Self, E. (1989). The intensity of motivation. In M. R. Rozenweig and L. W. Porter (Eds.), *Annual review of psychology* (pp. 109–131). Palo Alto: Annual Reviews.

Brehm, J. W., Wright, R. A., Solomon, S., Silka, L., & Greenberg, J. (1983). Perceived difficulty, energization, and the magnitude of goal valence. *Journal of Experimental Social Psychology, 19,* 21–48.

Brown, P. C., & Smith, T. W. (1992). Social influence, marriage, and the heart: Cardiovascular consequences of interpersonal control in husbands and wives. *Health Psychology, 11,* 88–96.

Burger, J. M. (1989). Negative reactions to increases in perceived personal control. *Journal of Personality and Social Psychology, 56,* 246–256.

Carrier, D. (1996). The specificity of cardiovascular ability effects. Undergraduate honors thesis, University of Alabama at Birmingham.

Cervone, D. (1989). Effects of envisioning future activities on self-efficacy judgments and motivation: An availability heuristic interpretation. *Cognitive Therapy and Research, 13*, 247–261.

Cervone, D., & Peake, P. K. (1986). Anchoring, efficacy, and action: The influence of judgmental heuristics on self-efficacy judgments and behavior. *Journal of Personality and Social Psychology, 50*, 492–501.

Clark, L. A., Denby, L., Pregibon, D., Harshfield, G. A., Pickering, T. G., Blank, S., & Laragh, J. H. (1987). A data-based method for bivariate outlier detection: Application to automatic blood pressure recording devices. *Psychophysiology, 24*, 119–125.

Collins, A., & Frankenhauser, M. (1978). Stress responses in male and female engineering students. *Journal of Human Stress, 4*, 43–48.

Cox, T. (1978). *Stress*. Baltimore, MD: University Park Press.

Davis, M. C., & Matthews, K. A. (1996). Do gender-relevant characteristics determine cardiovascular reactivity? Match versus mismatch of traits and situations. *Journal of Personality and Social Psychology, 71*, 527–535.

Eisenberg, N., Fabes, R., Miller, P. A., Fultz, J., Shell, R., Mathy, R. M., & Reno, R. (1989). Relation of sympathy and personal distress to prosocial behavior: A multimethod study. *Journal of Personality and Social Psychology, 57*, 55–66.

Elliott, R. (1969). Tonic heart rate: Experiments on the effects of collative variables lead to a hypothesis about its motivational significance. *Journal of Personality and Social Psychology, 12*, 211–228.

Ewart, C. K. (1995). Self-efficacy and recovery from heart attack: Implications for a social-cognitive analysis of exercise and emotion. In J. E. Maddux (Ed.), *Self-efficacy, adaptation, and adjustment: Theory, research, and application* (pp. 203–224). New York: Plenum.

Falkner, B., & Kushner, H. (1989). Race differences in stress-induced reactivity in young adults. *Health Psychology, 8*, 613–627.

Ford, C. E., & Brehm, J. W. (1987). Effort expenditure following failure. In C. R. Snyder & C. E. Ford (Eds.), *Coping with negative life events: Clinical and social psychological perspectives* (pp. 51–79). New York: Plenum.

Fowles, D. C. (1982). Heart rate as an index of anxiety: Failure of a hypothesis. In J. T. Cacioppo & R. E. Petty (Eds.), *Perspectives in cardiovascular psychophysiology* (pp. 93–126). New York: Guilford Press.

Frankenhauser, M. (1983). The sympathetic-adrenal and pituitary-adrenal response to challenge: Comparisons between the sexes. In T. M. Dembroski, T. H. Schmidt, & G. Blumchen (Eds.), *Biobehavioral bases of coronary heart disease* (pp. 91–105). Basel, Switzerland: Karger.

Geer, J. H., Davidson, G. C., & Gatchel, R. I. (1970). Reduction of stress in humans through nonveridical perceived control of aversive stimulation. *Journal of Personality and Social Psychology, 16*, 731–738.

Gellatly, I. R., & Meyer, J. P. (1992). The effects of goal difficulty on physiological arousal, cognition, and task performance. *Journal of Applied Psychology, 77*, 694–704.

Gendolla, G. H. E. (1995). Motivationale erregung und statisches denken. Aschen: Shaker-Verlag. Doctoral dissertation, University of Bielefeld, Bielefeld, Germany.

Glass, D. C., Reim, B., & Singer, J. (1971). Behavioral consequences of adaptation to controllable and uncontrollable noise. *Journal of Experimental Social Psychology, 7*, 244–257.

Gollwitzer, P. M., Wicklund, R. A., & Hilton, J. L. (1982). Admission of failure and symbolic self-completion: Extending Lewinian theory. *Journal of Personality and Social Psychology, 43*, 358–371.

Hackett, G., & Betz, N. (1995). Self-efficacy and career choice and development. In J. E. Maddux (Ed.), *Self-efficacy, adaptation, and adjustment: Theory, research, and application* (pp. 249–276). New York: Plenum.

Hassett, J., & Danforth, D. (1982). An introduction to the cardiovascular system. In J. T. Cacioppo & R. E. Petty (Eds.), *Perspectives in cardiovascular psychophysiology* (pp. 4–18). New York: Guilford.

Heckhausen, H. (1991). *Motivation and action* (P. K. Leppman, Trans.). Berlin: Springer-Verlag. (Original work published in 1989)

Heider, F. (1958). *The psychology of interpersonal relations*. New York: Wiley.

Jacob, R. G., & Chesney, M. A. (1986). Psychological and behavioral methods to reduce cardiovascular reactivity. In K. A. Matthews, S. M. Weiss, T. Detre, T. M. Demobroski, B. Falkner, S. B. Manuck, & R. B. Williams (Eds.), *Handbook of stress, reactivity, and cardiovascular disease* (pp. 417–457). New York: Wiley.

Jacobs, B., Prentice-Dunn, S., & Rogers, R. W. (1984). Understanding persistence: An interface of control theory and self-efficacy theory. *Basic and Applied Social Psychology, 5,* 333–347.

James, S. A., Hartnett, S. A., Kalsbeck, W. D. (1983). John Henryism and blood pressure differences among black men. *Journal of Behavioral Medicine, 6,* 259–277.

Kahneman, D. (1973). *Attention and effort*. Englewood Cliffs, NJ: Prentice-Hall.

Kamarck, T. W. (1992). Recent developments in the study of cardiovascular reactivity: Contributions of psychometric theory and social psychology. *Psychophysiology, 29,* 491–503.

Kukla, A. (1972). Foundations of an attributional theory of performance. *Psychological Review, 79,* 454–470.

Kukla, A. (1974). Performance as a function of resultant achievement motivation (perceived ability) and perceived difficulty. *Journal of Research in Personality, 7,* 374–383.

Lash, S. J., Eisler, R. M., & Schulman, R. S. (1990). Cardiovascular reactivity to stress in men: Effects of masculine gender role stress appraisal and masculine performance challenge. *Behavior Modification, 14,* 3–20.

Lash, S. J., Eisler, R. M., & Southard, D. R. (1995). Sex differences in cardiovascular reactivity as a function of the appraised gender relevance of the stressor. *Behavioral Medicine, 21,* 86–94.

Lash, S. J., Gillespie, B. L., Eisler, R. M., & Southard, D. R. (1991). Sex differences in cardiovascular reactivity: Effects of gender relevance of the stressor. *Health Psychology, 10,* 392–398.

Lazarus, R. S. (1966). *Psychological stress and the coping process*. New York: McGraw-Hill.

Lazarus, R. S. (1968). Emotion and adaptation: Conceptual and empirical relations. In W. J. Arnold (Ed.), *Nebraska symposium on motivation* (pp. 175–270). Lincoln, NE: University of Nebraska Press.

Liberson, C. W., & Liberson, W. T. (1975). Sex differences in autonomic responses to electric shock. *Psychophysiology, 17,* 243–252.

Light, K. C. (1981). Cardiovascular responses to effortful active coping: Implications for the role of stress in hypertension development. *Psychophysiology, 17,* 243–252.

Light, K. C., & Obrist, P. A. (1980). Cardiovascular response to stress: Effects of the opportunity to avoid shock, shock experience, and performance feedback. *Psychophysiology, 17,* 243–252.

Light, K. C., & Obrist, P. A. (1983). Task difficulty, heart rate reactivity, and cardiovascular responses to an appetitive reaction time task. *Psychophysiology, 20,* 301–312.

Light, K. C., Turner, J. R., Hinderliter, A. L., & Sherwood, A. (1993). Race and gender comparisons: I. Hemodynamic responses to a series of stressors. *Health Psychology, 12,* 354–365.

Locke, E. A., Frederick, E., Lee, C., & Bobko, P. (1984). Effects of self-efficacy, goals, and task strategies on task performance. *Journal of Applied Psychology, 69,* 241–251.

Locke, E. A., & Kristof, A. L. (1996). Volitional choices in the goal achievement process. In P. M. Gollwitzer & J. A. Bargh (Eds.), *The psychology of action: Linking cognition and action to behavior* (pp. 365–384). New York: Guilford Press.

Locke, E. A., & Latham, G. P. (1990). *A theory of goal setting and task performance.* New York: Prentice-Hall.

Locke, E. A., & Latham, G. P. (1994). Goal setting theory. In H. F. O'Neal & M. Drillings (Eds.), *Motivation: Theory and research* (pp. 13–29). Hillsdale, NJ: Erlbaum.

Maddux, J. E. (1995). Self-efficacy theory: An introduction. In J. E. Maddux (Ed.), *Self-efficacy, adaptation, and adjustment: Theory, research, and application* (pp. 3–27). New York: Plenum.

Manuck, S. B., Harvey, S. H., Lechleiter, S. L., & Neal, K. S. (1978). Effects of coping on blood pressure responses to threat of aversive stimulation. *Psychophysiology, 20,* 301–312.

Manuck, S. B., Morrison, R. L., Bellack, A. S., & Polefrone, J. M. (1985). Behavioral factors in hypertension: Cardiovascular responsivity, anger, and social competence. In M. A. Chesney & R. H. Rosenman (Eds.), *Anger and hostility in cardiovascular and behavioral disorders* (pp. 149–172). Washington, DC: Hemisphere.

Matthews, K. M., Davis, M. C., Stoney, C. M., Owens, J. F., & Caggiula, A. R. (1991). Does the gender relevance of the stressor influence sex differences in psychophysiological responses? *Health Psychology, 10,* 112–120.

Meyer, W. U. (1987). Perceived ability and achievement-related behavior. In F. Halisch and J. Kuhl (Eds.), *Motivation, intention, and volition.* Berlin: Springer-Verlag.

Meyer, W. U., & Hallermann, R. (1977). Intended effort and informational value of task outcome. *Archives of Psychology, 129,* 131–140.

Miller, S. M. (1980). Why having control reduces stress: If I can stop the roller coaster, I don't want to get off. In J. Garber & M. E. P. Seligman (Eds.), *Human helplessness: Theory and applications* (pp. 71–95). San Diego, CA: Academic Press.

Mower, O. H., & Viek, P. (1948). An experimental analogue of fear from a sense of helplessness. *Journal of Abnormal and Social Psychology, 43,* 193–200.

Murray, J. B. (1994). Gender relevant tasks and the elicitation of sex differences in cardiovascular response. Unpublished doctoral dissertation, University of Alabama at Birmingham.

Murray, J. B., Wright, R. A., & Williams, B. J. (1993). Difficulty as a determinant of cardiovascular response: Moderating effect of instrumentality in an alleviation paradigm. *International Journal of Psychophysiology, 15,* 135–145.

Obrist, P. A. (1976). The cardiovascular-behavioral interaction as it appears today. *Psychophysiology, 13,* 95–107.

Obrist, P. A. (1981). *Cardiovascular psychophysiology: A perspective.* New York: Plenum.

Obrist, P. A., Webb, R. A., Sutterer, J. R., & Howard, J. L. (1970). The cardiac–somatin relationship: Some reformulations. *Psychophysiology, 6,* 569–587.

Obrist, P. A., Gaebelein, C. J., Teller, E. S., Langer, A. W., Grignolo, A., Light, K. C., & McCubbin, J. A. (1978). The relationship among heart rate, carotid dp/dt, and blood pressure in humans as a function of type of stress. *Psychophysiology, 15,* 102–115.

O'Leary, A., & Brown, S. (1995). Self-efficacy and the physiological stress response. In J. E. Maddux (Ed.), *Self-efficacy, adaptation, and adjustment: Theory, research, and application* (pp. 227–246). New York: Plenum.

Overmier, J. B., & Seligman, M. E. P. (1967). Effects of inescapable shock upon subsequent escape and avoidance responding. *Journal of Comparative and Physiological Psychology, 63,* 28–33.

Papillo, J. F., & Shapiro, D. (1990). The cardiovascular system. In J. T. Cacioppo, & L. G. Tassinary (Eds.), *Principles of psychophysiology: Psychical, social, and inferential elements* (pp. 456–512). New York: Cambridge University Press.

Peake, P. K., & Cervone, D. (1989). Sequence anchoring and self-efficacy: Primacy effects in the consideration of possibilities. *Social Cognition, 7*, 31–50.

Pecchinenda, A., & Smith, C. A. (1996). The affective significance of skin conductance activity during a difficult problem-solving task. *Cognition and Emotion, 10*, 481–503.

Polefrone, J. M., & Manuck, S. B. (1987). Gender differences in cardiovascular and neuroendocrine response to stressors. In R. C. Barnett, L. Biener, and G. K. Baruch (Eds.), *Gender and stress* (pp. 13–38). New York: Free Press.

Saab, P. G. (1989). Cardiovascular and neuroendocrine response to challenge in males and females. In N. Schneiderman, S. M. Weiss, and P. G. Kaufmann (Eds.), *Handbook of research methods in cardiovascular behavioral medicine* (pp. 453–481). New York: Plenum.

Schönpflug, W. (1983). Coping efficiency and situational demands. In G. R. J. Hockey (Ed.), *Stress and fatigue in human performance* (pp. 299–330). New York: Wiley.

Schunk, D. M. (1995). Self-efficacy and education and instruction. In J. E. Maddux (Ed.), *Self-efficacy, adaptation, and adjustment: Theory, research, and application* (pp. 281–300). New York: Plenum.

Shepperd, J. A., Arkin, R. M., Strathman, A., & Baker, S. M. (1994). Dysphoria as a moderator of the relationship between perceived effort and perceived ability. *Journal of Personality and Social Psychology, 66*, 559–569.

Sigall, H., & Gould, R. (1977). The effects of self-esteem and evaluator demandingness on effort expenditure. *Journal of Personality and Social Psychology, 35*, 12–20.

Skinner, E. A. (1996). A guide to constructs of control. *Journal of Personality and Social Psychology, 71*, 549–570.

Smith, C. A., & Pope, L. K. (1992). Appraisal and emotion: The interactional contributions of situational and dispositional factors. In M. S. Clark (Ed.), *Review of personality and social psychology, Vol. 14: Emotion and social behavior* (pp. 32–62). Newbury Park, CA: Sage.

Smith, T. W., Baldwin, M., & Christenson, A. J. (1990). Interpersonal influence as active coping: Effects of task difficulty on cardiovascular reactivity. *Psychophysiology, 24*, 127–131.

Smith, T. W., Limon, J. P., Gallo, L. C., & Ngu, L. Q. (1996). Interpersonal control and cardiovascular activity: Goals, behavioral expression, and the moderating effects of sex. *Journal of Personality and Social Psychology, 70*, 1012–1024.

Staub, E., Tursky, B., & Schwartz, G. E. (1971). Self-control and predictability: Their effects on reactions to aversive stimulation. *Journal of Personality and Social Psychology, 18*, 157–162.

Steptoe, A., Moses, J., Mathews, A., & Edwards, S. (1990). Aerobic fitness, physical activity and psychophysiological reactions to mental tasks. *Psychophysiology, 27*, 264–274.

Stoney, C. M., Davis, M. C., & Matthews, K. A. (1987). Sex difference in physiological responses to stress and in coronary disease: A causal link? *Psychophysiology, 24*, 127–131.

Stoney, C. M., Matthews, K. A., McDonald, R. H., & Johnson, C. A. (1988). Sex differences in lipid, lipoprotein, cardiovascular and neuroendocrine responses to acute stress. *Psychophysiology, 27*, 125–135.

Storey, P. L. (1996). Cardiovascular gender effects as a function of task difficulty and the gender relevance of a behavioral challenge. Unpublished doctoral dissertation, University of Alabama at Birmingham.

Storey, P. L., Wright, R. A., & Williams, B. J. (1996). Need as a moderator of the difficulty-cardiovascular response relation: The case of fluid deprivation. *Journal of Psychophysiology, 10*, 228–238.

Thompson, S. C. (1981). Will it hurt less if I can control it? A complex answer to a simple question. *Psychological Bulletin, 90*, 89–101.

Tomaka, J., Blascovich, J., Kelsey, R. M., & Leitten, C. L. (1993). Subjective, physiological, and behavioral effects of threat and challenge appraisal. *Journal of Personality and Social Psychology, 65*, 248–260.

Turner, J. R. (1994). *Cardiovascular reactivity and stress: Patterns of physiological response.* New York: Plenum.

Van Schijndel, M., DeMey, H., & Näring, G. (1984). Effects of behavioral control and Type A behavior on cardiovascular responses. *Psychophysiology, 21*, 501–509.

Vroom, V. H. (1964). *Work and motivation.* New York: Wiley.

Weiss, J. M. (1971). Somatic effects of predictable and unpredictable shock. *Psychosomatic Medicine, 32*, 397–408.

Wicklund, R. A., & Braun, O. L. (1987). Incompetence and the concern with human categories. *Journal of Personality and Social Psychology, 53*, 373–382.

Wicklund, R. A., & Gollwitzer, P. M. (1982). *Symbolic self-completion.* Hillsdale, NJ: Erlbaum.

Wiedenfeld, S. A., O'Leary, A., Bandura, A., Brown, S., Levine, S., & Raska, K. (1990). Impact of perceived coping efficacy on components of the immune system. *Journal of Personality and Social Psychology, 59*, 1082–1094.

Williams, S. L. (1995). Self-efficacy and anxiety and phobic disorders. In J. E. Maddux (Ed.), *Self-efficacy, adaptation, and adjustment: Theory, research, and application* (pp. 69–102). New York: Plenum.

Wright, R. A. (1996). Brehm's theory of motivation as a model of effort and cardiovascular response. In P. M. Gollwitzer & J. A. Bargh (Eds.), *The psychology of action: Linking cognition and motivation to behavior* (pp. 424–453). New York: Guilford.

Wright, R. A., & Brehm, J. W. (1989). Energization and goal attractiveness. In L. A. Pervin (Ed.), *Goal concepts in personality and social psychology* (pp. 169–210). Hillsdale, NJ: Erlbaum.

Wright, R. A., Brehm, J. W., Crutcher, W., Evans, M. T., & Jones, A. (1990). Avoidant control difficulty and aversive incentive appraisals: Additional evidence of an energization effect. *Motivation and Emotion, 14*, 5–73.

Wright, R. A., Caldwell, J. A., Evans, M. T., & Ritter, M. (1991). Effort, energy, and appraisals of an aversive incentive: Effects of self-esteem and avoidant task difficulty. *Journal of Research in Personality, 25*, 45–56.

Wright, R. A., & Dill, J. C. (1993). Blood pressure responses and incentive appraisals as a function of perceived ability and objective task demand. *Psychophysiology, 30*, 152–160.

Wright, R. A., Dill, J. C., Geen, R. G., & Anderson, C. A. (in press). Social evaluation influence on cardiovascular response to a behavioral challenge: Effects across a range of difficulty levels. *Annals of Behavioral Medicine.*

Wright, R. A., & Dismukes, A. (1995). Cardiovascular effects of experimentally-induced efficacy (ability) appraisals at low and high levels of avoidant task demand. *Psychophysiology, 32*, 172–176.

Wright, R. A., & Gregorich, S. (1989). Difficulty and instrumentality of imminent behavior as determinants of cardiovascular response and self-reported energy. *Psychophysiology, 26*, 586–592.

Wright, R. A., Murray, J. B., Storey, P. L., & Williams, B. J. (1997). Ability analysis of gender relevance and sex differences in cardiovascular response. *Journal of Personality and Social Psychology., 73, 405–417*

Wright, R. A., Shaw, L. L., & Jones, C. R. (1990). Task demand and cardiovascular response magnitude: Further evidence of the mediating role of success importance. *Journal of Personality and Social Psychology, 59*, 1250–1260.

Wright, R. A., Tunstall, A. M., Williams, B. J., Goodwin, J. S., & Harmon-Jones, E. (1995). Social evaluation and cardiovascular response: An active coping approach. *Journal of Personality and Social Psychology, 69*, 530–543.

Wright, R. A., Wadley, V. G., Pharr, R. P., & Butler, M. (1994). Interactive influence of self-reported ability and avoidant task demand on anticipatory cardiovascular reactivity. *Journal of Research in Personality, 28*, 68–86.

Wright, R. A., Williams, B. J., & Dill, J. C. (1992). Interactive effects of difficulty and instrumentality of avoidant behavior on cardiovascular reactivity. *Psychophysiology, 29*, 677–689.

CHAPTER 9

CONFIRMATION BIAS

COGNITIVE ERROR OR ADAPTIVE STRATEGY OF ACTION CONTROL?

MARIA LEWICKA

INTRODUCTION

Robert Zajonc once wrote that opinions of psychologists about people's rationality tend to vary with every decade (Zajonc, 1989). The "irrational" New Look approach of the fifties was thus duly replaced by the rational "lay scientist metaphor" of the sixties, to be followed by the boom of interest in "nonrational" biases and errors of the seventies. Here, however, the regularity seems to end. While the next two decades witnessed the undiminished interest in the nature of biased cognition, manifested in growing number of monographs and collectively edited books (Evans, 1989; Hogarth, 1980; Kahneman, Slovic, & Tversky, 1982; Manktelow & Over, 1993; Nisbett & Ross, 1980), the preferred theoretical approaches appeared to lose their pendulumlike character and suggested some form of a compromise. This means that while nobody nowadays denies the existence of biases in lay cognition (it can hardly be done in the face of the amassed evidence), the focus of interest apparently has shifted from their evaluation (whether the biases testify or not to human rationality) to explanation.

MARIA LEWICKA • Faculty of Psychology, University of Warsaw, 00-183 Warsaw, Poland. E-mail: marlew@sci.psych.uw.edu.pl

Personal Control in Action, edited by Kofta et al., Plenum Press, New York, 1998.

The majority of the proposed alternative explanations tend to cast a benevolent look at lay reasoning either by challenging the normative character of existent models of rationality (Cohen, 1981, Kruglanski and Ajzen, 1983) or by pointing to the adaptive, action-promoting functions of biases and errors. The latter concerns both "hot" or affect-laden biases like positivity bias, illusion of control, or some of the egotistic attributional biases (Taylor & Brown, 1988), and the tendencies traditionally associated with "cold," deductive or inductive, types of error, e.g., confirmation bias, base-rate neglect, or incorrect understanding of logical implication (Cosmides, 1989; Klayman & Ha, 1987; Lewicka, 1988a, 1992). As a consequence of these tendencies, the nineties without any doubt must be called the "decade of pragmatic cognition" (see Anderson, 1990, Friedrich, 1993; Lewicka, 1993).

I have long favored the view that thinking is, first of all, the instrument of action. To understand human biased reasoning implies understanding the role that reasoning plays in everyday activity (Lewicka, 1985, 1988a). However, in contrast to some adherents of the pragmatic approach, I try to avoid the pitfalls of its extreme version and do not believe that any cognition is adaptive or that irrationality is a precondition of mental health. Nor do I question the view that normative models of rational reasoning (e.g., inductive logic) do provide guidelines for rational conclusions. The fact that they are not always followed or that sometimes efficiency cannot be reconciled with rationality does not change this view.

The third point that I wish to make concerns the conditions under which lay reasoning naturally conforms to normative prescriptions, that is, becomes rational. According to the present author, the conditions are neither unusual nor infrequent. The pragmatic framework proposed in this chapter makes some preliminary suggestions as to when reasoning is biased and when the normatively correct cognition ensures the most efficient behavior.

The chapter specifically focuses on confirmation bias. The choice of the confirmation bias is not accidental. In my opinion, this is the "bias of biases," a "metabias" so to speak. Based on the logical error of "affirmation of the consequent," its underlying mechanism helps to understand deviations from rationality in the majority of areas in which these have been detected, e.g., deductive reasoning, hypothesis testing, causal reasoning, covariation detection, control judgment, judgment under uncertainty, etc. The disproportionately greater attention devoted in the literature to the confirmation bias, compared to any other single bias, implies that this view is shared, at least implicitly, by a number of other authors in the area.

The structure of the chapter is as follows. First I discuss the two concurrently used and often confused meanings of the "confirmation bias"—tendentious handling of evidence and a confirmatory strategy of hypothesis testing,—and focus on the latter. Next I present classical research that demonstrates occurrence of the confirmation bias and discuss numerous attempts (mostly unsuccessful) at its removal. The next section is devoted to discussion of possible mechanisms of the confirmation bias with special focus on these explanations that make use of the signal detection framework and that show how confirmation bias follows from the (undue) attention paid to the error of commission (false positives) at the expense of omissions (false negatives). I also focus on the function that the bias plays in the overall action pragmatics. In the last two sections I argue that incidence of confirmation bias will depend on the affective value of a goal (positive or negative). Desirable goals (approachable targets), which sensitize people to the error of commission, should favor biased hypothesis testing to a higher degree than undesirable goals (targets to be avoided), which make salient the danger of omission. The last section presents a selection of my own data that corroborate this view. Finally, in the conclusion I discuss the issue of the adaptive character of confirmation bias.

TWO TYPES OF CONFIRMATION BIAS

Two meanings of the "confirmation bias" are used concurrently in the literature. The first, which will be termed confirmation bias I, follows from the everyday understanding of the term and it means preference for confirming information, i.e., selective attention to the evidence that may confirm the hypothesis and neglect of the data that may refute it (cf. Gorman, 1989; Snyder, 1980; Snyder & Swann, 1978; Trope & Bassock, 1983). Its manifestations include selective vigilance favoring positive evidence and ignoring, distorting, or reinterpreting negative evidence in such a way that it might fit the hypothesis. For instance, a person may believe that fate is unfair to him, as proven by a series of observations showing that whenever he waits for a bus the bus is always late. He will then tend to register as "evidence" only those cases when the bus comes late but not those when it arrives on time. Confirmation bias I makes it hard to refute a hypothesis and therefore may be responsible for the frequently discussed unfounded perseverance and conservatism of beliefs (Jelalian & Miller, 1984; Snyder, 1980).

The other understanding of "confirmation bias," confirmation bias II, has its rationale in the principles of inductive logic. Instead of a tendentious handling of (negative) evidence, confirmation bias II describes a focus on positive instances of a hypothesis, known as confirmatory *strategy* of hypotheses testing. This is defined as a way of testing a hypothesis on the basis of instances that are predicted by the hypothesis while ignoring instances beyond its scope (and thus ignoring alternative explanations of the predicted/explained phenomena)(cf. Wason, 1960, 1968).

We can again use the example of our pessimistic friend who is convinced that buses that he is expecting always come late. If he is committing confirmation bias II he will be inclined to check only those buses that he himself is waiting for while ignoring the fact that other persons who are waiting at the same bus stop may face identical problems. Accordingly, he will fail to realize that his person probably has very little influence over the sad state of city transportation. It can be seen that, in contrast to confirmation bias I, what is subject to a bias in this case is not the validity of the *evidence* but of its *reason*. Confirmation bias II therefore does not exclude receiving disconfirmatory evidence to the hypothesis. On the contrary, our mournful friend, deeply convinced about his permanent bad luck, may be nicely surprised when the bus arrives exactly on schedule and may even attribute this fact to the sudden lucky turn in his life affairs. He will still be (egocentrically) biased, but the biased interpretation will concern not the evidence to the hypothesis but the hypothesis itself (i.e., the hypothetical premise for this evidence).

We can put the difference between the two types of confirmation bias in a somewhat different way and say that while confirmation bias I makes it difficult to check whether the hypothetical factor is a sufficiently good reason for the observed evidence (e.g, if it is really true that whenever our friend waits for the bus it is always late), confirmation bias II makes it difficult to establish the factor's necessity for the phenomena observed (e.g., to check if our friend's presence at the bus stop is the sole reason for the bus being late). As we can see, these two types of neglect lead to totally different consequences and therefore should not be confused. Unfortunately, such confusion is presently rampant in psychological research in this area.

Confirmation bias is an extensively studied phenomenon in the literature on lay cognitive functioning. A review of the pertinent literature shows that its two forms have drawn unequal attention from different areas of research in human cognition. While confirmation bias I has usually been studied within the domain of social cognition in which the self-perpetuating nature of social stereotypes is a particularly salient phenomenon (cf. Snyder, 1980; Snyder & Swann, 1978; Swann & Guliano, 1987), confirmation bias II appears interesting mainly to cognitive psychologists and to philosophers of science (Gorman, Gorman, Latta, & Cunningham, 1984; Klayman & Ha, 1987; Mynatt, Doherty, & Tweney, 1977, 1979; Tukey, 1986; Wason, 1960; Wetherick, 1962).

In both cases, the bias is usually treated as a methodologically incorrect way of testing hypotheses, equivalent to an error. However, it seems that, of its two forms, only confirmation bias I may be justly considered an error because it involves tendentious handling of *evidence* and hence may lead to distorted and inaccurate cognitions. Let us however note that, much against popular conviction about the omnipresence of confirmation bias I, a considerable portion of research in social hypothesis testing demonstrates that people tend to prefer information that is diagnostic, i.e., which allows them to choose between several competing hypotheses, over a simple confirmation of the previously held beliefs (cf. Devine, Hirt, & Gehrke, 1990; Skov & Sherman, 1986; Trope & Bassock, 1983; Trope, Bassock, & Alon, 1984). Also, Evans (1989), drawing from another research area, emphasizes the fact that even though people may not be willing to actively seek disconfirming evidence, they seem perfectly able to appreciate its significance once it is presented to them. It seems then that the issue of whether the held belief is or is not a sufficiently good predictor of events is important to the majority of people. This finding may cast doubt on the generality of confirmation bias I.

WASON'S 2-4-6 TASK AND CONFIRMATION BIAS II

Confirmation bias II is a *strategy of hypothesis testing*. The fact that people tend to check the truth of their hypotheses on positive and not on negative instances of their preliminary guesses was first empirically demonstrated by Bruner, Goodnow, and Austin (1956) in their classical investigations of processes involved in rule discovery (concept formation) tasks. In a series of analogous experiments on artificial concept formation, A. Lewicki (1957) observed a similar phenomenon and noticed that its usual outcome is categories that are overly restricted compared to the rule held by the experimenter. Lewicki called this phenomenon the "error of insufficient negative abstraction" and considered it a general feature of the human conceptual representation system. However, Lewicki ascribed the reasons for this overconcreteness primarily to properties of the natural environment in which conceptual learning takes place, namely to the restricted range of the exemplars available to a person. In other words, in so-called real life we are often placed in the situation of a man who is the only passenger waiting for a bus at a certain bus stop. Most probably both mechanisms, the objectively low variance of the concept's exemplars in our environment and the psychological unwillingness to actively seek instances that go beyond our hypotheses, may be responsible for the phenomenon of conceptual overconcreteness.

Further investigations of the undue focusing on positive instances of a hypothetical rule were undertaken by Wason (1960, 1968) in an experimental context that is an extension of the work of Bruner et al. (1956). In a series of now classical experiments he asked participants to discover a rule—chosen in advance by the experimenter—for generating three-number series. Participants were first presented with a single triplet (2-4-6), informed that the triplet was a positive instance of the rule, and next asked to generate other triplets, one at a time. After each triplet they were informed whether the generated sequence conformed or not to the rule that the experimenter had in mind. They were asked to generate as many and as different triplets as necessary to discover the nature of the rule. The main result in this experiment and in its numerous replications was a clear preference for triplets that were positive instances of participants' initial hypotheses (e.g., 8-10-12 when the guess was "even ascending by two" or 17-21-25 when it was "ascending in even intervals" etc.), that is, the confirmation bias. This performance could in theory lead to falsification of the hypothesis (receiving the "No" answer from an experimenter) but only in those cases where the experimenter's rule was not broader than the hypothetical rule held by the participant (i.e., when it was either surrounded by or overlapped the participant's hypothesis). However, this was not the case in the classical version of the task, because the experimenter's rule here was deliberately made very broad ("any three ascending numbers") while the participant's first guesses, inferred from the salient properties of the initial triplet (2-4-6), were usually very concrete (e.g., "even numbers ascending by two" or "even numbers ascending in equal intervals"). Generating positive instances of this embedded hypothetical rule could thus bring only positive feedback and hence would fortify the participant in the conviction that the "real" rule coincided with the initial guess. In clear analogy to the concept formation tasks, the usual outcome in these experiments was thus the overly concrete nature of the finally "discovered" rule.

Subsequent modifications of the 2-4-6 task introduced a number of changes into both its form and content e.g., different set relations or verbal and graphical, along with the arithmetic, content of the tasks (Gorman, 1986, 1989; Gorman, Gorman, Latta, & Cunningham, 1984; Kareev & Avrahami, 1995; Klayman & Ha, 1989). Neither of these changes seem to have greatly improved performance.

Other modifications were introduced in order to make participants pay more attention to *noninstances* of their initial guesses and thus to reduce the confirmation bias. For example, Wetherick (1962) presented participants with an initial triplet that *was not* an instance of the rule (4-2-6), thus successfully reducing the number of generated positive instances. However, Stock and Freitag (1991), who provided participants with varying proportions of evidence inconsistent with the experimenter's rule, obtained a paradoxical effect of generally decreased performance (fewer correct guesses) under conditions of exposure to disconfirming relative to confirming evidence. Tweney et al. (1980) explicitly instructed participants to use disconfirmatory strategies of testing hypotheses and failed to find any improvement on the task. However, the same modification replicated by Gorman et al. (1984) in the conditions of group problem solving gave positive results. Another modification employed by Wetherick (1962), Tweney et al. (1980), and Gorman, Stafford, and Gorman (1987) consisted of asking participants to find two, instead of one, complementary rules, arbitrarily labeled DAX and MED. This modification led to a successful increase in the number of correct guesses but it also positively influenced the number of confirmatory tests employed. Finally, Kareev and Avrahami (1995) instructed participants to generate examples in order to teach someone else a rule when both the correct rule and the trainee's hypothesis were known to the participant. Results showed that when the participants were aware of the correct rule they were also perfectly able to appreciate the importance of negative instances.

Overall, the attempts to make participants focus on negative instances and hence to reduce the confirmation bias have met with varying success. It should be made clear, however, that these results do not undermine the basic finding of Wason's research, namely, that confirmation bias is a very robust phenomenon. At most they show that under some circumstances, which are mostly artificially created by an experimenter, people can be made aware of the existence of counterexamples to their hypotheses and they can be taught the disconfirming strategies of testing these hypotheses. Whether these efforts lead to a better performance (i.e., to a higher incidence of correct guesses in rule discovery tasks) is again an open question and the respective evidence is by no means unequivocal.

EXPLANATIONS OF CONFIRMATION BIAS

Why are people so stubborn in their reluctance to consider alternative hypotheses? Why do they prefer narrow hypotheses to broader and more encompassing ones? Why are they unwilling to investigate facts that fall beyond the scope of their predictions? If confirmation bias II is so resistant to modifications, then we should guess that its psychological mechanisms indeed must be very deep.

Three hypotheses directly address this issue: the positivity bias hypothesis, the positive test strategy hypothesis, and the error minimization/sufficiency seeking hypothesis. I will describe each of them below.

Confirmation Bias and Positivity Bias

This explanation of confirmation bias has been proposed by Evans (1989). According to it, the bias is another manifestation of the robust "positivity bias"—the preference for positive over negative information. "The cognitive failure is caused by a form of selective processing which is very fundamental indeed in cognition—a bias to think about positive rather than negative information..." (p. 42). By this, Evans means that confirmation bias is a cognitive rather than motivational phenomenon (i.e., it is due not to the lack of willingness on the part of a person to look for disconfirming evidence, but to the difficulties experienced during processing of logically negative material). This phenomenon is known both in cognitive psychology and in studies on language (Clark & Clark, 1977). Semantically or syntactically negative material takes longer to process than positive material, and linguistic forms with inherent negation, such as linguistically negative verbs, are acquired later in childhood than linguistically positive grammatical forms (De Boysson-Bardies, 1970). As a consequence, people may find it easier to think about logically affirmative (confirming) instances to their hypotheses than about logically negative (disconfirming) instances.

Confirmation Bias and Positive Test Strategies

This explanation, which was advanced by Klayman and Ha (1987), makes use of the logic of conditions (sufficient versus necessary) and of signal detection theory. The main point of this explanation is that confirmation bias is not an error but a purposeful strategy of hypothesis testing, chosen for the sake of its cognitive simplicity and generally positive cognitive results.

Klayman and Ha suggest four possible strategies of testing a hypothesis, two of which consist in checking positive examples of the hypothesis (H+ strategy) or the target (T+ strategy), while the remaining two check counterexamples—to the hypothesis (H– strategy) or to the predicted target (T– strategy). Klayman and Ha's ideas are best described with the help of a contingency table depicting possible relations between H (hypothesis held by a participant), non-H (alternative hypotheses), T (target), and non-T (alternative targets) (Figure 1).

According to the theory, confirmation bias is an example of a positive test strategy (called H+ test) that checks cases predicted by the temporarily accepted hypothesis H+ (it compares number of hits with number of commissions) (see Figure 1). As a consequence, it helps to eliminate errors of false positives (commissions) and safeguards people against rules of categorization (H) that may be overly broad compared to the predicted phenomena (T).

The H+ test is the most popular of available tests. For instance, it will be used by a job committee who tests the validity of the accepted decision criteria by checking how many of the accepted candidates consequently succeed (number of hits) and how many fail (number of commissions) on the job. If an undue number of unsuitable candidates has been accepted,

	H	non-H	
T	(a) p(H and T) hits	(c) p(non-H and T) omissions	p(T)
non-T	(b) p(non-T and H) commissions	(d) p(non-T and non-H) correct rejections	p(non-T)
	p(H)	p(non-H)	

Strategies for assessing sufficiency of H for T:
- H+ strategy: p(T/H)
- T− strategy: p(−H/−T)

Strategies for assessing necessity of H for T:
- H− strategy: p(−T/−H)
- T+ strategy: p(H/T)

FIGURE 1 Two-by-two contingency table depicting possible relations between hypothetical factors (H), alternative hypotheses (non-H), predicted targets (T), and alternative targets (non-T).

the committee may in the future want to introduce stricter acceptance criteria and thus safeguard against the possible error of commission (although not necessarily against omissions; that is, if the criterion becomes overly strict it may screen out some really good candidates).

Another "positive test" strategy is the T+ test. In contrast to the former, its focus is on target cases that is, it compares the number of hits with the number of omissions (see Figure 1). Hence a medical committee may be interested in developing a screening test that identifies possibly many cases of a particularly dangerous disease X. One possibility is to test all known cases of disease X (T+ cases) with the known screening tests (H+), and to compare the number of sick patients who score positively on the test (number of hits) with those who score negatively (omissions). The ensuing modification of the hypothetical screening criterion should make it broad enough to minimize omissions even at the expense of some commissions (diagnosing as "sick" people who are really quite healthy).

To use other language, we may say that while the H+ strategy helps to establish a sufficient (although not necessary) condition of the predicted target, the T+ strategy aims at identifying a necessary (although not sufficient) condition of the target case (see Figure 1).

The T+ strategy should in theory be as easy cognitively as the H+ strategy (both are positive test strategies); however, it is applied infrequently for purely objective reasons: Rarely can people have access to all positive instances of the rule (all T+ cases). In Wason's task this strategy would be registered, if participants approached the task in a purely exploratory way, by first generating at random a set of different triplets, then checking how many of them classified as positive instances of the experimenter's rule and next finding out how well they fitted their hypothetical guess. In some modifications of Wason's task, such examples of the attribute-based or exploratory behavior were observed, but they were significantly less frequent than examples of behavior guided by specific hypotheses (cf. Tukey, 1986).

According to Klayman and Ha (1987), positive test strategies are cognitively easier than the two remaining negative test strategies, called, respectively, H– and T–, which consist either in checking cases predicted by alternative hypotheses (H– strategy) or in checking alternative outcomes (T– strategy). Moreover, each positive strategy has its functional equivalent in one of the two negative strategies: The H+ and T– strategies are equivalent in safeguarding against commissions (identifying sufficient reasons); the H– and T+ strategies safeguard against omissions (identify reasons which are necessary). However, according to Klayman and Ha, despite this equivalence, people prefer positive to negative tests; that is, they use H+ rather than T– and T+ rather than H–. And since the strategy T+ is diffcult to apply in a life setting, the obvious choice is a restriction to H+ tests. This strategy is highly efficient in the majority of life situations (it can lead to correct identification of the rule), the only exception being those cases when the individual's hypothesis happens to be embedded within the "real" rule (when it is overly narrow). According to the authors, however, this situation rarely happens outside the laboratory.

CONFIRMATION BIAS AND ERROR MINIMIZATION/SUFFICIENCY SEEKING

The third explanation of confirmation bias was proposed by Lewicka (1985, 1988a, 1993); several years later a very similar approach was presented independently by Friedrich (1993) in a model called PEDMIN (primary error detection and minimization).

Both Lewicka and Friedrich propose an approach to cognition that is pragmatic; that is, they assume that cognitive processes are, first of all, instruments of action. This, implies, among other things, that outside the laboratory an individual (who does not happen to be a scientist) is rarely faced with the demand to contemplate reality by discovering its "real" rules or "objective" truths. In daily circumstances this idealized scientific goal is replaced by a number of specific action-oriented goals; that is, an organism attempts to maximize gains (obtain outcomes that are gratifying) and minimize losses (avoid events that are harmful). These adaptive demands have shaped our minds: Certain ways of reasoning (reasoning strategies, inference rules, etc.) proved in the past to be more beneficial than others; they ensured higher survival ability to the species and thus became reinforced in the evolution of mind. Therefore if people now prefer certain cognitive strategies over others, this is caused not so much by processing demands placed on a cognitive system or by the availability of test cases (as the two other explanations would suggest) but by the pragmatic significance of the obtained outcomes.

This explanation shares a number of common points with that of Klayman and Ha (1987) but it also differs in a number of respects. Like the former, its theoretical background is the logic of conditions, contingency tables, and the terminology proposed by signal detection theory. Like Klayman and Ha, Lewicka and Friedrich also suggest that confirmation bias should be looked at not as an error but as a strategy aimed at avoiding commissions (false positives) and hence as a safeguard against overly broad categorization rules. However, in contrast to Klayman and Ha, the main emphasis of this explanation is not on whether the employed strategy makes use of positive or negative instances but on its psychological consequences for the person, namely, on whether the focus is on elimination of commissions or omissions, and hence whether the product is a correct identification of sufficient or necessary conditions of the predicted/explained phenomena.

The model assumes that the sufficiency-oriented reasoning predominates in lay thinking because of its higher survival value. In Klayman's and Ha's terms this would mean that in the majority of situations, the H+ strategies should predominate over T+, and that within the negative test strategies, the T– should be more popular than the H–. It is further claimed that the focus on sufficient at the expense of necessary conditions, accounts for a considerable portion of existent biases and errors in the domains of inductive reasoning, attributional inference, and judgment under uncertainty (for a review, see Lewicka, 1989, 1993). The cause of this asymmetrical preference is greater negative utility attached to the error of commission (cell H+ & T–) than to the error of omission (cell H– & T+). This phenomenon is highly adaptive because for the majority of categorization targets, particularly those that have a positive affective value, commission can lead to more disastrous and irreversible consequences than the error of omission. In other words successful avoidance of a harmful event is more important for the survival of an organism than potential contact with an additional beneficial event (Friedrich, 1993; Lewicka, 1988a). To use a different phrasing, we can say that a living organism is acting according to the old medical principle *primum non nocere*: It is more interested in not making its own situation worse than in making it better. This phenomenon is known as the negativity effect in evaluations, and it consists of higher weighting of undesirable than of respective desirable outcomes (Kanouse and Hanson, 1971; Peeters, 1971; Peeters & Czapinski, 1990). Its existence has been documented in a large variety of behavioral domains (e.g., person perception, moral judgments, decision making, animal behavior, etc.) (for a review and interpretation, see Czapinski, 1988).

Sufficiency testing, aimed at the elimination of potentially lethal commissions, and thus confirmation bias, appears then to belong to very elementary reasoning schemata, reinforced early in the processes of the evolution of the mind. In another place (Lewicka, 1988a, 1993) I have argued that the sufficiency driven confirmation bias is part and parcel of the epistemological attitude of an *actor*, and can be contrasted with the necessity oriented attitude of an *observer*. The actor reasons *prospectively*, from hypothetical premises to the hypothetical outcomes (H $\rightarrow$ T). This forward reasoning is focused on alternative outcomes rather than on alternative premises since the latter are taken for granted. "What follows from H?" rather than "Why did T happen?" is the habitual question asked by an actor. The actor is thus interested in if H is sufficient for T and much less in if it is also necessary, hence, confirmation bias with its disregard for alternative explanations.

In contrast, the observer reasons backward (T $\rightarrow$ H) and tries to *explain* the observed target phenomena. "Why did T happen?" rather than "What follows from H?" is the habitual question. The observer therefore looks for alternative premises (reasons) rather than for alternative outcomes since now it is the outcome that is taken for granted. The observer is thus mostly interested if the hypothetical premise H is a necessary condition of T, the interest that coincides with normative prescriptions. The observer is thus more rational—and less prone to confirmation bias.

Notwithstanding the well-documented claim that the attitude of an actor is both filogenetically older and more natural for the majority of people, we assume that humans have been endowed with considerable cognitive flexibility, the product of the unmet development of the brain, which is manifested in the ability to shift from subjectively to objectively anchored reasoning, in answer to pragmatic demands. The next section discusses this issue.

SUFFICIENCY/NECESSITY TESTS AND THE PRAGMATICS OF APPROACH AND AVOIDANCE

Preference for sufficiency-oriented thinking does not mean that the human mind is incapable of spontaneous use of necessity-oriented strategies. The theoretical explanation advanced here suggests that these evolutionarily younger and thus less natural inferences that happen to coincide better with the demands placed by normative models of rational inference (cf. Friedrich 1993; Lewicka, 1989, 1993) will be spontaneously triggered in all the circumstances where omissions are weighted at least as high as commissions.

Some time ago I (Lewicka, 1985, 1988a) presented a theoretical hypothesis that predicts that the relative weight of the two types of categorization error may be highly correlated with the desirability of the target outcome. This hypothesis is based on a purely logical analysis of the preconditions of successful approach and avoidance. These may be summarized as follows: Whereas the approach reaction can be successfully performed even if an individual masters only a single sufficient condition of the beneficial outcome, the successful avoidance of a harmful event requires identification of at least one of its necessary conditions. Knowledge of its single sufficient reason does not suffice, since the event may be caused by many other factors as well, and its resulting neglect (omission) may lead to detrimental consequences.

It has been further assumed that people have been endowed with sufficient cognitive skills to process conditions of efficient reactions. Thus the necessity-oriented strategies, in the form of either the T+ strategy (e.g., a retrospective analysis of a target's possible causes) or the H− strategy (e.g., counterfactual thinking about alternative scenarios or search for counterexamples to the hypothetical negative category), should be triggered significantly more often when the target is undesirable rather than desirable (Lewicka, 1988a, 1993), thus enabling a successful future elimination of false negatives (omissions).

An analogous prediction follows from the area of research known as positive-negative asymmetry (PNA) in evaluations (Czapinski, 1985, 1988; Matlin & Stang, 1978; Peeters, 1971). One of the manifestations of PNA is the so-called informational negativity effect (Peeters & Czapinski, 1990), which is defined as higher informativeness of negative compared to positive evaluations. For example, negative events have been shown to attract more attention, stimulate more interest in their causes, and be processed on a deeper cognitive level than positive events. Undesirable occurrences instigate more counterfactual thinking, thus leading to a more sophisticated knowledge of "what might have been" than desirable events (Miller, Turnbull, & McFarland, 1990; Teigen, 1995, 1996). Negative judgments call for more justification than positive judgments, and negative evaluative labels are found to be more diagnostic and descriptive of reality than respective positive labels (Peeters & Czapinski, 1990).

On the basis of these findings, Lewicka (1988a) suggested that positive and negative evaluative judgments may be asymmetrically anchored: Positive evaluations are anchored subjectively in a hypothesis held by a person ($H \rightarrow T$), and thus can vary from individual to individual, whereas negative evaluations are mostly products of "objective" anchoring ($T \rightarrow H$) and hence should show a much higher interpersonal consistency. These differences in anchoring should have consequences for hypotheses-testing strategies: H+ tests are expected more often when the hypothesis concerns reasons for desirable than undesirable outcomes, and T+ tests should prevail when a person tests reasons of undesirable rather than desirable outcomes. In other words, we can say that people are more interested in "how to do it?" when thinking about desirable outcomes, and in "why did it happen?" when the target is undesirable, than the other way round (Lewicka, 1989). The result is a relatively higher focus on necessity when the target is negatively rather than positively evaluated, which in turn should coincide better with normative requirements of rational judgement, another manifestation of the informational negativity effect.

According to the explanation presented by Lewicka, the fact that processing of undesirable outcomes may conform better to rational requirements than processing of desirable outcomes does not result from a pure coincidence of pragmatic and normative demands but is in fact an adaptive "must." In other words, we can allow ourselves to be "nonrational" and "subjective" when we define rewards, but we feel that reality must be taken seriously into account when it signals dangers. In other words, the negative will affect us independently of how we construct it. It is simply "out there," very palpable and real, waiting for us to assess its scope realistically and master the suitable avoidance strategy.

One strong implication of this approach is that the existent models of rationality should not be perceived as a scientific convention, a set of idealized prescriptions, unrelated to the requirements of efficiency (see, for instance, Evans & Over, 1997), but as intellectual tools that guarantee veridicality of our judgments and hence efficiency in the long run. This realistic attitude happens to be more pronounced when the judgmental targets are undesirable than desirable, a straightforward implication of our pragmatic approach to cognition.

ASYMMETRICAL LOGIC OF APPROACH AND AVOIDANCE: EMPIRICAL EVIDENCE

This section contains a review of selected studies, mostly conducted by the author, that tested the predicted link between evaluative meaning of a target and the asymmetry of reasoning schemata. The first part describes reasoning in decision-making situations and demonstrates that positive choices tend to be preceded by a more biased information search than negative choices. The second set of data concerns deductive reasoning and shows how desirability of a consequent of logical implication may influence the choice of a logical test: the sufficiency test is typically chosen for desirable, and the necessity test for undesirable, reasoning targets. The third section summarizes data concerning behavior in rule discovery tasks carried out under two conditions: when the rule concerns targets of approach (gains) and of avoidance (losses) and demonstrates that the habitual confirmation bias and ensuing overconcreteness of the final rule are more pronounced when the hypothetical rule concerns reasons for desirable than for undesirable outcomes.

Accept and Reject Decisions

In a series of six experiments involving choice (Lewicka, 1997), desirability of an outcome was manipulated explicitly by positive or negative framing of the choice situation. In all experiments, participants were asked either to choose (positive framing) or to reject (negative framing) one out of several alternatives representing potential candidates for future cooperation. Tasks in different experiments varied with respect to (1) number of available alternatives to select from (three to nine); (2) ratio of positive to negative traits on each alternative (i.e., the overall evaluation of the candidates—positive, ambivalent, negative alternatives); (3) how different the alternatives were from each other on general attractiveness (matched vs. differentiated on overall attractiveness); and (4) allowed ways of collecting information about the alternatives (attribute-wise vs. alternative-wise vs. mixed). Framing of the instructions (accept vs. reject) significantly influenced the predecisional information search. In all six experiments, independent of additional variables, the rejecting participants manifested a significantly more careful predecisional behavior by spreading their attention more evenly over different candidates and displaying a less biased information search then they did in the accept condition. In contrast to the rejecting participants, the accepting ones devoted disproportionately more attention to their first choices, which also turned out to be the selected ones (see Montgomery, 1983, 1989, for a more detailed description of the phenomenon of precommitment in decision making). Thus, it appears that while the accepting persons satisfied themselves with an alternative that was sufficiently good, the rejecting participants collected their information in a way that made it possible to eliminate the objectively worst candidate. The ensuing, more balanced picture of the candidates when their drawbacks rather than their merits were scrutinized may be viewed as another manifestation of the informational negativity effect.

The strategies of predecisional information search for reject and accept decisions appear to differ also in other respects. In a decision task simulating a publication review procedure, Westenberg and Koele (1989) asked participants either to choose manuscripts that they thought were suitable for publication or to reject manuscripts that were unsuitable. Rejecting persons used a significantly more attribute-wise search than accepting persons, who used a more alternative-wise search. In other words, participants who were asked to choose tended to pick out one alternative and check its position on consecutive attributes, whereas participants who were asked to reject preferred to compare several alternatives on one attribute. If we denote the hypothetical object of choice as H+ and its position on an attribute as T+, then these data can be reinterpreted as higher interest for T+ anchored tests in the reject than in the accept conditions and higher use of H+ anchored tests in the accept than in the reject conditions.

These data find corroboration in another study (Lewicka and Wojcik, 1989) in which participants who were asked either to choose or to reject a candidate for future cooperation could do it by asking a question either explicitly anchored in some property of the target (i.e., description of his behavior—"Who did X?") or explicitly anchored in one of the alternatives ("How did Y behave with respect to Z?"). Participants in the reject condition asked significantly more attribute-anchored questions than participants in the choice condition. The choosing persons preferred alternative-anchored questions. All this seems to confirm the prevalence of T+ over H+ tests when the decision is negative, and H+ over T+ tests when it is framed positively.

Deductive Reasoning about Desirable and Undesirable Targets

An interesting group of data closely bearing on the issue of the relations between sufficiency versus necessity testing (error minimization) and desirability of the target of inference comes from studies carried within the paradigm of the "selection task" (Wason, 1968). Traditionally, participants in this task are shown four cards representing a logical antecedent (P), negation of the antecedent (non-P), a consequent (Q), and negation of the consequent (non-Q) and told that the reverse side of each card has one of the two complementary terms (Q or not-Q in the case of the first two cards and P or not-P in the case of the remaining two cards). Participants are next provided with a verbally phrased implication (e.g., "Each time you do P you do Q") and asked to turn those and only those cards that they think necessary to check for violation of this rule.

The selection task was originally used to demonstrate people's (in)ability to test the truth of a logical implication (Wason, 1968); however, it has recently evolved into a fascinating domain of investigations into the pragmatics of human cognition (Cheng & Holyoak, 1985; Cosmides, 1989, Gigerenzer & Hug, 1992; Manktelow & Over, 1991, for a review see Evans, Newstead, & Byrne, 1993). In a series of modifications of the task, it has not only been shown that people are perfectly able to reason in terms of the simple $P \rightarrow Q$ implication (i.e., they are able to test how sufficient the antecedent term is for its consequent, as evidenced by checking P and non-Q), but also that under some circumstances they tend spontaneously to reverse their understanding of the tested rule ($Q \rightarrow P$) and switch instead to testing how necessary the antecedent term is for its consequent (they check the two remaining cards, non-P and Q) (Cosmides, 1989; Gigerenzer & Hug, 1992; Lewicka, 1988b; Manktelow & Over, 1991). This shift appears to be strongly related to the desirability of the terms used in the implication.

This shift was first demonstrated by Lewicka (1988b, 1992) in a modification of the selection task that introduced the affective value of the consequent into the phrasing of the rule. More precisely, in one condition the rule was phrased as "if one does P one will get benefit Q" (desirable outcome), while in another, "if one does P one will pay penalty Q" (undesirable outcome). Three additional conditions manipulated significance of the outcome for the person (i.e., "personal" described participant's personal gain or loss, "impersonal" described somebody else's outcomes, and "personal reversed" indicated that somebody else's gain meant the participant's loss and somebody else's loss meant the participant's gain). As predicted, the data showed a strong preference for sufficiency tests over necessity tests (i.e., participants checked more P and non-Q combinations than non-P and Q combinations) in four out of six experimental conditions (personal gains, impersonal gains, reversed gains, and reversed losses). This preference was particularly pronounced in the conditions of personal and impersonal gains (desirable outcomes). Reversed losses and reversed gains (i.e., the conditions where interests conflicted) also produced a considerable number of sufficiency tests, higher in both cases than the analogous number of necessity tests, although lower than in the remaining "gains" conditions. In all these conditions, the "natural" performance consisted of checking whether the fulfillment of the criterion (P) did not go unrewarded (non-Q). However, in the remaining two conditions, when explicit losses were mentioned, particularly where they were also personally relevant, the majority of participants tended to switch to the necessity tests (checking non-P and Q cards). They were thus more interested in checking whether the received penalty (Q) was not undeserved (non-P) than in checking whether the deserved penalty (P) did not go unnoticed (non-Q). As can be seen, when undesirable outcomes were involved, people tried first of all to eliminate the error of omission and hence applied necessity tests. However, the data from this experiment also point to a considerable asymmetry in processing desirable and undesirable outcomes: Whereas the preconditions of positive outcomes are mostly tested with respect to their sufficiency, negative outcomes apart from the pragmatically useful necessity tests also tend to trigger sufficiency tests, thus contributing to higher complexity of the overall pattern for losses than for gains. I will come back to this complexity in the next section when I present data from hypothesis-testing experiments.

Asymmetry of Approach and Avoidance and Confirmation Bias

In the two research domains (decision making and deductive reasoning) described above, respective framing of a task (triggering approach or avoidance) tended to change participants' choices from sufficiency tests under positive framing to necessity tests under negative framing. Would the respective shift also occur in typical rule discovery tasks where the concept of "confirmation bias" originated? Are processes of rule discovery different when they serve to identify positive and negative targets? These issues were addressed in a series of experiments (Lewicka, 1996), of which one is described in more detail below.

The experiment was a modification of Wason's 2-4-6 task. The task was made pragmatically meaningful to participants in that instances and noninstances of the rule were presented as sources of either financial gain or financial loss. The task therefore had the form of a game in which participants could earn or lose real money.

For the sake of comparison we have introduced a third, "cognitive," condition in which participants were simply asked to guess the true rule. This condition closely resembled the classical Wason's procedure.

It was predicted that undesirable instances would instigate avoidance and thus stimulate natural search for noninstances. This should correspond to "falsification" in hypothesis-testing behavior and facilitate rule discovery. In the case of desirable instances, we predicted the well-known conservative focus on profit-bringing targets and the ensuing overconcreteness of the rule. The cognitive condition was predicted to resemble the situation of "gains" more than the situation of "losses."

Participants were thus expected to end the task with significantly broader rules for identifying emotionally negative than emotionally positive targets, with the cognitive condition falling in between. By the same token, we expected that the rules used to identify desirable targets would consist of more sufficient than necessary criteria, and rules used to identify undesirable targets of necessary rather than sufficient criteria. The cognitive condition was again predicted to resemble the "desirable target" condition.

The task was run on a computer, which registered all consecutive steps taken by a participant. The procedure was as follows:

At the beginning, participants were shown a logically positive instance of a rule and told that for "instances like this one" they would earn ("gain" condition) or lose ("loss" condition) a certain amount of money. In the cognitive condition the instance was presented as a positive example of the rule. We kept close to the original task and hence the initial instance used was the 2-4-6 triplet while the rule to be discovered was "any ascending three numbers." Since the most plausible initial guess was more concrete than the "real" rule, the correct identification of the rule always required falsification (i.e., focus on noninstances).

The task consisted of two stages. In the first, experimental, stage, the participants were allowed to select targets that they wished to check and thus either earned or lost money for respective choices (in the cognitive condition no money was involved). The financial outcome of the choice (respective payoff) was shown after each step in the upper-right corner of the screen. In the "gain" condition, choice of a positive instance was accompanied by the profit while choice of a negative instance by the respective loss. The reverse payoff matrix was applied in the "loss" condition. In the cognitive condition the feedback information had the form of the "yes" or "no" answer shown on the screen.

Additional manipulation concerned mode of search. In one condition participants could generate respective triplets, in clear analogy to the classical Wason's task; in another condition they were asked to select the triplets from a larger set of 13 subsets, one at a time. The experimental phase included 13 consecutive trials.

The experimental phase was followed by a test phase that tested formal properties of the acquired rule. At this stage participants were displayed exemplary instances and noninstances of the rule and asked to select those triplets that they associated with profits (gain condition) or with losses (loss condition). In the cognitive condition we asked for identification of positive examples of the rule.

From these responses we computed frequencies of four kinds of categorization decisions (hits, commissions, omissions, and correct rejections), width of the final rule (hits + commissions), and sufficiency [hits/(hits + commissions)] and necessity [hits/(hits + omissions)] of the final categorization criterion.

TABLE 1 Mean Number of Choices of Instances and Noninstances in Conditions of Approach (Gains), Avoidance (Losses), and Cognitive

	Approach	Avoidance	Cognitive	F	p
Instances	10.56_a	3.42_b	9.42_a	360.69	.000
Noninstances	2.44_a	9.58_b	3.58_a		
Money earned	10.10_a	6.07_b		25.89	.000

Note. Conditions that do not share a common subscript differ at at least $p < .05$.

TABLE 2 Formal Properties of Positive Categories (Approach Targets), Negative Categories (Avoidance Targets), and Neutral Categories (Cognitive Targets)

	Gains	Losses	Cognitive	F	p
Sufficiency	$.884_{ac}$	$.808_{a}$	$.915_{cb}$	5.42	.005
Necessity	$.633_{d}$	$.819_{ae}$	$.791_{ae}$	10.68	.000
Category width	4.54_{a}	6.60_{b}	5.35_{c}	18.71	.000
Rule ident.	$.125_{a}$	$.250_{a}$	$.275_{a}$	2.65	.074

Note. Conditions that do not share a common subscript differ at least $p < .05$.

As can be seen from Table 1, the affective value of the category instance strongly influenced participant's categorization behavior. Significant differences between approaching (gain condition) and avoiding (loss condition) participants were obtained in the experimental phase: Participants shown the undesirable initial instance (example of a loss) chose to contact noninstances significantly more often than participants shown a desirable instance (example of a gain). Participants placed in the cognitive condition resembled the gain condition significantly more than the loss cognition. Mode of selecting instances did not influence these results.

The strong main effects are a good proof of the effectiveness of our manipulation: Approaching participants indeed approached and avoiding participants indeed avoided the category instances. However, apart from this effect we also noted a visible asymmetry in the pattern of choices in the two conditions. The "avoiding" participants appeared to select instances (undesirable targets) more often than the approaching participants selected the noninstances (and hence also the undesirable targets). The avoiding participants thus had more contacts with undesirable targets and in effect lost more money during the experiment than the approaching participants.

This observation was confirmed by highly significant differences in the overall profit in the two conditions (Table 1). There is no doubt, then, that the consistently conservative strategy of approaching participants was pragmatically more efficient than the risk-taking, or perhaps more chaotic, behavior of the avoiding participants. Did these differences reflect on the nature of the final categories? The respective data are shown in Table 2.

As predicted, the final rules were significantly broader when they described criteria of losses than those of gains, and they included more sufficient and less necessary categorization criteria of gains than losses. Again, the mode of search did not influence this general pattern and hence the respective means were collapsed across all other variables.

Avoiding participants also had more correct guesses of the final rule than the approaching participants, although the difference did not approach significance. Unexpectedly, the cognitive condition exceeded (insignificantly) the remaining two conditions in the number of correct guesses, the result associated with the overall very high measures of both sufficiency and necessity of final categories obtained in this condition.

As we can see, the "pragmatic" modification of Wason's task by introducing a condition of "avoidance" succeeded in making participants switch from a conservative, sufficiency-only strategy to the strategy focused also on necessity of the final categorization rule. These results have been replicated in an independent series of five experiments (Lewicka, 1996) using nonarithmetic material (participants were "discovering" rules underlying combinations of facial features). The experiments manipulated both the pragmatic value of the category instances (signifying financial gains or losses) and a number of other factors that were hypothesized to influence performance (logical structure of categories, category concreteness, utilities attached to categorization decisions, etc.). Independently of the additional factors, in analogy to the former task, the "approaching" participants displayed consistent preferences for more conservative and more sufficiency oriented search strategies and formed significantly narrower final categorizations rules then did the "avoiding" participants. Also replicated was the result pointing to the overall higher "financial efficiency" shown by participants placed in the gain conditions.

CONCLUSION: ON USES AND DISUSES OF CONFIRMATION BIAS

Is confirmation bias adaptive or disadvantagous? Should we teach people to overcome it or, perhaps, should it be viewed as a precondition of efficient behavior? The answer to both questions is simultaneously "yes" and "no." The proposed interpretation of confirmation bias as a product of focus on sufficient rather than necessary conditions of predicted target events or, in another language, as a manifestation of attention paid to the error of commission instead of omission makes it clear why the answer cannot be univocal.

Confirmation bias is part and parcel of human "survival equipment": It ensures sure profits without undue exposure to uncertainty and risk. It first of all eliminates loss and in doing so guarantees survival. This is adaptive and positive.

Second, confirmation bias underlies habit acquirement and automatization of routine activities. Mastering a sufficiently good way to obtain a desirable result frees our consciousness from unnecessary deliberation, leaving space for important life decisions.

Finally, confirmation bias facilitates commitment: Attachment to one possibility (hypothesis, decision option) helps to devalue alternative (perhaps better) possibilities. The elusive phenomenon of commitment has been nicely defined by Phillip Brickman (1987) as "the point in decision making where rationality ends and something else begins." The "nonrational" confirmation bias with its focus on positive instances and disregard of alternative hypotheses seems to guarantee that this "something else" will indeed take place and hence that the chosen option will not prematurely lose its attractiveness. According to a number of authors, this is a precondition for an action to be taken at all (see Beckmann & Irle, 1985; Kuhl, 1984; Lewicka, 1985, 1997; Montgomery, 1983).

Does the above mean that in order to be efficient, it is enough to take on the attitude of an actor, of which confirmation bias is the essential cognitive equipment? By no means. The theoretical analysis presented above should make it clear that actors' efficiency means efficiency in the short run, confined mostly to the limits of the environment that is stable and provides inexhaustible resources. Actors satisfy but do not optimize. They don't look for better means to achieve better ends. They apply the sure-thing principle and prefer a sparrow in a hand to the two in the bush. They don't change unless forced to do so by objective circumstances. Traditional rituals no doubt make our life easier and our decisions more automatic, but they ensure little personal development and change.

As an example of the advantage of scientific over traditional thinking, Robin Dunbar (1995) describes the sad fate of the Norwegian Vikings who invaded Greenland in the tenth century. The group was able to survive on the island for over 400 years, using the tools and habits acquired in their homeland. However, when the climate became more severe, their unwillingness to learn from the native Eskimo people led to their gradual extinction. Inability to test alternative hypotheses in a stable environment is the enemy of progress in a changing environment.

What seems to ensure our ability to learn, and thus in the majority of natural circumstances can help us overcome attachment to old hypotheses, are encounters with undesirable outcomes that spontaneously trigger the attitude of an observer. Search for necessary causes of threatening events leads to elaboration of abstract knowledge about causes of dangers, diseases, and calamities, and to development of efficient prevention programs. This is done through processes of reasoning, which both conform better to the demands of rational judgment and lead to the conclusions that, in the long run, may better serve the demands of action pragmatics.

Acknowledgments

This chapter was prepared with the financial means provided by grant BST 505/4 given to the author. The presented research was financed from BST 505/4 and from grant nr 1P106 013 04 offered by the Committee for Scientific Research.

REFERENCES

Anderson, J. R. (1990). *The adaptive character of thought.* Hillsdale, NJ: Lawrence Erlbaum.

Beckmann, J., & Irle, M. (1985). Dissonance and action control. In J. Kuhl & J. Beckmann (Eds.), *Action control: From cognition to behavior* (pp. 129–150). Berlin: Springer-Verlag.

Brickman, P. (1987). *Commitment, conflict and caring.* Englewood Cliffs, NJ: Prentice-Hall.

Bruner, J. S., Goodnow, J. J., & Austin, G. A. (1956). *The study of thinking.* New York: Wiley.

Cheng, P. W., & Holyoak, K. J. (1985). Pragmatic reasoning schemas. *Cognitive Psychology, 17,* 391–416.

Clark, H. H., & Clark, E. V. (1977). *Psychology and language: An introduction to psycholinguistics.* New York: Harcourt.

Cohen, J. L. (1981). Can human irrationality be experimentally demonstrated? *The Behavioral and Brain Sciences, 4,* 317–331.

Cosmides, L (1989). The logic of social exchange: Has natural selection shaped how humans reason? Studies with the Wason selection task. *Cognition, 31,* 187–286.

Czapinski, J. (1985). *Wartosciowanie—Zjawisko inklinacji pozytywnej. O naturze optymizmu.* (Valuation–positivity bias. On the nature of optimism). Wroclaw: Ossolineum.

Czapinski, J. (1988). *Wartosciowanie—Efekt negatywnosci. O naturze realizmu.* (Valuation–negativity effect. On the nature of realism). Wroclaw: Ossolineum.

De Boysson-Bardies, B. (1970). Syntax and semantix in memorization of negations. In G. B. Flores d'Arcais & W. J. M. Levelt (Eds.), *Advances in psycholinguistics* (pp. 237–246). Amsterdam: North Holland.

Devine, P. G., Hirt, E. R., & Gehrke, E. M. (1990). Diagnostic and confirmation strategies in trait hypothesis testing. *Journal of Personality and Social Psychology, 58,* 952–963.

Dunbar, R. (1995). *The trouble with science.* London: Faber and Faber.

Evans, J. St. B. (1989). *Bias in human reasoning. Causes and consequences.* London: Lawrence Erlbaum.

Evans, J. St. B., Newstead, S. E., & Byrne, R. M. J. (1993). *Human reasoning. The psychology of deduction.* Hillsdale, NJ: Lawrence Erlbaum.

Evans, J.St.B., & Over, D. (1997). Rationality in reasoning. The problem of deductive competence. *Cahiers de Psychologie Cognitive, 16(1),* 3–38.

Farris, H. H., & Revlin, R. (1989). Sensible reasoning in two tasks: Rule discovery and hypothesis evaluation. *Memory and Cognition, 17,* 221–232.

Friedrich, J. (1993). Primary error detection and minimization (PEDMIN) strategies in social cognition: A reinterpretation of confirmation bias phenomena. *Psychological Review, 100,* 298–319.

Gigerenzer, G., & Hug, K. (1992). Domain-specific reasoning: Social contracts, cheating and perspective taking. *Cognition, 43,* 127–171.

Gorman, M. E., Gorman, M. E., Latta, M., & Cunningham, G. (1984). How disconfirmatory, confirmatory and combined strategies affect group problem solving. *British Journal of Psychology, 75,* 65–79.

Gorman, M. E., Stafford, A., & Gorman, M. E. (1987). Disconfirmation and dual hypotheses on a more difficult version of Wason's 2-4-6 task. *The Quarterly Journal of Experimental Psychology, 39A,* 1–28.

Gorman, M. F. (1986). How the possibility of error affects falsification on a task that models scientific problem solving. *British Journal of Psychology, 77,* 85–96.

Gorman, M. F. (1989). Error, falsification and scientific inference: An experimental investigation. *The Quarterly Journal of Experimental Psychology, 41A*, 385–412.

Hogarth, R. (1980). *Judgment and choice*. New York: Wiley.

Jelalian, E., & Miller, A. G. (1984). The perseverance of beliefs: Conceptual perspectives and research developments. *Journal of Social and Clinical Psychology, 2*, 25–56.

Kahneman, D., Slovic, P., & Tversky, A. (Eds.) (1982). *Judgment under uncertainty: Heuristics and biases*. Cambridge: Cambridge University Press.

Kanouse, D. E., & Hanson, L. R., Jr. (1971). Negativity in evaluations. In E. E. Jones et al. (Eds.), *Attribution: Perceiving the causes of behavior*. Morriston: General Learning Press.

Kareev, Y., & Avrahami. J. (1995). Teaching by examples: The case of number series. *British Journal of Psychology, 86*, 41–54.

Klayman, J., & Ha, Y.-W. (1987). Confirmation, disconfirmation, and information in hypothesis testing. *Psychological Review, 94*, 211–228.

Klayman, J., & Ha, Y.-W. (1989). Hypothesis testing in rule discovery: Strategy, structure, and content. *Journal of Experimental Psychology: Learning, Memory and Cognition, 15*, 596–604.

Kruglanski, A. W., & Ajzen, I. (1983). Bias and error in human judgment. *European Journal of Social Psychology, 13*, 1–44.

Kuhl, J. (1984). Volitional aspects of achievement motivation and learned helplessness: Toward a comprehensive theory of action control. In B. A. Maher (Ed.), *Progress in experimental personality research* (Vol. 12, pp. 99–170). New York: Academic Press.

Lewicka, M. (1985). Towards a motivational account of human cognitive biases. Paper presented at the 10th Research Conference on Subjective Probability, Utility and Decision Making, Helsinki, Finland.

Lewicka, M. (1988a). On subjective and objective anchoring of cognitive acts. How behavioral valence modifies reasoning schemata. In W. J. Baker, L. P. Mos, H. V. Rappard, & H. J. Stam (Eds.), *Recent trends in theoretical psychology* (pp. 285–301). Springer-Verlag.

Lewicka (1988b). Pragmatic reasoning schemata with differing affective value of a consequent of logical implication. Paper presented at the Conference on Cognitive Biases, Aix-en-Provence, France.

Lewicka, M. (1989). Toward a pragmatic perspective on cognition. Does evaluative meaning influence rationality of lay inferences? *Polish Psychological Bulletin, 23*, 237–252.

Lewicka, M. (1992). Pragmatic reasoning schemata with differing affective value of a consequent of logical implication. *Polish Psychological Bulletin, 23*, 237–252.

Lewicka, M. (1993). *Aktor czy obserwator? Psychologiczne mechanizmy odchylen od racjonalnosci w mysleniu potocznym* (Actor or observer? Psychological mechanisms of deviations from rationality). PTP: Warszawa.

Lewicka, M. (1996). Asymetria pozytywno-negatywna w wartosciowaniu, a struktura kategorii pojeciowych (Positive negative asymmetry in evaluations and structure of conceptual categories). Unpublished research report. University of Warsaw.

Lewicka, M. (1997). Is hate wiser than love? Cognitive and emotional utilities in decision making. In R. Ranyard, R. Crozier, & O. Svenson (Eds.), *Decision making: Cognitive models and explanations* (pp. 90–106). London: Routledge & Kegan Paul.

Lewicka, M., & Wojcik, P. (1989). Affective and evaluative factors in decision making. Paper presented at the East-West Meeting of the European Association of Experimental Social Psychology, Jablonna, Poland.

Lewicki, A. (1957). Abstrakcja i analiza w procesie powstawania pojec (badania eksperymentalne) (Abstraction and analysis in concept formation). *Studia Psychologiczne, 2*, 96–125.

Manktelow, K. I., & Over, D.E (1991). Social roles and utilities in reasoning with deontic conditionals. *Cognition, 39*, 85–105.

Manktelow, K. I., & Over, D. (Eds.) (1993). *Rationality.* London: Routledge & Kegan Paul.

Matlin, M. W., & Stang, D. J. (1978). *The Pollyanna principle. Selectivity in language, memory and thought.* Cambridge, MA: Schenkman Publishing.

Miller, D. T., Turnbull, W., & McFarland, C. (1990). Counterfactual thinking and social perception: Thinking about what might have been. In M. P. Zanna (Ed.), *Advances in experimental social psychology* (Vol. 23, pp. 305–331). Orlando, FL: Academic Press.

Montgomery, H. (1983). Decision rules and the search for the dominance structure: Towards a process model of decision making. In P. Humphreys, O. Svenson, & A. Vari (Eds.), *Analyzing and aiding decision processes.* Budapest: Publishing House of the Hungarian Academy of Sciences.

Montgomery, H. (1989). From cognition to action: The search for dominance in decision making. In H. Montgomery & O. Svenson (Eds.), *Process and structure in human decision making.* Chichester: Wiley.

Mynatt, C. R., Doherty, M. E., & Tweney, R. D. (1977). Confirmation bias in a simulated research environment: An experimental study of scientific inference. *Quartely Journal of Experimental Psychology, 29,* 85–95.

Mynatt, C. R., Doherty, M. E., & Tweney, R. D. (1979). Consequences of confirmation and disconfirmation in a simulated research environment. *Quarterly Journal of Experimental Psychology, 30,* 395–406.

Nisbett, R. E., & Ross, L. (1980). *Human inference: Strategies and shotcomings of social judgment.* Englewood Cliffs, NJ: Prentice-Hall.

Peeters, G. (1971). The positive-negative asymmetry: On cognitive consistency and positivity bias. *European Journal of Social Psychology, 1,* 455–474.

Peeters, G., & Czapinski, J. (1990). Positive-negative asymmetry in evaluations. The distinction between affective and informational effects. In W. Stroebe & M. Hewstone (Eds.), *European Review of Social Psychology* (Vol. 1, pp. 33–60).

Skov, R. B., & Sherman, S. J. (1986). Information-gathering processes: Diagnosticity, hypothesis-confirmatory strategies, and perceived hypothesis confirmation. *Journal of Experimental Social Psychology, 22,* 93–121.

Snyder, M. (1980). On the self-perpetuating nature of social stereotypes. In D. L. Hamilton (Ed.), *Cognitive processes in stereotyping and intergroup behavior.* Hillsdale, NJ:Erlbaum.

Snyder, M., & Swann, W. B., Jr. (1978). Hypothesis-testing processing in social interaction. *Journal of Personality and Social Psychology, 36,* 1202–1212.

Stock, W. A., & Freitag, E. (1991). The use of consistent and inconsistent evidence with a set of 2-4-6 problems. *Bulletin of the Psychonomic Society, 29,* 4–6.

Swann, W. B., & Guliano, T. (1987). Confirmatory search strategies in social interaction: How, when, why and with what questions. *Journal of Social and Clinical Psychology, 5,* 511–524.

Taylor, S. E., & Brown, J. D. (1988). Illusion and well-being: A social psychological perspective on mental health. *Psychological Bulletin, 103,* 193–210.

Teigen, K. H. (1995). How good is good luck? The role of counterfactual thinking in the perception of lucky and unlucky events. *European Journal of Social Psychology, 25,* 281–302.

Teigen, K. H. (1996). Luck: The art of near miss. *Scandinavian Journal of Psychology, 37,* 156–171.

Trope, T., Bassok, M., & Alon, E. (1984). The questions lay interviewers ask. *Journal of Personality, 52,* 90–106.

Trope, Y., & Bassok, M. (1983). Information gathering strategies in hypothesis-testing. *Journal of Experimental Social Psychology, 19,* 560–576.

Tukey, D. D. (1986). A philosophical and empirical analysis of subjects' modes of inquiry in Wason's 2-4-6 task. *The Quarterly Journal of Experimental Psychology, 38A,* 5–33.

Tweney, R. D., Doherty, M. E., Werner, W. J., Pliske, D. B., Mynatt, C. R., Gross, K. A., & Arkelin, D. L. (1980). Strategies of rule discovery on an inference task. *Quarterly Journal of Experimental Psychology, 32*, 109–123.

Wason, P. C. (1960). On the failure to eliminate hypotheses in a conceptual task. *Quarterly Journal of Experimental Psychology, 12*, 129–140.

Wason, P. C. (1968). "On the failure to eliminate hypotheses..."—A second look. In P. C. Wason & P. N. Johnson-Laird (Eds.), *Thinking and reasoning*. Middlex, England: Penguin Books.

Westenberg, M., & Koele, P. (1989). Response modes and decision strategies. Paper presented at the XII Conference on Subjective Probability, Utility and Decision Making. Moscow, Russia.

Wetherick, N. E. (1962). Eliminative and enumerative behavior in a conceptual task. *Quarterly Journal of Experimental Psychology, 14*, 246–249.

Zajonc, R. (1989). Styles of explanation in social psychology. *European Journal of Social Psychology, 19*, 345–368.

CHAPTER 10

INTRUSIVE THOUGHTS, RUMINATION, AND INCOMPLETE INTENTIONS

JÜRGEN BECKMANN

Sometimes we find it hard to remember things that we should not forget. At other times thoughts about completely unimportant or even ridiculous matters linger on in our minds. Thoughts intruding into our conscious attention can severely impair or even completely block what we are currently trying to achieve. I may not be able to concentrate on reading if I am continuously harassed by thoughts of how stupid I looked yesterday when I tried to repair the dishwasher and a plumber had to come to fix the disaster I caused. We may then want to suppress these thoughts but fail. Wegner, Schneider, Carter, and White (1987) have shown that the instruction not to think about a white bear actually provokes repeated intrusions of this rather far-fetched thought into consciousness.

The major focus of this chapter is on explaining how different contents unintendedly intrude into consciousness. Attention control mechanisms usually maintain conscious attention focused on whatever an individual is trying to achieve at that moment. Sometimes, however, contents not related to the pursued goal manage to pass these control mechanisms, interrupt the thought flow, and intrude into conscious attention.

JÜRGEN BECKMANN • Insitute for Sports Science, University of Potsdam, 14469 Potsdam, Germany. E-mail: jbeck@rz.uni-potsdam.de

Personal Control in Action, edited by Kofta et al., Plenum Press, New York, 1998.

This interruption of the current thought flow can be functional as well as dysfunctional. A startling reflex that focuses attention on a threatening input can be a life saver. But ruminations about something that we can do nothing about can interfere with the achievement of the goal at hand. A basketball player who abides under the opponent's basket buried in rumination about missing a shot fails to prevent the opponent from scoring. There are a number of sources for intrusions. Rumination is discussed as a very potent source that has especially strong effects when it is based on incomplete intentions.

RUMINATIVE THOUGHT AND INTRUSIONS

When I speak of intrusions I mean thoughts that enter consciousness unintentionally. I differentiate between intrusions and rumination. Intrusions can be the result of ruminations. Broadly defined, rumination refers to thinking that circles around the same content over and over again. Not all intrusions are caused by ruminations. But all intrusions interfere with what one is currently doing.

From my point of view, information processing that may eventually result in intrusions is not necessarily consciously represented. Often when we are, for example, in a conversation with colleagues searching for the name of a person who made an essential contribution to psychology, we have the feeling that the name is at the tip of our tongues but just won't come to mind. We continue the conversation and the search for the name may go on unconsciously. Trying to solve a difficult intellectual problem can be consciously postponed but may be continued unconsciously and unintentionally. Once we find the name or the solution to the intellectual problem, the unconscious search routine will come forward and its result intrudes into conscious attention (cf. Bühler, 1907–1908). These intrusions seem to be so powerful that they can even wake a person up in the middle of the night when a solution is found.

I consider these examples as instances of an unconscious completion of an incomplete task. I would not refer to them as ruminations. Characteristic of ruminations is the unsystematic repetition of some content. The same content is "re-chewed" over and over again. This is not the case in the above examples. Problem solving can acquire, for example, the characteristics of ruminations if conscious or unconscious processing exclusively circles around the unsatisfactory present state (a present state that falls short of a standard we have) or the desired future state (the positive effects of reaching the standard) without including a consideration of how to move from the present to the future state (cf. Kuhl's, 1984, characterization of "state orientation"). Thus, according to my view ruminations are static contemplations that lack a change orientation.

This does not imply that ruminations will never help to attain goals. The repeated contemplations of the state may (or may not) have adaptive value for long-term coping. A critical life event may render former goals inappropriate and may require a person to reevaluate and to redefine these goals (cf. Herrmann & Wortman, 1985). Some goals that carry commitment may be characterized as "degenerated intentions" that persist in spite of the fact that they cannot be carried out or are no longer appropriate (Kuhl, 1984). Going through a phase of ruminations may be required to overwrite these no longer appropriate motivational structures or underlying self schemas (cf. Horowitz, 1990). Like Clark (1996) and King and Pennebaker (1996), I see the basic function of rumination as making sense of a certain state of the organism (e.g., after a critical life event) rather than as serving the attainment of a specific goal, as Martin and Tesser (1996a,b) do. Consequently, in contrast to Martin and Tesser (1996b, p. 192) who refer to ruminations as "the entire class of thoughts that have a tendency to recur," I consider the distinction between rumination and problem solving, or systematic deliberation on which goal to pursue and how to attain it, as essential (cf. Nolen-Hoeksema, 1996).

But I agree with the following characteristics of ruminations specified by Martin and Tesser (1989, p. 306): (1) They occur over relatively long periods of time, (2) they often appear to be counterproductive, and (3) they involve both automatic and controlled processes.

What Causes Intrusions?

What are the sources for intrusions? The general assumption is that some activated structure generates inputs that can gain access to conscious attention. There are different assumptions about what keeps structures in a state of activation. All kinds of contents can become intrusive. Most persistent and most vigorous should be the intrusions resulting from incomplete intentions that cause ruminations about the unattained goal. A person desperately in love who is rejected by the object of affection is likely to be unable to think of anything other than the loved one. For some people the unfulfilled love can become an obsession for a lifetime. As stated above, ruminations cause the counterproductive type of intrusion that just blocks attentional capacity without providing a solution to a problem of immediate interest. But there is also a productive type of intrusion that is not based on rumination. Here, as described above, the intrusion is a conscious representation of the result of an unconscious problem-solving routine.

Obviously there are different sources for intrusions with different functional consequences. The literature lists mainly three such sources:

spreading activation, outcome-resultant affect, and motivationally driven activation.

Spreading activation is discussed by Martin and Tesser (1989, 1996a,b) as repetition that channelizes thought as a string of thoughts over time. Even in the absence of motivation, many ruminationlike processes may be triggered. Thinking about one thing simply cues thoughts about another. Sometimes this channelization of thought appears rather automatic and may even go unregistered, as in the case of a 35-year-old student described by Hurlburt (1990, p. 111): "Sonja repeatedly experienced a type of thinking that included a mindless inner repeating of words, sentence fragments, or even whole sentences. These words had lost their original meaning, and sometimes the words themselves had become altered, but she was nonetheless repeating them silently."

Obtaining an outcome on a task (positive or negative) has usually more or less strong affective consequences (see also Martin & Tesser, 1996a, p. 17, 1996b, p. 196). I refer to these affective consequences as outcome-resultant affect. Failing on an important task produces negative affect, whereas succeeding on the task results in positive affect. The outcome-resultant affect can maintain a content structure in an activated state as long as the affect lasts (cf. Singer, 1988). Presumably, the primary function of the outcome-resultant affect is to stimulate postactional evaluation processes.

Negative outcome-resultant affect indicates that one fell short of the standard that was set. It thus instigates an evaluation of the performance to find out why one failed and how the standard can possibly be attained in future performances. If the postactional evaluation shows that meeting the standard is impossible, the standard should either be lowered or, if that is not possible, the person should attempt to disengage from that particular goal during the postactional evaluation (cf. Beckmann, 1994; Klinger, 1975, 1977). There is no need for this kind of evaluation in the case of an outcome that meets the set standard. However, usually we do not turn immediately away from a successful action after obtaining the outcome but keep focused on it for at least a little while. In this case the resulting positive affect and the basking it stimulates has probably primarily a self-reinforcing function (cf. Heckhausen, 1991; Weiner, 1985).

The third and presumably most powerful source of intrusions is motivationally driven activation. Motivationally driven activation is based on an instigated motivational structure. It is assumed that such a structure persists until the respective goal is attained or until it is abandoned as inaccessible or as too costly (cf. Atkinson & Birch, 1970; Freud, 1949; Klinger, 1977, Martin & Tesser, 1996a). Since Zeigarnik (1927) and Ovsiankina's (1928) classical studies, a number of experiments have shown that incomplete intentions persist in memory and strive toward resumption (see Beckmann, 1996).

As discussed above, I see two types of information processing associated with motivationally driven activation: goal-oriented deliberation (problem solving) and rumination. The former can have tangible results that allow deactivation of the structure temporarily. Deactivation means that the activation and consequent accessibility of the structure is reduced to a kind of stand-by mode that allows monitoring of inputs for goal-relevant cues without making demands for cognitive capacity. According to my definition of rumination, the latter cannot achieve tangible results. Consequently, a deactivation of the motivational structure is not possible in the case of rumination.

The primary energetic resource that maintains the flow of mental events related to the goal specified in the motivation is affective. But this kind of affect is different from the above mentioned outcome-resultant affect that stimulates postactional evaluation. It may be referred to as goal affect since it originates from the anticipated consequences of the outcome of an action (cf. McClelland, Atkinson, Clark, & Lowell, 1953). As a core element in motivation, it is the director of behavior (Klinger, 1977, p. 82).

All three mechanisms discussed above can account for the persistence of the activation of content structures, and thus, for intrusions. But the intrusive potential should be highest for motivationally driven activation and lowest for spreading activation. The intrusive thought caused by spreading activation has no motivational base that can activate the thoughts by itself, as is the case for outcome-resultant affect and incomplete intentions. Spreading activation needs a cue to start with, and the intrusions remain active in the absence of motivation only if one thought can cue another. If the string of thoughts is interrupted, the intrusive potential is eliminated. Outcome-resultant affect actually motivates thinking about the past action. Its effect is assumed to wane over time. But intentions that have not been completed and still carry a person's commitment would be a persistent source for intrusions for a long time (cf. Klinger's research on "current concerns"; Klinger 1975, 1977; Klinger, Barta, & Maxeiner, 1980).

Functional and Dysfunctional Aspects of Intrusions

The term "intrusion" usually has a negative connotation. Yet sometimes intrusions can be beneficial. The research literature, however, mainly supports the negative aspect. Rumination about failing on an ego-involving task can generate intrusions while one tries to concentrate on a new task. These intrusions constitute a functional deficit that impairs performance on the new task (Kuhl, 1981). The rumination can eventually result in depression (Kuhl & Helle, 1994; Pyszczynski & Greenberg, 1987).

As mentioned above, sometimes the intrusions can announce that some unconsciously operating subroutine found the solution to a problem that could not be solved consciously. For example, the name that could not be retrieved will suddenly pop up. Or, during a conversation the solution to an unrelated problem that one long thought about will enter the mind. Even in theses cases the intrusions interrupt or interfere with what we are currently doing. However, we certainly benefit from these interruptions. Maybe what we were currently doing was not that important. Actually, it is assumed here that whether or not intrusions occur is a function of both the valence of what we are currently doing as well as the valence of the intrusive content.

Often we try to suppress unwanted thought. But this attempt at mental control may have negative effects. Clinical research suggests that trying to suppress motivational tendencies may actually increase the likelihood that they will intrude. In the case of an attempt to lose weight, for example, a self-restraining diet in which one forces oneself to stay away from food actually drags attention toward food, which eventually results in increased ingestion (Nisbett, 1972). Self-restraining strategies (self-control) can have short-term benefits at the possible cost of long-term disadvantages (cf. Kuhl & Beckmann, 1994b).

To Control or Not to Control: The Difficulties in Trying to Suppress Unintended Thoughts

Wegner et al. (1987) found that when they asked their subjects not to think about a white bear a rebound effect actually occurred. The subjects thought about a white bear more often than subjects who did not try to suppress that thought.

Kelly and Kahn (1994) point out that there is a paradox inherent in thought suppression. They state that "It is logically impossible to not have a thought without having it" (p. 999). This seems right only at first glance, if one thinks of direct attempts at thought suppression. But as we shall see, there are more sophisticated, indirect routes to getting rid of unwanted thoughts.

Research findings seem to suggest that personally relevant emotional thoughts can be suppressed more easily than relatively neutral or unfamiliar contents, such as the white bear (Kelly & Kahn, 1994; Wegner & Gold, 1995). This contradicts everyday experience. We certainly do have the most trouble trying to keep thoughts out of our minds that remind us of a failure experience on an ego-involving task or even more so about losing a loved one. In fact, it is maintained here that rumination is caused by unfulfilled goals, and those ruminations tend to intrude into conscious attention. How can this be reconciled with the above mentioned research findings? In the experiments by Kelly and Kahn (1994) and Wegner and Gold (1995), the measures of thinking about some contents were taken immediately after the instructions were given (to think or not to think about them). Other research (Martin & Tesser, 1996a; Pyszczynski & Greenberg, 1987) suggests that especially for emotionally relevant contents, after primes for these contents are given, initial attempts at suppressing thoughts about them are quite successful. However, sometime later a rebound effect occurs. Thus, suppressing does not appear to be a suitable strategy to get rid of intrusive potential for a prolonged period of time. Suppression may even prove to be detrimental, as it may amplify the underlying motivational tendency, as in the case of hunger described above. The route that leads to at least temporary relief from intrusions, for instance, until the current intention is realized, is not an effortful suppression of the unwanted thoughts. Rather, unintended, intrusive thought is stopped through a selective strengthening of the motivational tendency underlying the intended stream of thought. The latter can be called self regulation in contrast to the former attempt at self-control (cf. Kuhl & Beckmann, 1994a). The mechanisms underlying the self regulation route will now be addressed.

APPROACHING A THEORY OF INTRUSIVE CONTENTS

I agree with Wegner and Pennebaker (1993, p. 5) that mental control is a function of attention. When Wegner and Pennebaker (1993) speak about mental control they focus only on coercive strategies to control the focus of attention directly. Relating to William James's (1890) ideas, they suggest that in order to determine what gets into the focus of attention (and what not) and is "held fast before the mind" some "effort of attention" is required. But they realize this mental control strategy can turn out to be a double-edged sword. The control attempts might actually increase the likelihood that the contents that are intended to be suppressed intrude (Wegner et al., 1987); this self-controlling kind of mental control "can lead to a host of physical and psychological problems" (Wegner & Pennebaker, 1993, p. 3).

There are different routes to determining what gets into and what is maintained in the focus of conscious attention. The authoritarian self-control mode is only one of those and a not very sophisticated one. A route that is more successful in maintaining the attentional focus on intended contents and keeping unwanted thoughts from intruding into conscious attention is what I refer to as "intense attention," in contrast to the "strained attention" strategy (Beckmann, 1991). Intense attention is experienced as an effortlessly achieved, perfect concentration on the performed task. It is typical for the "flow experience" described by Csikszentmihalyi (1975). As shall be seen later, there is some chance of combining both strategies successfully. In what follows, I will describe some assumptions about the fundamentals of the dynamics of conscious attention.

THE CONSTANTLY ACTIVE MIND

The initial premise in this approach is that the subject of study is constantly active: The mind is never silent; we cannot stop thinking; one thought gives way to another. This assumption is at the core of Atkinson and Birch's (1970) dynamics of action:

> There are no behavioral vacuums except when the individual is literally inactive and unconscious—yet still alive in a medical sense—as in the case of extreme illness or after a severe blow on the head. Otherwise, his behavioral life (which constitutes the subject matter of psychology) is, as Barker (1963) has described it: a continuous stream characterized by change from one activity to another without pause from birth until death. (p. 1)

This especially applies to conscious attention.

THE GATEKEEPER MODEL OF MAINTENANCE AND REPLACEMENT

The questions here are how and when does a change of thought content occur, and how and when is it prevented: How does one line of thinking give way to another and why does it do so at some times but not at others? In addressing this question, I postulate that there is a gatekeeper function that mediates changes in thought contents. This assumption is derived from Glass, Holyoak, and Santa's (1979, p.183) model of attention. The modified gatekeeper version of this model is depicted in Figure 1.

According to the model there are several inputs of various sources (external and internal) to an organism at a certain point in time. Unconscious monitoring procedures constantly monitor all kinds of inputs. But only one input goes directly to the conscious decision procedure that initiates and directs voluntary, intended actions. While conscious attention deals with this input, the unconscious monitoring procedures register all kinds of changes in the external and internal environments that we are not paying (conscious) attention to. The unconscious monitoring procedures pass along information to the attention controller, which is the gatekeeper in this model. This gatekeeper determines whether or not and which of the currently-not-consciously-attended-to inputs will gain access to conscious attention.

The gatekeeper is no decision-making homunculus. It can be conceptualized as a hierarchy of attention controllers with the top level attention controller residing on the verge of consciousness. Each controller has a certain threshold that inputs must exceed in order to pass the controller and proceed on the way into consciousness. Gray (1982) identifies the subiculum as a very basic gatekeeper in the brain that determines whether or not an input will be processed further. Gate opening by the subiculum is assumed to be authorized by the hippocampal circuit. Even if inputs are

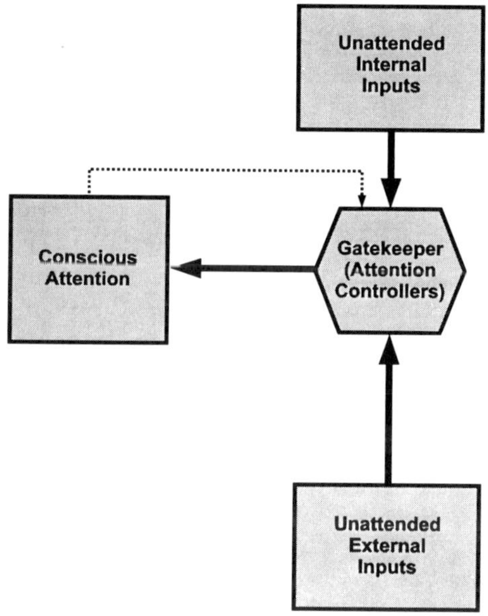

FIGURE 1 The gatekeeper model.

passed on for further processing here, whether or not they will reach consciousness is probably decided along pathways through the prefrontal cortex (cf. Crick & Koch, 1995; Damasio, 1995). The lower-level controllers are beyond the level of conscious control. They do not require cognitive resources. The top-level controller, i.e., the controller on the verge of conscious attention, is likely to involve controlled processes that require cognitive resources.

Linville (1996, p. 122) states: "Attentional inhibition acts as an automatic cognitive gatekeeper, hindering access to consciousness of marginally relevant or irrelevant external information and internal thoughts, thus focusing attention on current task goals." According to my view, there is a consciously addressable top-level gatekeeper and automatic lower-level attention controllers. All controllers can make use of inhibition to screen out irrelevant inputs.

Thus, in order to pass into consciousness, the unattended inputs require a certain strength above the threshold of the controller. Inputs that have a strength below that threshold are inhibited.

The controller's threshold has no constant value but is determined by a number of factors. For example, if we are tired we seem to get more easily distracted even by not very strong stimuli. Most important seems to be the current content of the conscious decision procedure. If it contains something that is intrinsically very interesting, almost no other inputs have a chance of intruding into consciousness. An extreme example is a "flow experience" (Csikszentmihalyi, 1975), in which case we do not even seem to notice otherwise strong inputs such as feelings of exhaustion or the passing of time. If the content that currently is in consciousness is not intrinsically very interesting or is not very demanding regarding resources of conscious attention, other contents will intrude. This is described by Hurlburt (1990, p. 112): The student who was found to engage in mindless repeating of words and sentences did so when she was "usually both concentrating on a manual task, such as driving, buttering toast, etc., and engaging in some unknown daydream or Reverie...which may or may not have been related to the sampled words."

Thus, expressed more technically, the likelihood that attentional space used by a current activity will be occupied by competing contents is a negative function of the strength of the current activity and a positive function of the strength of the competing contents. Strength of an activity includes motivational strength as well as an action's strength of captivating attention (cf. Hoffmann's, 1993, idea of a closed anticipatory structure that guides attention and James, 1890, cited above). If there is nothing interesting to turn to, the probability increases that thinking will be flooded by ruminations about some past event, especially a case of failure that left an intention uncompleted. So far, the only discussed attention-controlling mechanism was inhibition. But in contrast to Linville (1996) I assume that another mechanism, which can be referred to as "excitation," plays an important role in the control of conscious attention.

The Auxiliary Function of Volition

We are not necessarily the passive victims of the forces competing over the limited space of conscious attention. This is where volition or action control comes into play. These strategies help to maintain the intended content of attention in the case of strong distractions. They are an auxiliary function to the attention controller working in favor of what currently is intended to be in the focus of attention. One strategy consists of trying to suppress or inhibit whatever content is likely to pass the attention controller. This strategy is referred to as self-control (Kuhl & Beckmann, 1994a). The other strategy, self-regulation, attempts to strengthen what is intended to be in the focus of attention. This can be equated with an excitation of relevant information. Several strategies can be used to achieve the latter: motivation control, trying to increase the incentive value of what one intends to do (Beckmann & Kuhl, 1984); emotion control, trying to set up a state of emotion that supports enactment of the current intention (Kuhl & Schneider, 1987); environmental control, trying to seek out an environment or change the environment in a way that reduces distraction and supports the current intention (see Kuhl & Beckmann, 1994b, for more details).

Self-control tries to restrain attention in a self-disciplined, effortful way that, as we have seen in the discussion of mental control, may only be effective in the short run if no immediate rebound effect occurs. Via self-regulation, involvement in the current activity can become sufficiently high to guarantee that no intrusions will occur during task performance (see Kuhl & Beckmann, 1994b, for an overview of the research supporting these assumptions).

People with a personality disposition toward state orientation who in stressful situations block access to other personal subsystems such as, for instance, their affective sources (Kuhl, 1994), are unable to make use of self-regulation in those situations. They attempt mental control via the self-control strategy. A large body of research has shown that state-oriented individuals suffer from distraction and rumination (see Kuhl & Beckmann, 1994b). Recent neurophysiological findings show that early detection of threatening inputs (at a low level in the hierarchy of attention controllers) fails in state-oriented individuals. Action-oriented individuals, in contrast to state-oriented individuals, identify threatening inputs long before they reach consciousness, as indicated by large reactions in the N100 component of the EEG to words related to negative emotions in a study by Rosahl, Tennigkeit, Kuhl, and Haschke (1993). This allows repression of these inputs long before they can start to compete with what currently is in consciousness. State-oriented individuals, on the other hand, do not seem to identify stimuli as threatening until they are on the verge of consciousness, which leaves them with only the self-restraining control strategies that do not work all that well.

EMPIRICAL EVIDENCE

FINDINGS ON THE ASSUMPTION OF A CONSTANTLY ACTIVE MIND AND THE GATEKEEPER FUNCTIONS

The first study to be reported addresses the basic assumption of a constantly active mind that will be filled with whatever contents are available. In this study (Beckmann, 1994) half of the subjects received failure feedback on all six trials of an alleged intelligence test (failure condition). For the other half of the subjects the intelligence test task was introduced as testing material for a new test. No performance feedback was given in this control condition. The task was followed by a short waiting period (90 s). At the beginning of this waiting period half of the subjects were given specific information about another task that they expected to come up sub-

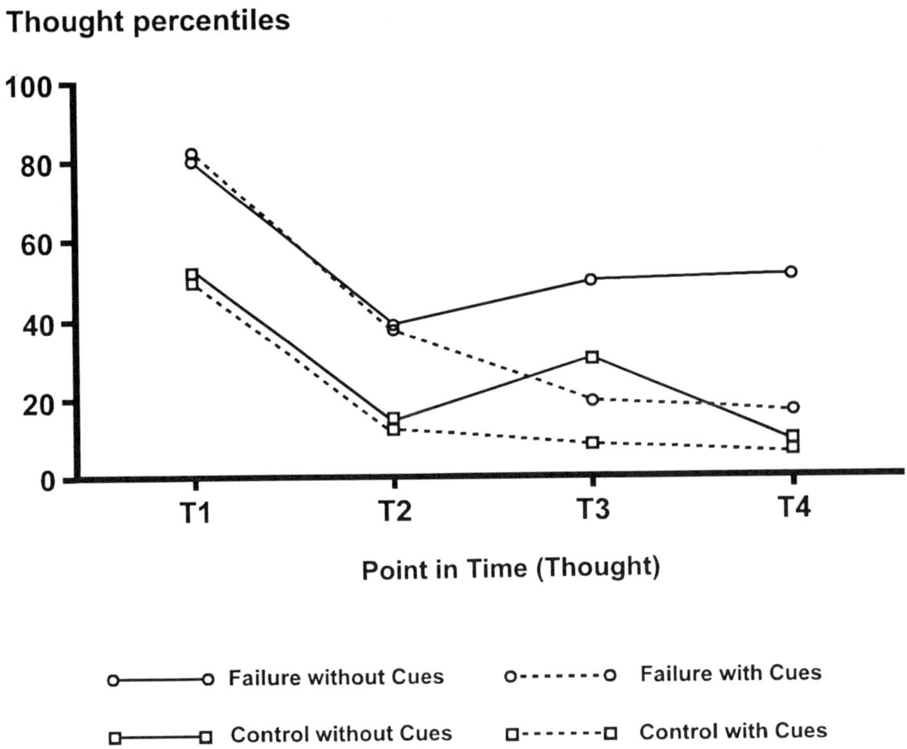

FIGURE 2 Distribution of percentages of thinking related to the past task in the four experimental conditions over the four points in time during the waiting period (taken from Beckmann, 1994).

sequent to the waiting period (conditions with cues). The other half of the subjects were not provided with these cues. After the waiting period was over, the subjects listed the thoughts they had had during the waiting period, writing down their last thought first, then the second to last thought, then the first, and finally the thoughts in between.

As Figure 2 shows, thoughts regarding the intelligence test steadily decreased during the waiting period in the control condition as well as in the failure condition, when the upcoming task was introduced at the beginning of the waiting period (conditions "with cues"). At the end of the waiting period, only a small percentage of the overall stated thoughts related to the intelligence test in these two conditions. In the failure condition without cues for the new task, thoughts about the past failure experience still occupied the thoughts at the end of the waiting period to a large degree. Interestingly, a similar decrease in retrospective thinking is observed in all four conditions for the first two thoughts during the waiting period. Subjects seem to move away from the past task. Whereas this decrease continues in the two conditions with cues for the new task, a rebound of thoughts about the intelligence test occurs if nothing is introduced that subjects could think about.

Thus, space in consciousness that is not occupied by strong content is immediately filled with that content that currently has the highest strength. In the reported experiment the intelligence test was a content low in strength when no performance feedback was given, i.e., in the control conditions. Obviously, in these conditions it was not strong enough to fill consciousness until the end of the break. There were more important matters outside the laboratory that entered subjects' thinking. In the failure condition without cues for the new task, all the outside matters were comparatively less strong than the intelligence test on which the subjects fell short of their standards. Subjects' thinking in this condition was characterized by self-evaluation loops with respect to their performance on the intelligence test. These ruminations managed to hold fast their conscious attention until the end of the waiting period and probably until they were debriefed.

FINDINGS ON THE THREE SOURCES OF INTRUSIONS

Further studies tested the assumptions about the sources of rumination and intrusions. As mentioned above, three sources of intrusions are suggested in the literature: spreading activation, outcome-resultant affect, and motivationally driven activation (incomplete intentions). All three sources should contribute to rumination and the occurrence of intrusions. Motivationally driven activation is assumed to have the highest intrusive potential; that is, incomplete intentions represent strong inputs that are more likely to pass the gatekeeper than contents related to the other two sources. It is assumed that disruption would remove the intrusive potential of spreading activation and the charge from outcome-resultant affect would wane over time, but incomplete intentions would be a persistent source for intrusions for a relatively long period of time.

These assumptions were tested in a number of experiments in which subjects worked on a series of analogy tasks. For every analogy problem they had to select the optimal solution from a list of 12 suggestions. Each analogy task was followed by an instruction that should affect thought flow (Beckmann, 1995). The first experiment contained two types of instructions. One asked subjects to evaluate their performance immediately after receiving failure feedback and to start the next task when they had brought that evaluation to an end. The second instruction asked subjects to count backward by 3 beginning with 999 immediately after they had received the failure feedback. This second instruction should effectively interrupt spreading activation and thus rule it out as an explanation for the perseverance of the respective task in a state of heightened activation. Nevertheless, higher persevering activation of the task and thus higher intrusive potential was expected in this condition than in the task evaluation condition. Subjects in the counting backward condition should be unable to come to terms with their performance and thus be unable to evaluate their performance to find out how they could have done better. Without having found this solution, the task should remain in a state of heightened activation. According to this reasoning, a seemingly paradoxical data pattern was expected, namely, less easy accessibility of tasks in memory about which subjects had thought more.

This assumption was clearly supported. Recognition latencies for words taken from the analogy tasks followed by the task evaluation instruction were significantly longer in a word recognition test than for words taken from the tasks followed by the counting instruction. Thus, as predicted, the latter were much more accessible, that is, more strongly activated in memory, than the former. Because a blocking of thinking about the task interrupted spreading activation, this source cannot account for the perseverance of the contents of the incomplete tasks that was found in this study.

Another experiment tested the contribution of outcome-resultant affect to the perseverance of the contents of incomplete tasks. As stated above, the effects of outcome-resultant affect should wane over time. In the case of failure, the affect is of course confounded with the incompleteness of the task. This is not the case for successes. If outcome-resultant affect is responsible for the perseverance, tasks on which successes and failures were experienced should both be easily accessible in the recognition test. This should not be the case if motivational charge rather than outcome-resultant affect was the most potent source for intrusions. Therefore, the assumption was that shorter recognition latencies should be found for failure tasks on which the postactional evaluation was blocked than for tasks with blocked postactional evaluation on which subjects succeeded. But the data showed a different pattern.

Whereas for the failure trials the results of Study 1 were replicated, recognition latencies in the case of successfully completed tasks with and without postactional evaluation were the same. And contradicting the hypothesis, these recognition latencies did not differ from the ones for the failure tasks with blocked evaluation. Thus, the success tasks, regardless of whether a postactional evaluation occurred or not, were as strongly activated as the failure tasks without a postactional evaluation. Obviously, outcome-resultant affect plays a role in the perseverance of contents.

However, the outcome-resultant affect should not have the potential for generating intrusions over a longer period of time. The general hypothesis stated earlier was that in contrast to outcome-resultant affect, the motivational charge from incomplete intentions constitutes a very persis-

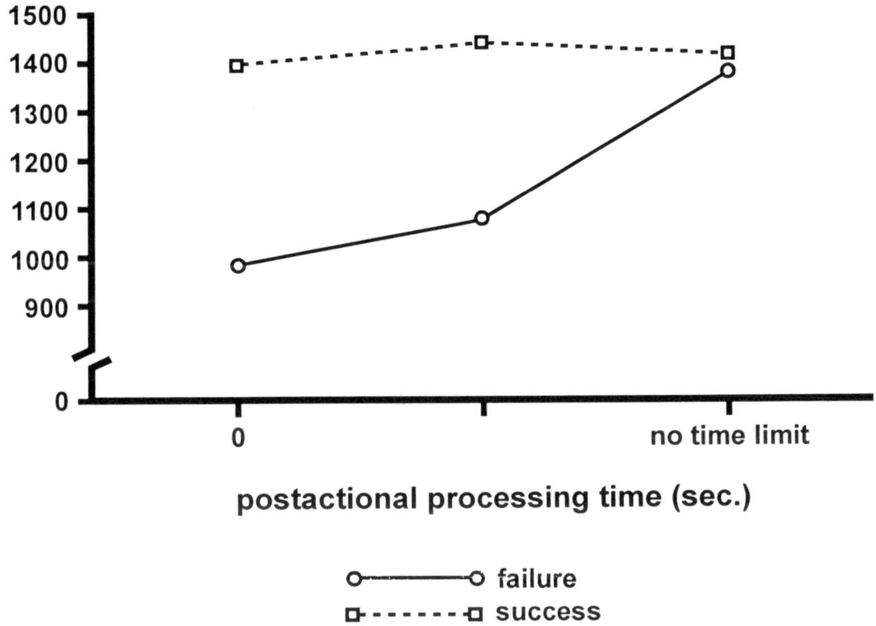

FIGURE 3 Recognition latencies for words from tasks with different opportunities for postactional evaluation (0 = postactional evaluation blocked immediately after feedback; 5 = postactional evaluation blocked after 5 s; no time limit = postactional evaluation could be brought to an end) separated for success and failure tasks.

tent source of intrusions. We all know that the warm glow of success diminishes all too soon, but failing on an important exam can haunt us for a lifetime. Therefore, a third study included a 10-min distractor task between working on the analogy tasks and the recognition test. It was expected that the warm glow of success would fade during the distractor task and make the memory contents related to the successfully completed tasks less easily accessible. If motivational charge is responsible for the perseverance of a high level of activation of the failure tasks, the introduction of the distractor tasks should not affect the accessibility of failure task words. As Figure 3 shows this was indeed the case.

CONCLUSION: GETTING RID OF INTRUSIVE POTENTIAL

Of interest to those who suffer from ruminations and intrusive thoughts is how to get rid of the intrusions. To find an answer to this question I will return to the very first study I mentioned. In that study (Beckmann, 1994) we gave subjects something that could fill their conscious attention, something to look forward to—a new task. This task obviously was interesting enough to capture the subjects' attention and hold it fast—as William James (1890) put it. Relapses into ruminations about the failure experience were prevented by that new task.

The cues for the new task diminished the proportion of retrospective orientation after the failure experience but did not eliminate postactional evaluation. During the break following the performance of the first task subjects addressed their past performance first. But anticipating the performance of another task related to a high-priority goal obviously restricted the postactional evaluation to a low, performance-related level[1] of analysis of the past task rather than provoking self-evaluation. With cues, subjects became occupied to a much lesser degree by self-evaluation and were prevented from being caught in self-evaluation loops. Once people get trapped in such self-evaluation loops, it is much more difficult to deactivate incomplete intentions than when they focus on the low identification level of how they failed. Finding a reason for the failure on that level of task analysis can help to get rid of, at least temporarily, this source for intrusions because one knows now how to deal with the task on a next encounter (cf. Silver, Boon, & Stones, 1983; Tait & Silver, 1989).

However, attending to something interesting that can hold attention fast may not suffice to keep incomplete intentions from intruding forever. Situational cues can easily make us think of the unattained goal again. In some cases strong associations may have built up as a result of prolonged rumination. Martin and Tesser (1996b, p. 194) point out that, if, for example, a woman ruminates about her deceased husband for a long time, she is not likely to stop doing so even when the motivation to ruminate is eliminated. This is because her husband-related thoughts are not only well practiced (e.g., automatic) but are also deeply enmeshed in her network of thoughts. As a result, the thoughts can be easily activated by a variety of environmental cues. This is an example for the possibility that spreading activation can be a source of repeated intrusions over years. However, these intrusions are respondent to situational cues. In contrast, incomplete goals for which the motivation is not eliminated do not require situational cues to intrude into consciousness. Furthermore, they should be less easily replaceable by other contents than the string of thoughts that is merely caused by spreading activation.

Klinger (1977) postulated that to free oneself ultimately from an intention that cannot be completed, one has to go through a disengagement cycle that systematically disengages one from the incentives related to the intentional goal. Singer and Singer (1992) describe how summary memories that may have the form of global self-evaluations with respect to an unattained goal can be "unpacked" and transformed into concrete memories. This procedure establishes a basis "for more extensive guided imagery or for direct exploration of alternatives such as 'possible selves' (Markus & Nurius, 1986) with fantasies that are not initially rule-founded gradually being reshaped in the direction of more realistic possible courses of action" (Bonanno & Singer, 1993, p. 165). This therapeutic approach is very similar to the systematic deactivation that was found to be effective in the study by Beckmann (1994). The general conclusion is that to avoid intrusions, sometimes just interrupting spreading activation may work, and sometimes outcome-resultant affect has to fade. To get rid of the intrusive potential of incomplete intentions and avoid possible interference during the execution of another intention, one may use self-regulation to improve the strength of the task at hand. But to get rid of the intrusive potential of incomplete intentions in the long run, one has to either complete them or, if that is not feasible, disengage from them.

SUMMARY

All kinds of contents can intrude into consciousness. Access to conscious attention is controlled by a gatekeeper (a hierarchy of attention controllers). Only unattended inputs with strengths above the controllers' thresholds can pass on to consciousness. The thresholds of the controllers are partly determined by the strength of the content that is currently in the focus of attention. Two types of auxiliary functions can be employed to avoid intrusions: self control and self-regulation. The coercive type, self-control, can temporarily inhibit intrusions but may evoke even more intrusions in the longer run. Self-regulation can increase the strength of the content that is already in the focus of attention and, thereby, block access of unattended inputs to higher processing levels already at low levels in the hierarchy of attention controllers. The most powerful and persistent sources of intrusions are incomplete intentions. Their intrusive potential can be eliminated by either completion or disengagement from them.

NOTE

1. According to Vallacher & Wegner (1987) actions can be identified at different levels. Whereas the higher levels of action identification reflect the action goal, the lowest level focuses on the execution of the action.

ACKNOWLEDGMENTS

I am grateful to Ralph Hertwig, Leonard L. Martin, Thomas A. Pyszczynski, and the editors for valuable comments on an earlier version of this chapter. The chapter was written while the author was on a Heisenberg scholarship of the German Science Foundation (DFG).

REFERENCES

Atkinson, J. W., & Birch, D. (1970). *A dynamic theory of action.* New York: Wiley.

Barker, R. G. (1963). *The stream of behavior.* New York: Appleton-Century-Crofts.

Beckmann, J. (1991). Erhöhte Konzentration als Folge von Aufmerksamkeitsstörungen: Ein Zwei-Phasen-Modell. In J. Janssen, E. Hahn, & H. Strang (Eds.), *Konzentration und Leistung* (pp. 75–85). Göttingen: Hogrefe.

Beckmann, J. (1994). Ruminative thought and the deactivation of an intention. *Motivation and Emotion, 18,* 317–334.

Beckmann, J. (1995). Unerledigte Absichten und unkontrollierbare Gedanken. In K. Pawlik (Ed.), Bericht über den 39. Kongreß der Deutschen Gesellschaft für Psychologie in Hamburg 1994 (pp. 503–507). Göttingen: Hogrefe.

Beckmann, J. (1996). Self-presentation and the Zeigarnik effect. In T. Gjesme & R. Nygard (Eds.), *Advances in motivation* (pp. 35–45). Oslo: Oslo University Press.

Beckmann, J., & Kuhl, J. (1984). Altering information to gain action control: Functional aspects of human information-processing in decision-making. *Journal of Research in Personality, 18,* 224–237.

Bonanno, G. A., & Singer, J. L. (1993). Controlling one's stream of thought through perceptual and reflective processing. In D. M. Wegner and J. W. Pennebaker (Eds.), *Handbook of mental control* (pp. 149–170). Englewood Cliffs, NJ: Prentice-Hall.

Bühler, K. (1907–1908). Tatsachen und Probleme zu einer Psychologie der Denkvorgänge: I. Über Gedanken. *Archiv für die gesamte Psychologie, 9,* 297–305. II. Über Gedankenzusammenhänge. *Archiv für die gesamte Psychologie, 12,* 1–23. III. Über Gedankenerinnerungen. *Archiv für die gesamte Psychologie, 12,* 24–92.

Cervone, D., Kopp, D. A., Schaumann, L., & Scott, W. D. (1994). Mood, self-efficacy, and performance standards: Lower moods induce higher standards for performance. *Journal of Personality and Social Psychology, 67,* 499–512.

Clark, L. F. (1996). Restructuring and realigning mental models: Rumination as guides to cognitive home repair. In R. S. Wyer (Ed.), *Advances in Social Cognition* (Vol. IX, pp. 63–72). Mahwah, NJ: Erlbaum.

Crick, F., & Koch, C. (1995). Are we aware of neural activity in primary visual cortex? *Nature, 375,* 121–123.

Csikszentmihalyi, M. (1975). *Beyond boredom and anxiety.* San Francisco: Jossey-Bass.

Damasio, A. R. (1995). Knowing how, knowing where. *Nature, 375,* 106–107.

Freud, S. (1949). Instincts and their vicissitudes. In *Collected papers* (Vol. 4). New York: Basic Books. (Original work published 1915.)

Glass, A. L., Holyoak, K. J., & Santa, J. L. (1979). *Cognition.* Reading, MA: Addison-Wesley.

Gray, J. A. (1982). *The neurophysiology of anxiety.* New York: Oxford University Press.

Heckhausen, H. (1991). *Motivation and action.* Berlin: Springer.

Herrmann, C., & Wortman, C. B.(1985). Action control and the coping process. In J. Kuhl & J. Beckmann (Eds.), *Action control: From cognition to behavior* (pp. 151–180). Berlin: Springer.

Hoffmann, J. (1993). Vorhersage und Erkenntnis. Die Funktion von Antizipationen in der menschlichen Verhaltenssteuerung und Wahrnehmung. Göttingen: Hogrefe.

Horowitz, M. J. (1990). A model of mourning: Change in schemas of self and other. *Journal of the American Psychoanalytic Association, 38,* 297–324.

Hurlburt, R. T. (1990). *People thinking*. New York: Plenum.

James, W. (1890). *The principles of psychology*. New York: Holt.

Kelly, A. E., & Kahn, J. H. (1994). Effects of suppression of personal intrusive thoughts. *Journal of Personality and Social Psychology, 66*, 998–1006.

King, L. A., & Pennebaker, J. W. (1996). Thinking about goals, glue, and the meaning of life. In R. S. Wyer (Ed.), *Advances in social cognition* (Vol. IX, pp. 97–106). Mahwah, NJ: Erlbaum.

Klinger, E. (1975). Consequences of commitment to and disengagement from incentives. *Psychological Review, 82*, 1–25.

Klinger, E. (1977). *Meaning and void. Inner experiences and the incentives in people's lives*. Minneapolis: University of Minnesota Press.

Klinger, E., Barta, S. G., & Maxeiner, M. E. (1980). Motivational correlates of thought content frequency and commitment. *Journal of Personality and Social Psychology, 39*, 1222–1237.

Kuhl, J. (1981). Motivational and functional helplessness: The moderating effect of state versus action orientation. *Journal of Personality and Social Psychology, 40*, 155–170.

Kuhl, J. (1984). Volitional aspects of achievement motivation and learned helplessness: Toward a comprehensive theory of action control. In B. A. Maher (Ed.), *Progress in experimental personality research* (pp. 99–171). New York: Academic Press.

Kuhl, J. (1994). A theory of action and state orientations. In J. Kuhl & J. Beckmann (Eds.), *Volition and personality. Action versus state orientation* (pp. 9–46). Seattle: Hogrefe & Huber.

Kuhl, J., & Beckmann, J. (1994a). Alienation. Ignoring one's preferences. In J. Kuhl & J. Beckmann (Eds.), *Volition and personality. Action- and state of orientation* (pp. 375–390). Seattle: Hogrefe & Huber.

Kuhl, J., & Beckmann, J. (Eds.) (1994b). *Volition and personality. Action versus state orientation*. Seattle: Hogrefe & Huber.

Kuhl, J., & Helle, P. (1994). Motivational and volitional determinants of depression: The degenerated intention hypothesis. In J. Kuhl & J. Beckmann (Eds.), *Volition and personality. Action versus state orientation* (pp. 283–296). Seattle: Hogrefe & Huber.

Kuhl, J., & Schneider, W. (1987). Emotion control and self-regulation in children: Avoidance of sadness-inducing stimuli while resisting temptation. Unpublished manuscript, Max-Planck-Institute for Psychological Research, Munich.

Linville, P. (1996). Attention inhibition: Does it underlie ruminative thought? In R. S. Wyer (Ed.), *Advances in social cognition* (Vol. IX, pp. 121–133). Mahwah, NJ: Erlbaum.

Martin, L. L., & Tesser, A. (1989). Toward a motivational structural theory of ruminative thought. In J. S. Uleman & J. A. Bargh (Eds.), *Unintended thought* (pp. 306–326). New York: Guilford Press.

Martin, L. L., & Tesser, A. (1996a). Some ruminative thoughts. In R. S. Wyer (Ed.), *Advances in social cognition* (Vol. IX, pp. 1–47). Mahwah, NJ: Erlbaum.

Martin, L. L., & Tesser, A. (1996b). Clarifying our thoughts. In R. S. Wyer (Ed.), *Advances in social cognition* (Vol. IX, pp. 189–208). Mahwah, NJ: Erlbaum.

McClelland, D. C., Atkinson, J. W., Clark, R. A., & Lowell, E. L. (1953). *The achievement motive*. New York: Appleton-Century-Crofts.

Nisbett, R. E. (1972). Hunger, obesity, and the ventromedial hypothalamus. *Psychological Review, 79*, 433–453.

Nolen-Hoeksema, S. (1996). Chewing the cud and other ruminations. In R. S. Wyer (Ed.), *Advances in social cognition* (Vol. IX, pp. 135–144). Mahwah, NJ: Erlbaum.

Ovsiankina, M. (1928). Die Wiederaufnahme unterbrochener Handlungen. *Psychologische Forschung, 11*, 302–397.

Pyszczynski, T., & Greenberg, J. (1987). Self-regulatory perseveration and the depressive self-focusing style: A self-awareness theory of reactive depression. *Psychological Bulletin, 102*, 122–138.

Rosahl, S. K., Tennigkeit, M., Kuhl, J., & Haschke, R. (1993). Handlungskontrolle und langsame Hirnpotentiale: Untersuchungen zum Einfluß subjektiv kritischer Wörter. *Zeitschrift für Medizinische Psychologie, 2,* 172–180.
Silver, R. L., Boon, C., & Stones, M. H. (1983). Searching for meaning in misfortune: Making sense of incest. *Journal of Social Issues, 39,* 81–102.
Singer, J. A., & Singer, J. L. (1992). Transference in psychotherapy and daily life: Implications of current memory and social cognition research. In D. Barron, M. Eagle, & D. Wolitzky (Eds.), *The interface of psychoanalysis and psychology* (pp. 516–538). Washington, DC: American Psychological Association.
Singer, J. L. (1988). Sampling ongoing consciousness and emotional experience. Implications for health. In M. J. Horowitz (Ed.), *Psychodynamics and cognition* (pp. 297–346). Chicago: University of Chicago Press.
Tait, R., & Silver, R. (1989). Coming to terms with major negative life events. In J. S. Uleman & J. A. Bargh (Eds.), *Unintended thought* (pp. 351–382). New York: Guilford.
Vallacher, R. R., & Wegner, D. M. (1987). What do people think they're doing? Action identification and human behavior. *Psychological Review, 94,* 3–15.
Wegner, D. M., & Gold, D. B. (1995). Fanning old flames: Emotional and cognitive effects of suppression of thoughts of a past relationship. *Journal of Personality and Social Psychology, 68,* 782–792.
Wegner, D. M., & Pennebaker, J. W. (1993). Changing our minds: An introduction to mental control. In D. M. Wegner & J. W. Pennebaker (Eds.), *Handbook of mental control* (pp. 1–12). Englewood Cliffs, NJ: Prentice-Hall.
Wegner, D. M., Schneider, D. J., Carter, S. R., & White, T. L. (1987). Paradoxical effects of thought suppression. *Journal of Personality and Social Psychology, 47,* 237–252.
Weiner, B. (1985). An attributional theory of achievement motivation and emotion. *Psychological Review, 92,* 548–573.
Zeigarnik, B. (1927). Über das Behalten von erledigten und unerledigten Handlungen. *Psychologische Forschung, 9,* 1–85.

CHAPTER 11

DECISION MAKING AND ACTION

THE SEARCH FOR A DOMINANCE STRUCTURE

HENRY MONTGOMERY

INTRODUCTION

There is a close link between decision making and action. By making a decision a person commits herself to act in a certain way. However, in behavioral decision research, the link between decision making and action is largely neglected. The reason may be that decision making primarily is seen as a question of forming preferences, i.e., a question of finding the better or best alternative. However, in contrast to decisions preferences are not necessarily linked to actions. An individual may prefer alternative *x* to alternative *y* without committing herself to any action. That is, the alternatives in preferences need not be action alternatives (e.g., preferences among articles of consumption), which always is true in a decision situation (e.g., in decisions to buy an article of consumption).

As a consequence of a large number of empirical findings, the presumed synonymy between preferences and decisions or choices has become problematic. First, it has been found that preferences in a nonchoice context may be inconsistent with people's choices (Lichtenstein & Slovic, 1971;

HENRY MONTGOMERY • Department of Psychology, Stockholm University, S-10691 Stockholm, Sweden. E-mail hmy@psychology.su.se

Personal Control in Action, edited by Kofta et al., Plenum Press, New York, 1998.

Slovic & Lichtenstein, 1983, Tversky, Sattah, & Slovic, 1988). Second, it has been shown that people's preferences may be practically unrelated to people's actions (Rohrman & Borcherding, 1988; Lindberg, Gärling, & Montgomery, 1990; Montgomery, 1993). That is, people do not necessarily enact an alternative that they prefer. The reason may be that the preference has been formed without making a decision to enact the preferred alternative.

The research findings cited above emphasize the necessity to distinguish between preferences and decisions. Below, a decision making theory—search for dominance structure (SDS) theory (Montgomery, 1983, 1989)—is presented that highlights this distinction, as well as how predecisonal processes prepare the decision maker for action. The latter feature of the theory contrasts with assumptions in other theories of decision making and action control. After having presented SDS theory, I will review empirical data that bear on the validity of the theory. Thereafter, I will compare SDS theory with other approaches to decision making that invite discussion of how SDS be developed or changed. Finally, I will use the literature reviewed in this article as a platform for discussing relationships between decision making and action.

SDS THEORY

Decision Making Phases

SDS theory describes the cognitive process that starts when an individual faces a decision conflict between a number of alternatives and that ends when a decision is made. Each alternative is experienced in terms of its attractiveness on a number of subjectively defined dimensions or attributes. The key idea in the theory is that the decision maker attempts to structure and restructure given information about attributes in such a way that one alternative becomes the self-evident choice. More precisely, the decision maker attempts to find a dominance structure, i.e., a cognitive structure in which the to-be-chosen alternative dominates other alternatives on relevant attributes. In a dominance structure the to-be-chosen alternative has at least one clear advantage to other alternatives, and all disadvantages, if any, of that alternative are neutralized or deemphasized.

The search for a dominance structure is assumed to go through four phases, viz., pre-editing, finding a promising alternative, dominance testing, and dominance structuring. Figure 1 shows how the process is organized in terms of the four phases.

In the pre-editing phase, which typically occurs early in the decision process, the decision maker attempts to simplify the decision problem by

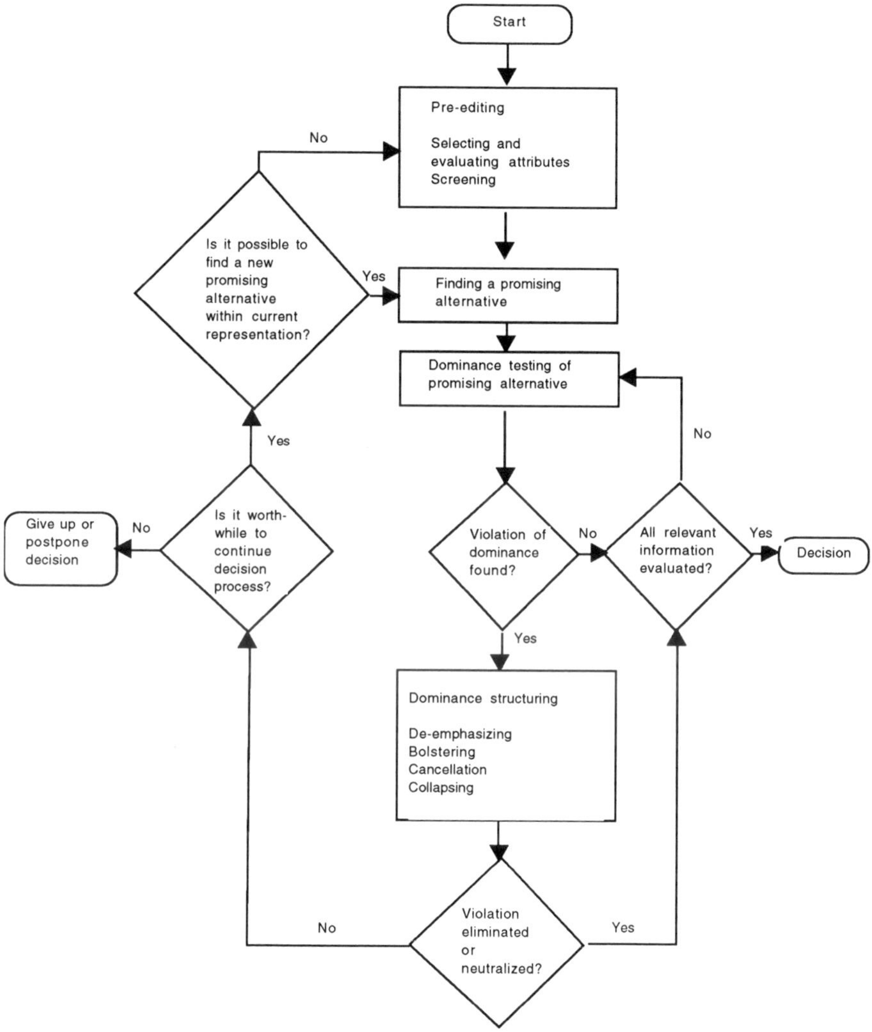

FIGURE 1 The search for a dominance structure theory of decision making.

selecting those alternatives and attributes that should be included in the representation of the decision situation.

In the finding-a-promising-alternative phase the decision maker finds a candidate for his or her final choice. An alternative that is more attractive than other alternatives on an important attribute may be selected as a promising alternative. When a promising alternative has been found the decision maker has formed a preference, albeit a temporary one, for a particular alternative. The question now arises as to whether the decision maker can decide to choose this alternative. This question is dealt with in subsequent phases of the decision making process.

The dominance testing phase implies that the decision maker tests whether a promising alternative dominates the other alternatives. These tests could be more or less systematic or exhaustive. If the promising alternative is found to be dominant, it is chosen and the decision process ends.

If, on the other hand, a violation of dominance is found, the decision maker continues to the dominance structuring phase. In this phase the decision maker attempts to neutralize or counterbalance the disadvantage(s) found for the promising alternative. These attempts are based on various operations. The decision maker may de-emphasize a disadvantage by arguing that the probability of the disadvantage is very low and that it could be controlled or avoided in one way or another. Another possibility is to bolster the advantages of the promising alternative and in this way indirectly de-emphasize the disadvantages. In the cancellation operation the decision maker attempts to find dominance by canceling a disadvantage by relating it to an advantage that has some natural connection to the disadvantage in question. Finally, the decision maker may find a dominance structure by collapsing two or more attributes into a new, more comprehensive attribute.

If the decision maker fails to find a dominance structure he or she may go back to a previous phase and make a new start in the search for dominance or he or she may postpone the decision, if possible.

SDS Theory and Action

To decide is to commit oneself to follow a line of action. The commitment means that the decision maker is ready to defend the decision and stick to it in the face of adverse circumstances. This means that there will be a certain degree of consistency in the decision maker's pattern of behavior. It may be speculated that such a consistency will promote the individual's possibility to reach his or her long-term goals even if the defence of the decision may involve a biased view of the external world.

This view of decision making suggests that it will be important for the individual in his or her predecisional processes to build up a basis that may promote postdecisional commitment. In line with this suggestion, Montgomery (1989) assumed that SDS theory portrays the decision-making process as a preparation for action. The search for a dominance structure implies that the decision maker prepares himself or herself for coping with problems that may arise when implementing a tentatively chosen alternative. In other words, a dominance structure implies that the decision maker has access to counterarguments to any drawbacks of the chosen alternative that have been considered in the decision making process. In this way, the decision maker will have resources to maintain his or her commitment to the chosen line of action.

SDS THEORY AND MIND-SETS

SDS theory deviates from other theories that assume that predecisional processes involve a careful and impartial weighing of pros and cons of different choice alternatives (Edwards, 1954; Festinger, 1957; Gollwitzer, Heckhausen, & Ratajczak, 1990). In a series of recent papers, Gollwitzer and his associates argued that predecisional processes are characterized by a deliberative mind-set, which is expected to foster a relatively evenhanded and accurate appraisal of evidence (e.g., Gollitzer et al., 1990; Taylor & Gollitzer, 1996). These theorists offer a contrasting view of the postdecisional phase, where people plan to implement a chosen alternative. This phase is characterized by an implemental mind-set, in which the individual musters motivation, resources, and cognition that favor the achievement of chosen goals.

SDS theory's view of predecisional processes is similar to mind-set theory's view of postdecisional processes. Dominance structuring may be seen as an implemental activity. The decision maker "runs" the tentatively chosen alternative and looks for possibilities of solving problems associated with its implementation. However, in contrast to mind-set theory the implemental activities in dominance structuring are provisional. Their purpose is not purely implemental but also concerned with testing the feasibility of the tentatively chosen alternative, which occurs in the dominance-testing phase. That is, SDS theory states that if the decision maker does not succeed in constructing a dominance structure he or she abandons the promising alternative. In this way, the search for a dominance structure affords a "window of realism" (Taylor & Gollwitzer, 1996) the size of which is negatively related to the decision maker's motivation to stick to the promising alternative.

The distinction between deliberative and implemental mind-sets is strongly supported by empirical data (Gollwitzer, 1990). The same is true for the similar distinction between state and action orientation (Kuhl, 1992). However, the support for the assumption that predecisional processes are primarily deliberative is indirect and meagre. For example, Taylor and Gollwitzer (1996) asked subjects to report their recent thoughts related to an unsolved personal problem and found that subjects divided their attention about equally between positive and negative consequences of a change decision. Obviously, the request to think of an unsolved problem may have stimulated subjects to answer in a way that is consonant with this request, for example, by listing an equal amount of positive and negative consequences. Moreover, subjects' sensitivity to the demand characteristics of their task may have been further accentuated by the fact that subjects were asked to make retrospective rather than concurrent reports on their thoughts (Ericsson & Simon, 1980). In the following, we will review data that may give a clearer picture of the nature of predecisional processes and their compatibility with SDS theory and, hence, the notion that decision making can be seen as preparation for action.

EMPIRICAL VALIDITY OF SDS THEORY

I will now discuss a body of research findings that are all related to, or compatible with, the key idea of SDS theory, viz., the notion of decision making as a search for a "good" structure that makes one alternative the self-evident choice. Some of this research deals with limited aspects of the decision making process, whereas other findings highlight the decision process as a whole. The research findings also vary with respect to how explicitly they assume that a "good" decision making structure is a dominance structure. The review includes research that clearly supports SDS theory but also data that are less supportive or even appear to be at odds with the theory.

PREEDITING

There is ample evidence for the hypothesis that decision makers attempt to simplify a given decision problem by focusing on a limited subset of attributes (Svenson, 1979), by rounding off information about attribute levels (Kahneman & Tversky, 1979), and by screening out alternatives that fall short on important attributes (Beach, 1990). However, these research findings belong to those that illustrate a limited aspect of SDS theory, and that also support other decision-making models such as prospect theory (Kahneman & Tversky, 1979 and image theory (Beach, 1990).

FINDING AND DEFENDING A PROMISING ALTERNATIVE

Research that has examined decision making as a process across time has shown that before an alternative is definitely chosen it draws more attention than other alternatives and is judged as more and more attractive as compared with its competing alternatives (Dahlstrand & Montgomery, 1984; Lewicka, 1997; Montgomery & Svenson, 1989; Sedek, Kofta, & Tyszka, 1993). The tendency to an increasing attractiveness gap between chosen and nonchosen alternatives as time proceeds has been demon-

strated in a number of additional experimental studies (Beckmann & Kuhl, 1984; Mann, Janis, & Chaplin, 1969; Tyszka & Wielochovski, 1991). The same phenomenon has also been found in research on decision making in naturalistic contexts such as career decisions (Soelberg, 1967), various decisions in people's private lives (Blom Kemdal & Montgomery, 1997), residential choices (Lindberg, Gärling, & Montgomery, 1990), and in a case study of a military decision (Montgomery, 1997).

It seems safe to conclude that predecisional processes often deviate from the picture of an impartial decision maker who carefully weighs pros against cons before making his or her decision. On the contrary, we are faced with the picture of a deeply committed decision maker who attempts to prove that a particular alternative definitely is better than its competing alternatives. The validity of this picture is further substantiated in studies of the decision-making processes of depressed people (Lewicka, 1990) and persons who have undergone learned helplessness training (Sedek, Kofta, & Tyszka, 1993). In line with the assumption that persons in this precondition lack cognitive resources or motivation to build up support for a to-be-chosen alternative, it was found that they examined choice alternatives in a more balanced and impartial manner than was true for nondepressed or no-helplessness training control subjects (Lewicka, 1997; Sedek, Kofta, & Tyszka, 1993).

Existence of Dominance Structures

The fact that the decision maker manages to increase the support for the chosen alternative does not necessarily mean that the alternative dominates its rivals. Montgomery (1994), however, found strict dominance or close to strict dominance for the chosen alternative in a great majority of think-aloud protocols collected in a previous study of housing choices (Montgomery & Svenson, 1989). In the same vein, Lindberg, Gärling, and Montgomery (1989a) found that when information was missing about choice alternatives, subjects tended to bolster (enhance) the value of inferred aspects of the finally chosen alternative in such a way that more than 90% of the inferences supported or did not speak against the finally chosen alternative. Other studies have identified dominance structures in postdecisional justifications in a political discourse (Axelrod, 1976; Biel & Montgomery, 1986; Gallhofer & Saris, 1989), and in justifications of professorial appointments (Montgomery & Hemlin, 1991).

Dominance-Structuring Operations

Many of the process tracing studies that concerned the validity of SDS theory did not closely examine the particular operations that led to the representation supporting the finally chosen alternative. However, the overall pattern in the think-aloud protocols analyzed by Montgomery and Svenson (1989) suggests that subjects would rather de-emphasize the value of nonchosen alternatives than bolster the value of the chosen alternative. On the other hand, rating data collected in other studies suggest the opposite pattern, i.e., more bolstering than de-emphasizing (Lewicka, 1997; Sedek, Kofta, & Tyszka, 1993), as also was true in Lindberg et al.'s study (1989a) of inferences of missing information about choice alternatives. Lindberg et al.'s (1990) naturalistic field study (interviews) of persons looking for a new home evidenced a combined usage of bolstering and de-emphasizing operations. The data suggested that in order to facilitate the choice of a new home, attributes favoring the new dwelling were seen as more important (bolstering), whereas attributes favoring the old dwelling were perceived as less important (de-emphasizing).

In a reanalysis of the think-aloud data previously analyzed by Montgomery and Svenson (1989) on choices between homes Montgomery (1994) found support for the cancellation operation (canceling disadvantages by relating them to advantages that have some natural connection with the disadvantage). For example, a long traveling time to downtown (disadvantage) was seen as providing an opportunity for to relax during the journey (advantage). The realism of the collapsing operation (collapsing of two or more attributes to a more comprehensive attribute) is supported by studies showing that housing choices could be predicted from the respondents' beliefs about how the alternatives relate to various general life values such as freedom and security (e.g., Lindberg, Gärling, & Montgomery, 1988; 1989c). We also found that at least 50% of the choice situations were associated with dominance structures on the level of life values (e.g., a chosen alternative is seen as better than or equal to its competitors with respect to freedom, security, family, etc.), whereas on the level of attributes (e.g., size, location, standard) pure dominance structures were rare (Garvill, Gärling, Lindberg, & Montgomery, 1991). The fact that subjects' choices appear to have been guided by life values suggests that dominance structures on this level may have facilitated the respondents' choices.

It may be concluded that there exists empirical support for each of the four dominance-structuring operations (i.e., de-emphasizing, bolstering, cancellation, and collapsing). In addition, recent evidence suggests that dominance structures may also be attained by changing the external the situation, i.e., with a more direct link to overt action than is assumed in the dominance structuring operations described above. Montgomery (1993) reported data showing that decision makers may not accept negative information about a promising alternative, but instead figure out actions that will improve the alternative. Other studies have shown that the individual may also intervene in the external world before the decision to increase the support for a promising alternative (Blom, Kemdal, & Montgomery, 1997; Willén, 1994).

Preferences versus Choices

SDS theory assumes that our preferences should be backed up more by dominance structuring when we anticipate a decision and engage in the search of support for the promising alternative. Hence, SDS theory implies that options should be less differentiated in attractiveness with no requirements to choose as compared to a situation where subjects are to make a choice between the same options. This prediction has been only partially validated. It is supported by think-aloud data in terms of an evaluation index that was calculated for each alternative from the number of positive and negative evaluations of the alternative on specific attributes (Montgomery, Selart, Gärling, & Lindberg, 1994; Selart, Montgomery, Romanus, & Gärling, 1994) whereas ratings of specific attributes (e.g., size or cost of housing alternatives) and more general values (life values) associated with the options (e. g, health or freedom) gave mixed support (Garvill, Gärling, Lindberg, & Montgomery, 1991; Lindberg, Gärling, & Montgomery, 1989b). Attractiveness on the level of life value is assumed to result from the collapsing operation since life values are assumed to integrate attractiveness on specific attributes. In line with our prediction, we found a greater mean difference between life value ratings of chosen and nonchosen options than between life value ratings of preferred and nonpreferred options (preference ratings). However, there was no difference between the two tasks with respect to the proportion of cases where the chosen or preferred alternative was dominant on the level of life values (Garvill et al., 1991). On the other hand, approximately 50% of the choice situations included an alternative that was already dominant on the level-of-life values before subjects were asked to make a choice. Evidently, in these cases there was no need to restructure information in order to attain dominance, but of course there are still 50% of the choice situations that have a nondominant structure.

In a series of studies, SDS theory was used as a point of departure for elucidating the nature of the so called prominence effect (Montgomery, Gärling, Lindberg, & Selart, 1990; Montgomery, Selart, Gärling, & Lindberg, 1994). This effect concerns the case where a choice has to be made between two alternatives that are described on two attributes (e.g., effectiveness and painfulness of two medical treatments). The effect implies that the more important attribute (e.g., effectiveness) looms larger in the choice than in a task where subjects have matched the two alternatives to be equally attractive. That is, in choices between two options judged as equally attractive, subjects tend to choose the option that is superior on the more important attribute (e.g., a treatment that is more effective but also more painful) (Slovic, 1975; Tversky, Sattah, & Slovic, 1988). SDS theory predicts that in the choice situation subjects will attempt to restructure the given alternative in such a way that one of the alternatives will be seen as clearly better. In the present case this could mean that subjects, in order to attain dominance, emphasize differences between alternatives on the prominent attribute, and de-emphasize differences on the nonprominent attribute. This prediction was indeed confirmed in think-aloud data collected from choices between two alternatives as compared to think-aloud data from preference judgments of the same alternative with no choice requirement (Montgomery et al., 1994). It was also predicted from SDS theory that there would be no prominence effect for preference judgments since in this task subjects would not need to restructure the alternatives in order to be able to make a choice. However, also in preference judgments subjects tended to emphasize the prominent attribute more than they did in the matching task (see also Fischer & Hawkins, 1993; Selart, 1996; Selart et al., 1994). Obviously, SDS theory does not seem able to explain the prominence effect, although the theory itself was supported by the think aloud data obtained for choices.

Dominance Violations and Dominance Structuring

A straightforward prediction from SDS theory is that if a promising alternative does not dominate a competing alternative then the decision maker will restructure available information in order to attain dominance. If, on the other hand, the promising alternative is dominant there is no reason to restructure the information. In Garvill et al.'s (1991) study these predictions were only partially borne out when ratings of levels of life values associated with choice housing alternatives were compared between dominated and nondominated choice sets. In line with the predictions it was found that in the nondominated choice sets subjects tended to increase the differentiation between the alternatives when making the choice, whereas there was no such tendency in the dominated choice sets. In a recent study of real-life decision processes concerning career choices (Svenson & Hill, 1997), it was found that subjects who experienced goal conflicts (i. e., dominance violations) tended to reverse the conflict into an advantage favoring the chosen alternative. In line with SDS theory, it can be concluded that decision makers encountering a dominance violation may increase the differential support for the to-be-chosen alternative. However, the resulting cognitive structure may either fall short of strict dominance or be changed more than is needed to attain dominance.

Other studies have demonstrated that decision making strategies seem to be sensitive to dominance structures or close-to dominance structures in given information. That is, when one option dominates another one, subjects tend to choose the former rather than a third alternative that is not dominant (Ariely & Wallsten, 1995; Huber, Payne & Puto, 1982; Tyszka, 1980), and they are less interested in looking for additional options or additional information about the given options (Bockenholt, Albert, Aschenbrenner, & Schmalhofer, 1991; Shafir, Simonson, & Tversky, 1993). Thus, in line with SDS theory, it appears that subjects do less in order to make a decision when dominance is at hand. Also in line with SDS theory, Ariely and Wallsten (1995) reported data that are compatible with the notion that subjects restructure (or categorize) close-to-dominance as being equivalent to dominance. Ariely and Wallsten coined the term "subjective dominance" to denote how decision makers conceive of close-to-dominance.

DEVELOPING AND CONSTRAINING SDS THEORY: A COMPARISON WITH OTHER APPROACHES TO DECISION MAKING

By and large, it appears that SDS theory is congruent with process data on human decision making. In particular, many observations are in line with the key idea in the model that the decision maker attempts to structure and restructure given information about attributes in such a way that one alternative becomes the self-evident choice. Data also support the existence of decision making stages and operations that are largely in line with the model. Apparently, the findings reviewed above are sufficiently encouraging to justify using SDS theory as a platform for further theory development on the nature of human decision making. However, the fact that some predictions from the model have been unsuccessful invites thinking about how the model may be developed or changed. Below I discuss two approaches to decision making that invite a discussion of how SDS theory may be modified or constrained.

Dominance Structuring or Differentiation?

The concept of dominance is central in the two final stages of SDS theory. In the dominance testing phase the decision maker will react differently depending on whether he or she finds dominance or not. In the dominance structuring phase he or she attempts to attain dominance. However, as noted above, in both contexts empirical data suggest that subjects do not make a clear distinction between dominance and what may be interpreted as close-to-dominance. Moreover, it might be conjectured that in situations when a dominating alternative is only marginally better than its rivals, decision makers want to increase the differentiation between the alternatives in order to have a safety margin against preference reversals in the postdecision future (Svenson, 1992). In other words, it may be questioned whether the attainment of a dominance structure is a necessary and sufficient condition for getting to the decision point. Still, dominance as such seems to be an important decision criterion also in cases when one might expect the decision maker to look for more information before making the final decision (Bockenholt, Albert, Aschenbrenner, & Schmalhofer, 1991; Shafir, Simonson, & Tversky, 1993).

In his differention and consolidation theory of decision making (Diff Con theory), Svenson (1992, 1996) suggested that when a sufficiently high degree of differentiation, rather than dominance, between a chosen and nonchosen alternative is at hand, then the decision maker is ready to make a decision. The rationale for this decision criterion is to choose an alternative that can withstand threats that may appear in the postdecision future. Differentiation may be achieved by three processes, viz., holistic differentiation (which includes matching to previous prototypical decision situations), process differentiation (using decision rules that support the decision), and structural differentiation (which includes changes in the representation of attractiveness, attribute importance, facts, or the decision problem as a whole). Diff Con theory posits that these subprocesses continue after the decision to consolidate the support for the chosen alternative.

Diff Con theory implies that dominance is neither a sufficient nor a necessary decision criterion. The notion of sufficient differentiation offers a more flexible, but also a more loosely defined, decision criterion. However, the problems with validating predictions from SDS theory regarding the role of dominance could be handled, I think, by introducing subjective dominance, rather than strict dominance as the decision criterion. Ariely and Wallsten (1995) define subjective dominance as "a perceived relationship in which a certain difference on some dimension, although noticeable, is considered unimportant and the values on this dimension are considered to be subjectively equal, while simultaneously all other dimensions are clearly perceived as better for one of the items" (p. 224). Subjective dominance differs from strict dominance by excluding cases where a strictly dominating alternative is only slightly better than its competitors on favorable attributes. In this situation the decision maker will view the alternatives as being practically the same. Subjective dominance also differs from strict dominance by including cases when one alternative has a decisive advantage, although it is not strictly dominant. However, the notion of subjective dominance implies that SDS theory comes closer to Diff Con theory inasmuch as a more vaguely defined decision criterion is introduced. That is, the well defined notion of dominance is replaced by the less well defined notion of subjective dominance.

There are a number of reasons for keeping (subjective) dominance as a decision criterion. First, as discussed above, empirical studies show that decision makers are very sensitive to dominance relations. Second, as also discussed above, people appear to have access to dominance structures in a variety of situations. Third, and most important, having access to a dominance structure implies that the decision maker has built up a cognitive basis for acting in line with the decision, i.e., to implement the decision. This is because a dominance structure implies that a counterargument is available against any drawback that may be associated with the chosen alternative in the decision maker's representation of the decision problem. Hence, if a drawback that has been taken into account in a dominance structure emerges after the decision is made, the decision maker will be able to defend his or her decision and continue implementing it (Montgomery, 1989). Svenson (1992) himself assumes that an important aim of differentiation is to defend the decision against future threats. Obviously, this goal is facilitated by having access to a dominance structure in the postdecision phase.

Another important difference between SDS theory and Diff Con theory, besides the role of dominance, is that the former model stresses that differentiation is accomplished by a kind of structuring, i.e., dominance structuring, whereas Diff Con theory regards structuring as one of several possible ways of attaining differentiation. SDS theory regards the other types of differentiation as subordinate to structuring. By using different decision rules (rule differentiation) the decision maker changes his or her representation of the decision situation (e.g., using the conjunctive rule means that attribute levels are classified as acceptable or not), which in turn is equivalent to or facilitates dominance structuring. Similarly, what Svenson (1992, p. 154) calls holistic differentiation leads either to a decision or to the finding of a promising alternative, which in turn may provide an input to the dominance structuring phase.

Further research is needed to evaluate the validity of the two theories on these discrepant points.

SDS Theory and Naturalistic Decision Making

SDS theory starts out from a general model of human decision making that for many years has been prevalent in behavioral decision-making research. In recent years doubts have been raised about the applicability of this model to decision making in a naturalistic context (e.g., Klein, Orasanu, Calderwood, & Zsambok, 1993). The criticism has concerned the following assumptions: (1) that decision making involves a choice among several options, (2) that choice is equivalent to conflict resolution, (3) that decision problems are represented in terms of attributes or dimensions, and (4) that the description of decision making is restricted to mental processes and structures. An alternative picture has emerged in which decision making is seen as (1) typically involving just one option, which has to be accepted or not (Beach & Lipshitz, 1993), (2) being largely automatic and being based on recognition of prototypical choice situations (Klein, 1993a), (3) involving attempts to use available information to form coherent stories or scenarios (Beach, 1990; Cohen, Freeman, & Wolf, 1996; Pennington & Hastie, 1993), and (4) taking place in a dynamic environment with which the decision maker interacts (Brehmer, 1990; Orasanu & Connoly, 1993, Rasmussen, 1993). This picture simultaneously plays down the idea of decision making as conflict resolution between alternative courses of action and the idea that decision making can be studied under well controlled laboratory conditions.

What are the implications of this picture of naturalistic decision making for SDS theory? Admittedly, in previous research I have overestimated the role of conflict resolution in decision making. Decisions do not differ from preference judgments in this respect as much as I thought. Our own research (e.g., Garvill, Gärling, Lindberg, & Montgomery, 1991; Montgomery, 1994) illustrates that people often have access to ready-made cognitive structures that relieve them from the burden of solving conflicts. On the other hand, SDS theory definitely deals with conflict resolution. However, even if it is true that human decision making very often does not involve conflict resolution, in the sense assumed by researchers in behavioral decision making, these situations still exist and people's decisions in these situations may be of great importance for themselves and for other people. Actually, researchers advocating a naturalistic approach to decision making have reserved a niche for SDS theory in situations involving conflicts between different goals (Cohen, 1993; Klein, 1993b; Lipshitz, 1993).

The holistic and dynamic aspects of human decision making , which could be difficult to study in the laboratory, definitely pose a challenge to SDS theory. However, I regard SDS theory as having taken a step in that direction inasmuch as (1) dominance structures can be seen as good "gestalts" and (2) the theory's ambition to understand the link between decision making and action may facilitate further modeling on how decision makers interact with the external world.

ACTING AND DECIDING—HOW MAY THEY BE RELATED?

The literature reviewed in the present chapter shows that the concept of action is prominent in current research on decision making. In this final section, I will in the light of this literature discuss how action may be related to decision making.

Preparation for Action

SDS theory, as well as Diff Con theory, stresses the link between predecisional processes and the commitment to act in line with the chosen alternative in postdecisional processes. Both theories assume that predecisional processes aim at building up a firm ground for defending the to-be-chosen alternative in a postdecisonal future. The validity of this assumption is backed up by empirical support for the four phases of SDS theory as well as for the differentiation assumption in Diff Con theory. It seems clear that people in their decision-making processes often manage to increase the cognitive support for the to-be-chosen alternative, which in turn means that later on it will become easier to defend that alternative. That the predecisonal process indeed may be oriented toward facilitating ensuing action is shown by the finding that decision makers may not accept the character of given alternatives, but instead try to figure out how they could improve the to-be-chosen alternative (Montgomery, 1993). On the other hand, it appears that research is lacking on the extent to which decision makers in postdecisional processes actually employ the support built up in predecisional processes to defend their decision.

Interventions in the External World

The earlier formulations of SDS theory focused on the decision maker's cognitive processes. However, on his or her way to the decision, the individual may also intervene in the external world to increase the support for the to-be-chosen alternative (Blom Kemdal, & Montgomery, 1997; Willen, 1994). Similarily,. naturalistic decision theories stress that decision makers interact with a dynamic environment, although the research in this tradition does not seem to be concerned with the support that predecisional action may give to the final decision.

Thoughts as Actions

The empirical support for dominance structuring is not unequivocal. In general, the support is stronger when think-aloud data rather than quantitative ratings were used. Think-aloud data also differentiate more clearly between preferences and choices than is true for rating data. It may be speculated that think-aloud reports reflect an internal argumentation process. In line with the view of thinking advanced in so-called rhetoric psychology (Billig, 1991), dominance structuring may be analogous to arguing with a defender of a competing alternative. Assuming that the argumentation process primarily is expressed in words, it follows that verbal data will reflect this process more closely than is the case for ratings.

A stress on the rhetorical and argumentative character of thinking implies that thinking may be seen as a kind of acting. Just as is the case in conflicts between individuals acting in the external world, the individual decision maker uses his or her thoughts as weapons against an opponent. In this fight the individual may be more or less successful, which will be manifested in the choice or the rejection of a tentatively chosen alternative.

The Control of the Control

SDS theory as well as Diff Con theory may be seen as models of how the individual attempts to control his or her thinking when confronted with a decision problem. The decision maker avoids certain thoughts and entertains others in his or her search for a "good gestalt." But what controls the control? To be sure, the individual does not have unlimited freedom to construct any degree of differentiation or any kind of dominance structure. Obviously, the makeup of the individual as well as of his or her environment provides constraints for differentiation or dominance structuring. Moreover, within these constraints the individual at any given moment may be further limited by his or her perspective on the choice situation (Montgomery, 1994). For example, the choice between giving money or not to a beggar will be experienced differently from an ego-protective or altruistic perspective.

However, as suggested by Kant (1785/1959), the individual may have some freedom to choose the principles (i.e., the perspective) he or she will follow. In other words, the individual will be free to decide how to decide. Knowledge of how people make such metadecisions may provide a deeper understanding of how people control their actions.

Acknowledgments

This chapter was supported by a grant from the Swedish Council for Research in the Humanities and Social Sciences. I thank Ola Svenson for his comments on a previous draft.

REFERENCES

Ariely, D., & Wallsten, T. (1995). Seeking subjective dominance in multidimensional space: An explanation of the asymmetric dominance effect. *Organizational Behavior and Human Decision Processes*, 63, 223–232.

Axelrod, P. (Ed.), (1976). *Structure of decision: The cognitive maps of political elites*. Princeton, NJ: Princeton University.

Beach, L. R. (1990). *Image theory: Decision making in personal and organizational contexts.* Chichester, Eng.: Wiley.

Beach, L. R., & Lipshitz, R. (1993). Why classical decision theory is an appropriate standard for evaluating and aiding most human decision making. In G. A. Klein, J. Orasanu, R. Calderwood, & C. E. Zsambok (Eds.), *Decision making in action: Models and methods* (pp. 21–35). Norwood, N J: Ablex.

Beckmann, J., & Kuhl, J. (1984). Altering information to gain action control: Functional aspects of human information processing in decision making. *Journal of Research in Personality, 18,* 224–237.

Biel, A., & Montgomery, H. (1986). Scenarios in energy planning. In B. Brehmer, H. Jungermann, P. Lourens, & G. Sevon (Eds.), *New directions in research on decision making* (pp. 205–218). Amsterdam: North-Holland.

Billig, M. (1991). *Ideology and opinions.* London: Sage.

Blom Kemdal, A., & Montgomery, H. (1997). Perspectives and emotions in personal decision making. In R. Ranyard, W. R. Crozier, & O. Svenson (Eds.), *Cognitive models and explanations* (pp. 72–89). London: Routledge.

Bockenholt, U., Albert, D., Aschenbrenner, M., & Schmalhofer, F. (1991). The effects of attractiveness, dominance, and attribute differences on information acquisition in multiattribute binary choice. *Organizational Behavior and Human Decision Processes, 49,* 258–281.

Brehmer, B. (1990). Strategies in real-time dynamic decision making. In R. Hogarth (Ed.), *Insights in decision making: A tribute to Hillel J. Einhorn* (pp. 262–279). Chicago: University of Chicago Press.

Cohen, M. S. (1993). The naturalistic basis of decision biases. In G. A. Klein, J. Orasanu, R. Calderwood, & C. E. Zsambok (Eds.), *Decision making in action: Models and methods* (pp. 51–99). Norwood, NJ: Ablex.

Cohen, M. S., Freeman, J. P., & Wolf, S. (1996). Metarecognition in time-stressed decision making: Recognizing, critiquing, and correcting. *Human Factors, 38,* 206–219.

Dahlstrand, U., & Montgomery, H. (1984). Information search and evaluative processes in decision making: A computer based process tracing study. *Acta Psychologica, 56,* 113–123.

Edwards, W. (1954). The theory of decision making. *Psychological Bulletin, 51,* 380–417.

Ericsson, K. A., & Simon, H. A. (1980). Verbal reports as data. *Psychological Review, 87,* 215–251.

Festinger, L. (1957). *A theory of cognitive dissonance.* Palo Alto, CA: Stanford University Press.

Fischer, G. W., & Hawkins, S. A. (1993). Strategy compatibility, scale compatibility, and the prominence effect. *Journal of Experimental Psychology: Human Perception and Performance, 19,* 580–597.

Gallhofer, I., & Saris, W. (1989). Decision trees and decision rules in politics: The empirical decision analysis procedure. In H. Montgomery & O. Svenson (Eds.), *Process and structure in human decision making* (pp. 293–311). Chichester: Wiley.

Garvill, J., Gärling, T., Lindberg, E., & Montgomery, H. (1991, August). In search of evidence for dominance structuring in decision making. Paper presented at the 13th European Research Conference of Subjective Probability, Utility, and Decision Making, Fribourg, Switzerland.

Gollwitzer, P. M. (1990). Action phases and mind-sets. In T. E. Higgins & R. M. Sorrentiono (Eds.), *Handbook of motivation and cognition: Foundations of social behavior* (Vol. 2, pp. 53–92). New York: Guiford Press.

Gollwitzer, P. M., Heckhausen, H., Ratajezah, H. (1990). From weighing to willing: Approaching a change decision through pre- or postdecisional mentation. *Organizational Behavior and Human Decision Processess, 45,* 41–65.

Huber, J., Payne, J. W., & Puto, C. (1980). Adding asymmetrically dominated alternatives: Violations of regularity and the similarity hypothesis. *Journal of Consumer Research, 9,* 90–98.

Kahneman, D., & Tversky, A. (1979). Prospect theory. *Psychometrica, 47,* 263–291.

Kant, I. (1959). *Foundations of the metaphysics of morals* (L. W. Beck, Trans.). New York: Bobbs-Merrill. (Original work published 1785.)

Kemdal, A. B., & Montgomery, H. (1995, August). Self reports of important real life decisions. Paper presented at the 15th conference on Subjective Probability, Utility, and Decision Making, Jerusalem.

Klein, G. A. (1993a). A recognition primed decision (RPD) model of rapid decision making. In G. A. Klein, J. Orasanu, R. Calderwood, & C. E. Zsambok (Eds.), *Decision making in action: Models and methods* (pp. 138–147). Norwood, NJ: Ablex.

Klein, G. A. (1993b). Twenty questions: Suggestions for research in naturalistic decision making. In G. A. Klein, J. Orasanu, R. Calderwood, & C. E. Zsambok (Eds.), *Decision making in action: Models and methods* (pp. 389–403). Norwood, NJ: Ablex.

Klein, G. A., Orasanu, J., Calderwood, R., & Zsambok, C. E. (1993) (Eds.), *Decision making in action: Models and methods.* Norwood, NJ: Ablex.

Kuhl, J. (1992). A theory of self-regulation: Action versus state orientation, self-discrimination, and some applications. *Applied Psychology: An International Review, 41,* 97–129.

Lewicka, M. (1997). Rational or uncommitted? Depression and indecisiveness in interpersonal decision making. *Scandinavian Journal of Psychology, 38,* 227–236.

Lichtenstein, S., & Slovic, P. (1971). Reversals of preference between bids and choices in gambling decisions. *Journal of Experimental Psychology, 101,* 16–20.

Lindberg, E., Gärling, T., & Montgomery, H. (1988). People's beliefs and values as determinants of housing preferences and simulated choices. *Scandinavian Housing and Planning Research, 5,* 181–197.

Lindberg, E., Gärling, T., & Montgomery, H. (1989a, August). Decisions with incompletely described alternatives. Paper presented at the 12th European Research Conference on Subjective Probability, Utility, and Decision Making, Moscow, SSSR.

Lindberg, E., Gärling, T., & Montgomery, H. (1989b). Differential predictability of preferences and choices. *Journal of Behavioral Decision Making, 2,* 205–219.

Lindberg, E., Gärling, T., & Montgomery, H. (1989c). Subjective belief-value structures as determinants of preferences for and choices among housing alternatives. *Journal of Consumer Policy, 12,* 119–137.

Lindberg, E., Gärling, T., & Montgomery, H. (1990). *Intra-urban residential mobility: Subjective belief-value structures as determinants of residential preferences and choices* (Umeå Psychological Reports, No. 197). Umeå: Department of Psychology, University of Umeå.

Lipshitz, R. (1993). Converging themes in the study of decision making in realistic settings. In G. A. Klein, J. Orasanu, R. Calderwood, & C. E. Zsambok (Eds.), *Decision making in action: Models and methods* (pp. 103–137). Norwood, NJ: Ablex.

Mann, L., Janis, I. L., & Chaplin, R. (1969). The effects of anticipation of forthcoming information on predecisional processes. *Journal of Personality and Social Psychology, 11,* 10–16.

Montgomery, H. (1983). Decision rules and the search for a dominance structure: Towards a process model of decision making. In P. C. Humphreys, O. Svenson, & A. Vari (Eds.), *Analyzing and aiding decision processes* (pp. 343–369). Amsterdam: North Holland.

Montgomery, H. (1989). From cognition to action: The search for dominance in decision making. In H. Montgomery & O. Svenson (Eds.), *Process and structure in human decision making* (pp. 23–49). Chichester: Wiley.

Montgomery, H. (1993). The choice of a home seen from the inside: Psychological contributions to the study of decision making in housing markets. In T. Gärling & R. G. Golledge (Eds.), *Behavior and environment* (pp. 317–341). Amsterdam: Elsevier.
Montgomery, H. (1994). Towards a perspective theory of decision making and judgment. *Acta Psychologica, 87*, 155–178.
Montgomery, H. (1997). Surrender at Perevolochna: A case study of perspective and action control in decision making under stress. In R. Flin, E. Salas, M. Strub, & L. Martin (Eds.), *Decision making under stress. Emerging themes and applications*. Aldershot: Ashgate.
Montgomery, H., & Hemlin, S. (1991). *Judging scientific quality: A cross-disciplinary investigation of professorial evaluation documents* (Göteborg Psychological Reports, Vol. 21, No. 4). Göteborg: Department of Psychology, University of Göteborg.
Montgomery, H., Gärling, T., Lindberg, E., & Selart, M. (1990). Preference judgments and choice: Is the prominence effect due to information integration or to information evaluation? In K. Borcherding, O. I. Larichev, & D. Messick (Eds.), *Contemporary issues in decision making* (pp. 149–157). Amsterdam: North Holland.
Montgomery, H., Selart, M., Gärling, T., & Lindberg, E. (1994). The judgment-choice discrepancy: Noncompatibility or restructuring? *Journal of Behavioral Decision Making, 7*, 145–155.
Montgomery, H., & Svenson, O. (1989). A think aloud study of dominance structuring in decision processes. In H. Montgomery and O. Svenson (Eds.), *Process and structure in human decision making* (pp. 135–150). Chichester: Wiley.
Orasanu, J., & Connoly, T. (1993). The reinvention of decision making. In G. A. Klein, J. Orasanu, R. Calderwood, & C. E. Zsambok (Eds.), *Decision making in action: Models and methods* (pp. 3–20). Norwood, NJ: Ablex.
Pennington, N., & Hastie, R. (1993). Reasoning in explanation-based decision making. *Cognition, 49*, 123–163.
Rasmussen, J. (1993). Deciding and doing: Decision making in natural contexts. In G. A. Klein, J. Orasanu, R. Calderwood, & C. E. Zsambok (Eds.), *Decision making in action: Models and methods* (pp. 158–171). Norwood, NJ: Ablex.
Rohrman, B., & Borcherding, K. (1988, August). The cognitive structure of residential decisions: A longitudinal field study. Paper presented at the XXIV International Congress of Psychology, Sydney.
Russo, J. E., Medvec, V. H., & Meloy, M. G. (1996). The distortion of information during decisions. *Organizational Behavior and Human Decision Processes, 66*, 102–110.
Sedek, G., Kofta, M., & Tyszka, T. (1993). Effects of uncontrollability on subsequent decision making: Testing the cognitive exhaustion hypothesis. *Journal of Personality and Social Psychology, 6*, 1270–1281.
Selart, M. (1996). Structure compatibility and restructuring in judgment and choice. *Organizational Behavior and Human Decision Processes, 65*, 106–116.
Selart, M., Montgomery, H., Romanus, J., & Gärling, T. (1994). Violations of procedural invariance in preference measurement: Cognitive explanations. *European Journal of Cognitive Psychology, 6*, 417–436.
Shafir, Simonson, & Tversky, T. (1993). Reason-based choice. *Cognition, 49*, 11–36.
Slovic, P. (1975). Choice between equally valued alternatives. *Journal of Experimental Psychology: Human Perception and Performance, 1*, 280–287.
Slovic, P., & Lichtenstein, S. (1983). Preference reversals: A broader perspective. *American Economic Review, 73*, 596–605.
Soelberg, P. (1967). Unprogrammed decision making. *Management Review, 3*, 19–29.
Svenson, O. (1979). Process descriptions of decision making. *Organizational Behavior and Human Performance, 23*, 86–112.

Svenson, O. (1992). Differentiation and consolidation theory of human decision making: A frame of reference for the study of pre- and post-decision processes. *Acta Psychologica, 80*, 143–168.

Svenson, O. (1996). Decision making and the search for fundamental psychological regularities: What can be learned from a process perspective? *Organizational Behavior and Human Decision Processes, 65*, 252–267.

Svenson, O., & Hill, T. (1997). Turning prior disadvantages into advantages: Decision making through the looking glass of differentiation and consolidation theory. In R. Ranyard, W. R. Crozier, & O. Svenson (Eds.), *Decision making: Cognitive models and explanations* (pp. 218–232). London: Routledge.

Taylor, S. E., & Gollwitzer, P. M. (1996). Effects of mindset on positive illusions. *Journal of Personality and Social Psychology, 69*, 213–226.

Tversky, A., Sattah, S., & Slovic, P. (1988). Contingent weighing in judgment and choice. *Psychological Review, 95*, 371–384.

Tyszka, T. (1980). Contextual multiattribute decision rules. In L. Sjöberg, T. Tyszka, & J. Wise (Eds.), *Decision processes and decision analysis*. Lund: Doxa.

Tyszka, T., & Wielochovski, M. (1991). Must boxing verdicts be partial? *Journal of Behavioral Decision Making, 4*, 283–295.

Willén, H. (1994). *How do couples decide about having their first child? An explorative study* (Göteborg Psychological Reports, Vol. 24, No. 1). Göteborg: Göteborg University, Department of Psychology.

CHAPTER 12

IMPROVING EFFICIENCY OF ACTION CONTROL THROUGH TECHNICAL AND SOCIAL RESOURCES

WOLFGANG SCHÖNPFLUG

ACTION CONTROL AND EFFICIENCY

PERSONAL CONTROL AND EXTERNAL RESOURCES

Theories of action share the supposition that persons construct representations of the world, set goals, and operate toward achievement of these goals (Airaksinen & Gasparski, 1993; Frese & Zapf, 1994). According to these theories, efficiency of action derives from the quality of representations, the appropriateness of goals, and the skills of planning and executing operations. Improving efficiency requires the acquisition of skills for superior planning and execution, as well as learning how to construct better representations and how to find more adequate goals. Such a view focuses on individuals as agents who exert direct personal control in domains of their concern.

The range for improving efficiency by individual learning may be considerable. However, the range is limited for each individual. Indi-

---

WOLFGANG SCHÖNPFLUG • Studiengang Psychologie, Freie Universität Berlin, Habelschwerdter Allee 45, D-14 195 Berlin-Dahlem, Germany. E-mail: wpflug@go-on.de

Personal Control in Action, edited by Kofta et al., Plenum Press, New York, 1998.

viduals who want to achieve beyond their personal limits, have to rely on external resources such as tools and friends. In general, the efficiency of human actions can only be maximized by employing external resources. This point had already been raised in an early stage of technological progress. To the British scholar and politician Francis Bacon (1620/1858, p. 157) we owe the following aphorism: *Nec manus unda nec intellectus sibi permissus multum valet; instrumentis et auxiliis res perficitur; quibus opus est non minus ad intellectum quam ad manum. Atque ut instrumenta manus motum aut cient aut regunt, ita et instrumenta mentis intellectui aut suggerunt aut cavent.* [Neither the bare hand nor the mind by itself is highly efficient. Control is only achieved by the use of tools and instruments; they are needed for both mental and manual work. And as manual instruments guide the hand's movement, the mental instruments control mental activity.] Nowadays, after 300 hundred years of increasingly sophisticated technological and organizational progress, it is inconceivable how modern women and men could carry out their ambitious cultural tasks, such as traffic, surgery, or entertainment, if not by employing technical and social systems.

Contemporary psychological action theories have not paid much attention to external resources. Some of them have not treated the phenomenon of external resources at all. Some have considered external resources only as agents that benefit a person, but are not controlled by that person. For example, research in applied and social psychology has elucidated the benefits of social support for buffering stress. However, social support may just provide benefits from outside, beyond the person's own control (e.g., medical care obtained during a fainting fit). External involvement may even interfere with a person's own involvement (e.g., if overprotective parents take a child by car when he could equally walk). In the former case, the person experiences the lack of personal control, in the latter the loss of personal control (cf. Lewis, Rook, & Schwarzer, 1994; Leppin & Schwarzer, 1990).

Psychological action theories should be complemented in two respects. First, mediated control should be distinguished from direct control. In the mode of direct control, the person operates on an object exclusively by means of her own personal resources, such as her fingers (e.g., when molding clay). In the mode of mediated control, the person operates on an object by means of an external resource such as a tool (e.g., when cutting wood), i.e., the external resource serves as a mediator between the person and the object of her operations. Second, external resources should be more carefully defined as agents or as objects *vis-á-vis* a person. In the role of agents, external resources are not controlled by the person; the person may even experience the loss of personal control if benefiting from the external agents (e.g., an elderly patient may feel patronized by a nurse). In the role of objects, external resources are controlled by the person; she can utilize the external resources as tools to serve her own intentions, and she may even experience an amplification of personal control (e.g., a speaker may sense more power if broadcasted nationwide).

Assignment of Control in Extended Control Systems

Ecological settings provide social resources (such as friends, co-workers, spouses), technical resources (such as telescopes, knives, engines), and natural resources (such as water, fruit, oil). Individuals may intentionally employ these resources for the advancement of their own actions. Then agents interact with technical or social support systems. Agents interacting with their supports will be designated as extended control systems. (Thus, the concept of extended control system encompasses both social and man–machine systems.)

A paradigmatic case of an extended control system is the extended memory system as analyzed by Schönpflug and Esser (1995). The authors have called their extended memory system *GRAECULUS*. *Graeculi* (from Latin "little Greeks") were Roman slaves of Greek origin who memorized socially relevant details (such as merits, ancestors, possessions) to prompt their masters during conventions, before court, etc. Thus, an extended memory system consists of an agent who benefits from information storage and retrieval (such as a Roman lawyer, or an American presidential candidate) and a person (such as a Graeculus, or a secretary) who supports him by storing and retrieving information. Given modern information technology, the supporting person can be replaced by a database.

A crucial point in an extended memory system is the assignment of control. Control can be assigned to the agent; then the agent—according to his needs and intentions—selects information for storage, assigns selected information to his own memory or to a supportive person or database, and initiates retrieval from the external store. For instance, a Roman master may decide that the estates of his opponent are worth remembering. Then he may memorize them himself, or he may ask his Graeculus to memorize them, or he may note them down on a papyrus; at a later occasion, the master may intentionally recall what he has memorized, or he may ask his Graeculus to recall from his memory, or he may return to his notes. As an alternative, control may be assigned to the support. Then the support system selects, stores, and retrieves information according to the needs of the agent as they are represented in the support system. For instance, a Graeculus may find that the estates of his master's opponents are worth remembering because knowledge of these estates may be relevant in an upcoming dispute over an inheritance; then he decides to memorize locations, sizes, etc., as he regards it to be salient for his master; later he conveys his knowledge to his master, whenever he believes this to be useful.

The distribution of tasks is different in extended memory systems, depending on the assignment of control. If control is assigned to the agent, he has to acquire knowledge about content and functional features of the support systems in order to operate them effectively. For instance, an active Roman master must remember what his Graeculus preserves in his memory before he can ask him a question. Similarly, a student who actively uses a database must know where to find the database, what is stored in that database, and how to retrieve the information available. On the other hand, appointing control to the support system is only functional if the support system monitors the agent's actual and forthcoming concerns, the progress he has made and the errors he has committed. For instance, the faithful Graeculus must be aware of the suits and controversies his master may become involved in. Or as an example from modern technology, an intelligent road information system must consider the location and direction of the driver. A general principle for extended support systems may be stated as follows: The assignment of control to an agent requires adequate knowledge about the support system on the part of the agent. Alternatively, the assignment of control to a support system requires adequate monitoring of the agent's needs and intentions on the side of the support system.

A special feature of analyses dealing with extended control systems should be the distinction between primary tasks (e.g., constructing an edifice) and secondary tasks of managing specific support systems (e.g., renting, operating a tower crane). In the hierarchical organization of action, the primary tasks should be superordinated to the secondary tasks. Intentions regarding the primary task should govern the intentions regarding the secondary task of controlling an external support system. Also, feedback from the primary task should be relevant for operating the support system.

In the analysis of primary and secondary tasks several complications can be observed. First, individuals may not be fully aware of the control they are imposing by employing support systems. They may misjudge the effects of their operations on the support system, or the effects of the support system on the primary task. Second, personal control may be jeopardized by effects of support systems that individuals do recognize but cannot control. The latter case is illustrated by some controversies about loss of control due to highly automatized support systems such as autopilots (Bainbridge, 1983).

The Economy of Extended Control Systems

Whereas theories of action traditionally emphasize the value of personal control, the economy of control should equally be pointed out. Full personal control enhances self-esteem but taxes personal resources (e.g., excessive personal control may lead to early physical exhaustion). In contrast, lack or loss of control lowers self-esteem but may save personal resources, particularly in a benign environment (as is reported from the legendary land of Cockaigne, the fool's paradise). The economy of mediated control is twofold. The employment of external resources may either permit the conservation of personal resources while maintaining the personal level of performance (e.g., when riding a bicycle one can maintain the speed of running and still save the effort of running) or, if personal resources are fully exploited, permit the attainment of higher performance (e.g., riding a bicycle with the same effort as running yields higher speed). It is mainly the economic aspect of mediated control that deserves attention when efficiency of action is the focus of analysis. Efficiency of action is not only defined by achievement but also by expenses. Since mediated control may affect both achievement and expenses, it becomes an attractive option in the regulation of human activity.

The issue of mediated control, or taking advantage of external support, is economically ambivalent. On the one hand, in many ecologically relevant tasks efficiency can only be maximized by external supports. On the other hand, the employment of external supports sets its own demands and includes its own risks. Therefore, initiation and maintenance of activity within extended control systems require careful planning and evaluation. One has especially to examine the costs and benefits of unsupported activity. What are the costs and benefits of external supports? How do costs and benefits of supported and unsupported activity compare? How do costs and benefits of alternative supports compare?

Benefits and costs of actions can be evaluated by the gains and losses of external resources, i.e., the social, technical, and natural resources mentioned above. By involvement in activities, a person may win or lose friends, or gadgets, or food, or gasoline, etc. These resources are evaluated according to several criteria. The main criterion seems to be the ease of restitution. Benefits and costs of actions can equally be defined as gains and losses of personal resources such as skills, stamina, and emotional states (Hobfoll, 1988; Schönpflug & Battmann, 1988; Schönpflug, 1986). Taking external and personal resources into account, comparisons can be made between (1) an action recruiting and utilizing specific external resources (e.g., preparing a party with the help of neighbors), (2) similar actions with alternative external resources (preparing a party through a catering service), (3) similar actions without external resources (preparing a party without help), and (4) renunciation (no party). Depending on actual conditions, a broad range of economic evaluations can be expected. In some cases, the benefits achieved by external resources may to be too low (e.g., a neighbor cheerfully offers his help to prepare a party, but is inefficient) or the cost invested may be too high (the neighbor is an efficient aid for preparing a party, but expects frequent baby-sitting in return); these cases will be rated as uneconomical. In other cases, rated as economical, the benefits of active involvement in the recruitment and utilization of external resources balance or outweigh the cost.

The economy of action seems to regulate both the intensity of personal involvement and the distribution of control within extended systems. Under some conditions, reducing personal control saves effort, preserves health, and obviates potential frustration from personal failure. Under other conditions, it is the active recruitment and utilization of external resources that serves the same purposes. Ecologically valid theories of action should more carefully investigate the demands that external resources impose on the user (e.g., manual skills for handling technical instruments, social skills for soliciting help), as well as the cost arising from external support (e.g., effort for handling technical instruments, social obligations after accepting support).

Against this theoretical background, some studies have been performed that investigate the benefits and costs of incorporating support into personal activity or the extension of personal control from primary tasks to external resources. Examples for two groups of studies will be reported in more detail; the first from the technical domain, the second from the social domain.

TECHNICAL SUPPORT: STUDIES ON MEMORY AIDS

Memorizing versus External Storage of Information

As has been explained with reference to the *GRAECULUS* model of Schönpflug and Esser (1995), there are several options for preserving information. One way to achieve this goal is to store information in and retrieve it from one's internal, personal memory. But an external storage in other people's memory (e.g., assistants), in realistic models (e.g., monuments), and in visible or audible documents (e.g., paintings, tape recordings) are frequent options. The following studies investigate task situations in which agents employ external memory aids. The main purpose of these studies is to corroborate some of the assumptions regarding the economy of mediated actions.

In the studies reported, agents and memory aids form an extended system where control is assigned to the agent. In order to take advantage of the external aid, the user has to acquire sufficient knowledge of the aid. In particular, the person needs knowledge about the contents of the store, its organization, the addresses of documents and similar characteristics.

Using an external store may yield benefits. However, acquiring knowledge about a memory aid results in costs that can be avoided if a person refrains from using the external aid. The cost of constructing a model of the external storage device may, but need not be, balanced by the benefits of external storage, especially the gain in storage capacity. Therefore, using an external information store presupposes an economic decision.

USING A DATABASE: A LABORATORY EXPERIMENT

Determinants of the decision to choose a technical aid were studied by means of behavior in a reconstruction task (Schönpflug & Esser, 1991). The experimental task for all participants was to read a text on Chinese history and subsequently to answer questions related to the text. For example, a sentence from the text read: "During his reign until 1722, emperor Kang-Tsi achieved for the first time a unification of his domain with lasting internal peace." The complete text was displayed sentence by sentence on a computer screen. After one complete presentation of the text, a series of questions followed; each referred to a different sentence from the text. For example, a question asked, "What were the political achievements of emperor Kang-Tsi?" The participants were asked to answer the questions; however, a verbatim text reproduction was not required.

The participants were assigned to a control group C, or to one of two experimental groups, E+ and E–. The control group underwent the same procedure as in a conventional learning experiment. The members of the group memorized the text and tried to answer the questions orally without having any aid at their disposal. The two experimental groups were offered an electronic database during the presentation of the text. During presentation, they could transfer single sentences to a personal file. For that purpose, they had to mark the sentence on the screen and type a keyword. All participants in the two experimental groups were instructed that entering the keyword during the quiz would bring back the corresponding sentence to the screen. This way, they had a choice of whether or not to support storage and retrieval by an external memory aid. Actually, only the participants in experimental group E+ were permitted to use the database during the reproduction test. The participants in experimental group E– did not have access to their database. In order to avoid reactance, anger, etc., this condition was explained as a real-life test, analogous to situations where a person wants to reproduce some items contained in a database, but is not able to find or to use it.

The database was an efficient tool for improving the reproduction. With a database available during learning and accessible during testing, group E+ reached a score of 63% correct answers. This was significantly greater than the score of group C, which learned and reproduced without a database. Group C achieved a score of only 31% correct answers. However, feeding materials into a database during learning alone did not benefit reproduction. The members of group E–, who entered sentences into a database that was not at their disposal during the reproduction task, achieved a score of only 12% correct answers. This score was significantly lower than the performance of the control group C.

Thus, the benefits of using a database are evident. However, for evaluating the payoff of external storage, cost must also be taken into account. In the experiment reported above, external storage caused an operational cost for marking the sentences. In addition, there was a mental cost for constructing and memorizing the keywords under which sentences were stored in the database; constructing and memorizing keywords was mandatory for retrieving from the external store but did not—in the present case—improve internal memory for the text.

Apparently, the balance of costs and benefits varied between experimental conditions. Both experimental groups, E+ and E–, memorized both the sentences they had entered into the database and the keywords attached to the sentences. These were the specific demands for using the database, or the cost of external storage. The experimental group E+ actually benefited from external storage. The members of this group were able to reduce the entries into their personal memories to the topics of the sentences, and retrieve the details from the database. Group E– obviously also elaborated a strategy of complementing recall with external retrieval; but that strategy became obsolete when the external memory aid was not accessible during the test. This group had the cost of external storage but did not benefit from it. As compared to the control group C that had no database at any time, experimental group E– had invested costs into a failing tool and suffered from low returns.

Comparing the cost and benefits of internal and external storage may constitute a specific type of memory control process. Memory control processes (such as calculating study time as related to text difficulty) establish the domain of metamemory (cf. Nelson & Narens, 1990). Therefore, estimating the economic features of external versus internal storage and retrieval may form another facet in the study of metamemory (Esser, 1996).

Notes as Memory Aids: A Field Experiment

The problem of internal resources as prerequisites for the efficient use of external support was investigated in a field experiment on memory for notes. Notes are among the most frequent and straightforward memory aids (Harris, 1980). Mostly, however, notes have to be actively approached in the case of demand. For that purpose, the availability, the location, and the content of a note must be represented in memory. Thus, notes may be an external resource for reconstruction. But memory for notes is an internal resource required for their use.

A pertinent study on memory for notes was conducted by Schönpflug and Fritsch (1994). The participants in this study varied in age from 30 to 80 years. Within this range, large differences in memory capacity can be expected, with the elderly suffering from a mild loss. Memory decrements can be compensated by notes, and, indeed, the elderly have been found in another study (Loewen, Shaw, & Craik, 1990) to engage frequently in note taking. However, notes as aids for reconstruction are only functional if sufficiently remembered. Therefore, the elderly may not take advantage of their notes because they do not remember them. The case could be generalized in the following paradox: External aids may be most valuable for compensating personal disadvantages. However, the same or similar personal disadvantages may prevent the effective use of compensatory external aids. In contrast, highly efficient persons will achieve the greatest benefits from external aids, thereby extending their personal efficiency.

All participants of the experiment conducted by Schönpflug and Fritsch had to read a list of 24 intentions. They were asked to adopt the role of a single person who prepares for a somewhat long journey. Each person faced a list of sentences describing intended errands, communications and so forth, such as "taking out a health insurance policy" and "putting the pet in a kennel." The participants were given free time to study the list. After an interval of 10 min, they were asked to reproduce the list as completely as possible.

Three experimental conditions were compared. In the first condition, E1, the participants were encouraged to take notes during the presentation of the list and to consult the notes during reproduction. In the second condition, E2, the participants received copies from half of the sentences presented. Under both conditions E1 and E2, the number of notes taken or copies collected, respectively, was limited to 12, i.e., 50% of the sentences presented. The third condition was a control condition C. Participants had to rely on their own memory; they were permitted neither to take notes nor to receive copies. There were also two groups of participants. A middle-aged group ranged between 30 and 45 years, and a senior group between 65 and 80. Although we expected a mild memory loss in the senior sample, all participants were healthy and socially active. The experimenter met the participants in their homes or in their senior clubs; all were run individually.

In both samples and under both experimental conditions E1 and E2, still another reproduction test was administered. After free recall of sentences as described above, the participants were tested for recall of notes.

The experimenter repeated all sentences from the list and the participants indicated whether a note or a copy of each sentence was available; the participants were encouraged to guess if they were uncertain about the correct answer. Since only a maximum of 12 notes were permitted for each participant, the chance probability for guessing was .5 or lower. In the control group C, the participants were not permitted to use notes. Therefore, they could only undergo a free recall test of sentences.

The main results appear in Table 1. As compared to the middle-aged, seniors remembered fewer sentences in free recall. Taking notes (condition E1) improved free recall of sentences. The effect of collecting copies (condition E2) on free recall of sentences was low and, compared to learning without notes (condition C), not significant. However, the recall scores in the middle-aged group benefited more from note taking than the recall scores of senior participants.

A more complicated issue was memory of available notes. Actually, the senior group had a high rate of hits and compared well with the middle-aged group when they were asked whether they had a pertinent note in their file. Assuming that a note was available could have permitted the seniors to consult their notes and compensate for their memory deficits. However, they also had a high false alarm rate of 38%; this was almost twice the rate of 18% found for the middle-aged. This means that more often than the middle-aged, the seniors believed that they had a note when actually no note was available.

In fact, the seniors could have compensated their memory deficit by utilizing notes. However, their assumptions of having a note available were based on a risky guessing strategy. The senior participants had a bias toward availability of notes. In the present experiment such a bias did no harm from the economical point of view. Hitting an available note enabled

Table 1. Recall of Sentences and Recall of Notes by Middle-Aged and Senior Participants[a]

	Age	
	30-45 years	65-80 years
Recall of sentences		
Condition E1: Note taking	39%	27%
Condition E2: Collecting notes	39%	18%
Condition C: No notes	31%	17%
Recall of notes		
Condition E1: Note taking	77%	70%
Condition E2: Collecting notes	71%	69%

[a]After Schönpflug & Fritsch (1994).

the complete retrieval of a sentence. Asking for a note not available just resulted in the polite reply of the experimenter: "Sorry, you don't have a note." Thus, the cost of false alarms was rather low. In other situations, among them real-life situations, the cost of false alarms may be much higher. The notion of having a note (or a memo, a letter, etc.) may initiate a lengthy and stressful search; if the notion is false, the time of search is wasted, and frustration arises.

From this field experiment the following conclusions can be drawn: Notes may be excellent external resources, but in order to utilize them, memory is needed as an internal resource. In some situations, externally stored information can be efficiently retrieved without a knowledge base, i.e., without being appropriately represented in the internal memory. A guessing strategy (as in the senior sample in this study) or other search strategies such as browsing may also prove to be efficient for retrieval from an external store. However, as compared to knowledge-based procedures, guessing and browsing yield low control. Employing a procedure with low control yields the risk of high unbalanced costs.

SOCIAL SUPPORT: STUDIES ON COOPERATION

Benefits and Cost of Cooperation

As has been explained above, social systems can also be analyzed as extended control systems. A minimal case of a social system is a dyad. Within a dyad, control is divided between two individuals. A straightforward option is that a dyad works exclusively toward the intentions of one agent, and control within the dyad is exclusively located with this agent. Eventually, a second agent within the dyad may share the first agent's intentions and may devote his or her own control potential to the service of the first agent.

Extending personal control in social systems poses similar economic problems as in man–machine systems. For efficient cooperation in a dyad, an agent needs a mental model of his or her partner, and he or she must monitor the interactions with the partner, the partner's internal state and external accomplishments. To acquire knowledge about the partner's state and his or her accomplishments necessitates the investment of skills, effort, and external resources. This investment must be compared with gains to be attributed to the partner. Cooperation can be evaluated as paying off if the operational and emotional costs that arise from modeling and monitoring the partner are outbalanced by his or her contributions to the outcome of the cooperation.

When and Why Cooperation Pays Off: Another Experiment

Several studies were conducted to examine the costs and benefits of social cooperation. Representative of these studies was a laboratory experiment by Battmann (1989). The experiment was designed to simulate an office environment and office tasks, and the participants were explicitly hired to do office work. Two participants formed a workgroup and were instructed to cooperate. They shared the same pool of tasks, which were divided into two groups, called "ordinary work tasks" and "revisions."

Ordinary work tasks consisted of two separate parts that had to be solved consecutively. For instance, one type of an ordinary work task was to figure out the total cost attached to an employee. This type of task consisted of two parts: first, to calculate the salary of the employee, considering his qualification, age, and so on; second, to calculate on the basis of his salary extra payments by the employer to social agencies, such as social security fees. Revisions, the other kinds of tasks, were similar to ordinary work tasks described above. But revisions were listed as "incomplete or incorrect tasks, returned by the supervisor." Since these tasks were new for the participants they believed that they resulted from their partners' failures, and taking care of revisions compensated for their partners' mistakes. Revisions had to be finished by one person.

The partners received credit for correct solutions. To receive credit for an ordinary task, each partner had to contribute a correct solutions of his portion of the task. However, if one partner failed to finish his share of an ordinary task, the other partner did not receive any credit for his share. For instance, if one partner calculated a wrong salary, the other partner had no chance to determine the correct amount of extra payments. Or, if the salary was correct but the calculation of extra payments incorrect, both partners missed the credit. Such cooperation turned out to be rather stressful (Schulz, 1987). As the tasks listed as revisions could be finished individually, one partner could earn the credit for this task without involvement of the other partner. The credit was calculated in points, which were later transformed into a financial premium. All credit points received were added to a joint pool. The resulting premium, including the payments that either person earned by taking care of revisions, was equally split between the partners of the same workgroup.

Members of the same workgroup were seated in different rooms but shared the same computer network. The total number of correct and incorrect solutions, the number of credits received, and the time spent on each task were registered. Each participant believed that he was able to monitor the work progress and both his own and his partner's performance (tasks completed, failures, time consumed etc.). However, the feedback given about the partner's performance was controlled by the experimenter.

Ninety-six paid volunteers participated in the study. They all were male, and experienced in office work. The experimental design was as follows: The participants were selected on the basis of a test of verbal intelligence (Amthauer, 1971) and split into two experimental groups of high and low intelligence, respectively. One half of each group received feedback from an allegedly high-efficient partner, the other half from an allegedly low-efficient partner. This resulted in an experimental design with four groups (high-intelligent with high-efficient partner; high-intelligent with low-efficient partner; low-intelligent with high-efficient partner; low-intelligent with low-efficient partner). Each of the four experimental groups consisted of 24 participants.

The concepts to be operationalized in this study were benefits and costs of cooperation. Table 2 shows some illustrative data. An obvious measure of benefits is the number of correct solutions. Participants of higher intelligence performed better than those of lower intelligence, but the impression of cooperating with a high-efficient partner enhanced the performance of both groups of participants. Two measures related to the cost of cooperation. One measure was the number of revisions; the other measure was the number of times information was retrieved about the partner's performance. Revisions are interpreted as indicating costs because they could be attributed to the partner's failures. Information about the partner was partially a requirement for coordinating work; beyond that, retrieval of information about the coworker was an additional social involvement that gave knowledge about the partner's performance and permitted conjectures about his state. Most relevant is the finding that both measures increased for low-intelligent persons who believed that they were cooperating with a highly efficient partner.

In conclusion, weak partners benefit more from social support, but have to invest more resources for maintaining cooperation with their part-

Table 2. Cooperative Behavior in Dyads as a Function of Intelligence and of the Belief in the Efficiency of the Work Partner[a]

	Efficiency of partner			
	Low		High	
	Low intelligence	High intelligence	Low intelligence	High intelligence
Correct solutions	51%	57%	59%	63%
Number of revisions	2.0	3.1	3.9	2.9
Information about partner[b]	21	20	27	23

[a]After Battmann (1989).
[b]Instances of information retrieval.

ners. They try harder to monitor the ongoing cooperation, as exhibited in the amount of information retrieved. They also try harder to satisfy their partners, as is exhibited in the number of revisions taken over. By investing resources for cooperation with a highly efficient partner, weak participants may reach their limits of exhaustion faster, a finding from a postexperimental questionnaire. After 4 hours of work, persons of lower intelligence assigned to a stronger partner typically commented that they enjoyed cooperating with their partner but would rather not continue their cooperation in another experiment.

SUMMARY AND OUTLOOK

The main principle advocated in this chapter was the extension of personal control. Construal of actions includes the option of taking advantage of social and technical supports or external resources. Employing external resources has been regarded as extension of personal control, and agents interacting with supports have been designated as extended support systems. The control achieved by employment of external resources has been called mediated control. Examples have been given as to how interactions between agents and their technical or social supports, or interactions within extended control systems, can be analyzed both theoretically and empirically.

Contemporary psychological models of action focus on the agent and show no systematic concern for the action space. However, action theory could be complemented to account for interactions in various kinds of extended control systems. Such models may augment the ecological validity of traditional action theories. This was an important reason underlying the recommendation that extended control systems be investigated further.

A special issue considered in this chapter was the economy of mediated control. Mediated control may have its benefits, but it inevitably has its costs. It is both the level of costs and benefits and their balance that count in the planning, execution and evaluation of actions. However, the psychological assessment of benefits and costs in human actions is a problem that can only be tackled within a specified ecological context. The psychological value of internal and external resources depends on availability as well as on the ease of restitution and substitution. Resources such as personal health and stamina, friends and tools, and food and gasoline may or may not be abundant, they may or may not easily be restored or replaced if consumed or lost. Availability, ease of restitution, and substitution are determined by the environment, but can also be submitted to the control of agents.

The regulation of both the demands and the supply of resources is the superordinate goal of human action. Demand and supply are core concepts of economics. Therefore, the present approach tries to bring psychological action theory closer to theories of economics that define themselves as theories of action as well. It should be pointed out that theories of economics mostly deal with monetary values and commercial commodities. But modern economics goes far beyond what is traded in financial terms. Since Becker's (1976) pioneering analyses, economists have considered goods that are differentially evaluated, but not on an explicit financial scale (e.g., health, job satisfaction). They have also analyzed the exchange of such goods as functions of supply and demand in social organizations that operate outside financially defined markets (e.g., families, educational systems). Psychological action theories could gain much by adopting some of the highly sophisticated models from modern economics and applying these models to the internal and external resources involved in human actions.

Applications should include a variety of cases in the private and public domain. Typically, an economic theory of action should assist in evaluation and counseling in cases where control, support, and delegation are or have been options. Examples from the private domain might include when or whether it is advisable for parents to do homework with a child, or to send him to a special course; when or whether a business person should rather run her own office, or hire an employee; when to buy a computer, and which computer programs to use; or when to have one's heart, liver, or kidney replaced. Analoguous problems arise in the public domain. Social problems include the distribution of responsibility: when to assign or to deny, to assume or to refuse, or to accumulate or to split responsibility, whether public education should be enforced, the welfare system expanded; how many competencies should be given to college deans—these are actual problems of distributing responsibility in democratic countries. Equally of public importance are the controversies on functional progress, change of life style and personality, and environmental effects due to the establishment of large technologies, such as development of high-speed trains and telecommunication in schools. All these problems can be submitted to a psychological cost–benefit analysis. Alternative solutions can be evaluated for individuals and groups, differentially, which should prove to be valuable for explaining and resolving social conflicts. In this way, better conceptualizations of action control may have an impact on the quality and rationality of reflections and decisions in the private and public domains.

REFERENCES

Airaksinen, T., & Gasparski, W. W. (Eds.) (1993). *Practical philosophy and action theory.* New Brunswick, NJ: Transaction Publishers.

Amthauer, R. (1971). *Der Intelligenz-Struktur-Test IST 70* [The intelligence structure test IST 70]. Göttingen: Hogrefe.
Bacon, F. (1858). *The works of Francis Bacon* (Vol. 1, J. Spedding, R. L. Ellis, & D. D. Heath, eds.). London: Longman. (originally published 1620).
Bainbridge, L. (1983). Ironies of automation. In G. Johannson & J. E. Rijnsdorp (Eds.), *Analysis, design and evaluation of man-machine systems* (pp. 151–157). Oxford: Pergamon.
Battmann, W. (1989). Regulation und Fehlregulation im Verhalten. XIII. Entlastung und Belastung durch Kooperation [Regulation and disregulation of behavior. XIII. Induction and reduction of load by cooperation]. *Psychologische Beiträge, 31*, 35–56.
Becker, G. S. (1976). *The economic approach to human behavior.* Chicago, IL: Chicago University Press.
Esser, K. B. (1996). What can I do to remember? Outline of a general model for preparing future retrieval. In W. Battmann & S. Dutke (Eds.), *Processes of the molar regulation of behavior* (pp. 73–88). Lengerich, Germany: Pabst.
Frese, M., & Zapf, D. (1994). Action as the core of work psychology: A German approach. In H. C. Triandis, M. D. Dunette & L. M. Hough (Eds.), *Handbook of industrial and organizational psychology* (Vol. 4, pp. 271–340). Palo Alto, CA: Consulting Psychologists Press.
Harris, J. E. (1980). Memory aids people use: Two interview studies. *Memory and Cognition, 8*, 31–38.
Hobfoll, S. E. (1988). *The ecology of stress.* New York: Hemisphere.
Leppin, A., & Schwarzer, R. (1990). Social support and physical health: An updated meta-analysis. In L. Schmidt, P. Schwenkmezger, J. Weinman, & S. Maes (Eds.), *Theoretical and applied aspects of health psychology* (pp. 185–202). London: Harwood.
Lewis, M.-A., Rook, K. S., & Schwarzer, R. (1994). Social support, social control, and health among the elderly. In G. N. Penny, P. Bennett, & M. Herbert (Eds.), *Health psychology. A lifespan perspective* (pp. 191–211). London: Harwood.
Loewen, E. R., Shaw, R. J., & Craik, F. I. M. (1990). Age differences in components of metamemory. *Experimental Aging Research, 16*, 43–48.
Nelson, T. O., & Narens, L. (1990). Metamemory: A theoretical framework and new findings. *Psychology of Learning and Motivation, 26*, 125–173.
Schönpflug, W. (1986). Effort regulation and individual differences in effort expenditure. In G. R. J. Hockey, A. W. K. Gaillard, & M. G. H. Coles (Eds.), *Energetics and human information processing* (pp. 271–284). Dordrecht: Nijhoff.
Schönpflug, W., & Battmann, W. (1988). The costs and benefits of coping. In S. Fisher & J. Reason (Eds.), *Handbook of life stress, cognition and health* (pp. 699–713). Chichester: Wiley.
Schönpflug, W., & Esser, K. B. (1991). Das Lernen von Texten bei tatsächlicher und vermeintlicher externer Speicherung [Learning of texts and the availability of external storage devices]. *Zeitschrift für Psychologie (Suppl. 11)*, 260–267.
Schönpflug, W., & Esser, K. B. (1995). Memory and its Graeculi: Metamemory and control in extended memory systems. In Ch. A. Weaver, III, S. Mannes, & C.R. Fletcher (Eds.), *Discourse comprehension.* Hillsdale, NJ: Lawrence Erlbaum.
Schönpflug, W., & Fritsch, E. (1994). Lernen mit Hilfe von Notizen: Gedächtnis und Metagedächtnis im mittleren und höheren Alter [Learning with notes: Memory and meta-memory in the middle-aged and the elderly]. *Zeitschrift für experimentelle und angewandte Psychologie, 41*, 279–294.
Schulz, P. (1987). Regulation und Fehlregulation im Verhalten. XII. Herausforderung und Bedrohung bei einer kooperativen Tätigkeit [Regulation and disregulation of behavior. XII. Challenge and threat during cooperation]. *Psychologische Beiträge, 29*, 198–220.

PART III

THREATENED PERSONAL CONTROL

MOBILIZATION VERSUS DEMOBILIZATION

The main topic of concern in all of the chapters of this final section is the human response to actual or threatened loss of control over important outcomes. The chapters in this section focus on specific mechanisms involved in control restoration and reflect the complexity of reactions to lost control. Whether one sees enhanced or reduced effort aimed at control restoration, for example, appears to depend on a host of factors including individual differences in chronically accessible constructs and competencies, the level or extent of control deprivation, concurrent cognitive demands, task characteristics, the availability of situational affordances for control restoration, and competing motives.

Although several of the earlier chapters have noted in passing that having control over outcomes is not always desirable or beneficial, the conditions surrounding, and the motivations underlying, the relinquishment of control are the major topics of concern in Dolinski's chapter. When and why do people relinquish control? Dolinski identifies several motives that may become operative in different situations and that may result in the delegation of control to others. For example, when negative outcomes are possible, individuals may yield control to others if a rational assessment indicates that doing so may minimize the maximum danger. Similarly, if positive outcomes are possible, they may relinquish control if doing so seems likely to maximize the probability of obtaining the desired outcomes. Dolinski also notes, however, that such rational analyses in situations of uncertain or low control over aversive and positive outcomes are not the only motives that may underlie individuals' abandonment of direct, primary control activity. A variety of social motives, such as the desire to avoid blame and guilt for negative outcomes that might befall others, equity concerns, or self-presentational motives, also may result in the delegation of control to others. Dolinski presents a series of studies designed to examine his analysis of the motives underlying decisions about the exercise of control. His chapter serves as an important reminder of the equifinality of human behavior.

Bugental and Lewis present in their chapter a provocative analysis of reactions to control loss that occur within the context of a particular kind of relationship and during interpersonal interactions. The particular kind of relationship with which they are concerned is one characterized by an asymmetrical power structure. As the authors note, such relationships are quite common in everyday life (e.g., parent–child, teacher–student, boss–employee) and can result in an anomalous response. That is, the person who veridically is in power may react as if he or she is a victim of the less powerful interactant. According to Bugental and Lewis, variations in reactions to threatened or actual control loss in such dependent relationships reflect chronic differences in relationship schemas. Those who chronically see themselves as having low power in dependency relationships are more likely to appraise a situation as entailing a threat to control and to defend against such threat compared to those who see themselves as having high power. However, strategic responses of individuals who possess low power schemas will depend on the situational affordances that are available for control. Those with low perceived power are more likely to overreact and engage in abusive or coercive power tactics if control opportunities are available and to respond with avoidance and ingratiation tactics if control opportunities are not available. The research reported by Bugental and Lewis demonstrates the potency of differences in interpretive schemas for organizing both cognitive processes and interactional styles, and they highlight a theme repeated in other chapters in this volume—namely, the necessity of considering both person and situation factors in explaining complex regulatory activities.

Whereas Dolinski and Bugental and Lewis focus on decisions about and enactment of primary, or direct action, control strategies in the face of task and social challenges, Markman and Weary turn readers' attention to secondary control strategies. Like Bugental and Lewis, they focus on the cognitive and motivational consequences of chronic interpretational schemas in reactions to threats to control. Specifically, Markman and Weary focus in two studies on the manner in which the generalized and chronic control concerns characteristic of depressed individuals influence the way they mentally "undo" or engage in counterfactual thinking about past negative events. The evidence from these studies provides support for the notion that such chronic control concerns result in the generation of counterfactuals that focus on controllable relative to uncontrollable features of the event. Moreover, both studies suggest that such counterfactual generation has several important functional consequences for depressed perceivers; mutating more controllable than uncontrollable aspects of negative life events enhances feelings of retrospective control over these events. At the same time, Markman and Weary suggest that negative affect and self-blame can be the undesirable by-products of cognitions directed toward the attainment and reestablishment of control perceptions.

The final two chapters are both based on the information-processing model of learned helplessness develop by Kofta and Sedek. This model suggests that prolonged exposure to uncontrollable events results in a state of cognitive exhaustion and, in turn, to the cognitive, motivational, and behavioral symptoms of learned helplessness. In their chapter, Kofta and Sedek review experimental evidence for the notion that experiences with uncontrollability result in prolonged cognitive effort without cognitive gain and, ultimately, to the symptoms of mental exhaustion (e.g., attentional distraction, inhibition of thinking, impaired generation of mental models of problem solutions). They also present new research findings that argue for a further refinement of their cognitive exhaustion notion. Kofta and Sedek suggest that during experiences with uncontrollable events, people learn that selective investment of attention is useless. Inhibition of effortful strategies of attentional control follow and result in informational overload and corresponding cognitive resource deficits. The implications of this theoretical reformulation for depression and for reconceptualization of the human psychological response to control threatening situations are discussed.

Sedek and McIntosh apply the information-processing model of learned helplessness to an important real-life setting and task: the acquisition of domain specific knowledge (e.g., math or language studies) in school settings. They argue that students' inability to understand new material despite prolonged effort results in states of intellectual helplessness or cognitive exhaustion. This state of intellectual helplessness consists of both a cognitive and a content-specific component. The cognitive component entails an impaired ability to engage in the kind of controlled information processing typically required by complex and difficult tasks. The content-specific component involves a grossly disorganized knowledge schema in the domain. Both result in an inability to study with any degree of comprehension, a loss of intrinsic motivation, and lowered academic achievement. Sedek and McIntosh report the results of an ambitious two-year longitudinal study and laboratory-based experiments that provide impressive support for their model of intellectual helplessness

CHAPTER 13

TO CONTROL OR NOT TO CONTROL

DARIUSZ DOLINSKI

To have control over an event means exercising authority and influence over it by directing and regulating it oneself. Obviously, events differ in their amenability to control. We cannot change the order of days in the week; our influence on our own health is greater but still limited. We may have almost total control over the amount of sugar and milk in our cup of coffee, but only if we prepare our breakfast ourselves. Regardless of the objective nature of the situation, however, people vary in their assessments of perceived control over particular events and their lives in general. Some feel they can do almost anything they set their minds to; others feel that events result mostly from the actions of others or good and bad luck.

However, in addition to differences in perceived control, there might also arise differences in control desirability. Undoubtedly, people often suffer from a lack of control over their environment. Nevertheless, in some cases personal control may dramatically lose its attractiveness. In this chapter, I will focus on conditions under which people are likely to relinquish rather than increase their control. Although control relinquishment is quite easily observable in everyday life, it has not been the focus of major psychological theories of control.

DARIUSZ DOLINSKI • Department of Psychology, University of Opole, Oleska 48, 45-951 Opole, Poland. E-mail: darek@uni.opole.pl

Personal Control in Action, edited by Kofta et al., Plenum Press, New York, 1998.

SENSE OF CONTROL AS A SUBJECT OF PSYCHOLOGY

Over the past few decades, the concept of perceived control has played a very important role in research and theory on a large number of topics in psychology and related disciplines. With only a few exceptions (e.g., Burger, 1989; Rodin, Rennert, & Solomon, 1980; Wong, 1992), writers on this topic have placed great emphasis on a human motive to seek out and maintain control. Adler (1930), for instance, proposes a striving to demonstrate one's competence and superiority over events as one's major motivational force. White (1959) argues that individuals have a need to manipulate and control their surroundings—to produce an effective change in the environment. Kelly (1955) describes man as a scientist, constantly matching expectancies against perceptions in an effort to obtain a satisfactory level of predictability and control. The desire to be personally effective in the environment is also present in Bandura's (1977) notion of self-efficacy, in deCharms's (1968) theory of personal causation, in Deci's (1975) intrinsic motivation concept, and in many other theories, which have had great influence on contemporary psychology.

In line with these theoretical considerations, laboratory researchers have found that having control is advantageous. It has been shown, for instance, that when subjects in stressful settings were led to believe they had control, whether they did or did not, stress responses were lessened (e.g., Baker & Kirsch, 1991; Geer, Davison, & Gatchel, 1970; Glass & Singer, 1972; Mills & Krantz, 1979). A lack of perceived control has also been tied to performance decrements (e.g., Hiroto & Seligman, 1975; Seligman, 1975) and aroused reactance (Brehm, 1966). In the applied settings, numerous investigations have demonstrated that a sense of control improves performance and achievement in school (e.g., Brewin & Shapiro, 1984), accelerates the growth of earnings and occupational status (Andrisani, 1978), facilitates learning processes (Perlmuter & Monty, 1977; Perlmuter, Scharff, Karsh, & Monty, 1980), and reduces depression (e.g., Benassi, Sweeney, & Dufor, 1988; Thompson, Sobolew-Shubin, Galbraith, Schwankovsky, & Cruzen, 1993) and paranoia (Mirowsky, & Ross, 1983). Further, there have been several successful attempts to influence health and longevity with manipulations intended to increase real or perceived control (Langer & Rodin, 1976; Rodin, 1986; Rodin, & Langer, 1977; Schultz, 1976). It would seem, therefore, that perceiving control over the course of events is universally beneficial.

Other research and theoretical analyses suggest, however, that sense of control might not always be desirable. Fromm (1941) was an early champion of the view that a sense of freedom and control may often be something to be avoided. In another classic book, Beck (1972) argues that one of the major problems in depression is an unrealistic and overwhelming tendency to blame oneself for undesirable events, which is a consequence of people's feeling that they cause the undesirable outcomes in their lives. Assumptions that control can be burdensome are present also in more recent papers. Folkman (1984), for example, claims that in some situations control can induce rather than reduce anxiety and stress.

A few years ago, Jerry Burger suggested that studies finding that people willingly relinquish control or respond in a negative manner to the perception that their personal control has been increased, although "occasionally...are predicted by the researchers..., more often are reported as unexpected results" (Burger, 1989, p. 246). This is, probably, no longer true. Recent years have seen a growing recognition that control is not always preferred and that it can have not only positive but also negative concomitants. In this chapter, I will briefly review some recent work on when and why people may decrease their desire for personal control. Subsequently, I will present the results of several studies that together suggest that under uncertainty people may be especially willing to relinquish their control. Finally, reasons why individuals may decrease their desire for personal control in particular situations will be reconsidered in the light of the results of the present studies.

WHY PEOPLE MAY DECREASE THEIR DESIRE FOR CONTROL

It is obvious that in real life people sometimes voluntarily yield control. Most drivers prefer to relinquish control over their car's engine to car mechanics. Soccer players very often refuse to take the penalty kick during matches and insist instead that their colleagues do so. A wife wants her husband to have control over a child who is 15, but the spouse is not very enthusiastic about this idea. All the above mentioned situations have something in common: Uncontrollability is preferred to controllability. However, the reason(s) why people voluntarily yield control in these and other situations may be quite different. For example, drivers usually believe that qualified car mechanics know better what should be done with a car engine. A soccer player probably knows that in the eyes of fans he is almost obliged to score a goal when he takes a penalty kick. If he succeeds, there is no reason for glory because it is common knowledge that a goalkeeper has little chance to defend a penalty kick. If he fails, however, his reputation will be tarnished forever. A father of a teenager, perhaps, may prefer watching television or reading a newspaper (which is relaxing) to having personal influence on his child (which is time consuming).

Minimax Hypothesis

Clearly, we may prefer relinquishing control to holding control for many different reasons. To explain how people develop control preferences in aversive environments, Suzanne Miller (1979, 1980) has proposed a *minimax hypothesis*. According to her approach, when faced with an aversive situation, "individuals want to minimize the maximum danger to themselves; that is, they are inclined to make the best of a bad situation" (Miller, 1980, p. 80). Relying on one's own resources and capabilities often allows a person to ensure that serious harm will be avoided. Sometimes, however, other people with their abilities, skills, and experience provide a much better guarantee of a maximum upper limit of harm. In such cases, yielding control may be a more profitable option than persistent enactment of personal control strategies. A person who decides to ask a proficient dentist to extract a painful wisdom tooth (instead of doing it himself at home) is obviously relinquishing some control, but at the same time is minimizing pain and the probability of serious medical complications.

In Miller's (1980) study, subjects worked in pairs on a reaction-time speed test and were subsequently informed of its result. The results were "rigged" so that subjects believed they were better than, comparable to, or inferior to their partner on this ability. Following this, both individuals were informed that they were now in the second phase of the reaction-time speed experiment, which additionally involved their reactions to stress (in the form of electric shocks). Only one of them, however, would take part in this phase. They were told that they were wired together and that both would receive the electric shock on trials where the participant in control did not react properly on a test. Subjects were then given a choice as to whom would be the representative of their "team." The results (i.e., participants' decisions) fully supported Miller's predictions. Although all of the superior ability subjects and the majority of the comparable ability subjects chose control, the majority of subjects in the inferior ability condition chose no control. In an additional experiment, it was shown that participants' choice of no control was not a consequence of having experienced failure in the first phase of the study.

Another demonstration of the minimax principle comes from the series of experiments conducted by Burger, McWard, and LaTorre (1989). The authors gave subjects an option of drawing a blood sample from themselves or having another person draw the sample. Some subjects were allowed to choose between themselves and the experimenter, whereas others were given a choice between themselves and a subject who expressed his intention to be the blood-sample taker, saying however, that he did not know anything about the procedure. It was found that subjects in the former condition tended to relinquish control to the (apparently more competent) experimenter, but subjects in the latter condition tended to retain personal control and refused to choose the confederate (who obviously was not qualified).

Thus, there is a compelling experimental evidence showing that, when people anticipate that control relinquishment will reduce aversiveness of an external stimulation, they are likely to give up control to others.

Maximax Hypothesis

If people are likely to give up control to more competent others in order to avoid serious harm to themselves, do they behave the same way in the case of positive outcomes? In other words, is it so that they are equally likely to relinquish control to maximize the probability of obtaining a desirable state of affairs (results)? Strube and Berry (1985) conducted an empirical study to answer this question. In its first part, experimenters led subjects to believe that their and another participant's choice discrimination abilities were being assessed by means of a test. After the test completion, the subject and confederate each received feedback about their own performances. False feedback was used to create four experimental conditions in which a subject believed, either that (1) both the subject and the other participant possessed pretty good ability; (2) both the subject and the other participant scored rather badly on this ability; (3) the subject was better than the other person; or (4) the subject inferior to the other person. Following this, both participants were told that they would be partners on a second task and that the best teams would be awarded valuable prizes. Finally, subjects were informed that the task consisted of 25 consecutive trials and each trial would be solved only by one member of the team. Before each trial, subjects had to decide who would try to cope with a task, they or their partners.

Subjects who believed they were better at the choice discrimination tasks, and thus probably better able to win a prize for both participants, more often tended to retain rather than relinquish control. When subjects believed their partner was better at the choice discrimination tasks, however, they more often tended to select the partner as the one to be tested. In the two comparable ability conditions, subjects selected themselves as the person to be tested approximately as often as they appointed their partners. A similar pattern of results emerged in several other experiments (Strube, Berry, & Moergen 1985; Strube & Werner, 1985).

Thus, Strube and his coworkers clearly demonstrated that people often relinquish control when that option, rather than retaining control is perceived as likely to lead to profits. Since it is argued that they do so to increase the probability of obtaining the most desirable outcome, the minimax rule, originally describing conditions where people are motivated to lower maximum danger, is not quite appropriate here. I suggest, therefore, using the term *maximax hypothesis*, instead of minimax, in similar cases.

The findings discussed above reveal that people may sometimes be more interested in avoiding aversive stimuli and obtaining desirable outcomes than in exerting personal control. In situations where personal control decreases the chance to avoid harm or to achieve success, an individual often makes a rational decision to delegate control to another, more competent, person. Apparently, control is not a goal, but the means to obtain a goal. If somebody else has a better means at his or her disposal (i.e., is more skilled), a person may give up control and take advantage of the other's capabilities. Perhaps, Rodin, Rennert, and Solomon (1980) were right in concluding that "though control may be motivating in many circumstances, this is not the result of an intrinsic need to manipulate the environment per se" (p. 137).

UNCERTAINTY AND RELINQUISHMENT OF CONTROL

In all the studies discussed so far, subjects were given a rational basis for their decision to retain or relinquish control: They learned who (they or somebody else) was the most competent or skillful at a particular task. The world we live in is very often more complicated and uncertain, however. Sometimes our knowledge about our own and our partners' abilities may be very limited. At other times, we have no adequate understanding of the nature of the task to be solved. In both situations, uncertainty makes it very difficult to predict who is better able to obtain a desirable or avoid an undesirable outcome.

The critical question arises, then, as to how uncertainty affects the tendency to retain or relinquish control. There are many forms of uncertainty. In the studies to be presented, I will focus on uncertainty emerging in situations where an individual has not enough knowledge to assess who (the individual or somebody else) has the best competence to exert control over the course of events.

Illusion of Control and Its Paradoxical Consequences

Numerous studies have shown that, even if positive outcomes are determined exclusively by chance people tend to perceive control over these outcomes (e.g., Biner, Angle, Park, Mellinger, & Barber, 1995; Gromski, Dolinski, 1987; Henslin, 1967; Wortman, 1975). The tendency to be overconfident in one's ability to attain outcomes in chance situations is called the *illusion of control* (Langer, 1975). Langer found that introducing such elements as competition, choice, or practice into an objectively uncontrollable situation (factors typical of the skill-determined situations) considerably increased subjects' expectancies of success on the task. Presumably, subjects in Langer's studies developed skill orientation (i.e., approached the event as dependent on their own efforts and intentions) and, consequently, exhibited more confidence in their ability to attain the outcome.

If this is so, however, individuals should also believe that they may *cause* a negative outcome, as the situation is objectively uncontrollable. Because people are likely to see themselves as causal agents of positive, but not negative, states (e.g., Bradley, 1978; Snyder, 1989; Snyder, & Higgins, 1988), they may prefer "having control" in an objectively uncontrollable situation if there is a chance to obtain a desirable outcome (to cause the effect) but to "relinquish control" if an undesirable outcome is possible (not to cause the effect).

To summarize: In an uncontrollable (chance) situation, people may show preference for control if desirable outcomes are likely, and preference for control relinquishment if undesirable outcomes are likely. The purpose of my first investigation was to test these predictions using a very simple procedure in a natural setting.

Study 1

Overview and Predictions. In this study, 120 ten-year-old boys were invited to play a game of dice. In half of the cases success in this game involved obtaining some profit; in the remaining cases, success meant avoiding discomfort. Thus, in the first case a lack of success did not result in a worse situation, and success improved it. In the latter, a lack of success resulted in a worse situation, and success ensured only that this undesirable situation would not occur. Additionally, the probability of success was manipulated. In some cases, chances for success in the game were low, whereas in others the chances for success were high. The boys were divided into pairs, and all of them learned that it was their two-person team that would determine what would happen to their entire class. Each pupil then was given an opportunity to present individually to the experimenter his own preferences—whether he wanted to throw a die himself or if he preferred his partner to do it. It was expected that conditions in which lack of success involved risk (changing the situation for the worse) would make subjects give up a throw, as compared to conditions in which a lack of success did not involve risk. It was also expected that a tendency to relinquish control would be modified by the probability of success. Selecting a partner for the throw should certainly be more frequent in conditions of a low rather than a high probability of success.

Method. In a separate room, two boys randomly selected from the class were informed that they would take part in a short game of dice. One throw would determine what the entire class would soon be doing. Depending on their assignment to experimental conditions, they also were told either that if they were lucky at throwing, within a few days the class would go to the cinema (conditions in which success involves obtaining profit, whereas failure does not bring negative consequences) or that if they did not succeed in getting a certain number of spots on the die, the class would have to come to school on Saturday and take a special test in mathematics (conditions in which failure involves negative consequences). At the same time, the probability of success was varied. Half of the boys were told that success (i.e., depending on a group, going to the cinema or avoiding a going to school on Saturday) required only getting a 6 (conditions of low probability of success), whereas the other half were told that success required getting any number between 2 and 6 (conditions of high probability of success). Subsequently, subjects were informed that what would happen to the whole class would be determined by one of them throwing a die. At this point, the boys were asked to write on pieces of paper whether they would prefer to throw a die themselves or whether they would rather like their partners to throw it. (Boys were unable to contact each other). After the test, regardless of the result of the test, subjects were informed that their class would not go to school on Saturday but would instead go to the cinema. (This had been previously arranged with headmasters of the school where the study was conducted).

Results. A 2 (probability of success—high vs. low) × 2 (nature of success—profit vs. avoiding loss) ANOVA revealed a significant main effect of probability of success [$F(1, 116)=8.529, p < .004$]. The proportion of subjects who decided to "take control over the situation" was greater (.73) in conditions of high probability of success than in conditions of low probability of success (.48). The ANOVA also revealed a significant main effect of the nature of success [$F(1, 116) = 4.587, p < .034$]. In conditions where success meant a chance to obtain a desirable outcome, more persons were willing to throw a dice (.70) than in conditions where it involved a chance to avoid an undesirable outcome (.52). To test the predicted interactional effect, a contrast analysis using orthogonal planned comparisons was performed. The analyses set the avoiding-loss/low-probability group as distinct from the avoiding-loss/high-probability group; the profit/low-probability condition was contrasted with the profit/high-probability condition. It was found that for the avoiding-loss contrast, the mean of the low-probability condition was only nonsignificantly different from the high-probability condition [$F(1, 116) = 1.90, p < .17$]. For the profit contrast, however, the two groups were virtually different [$F(1, 116) = 7.58, p < .007$].

TABLE 1 Proportions of Subjects Delegating Themselves to Throw a Die in Various Experimental Conditions

	Probability of success	
Nature of success	Low	High
Undesirable state will not occur	.43	.60
Desirable state will occur	.53	.87

The proportions of persons willing to throw a die in each of the four respective groups are presented in Table 1.

Discussion. The results of this initial study provided clear support to my hypothesis. In conditions of high probability of success, most boys wanted to influence the course of events by throwing a die. However, when the probability of success was low, about half the subjects preferred to relinquish this privilege in favor of another pupil. Likewise, when lack of success did not involve negative consequences, most subjects wanted to throw a die, but when it meant negative consequences, nearly half showed no willingness to "take control over the situation." Thus it seems that one of the paradoxical consequences of treating purely chance-determined tasks as if they were ability determined is a different reaction of subjects in various (yet always chance-determined) conditions. In a situation where negative consequences are possible, as well as in conditions where chances for success are low, a tendency to influence events is not a dominant reaction.

It might be expected that for negative outcomes, a tendency towards active determination of events in objectively chance-determined conditions will decrease the more severe and more likely the negative outcomes are. In order to examine this hypothesis, a second study was conducted.

Study 2

Overview and Predictions. Sixty 10-year-old boys were invited to play a game of dice. Success in all experimental conditions meant avoiding a negative state of affairs, and the probability of such success was varied. In half of the cases it was low, in the other half it was high. The significance of the negative consequences attendant to failure was also manipulated. It was expected that when the negative consequences were serious, subjects' tendency to avoid personal control would be greater than when negative consequences were relatively slight. As in Study 1, it also was expected that subjects' tendency to hold on to or avoid personal control would be modified by the probability of success.

Method. The procedure for this study was analogous to that of Study 1, except that all boys were informed that they would have a chance to avoid an undesirable outcome. They were told that throwing a die would determine what their class would be doing on Saturday. Manipulation of the significance of the negative consequences was accomplished by telling the boys that the result of the throw would determine whether they would have to come to school on Saturday and take a special test (consequences of low significance) or whether on six successive Saturdays, they would have to come to school and take various tests submitted by the local Board of Education (consequences of high significance). After deciding who would throw the die, the experimenter informed the boys that no one would really have to take any tests on Saturday; all of their Saturdays would be free. He was only trying to find out if pupils were afraid of such tests.

Results. A 2 (probability of success) × 2 (significance of negative consequences) ANOVA again revealed a main effect of probability of success [$F(1, 56) = 3.69, p < .06$]. In conditions where the probability of success was high, more than half of the boys (53%) wanted to "personally influence" the outcome. However, when the probability of success was low, the percentage of volunteers to throw the die declined to 30%. The ANOVA also revealed a main effect of significance of negative consequences [$F(1, 56) = 6.10, p < .02$]. If the negative consequences were relatively slight (a necessity to come to school on a single Saturday), 57% of subjects wanted to "personally determine the course of events." However, when the consequences were more serious (in case of failure, coming to school on six successive Saturdays), the percentage of volunteers to throw the die declined to 27%. To test an interaction predicted in a hypothesis, a contrast analysis using orthogonal planned comparisons was conducted. The analyses that were performed set the high-consequences/high-probability group as different from the high-consequences/low-probability group; and the low-consequences/high-probability group as distinct from the low-consequences/low-probability group. It was found for the high-consequences contrast that the mean of high probability of success was higher than the mean of low probability of success [$F(1, 56) = 3.76, p < .06$]. For the low-consequences contrast, however, the differences were nonsignificant [$F(1, 56) = 2.41, p < .13$]. The proportions of pupils in each condition who were willing to throw a dice are presented in Table 2.

Discussion. The results of Study 2, like the results of the previous study, reveal that in some cases a paradoxical consequence of the phenomenon of the illusion of control may consist of avoiding influence in chance-determined situations. More specifically, when the possible nega-

TABLE 2 Proportions of Subjects Delegating Themselves to Throw a Die in Various Experimental Conditions

	Probability of success	
Significance of consequences	Low	High
Low	.47	.67
High	.13	.40

tive outcome of a chance-determined task (here throwing a die) is very serious, a typical reaction is to *avoid control*. A reduction of the desire for personal influence is also observed when chances for success are slight.

Chance-determined situations are a specific class of events. It is worth considering whether conditions of uncertainty may prompt people to limit their own influence on the course of events also in the case of skill-determined tasks.

Lack of Knowledge of One's Own and Others' Abilities as a Basis for the Relinquishment of Control

In various armies the world over, commanders sometimes appeal to their subordinates to volunteer for a dangerous, secret mission. Since the mission is secret, the commanders cannot, obviously, for the time being reveal to their subordinates what it is all about. So soldiers are supposed to volunteer for the mission without knowing practically anything about it. It seems likely that a similar situation happens in various everyday-life contexts. Yet, it often happens that the task we face is not always so well defined that we can know whether we have adequate competence and skills to succeed at it. We may also not know if others, who could possibly do the task instead of us, have the requisite skills. Thus, in such cases, a decision about the retention of personal control is quite risky: We do not know whether the retention or delegation of control will result in a more negative state of affairs.

Past research has shown that if subjects find out that, as a result of their having voluntarily undertaken action, not only they but also other people experience something undesirable or become deprived of a possibility to experience something pleasant, they attribute *moral responsibility* for the outcome to themselves and experience a heightened *sense of guilt* (Gromski & Nawrat, 1984; Milgram, 1974). Indeed, people tend to avoid such actions presumably because of a desire to avoid such unpleasant attributions and feelings. Also, other people perceive a person who voluntarily undertakes actions resulting in unpleasant consequences as guilty for what happened (e.g., Arkkelin, Oakley, & Mynatt, 1979; Brewer, 1977; see also Shaver, 1985, for a review). Persons who suffer immediate harm are especially inclined to feel so (Dolinski, 1991; Dolinski, Gromski, & Szmajke, 1988).

A subject who decides to undertake an activity under total task uncertainty, then, has to take into account the possibility that he or she will take responsibility for bad outcomes and will also be blamed by others. All this may contribute to his or her relinquishment of personal control. Thus, these elements may additionally intensify the will to minimize the probability of a negative result and to maximize the probability of a positive one, assumed by the rules of minimax and maximax.

A tendency to retain versus avoid personal control under conditions of task uncertainty was tested in Study 3. An additional goal of this study also was to determine the conditions that intensify and reduce this tendency, as well as the motives that drive people to take decisions to relinquish personal influence over the course of events.

Study 3

Overview and Predictions. Subjects were informed that they were to participate in an experiment devoted to examining the processes of functioning of a small (two-person) group. They also learned that the consequences of one person's actions in the group would be borne by both members of the group. Subjects were not given any information about the nature of the task. Depending on their assignment to experimental groups, they were informed, respectively, that (1) successes on this task would be rewarded, (2) failures on this task would be punished, (3) successes would be rewarded and failures punished, or (4) nothing was said about the consequences of a good or bad performance on the task.

It was expected that decisions about control relinquishment would be more frequent in conditions of high risk (i.e., when lack of success would entail punishment of both members of a team) rather than in conditions of low risk (i.e., when lack of success would not cause a change of situation for the worse). The study also tested subjects' perceptions of the underlying motives that resulted in their delegation of personal control.

Subjects. The study involved 142 high school students, aged 15–18. The study was conducted in 6- to 12-person groups. Subjects volunteered for a psychological experiment of an unspecified nature. They were informed that at any moment they would be able to terminate their participation in the experiment. Since 2 persons did so, and 4 others did not fill in a questionnaire correctly, the analysis involved data from 136 persons (84 females and 52 males).

Method. On arrival students were informed that they would be randomly divided into two-person teams, that the teams would not be coeducational, and that the experiment would concern the functioning of small groups. The experimenter explained that it was typical of such groups that the actions of one member of such a team brought consequences that had to be borne not only by that member but by other group members as well. Subjects were subsequently informed that the experiment would involve such a situation. Only one member of the two-person team would work on a test consisting of a sequence of five tasks (the experimenter did not specify what tasks, and when asked by subjects replied that he could not reveal it yet), but the consequences of one member's action would be borne by both members of the team.

In the first experimental condition, subjects were asked to decide at that very moment whether they would like to work on the test themselves or whether they would prefer an as yet unknown partner to work on the baseline condition. In the remaining conditions, subjects were to make such a decision after listening to additional information concerning the consequences of good or bad performance on particular tasks. Some subjects were told that both members of the team would be rewarded for the successes of their representative at each of the five test samples (the reward was a sum of money, 0.75 zlotys—about 25 cents per each success). Others were told that failure on each sample would be punished by a very mild electric shock administered to both members of the team. Yet others learned that each success would be rewarded with money, whereas each failure would be punished by a mild electric shock.

After the decision on whether to designate themselves or their partners as the test taker, subjects filled out a brief questionnaire. It included a question designed to assess their thoughts about why an "average person" in a similar situation might decide to delegate responsibility for such tasks to his or her partner. More specifically, subjects evaluated (on a 7-point scale defined at the extremes "absolutely certain—no" and "absolutely certain—yes") the truth of the following three statements:

1. Such a person assumes that her/his partner will probably be more competent than herself/himself concerning skills required in the tasks.
2. Such a person knows that she/he would feel awkward if it turned out that her/his partner suffers because of her/his failures.
3. Such a person would not like to be blamed by her/his partner if she/he happened to commit mistakes.

Results. The major dependent variable was subjects' preferences concerning taking versus avoiding personal control. Table 3 presents the distri-

Table 3. Proportions of Subjects Who Decided to Participate in the Test in Various Experimental Conditions

	No information on consequences of success and failure	Promise of reward for success	Threat of punishment for failure	Promise of reward for success and threat of punishment for failure	Overall
Females	.45	.42	.28	.30	.37
Males	.64	.50	.40	.39	.46
All subjects	.51	.44	.33	.34	.40

bution of subjects' decisions in the experimental conditions. A 2 (subjects' sex) × 4 (experimental conditions) ANOVA did not show any main or interactional effects. Generally, however, it was evidently typical (especially of women) to relinquish personal influence over the course of events. This result is significant in as much as it confirms a hypothesis assuming that a state of uncertainty may constitute a sufficient condition for activating a tendency to relinquish control over one's own and a partner's fate.

Each of the measures of possible motives for the relinquishment of personal control as perceived by subjects was analyzed by means of a 2 (subjects' sex) × 2 (decision to delegate oneself for the tasks vs. decision to delegate one's partner) × 4 (experimental conditions) ANOVA. These analyses indicated that the evaluation of truth of all the three statements concerning motives for relinquishment of personal control was closely related to the decision made by a subject. Participants who had decided to take part in the test themselves saw the main reason for an average person's decision to delegate a partner for the tasks in his or her conviction that he or she was probably less competent than the other member of the team. The main effect of the decision taken by the subject to perform the test [$F(1, 120) = 57.15, p < .0001$] indicates that the truth of this statement was evaluated significantly higher by these participants (M=4.88) than by subjects who relinquished control (M=3.17). Participants who relinquished personal participation in the test cited as the main reasons, analogous to that of an average person, his or her fear of emotional and interpersonal consequences [$F(1, 120) = 39.67, p < .0001$; Ms = 5.01 and 3.47]. Finally, compared to those who elected to undertake the task themselves, subjects who assigned responsibility to their partners also cited as the more likely reason a fear of the partner's reproaches [$F(1, 120) = 42.92$; M = 4.79 vs. M = 3.26].

Discussion. Our experimental treatments have not significantly modified subjects' tendency to avoid personal control over the course of events. Interestingly, however, most participants in the experiment did prefer that an unknown partner do the tasks instead of themselves. Uncertainty about the nature of the task present in all experimental groups was, thus, for many subjects a sufficient reason to relinquish personal influence over the course of events. Subjects made such a decision despite the fact that they had no knowledge about their likely team partner. Consequently, they had no reason to think that they were less competent than their partners-to-be.

The results of this study raise an interesting question: Why in such cases of ignorance do people decide to delegate to their partners responsibility for task performance. Subjects' answers to all three questions concerning the reasons for such behavior of a hypothetical other depended closely on the decision they had made regarding their own performance. Although questions concerned an "average person," we may assume that subjects who delegated responsibility to their partners thought that a similar decision made by an abstract average person would likely be driven by the same motives that they took into account. This result likely reflects the operation of the well-known false consensus effect, i.e., the tendency to overestimate typicality and commonness of one's own judgments, feelings, and actions (Ross, Greene, & House, 1977). In this way one may assume that their emotional motives (a will to avoid taking responsibility for negative states of affairs and a related sense of guilt) as well as their interpersonal motives (a will to avoid being blamed by the partner) for relinquishing control may play a greater role than motives related to the analysis of gains and losses involved in the task itself. In other words, indirect potential negative consequences of the result may be more important for an individual than the result itself. Remarkably, at the same time the pattern of results showed that relinquishment of personal control did not necessarily derive from a relatively low estimate of one's own competence (although those who did not want to relinquish this control and who themselves accepted performance responsibilities seemed to think so).

Study 4

If people abandon personal control for emotional and interpersonal reasons and not out of a sense of relative incompetence at an as yet unspecified task, they will not relinquish control under conditions in which they would be the only one to face the results of failure. That another person would not suffer because of their mistakes should eliminate a motive for avoiding a sense of guilt for harm done to someone else and a motive for avoiding blame. The major remaining motive in such a situation would involve a desire to avoid bringing harm to oneself, as assumed by the minimax hypothesis. In order to test this notion, it was first necessary to examine whether the aforementioned emotional and interpersonal motives can keep people from taking personal control over the course of events.

Overview and Predictions. Subjects were informed that they were to participate in an experiment devoted to examining the processes of functioning of a small (two-person) group. Depending on their assignment to experimental groups, they were informed that successes on the task would be rewarded or that failures would be punished. (On the basis of the results obtained in Study 1, one could expect that subjects' tendency to relinquish control would be higher in the condition of possible harm and punishment than in the condition of possible gain). Additionally, one-half of the subjects learned that rewards or punishments would involve only them, whereas the other half were told that the consequences would also affect their partners.

Subjects. The study involved 72 high school students (39 women and 33 men), aged 16–18. The study was performed in 8- to 10-person groups. All subjects volunteered for a psychological experiment of unspecified nature. They were informed that at any moment they would be able to terminate their participation in the experiment, but none of them did so.

Method. As in the previous study, on arrival students were preliminarily informed that they would be randomly divided into two-person teams. Additionally, they were told that the teams would not be coeducational and that the experiment would be devoted to an examination of the functioning of small groups. It was explained that actions of one member of the team would bring consequences for that member or for both members of the group. Subsequently, subjects were informed that, in the experiment, only one member of the team would work on a test consisting of a sequence of five tasks (the experimenter did not specify what tasks and, when asked about it, said that he could not reveal them yet). Half of the subjects were told that successes on these tasks would be rewarded with money (0.75 zlotys—about 25 cents per each success), whereas others were told that failure would be punished with a very mild electric shock (manipulation of positive vs. negative outcome expectation). The second experimental treatment, orthogonal to the previous one, was the following. Subjects in one group learned that regardless of who would be doing the test, the consequences (i.e., depending on experimental conditions, rewards or punishments) would be assumed by both members of the team. In the second group, subjects learned that regardless of who would be doing the test, only they would assume the consequences. Subsequently, all participants were supposed to declare in writing whether they preferred to do the task themselves or whether they would rather like that as yet unknown partner do it.

If subjects relinquish control equally frequently when the rewards or punishments involve only them as compared to when they involve both members of the team, this would mean that a desire to minimize losses or maximize profits is a basic motive for avoiding personal control in such circumstances. Presumably, people delegate control to others because they believe that the others are more competent. However, if subjects relinquish control more often in the condition where consequences of a good or bad performance on the task involve both members of the team, it would mean that the decision to delegate control springs from their willingness to avoid a sense of guilt and/or blame from the partner.

Results. A 2 (Subjects' sex) × 2 (Consequences of a good/bad performance—punishment for failures vs. rewards for successes) × 2 (Bearer of consequences—subject only vs. subject and his/her partner) ANOVA revealed only a main effect of the bearer of consequence variable [$F(1,64) = 25.837$, $p < .0001$]. When a subject was to be the only person to assume the consequences of a bad or good test performance, a larger percentage (90%) of participants wanted to do the test themselves than when the consequences were to be assumed by both members of the group (42%). Although, as it was predicted, subjects relinquished personal control more frequently when the bad performance consequence involving both members of the team was a punishment than when it was a lack of reward, this effect did not reach a level of statistical significance. Table 4 presents the distribution of subjects' decisions in the experimental conditions.

Discussion. Subjects decided to relinquish personal control more frequently when the consequences of their actions involved both members of their group. Such a decision presumably resulted from emotional motives (prediction of a sense of guilt for discomfort experienced by someone else) and interpersonal ones (prediction of possibly being blamed by a victim).

TABLE 4 Proportions of Participants Who Delegated Themselves for the Test in Various Experimental Conditions

	Punishments for failures		Rewards for successes	
	Subject punished	Subject and partner punished	Subject rewarded	Subject and partner rewarded
Females	.85	.25	.91	.43
Males	1.0	.44	.86	.57
All subjects	.91	.35	.89	.50

When these motives were not operative (i.e., when the subject was the only person to assume the consequences of a good or bad task performance), participants accepted personal control far more frequently.

WHEN PEOPLE TEND TO RELINQUISH THEIR PERSONAL CONTROL: BEYOND THE MINIMAX AND MAXIMAX RULES

Numerous empirical studies consistently show that people may relinquish their personal control following a rational analysis of a situation. If results thereof suggest that chances for a desirable result are greater when it is not they but someone else who takes control, they may "put their fate" in this person's hands (Burger, 1989; Burger, McWard, LaTorre, 1989; Miller, 1980; Strube, & Berry, 1985; Strube, Berry, & Moergen, 1985; Strube, & Werner, 1984, 1985). The results of four studies presented in this chapter indicate, however, that a subject's awareness that he or she is less capable than someone else of producing the favorable outcome is not the only important factor in control relinquishment. Uncertainty itself may suffice to provoke such a reaction. The state of uncertainty created in the present studies, without altering the perception of partners' competence, appeared to be a significant determinant of control delegation.

The minimax and maximax rules imply that human beings are primarily interested in a direct effect of action, namely, the avoidance of loss or gain of profit. Undoubtedly, in many cases these motives may determine the intensity of personal control over the course of events that humans consider most desirable. However, these are not the only motives. *A desire to avoid attributing responsibility and guilt to oneself, as well as a desire to avoid being blamed by others, may also constitute reasons for relinquishing personal control.* Results of studies presented in this chapter indicate that these motives may be quite powerful. Humans, as social creatures, are entangled in a complex network of interpersonal relations. In action, they have to take into account not only their own but also other people's fate. They also have to consider what other people think about them and to what degree they may be blamed for outcomes attendant to their behaviors.

In various existential situations man finds himself in the position of a soccer player who at an important match is to decide if he wants to do a penalty kick. He may know from training sessions that he is the best player to do penalty kicks. Thus, he should do the kick because this maximizes his team's chances for success. On the other hand, if he scores a goal, in a few weeks' time no one will remember much about it. If he misses, however, his team will blame him, soccer fans will hate him for years, and he will feel a sense of guilt for a long time. To kick or not to kick? To control or not to control? People often have to solve such dilemmas in their everyday lives.

Moreover, unlike our hypothetical soccer player, they may not always know if they are really more able at or motivated to accomplish a task.

A lowered level of personal control over the course of events may also serve other people's needs. Abdication of personal performance of a task the result of which is diagnostic of a level of competence may protect an individual's *vulnerable self-esteem* and preserve his current, high self-assessment of his competence (Conolley, Gerard, & Kline, 1978; Sachs, 1982). He may achieve the same end by use of a self-handicapping strategy (Berglas, & Jones, 1978; Jones, & Berglas, 1978). A student who prior to an exam goes drinking, instead of studying, reduces her control over the results of an exam and runs the risk of failing. However, she has strategically provided for herself a comfortable interpretation of her failure: "I failed because I had a hangover"—if she fails, and "I'm so excellent that I passed despite a hangover"—if she does fine. Thus, the desire to protect public or private self-esteem can also be a reason for reducing personal control over the course of events.

Yet another reason for avoiding control over events may be found in a culture-bound norm of "sharing control." In situations of social interrelatedness, we must take into account not only our own but also other people's business. Therefore, we sometimes let them influence our own fate, even if their actions are not necessarily in accord with our personal interests; we may tolerate such a situation because we know that we often influence others' fate and not necessarily in accord with their personal interests. A spouse, for example, may agree to spend an evening engaged in some pursuit chosen by his wife, even if this involves going to an opera, an activity which he hates. He knows that a week ago she agreed to go to a party with people whom she dislikes.

Relinquishment of control may also be used as a social manipulation technique. Some people may let others influence their own fate to have a right (based on the reciprocity rule) to influence them in the future (Grzelak et al., 1996).

People take into account many factors "for" and "against" taking personal control. Undoubtedly they use the rules of minimax and maximax, although they certainly do not confine themselves solely to such considerations.

REFERENCES

Adler, A. (1930). Individual psychology. In C. Murchinson (Ed.), *Psychologies of 1930* (pp. 138–165). Worchester, MA: Clark University Press.

Andrisani, P. J. (1978). Internal-external attitudes, personal initiative, and labor market experience. In P. J. Andrisani (Ed.), *Work attitudes and labor market experience: Evidence from the national longitudinal surveys* (pp. 101–134). New York: Praeger.

Arkkelin, D., Oakley, T., & Mynatt, C. (1979). Effects of controllable versus uncontrollable factors on responsibility attributions. A single-subject approach. *Journal of Personality and Social Psychology, 37,* 110–115.

Baker, S. L., & Kirsch, I. (1991). Cognitive mediators of pain perception and tolerance. *Journal of Personality and Social Psychology, 61,* 504–510.

Bandura, A. (1977). Self-efficacy: Toward a unifying theory of behavioral change. *Psychological Review, 84,* 191–215.

Beck, A. (1972). *Depression: Causes and treatment.* Philadelphia: University of Pennsylvania.

Benassi, V. A., Sweeney, P. D., & Dufour, C. L. (1988). Is there a relation between locus of control orientation and depression? *Journal of Abnormal Psychology, 97,* 357–367.

Berglas, S., & Jones, E. E. (1978). Drug-choice as a self-handicapping strategy in response to noncontingent success. *Journal of Personality and Social Psychology, 36,* 405–417.

Biner, P. M., Angle, S. T., Park, J. H., Mellinger, A. E., & Barber, B. C. (1995). Need state and the illusion of control. *Personality and Social Psychology Bulletin, 21,* 899–907.

Bradley, G. W. (1978). Self-serving biases in the attribution process: A reexamination of the fact or fiction question. *Journal of Personality and Social Psychology, 36,* 405–417.

Brehm, J. W. (1966). *A theory of psychological reactance.* New York: Academic Press.

Brewer, M. (1977). An information-processing approach to attribution of responsibility. *Journal of Experimental Social Psychology, 13,* 58–69.

Brewin C. R., & Shapiro, D. A. (1984). Beyond locus of control: Attribution of responsibility for positive and negative outcomes. *British Journal of Psychology, 75,* 43–49.

Burger, J. M. (1989). Negative reactions to increases in perceived personal control. *Journal of Personality and Social Psychology, 56,* 246–256.

Burger, J. M., McWard, J., & LaTorre, D. (1989). Boundaries of self-control: Relinquishing control over aversive events. *Journal of Social and Clinical Psychology, 8,* 209–221.

deCharms, R. (1968). *Personal causation.* New York: Academic Press.

Conolley, E. S., Gerard, H. B., & Kline, T. (1978). Competitive behavior: A manifestation of motivation for ability comparison. *Journal of Experimental Social Psychology, 14,* 123–131.

Deci, E. L. (1975). *Intrinsic motivation.* New York: Plenum.

Dolinski, D. (1991) Perpetrator's freedom of choice as a determinant of attribution of responsibility from the perspective of the victim and a neutral observer. *Polish Psychological Bulletin, 22,* 81–90.

Dolinski, D., Gromski, W., & Szmajke, A. (1988). Perpetrator's freedom of choice as a determinant of responsibility attribution. *Journal of Social Psychology, 128,* 441–449.

Folkman, S. (1984). Personal control and stress and coping processes: A theoretical analysis. *Journal of Personality and Social Psychology, 46,* 839–852.

Fromm, E. (1941). *Escape from freedom.* New York: Avon.

Geer, J. H., Davison, G. C., & Gatchel, R. I. (1970). Reduction of stress in humans through nonverdical perceived control of aversive stimulation. *Journal of Personality and Social Psychology, 16,* 731–738.

Glass, D., & Singer, J. (1972). *Urban stress.* San Diego, CA: Academic Press.

Gromski, W., & Dolinski, D. (1987). Ascription of responsibility for others. *Journal of Social Psychology, 127,* 251–257.

Gromski, W., & Nawrat, R. (1984). Some determinants of perceived responsibility and guilt in a compliance situation. *Polish Psychological Bulletin, 15,* 235–244.

Grzelak, J., Wieczorkowska, G., Kuhlman, D., Joireman, J., Shelley, G., & Toshiaki, D. (1996). Control preferences in interpersonal and macro social settings. Paper presented at the meeting of the European Association of Experimental Social Psychology, Gmunden, Austria, July 1984.

Henslin, J. M.(1967). Craps and magic. *American Journal of Sociology, 73,* 316–330.

Hiroto, D. S., & Seligman, M. E. P. (1975). Generality of learned helplessness in man. *Journal of Personality and Social Psychology, 31*, 311–327.

Jones, E. E., & Berglas, S. (1978) Control of attributions about the self through self-handicapping strategies: The appeal of alcohol and the role of underachievement. *Personality and Social Psychology Bulletin, 4*, 200–206.

Kelly, G. A. (1955). *The psychology of personal constructs*. New York: Norton.

Langer, E. J. (1975). The illusion of control. *Journal of Personality and Social Psychology, 32*, 311–328.

Langer, E. J., & Rodin, J. (1976). The effects of choice and enhanced personal responsibility for the aged: A field experiment in an institutional setting. *Journal of Personality and Social Psychology, 34*, 191–198.

Milgram, S. (1974). *Obedience to authority*. New York: Harper and Row.

Miller, S. M. (1979). Controllability and human stress: Method, evidence and theory. *Behavior Research and Therapy, 17*, 287–304.

Miller, S. M. (1980). Why having control reduces stress: If I can stop the roller coaster, I don't want to get off. In J. Garber & M. E. P. Seligman (Eds.), *Human helplessness: Theory and applications* (pp. 71–95). New York: Academic Press.

Mills, R., & Krantz, D. (1979). Information, choice, and reactions to stress: A field experiment in a blood bank with laboratory analogue. *Journal of Personality and Social Psychology, 37*, 608–620.

Mirowsky, J., & Ross, C. E. (1983). Paranoia and the structure of powerlessness. *American Sociological Review, 48*, 228–239.

Mirowsky, J., & Ross, C. E. (1990). Control or defense? Depresssion and the sense of control over good and bad outcomes. *Journal of Health and Social Behavior, 31*, 71–86.

Perlmuter, L. C., & Monty, R. A. (1977). The importance of perceived control: Fact or fantasy? *American Scientist, 65*, 759–765.

Perlmuter, L. C., Scharff, K., Karsh, R., & Monty, R. A. (1980). Perceived control. A generalized state of motivation. *Motivation and Emotion, 4*, 35–45.

Rodin, J. (1986). Aging and health: Effects of the sense of control. *Science, 233*, 1271–1276.

Rodin, J., & Langer, E. (1977). Long-term effect of a control-relevant intervention. *Journal of Personality and Social Psychology, 35*, 897–902.

Rodin, J., Rennert, K., & Solomon, S. K. (1980). Intrinsic motivation for control: Fact or fiction. In A. Baum & J. E. Singer (Eds.), *Advances in environmental psychology: Vol. 2 Applications of personal control* (pp. 131–148). Hillsdale, NJ: Erlbaum.

Ross, L., Greene, D., & House, P. (1997). The 'false consensus effect': An egocentric bias in social perception and attribution processes. *Journal of Experimental Social Psychology, 13*, 279–301.

Sachs, P. R. (1982). Avoidance of diagnostic information in self-evaluation of ability. *Personality and Social Psychology Bulletin, 8*, 242–246.

Schulz, R. (1976). Effects of control and predictability on the physical and psychological well-being of the institutionalized aged. *Journal of Personality and Social Psychology, 33*, 563–573.

Seligman, M. E. P. (1975). *Helplessness*. San Francisco: Freeman.

Shaver, K. G. (1985). *The attribution of blame: Causality, responsibility, and blameworthiness*. New York: Springer-Verlag.

Snyder, C. R. (1989). Reality negotiation: From excuses to hope and beyond. *Journal of Social and Clinical Psychology, 8*, 130–157.

Snyder, C. R., & Higgins, R. L. (1988). Excuses: The effective role in the negotiation of reality. *Psychological Bulletin, 104*, 23–35.

Strube, M. J., & Berry, J. M. (1985). Attributional and emotional concomitants of control relinquishment. *Basic and Applied Social Psychology, 6*, 205–220.

Strube, M. J., Berry, J. M., & Moergen, S. (1985). Relinquishment of control and the type A behavior pattern. *Journal of Personality and Social Psychology, 49*, 831–842.
Strube, M. J., & Werner, C. (1984). Psychological reactance and the relinquishment of control. *Personality and Social Psychology Bulletin, 10*, 225–234.
Strube, M. J., & Werner, C. (1985). Relinquishment of control and the type A behavior pattern: The role of performance evaluation. *Journal of Personality and Social Psychology, 48*, 688–701.
Thompson, S. C., Sobolew-Shubin, A., Galbraith, M. E., Schwankovsky, L., & Cruzen, D. (1993). Maintaining perception of control: Finding perceived control in low-control circumstances. *Journal of Personality and Social Psychology, 64*, 293–304.
White, R. (1959). Motivation reconsidered: The concept of competence. *Psychological Review, 66*, 297–333.
Wong, P. T. P. (1992). Control is a double-edged sword. *Canadian Journal of Behavioural Science, 24*, 143–146.
Wortman, C. B. (1975). Some determinants of perceived control. *Journal of Personality and Social Psychology, 31*, 282–294.

CHAPTER 14

INTERPERSONAL POWER REPAIR IN RESPONSE TO THREATS TO CONTROL FROM DEPENDENT OTHERS

DAPHNE BLUNT BUGENTAL AND
JEFFREY CLAYTON LEWIS

INTRODUCTION

The presence of potential social challenge or threat is a ubiquitous process within human experience. However, the reactions to such experiences are as variable as the ways in which they are interpreted. A potential insult may be easily written off and disregarded by one individual but responded to by another as an affront requiring an in-kind response. We suggest here that variations in responses to social challenge reflect differences in the perceived social power or control of interactants. When exposed to situations that pose a potential social challenge, those who see themselves as "power disadvantaged" (having less power or control than others) are likely to engage in defensive activity at both the intra- and interpersonal

DAPHNE BLUNT BUGENTAL • Department of Psychology, University of California, Santa Barbara, California 93106. E-mail: bugental@psych.ucsb.edu. JEFFREY CLAYTON LEWIS • Department of Psychology, Pitzer College, Claremont, California 91711. Email: jlewis@pitzer.edu.

Personal Control in Action, edited by Kofta et al., Plenum Press, New York, 1998.

levels. Such responses are motivated by the perceived need to prevent further erosion of power or to regain power. We are specifically concerned here with the differential responses to loss of control as they occur *during* the course of interpersonal interaction.

Our focus here is on asymmetrical human relationships—relationships in which one individual has more power than another. Such relationships assume particular importance because of the anomalous situation created when those in power respond as if they were the "victims" of those who lack power. As a prototypical example, we focus on interaction between adults in a nominal position of authority and dependent children. We could just as easily discuss relationships between superiors and subordinates in a job setting. The shared feature is the presence of a relationship in which one individual has veridical power or formal authority in relationship to another. Caregiving or teaching relationships represent classic examples of authority- or power-based relationships. More experienced adults assume responsibility and control over those who are less competent and have less control within the relationship. Normatively, the lines of power or control are clear—adults are the experts, children are the novices. Adults are the purveyors of positive or negative consequences, and children are the recipients. Adults direct the interaction and children comply with those directions. What happens, however, when children appear to be unresponsive, challenging, or demanding within these relationships—thus threatening a reversal of power?

Reactions to the anomalous threat posed by those in a dependent relationship vary widely across individual caregivers or teachers (or bosses). That is, there are striking individual differences as a function of the ways in which interactive events are construed. In our program of research, we have observed that adults with low perceived power as caregivers are particularly vulnerable to threats to control, that is, they are more likely than others to react negatively to child behavior that might be interpreted as a threat to their control. Such adults may be thought of as ever-vigilant to the power implications of their interactions: Am I having a successful impact? Am I being ignored? Am I in danger of being overwhelmed by a "powerful other"? Consistent with this orientation, such adults are more likely to rely on coercive—and even abusive—tactics in their efforts to retain or regain their power or authority (Bugental, Blue, & Cruzcosa, 1989). Paradoxically, abusers regularly describe themselves as victims of their children. These perplexing and distressing reactions are, of course, consistent with early findings within the social power literature. That is, those who most doubt their power are most likely to rely on punishment or coercive means of control (Kipnis, 1976; Raven & Kruglanski, 1970).

PERCEPTIONS OF POWER AS RELATIONSHIP SCHEMAS

The suggested anomalies in use of power tactics may be better understood by considering the cognitive representations that underlie such processes. In recent years, we have seen increasing attention turn to the role of social knowledge structures as regulators of interaction. Different disciplines bring a different vocabulary to our consideration of such representations. In social and personality psychology, we speak of relationship schemas or self schemas, that is, the chronic ways in which we represent self in relationship to others (e.g., Andersen & Glasman, 1996; Aron, Aron, Tudor, & Nelson, 1991; Baldwin, 1992; Markus & Kitayama, 1991). Within developmental psychology, reference is made to Bowlby's notion of "working models" of relationships. Here the concern is with the ways in which young children come to understand and predict human relationships as a function of their earliest attachments to parents (Bowlby, 1980), along with the ways in which working models or attachment styles are carried forward to influence future relationships (Collins & Read, 1990; Shaver & Hazan, 1994).

Variations in ways of thinking about interpersonal power may be conceptualized as stable knowledge structures (e.g., Bargh, Raymond, Pryor, & Strack, 1995). Such structures are best understood as dyadic representations that include a role for self and others. Adults who are most "at risk" for problematic relationships with dependent children are those who have a low perceived "balance of power," that is, who see themselves as having low power and dependent children as having high power. Such adults more easily believe that children pose a source of threat or interpersonal confrontation by being intentionally resistant or troublesome. Consistent with this construal, they engage in an incessant struggle to defend themselves against the perceived challenges posed by others. In terms used by Hollander (1985) to describe this defensive process, they engage "counter power" against the presumed power of others.

The notion of social power has a venerable history within social psychology. French and Raven's (1959) original conceptualization of the bases of power first alerted the field to the complex nature of social power. We have seen a resurgent interest in social power reframed as a topic that bridges personality and social psychology (Fiske, Morling, & Stevens, 1996). Fiske et al. have proposed that social powerlessness fosters anxiety, which, in turn, may foster attempts to gain or restore control. At the same time, they suggest that there are individual differences in ways of coping with powerlessness-induced anxiety. Some individuals will respond with vigilance and close monitoring of those in power, whereas others may align with power holders.

In our program of research, we are concerned with the extent to which individuals believe that their shared outcomes are controlled by the actions of self or others. Although we are concerned with both perceived power and the manifestations of power (e.g., use of coercive power), we distinguish between the cognitive and behavioral manifestations of power. In operationalizing perceived power, we have relied primarily on parental responses to a self-report instrument (Parent Attribution Test; Bugental, Blue, & Cruzcosa, 1989) in which adults are asked about the causes of caregiving outcomes. Specifically, they are asked to describe the importance they assign to factors that are controllable (or uncontrollable) by self and controllable (or uncontrollable) by children. Adults who attribute high control to children and low control to self over caregiving outcomes (in particular, caregiving failure) are described as having low perceived control or a low perceived balance of power. Such individuals have very easy access to thoughts of themselves as less dominant or less powerful than children. For example, in providing open-ended narratives about the causes of caregiving problems, they provide a more extensive account of the sources of caregiving conflict than of conflict resolution. In similar fashion, they access thoughts about the causes of caregiving problems more quickly than do other adults (Bugental, 1992).

POWER SCHEMAS AS ORGANIZERS OF INTERACTIONS

In understanding the relationships that are characteristic of adults with high or low perceived power, we have proposed the processing pattern shown in Figure 1. The responses shown by parents are not conceptualized as traits that consistently guide responses within caregiving situations. Instead, they are shown as ways of responding when *triggered* by interpersonal events that are ambiguous, unclear, aversive, or demanding, that is, by events that might pose a threat. In contrast, few (if any) differences are expected between parent groupings in their response to caregiving settings that are "easy" or "benign."

Within the social cognition literature, stimuli that are ambiguous or negative have classically been found to lead to high levels of cognitive activity (e.g., Pratto & John, 1991; Wong & Weiner, 1981). Such events lead to cognitive activity of two types: preappraisal processes in which relevant knowledge structures are accessed spontaneously, and appraisal processes that involve an effortful, reflective search for meaning and response options. Consistent with a diathesis model, the same events do not pose an equivalent trigger for all adults. Adults with high perceived power can be thought of as playing out a challenge scenario, whereas adults with low perceived power play out a threat scenario when confronted with a caregiving event that is unclear, unusual, demanding, or difficult. What is seen

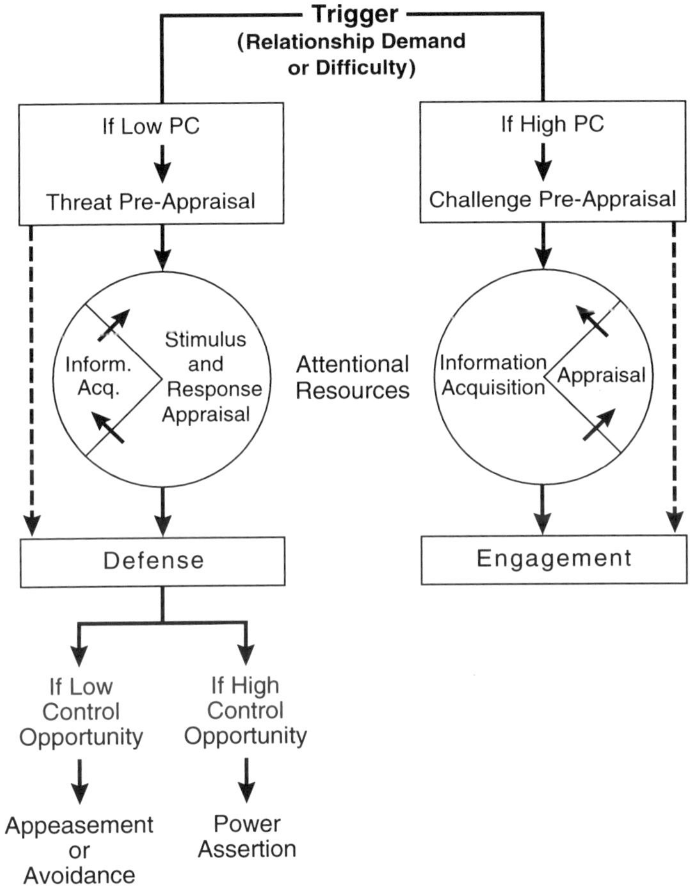

FIGURE 1 Partial model of processing and response patterns within difficult or demanding relationships (full model includes reciprocal or joint interpersonal processes).

as a confrontation by the latter group is seen as simply "interesting" or even "amusing" by the former.

The model has been tested in a program of research in which we have used a number of different research strategies to determine the ways in which adults with high or low perceived power respond to the demands associated with interaction with a dependent child. In field research, one of our early steps was to document that abusive parents are indeed more likely to show low perceived control or power, and that children whose behavior appeared to be unresponsive were more likely to be targeted for abuse or coercion (Bugental, Blue, & Lewis, 1990). We then conducted a series of experiments in naturalistic settings in which adults with high or low perceived power were paired with unrelated children who appeared to be responsive or unresponsive to them. The combined research strategy allowed us to assess the generality of observed processes while still affording the possibility of causal inference in the observed relationships. The predicted sequence of events for the combination of low power adults and "difficult" children is represented as follows:

STEP 1. PREAPPRAISAL PROCESSES

Low power adults have an easily accessible explanatory system that leads to sensitivity to the possibility of threat. If and when a child manifests behaviors or characteristics that are consistent with threat, there is a match between their explanatory system and the stimulus posed by the child.

We think of this original step primarily in terms of unaware processes that occur at an automatic level. That is, ways of thinking about relationships come to mind without reflection. As suggested earlier, knowledge structures concerning interpersonal power may be thought of as chronically accessible schemas. Associated with these schemas are associated affective responses (Fiske & Pavelchak, 1986).

Supporting this step, we have observed that low-power parents are more likely than other parents to access "threat" ideation when interacting with children who are relatively unresponsive to their influence attempts (Bugental et al., 1993). That is, their thoughts are more likely to include a negative appraisal of children's behavior. In order to assess the extent to which such adults access threat ideation *automatically*, we measured how quickly they were able to make social judgments in the presence or absence of a concurrent memory load (holding a number string in memory) (Bugental, Lyon, Krantz, & Cortez, 1997). Specifically, we asked them to make social comparison judgments about themselves versus their children on words that had implications for threat or dominance (negative-strong words), along with words that had no such implications (negative-weak, positive-strong, or positive-weak words). For example, they were shown a word such as "bossy" or "mean" and then asked to judge who this described better—themselves or one of their children. Low-power parents made "dominance" comparisons just as quickly in the presence or absence of a concurrent load. This suggests that low-power parents have an easily accessible representation of power or dominance; that is, making a decision as to who is more dominant does not require reflection. In contrast, high-power parents took longer to make such judgments under concurrent load than in the absence of concurrent load—suggesting that such judgments are *not* "precomputed" for them.

Step 2. Appraisal Processes

The next step involves a somewhat slower, more reflective appraisal of the stimulus situation and the possible coping options. As pointed out by Ingram and his colleagues (e.g., Ingram & Wisnicki, 1991), a distinction needs to be made between cognitive processes that occur automatically and the *products* of such automatic processes. That is, the thoughts that come to mind automatically (e.g., "This child is more dominant than I am") have implications for subsequent processing steps that occur more slowly. Ultimately, such individuals may reach the "corrected" decision that they are much more powerful than the child—as the final product of cognitive processes. For example, in the judgment study just described (Bugental et al., 1997), low power parents presented a very different picture of the power relationship between self and child in the presence or absence of a concurrent load. When constrained by the demands of dual tasks, they presented a schema-consistent judgment of the child as more dominant than the self. In the absence of this constraint, however, they described themselves as more dominant than the child. This combined pattern suggests a two-step process in which precomputed representations of the relationship are subsequently "corrected" by a cognitive repair process.

The ultimate consequence of the activation of a low-power schema is a reduction in cognitive processing capacity. For example, we have observed that low-power adults asked simply to think about negative caregiving interactions show subsequent difficulty in carrying out a cognitively demanding mental arithmetic task (Bugental, Brown, & Reis, 1996). In accounting for these deficits, two processes may be occurring. Elevated levels of stress that follow from schema activation (and associated biochemical changes at the neural level) may lead directly to reductions in cognitive capacity. For example, it has been suggested that certain kinds of biochemical changes may lead to selective impairment of effortful but not automatic processes (Roy-Byrne, Weingartner, Bierer, Thompson, & Post, 1986). Alternately, it may be that attentional resources are redirected to the imagined source of threat or the strategic defenses that may be engaged against an imagined threat. Such cognitive processes may then lead to a reduction in cognitive capacity (Hasher & Zacks, 1979), attentional narrowing (Christianson, 1992; Easterbrook, 1959), or a combination of these processes (Ellis & Ashbrook, 1989). As pointed out by Hartlage et al. (1993), reduced cognitive capacity and attentional narrowing are not necessarily mutually exclusive. Our research has suggested that perceived power disadvantage easily leads to reductions in cognitive capacity; on the other hand, we have not obtained evidence for attentional narrowing (Bugental, Brown, & Reis, 1996; Bugental, Lin, & Susskind, 1995). We anticipate that low-power adults do indeed show enhanced processing of potential threat—but only during *initial* phases of processing. That is, perceived power disadvantage is expected to serve as an initial sensitizer to particular kinds of stimuli but not as a continuing source of intruding thoughts.

Step 3. Response Activation

At the third step, adults display responses that follow from their reflective appraisal of the stimulus and their response options. Analysis now turns to consideration of the operation of an interdependent system in which there are reciprocal influences between the actions (as well as emotions and information processing) of parents and children. Such interdependent interactions are best thought of as representing a continuous flow system (Bugental & Goodnow, 1997; Crick & Dodge, 1994). Although we have described the initial processing that occurs in adult-child interaction in a linear fashion, it is important to recognize that there is continuous feedback within both intrapersonal and interpersonal systems.

The response patterns played out within these interdependent systems reveal regularities that follow from the differential pairing of adults and children and from the control options that are available to both. Low-power parents are particularly reactive to social cues to potential threat or challenge. It is predicted here that they are also highly reactive to control options. For example, if they have high control over the child's outcomes, they may become exceptionally forceful. A clear demonstration of this outcome is reflected in the higher levels of coercion and abuse demonstrated by low-power parents (Bugental, Blue, & Cruzcosa, 1989). Alternately, if they lack veridical control, an avoidant or ingratiating strategy may be selected. In short, the same individual who appears benign or even submissive when he or she lacks control may become very dominant or coercive when in a position of control. The predicted bifurcation is consistent with the notion that lost control has very different consequences based upon the opportunities available to regain control. That is, lost control may lead to either withdrawal of effort (consistent with the learned helplessness literature, e.g., Abramson, Seligman, & Teasdale, 1978) or intensification of effort (consistent with the findings of Pittman and his colleagues, e.g., Pittman & Pittman, 1980).

In most of our past research, we have observed situations in which there are constraints on the control options that are available to adults in their interactions. For example, the adult–child interaction was relatively public and few opportunities were provided for adults to influence the outcomes of children. Under these circumstances, we have observed that low power parents show an inconsistent pattern of response that may be thought of as reflecting the ambivalence between their motives and the situational opportunities. For example, we have observed that low-power adults respond with an immediate burst of smiles to unrelated children who are "difficult" or "odd" (Bugental et al., 1990); that is, they respond with amazing speed to the subtle response characteristics of children. As might be anticipated, the superficially positive behavior of such adults contains cues to dissimulation (e.g., Bugental, 1986; Bugental et al., 1990). They are also more likely than other parents to manifest a combination of strong evaluative comments voiced in a very unassertive fashion (e.g., Bugental & Shennum, 1984).

Not surprisingly, children respond to the communication style of low-power adults with an overall pattern of social and cognitive disengagement (Bugental & Shennum, 1984). Disengagement may take many different forms. For example, in our observations of face-to-face interaction, we found a consistent pattern of social avoidance. Specifically, children were likely to look down or look away in response to the disingenuous smiles of such women (Bugental, Kopeikin, & Lazowski, 1991). In teaching interactions, children showed increasing indications of distress in response to such women, along with deficits in their performance on cognitively demanding tasks (Bugental, Lyon, McGrath, & Bimbela, 1996). These child responses may in turn be (mis)interpreted by low-power adults as defiant.

As interaction continues within "mismatched" pairings, parental strategies may easily come to be understood as "failed." The apparent unresponsiveness of children may be construed by low-power parents as confirmation of their initial appraisal of the situation as confrontational or threatening. Early manifestations of parental positivity by low power parents are quickly replaced with neutral and then negative affect. No such interactional pattern emerges when low-power parents are paired with "easy" children or when high-power parents are paired with either "difficult" or "easy" children.

The deteriorating interaction patterns that emerge for "mismatched" pairings of adults and children are also reflected at a physiological level. That is, as child unresponsiveness continues, parents show autonomic changes that are consistent with defensive arousal or mobilization (e.g., increases in heart rate and electrodermal activity). Such reactions reflect the kinds of autonomic changes that are observed in response to tasks seen as effortful, either at a cognitive level (e.g., Wright, 1996) or a physical level (e.g., Obrist, 1981). This pattern of mobilization has been found to be a common reaction of abusive parents to stimuli that have implications for caregiving challenge (e.g., Frodi & Lamb, 1980; Wolfe, Fairbanks, Kelly & Bradlyn, 1983).

In summary, we have proposed that parent–child relationships are strongly influenced by the management of power and control. Parents who believe they lack power within the relationship easily perceive threats to their sense of control and respond in ways that "defend" against such threat. Ultimately, however, the strategic options they select will depend on the situational affordances that are available for control. If their environment allows them direct control over children, this is the option they will take. If their environment precludes the possibility of control, they will seek more passive means of defense.

PREDICTIONS

In the research described here, we focus on the bifurcated response pattern predicted at Step 3. That is, we are concerned with the alternate response patterns expected to be shown by low-power adults as a function of control opportunities. Although we have obtained suggestive evidence for this response polarization, we have not made a direct test of the expected pattern of response to situational opportunities for control.

We predicted that low-power adults demonstrate exceptionally high levels of assertion when the interaction setting facilitates control but exceptionally low levels of assertion when the interaction setting limits control. To test these predictions, we conducted two studies in which we systematically varied the extent to which adults were given the opportunity to provide evaluative feedback to children during a training procedure. That is, they were given high or low opportunities to show their approval or disapproval of children's performance.

EMPIRICAL TEST OF PREDICTIONS

STUDY 1

Procedures

In an initial study, we brought 58 undergraduate women into the lab to provide training to children on a maze task (learning how to successfully negotiate a maze displayed on a computer screen). Research participants were simply told that they would be teaching an 8-year-old boy (at a distant location) via closed-circuit TV. In actuality, "children's" performances were preprogrammed to simulate responsive and unresponsive behavior. All women were given the opportunity to provide verbal instructions to children at several points during the course of the interaction. However, systematic differences were introduced in the extent to which they had "evaluative control" over the child. In the high-control condition, they could provide continuous evaluation of children's performance. That is, as children progressed through the maze, "teachers" had access to computer controls that displayed "happy" or "mad" faces on the screen as a way of indicating positive or negative evaluation of child actions. In the low control condition, they had no way of providing evaluative feedback during children's performance; their opportunities for "control" were limited to verbal feedback to the child after an entire "game" was completed—an option also available to "teachers" in the high control condition.

We predicted that low-power women, in particular during interactions with unresponsive children, would be maximally reactive to the control possibilities within the situation. That is, the degree of assertiveness they showed was expected to closely reflect control options. We used vocal amplitude as our measure of power assertion, i.e., how loudly adults spoke during their instructions to children. Vocal amplitude provides an index of social effort, and has been found to be a reliable indicator of power assertion or dominance (Pittam, 1994; Scherer, 1986). We expected that low-power adults interacting with unresponsive children would show the highest levels of assertion when they were given the opportunity for control; at the same time, we anticipated that this same grouping would manifest the *lowest* levels of vocal assertion when they lacked access to the opportunity for control.

Results

Although the predicted interaction between variables did not reach significance, a significant main effect was found for access to evaluative control, $F(1, 49) = 6.31, p = .015$. As shown in Figure 2, women allowed high evaluative control showed higher levels of vocal assertiveness than did women placed in a situation in which they could only use instructions as a means of influence. A planned contrast testing the predicted pattern of effects reached significance, $t(50) = 2.21, p = .032$. Low-power women paired with unresponsive trainees, when provided *high* evaluative control, spoke very loudly (mean = 74 decibels). In contrast, low-power women with unresponsive trainees, when provided *low* evaluative control, spoke relatively softly (mean = 65 decibels). "Teachers" in other groupings showed moderate levels of vocal assertion (mean = 70 decibels).

A number of reasonable questions could be asked about our findings—primarily focused on its ecological validity. For example, we used undergraduate women, not parents. In order to test the extent to which similar effects could be observed with mothers (again paired with unrelated children), we conducted a second study that was limited to mothers.

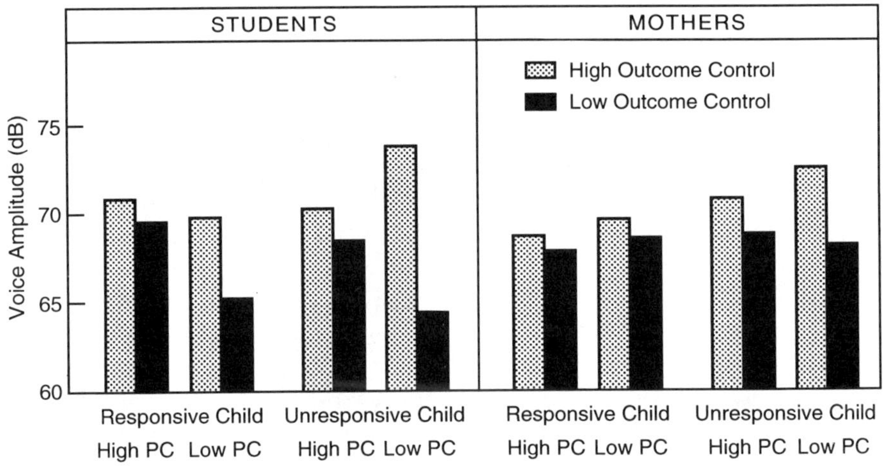

FIGURE 2 Vocal amplitude shown in response to high versus low outcome control.

We also obtained information on the kinds of ideation that parents brought to mind during the training situation.

STUDY 2

Procedures

In a second study, research participants were 160 mothers of school-aged children recruited from the general community.[1] Using the same essential paradigm that was employed in Study 1, women were initially shown one of 20 different videotapes (of boys between the ages of 5 and 12) with whom they believed they would interact.

As in Study 1, we systematically varied the extent of evaluative control that mothers were allowed in interaction with children. In order to provide a more stringent test of the effects of evaluative control, we provided all mothers the opportunity to display "happy faces" and "mad faces" to children in response to their performance. However, "teachers" in the high-control condition had continuous access to such evaluative feedback, whereas teachers in the low-control condition only had access to such evaluative feedback after games were concluded.

As in Study 1, we expected maximum vocal amplitude among low-power women interacting with unresponsive children but only when they had maximum access to control. Conversely, we expected the lowest levels of vocal amplitude for low-power women with unresponsive children when they had relatively low access to control.

In order to test the extent to which low-power parents actually differed in their appraisals of children in the different conditions, we replayed videotapes for them at the end of the interaction. We asked them to write down what they believed the child had been thinking during the game interactions. This allowed us to assess the extent to which adults construed the unresponsive child's behavior as competitive (i.e., a potential threat). Parental statements were coded as attributing "competitive," "cooperative," and/or "individualistic" motives to the child (consistent with the social values orientations studied by McClintock and his colleagues (e.g., McClintock & Liebrand, 1988).

Results

Predictions were tested by an ANOVA that included parental power, child responsiveness, and evaluative control as grouping variables and vocal intensity (in decibels) as the dependent variable. Although the predicted 3-way interaction between variables did not reach significance, the interaction between perceived power and experimental control was significant, $F(1, 117) = 4.41$, $p = .038$. A planned comparison testing the predicted difference between groupings approached significance, $t(118) = 1.78$, $p = .08$. As shown in Figure 2, low-power parents who interacted with unresponsive children, when allowed high evaluative control, gave instructions with a relatively loud voice (mean = 72 decibels). In contrast, low-power parents with unresponsive children, when allowed little evaluative control, displayed relatively soft voices (mean = 68 decibels). Other parental grouping showed moderate vocal intensity (mean = 69 decibels).

Predictions concerning the types of motives attributed to children were tested in chi-square analyses. Specifically, a comparison was made of the frequency with which "teachers" attributed competitive motives (as opposed to cooperative, individualistic, or mixed motives) to child trainees. A comparison was made of the different types of attributions made in the "lost control" condition (unresponsive child/low access to evaluative control) versus all other conditions. In the lost control condition, 71% of low-power parents attributed competitive motives to child trainees; in all other conditions, none of the low-power parents attributed competitive motives to child trainees. A chi-square testing these differences yielded a coefficient of 7.34 ($p < .01$). In contrast, 29% of high-power parents in the lost control condition and 8% of high-power parents in other conditions attributed competitive motives to child trainees. A chi-square testing these differences did not approach significance (chi-square = 2.18).

IMPLICATIONS OF EMPIRICAL FINDINGS

SUPPORT FOR MODEL

The findings reported here, combined with past research within this program, provide support for the proposed model. The ways in which adults chronically construe their relationships with children serve to organize their responses to those relationships. In research reported here, adults who thought of themselves as lacking power were found to be highly reactive to the possibility of lost control. When confronted with an unresponsive child "trainee" and a situation that gave them little control over that child, they made the interpretation that the child was competing with them. For example, they often reported that child "trainees" were trying to outdo them. Under these circumstances, they withdrew effort—as reflected in their unassertive voice quality.

A very different response was shown to unresponsive "trainees" when low-power "teachers" were afforded the opportunity to provide continuous evaluative feedback to them. Under these circumstances, they did not report believing that the child was competing with them. Additionally, they employed a communication strategy that was characterized by exaggerated assertion. Specifically, they spoke to children in an exceptionally loud voice—a well-documented manifestation of power assertion (Pittam, 1994: Scherer, 1986).

Adults with low perceived power within power-asymmetric relationships appear to have a somewhat chameleonlike quality. That is, they present a polarized pattern of very high dominance or very low dominance, based on the opportunities for control that are immediately available in the situation. When there are low opportunities for control, they may be thought of as displaying a schema-consistent "default" response of low assertion. If, on the other hand, there are clear opportunities for power assertion (i.e., evaluative control), they display a counterschematic and exaggerated display of force that may be thought of as reflecting a stereotyped enactment of behavior seen as characteristic of powerful others. In contrast, adults with higher levels of perceived control are less reactive to control opportunities. They present a picture of moderate levels of assertion that is little influenced by the characteristics of children or the opportunities for evaluative control.

When these observations are combined with past findings, we see that the interpretive systems that adults bring to relationships serve as powerful organizers not only of cognitive processes but also of interactional style. Low-power women do *not*, however, reveal response patterns that appear as traits. That is, they do not show any characteristic response pattern that transcends settings. Instead, they show an exaggerated pattern of reactivity to situational cues that are relevant for power. They are highly reactive to the potential threat suggested by children's behavior and to the situational opportunities for control over the child.

The exaggerated reactivity of low-power parents is consistent with the literature on abusive parents (or batterers). Although abusive parents are rarely characterized by any particular pattern of psychopathology, they show exaggerated reactivity to a variety of life stressors (e.g., job stress, illness) (Wolfe, 1985). In the same way, they are sensitive to the availability of power repair possibilities. The process involved is similar to that observed in authority-based relationships in the work environment. That is, the passive subordinate may reveal unexpectedly tyrannical properties when placed in a position of authority over others (Kipnis, 1976). It is also similar to the pattern reported for unusually aggressive children. That is, aggressive children have been found to place an unusually high degree of value on control over the victim (Boldizar, Perry, & Perry, 1989). Powerless-prone individuals may be thought of as having unique outcome values; that is, they obtain exceptional "benefits" from the opportunities for control over those in a position of lesser power.

Self-Maintenance Patterns

Adults who show "power reversals" in their perceptions of children may ultimately come to foster and maintain relationships in which they genuinely lack control. These self-maintenance processes operate at two different levels. The first self-maintaining pattern occurs at a *cognitive* level. When low-power adults are placed in a position of nominal authority, there is an implicit contradiction between their perceptions of their veridical power and cultural expectations that are associated with an authority role. This explanation is consistent with the views of Sedek and Kofta (1990), who have suggested that uncontrollable situations may generate symptoms of helplessness because of the self-contradictory task information that comes into play during problem-solving activity. As pointed out earlier, such parents are likely to show a reduction in cognitive capacity under these circumstances (Bugental et al., 1996). As a result, they are unlikely to broadly process events that occur during challenging interactions. Thus few inroads are made on their preexisting ways of conceptualizing parenting interactions.

As a second self-maintenance pattern, the communication style shown by low-power adults in response to perceived threat is likely to be ineffective. The lability of their assertiveness (demonstrated here), combined with the unreliability of their affect (e.g., Bugental, Blue, & Lewis, 1990), provides an inconsistent stimulus for children. As noted earlier, children frequently show a social avoidance pattern in response to such adult communication patterns. Ultimately, the unreliability of adult messages serves to foster and maintain child unresponsiveness—thus confirming adult expectations of low control.

We have applied the proposed model to abusive relationships, in particular those relationships characterized by physical or emotional abuse (e.g., Bugental, 1993). More generally, this pattern is characteristic of those who abuse others in a position of lesser power. Appeasement/avoidance and coercion are two sides of the same coin—alternately turned to respond to the immediate situational opportunities for control. In lay terms, we see the picture of a "bully."

Interventions attempting to alter entrenched patterns of child abuse have had modest success at best (e.g., Wekerle & Wolfe, 1993). Although abuse is caused by a complex interaction of factors (e.g., Wolfe, 1985), the elevated risk that is associated with perceived power disadvantage suggests some of the reasons why abuse may be resistant to change. The expectations of low power parents easily set self-fulfilling prophecies into place. Such individuals easily misconstrue the benign responses of children as confrontations, challenges, or threats. Subsequent increases in autonomic mobilization and reductions in cognitive capacity further limit parents' ability to accurately process the responses of their children. A child who misunderstands them may be interpreted as disobeying them. A fearful child who looks away may be interpreted as ignoring them. The labile responses of "powerless" parents (vacillating between avoidance and exaggerated power assertion) contribute additional fuel to escalating conflict and stress. The relative intractability of such systems provides a convincing rationale for current efforts to make greater use of child abuse prevention efforts (Wekerle & Wolfe, 1993).

Implications for Lost Control

Our findings also may be interpreted from the framework of the broader literature concerning reactions to loss of control. Within this literature, quite different outcomes have been observed as a function of levels and circumstances of lost control and the opportunities to regain control. From the standpoint of the learned helplessness literature, it has been suggested that those who are deprived of control will show increased withdrawal and reduced efforts to attempt control (Abramson, Seligman, & Teasdale, 1978). Others have suggested that *low* levels of lack of control may lead to very active efforts to regain control (Pittman & Pittman, 1980; Wortman & Brehm, 1975), whereas only very high levels of lost control may lead to helplessness and effort withdrawal.

Our findings suggest that individuals respond quite differently to lost control based on the implicit opportunities for regaining control.

Low-power parents may be thought of as experiencing loss of control when confronted with an unresponsive child. When these individuals were placed in a teaching setting that afforded them little control (and thus few repair opportunities), they withdrew vocal effort—a pattern that is consistent with the formulations of learned helplessness. If, however, they were afforded the opportunity for regaining control (evaluative control over child), their high levels of vocal effort were consistent with the *motivating* effects of lost control.

Our focus here has been on repair efforts that occur in response to lost control in social settings. In contrast, most research on reactions to lost control have involved noninteractive tasks. As a result, it is not easy to relate our findings directly to the broader literature. The exertion of strategic effort to regain control during interaction can be seen as actively competing with the demands of processing other ongoing events. For example, the individual who is attempting to regain their power in interaction with a resistant child may not easily process details of that interaction. Such may not be the case if opportunities to regain control lack such dual processing demands; under these circumstances, efforts to repair lost control may more easily lead to enhanced processing accuracy (e.g., Gleicher & Weary, 1991; Pittman & D'Agostino, 1989). Consistent with this explanation, we have observed that low-power adults—following loss of control in a teaching setting—showed increased unitizing responses on a subsequent noninteractive task (Lewis, Bugental, & Fleck, 1991). Unitizing activity has typically been interpreted as reflecting efforts to obtain cognitive control (Newtson, 1973). In short, the implications of exaggerated repair efforts for performance effectiveness or processing accuracy may be greatly influenced by task characteristics.

As a final note, it is important to consider the amount of overlap between the constructs of low perceived power, depression, and anxiety. Those who are characterized as "powerless," depressed, or anxious all reveal the presence of cognitive deficits in response to salient events (Hartlage et al., 1993). Somewhat surprisingly, individuals with low perceived power have *not* been found to show elevated levels of depression (on the Beck Depression Inventory).[2] Although low power adults are exceptionally autonomically reactive and they report relatively high negative ideation, we have no information that suggests they experience any particular pattern of negative affect (Bugental et al., 1990). Thus there is no reason to believe that the processes observed here are associated with specific affective patterns. At the same time, low-power parents do report higher levels of chronic stress.[3] To the extent such chronic stress reactions reflect anxiety, the reduced cognitive capacity they show in response to threat is consistent with the literature on anxiety (e.g., Hartlage et al., 1993). Additionally, the exaggerated vigilance we have suggested for those with low perceived power parallels the automatic attention response given to threat stimuli by anxious individuals (e.g., MacLeod, Mathews, & Tata, 1986; Shiffrin & Schneider, 1977). However, we have no evidence suggesting that observed reductions in cognitive capacity occur in response to intruding negative thoughts—a pattern that has been observed in response to depression (Hartlage et al., 1993) and anxiety (e.g., Eysenck, 1982; Schlenker & Leary, 1982). Indeed, low-power parents—when stressed—have been found to have unusual difficulty in recalling their thoughts (Bugental, Brown, & Reiss, 1996). In future research, we hope to determine the extent to which the cognitive deficits demonstrated by low-power individuals reflect initial attentional biases, cognitive interference produced by strategy generation, or biologically mediated changes in cognitive capacity.

SUMMARY AND CONCLUSIONS

We have suggested some of the ways that cognitive representations of relationships act to organize processes that occur *during* interpersonal interaction. Adults who chronically see themselves as power disadvantaged are highly reactive to the threat potential of dependent others. When confronted with a child who might be interpreted as challenging their authority, they respond with intrapersonal and interpersonal processes that appear to be both defensive and maladaptive in nature. They easily construe relationships as power contests. In their interactional style, they respond alternately as purveyors of power or as appeasers/avoiders of "powerful others." Rather than responding in any consistent fashion within their relationships, they are highly sensitive to the immediate power implications of relationships and settings. They respond easily to triggering information that directs the pathway of their reactions toward dominance (exaggerated efforts to regain control) or submission (appeasement or reduction in efforts to regain control). At a theoretical level, these findings suggest the combined importance of considering individual variations in sensitivity to loss of control, situational variations in threats to control, and situational opportunities for repair of lost control. At an applied level, the processes observed are useful for the conceptualization and prevention of power misuse within dependent relationships.

NOTES

1. Study 2 reports new data obtained as part of a larger study (Bugental et al., 1993). The sound quality was not suitable for acoustical analysis on 35 cases. The second measure (appraisal) was introduced only during the second half of the study. Therefore, analyses are not based on the same number of cases for the two different measures.
2. The correlation (*r*) between perceived power and the BDI was .06 among individuals participating in Study 1.

3. On an 8-point scale (where 7 is high), low-power mothers participating in Study 1 reported a higher level of chronic stress (mean = 3.73) than did high-power mothers (mean = 2.70), $F(1, 134) = 5.01$, $p = .027$.

REFERENCES

Abramson, L. Y., Seligman, M. E. P., & Teasdale, J. D. (1978). Learned helplessness in humans: Critique and reformulation. *Journal of Abnormal Psychology, 87,* 49–74.

Andersen, S. M., & Glassman, N. S. (1996). Responding to significant others when they are not there: Effects on interpersonal inference, motivation, and affect. In R. M. Sorrentino & E. T. Higgins (Eds.), *Handbook of motivation and cognition* (Vol. 3, pp. 262–321). New York: Guilford.

Aron, A., Aron, E. N., Tudor, M., & Nelson, G. (1991). Close relationships as including other in self. *Journal of Personality and Social Psychology, 60,* 241–253.

Baldwin, M. W. (1992). Relational schemas and the processing of social information. *Psychological Bulletin, 112,* 461–484.

Bargh, J. A., Lombardi, W. J., & Higgins, E. T. (1988). Automaticity of chronically accessible constructs in person situation effects on person perception: It's just a matter of time. *Journal of Personality and Social Psychology, 55,* 559–605.

Bargh, J. A., Raymond, P., Pryor, J. B., & Strack, F. (1995). Attractiveness of the underling: An automatic power-sex association and its consequence for sexual harrassment and aggression. *Journal of Personality and Social Psychology, 68,* 768–781.

Boldizar, J. P., Perry, D. G., & Perry, L. C. (1989). Outcome values and aggression. *Child Development, 60,* 571–579.

Bowlby, J. (1980). *Attachment and loss. Vol. III. Loss.* New York: Basic Books.

Bugental, D. B. (1986). Unmasking the "polite smile": Situational and personal determinants of managed affect in adult-child interaction. *Personality and Social Psychology Bulletin, 12,* 7–16.

Bugental, D. B. (1992). Affective and cognitive processes within threat-oriented family systems. In I. E. Sigel, A. McGillicuddy-DeLisi, & J. Goodnow (Eds.), *Parental belief systems: The psychological consequences for children.* Hillsdale, NJ: Erlbaum.

Bugental, D. B. (1993) Communication in abusive relationships: Cognitive constructions of interpersonal power. *American Behavioral Scientist, 36,* 288–308.

Bugental, D. B., & Goodnow, J. G. (1997). Socialization processes. In N. Eisenberg (Ed.), *Handbook of child psychology. Volume 3: Social, emotional, and personality development* (pp. 389–462). New York: Wiley.

Bugental, D. B., & Shennum, W. A. (1984). "Difficult" children as elicitors and targets of adult communication patterns: An attributional-behavioral transactional analysis. *Monographs of the Society for Research in Child Development, 49* (1, Serial No. 205).

Bugental, D. B., Blue, J. B., & Cruzcosa, M. (1989) Perceived control over caregiving outcomes: Implications for child abuse. *Developmental Psychology, 25,* 532–539.

Bugental, D. B., Blue, J., & Lewis, J. (1990). Caregiver cognitions as moderators of affective reactions to "difficult" children. *Developmental Psychology, 26,* 631–638.

Bugental, D. B., Kopeikin, H., & Lazowski, l. (1991). Children's responses to authentic versus polite smiles. In K. J. Rotenberg (Ed.), *Children's interpersonal trust.* New York: Springer-Verlag.

Bugental, D. B., Blue, J., Cortez, V., Fleck, K., Kopeikin, H., Lewis, J. C., & Lyon, J. (1993). Social cognitions as organizers of autonomic and affective responses to social challenge. *Journal of Personality and Social Psychology, 64,* 1–9.

Bugental, D. B., Lin, E. K., & Susskind, J. E. (1995). Influences of affect on cognitive processes at different ages: Why the change? In N. Eisenberg (Ed.), *Social development. Review of personality and social psychology* (Vol. 15, pp. 159–184). Thousand Oaks, CA: Sage.

Bugental, D. B., Bimbela, A., & McGrath, E. (1996). Child responses to communication patterns characteristic of parents with low perceived control. Unpublished paper.

Bugental, D. B., Brown, M., & Reiss, C. (1996). Cognitive representations of power in caregiving relationships: Biasing effects on interpersonal interaction and information-processing. *Journal of Family Psychology, 10*, 397–407.

Bugental, D. B., Lyon, J. E., McGrath, E., & Bimbela, A. (1996). Performance deficits shown by children when instructed by teachers with high versus low perceived power. Unpublished paper.

Bugental, D. B., Lyon, J. E., Cortez, V., & Krantz, J. (1997). Who's the boss? Accessibility of dominance ideation among individuals with low perceptions of interpersonal power. *Journal of Personality and Social Psychology, 72*, 1297–1309

Christianson, S-A (1992). Emotional stress and eyewitness memory: A critical review. *Psychological Bulletin, 112*, 284–309.

Collins, N. L., & Read, S. J. (1990). Adult attachment, working models, and relationship quality in dating couples. *Journal of Personality and Social Psychology, 58*, 644–663.

Crick, N. R., & Dodge, K. A. (1994). A review and reformulation of social information-processing mechanisms in children's social adjustment. *Child Development, 52*, 857–865.

Donovan, W. L., Leavitt, L. A., & Walsh, R. O. (1990). Maternal self-efficacy: Illusory control and its effect on susceptibility to learned helplessness. *Child Development, 61*, 1638–1647.

Easterbrook, J. A. (1959). The effect of emotion on cue utilization and the organization of behavior. *Psychological Review, 66*, 183–201.

Ellis, H. C., & Ashbrook, W. (1989). The "state" of mood and memory research: A selective review. Special issue: Mood and memory: Theory, research and applications. *Journal of Social Behavior and Personality, 4*, 1–21.

Eysenck, M. W. (1982). Attention and arousal: cognition and performance. Berlin: Springer-Verlag.

Fiske, S. T., Morling, B., & Stevens, L. E. (1996). Controlling self and others: A theory of anxiety, mental control, and social control. *Personality and Social Psychology Bulletin, 22*, 115–123.

Fiske, S. T., & Pavelchak, M. A. (1986). Category-based versus piecemeal-based affective responses: Developments in schema-triggered affect. In R. M. Sorrentino, & E. T. Higgins (Eds.), *Motivation and cognition* (pp. 167–203). New York: Guilford.

French, J. R.P., Jr., & Raven, B. H. (1959). The bases of social power. In D. Cartwright (Ed.), *Studies in social power* (pp. 118–149). Ann Arbor: University of Michigan Press.

Frodi, A. M., & Lamb, M. E. (1980). Child abusers' responses to infant smiles and cries. *Child Development, 51*, 238–241.

Gilbert, D. T., & Osborne, R. E. (1989). Thinking backward: Some curable and incurable consequences of cognitive busyness. *Journal of Personality and Social Psychology, 57*, 940–949.

Gleicher, F., & Weary, G. (1991). Effects of depression on quantity and quality of social inference. *Journal of Personality and Social Psychology, 61*, 105–114.

Grusec, J. E., & Mammone, N. (1995). Features and sources of parents' attributions about themselves and their children. In N. Eisenberg (Ed.), *Review of personality and social psychology* (Vol. 15). Thousand Oaks, CA: Sage.

Hartlage, S., Alloy, L. B., Vazquez, C., & Dykman, B. (1993). Automatic and effortful processing in depression. *Psychological Bulletin, 113*, 247–278.

Hasher, L., & Zacks, R. T. (1979). Automatic and effortful processes in memory. *Journal of Experimental Psychology: General, 108*, 356–389.
Hazan, C., & Shaver, P. (1987). Romantic love conceptualized as an attachment process. *Journal of Personality and Social Psychology, 52*, 511–524.
Hollander, E. P. (1985). Leadership and power. In G. Lindzey & E. Aronson (Eds.), *Handbook of social psychology* (Vol. 2, pp. 485–538). New York: Random House.
Ingram, R. E., & Wisnicke, K. (1991). Cognition in depression. In P. A. Magaro (Ed.), *Annual review of psychopathology* (Vol. I, pp. 187–230). Newbury Park: Sage.
Kahneman, D. (1973). *Attention and effort*. Englewood Cliffs, NJ: Prentice-Hall.
Kipnis, D. (1976). *The powerholders*. Chicago, IL: University of Chicago Press.
Lewis, J. C., Bugental, D. B., & Fleck, K. (1991). Attributions as moderators of reactions to computer-simulated responsive and unresponsive children. *Social Cognition, 9*, 277–293.
MacLeod, C., Mathews, A., & Tata, P. (1986). Attentional bias in emotional disorders. *Journal of Abnormal Psychology, 95*, 15–20.
Markus, H. M., & Kitayama, S. (1991). Culture and the self: Implications for cognition, emotion, and motivation. *Psychological Review, 98*, 234–253.
Newtson, D. (1973). Attribution of the unit of perception of ongoing behavior. *Journal of Personality and Social Psychology, 28*, 28–38.
Obrist, P. A. (1981). *Cardiovascular psychophysiology: A perspective*. New York: Plenum.
Pittam, J. (1994). *Voice in social interaction: An interdisciplinary approach*. Thousand Oaks, CA: Sage.
Pittman, T. S., & D'Agostino, P. R. (1989). Motivation and cognition: Control deprivation and the nature of subsequent information-processing. *Journal of Experimental Social Psychology, 25*, 465–480.
Pittman, T. S., & Pittman, N. L. (1980). Deprivation of control and the attribution process. *Journal of Personality and Social Psychology, 39*, 377–389.
Pratto, F., & John, O. P. (1991). Automatic vigilance: The attention-grabbing power of negative social information. *Journal of Personality and Social Psychology, 61*, 380–391.
Raven, B. H., & Kruglanski, A. W. (1970). Conflict and power. In P. Swingle (Ed.), *The structure of conflict* (pp. 69–110). San Diego, CA: Academic Press.
Roy-Byrne, P. P., Weingartner, H., Bierer, L. M., Thompson, K., & Post, R. M. (1986). Effortful and automatic cognitive processes in depression. *Archives of General Psychiatry, 43*, 265–267.
Scherer, K. R. (1986). Vocal affect expression: A review and model for future research. *Psychological Bulletin, 99*, 143–165.
Schlenker, B. R., & Leary, M. R. (1982). Social anxiety and self-presentation: A conceptualization model. *Psychological Bulletin, 92*, 641–669.
Sedek, G., & Kofta, M. (1990). When cognitive exertion does not yield cognitive gain: Toward an informational explanation of learned helplessness. *Journal of Personality and Social Psychology, 58*, 729–743.
Shaver, P. R., & Hazan, C. (1994). Adult romantic attachment: Theory and evidence. In A. L. Weber & J. H. Harry (Eds.), *Perspectives on close relationships* (pp. 110–130). Boston, MA: Allyn & Bacon.
Shiffrin, R. M., & Schneider, W. (1977). Controlled and automatic information process: II. Perceptual learning, automatic attending, and a general theory. *Psychological Review, 84*, 127–188.
Wekerle, C., & Wolfe, D. A. (1993). Prevention of child physical abuse and neglect: Promising new directions. *Clinical Psychology Review, 13*, 501–540.
Wolfe, D. A. (1985). Child-abusive parents: An empirical review and analysis. *Psychological Bulletin, 97*, 462–482.

Wolfe, D. A., Fairbanks, J. A., Kelly, J. A., & Bradlyn, A. S. (1983). Child abusive parents' physiological responses to stressful and nonstressful behavior to children. *Behavioral Assessment*, *5*, 363–372.

Wong, P. T., & Weiner, B. (1981). When people ask "why" questions, and the heuristics of attributional search. *Journal of Personality and Social Psychology*, *40*, 650–663.

Wortman, C. B., & Brehm, J. W. (1975). Responses to uncontrollable outcomes: An integration of reactance theory and the learned helplessness model. In L. Berkowitz (Ed.), *Advances in experimental social psychology* (Vol. 8, pp. 277–336). San Diego, CA: Academic Press.

Wright, R. (1996) Brehm's theory of motivation as a model of effort and cardiovascular response. In J. M. Gollwitzer & J. A. Bargh (Eds.), *The psychology of action: Linking cognition and motivation to behavior* (pp. 424–453). New York: Guilford.

CHAPTER 15

CONTROL MOTIVATION, DEPRESSION, AND COUNTERFACTUAL THOUGHT

KEITH D. MARKMAN AND GIFFORD WEARY

INTRODUCTION

The notion that there exists a fundamental need to exert control over or to influence one's environment has enjoyed a long history in psychology (e.g., DeCharms, 1968; Heider, 1958) and has stimulated considerable theoretical work. Such a need has been characterized by theorists at multiple levels of analysis. Control motivation, for example, has been characterized broadly in terms of proactive (White, 1959) or reactive (e.g., Abramson, Seligman, & Teasdale, 1978; Brehm, 1966; Brehm & Brehm, 1981) strivings for control over general or specific (Brehm & Brehm, 1981) and central or peripheral outcomes (Thompson, 1993). Additionally, various types of control strategies used to gain or maintain a sense of personal control have been proposed (e.g., Averill, 1973; Heckhausen & Schulz, 1995; Rothbaum, Weisz, & Snyder, 1982; Thompson, 1981). Modes of control, for instance, have been categorized as either primary or secon-

KEITH D. MARKMAN • Department of Psychology, Marywood University, Scranton, Pennsylvania 18509. E-mail: markman@ac.marywood.edu. GIFFORD WEARY • Department of Psychology, Ohio State University, Columbus, Ohio 43210. E-mail: gweary@pop.service.ohio-state.edu

Personal Control in Action, edited by Kofta et al., Plenum Press, New York, 1998.

dary. Primary strategies involve direct action undertaken to produce desirable and avoid undesirable outcomes in the external world, whereas secondary strategies employ primarily cognitive processes undertaken to produce a change within the person. Recently, Heckhausen and Schulz (1995) have further delineated these primary and secondary forms of control according to whether they are based on veridical or illusory causal understandings of the world and whether they are functional or dysfunctional. While most control theorists view primary control as preferable to secondary control, the latter is viewed as critical in the process of adaptation to control failures and in the promotion of future primary control attempts.

However conceptualized and achieved, there can be little doubt that a need for control plays a critical role in a variety of motivational, behavioral, and emotional processes (Weary, Gleicher, & Marsh, 1993). Threats to or decrements in individuals' beliefs that they can achieve desired outcomes have been associated with psychological reactance, motivational impairments, adaptive and maladaptive coping behaviors, depressed and anxious affect, metacognitive feelings of causal uncertainty, and immunological responses to stress.

In this chapter, we focus on a particular consequence of generalized control concerns for a secondary control strategy. More specifically, we examine the role of chronic control concerns in individuals' attempts to render their social environments more understandable, predictable, and controllable. Because chronic control concerns and resultant levels of chronic, heightened control motivation have been shown to be associated with mild and moderate levels of depressive symptomatology, we examine the sense-making activities of individuals suffering from subclinical levels of depression.

While other investigators have examined the attributional inferences that relatively depressed and nondepressed individuals typically employ in their quest for enhanced understanding, prediction, and control, here we focus on an alternative cognitive process. Specifically, in two studies we focus on the manner in which relatively depressed and nondepressed people mentally "undo" or engage in counterfactual thinking (Kahneman & Tversky, 1982) about a past negative event. We will argue that the control concerns characteristic of depressed individuals are important determinants of the content of their counterfactual thoughts. We also will present evidence suggesting that these counterfactuals have important implications for the retrospective control perceptions, of and control restoration behaviors likely to be employed by, depressed individuals. At the same time, however, we will suggest that negative affect and self-blame can be the undesirable by-products of cognitions directed toward the attainment and reestablishment of control perceptions.

CONTROL BELIEFS, DEPRESSION, AND SOCIAL INFERENCES

Over the past fifteen years or so, researchers have become increasingly interested in exploring the impact of depression on various social cognitive processes (for a recent review, see Weary & Edwards, 1994). Much of this work has consisted of demonstrations of the existence of the structural elements theorized (e.g., Abramson, Metalsky, & Alloy, 1989; Abramson, Seligman, & Teasdale, 1978; Alloy, Kelly, Mineka, & Clements, 1990; Beck, 1976) to be critical antecedents of depression (e.g., depressogenic schemata and attributional control styles) and the influence of these elements on subsequent emotional, motivational, and cognitive processes. Of particular importance for this chapter is research that has examined the role of depressed and nondepressed perceivers' stylized expectations of response-outcome contingency on the content of their social inferences. We will now turn our attention to a brief examination of two lines of work that have addressed such issues.

The first line of work focusing on the inferential effects of generalized control expectations concerns depressed and nondepressed perceivers' causal attributions for their behavioral outcomes. Although there appears to be less consistency in the attributions of nondepressed and depressed individuals for their positive outcomes, numerous studies have demonstrated consistent patterns of their self-attributions for negative outcomes. Nondepressed individuals tend to ascribe their negative outcomes to internal, unstable, and controllable factors (e.g., modifiable behavioral strategies, mood states). Depressed individuals, on the other hand, tend to implicate internal, stable, and uncontrollable factors (e.g., character, dispositions, native abilities) as causes of their negative outcomes (for reviews see Anderson, 1985; Sweeney, Anderson, & Bailey, 1986; Weary & Edwards, 1994). These attributional patterns of nondepressed and depressed perceivers correspond to the conceptualizations of behavioral and characterological self-blame attributions first identified by Janoff-Bulman (1979) and recently refined by Anderson, Miller, Riger, Dill, and Sedikides (1994).

The second body of relevant research has developed in parallel to the psychopathology theory and research discussed above. This work, based more on control-deprivation models of social information processing (Pittman & D'Agostino, 1985; Pittman, 1993), stresses the potentially positive motivational functions of mild and moderate expectations of uncontrollability in depressives' social inference processes.

Perhaps a major example of this approach to depression and social perception is the work of Weary and her colleagues (for reviews see Weary, Marsh, Gleicher, & Edwards, 1993; Weary & Gannon, 1996). They have developed a model of the social-cognitive consequences of the chronic control concerns known to characterize depressed perceivers (Garber, Miller, & Seaman, 1979; Warren & McEachren, 1983; Weary, Elbin, & Hill, 1987; Weisz, Weiss, Wasserman, & Rintoul, 1987). Briefly, their model posits that mild and moderate perceptions and expectations of control loss associated with mild and moderate levels of depression engender feelings of uncertainty about one's ability to understand causal relations in the social world; often these feelings are thought to motivate depressed individuals to (1) selectively attend to information that might reasonably render their social environments more understandable, predictable, and controllable and (2) process the available social information more extensively in an effort to restore interpretive and predictive control (Rothbaum et al., 1982).

A number of studies have provided support for this model. Of most relevance here are studies that have demonstrated an enhanced sensitivity to control-relevant features of the social environment. In this regard, research has indicated that, compared to nondepressives, individuals experiencing moderate levels of depressive symptomatology are more interested in and use more information about the potential causes of their outcomes (Marsh & Weary, 1989), and are more responsive to social comparison feedback (Weary et al., 1987), negative or unexpected events (Gleicher & Weary, 1991; Weary, Jordan, & Hill, 1985), and particularly diagnostic social information (Edwards & Weary, 1993; Hildebrand-Saints & Weary, 1989). Moreover, at least two studies have provided some evidence that depressives' greater sensitivity to such types of social information result from their generalized expectations of control loss (Edwards & Weary, 1993; Yost & Weary, 1996).

In the present set of studies, we set out to document the underlying role of depressives' chronic control beliefs on their counterfactual thought processes. In particular, we examine the influence of depression-related control beliefs on the generation of counterfactuals that focus on controllable relative to uncontrollable features of a past event. We also examine how such thought might alter a sense of retrospective control (Thompson, 1981). Although the work we reviewed by Weary and her colleagues assumes that a differential sensitivity to control-relevant social information in certain situations is in the service of control restoration, their research has not documented actual increases in perceived control.

COUNTERFACTUALS AND CONTROL

The phenomenon of counterfactual or "if only..." thinking (e.g., "If only I had taken a different exit, I wouldn't be caught in this traffic jam") has generated a great deal of research interest in recent years (see Miller, Turnbull, & McFarland, 1990; Roese & Olson, 1995b, for reviews). Counterfactuals are often conditional statements, containing both an antecedent (e.g., taking a different exit) and a consequent (e.g., not being in a traffic jam). Once in mind, these alternative versions of past events have been shown to influence a wide range of social judgments, including attributions of causality (Wells & Gavanski, 1989), victim compensation (Miller & McFarland, 1986), suspicion (Miller, Turnbull, & McFarland, 1989), and regret (Gilovich & Medvec, 1995; Landman, 1987).

Researchers recently have begun to explore the motivational and functional implications of counterfactual thought (e.g., Johnson & Sherman, 1990; Markman, Gavanski, Sherman, & McMullen, 1993; McMullen et al., 1995; Roese, 1994; Roese & Olson, 1995c; Taylor & Pham, 1996). For instance, Markman et al. (1993) and Roese (1994) have drawn a distinction between *upward* ("it could have been better") counterfactuals and *downward* ("it could have been worse") counterfactuals. They also have obtained empirical evidence suggesting that upward counterfactuals can prepare one for the future, whereas downward counterfactuals can engender positive affect.

The results of several recent studies have provided some support for an empirical relationship between control motivation and counterfactual thought. Girotto, Legrenzi, and Rizzo (1991) presented participants with a scenario in which the protagonists' drive home is interrupted by several events. The counterfactuals participants generated tended to focus on controllable rather than uncontrollable aspects of the scenario (see also N'Gbala & Branscombe, 1995, for a replication of this effect). Similarly, Markman, Gavanski, Sherman, and McMullen (1995) found that participants were more likely to make counterfactuals about controllable than uncontrollable antecedents of their performance outcomes. According to Markman et al. (1995), people may focus attention on the controllable aspects of events in an effort to instill feelings of control over both past and future outcomes.

Recent work by Roese and Olson (1995a) also has found that controllability can influence the *direction* of counterfactual comparison. Specifically, participants in their study made more upward counterfactuals about a story character placed in a controllable situation, but made more downward counterfactuals about the same story character placed in an uncontrollable situation. These authors reasoned that upward counterfactuals, because they serve a preparative function, are more relevant in controllable circumstances where the opportunity for future improvement is a possibility.

Depression

The results of these studies, then, have established perceived control as one determinant of the types of counterfactuals people generate. As opposed to these studies that examined counterfactual generation in situations where control perceptions were manipulated or temporarily aroused, the work we will be discussing here focuses on how *chronic* control perceptions influence the nature of counterfactual thought. Just as chronic perceptions of control loss motivate depressives to attend more to control-relevant features of social situations (Weary, Marsh, Gleicher, & Edwards, 1993), we also expect that depressed individuals will be more likely than nondepressed individuals to make counterfactuals about controllable aspects of life events in an effort to restore perceived control. In other words, we suggest that when individuals reflect back on "what could have been different" about a negative life event, the depressed individual is more likely than the nondepressed individual to focus on a controllable aspect of that event because of the former's greater need to minimize control losses and maintain and possibly expand future levels of primary control.[1] An important implication, then, is that the relationship between depression and controllable counterfactuals should be mediated or driven by generalized perceptions of control loss. A second implication is that making counterfactuals about controllable aspects of events should be more likely to enhance the sense that one "could have" controlled an event in the past (cf. Thompson, 1981) than making counterfactuals about uncontrollable aspects.

Event Repeatability

A potential moderator of the effects of control motivation on counterfactual thinking, as well as the effects of counterfactual thinking on perceived control, is whether one believes that the event in question might happen again in the future. In a relevant study, Markman et al. (1993) found that a potentially repeatable event was more likely to engender upward counterfactual thought than a nonrepeatable event. According to these researchers, a potentially repeatable event presents one with the opportunity to improve upon the outcome in the future, and should, therefore, stimulate the generation of upward counterfactuals. On the other hand, nonrepeatable events should not engender as many upward counterfactuals because preparation for the future is largely irrelevant.[2]

Because the potential repeatability of an event presents one with the opportunity for future improvement, we also suggest that a repeatable event affords individuals with the opportunity to satisfy their control motivations. That is, it is functional to think about how one could have controlled a repeatable event in the past because it suggests that one might be better able to control things in the future. On the other hand, because the opportunity to exercise control over the future is largely irrelevant for nonrepeatable events, it is perhaps less functional to think about how one could have controlled such an event in the past (cf. Silver, Boon, & Stones, 1983).

These notions, in turn, allow us to generate hypotheses regarding how event repeatability might moderate the manner in which depressed and nondepressed individuals engage in counterfactual thinking about negative life events. Earlier, we suggested that depressives may be more likely than nondepressives to focus on controllable aspects when engaging in counterfactual thinking and, furthermore, that this relationship should be mediated by generalized control loss perceptions. At this point, however, we also suggest that the mediating effects of control loss perceptions will only be seen in the case of repeatable events, where future control is a possibility. Because the opportunity for future control does not exist for nonrepeatable events, on the other hand, control loss perceptions should not mediate the effects of depression on counterfactual generation in such cases. In other words, even if depression, at least as measured by the Beck Depression Inventory (BDI; Beck, 1967), includes symptom components *other* than control concerns that might also lead to a relative focus on controllable aspects, the effects of depression on counterfactual generation for nonrepeatable events should not be mediated by control loss perceptions.[3] Second, because only repeatable events present individuals with future opportunities to reexert control, a tendency to mutate controllable aspects should be likely to enhance control perceptions for repeatable but not for nonrepeatable events.

DEPRESSION AND COUNTERFACTUALS FOR NEGATIVE LIFE EVENTS: STUDY 1

We conducted our first study (Markman & Weary, 1996) with four goals in mind: (1) To examine differences between depressed and nondepressed individuals in the types of counterfactuals they make about negative life events; (2) to examine whether control loss perceptions mediate the relationship between depression and the generation of different types of counterfactuals; (3) to examine the subsequent effects of these different types of counterfactuals on feelings of control; and (4) to examine how event repeatability might moderate all of these relationships. In order to explore these issues, we developed a relatively straightforward paradigm that allowed us to examine counterfactuals generated about real life events.

Participants in the study were selected from a pool of introductory psychology students at Ohio State University who completed the BDI. From this initial pool, a random sample of students who scored less than 6 or above 9 on the BDI were selected for participation in the experiment and were classified as nondepressed or depressed, respectively. The final sample consisted of 60 depressed participants and 61 nondepressed participants.[4]

After being told that the study concerned "thinking about life events," participants were given the Edwards and Weary (1996) Perceptions of Control Scale (PCS) to complete. This scale is a 13-item measure of generalized perceived lack of control (i.e., higher scores indicate greater feelings of lack of control), and employs six response options (1 = "strongly disagree"; 6 = "strongly agree"). Examples of items include "I can do anything I set my mind to" and "I have little control over the bad things that happen to me." Edwards and Weary (1997) found the scale to demonstrate adequate test–retest reliability over a six-week period (r = .58). As evidence for the validity of the control scale, the scale was found to correlate with measures of other constructs in a manner consistent with what would be theoretically expected for a measure of generalized perceived lack of control. In the present sample, the scale demonstrated adequate internal consistency (Cronbach's α = .75).

After completing the PCS, participants were given a packet of instructions and questions. Upon opening the packet, half of the participants—those assigned to the repeatable event condition—were given the following instructions (see also McMullen et al., 1995):

> We would like you to take a moment and recall a *negative* event that has happened to you in your life. The event should have these characteristics:
>
> 1. It should be a *very negative event* (it should have made you unhappy or upset you in some way).
> 2. It should involve *you* (events you only heard about, for example, don't count).
> 3. It should have *happened recently* (within the last year or so).
> 4. It should be an event that could possibly *happen to you again in the future* (e.g., taking an exam).

The other half of the participants—those assigned to the nonrepeatable event condition—received the same instructions, with the exception that the event they recalled "...should be an event that will probably *not happen again in the future* (e.g., your only trip to a far away country)." All participants then were told to provide a written description of the event. Examples of events described in the repeatable event condition included "not studying hard enough and failing an exam" and "fighting with parents," whereas examples of events described in the nonrepeatable event condition included "missing a final year of high school football due to an injury" and "not spending enough time with a terminally ill relative."

After describing the event, participants indicated how negative they thought the event was and how much control they felt they had over what happened to them on 9-point scales—the latter measure constituted an index of precounterfactual control. Participants then were told to once again "vividly imagine" the event they had described and then respond to the following question (see Roese & Olson, 1993):

People often have thoughts like "if only" or "what if" after experiences like the one that you described. In the space below, please list any things that, had they been different, could have changed the outcome of the event you described (i.e., that could have made the outcome of the event *better*). List as many things as come to mind.

Following this counterfactual-listing task, participants once again rated how much control they felt they had over what happened to them—this measure constituted an index of postcounterfactual control (i.e., over the specific event that they recalled).

Counterfactual statements derived from the listing task were coded by two independent judges. Our coding scheme was designed to be consistent with the way attribution theorists previously have conceptualized the controllability dimension (e.g., Anderson & Deuser, 1993; Bulman & Wortman, 1977; Weiner, 1986). The general guideline for coding was that if the counterfactual focused on an aspect of the event that, in the opinion of the judge, "could have been controlled by the actor at that time," it should be categorized as controllable. On the other hand, if the judge deemed that the counterfactual focused on an aspect that "could not have been controlled by the actor at that time," it should be categorized as uncontrollable. Thus, counterfactuals that focused on specific behaviors or failures to act (e.g., "If only I had studied harder...") or transient qualities of the self (e.g., "If only I had been paying more attention...") were coded as controllable, whereas counterfactuals that focused on chronic and enduring aspects of the self (e.g., "If only I wasn't so stupid...") or external forces (e.g., If only it hadn't been raining...") were coded as uncontrollable (Niedenthal, Tangney, & Gavanski, 1994).[5]

COUNTERFACTUALS

Our prediction was that depressed compared to nondepressed individuals would mutate relatively more controllable than uncontrollable aspects of the events they described. Thus, we predicted a two-way interaction between level of depression and the type of counterfactual generated. In order to test this prediction, we initially performed a 2 (Depression) × 2 (Event Type: repeatable vs. nonrepeatable) × 2 (Counterfactual Type: controllable vs. uncontrollable) analysis of variance (ANOVA),

Table 1. Study 1: Number of Controllable and Uncontrollable Aspects Mutated

Depression	Counterfactual type: Controllable	Counterfactual type: Uncontrollable
Nondepressed		
Repeatable event ($n = 28$)	1.64	1.50
Nonrepeatable event ($n = 33$)	1.64	1.48
Depressed		
Repeatable event ($n = 32$)	2.75	1.22
Nonrepeatable event ($n = 28$)	2.18	0.79

with counterfactual type serving as a within-subjects variable. Table 1 shows the number of each type of counterfactual generated by participants in all conditions.[6]

According to the analysis, the predicted Depression × Counterfactual Type interaction was obtained ($p = .006$). Planned comparisons of the means involved in this interaction revealed that depressed participants mutated more controllable aspects ($M = 2.48$) than did nondepressed participants ($M = 1.64$), but they did not differ from nondepressed participants in terms of the number of uncontrollable aspects mutated (Ms = 1.02 and 1.49, respectively). Furthermore, it appeared that only depressed participants mutated more controllable than uncontrollable aspects; nondepressed participants showed no preference for either type of counterfactual. The Depression × Event Type × Counterfactual Type interaction was not significant.

Relationships between Depression, Counterfactual Thinking, and Perceived Control

Earlier, we predicted that event repeatability would moderate some of the relationships between depression, counterfactual thinking, and the measures of generalized and specific control perceptions. Consequently, we performed separate regression analyses on the repeatable and nonrepeatable event subsamples. For all path models, we decided that it was important to focus on the number of controllable aspects mutated *relative* to the number of uncontrollable aspects mutated (controllable counterfactual thought index—CCT). We reasoned that while mutating controllable aspects should enhance perceived control, mutating uncontrollable aspects should, if anything, *decrease* perceived control, as the latter is a particularly undesirable goal for depressed individuals. A difference score, therefore, was computed by subtracting the number of uncontrollable aspect mutations coded from the number of controllable aspect mutations coded for each judge. The difference scores from both judges then were averaged for each participant, and this average difference score constituted an index of participants' relative tendency to mutate controllable over uncontrollable aspects.

According to our a priori arguments, generalized control perceptions (higher scores on the PCS indicating greater lack of control perceptions) should statistically account for the relationship between level of depression (dummy coded as "0" = nondepressed, "1" = depressed) and controllable counterfactual thought (CCT) only in the repeatable event condition. Additionally, we posited that specific feelings of control over both repeatable and nonrepeatable events (i.e., greater feelings of precounterfactual control) would predict CCT; greater feelings of control over an event should make controllable aspects more available for mutation than uncontrollable aspects (Kahneman & Miller, 1986; Markman et al., 1995). In turn, mutating more controllable than uncontrollable aspects should be associated with increases in feelings of control over the event (i.e., increases from pre- to postcounterfactual control) only in the repeatable event condition; controllable counterfactual thought should not enhance control for nonrepeatable events because the opportunity for future improvement is largely irrelevant.

Repeatable Event Condition

A major hypothesis, then, was that generalized control loss perceptions would mediate the relationship between depression and counterfactual type for potentially repeatable events. In order to examine this hypothesis, we employed the procedure suggested by Baron and Kenny (1986) for testing mediation.[7] An initial regression analysis indicated that depression was significantly related to higher scores on the PCS ($p < .001$). Next, an analysis involving the regression of depression on CCT found that depressed compared to nondepressed individuals mutated relatively more controllable than uncontrollable aspects of the events, $p = .05$. The third step involved a simultaneous regression of depression and PCS scores on CCT. Importantly, and as predicted, PCS scores significantly predicted CCT ($p = .02$), whereas the effect of depression on CCT became nonsignificant ($p > .20$). This analysis suggests, then, that generalized control loss perceptions are the component of depression that drives depressed individuals to mutate more controllable than uncontrollable aspects of repeatable events.

The second major hypothesis was that mutating more controllable than uncontrollable aspects should enhance control perceptions, but only in the repeatable event condition. As can be seen in Figure 1, mutating more controllable than uncontrollable aspects did indeed enhance feelings of (postcounterfactual) control over repeatable events, above and beyond the influence of precounterfactual control ($p = .01$).

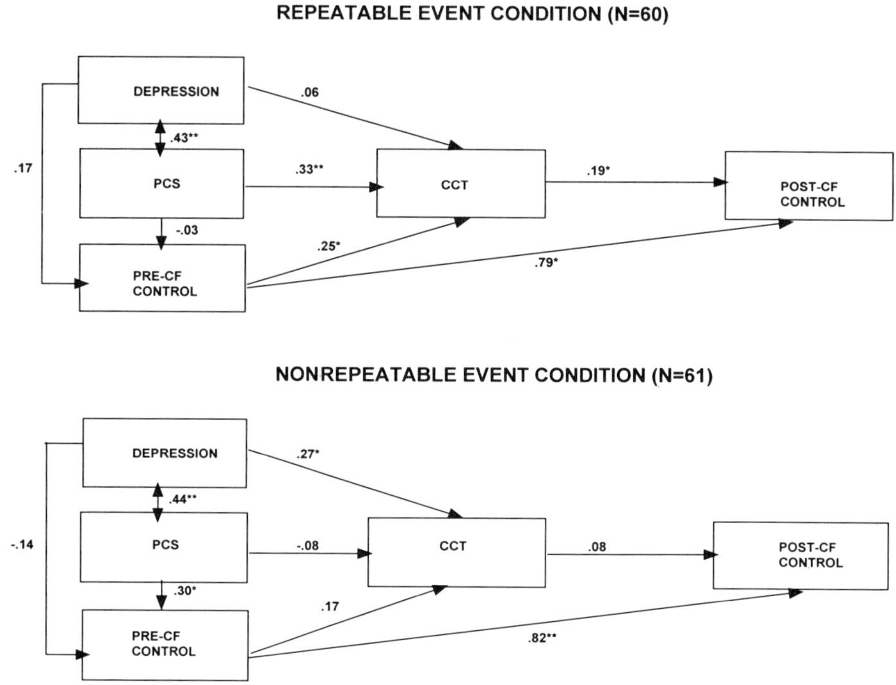

FIGURE 1 Results of the Study 1 separate path analyses for the repeatable and nonrepeatable event condition models. Path coefficients are standardized regression weights (* $p < .05$, ** $p < .01$).

Nonrepeatable Event Condition

Because the opportunity to satisfy one's control motivation should be lowered when thinking about nonrepeatable events, we predicted that generalized perceptions of control loss would not mediate the relationship between depression and counterfactual type for the nonrepeatable event subsample. An initial analysis indicated that depression predicted a relative tendency to mutate controllable over uncontrollable aspects ($p = .05$). On the other hand, and as depicted in Figure 1, participants who scored higher on the PCS did not mutate more controllable than uncontrollable aspects ($p > .50$). Thus, generalized control loss perceptions could not have mediated the relationship between depression and CCT in the nonrepeatable event condition.

Because nonrepeatable events do not present an opportunity to satisfy one's control motivation, we also predicted that participants in the nonrepeatable event condition would not gain perceived control from mutating more controllable than uncontrollable aspects. As can be seen in Figure 1, the relationship between CCT and postcounterfactual control was nonsignificant ($p > .20$), indicating that a greater tendency to mutate controllable over uncontrollable aspects did not lead to significant increases in retrospective control over nonrepeatable events.

Finally, we should note the unexpected positive relationship between high PCS scores and precounterfactual control (see Figure 1—$p < .05$). While admittedly speculative, it may be that participants suffering from greater perceptions of lack of control attempted to compensate for these feelings by recalling events over which they felt they had more control. These participants may not have attempted to compensate by mutating relatively more controllable aspects, however, because the motivation to control such events in the future was irrelevant in this condition.

The results of this study demonstrated that when individuals engaged in counterfactual thought about negative life events, those who were mildly depressed were more likely to mutate controllable than uncontrollable aspects of those events. Moreover, this effect appeared attributable, in the repeatable event condition at least, to the control loss concerns that are known to characterize mildly depressed individuals. Finally, mutating more controllable than uncontrollable aspects led to enhanced beliefs that one had control over the event in the past, although this was more likely to be the case for potentially repeatable events.

As we noted earlier, however, there was a significant and positive relationship between depression and counterfactual type in the nonrepeatable event condition. Thus, there appear to be other aspects of depression above and beyond control concerns that can result in the mutation of more controllable than uncontrollable aspects. Although further research will be needed to determine exactly what these may be, one possibility is the feelings of guilt associated with depression. According to a number of researchers (e.g., Niedenthal et al., 1994; Weiner, 1986; Weiner, Graham, & Chandler, 1982; Wicker, Payne, & Morgan, 1983), feelings of guilt over negative occurrences result from attributions to personally controllable causes and self-responsibility. In our estimation, although nonrepeatable events may not present the opportunity to satisfy one's control motivation, they may still lead to the ascriptions of self-responsibility and personal controllability that engender the guilt so often experienced by depressed individuals. Driven by these feelings of guilt, depressed individuals may then focus on controllable relative to uncontrollable aspects in an effort to make amends for their past actions. As our results demonstrate, however, such thinking may not enhance perceived control when an event will not be repeated.

DEPRESSION AND COUNTERFACTUALS FOR NEGATIVE LIFE EVENTS: STUDY 2

Our first study demonstrated that chronic control loss concerns can be an important antecedent of the type of counterfactual generated and that counterfactuals can enhance perceptions of control over the past. For our next study, we decided to examine a potential moderator of the control function of counterfactual thought. Although recent work has suggested that individuals may engage in counterfactual thinking in order to satisfy particular goal states (e.g., Markman et al., 1993; Roese, 1994), none of this work has examined individual beliefs in the ability of counterfactuals to do so. In our view, individuals who possess such beliefs may derive more psychological benefits from counterfactual thought than individuals who do not. Thus, we suggest that idiosyncratic beliefs in the ability of particular types of counterfactuals to help bring about particular goal states may actually moderate the success of such counterfactuals in goal attainment (cf. Carver & Scheier, 1990; Weary & Edwards, 1996).

The specific goal state we chose to focus on in our second study was the need for meaning (Silver et al., 1983). Our interest in this variable stemmed from Thompson's (1981) suggestion that the underlying goal of establishing retrospective control is to satisfy a need for meaning—to understand the event. In our second study, we predicted that mutating controllable relative to uncontrollable aspects of negative events would be especially likely to enhance control perceptions to the extent that one believes in the ability of counterfactuals to provide a sense of meaning or insight into these life events. Such a finding would also begin to establish an empirical relationship between the need for meaning and perceived control.

In Study 2 (Markman & Weary, 1997), participants once again recalled negative life events and made counterfactuals about them. Because control perceptions were only enhanced in the repeatable event condition of Study 1, participants were only asked to describe potentially repeatable events. Our main goal was to demonstrate the moderating effects of beliefs in the ability of counterfactuals to provide meaning on the relationship between counterfactual generation and perceived control.

Participants, preselected on the basis of their BDI scores ($N = 64$), were given the same cover story employed in Study 1. They then received a packet of instructions and questions and were given the same set of instructions that were used in the repeatable event condition of Study 1 (i.e., to recall a very negative event that could potentially happen again). After providing a written description of the event, participants indicated, as they did in Study 1, how negative they thought the event was and how much control they felt they had over what happened to them (precounterfactual control). Participants then performed the same counterfactual-listing exercise that was used in Study 1.

After listing their counterfactuals, participants once again rated how much control they felt they had over what happened to them (postcounterfactual control). Finally, and importantly, participants responded to the question "To what extent does engaging in 'if only' thinking help provide you with a sense of 'meaning' or 'insight' into negative events that have occurred to you in the past?" on a 1 (not to any extent) to 9 (to a great extent) scale. This measure constituted an index of individual beliefs in the ability of counterfactuals to provide meaning. The counterfactuals derived from the listing exercise were later coded in the same manner as before.[8]

For our primary analysis, we proposed a regression model that specified interrelationships among CCT, beliefs in meaning, and changes in pre- to postcounterfactual control. Our major hypothesis was that the CCT main effect and the Meaning × CCT interaction would independently predict increases in perceived control. As predicted, the Meaning × CCT interaction independently predicted increases in pre- to postcounterfactual control ($p = .05$). Beyond this, the CCT main effect was significant as well ($p = .04$), showing once again that a relative tendency to mutate controllable over uncontrollable aspects enhances feelings of retrospective control. On the other hand, meaning, by itself, did not predict increases in perceived control ($p > .50$). Rather, it appears that meaning moderated the relationship between counterfactual type and perceived control (Baron & Kenny, 1986).[9]

To clarify the meaning of the interaction, we divided our participants at the median into those scoring high and low on beliefs in meaning and performed separate regression analyses for each set of participants (for a similar procedure, see Andersen & Schwartz, 1992). The analysis showed that for participants who had relatively high beliefs in meaning, mutating more controllable than uncontrollable aspects predicted increases in perceived control ($p < .001$). On the other hand, mutating more controllable than uncontrollable aspects did not predict increases in perceived control for participants who had relatively low beliefs in meaning ($p = .30$). Thus, this analysis suggests that mutating more controllable than uncontrollable aspects enhances perceived control over negative life events to the extent that one believes that counterfactual thinking can provide a sense of meaning or insight into these events.

IMPLICATIONS

The results of two studies reveal differences in the way moderately depressed and nondepressed individuals generate counterfactual alternatives in response to negative life events. Depressed participants were more likely than nondepressed participants to generate counterfactuals that focused on more of the controllable than uncontrollable aspects of such negative events. Moreover, mediational analyses suggested that this greater relative tendency was driven by general perceptions of control loss in the case of potentially repeatable events. The results of both studies also indicated that mutating more controllable than uncontrollable aspects was associated with increases in perceived control over repeatable events. In our view, the results of these two studies suggest the operation of a *compensatory mechanism* (cf. Thompson, 1993)—that depressed individuals may attempt to compensate for their *general* perceptions of control loss by enhancing their perceptions of control over *specific* events through counterfactual thought.

To the best of our knowledge, the current studies are the first in the published literature to document individual differences in counterfactual thinking as a function of depression. In a related series of studies, Roese and Olson (1993) focused on individual differences in counterfactual thinking and a component of depression—self-esteem. In their work, participants with either high (HSEs) or low (LSEs) self-esteem were asked to imagine themselves performing behaviors with another person that resulted in either a successful outcome or failure. The counterfactuals participants generated about these outcomes were then coded as focusing on either actions taken by the self or actions taken by the other. Relevant to the present work, the results indicated that following failure, LSEs were more likely than HSEs to mutate their *own* actions. Although Roese and Olson (1993) were concerned with self- versus other-referent counterfactuals as opposed to controllability per se, their finding that LSEs were more likely to mutate their own (controllable) actions than the actions of another (uncontrollable) is certainly consistent with our results. These authors also went on to suggest a number of potential explanations for their findings, including differences between HSEs and LSEs in terms of their self-enhancement and self-presentation needs, and differences between these two groups in terms of the relative accessibility of positive versus negative self-schematic information. In general, future research might also examine the extent to which these aspects of self-esteem moderate or mediate the relationship between depression and counterfactual thinking.

Reconciling Our Findings with Those of Learned Helplessness Theory

The finding that depressed individuals mutated more controllable than uncontrollable aspects may seem surprising in light of Janoff-Bulman's (1979) finding that depressed individuals tend to engage in

characterological self-blame—a form of self-blame that focuses on unmodifiable (and thus uncontrollable) aspects of the self. Similarly, learned helplessness theory (Abramson et al., 1978; Alloy et al., 1990; Anderson, 1985; Seligman, 1975) suggests that depressed individuals will tend to ascribe blame to uncontrollable factors. We suggest three ways of reconciling the findings of learned helplessness theory with our own.

There May Be No Contradiction

It may be that direct causal questioning focuses the individual on a different level of analysis than asking "what could have been different." For example, when moderately depressed individuals make a characterological attribution, they are emphasizing that it is something about themselves that they could not or did not control, not that other people could not have controlled it. Thus, they may readily agree with both the statement "It was my own stupidity" (a characterological attribution) and the statement "If only I had done X, the event would have been avoided" (a controllable counterfactual); causal questioning focuses the individual on the former type of answer, whereas counterfactual questioning focuses the individual on the latter. The depressed individual would not see these two answers as contradictory.[10]

Causal Attribution and Undoing May Be Independent Processes

Although past research has implicated the role of counterfactual thinking in influencing causal ascriptions (e.g., Hilton, 1990; Lipe, 1991; Wells & Gavanski, 1989), recent theorizing has suggested that important distinctions can also be made between the two processes. For instance, Davis, Lehman, Silver, Wortman, and Ellard (1996) and N'Gbala and Branscombe (1995) have suggested that causal attribution is a process whereby possible causes are identified and evaluated with reference to the extent to which they were necessary and/or sufficient to produce a given outcome, whereas counterfactual thinking is a process whereby antecedents are evaluated in terms of the relative ease with which they could have been undone or avoided (see also Mandel and Lehman, 1996). Empirical support for this distinction comes from a study of parents who had lost a child to sudden infant death syndrome conducted by Davis et al. (1995). According to their findings, although most parents did not feel that they *caused* the death, the vast majority did feel that the death could have been *avoided* if they had done something differently.

In turn, this distinction may help us to accommodate our results with the large body of findings that support learned helplessness theory. In the present studies, participants were asked to think about "what might have been different" about the events they described. In our view, the greater control loss perceptions of our depressed compared to nondepressed participants resulted in their greater attention to controllable features of the described events. Since controllable features were by their nature avoidable, they were easier to mutate. When depressives are asked to attribute cause for a particular event, they may go through an entirely different cognitive process, i.e., one in which they evaluate the necessity and sufficiency of various possible causes. In so doing, uncontrollable antecedents may be afforded more causal weight by depressed than nondepressed individuals because they are evaluated as more necessary and/or sufficient for producing a particular outcome.

Causal Attribution versus Undoing as Passive versus Problem-Solving Processes

Causal attribution, or focusing on reasons, is often conceptualized as a posthoc analysis of what happened before, during, and after an event for the purpose of identifying cause–effect covariances. When attributing cause, depressed individuals often may rely on what they know about themselves and the world around them—negative cognitive schemata (Andersen, Spielman, & Bargh, 1992; Beck, 1967)—to come to the conclusion that causality rests with something unmodifiable about themselves. On the other hand, undoing may be more of a problem-solving oriented process (Lazarus & Folkman, 1984) that leads the individual to think about what could have been different about the event. Undoing the various features of an event may allow the individual to view the event from different perspectives and develop strategies for dealing with a similar event in the future. Consistent with this notion, Pennebaker and Beall (1986) find that the process of writing and organizing one's thoughts about a traumatic experience is more likely to produce positive health benefits than is merely focusing on the facts of the experience. In our view, the problem-solving nature of the undoing process may give depressed individuals a greater opportunity to satisfy their secondary control motivations than might the reasons-oriented nature of the causal attribution process (cf. Wilson & Schooler, 1991). It may be for this reason, then, that depressed individuals show more of a tendency to focus on controllable than uncontrollable aspects when they undo an event than when they ascribe cause for an event.

Depressed compared to nondepressed individuals also have been found to ruminate and self-focus in reaction to negative outcomes (e.g., Nolen-Hoeksema, 1991; Pyszczynski & Greenberg, 1987; Wood, Saltzberg, Neale, Stone, & Rachmiel, 1990). Nolen-Hoeksema and her colleagues (e.g., Lyubomirsky & Nolen-Hoeksema, 1993, 1995; Morrow & Nolen-Hoeksema, 1990) have described ruminative responses to depressed mood as thoughts and behaviors that focus individuals' attention on their depressive symptoms and on the causes and consequences of those symptoms. In a recent set of studies, Lyubomirsky and Nolen-Hoeksema (1995) induced some depressed individuals to ruminate by focusing their attention on their current feeling states, and other depressed individuals to distract themselves from their current feeling states. According to their findings, depressed individuals induced to ruminate gave more pessimistic attributions for hypothetical events and interpersonal problems, and generated poorer-quality solutions to these problems than depressed individuals who first distracted themselves from their current mood. Thus, rumination also appears to be a passive reaction to negative outcomes that inhibits problem-focused coping and, indeed, may also lead depressed individuals to believe that their problems are less controllable than they really are (Lyubomirsky & Nolen-Hoeksema, 1995). Similarly, brooding about the negative aspects of a problem corresponds to Kuhl's (1981) notion of "state orientation," a condition of perseveration on one's past, present, or future state that inhibits one from taking direct action to deal with the problem.

It is quite reasonable to characterize counterfactual undoing as a form of rumination (cf. Martin & Tesser, 1989; Tait & Silver, 1989). Of all the various forms of ruminative thought, however, counterfactual thought—especially *controllable* counterfactual thought—may be the most functional. Indeed, focusing individuals on what they "could have done differently" should be more likely to enhance control perceptions than focusing them on their feelings. Thus, just as rumination corresponds to state orientation, controllable counterfactual thought may more closely correspond to "action orientation," described by Kuhl (1981) as a tendency to focus on *alternative* plans of action for the purposes of achieving a goal.

Why Do Depressives Still Suffer from Control Loss Perceptions?

The results of the present studies raise an interesting question: If mildly depressed individuals routinely restore perceived control over negative life events by mutating more controllable than uncontrollable aspects, then why do they suffer from control loss perceptions relative to nondepressed individuals? Moreover, if counterfactual thinking focuses individuals on alternative solutions to problematic situations, then why do depressed individuals suffer from marked deficits in problem-solving ability relative to nondepressed individuals (e.g., Conway & Giannopolous, 1993; Marx, Williams, & Claridge, 1992)?

Although we can only speculate at this point, we suggest several possibilities. First, although depressed individuals may be capable of enhancing perceived control over a number of specific life events, they simply may be bombarded by too many seemingly aversive and uncontrollable events to be able to restore any generalized feelings of control. Second, although depressed individuals may feel like they have control over an impending event, they may experience "breakdowns" in the implementation of behavioral strategies designed to deal with a recurrence of the event. As recent reviews by Gollwitzer (1990, 1993) suggest, depressed affect and ruminative or self-focused thought can sap the cognitive resources needed for the effective implementation of goal intentions. Likewise, Lyubomirsky and Nolen-Hoeksema (1995) suggest that ruminating on one's depressed mood can prevent individuals from effectively carrying out problem solutions by sapping their energy and motivation and impairing their concentration. Additionally, depressed individuals have been shown to be less likely or willing to take actions that might expose them to social risk (Pietromonaco & Markus, 1985; Pietromonaco & Rook, 1987). Also, Beck, Rush, Shaw, and Emery (1979) have suggested that depressed individuals' greater requirement for certainty of the correctness of a decision before committing to it contributes to their failure to make the appropriate response (Coyne, Aldwin, & Lazarus, 1981); Miller & Lewis, 1977). Thus, although depressed individuals may be able to develop constructive thoughts and strategies, their difficulties in converting those thoughts into action may leave them feeling as frustrated and control deprived as ever. Clearly, future research would benefit from an analysis of the action phases (Heckhausen, 1991) most influenced by depressives' counterfactual thought. It may well be that the restoration of secondary control engendered by depressives' counterfactual thought influences primarily the predecisional and postactional phases, but has relatively little impact on the actional phase. In a similar vein, it also would be useful to examine how feelings of self-efficacy (i.e., expectations of being able to successfully implement specific courses of action—Bandura, 1996) might moderate the relationship between depressive controllable counterfactual thought and control perceptions. For instance, controllable counterfactual thought may only impact the actional phase when self-efficacy expectations are high (cf. Sanna, 1997).

Finally, a third possibility is that depressed individuals do not always mutate controllable over uncontrollable aspects spontaneously. Rather, the initial reaction to a negative outcome may be to ruminate about one's depressed mood, as well as the causes and consequences of that mood. However, it should be noted that the simple instruction used in the present studies to "think about how the event could have been different" was enough to engage depressed individuals in a control restoration process. Thus, therapies designed to distract individuals from their moods by engaging them in counterfactual-listing exercises might be beneficial, at least on a short-term basis, for restoring control perceptions.

IMPLICATIONS FOR NEGATIVE AFFECT, SELF-BLAME, AND SENSE-MAKING

Elsewhere in the literature, we (Markman et al., 1993; McMullen et al., 1995) have characterized upward counterfactual thinking as holding psychological "trade-offs" for the individual—upward counterfactuals prepare one for the future, but this preparative value may obtain at the expense of engendering "unnecessary negative affect" (Sherman & McConnell, 1995). In a similar vein, although depressives may experience a "boost" in control perceptions after mutating controllable aspects of negative events, this focus on controllable aspects may also lead depressives to blame themselves, perhaps unduly so, for failures or negative outcomes. In fact, recent research by Davis et al. (1996) suggests that the more people believe that they could have avoided a traumatic life event, the more they blame themselves for the event. In turn, these feelings of self-blame will engender negative affect. In terms of the present research, then, we suggest that the depressogenic tendency to focus on controllable aspects may actually be a major source of the feelings of self-blame, guilt, and negative affect that characterize the depressed individual.

Study 2 suggested a potential moderator of the relationship between counterfactual thinking and perceived control—beliefs that counterfactuals can provide a sense of meaning and insight into negative events. Specifically, participants who mutated more controllable than uncontrollable aspects experienced increases in perceived control to the extent that they believed that counterfactuals provide them with a sense of meaning and insight; this finding also established an empirical relationship between the need for meaning and perceived control. Participants who did not possess such beliefs, on the other hand, did not experience gains in perceived control from mutating more controllable than uncontrollable aspects. Relatedly, Davis and Lehman (1995) have suggested that the search for meaning may be an important goal of counterfactual thinking. In a set of studies examining victims of traumatic events, Davis, Lehman, and their colleagues (Davis et al., 1995; Davis et al., 1996) have documented the pervasive tendency to generate counterfactuals about extremely negative events that are very unlikely to recur and, thus, are bereft of any future control concerns. According to these researchers, individuals possess implicit or explicit expectations or assumptions regarding their daily life events. When a negative outcome shatters their implicit or explicit assumptions, however, individuals then become motivated to find meaning in the traumatic event, and counterfactual thinking may be one way they attempt to do this. In general, then, the relationship between the need for meaning and counterfactual thinking would seem to be an important area for future research to explore, as sense-making may be one of the overarching motivations behind counterfactual thinking.

Before concluding, we should note that our results may well not be specific to individuals experiencing mild and moderate levels of depression. Indeed, the specific component of depression in which we were interested, control loss perceptions, also is known to be a feature of anxiety disorders (Alloy et al., 1990; Garber, Miller, & Abramson, 1980; Marsh & Weary, 1994). Just as we have shown that the relationship between level of depressive symptomatology and type of counterfactual thought is mediated by control loss perceptions, we would expect future research to demonstrate that they also mediate the relationship between the level of anxiety and counterfactual type.

CONCLUSION

In conclusion, the present studies support the notion that depressed compared to nondepressed persons are more likely to mutate controllable than uncontrollable aspects of life events in an effort to restore generalized perceptions of control loss. Moreover, it appears that mutating more controllable than uncontrollable aspects of negative life events enhances feelings of control over these events, particularly if they are repeatable. In general, these results represent an initial step toward describing the manner in which depressed persons engage in counterfactual thinking about negative life events, as well as the manner in which perceived control can be attained through such counterfactual thought. We believe that a further integration of research on depressive symptomatology, counterfactual thinking, and action control will be extremely beneficial for the advancement of theory in all three domains. In turn, such advancements also may increase the potential for clinical applications.

NOTES

1. One caveat we should mention, however, is that individuals who are severely depressed might have low motivation to make counterfactuals about controllable aspects. At extreme levels of depression, individuals' general perceptions of control may be so low that they would be unlikely to believe that there is anything they can do to control their outcomes (see Marsh & Weary, 1989). Such extreme levels of uncontrollability could be expected to result in a helplessness pattern of behavior (i.e., passivity and withdrawal) rather than the active attempts to regain control that we expected to be demonstrated by the mildly depressed participants in the present studies.
2. We would not want to suggest, however, that negative and nonrepeatable events never result in the generation of upward counterfactuals. For instance, Davis, Lehman, Wortman, Silver, and Thompson (1995) found that people suffering the traumatic loss of a loved one—a nonrepeatable event—generated a great many upward counterfactuals. In our view, the strong degree of personal and emotional involvement in these events and

the absence of plausible downward counterfactual alternatives overwhelmingly favor the generation of upward counterfactuals under such circumstances.

3. In light of the possibility that components of depression unrelated to control concerns might also lead to a focus on controllable aspects, we decided not to make any firm predictions regarding how event repeatability might moderate the relationship between depression and the content of counterfactual thought.
4. The BDI was readministered to participants at the end of the experiment, after they had completed all of the experimental materials. Only those participants whose scores remained in their appropriate category were included in the final analyses. Participants who changed category were excluded from the sample because they may have been experiencing a transient mood state.
5. Preliminary analyses revealed no differences between depressed and nondepressed participants in terms of how negatively they rated the events they described (*M*s = 7.54 and 7.36, respectively), or in terms of how much precounterfactual control they felt they had over the event (*M*s = 6.20 and 5.72, respectively). Additionally, there were no differences between repeatable and nonrepeatable events in terms of how negatively participants rated the events they described (*M*s = 7.41 and 7.50, respectively), or in terms of how much pre-counterfactual control they felt they had over the event (*M*s = 6.11 and 5.81, respectively). In general, there were no differences between these two groups in terms of the context of negative life events they chose to describe—academic, work, interpersonal, health, or other.
6. There was no overall effect of depression or repeatability on the sheer number of counterfactuals generated, and the interaction between these factors also was not significant. Participants, overall, did mutate more controllable (M = 2.06) than uncontrollable aspects (M = 1.26), replicating previous findings (Davis et al., 1995; Girotto et al., 1991; Markman et al., 1995; N'Gbala & Branscombe, 1995; Niedenthal et al., 1994; Roese & Olson, 1995a).
7. In order to provide evidence of mediation by employing this procedure, it is necessary to demonstrate three patterns of relationships: (1) the predictor (depression) and the mediator (PCS) should be related; (2) the predictor and mediator should be independently related to the criterion (CCT); and (3) the effects of the predictor on the criterion should become nonsignificant when the effects of the mediator are controlled.
8. Once again, there were no differences between depressed and nondepressed participants in terms of how negatively they rated the event, how much control they felt they had over the events, or the general context of the events they chose to describe. Additionally, there were no differences between depressed and nondepressed participants in terms of their beliefs in meaning (*M*s = 5.99 and 5.62, respectively). In a replication of Study 1, an ANOVA revealed a Depression × Counterfactual Type interaction—depressed participants mutated more controllable aspects (M = 2.34) than did nondepressed participants (M = 1.43), and somewhat fewer uncontrollable aspects (M = 1.22) than did nondepressed participants (M = 1.67).
9. Meaning and CCT were not significantly related to one another (p >.10).
10. This insightful possibility was suggested by an anonymous reviewer of the Markman and Weary (1996) paper.

ACKNOWLEDGMENTS

We thank C. R. Snyder, M. Kofta, and G. Sedek for helpful comments.

The research reported herein and preparation of this chapter were supported in part by National Science Foundation research grant SBR-

9631858 awarded to the second author and by National Institute of Mental Health Postdoctoral Training Fellowship T32MH19728 awarded to the first author.

REFERENCES

Abramson, L. Y., Seligman, M. E. P., & Teasdale, J. (1978). Learned helplessness in humans: Critique and reformulation. *Journal of Abnormal Psychology, 87*, 49–74.

Alloy, L. B., Kelly, K. A., Mineka, S., & Clements, C. M. (1990). Comorbidity in anxiety and depressive disorders: A helplessness/hopelessness perspective. In J. D. Maser & C. R. Cloninger (Eds.), *Comorbidity in anxiety and mood disorders* (pp. 499–543). Washington, DC: American Psychiatric Press.

Andersen, S. M., & Schwartz, A. H. (1992). Intolerance of ambiguity and depression: A cognitive vulnerability factor linked to hopelessness. *Social Cognition, 10*, 271–298.

Andersen, S. M., Spielman, L. A., & Bargh, J. A. (1992). Future-event schemas and certainty about the future: Automaticity in depressives' future-event predictions. *Journal of Personality and Social Psychology, 63*, 711–723.

Anderson, C. A. (1985). Actor and observer attributions for different types of situations: Causal structure effects, individual differences, and the dimensionality of causes. *Social Cognition, 3*, 323–340.

Anderson, C. A., & Deuser, W. E. (1993). The primacy of control in causal thinking and attributional style: An attributional functionalism perspective. In G. Weary, F. Gleicher, & K. L. Marsh (Eds.), *Control motivation and social cognition* (pp. 94–121). New York: Springer-Verlag.

Anderson, C. A., Miller, R. S., Riger, A. L., Dill, J. C., & Sedikides, C. (1994). Behavioral and characterological attributional styles as predictors of depression and loneliness: Review, refinement, and test. *Journal of Personality and Social Psychology, 66* 549–559.

Averill, J. R. (1973). Personal control over aversive stimuli and its relationship to stress. *Psychological Bulletin, 80*, 286–303.

Bandura, A. (1996). *Self-efficacy: The exercise of control*. New York: W. H. Freeman.

Baron, R. M., & Kenny, D. A. (1986). The moderator-mediator variable distinction in social psychological research: Conceptual, strategic, and statistical considerations. *Journal of Personality and Social Psychology, 51*, 1173–1182.

Beck, A. T. (1967). *Depression: Clinical, experimental, and theoretical aspects*. New York: Harper & Row.

Beck, A. T. (1976). *Cognitive therapy and the emotional disorders*. New York: International Universities Press.

Beck, A. T., Rush, A. J., Shaw, B. F., & Emery, G. (1979). *Cognitive therapy of depression*. New York: Guilford.

Brehm, J. W. (1966). *A theory of psychological reactance*. New York: Academic Press.

Brehm, S. S., & Brehm, J. W. (1981). *Psychological reactance: A theory of freedom and control*. New York: Academic Press.

Bulman, R., & Wortman, C. (1977). Attributions of blame and coping in the "real world": Severe accident victims respond to their lot. *Journal of Personality and Social Psychology, 35*, 351–363.

Carver, C. S., & Scheier, M. F. (1990). Principles of self-regulation: Action and emotion. In E. T. Higgins & R. M. Sorrentino (Eds.), *Handbook of motivation and cognition: Foundations of social behavior* (Vol. 2, pp. 3–52). New York: Guilford Press.

Conway, M., & Giannopolous, C. (1993). Dysphoria and decision making: Limited information use for evaluations of multiattribute targets. *Journal of Personality and Social Psychology, 64*, 613–623.

Coyne, J. C., Aldwin, C., & Lazarus, R. S. (1981). Depression and coping in stressful episodes. *Journal of Personality and Social Psychology, 90*, 439–447.

Davis, C. G., & Lehman, D. R. (1995). Counterfactual thinking and coping with traumatic life events. In N. J. Roese & J. M. Olson (Eds.), *What might have been: The social psychology of counterfactual thinking* (pp. 353–374). Hillsdale, NJ: Erlbaum.

Davis, C. G., Lehman, D. R., Silver, R. C., Wortman, C. B., & Ellard, J. H. (1996). Self-blame following a traumatic event: The role of perceived avoidability. *Personality and Social Psychology Bulletin, 22*, 557–567.

Davis, C. G., Lehman, D. R., Wortman, C. B., Silver, R. C., & Thompson, S. C. (1995). The undoing of traumatic life events. *Personality and Social Psychology Bulletin, 21*, 109–124.

DeCharms, R. (1968). *Personal causation: The internal affective determinants of behavior.* New York: Academic Press.

Edwards, J. A., & Weary, G. (1993). Depression and the impression formation continuum: Piecemeal processing despite the availability of category information. *Journal of Personality and Social Psychology, 64*, 636–645.

Edwards, J. A., & Weary, G. (1997). The relationships among perceived control, causal uncertainty, and depressive symptomatology: A prospective study. Unpublished manuscript.

Garber, J., Miller, W. R., & Abramson, L. Y. (1980). On the distinction between anxiety states and depression: Perceived control, certainty, and probability of goal attainment. In J. Garber & M. E. P. Seligman (Eds.), *Human helplessness: Theory and applications* (pp. 131–171). New York: Academic Press.

Garber, J., Miller, W. R., & Seaman, S. F. (1979). Learned helplessness, stress, and the depressive disorders. In R. A. Depue (Ed.), *The psychobiology of the depressive disorders: Implications for the effects of stress* (pp. 335–364). New York Academic Press.

Gilovich, T., & Medvec, V. H. (1995). The experience of regret: What, when, and why. *Psychological Review, 102*, 379–395.

Girotto, V., Legrenzi, P., & Rizzo, A. (1991). Event controllability and counterfactual thinking. *Acta Psychologica, 78*, 111–133.

Gleicher, F., & Weary, G. (1991). The effect of depression on the quantity and quality of social inferences. *Journal of Personality and Social Psychology, 61*, 105–114.

Gollwitzer, P. M. (1990). Action phases and mind-sets. In E. T. Higgins & R. M. Sorrentino (Eds.), *Handbook of motivation and cognition: Foundations of social behavior* (Vol. 2, pp. 53–92). New York: Guilford Press.

Gollwitzer, P. M. (1993). Goal achievement: The role of intentions. In W. Stroebe & M. Hewstone (Eds.), *European review of social psychology* (Vol. 4, pp. 141–185). Wiley & Sons.

Heckhausen, J. (1991). *Motivation and action.* New York: Springer.

Heckhausen, J., & Schulz, R. (1995). A life-span theory of control. *Psychological Review, 102*, 284–304.

Heider, F. (1958). *The psychology of interpersonal relations.* New York: Wiley.

Hildebrand-Saints, L., & Weary, G. (1989). Depression and social information gathering. *Personality and Social Psychology Bulletin, 15*, 150–160.

Hilton, D. J. (1990). Conversational processes and causal explanations. *Psychological Bulletin, 93*, 65–81.

Janoff-Bulman, R. (1979). Characterological versus behavioral self-blame: Inquiries into depression and rape. *Journal of Personality and Social Psychology, 37*, 1798–1809.

Johnson, M. K., & Sherman, S. J. (1990). Constructing and reconstructing the past and future in the present. In E. T. Higgins & R. M. Sorrentino (Eds.), *Handbook of motivation and cognition: Foundations of social behavior* (Vol. 2, pp. 482–526). New York: Guilford.

Kahneman, D., & Miller, D. T. (1986). Norm theory: Comparing reality to its alternatives. *Psychological Review, 93*, 136–153.

Kahneman, D., & Tversky, A. (1982). The simulation heuristic. In D. Kahneman, P. Slovic, & A. Tversky (Eds.), *Judgment under uncertainty: Heuristics and biases* (pp. 201–208). New York: Cambridge University Press.

Kuhl, J. (1981). Motivational and functional helplessness: The moderating effect of state versus action orientation. *Journal of Personality and Social Psychology, 40*, 155–170.

Landman, J. (1987). Regret and elation following action and inaction: Affective responses to positive versus negative outcomes. *Personality and Social Psychology Bulletin, 13*, 524–536.

Lazarus, R., & Folkman, S. (1984). *Stress, appraisal, and coping*. New York: Springer-Verlag.

Lipe, M. G. (1991). Counterfactual reasoning as a framework for attribution theories. *Psychological Bulletin, 109*, 456–471.

Lyubomirsky, S., & Nolen-Hoeksema, S. (1993). Self-perpetuating properties of dysphoric rumination. *Journal of Personality and Social Psychology, 65*, 339–349.

Lyubomirsky, S., & Nolen-Hoeksema, S. (1995). Effects of self-focused rumination on negative thinking and interpersonal problem solving. *Journal of Personality and Social Psychology, 69*, 176–190.

Mandel, D. R., & Lehman, D. R. (1996). Counterfactual thinking and ascriptions of cause and preventability. *Journal of Personality and Social Psychology, 71*, 450–463.

Markman, K. D., & Weary, G. (1996). The influence of chronic control concerns on counterfactual thought. *Social Cognition, 14*, 292–316.

Markman, K. D., & Weary, G. (1997). Unpublished raw data.

Markman, K. D., Gavanski, I., Sherman, S. J., & McMullen, M. N. (1993). The mental simulation of better and worse possible worlds. *Journal of Experimental Social Psychology, 29*, 87–109.

Markman, K. D., Gavanski, I., Sherman, S. J., & McMullen, M. N. (1995). The impact of perceived control on the imagination of better and worse possible worlds. *Personality and Social Psychology Bulletin, 21*, 588–595.

Marsh, K. L., & Weary, G. (1989). Depression and attributional complexity. *Personality and Social Psychology Bulletin, 15*, 325–336.

Marsh, K. L., & Weary, G. (1994). Severity of depression and responsiveness to attributional information. *Journal of Social and Clinical Psychology, 13*, 15–32.

Martin, L. L., & Tesser, A. (1989). Toward a motivational and structural theory of ruminative thought. In J. S. Uleman & J. A. Bargh (Eds.), *Unintended thought* (pp. 306–326). New York: Guilford Press.

Marx, E. M., Williams, J. M., & Claridge, G. C. (1992). Depression and social problem solving. *Journal of Abnormal Psychology, 101*, 78–86.

McMullen, M. N., Markman, K. D., & Gavanski, I. (1995). Living in neither the best nor worst of all possible worlds: Antecedents and consequences of upward and downward counterfactual thinking. In N. J. Roese & J. M. Olson (Eds.), *What might have been: The social psychology of counterfactual thinking* (pp. 133–167). Hillsdale, NJ: Lawrence Erlbaum.

Miller, D. T., & McFarland, C. (1986). Counterfactual thinking and victim compensation: A test of norm theory. *Personality and Social Psychology, 12*, 513–519.

Miller, D. T., Turnbull, W., & McFarland, C. (1989). When a coincidence is suspicious: The role of mental simulation. *Journal of Personality and Social Psychology, 57*, 581–589.

Miller, D. T., Turnbull, W., & McFarland, C. (1990). Counterfactual thinking and social perception: Thinking about what might have been. In M. P. Zanna (Ed.), *Advances in experimental social psychology* (Vol. 23, pp. 305–331). New York: Academic Press.

Miller, E., & Lewis, P. (1977). Recognition memory in elderly patients with depression and dementia: A signal detection analysis. *Journal of Abnormal Psychology, 86*, 84–86.

Morrow, J., & Nolen-Hoeksema, S. (1990). Effects of responses to depression on the remediation of depressive affect. *Journal of Personality and Social Psychology, 58*, 519–527.

N'Gbala, A., & Branscombe, N. R. (1995). Mental simulation and causal attribution: When simulating an event does not effect fault assignment. *Journal of Experimental Social Psychology, 31*, 139–162.

Niedenthal, P. M., Tangney, J. P., & Gavanski, I. (1994). "If only I weren't versus "If only I hadn't": Distinguishing shame and guilt in counterfactual thinking. *Journal of Personality and Social Psychology, 67*, 585–595.

Nolen-Hoeksema, S. (1991). Responses to depression and their effects on the duration of depressive episodes. *Journal of Abnormal Psychology, 100*, 569–582.

Pietromonaco, P. R., & Markus, H. (1985). The nature of negative thoughts in depression. *Journal of Personality and Social Psychology, 48*, 799–807.

Pietromonaco, P. R., & Rook, K. S. (1987). Decision style in depression: The contribution of perceived risks versus benefits. *Journal of Personality and Social Psychology, 52*, 399–408.

Pennebaker, J. W., & Beall, S. K. (1986). Confronting a traumatic event: Toward an understanding of inhibition and disease. *Journal of Abnormal Psychology, 95*, 272–281.

Pittman, T. S. (1993). Control motivation and attitude change. In G. Weary, F. Gleicher, & K. L. Marsh (Eds.), *Control motivation and social cognition* (pp. 157–175). New York: Springer-Verlag.

Pittman, T. S., & D'Agostino, P. R. (1985). Motivation and attribution: The effects of control deprivation on subsequent information processing. In J. H. Harvey & G. Weary (Eds.), *Attribution: Basic issues and applications* (pp. 117–141). New York: Academic Press.

Pyszczynski, T., & Greenberg, J. (1987). Self-regulatory perseveration and the depressive self-focusing style: A self-awareness theory of reactive depression. *Psychological Bulletin, 102*, 122–138.

Roese, N. J. (1994). The functional basis of counterfactual thinking. *Journal of Personality and Social Psychology, 66*, 805–818.

Roese, N. J., & Olson, J. M. (1993). Self-esteem and counterfactual thinking. *Journal of Personality and Social Psychology, 65*, 199–206.

Roese, N. J., & Olson, J. M. (1995a). Outcome controllability and counterfactual thinking. *Personality and Social Psychology Bulletin, 21*, 620–628.

Roese, N. J., & Olson, J. M. (1995b). Counterfactual thinking: A critical overview. In N. J. Roese & J. M. Olson (Eds.), *What might have been: The social psychology of counterfactual thinking* (pp. 1–55). Hillsdale, NJ: Erlbaum.

Roese, N. J., & Olson, J. M. (1995c). Functions of counterfactual thinking. In N. J. Roese & J. M. Olson (Eds.), *What might have been: The social psychology of counterfactual thinking* (pp. 169–197). Hillsdale, NJ: Erlbaum.

Rothbaum, F., Weisz, J. R., & Snyder, S. S. (1982). Changing the world and changing the self: A two-process model of perceived control. *Journal of Personality and Social Psychology, 42*, 5–37.

Sanna, L. J. (1997). Self-efficacy and counterfactual thinking: Up a creek with and without a paddle. *Personality and Social Psychology Bulletin, 23*, 654–666.

Seligman, M. E. P. (1975). *Helplessness: On depression, development, and death.* San Francisco: Freeman.

Sherman, S. J., & McConnell, A. R. (1995). Dysfunctional implications of counterfactual thinking: When alternatives to reality fail us. In N. J. Roese & J. M. Olson (Eds.), *What might have been: The social psychology of counterfactual thinking* (pp. 199–231). Hillsdale, NJ: Erlbaum.

Silver, R. L., Boon, C., & Stones, M. H. (1983). Searching for meaning in misfortune: Making sense of incest. *Journal of Social Issues, 39*, 81–102.

Sweeney, P. D., Anderson, K., & Bailey, S. (1986). Attributional style in depression: A meta-analytic review. *Journal of Personality and Social Psychology, 50*, 974–991.

Tait, R., & Silver, R. C. (1989). Coming to terms with major life events. In J. S. Uleman & J. A. Bargh (Eds.), *Unintended thought* (pp. 352–382). New York: Guilford Press.

Taylor, S. E., & Pham, L. B. (1996). Mental simulation, motivation, and action. In J. A. Bargh & P. M. Gollwitzer (Eds.), *The psychology of action* (pp. 219–235). New York: Guilford Press.

Thompson, S. C. (1981). Will it hurt less if I can control it? A complex answer to a simple question. *Psychological Bulletin, 90,* 89–101.

Thompson, S. C. (1993). Naturally occurring perceptions of control: A model of bounded flexibility. In G. Weary F., Gleicher, & K. L. Marsh (Eds.), *Control motivation and social cognition* (pp. 74–93). New York: Springer-Verlag.

Warren, L. W., & McEachren, L. (1983). Psychosocial correlates of depressive symptomatology in adult women. *Journal of Abnormal Psychology, 92,* 151–160.

Weary, G., & Edwards, J. A. (1994). Social cognition and clinical psychology: Anxiety, depression, and the processing of social information. In R. S. Wyer, Jr, and T. K. Srull (Eds.), *Handbook of social cognition* (Vol. 2, pp. 289–338). Hillsdale, NJ: Erlbaum.

Weary, G., & Edwards, J. A. (1996). Causal uncertainty beliefs and related goal structures. In E. T. Higgins & R. M. Sorrentino (Eds.), *Handbook of motivation and cognition: The interpersonal context* (Vol. 3, pp. 148–181). New York: Guilford Press.

Weary, G., Elbin, S., & Hill, M. G. (1987). Attributional and social comparison processes in depression. *Journal of Personality and Social Psychology, 52,* 605–610.

Weary, G., & Gannon, K. (1996). Depression, control motivation, and person perception. In J. A. Bargh & P. M. Gollwitzer (Eds.), *The psychology of action* (pp. 146–163). New York: Guilford Press.

Weary, G., Gleicher, F., & Marsh, K. L. (1993). *Control motivation and social cognition.* New York: Springer-Verlag.

Weary, G., Jordan, J. S., & Hill, M. G. (1985). The attributional norm of internality and depressive sensitivity to social information. *Journal of Personality and Social Psychology, 52,* 605–610.

Weary, G., Marsh, K. L., Gleicher, F., & Edwards, J. A. (1993). Depression, control motivation, and the processing of information about others. In G. Weary, F Gleicher, & K. L. Marsh (Eds.), *Control motivation and social cognition* (pp. 255–287). New York: Springer-Verlag.

Weiner, B. (1986). *An attributional theory of motivation and emotion.* New York: Springer-Verlag.

Weiner, B., Graham, S., & Chandler, C. (1982). Pity, anger, and guilt: An attributional analysis. *Personality and Social Psychology Bulletin, 8,* 226–232.

Weisz, J. R., Weiss, B., Wasserman, A. A., & Rintoul, B. (1987). Control-related beliefs and depression among clinic-referred children and adolescents. *Journal of Abnormal Psychology, 96,* 58–63.

Wells, G. L., & Gavanski, I. (1989). Mental simulation of causality. *Journal of Personality and Social Psychology, 56,* 161–169.

White, R. W. (1959). Motivation reconsidered: The concept of competence. *Psychological Review, 66,* 297–332.

Wicker, F. W., Payne, G. C., & Morgan, R. D. (1983). Participants descriptions of guilt and shame. *Motivation and Emotion, 7,* 25–39.

Wilson, T. D., & Schooler, J. (1991). Thinking too much: Introspection can reduce the quality of preferences and decisions. *Journal of Personality and Social Psychology, 60,* 181–192.

Wood, J. V., Saltzberg, J. A., Neale, J. M., Stone, A. A., & Rachmiel, T. B. (1990). Self-focused attention, coping responses, and distressed mood in everyday life. *Journal of Personality and Social Psychology, 58,* 1027–1036.

Yost, J. H., & Weary, G. (1996). Depression and the correspondent inference bias: Evidence for more careful cognitive processing. *Personality and Social Psychology Bulletin, 22,* 192–200.

CHAPTER 16

UNCONTROLLABILITY AS A SOURCE OF COGNITIVE EXHAUSTION

IMPLICATIONS FOR HELPLESSNESS AND DEPRESSION

MIROSLAW KOFTA AND GRZEGORZ SEDEK

INTRODUCTION

In the last three decades, a psychological response to circumstances that jeopardize human striving for control has emerged as a prominent topic in psychological inquiry. Researchers increasingly have asked how loss of control affects human motivation, mood, and cognitive processing. In addition, attention has been directed to the effects of loss of control on psychological well-being, adaptation, and interpersonal relationships.

Of considerable interest, two divergent metatheoretical perspectives have emerged in the psychological literature to account for reactions to loss of control. Essentially, the first perspective frames control loss as a "mobilizer" (an experience that instigates active coping), whereas the second perspective views control loss as a "demobilizer" (an experience that severely undermines active coping).

MIROSLAW KOFTA • Faculty of Psychology, University of Warsaw, 00-183 Warsaw, Poland. E-mail: kofta@sci.psych.uw.edu.pl GRZEGORZ SEDEK • University of Warsaw and Polish Academy of Science Faculty of Psychology, 00-183 Warsaw, Poland. E-mail sedek@sci.psych.uw.edu.pl

Personal Control in Action, edited by Kofta et al., Plenum Press, New York, 1998.

According to the former view, people are endowed with motivational and ability resources, and control loss (actual or anticipated) impels them to make use of these resources for regaining control. Several phenomena seem to support this general view. For example, threat to perceived choice arouses reactance, that is, motivation to reestablish endangered "behavioral freedoms" (Brehm, 1966, 1993). Within limits, increased goal difficulty (undermining perceived control) results in energization effects, that is, in more sympathetic arousal and heightened goal attractiveness (Wright & Brehm, 1989). In addition to releasing "energetic" reserves, loss of control may also liberate cognitive reserves: Following control deprivation, people typically switch to a more systematic and accurate mode of processing social information (e.g., Pittman, 1993; Weary, Gleicher, & Marsh, 1993; see also Markman & Weary, Chapter 15, this volume). Also, threats to control may mobilize more fundamental personality resources: For instance, experience of severe illness may result in more meaning being attributed to life in general, an increased sense of control over the present and the future, and heightened self-affirmation (Taylor, 1983).

As already stated, however, the notion of control loss as a demobilizer seems equally plausible: There is considerable support for the idea that control deprivation leads to drainage of motivational, affective, and mental reserves, or, at least, to a lessened accesss to these reserves. For instance, research in the learned helplessness paradigm (e.g., Abramson, Seligman, & Teasdale, 1978; Maier & Seligman, 1976; Maier & Jackson, 1979; Miller & Seligman; 1982; Seligman, 1975) frequently reveals various psychological deficits as a major consequence of control loss, including deficits of initiative (behavioral passivity), lowered mood, cognitive malfunctioning, severe disturbance in learning new, more adaptive ways of behavior, and lowered self-esteem. Also, findings from other conceptual paradigms support a general view of control loss as a demobilizer (e.g., Glass & Singer, 1972; Rosenbaum, 1988). The existence of a well-documented link between control loss and psychological deficits explains why health psychologists refer to uncontrollability as one of the major factors in reactive depression, anxiety states, psychosomatic symptoms, and even physical illness.

In this chapter, we develop ideas pertinent to the notion of control as a demobilizer. In particular, we will present and discuss new findings regarding the phenomenon of *cognitive exhaustion*—a hypothetical sequel of loss of control that accounts for cognitive, motivational, and behavioral symptoms of learned helplessness. Further, the usefulness of this notion in explaining cognitive deficits in depression will be analyzed.

However, we will suggest in addition how competing perspectives on control loss as mobilizing versus demobilizing experience could be integrated. In particular, we will analyze the relationship between the control motivation theory (assuming the former perspective) and the cognitive exhaustion theory (assuming the latter perspective). We hypothesize that these two theories are not incompatible: They may refer to simultaneously developing phenomena that emerge at different levels of information processing and are manifested in different contexts.

THE LEARNED HELPLESSNESS VERSUS COGNITIVE EXHAUSTION VIEWS OF UNCONTROLLABILITY AND ITS CONSEQUENCES

Prolonged contact with uncontrollable events often results in an important psychological change known as learned helplessness (LH). This syndromatic change is a composite of cognitive, motivational, and affective deficits (e.g., Hiroto & Seligman, 1975; Maier & Seligman, 1976).

Classical LH theory (Maier & Seligman, 1976; Seligman, 1975) explains the process of helplessness development in terms of a transfer of action-outcome noncontingency. In the uncontrollable situation, an organism develops a generalized expectation of noncontingency that interferes with learning new action-outcome associations. This interference is a major symptom of a cognitive (associative) deficit. In addition, uncontrollability produces a motivational (or activity) deficit, that is, a lowered readiness to initiate voluntary behavior, and an emotional deficit—a sad mood (e.g., Maier & Seligman, 1976; Miller & Seligman, 1982). Cognitive and motivational LH deficits account for an impaired performance in the test phase of numerous LH experiments conducted with both human and infrahuman subjects (e.g., Maier & Jackson, 1979; Maier & Seligman, 1976).

A recently developed, information-processing model of helplessness approaches uncontrollability and its consequences from a different angle (e.g., Kofta, 1993; Kofta & Sedek, 1989b, 1997; Sedek & Kofta, 1990; Sedek, Kofta & Tyszka, 1993). This model assumes that people tend to engage in a vigorous mental activity in problem-solving situations. They try to understand the meaning of task demands, select and memorize important data and categorize them properly, detect regularities (e.g., stimulus contingencies), draw correct inferences, and so forth.

In controllable situations, activity of this sort facilitates the construction of mental models—cognitive devices for structuring and active processing of new information in terms of inferential rules the models comprise. These cognitive devices allow one to predict and control future events and to provide explanations for past events (e.g., Brewer, 1987; Johnson-Laird, 1983; Greeno, 1989; Holland, Holyoak, Nisbett, & Thagard, 1986). The primary sign of a mental model's emergence is the generation of hypotheses for problem solutions.

However, in uncontrollable situations, this intense mental activity remains futile because it cannot lead to real progress in problem solving. Even if many hypotheses are generated, the person cannot effectively differentiate between good ideas and poor ideas in seeking a solution. As a result, cognitive effort fails to reduce uncertainty.[1]

We hypothesize that prolonged cognitive effort without "cognitive gain" results in an altered psychological state: cognitive (mental) exhaustion. In this state, the generation of mental models is inhibited (see von Hecker & Sedek, 1996). Therefore, insight processes (a discovery of task solutions despite incomplete data, e.g., Johnson-Laird, 1988; Perkins, 1988), critical for creative problem solving, seem likely to be affected. Thus, people turn from genuine problem solvers who go "beyond the data given" to passive collectors of task information. In general, such a state of cognitive exhaustion seems especially destructive for more complex problems requiring nonroutine, flexible adaptations, in either achievement or interpersonal realms.

Research Evidence

Let us summarize briefly the empirical support for this model from our own program of research. We begin with a question concerning the critical ingredients of uncontrollable situations that presumably account for subsequent deterioration of performance. Then we review the available evidence concerning the hypothetical mediator of these effects—the state of cognitive exhaustion.

As expected, we found that uncontrollability is associated with irreducible uncertainty. In one study, subjects' hypotheses of problem solution were recorded during a discrimination (concept formation) task. When this task consisted of controllable (solvable) problems, subjects showed a graduate decrease of uncertainty of the hypothesis set during the problem's progress. However, virtually no changes in the (high) uncertainty level were observed among subjects exposed to the uncontrollable problems (Kofta, 1993; see also Kofta & Sedek, 1997).

Second, results of several of our studies demonstrated that inefficient mental exertion (due to engagement in unsolvable problems requesting on-line integration of inconsistent cues) led to performance impairment on subsequent tasks and lowered mood (Sedek & Kofta, 1990; see also Kofta, 1993). Of importance, these deficits emerged in the conditions minimizing the likelihood of effort withdrawal as an ego-protective maneuvering—in the absence of failure feedback and ego-involving instructions[2] (for related findings, see Kofta & Sedek, 1989c; see also Snyder

& Frankel, 1989, and Kofta & Sedek, 1989a, for further discussion of these findings). In addition, performance deficits remained significant after statistically controlling for decreased mood (Sedek & Kofta, 1990, Experiment 3). Taken together, the results of this series of studies consistently support the present model's claim that it is deficient integration of task information during contact with uncontrollability—not accompanying affective or motivational changes—that is mainly responsible for subsequent impairment of performance in the laboratory.

Let us turn now to research in which we investigated the postulated mediating process. We found that subjective symptoms of mental exhaustion (like attentional distraction, inhibition of thinking, and lack of ideas of how to solve the problem) were reliably associated with performance impairment on the test task (Sedek & Kofta, 1990, Experiment 3; see also studies reported further on in this chapter). In another study, predecisional information search following uncontrollability was altered in a way suggesting cognitive exhaustion: Research participants tended to avoid effortful information-gathering strategies (Sedek et al., 1993). In still another study (Kofta & Narkiewicz-Jodko, 1996), students performed a control judgment task using the modified experimental paradigm of Alloy and Abramson (1979). During a sequence of trials presenting information on a response-outcome contingency, participants could signal the moment they arrived at a preliminary hypothesis about the degree of exercised control. Supportive of the notion of mental exhaustion as insufficient cognitive structuring, preexposure to uncontrollability led to a substantial delay in hypothesis generation, and this effect appeared independent of mood changes.

Most recently, compelling evidence was found for the hypothesized link between uncontrollability and an impaired mental modeling, which is assumed here to be a critical component of the state of cognitive exhaustion. In this research (von Hecker & Sedek, 1996), a computerized procedure was applied that allowed us to trace the process of mental model production in the social domain. On the basis of incomplete information about the distribution of likes and dislikes between the target persons, the participants were asked to categorize these persons into smaller groups: The task required them to generate two kinds of categorization models. It appeared that depressed subjects, as well as participants preexposed to uncontrollability, showed considerable impairment on this task.

Mental Exhaustion and Deficit of Cognitive Resources

In the present chapter, an attempt is made to deepen our understanding of cognitive exhaustion. Let us note that its core feature—deficient mental modeling—may have profound consequences for substantive processing of information (Bower, 1991). First and foremost, it may decrease *selectivity* in the intake of input data. Once generated, a mental model defines some aspects of the immediate environment as important and some others as unimportant and, in so doing, permits allocation of attention in more economic and efficient ways. Therefore, when there are deficits in model construction (e.g., when, during problem solving attempts, no ideas come to mind as to the correct solution), attention is diffused and new data are processed in a highly nonselective manner.[3]

An uncontrollable experience may impair subsequent filtering of input data for a second reason. An essential feature of this experience is that people are exposed to a stream of inconsistent task cues during strenuous cognitive exertion (Sedek & Kofta, 1990). In a way analogous to the learned irrelevance hypothesis (e.g., Barber & Winefield, 1986) one could argue that, during such an experience, people may learn that selective investment of attention is useless. This process may lead to a transient inhibition of effortful strategies of attention control (e.g., Gopher, 1993), which would impair processing selectivity.

Both lines of reasoning lead us to a major prediction examined in this chapter. We hypothesize that contact with uncontrollable events—presumably through loss of selectivity in data intake—results in a *deficit of cognitive resources*.

According to the cognitive economy view (e.g., Navon & Gopher, 1979; Shiffrin, 1976), people have finite cognitive resources for processing information. Of importance, resources may be flexibly allocated for "fueling" very different aspects or stages of our mental operations (e.g., Hasher & Zacks, 1979; Kahneman, 1973; Navon & Gopher, 1979; Shiffrin & Schneider, 1977). Utilization of these limited resources (for attending, memorizing, executing control or metacognitive strategies) results in effortful (or controlled) processing.

Why should loss of control deplete cognitive resources? Uncontrollability is hypothesized to impair the filtering of input data. When motivated to solve a problem, a person may attempt to attend to nearly everything. This strategy could be efficient in cognitively undemanding situations. However, with more demanding tasks, it will quickly result in mental overload; cognitive resources, utilized in a highly wasteful manner, will be insufficient for adequate processing of task information.

To test our major hypothesis, a dual-task procedure was employed in the studies reported below. This experimental paradigm allows a direct test of the resource allocation process (e.g., Gopher, 1993; Navon & Gopher, 1979), thus providing a stringent test for the considered hypothesis.

A deficit of general-purpose resources should be manifested in different performance on single versus dual tasks. Imagine that person A but not person B suffers from a resource deficit, but that the cognitive demands of the primary task do not exceed the resources of person A. Thus, one would not expect any difference between A and B in performance of a primary task when it is a single one. However, the same individuals should behave differently when a secondary task is simultaneously conducted. Person A's performance should now deteriorate on the primary task, because some part of his or her (small) resources has to be allocated for the secondary task. In the same situation, person B still has a reserve of "free" resources, which could now be applied for processing the secondary task. As a consequence, person B's performance should not deteriorate on the primary task (or the degree of deterioration should be very modest in comparison to person A). Given this reasoning, one should expect an *interaction*, on the primary task performance, between the deficit-producing treatment (in the reported experiments—uncontrollability) and single- versus dual-task conditions.

RESEARCH ON UNCONTROLLABILITY AND DUAL-TASK PERFORMANCE

Twenty eight high-school students participated in an experiment to be briefly reported here (Sedek & McIntosh, 1996).

Uncontrollability Treatment

To induce uncontrollability, a computerized version of informational helplessness training was applied in this and subsequent studies (for a full description, see Sedek & Kofta, 1990). The task consisted of four discrimination problems with eight trials per problem (see Figure 1). For each problem, the participant had to find a target element (feature) of the figure by examining successively presented slides. Figures varied on five dimensions: size, shape, surface, position of line (at the top or bottom), and size of the letter *r*. Students were told that by attending to "yes" or "no" cues they could determine the element to be discovered (in a given trial, "yes" meant that the target element was present, and "no" meant that the target element was absent).

In the uncontrollable condition, the cues were delivered in such a way that, on each problem, each feature was paired twice with positive ("yes") and twice with negative ("no") information (see Figure 1). Thus, whatever the hypothesis formulated, it was associated with conflicting, inconsistent cues. Immediately after each problem completion participants were requested to report its solution, but were not informed whether they succeeded or failed.

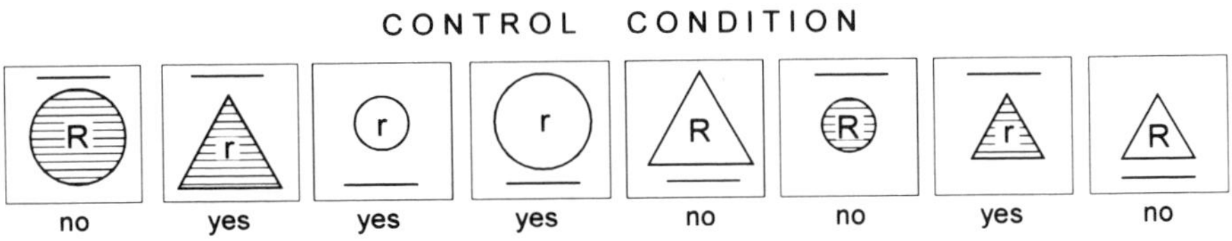

FIGURE 1 A set of patterns presented as Problem 1 in the uncontrollable condition (helplessness training) and the controllable condition (in the latter condition, the letter *r* is the correct solution).

In the controllable condition, the cues were delivered in a fully consistent way: "yes" appeared whenever a target element was present in the figure and "no" whenever it was absent (see Figure 1). Thus, given that the proper hypothesis was formulated by a subject, it received systematic support. In no other respects did the controllable condition differ from the uncontrollable condition.

Subsequently, all students performed the attentional task in the dual-task paradigm.[4] The primary task was a letter recognition task (see Figure 2). A capital letter was fixed centrally in a small frame. Within a broader frame, small letters appeared for 1 s. Participants had to press the

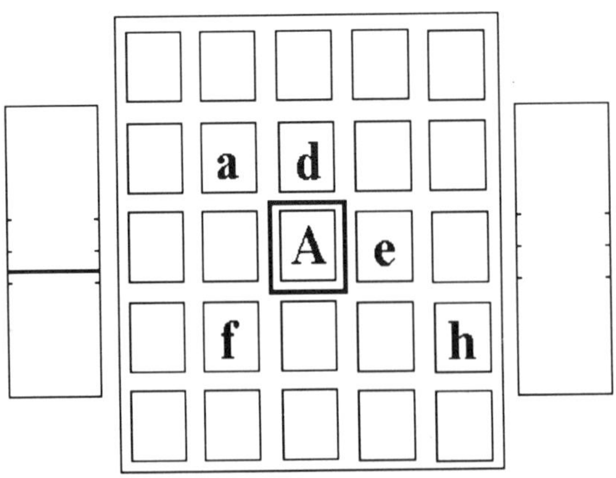

FIGURE 2 Dual-task paradigm. The primary task requires subjects to recognize as quickly as possible a small letter identical to the capital letter in the central frame. The secondary task requires subjects to keep the horizontal line (appearing in either the left or right frame) within boundaries.

left mousekey as quickly as possible whenever the lowercase version of the capital letter was present among other small letters (distractors), or they had to refrain from responding when the target small letter was absent. The number of hits was the main dependent measure of primary task performance.

The secondary task (see Figure 2) required keeping the horizontal line (emerging at the left or right side of the letter field) within the boundaries. Line movement was programmed to come down "spontaneously." The participant could control the line movement by pressing the right mousekey (when the line went down) or by releasing the key (when the line went up). Crossing the prohibited (lower or higher) boundary resulted in an unpleasant noise.

A single- vs. dual-task treatment was manipulated within subjects: They were first given the two series of seven trials with a single task, and next two series of seven trials with a dual task.

The major findings—for number of hits as a dependent variable—are shown in Figure 3. As can be seen, the expected interactional pattern emerged. Planned comparisons showed a significant decrease on primary task performance in the dual-task condition only for the group with uncontrollable preexposure, $F(1, 26) = 12.71$, $p < .001$, but not with controllable preexposure. Also, there was a significant difference between groups with controllable and uncontrollable preexposure for the dual-task condition, $F(1, 26) = 4.91$, $p < .05$, but not for the single task condition. Thus, results show that exposure to uncontrollable events produces deficits of nonspecific cognitive resources.

Further, we analyzed results for false alarms (erroneous recognition of distractors as target letters). Production of this type of error may indicate impaired data filtering: Irrelevant stimuli tend to be categorized as relevant ones. Of considerable interest, there was a main effect for uncontrollability on this measure, $F(1, 26) = 4.70$, $p < .05$ (uncontrollability increased the false alarms' rate). However, the interaction between uncontrollability and task conditions was not significant. Lack of this interaction suggests that an increment in false alarms after control loss was not just a consequence of cognitive overload. This is consistent with the idea that an impaired filtering—postulated here to be a direct consequence of uncontrollability—may emerge earlier and, possibly, may play a causal role in generating resource deficits.

In line with previous findings (Sedek & Kofta, 1990), participants in the uncontrollable preexposure condition reported a variety of generalized cognitive dysfunctions during the test task (e.g., diffused attention, mind blanks, general feelings of inadequate handling of the task). These dysfunctions may reflect the state of cognitive exhaustion at the subjective level. Participants also complained of more specific difficulties (in giving

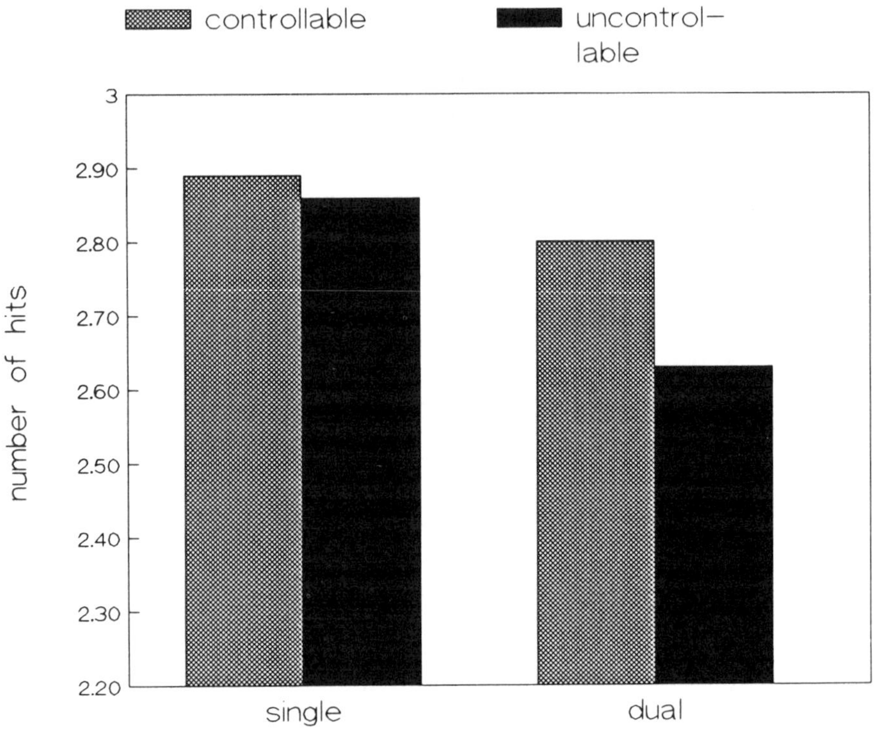

FIGURE 3 Number of hits in the primary task during single- versus dual task performance: Effects of controllable versus uncontrollable preexposure (Study 1).

fast responses to the letters, in coordinating line management and letter responding).

To check the stability of these findings, a study was conducted with a second set of 28 high school students (Sedek & McIntosh, 1996). In a slightly modified procedure, one highly difficult trial was introduced in the midst of each seven-trial series on the primary task (for both single- and dual-task conditions).[5]

The major findings, for number of hits, are presented in Figure 4. As can be seen, the previous interactional pattern was replicated, but the effects appeared stronger. Planned comparisons revealed a significant decrease in primary task performance in the dual-task condition only for the group with uncontrollable preexposure, $F(1, 54) = 44.90$, $p < .001$, but not with controllable preexposure. Also, there was a significant difference between groups with controllable and uncontrollable preexposure for the

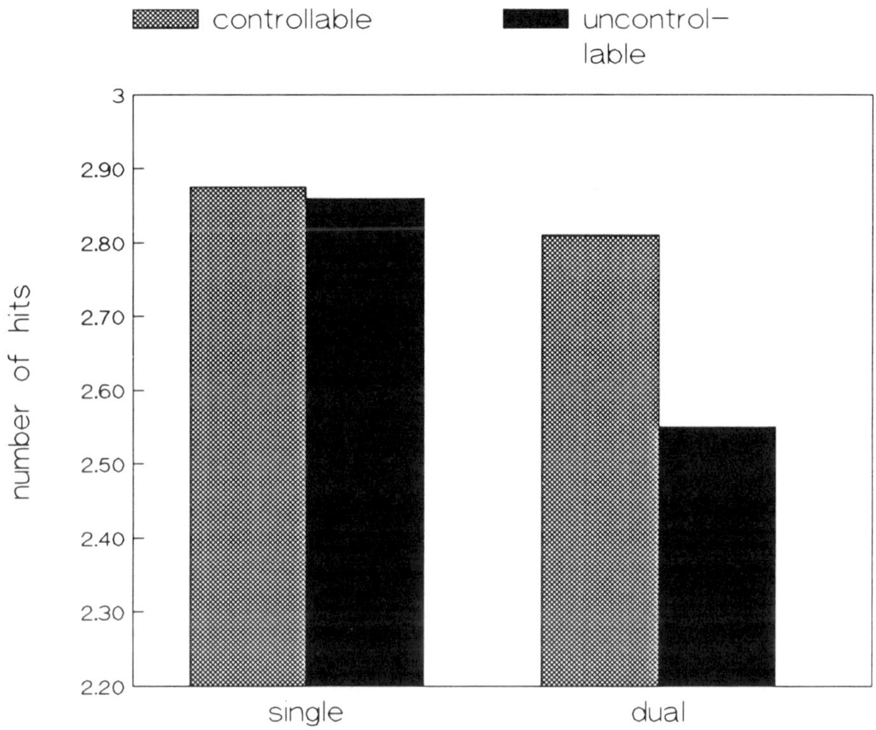

FIGURE 4 Number of hits in the primary task during single- versus dual task performance: Effects of controllable versus uncontrollable preexposure (Study 2).

dual-task (but not the single-task) condition, $F(1, 54) = 14.06, p < .001$. This pattern is highly supportive of the theory that uncontrollability brings about a deficit of general-purpose cognitive resources.

As found previously, uncontrollability also increased false alarms, $F(1, 26) = 3.69, p < .05$ (one-sided test), and did not significantly interact on this measure with a single versus dual task. In addition, as shown by separate analysis of the responses to highly difficult trials (inserted in each series), there was a substantial increment in false alarms after uncontrollability, $F(1, 26) = 12.35, p < .005$, and no significant interaction of uncontrollability with the task type. Again, findings for false alarms imply that impaired data filtering might be a direct consequence of uncontrollability, not the aftereffect of resource depletion. As in the former study, we also found that uncontrollability augmented subjective perceptions of cognitive exhaustion during subsequent task performance.

RESEARCH ON UNCONTROLLABILITY, INDUCTIVE REASONING, AND MENTAL ARITHMETIC

To cope with challenges in repeatable situations, it is enough to use previously acquired routines, that is, ready-made programs for cognitive operations and behavior control. However, one may also be faced by situations that are atypical, novel, and require creative mental operations for successful adaptation. Instead of application of programs already available in the person's repertoire, these situations demand the generation of new programs.

Assuming that uncontrollability produces a deficit of cognitive resources, an interesting question arises as to how this deficit will affect processing in novel as opposed to routine situations. On the one hand, coping with novel tasks engages a great deal of effortful processing (e.g., Hasher & Zacks, 1979; Shiffrin & Schneider, 1977). Therefore, to the extent that uncontrollability drains cognitive resources, one could expect more deterioration on novel than routine tasks. On the other hand, available evidence suggests that effortful processing is not inherently associated with performance of novel (problem-solving) tasks, but may occur in routine tasks as well, given that they impose high demands on working memory (e.g., Ackerman, 1986; Fisk & Schneider, 1983).

To operationalize our problem, two types of tasks were selected in the reported study: The task on series completion and the task on mental arithmetic.

The series completion task belongs to a broad class of tasks engaging inductive reasoning, considered to be a core component of fluid intelligence (e.g., Greeno, 1968; Pellegrino & Glaser, 1980; Simon, 1976; Sternberg, 1985). This task requires creative problem solving: One has to discover a rule "hidden" in the series of cases available and use this rule for correct generation (or recognition) of new cases. Series completion problems involve sophisticated cognitive strategies (e.g., Sternberg, 1985) and are likely to engage mental capacity.

In contrast, the task on mental arithmetic, engaging elementary operations acquired early in school, represents the class of routine tasks (which require an application of well-trained, ready-made cognitive programs to stimulus material). However, mental arithmetic may also impose a high load on working memory when one performs arithmetic operations in one's head on two- or three-digit numbers (as in the present research).

In the study reported below (Sosnowski, Krzywosz, Kofta, & Sedek, 1996), following exposure to uncontrollability, participants were presented with either a series completion task or a mental arithmetic task. The tasks were carefully matched with regard to (medium) difficulty, kind of input material (numbers), number of problems, length of task performance, and variability of cognitive operations needed. Uncontrollability treatment was identical to that described earlier (see Figure 1) with an exception that slides (not a computer) were used.

Test Tasks

In the series completion task, there were 16 series completion problems arranged according to four general rules (with four problems per rule): sequence of increasing numbers (e.g., 4, 7, 11, 16, 22, 29, 37, ...), sequence of decreasing numbers (e.g., 98, 87, 76, 65, 54, 43, 32, ...), two sequences of numbers in alternating order (e.g., 8, 4, 9, 3, 10, 2, 11, ...), and sequence of number pairs, the second number in each pair formed from the first by reversing the digit order (29, 92, 28, 82, 27, 72, 26, ...). Participants had to discover the hidden rule and report the solution (the missing number).

In the mental arithmetic task, there were 16 mental arithmetic problems arranged according to four rules of arithmetic operations: addition, subtraction, multiplication, or division (e.g., 494 + 289; 133 – 57; 15 × 11; 84 ÷ 6). Participants had to perform the arithmetic operation requested in a given trial and report the solution (the proper number).

For both tasks, the 16 problems were presented in four blocks, with four rules per block.

Major results were the following. An ANOVA yielded a very strong main effect for uncontrollability, $F(1, 96) = 96.77$, $p < .0001$, $\omega^2 = .49$,[6] whereas effects for task (arithmetic vs. series completion), and for Uncontrollability × Task interaction, were nonsignificant (see Figure 5). Further, uncontrollability accounted for a comparable proportion of variance in performance of the arithmetic task, $\omega^2 = .52$, and series completion task, $\omega^2 = .46$.

Confirming the previous results, it also appeared that, after loss of control, participants complained of diffuse cognitive dysfunctions in attention, memory, and idea generation regardless of the type of task solved. These subjective symptoms of cognitive exhaustion were inversely related to performance.

In the reported study, uncontrollability strongly impaired performance of a series completion and arithmetic task as well (remember that the tasks were carefully matched in difficulty and structural features). These findings (as well as results for subjective measures) provide further support to our hypothesis that uncontrollability induces a nonspecific deficit of cognitive resources. In addition, the discussed findings clarify that the adverse consequences of uncontrollability are not limited to more creative mental operations, but may also emerge in contexts that engage ready-made, routine operations. The question arises, under which conditions is the latter effect likely.

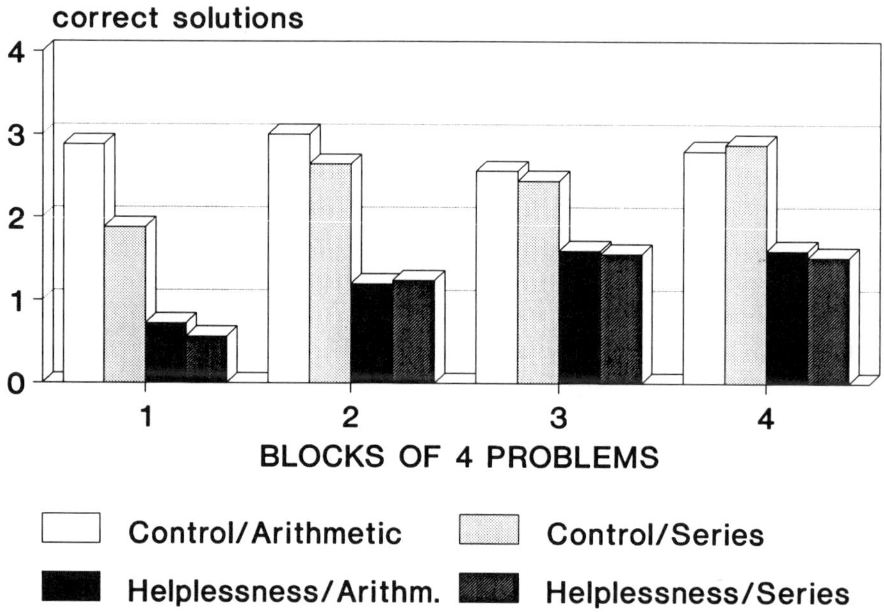

FIGURE 5 Mean number of correctly solved problems on mental arithmetic and series completion after controllable versus uncontrollable preexposure.

New developments in the theory of controlled processing help us to identify one such important condition. Besides situation novelty suggested earlier (e.g., Hasher & Zacks, 1979; Shiffrin & Schneider, 1977), inconsistency (variability) of cognitive operations is a powerful releaser of effortful processing (e.g., Ackerman, 1986, 1987; Fisk & Schneider, 1983). Thus, it is possible that resource depletion may also disturb the performance of routine (program-application) tasks if they are highly varied and require one to switch at a high pace from one operation type to another. Note that our task on mental arithmetic represents well the category of varied tasks: From trial to trial, participants had to change the kind of mathematical operation employed.

COGNITIVE EXHAUSTION AS A CONSEQUENCE OF CONTROL LOSS

Overall, the reported findings consistently support the cognitive exhaustion prediction that uncontrollability generates a deficit of nonspecific cognitive resources. Generalized decrements in performance following uncontrollability, the major finding in LH research (e.g., Dweck & Wortman, 1982; Maier & Seligman, 1976), may then stem from resource depletion. However, this deficit is particularly hazardous for tasks that are cognitively demanding. This would explain why LH performance decrements are more probable in complex than simple tasks, in animals and humans as well (Maier & Seligman, 1976; see also Sedek & Kofta, 1990).

At a more abstract level, our findings may help to reveal the adaptive meaning of the experience of control loss. They also allow us to place this experience into the broader context of a current discourse on mind and action. Cognitive control of action is a continuous interplay of effortful and automatic processing (e.g., Ackerman, 1987; Bargh, 1994; Hasher & Zacks, 1979; Shiffrin & Schneider, 1977). If uncontrollability limits access to general-purpose resources, as the present findings seem to imply, it should have detrimental consequences for effortful processing. To paraphrase Hasher and Zacks (1979), effortful processing is a specialized mode of operation for handling novelty, that is, for detecting new information, for encoding it in memory and assimilating it into preexisting knowledge structures, and—most of all—for changing earlier schemata. When a new schema is already established, repetition of schema-relevant experience will lead to knowledge proceduralization (e.g., Ackerman, 1987; Fisk & Schneider, 1983), and effortful processing—now no longer necessary—will be replaced by automatic processing.

Thus, the loss-of-control experience—particularly when occurring in a vital life domain—may be highly detrimental for coping with novel (current and long-term) tasks in the achievement and social areas as well (Kofta, 1993; see also Sedek and McIntosh, Chapter 17, this volume). Tasks requiring the generation of new ideas, the assimilation of new concepts, and the alteration of views to produce nonstandard solutions to cognitive or interpersonal problems seem likely to be affected. The risk of such a happening increases enormously when these tasks are complex, cognitively demanding, and loosely structured. In addition, however, our last study suggests that performance of routine cognitive tasks—given that they are highly varied—might also be disturbed. In contrast, there is no reason to expect that activity regulated at the automatic level of processing will be affected by uncontrollability.

Uncontrollability: Direct or Indirect Cause of Resource Deficit?

An interesting, and potentially critical question arises as to whether uncontrollability produces resource deficits directly or indirectly, via some mediating process.

Notwithstanding the former possibility,[7] we argue in this chapter in favor of a second scenario. We hypothesize that uncontrollability engenders a state of cognitive exhaustion: Its primary manifestation is a loss of processing selectivity, which leads in turn to resource deficit. Such a mediational schema seems theoretically fertile: Besides providing a better fit to the present findings, it also appears useful for creating conceptual links between helplessness and depression and for resolving some apparent inconsistencies in the depressive processing literature (see later).

In short, we hypothesize that uncontrollability impairs production of mental models—working "theories" of a situation constructed at the time of use. Such models simplify processing, promote understanding and prediction, and improve practical control over the course of events (e.g., Brewer, 1987; Greeno, 1989; Holland et al., 1986; Johnson-Laird, 1983). Supportive of this assumption, the most recent findings of von Hecker and Sedek (1996) have shown that the process of generating and applying mental models may be heavily impaired after an uncontrollable experience in the laboratory, as well as by a state of mild depression.

Importantly, active mental models impose priorities on data processing, that is to say, they serve to implement a selective set. When, for whatever reasons, model construction is inhibited or delayed in the course of the problem-solving attempts, this should impair selective attention. However, novel and complex problem-solving tasks are inherently rich (multidimensional): In the absence of criteria regarding the relative importance of different stimulus dimensions, a person might be tempted to attend to nearly everything, a strategy likely to lead to information overload.

Alternatively, impaired selection of input data might be a direct consequence of an experience of control loss. As suggested earlier (see also Kofta, 1993; Sedek & Kofta, 1990), a critical aspect of this experience is that people invest cognitive effort without cognitive gain in their problem-solving attempts. This may promote learning that the application of effortful strategies of attention control (Gopher, 1993) is meaningless. As a consequence, people may refrain from using such strategies in new situations.

The present findings (see studies 1 and 2) are consistent with the theory that uncontrollability may impair data selection: Following unsolvable problems, the rate of false alarms increased for both single- and dual-task conditions. Of considerable interest, this theoretical possibility is also supported by the recent research on animal helplessness and by laboratory studies on information processing in depression (see later). Minor and his associates (Minor, Dess, & Overmier, 1991; Minor, Jackson, & Maier, 1984; Minor, Pellymounter, & Maier, 1988) have found that choice accuracy deficit ("pure" associative deficit studied in animal helplessness) emerges only when reinforcements after correct responses are delayed, and in the presence of task-irrelevant cues. Minor et al. (1991) comment: "Thus, while learned helplessness theory predicts that exposure to inescapable shock should interfere with the formation of response-outcome associations, the actual difficulty appeared to arise at an earlier stage of information processing, perhaps at an attentional level" (p. 121).

In conclusion, the theoretical scenario developed in the present chapter implies that mental resources, rather than being reduced in an absolute sense, are inadequately invested following uncontrollability. In an enlightening paper, Gopher (1993) argues that an impaired dual-task performance does not necessarily reflect a genuine "capacity" deficit (i.e., decreased attentional/memory span). Such an impairment may well be due to the disturbance at the level of *strategic control of attention* (focusing attention, dividing attention, switching attention, etc.). In other words, deterioration on dual tasks may reflect deficient functioning of a "central executive" responsible for flexible allocation of cognitive resources in the face of dynamically changing demands of the task situation. Although our findings do not allow us to directly test Gopher's alternative, they nevertheless suggest that deficient attentional controls may play an important role in performance decrements on dual tasks after uncontrollability.

Cognitive Exhaustion versus Control Motivation

In the social cognition literature, the theory of control motivation offers a different perspective from the present approach on uncontrollable experience and its consequences. Control deprivation is hypothesized to lead to a more careful, systematic, and deep processing of information, apparently in the service of control restoration (Pittman & D'Agostino, 1985, 1989; Pittman, 1993). Also, chronic elevation of control concerns is assumed to be a distinct feature of mild depression (e.g., Gleicher & Weary,1991; Weary, Marsh, Gleicher, & Edwards, 1993; see also Markman & Weary, Chapter 15, this volume). Several studies on control-deprived and mildly depressed people provide evidence consistent with this theory (e.g., these subjects prefer systematic over heuristic strategies of information gathering and frequently show higher accuracy in social judgment; see Pittman, 1993; Weary et al., 1993).

Thus, whereas the control motivation approach views control loss as a source of cognitive arousal and performance increments, the mental exhaustion approach emphasizes cognitive deficits and performance decrements. The question arises as to whether these diverse understandings of uncontrollability are compatible or not (see also Bugental & Lewis, Chapter 14, this volume).

There is no space here for a thorough discussion of this intriguing issue. However, we suggest a general solution in the spirit of the former, not the latter alternative. Note that in different studies, very similar methods for uncontrollability induction resulted in deterioration on the problem-solving tasks (which is in line with the cognitive exhaustion approach) and improvement on social judgment tasks (which is in line with the control motivation approach). Sometimes, these divergent effects emerged in one experiment, after uncontrollable preexposure of the same length (as in the study by Pittman & Pittman, 1980: uncontrollability improved subsequent attributional processing in one condition and impaired performance of anagrams in another condition).

This implies that the juxtaposed theories describe parallel but different-level processes, which may overtly manifest (or not) depending on the type of stimulus context (e.g., processing demands) imposed by a situation. The cognitive exhaustion model seems to address an "ability factor," that is, a reduced mental capacity (interpreted here as a deficit of general-purpose cognitive resources due to the impaired data filtering). In contrast, the control motivation model seems to address a motivational process accounting for the mobilization of available resources (e.g., Yost & Weary, 1996). Within the limits of mental capacity, heightened control motivation may engage more resources and thereby lead to better performance.

Therefore, if people perform less cognitively demanding tasks (as seems to be the case with the social judgment tasks used in the control-deprivation experiments), uncontrollability may activate, still available, reserves of effortful processing that should improve performance. However, when the task is highly demanding (i.e., imposes a considerable load on attention and short-term memory), uncontrollability may result in impaired processing and performance deterioration (see Bugental & Lewis, Chapter 14, this volume, for similar arguments regarding loss of control in the context of interpersonal power repair).

THE MODEL OF COGNITIVE EXHAUSTION: SOME IMPLICATIONS FOR UNDERSTANDING DEPRESSION

Helplessness Training in the Mind and Depression

Psychologists frequently note interesting parallels between clinical depression and the psychological state resulting from control loss (see Seligman, 1975; see also Abramson et al., 1978; Gleicher & Weary, 1991; Healey & Williams, 1988; Sedek & Kofta, 1990). In the original LH theory (Seligman, 1975), these parallels were suggested not only for symptoms, but also for causal mechanisms: An experience of loss of control was assumed to be a common source of helplessness and reactive depression.

In addition to the importance of chronic problems (e.g., in marriage, in work), empirical research reveals the considerable role of singular, negative life events as antecedents of depression (e.g., Healey & Williams, 1988; Lewinsohn, Hoberman, Teri, & Hautzinger, 1985; Lloyd, 1980; Paykel, 1982): Sometimes depression develops from a separate highly stressful happening, like the death of a spouse or loss of a job. This would seem to be at odds with the classical LH framework for depression: On purely logical grounds, singularity of an event precludes learning action-outcome noncontingency.[8]

Assuming the cognitive exhaustion model, we would argue, however, that even in the case of a singular traumatic event an enduring and highly devastating helplessness training might actually be experienced by the person. This self-generated, mental helplessness training may substantially contribute to both affective and cognitive deficits in depression.

Recent research on counterfactual thought and control motivation will help to elaborate this idea. Counterfactual thinking, or mental undoing, refers to mental simulation of an alternative course of events resulting in a different outcome than that which occurred in reality. As several studies imply (e.g., Markman, Gavanski, Sherman, & McMullen, 1993; Roese, 1994), mental undoing of negative events may restore feelings of control and help generate more efficient, goal-oriented programs for future actions. This seems especially likely for events that are controllable and repeatable. However, counterfactual thinking may also become highly dysfunctional if mental undoing concerns a single traumatic event that has an irrevocable nature (e.g., sudden death of a child): Production of counterfactuals is then associated with self-blame, feelings of guilt, and depression (Davis, Wortman, Silver, & Thompson, 1995; Niedental, Tangney, & Gavanski, 1994; see also Markman & Weary, Chapter 15, this volume, for a thorough discussion of these and related findings).

Of considerable interest, Markman and Weary (Chapter 15, this volume) have shown that moderately depressed people tend to mutate the controllable (but not uncontrollable) aspects of negative life events. This finding is in line with the theory that mild depression is associated with chronic, heightened control concerns (Weary et al., 1993). In another study, it also was found that individuals with lowered self-esteem are more likely to mutate their actions following failure than are individuals with high self-esteem (Roese & Olson, 1993).

Let us imagine a scenario in which a person with chronic control concerns and lowered self-esteem is confronted by a traumatic, irreversible life event. In an attempt to find meaning in such event (Davis et al., 1995; Epstein, Chapter 1, this volume; see also Thompson, 1981; Wortman, 1976), the person may repeatedly return to this experience trying to construct still another hypothetical scenario that ends in a better outcome.

This lengthy mental engagement may have two types of after-effects. The first effect, as already noted, is emotional. Undoing of negative events (particularly when controllable counterfactuals are produced) will increase a sense of retrospective control over these events and lead to self-blame. As a consequence, dysphoric mood (e.g, feelings of guilt) might emerge. A prolonged involvement in this form of processing may then result in engendering and stabilization of a depressed mood.

However, as the cognitive exhaustion framework suggests, a second type of after-effect might also emerge, which is preeminently cognitive. In many respects, the described internal process seems analogous to informational helplessness training in the laboratory (e.g., Sedek & Kofta, 1990). Repeatable engagement in mental undoing of a negative event by mutating its controllable aspects means a prolonged investment of cognitive effort in unsuccessful problem-solving attempts. Obviously, these attempts cannot lead to the problem's solution, because one can do virtually nothing about a singular and irrevocable event (like the loss of a spouse in a car accident). Thus, in response to negative life events of critical importance, some people may engage in a sequence of mental operations identifiable as an on-line experience of loss of control, its essence being lengthy engagement in capacity-consuming processing that does not result in finding a remedy to the problem.

According to the cognitive exhaustion framework, such an experience should bring about a deficit of general-purpose cognitive resources. This deficit, as reasoned earlier, may impair problem-solving ability in a broad range of situations, including interpersonal challenges as well as cognitive tasks (e.g., Braff & Beck, 1974; Cole & Zarit, 1984; Ellis & Ashbrook, 1988; Hartlage, Alloy, Vazquez, & Dykman, 1993; Weingartner, 1986) and real-life academic problems (e.g., in school settings, see Sedek & McIntosh, Chapter 17, this volume). Interestingly, recent studies confirm that depression may destroy social problem solving as well (e.g., Marx, Williams, & Claridge, 1992; Nolen-Hoeksema, 1991). The suggested cognitive deficit may then contribute to the maintenance of depression, because the person's ability to cope with challenges in various life domains is not only subjectively (lowered perception of self-efficacy and control) but also objectively undermined.

To conclude, experience of control loss may accompany personal problems of a chronic nature that one cannot successfully resolve (e.g., in marriage, in school, in work). Obviously, such chronic problems in the important life domains may elevate vulnerability to depression. However, the live, on-line experience of control loss may also originate in a single traumatic life event. According to the present conceptual schema, the core of such experience is an enduring investment of cognitive effort without cognitive gain. In contrast to response-outcome noncontingency, this process does not require a real person–environment interaction and may proceed entirely "in the head," in the course of internal mental dynamics. We hypothesize that an essential aspect of these dynamics is the repeatable engagement in construing counterfactual scenarios for a singular negative, irrevocable event. As a consequence of this engagement, a global cognitive deficit (decreased access to general-purpose cognitive resources) may develop.

MENTAL EXHAUSTION AND COGNITIVE DEFICITS IN DEPRESSION

So far, we have focused on mental helplessness training as a hypothetical internal process intervening between the traumatic event and the onset of depression. Now we would like to discuss some (we believe) impressive analogies between the phenomenon of cognitive exhaustion (as measured in our laboratory) and the nature of cognitive deficits in depression.

From the present theoretical perspective, of great interest are the results of numerous studies on coping with cognitive tasks in depression (for a recent comprehensive review, see Hartlage et al., 1993). By and large, these studies show that clinical depression interferes with performance on tasks requiring a great deal of effortful processing, but not on tasks relying on automatic processing. For example, in addition to problem-solving tasks (involving primarily effortful processes, cf. Shiffrin, 1976), particularly impaired by depression are tasks of general learning (involving effortful operations of rehearsal, organization, and information transfer from short-term to long-term memory) and free recall (including effortful processes of organization, clustering, and semantic encoding). Moreover, this interference is deeper for more cognitively demanding tasks, and for more severe depression (see Hartlage et al., 1993).

However, controlled processing is, by definition, capacity demanding (e.g., Shiffrin & Schneider, 1977; Navon & Gopher, 1979). Thus, a deficit of nonspecific cognitive resources, which we obtained in the laboratory after uncontrollable preexposure, closely parallels the cognitive deficits of depressive patients. This convergence seems highly consistent with the cognitive exhaustion view of depression.

The cognitive exhaustion approach may also have interesting implications for a more specific issue: the recent controversy around memory dysfunctions in depression. Whereas Ellis and Ashbrook (1988; see also Ellis, 1990, 1991) explain them in terms of limited mental capacity, Hertel and Hardin (1990; see also Hertel & Rude, 1991) attribute these dysfunctions to reduced processing initiative. In short, the latter authors have shown that recognition deficits could be eliminated if depressive subjects are provided with strategies (for spelling and recognition) by an experimenter. Their findings support the theory that memory problems in depression may arise from lack of adequate strategies for structuring the input data (see also Weingartner, 1986; Weingartner et al., 1981) rather than from resource depletion.

The present conceptual perspective suggests that both approaches (reduced capacity and reduced initiative) might reveal important aspects of cognitive deterioration in depression; however, they focus on different stages of information processing. Reduced processing initiative may express more general problems with spontaneous structuring of input information (research in other paradigms also reveals insufficient cognitive structuring in depression, e.g., Abramson, Alloy, & Rosoff, 1981; Watts & Cooper, 1989).

However, impaired data structuring, presumably due to insufficient mental modeling (e.g., von Hecker & Sedek, 1996) and/or impaired attention control (see Gopher, 1993) will lead to a highly wasteful and inefficient investment of mental resources. As a consequence, a depressed person will suffer from deficits of mental capacity, which will adversely affect performance on cognitively demanding tasks.

CONCLUDING REMARKS

In conclusion, the studies presented in this chapter brought us to a better understanding of cognitive exhaustion, a hypothetical sequel of uncontrollability. We found that loss of control ends in a considerable deficit of general-purpose cognitive resources.

Paradoxically, though the phenomenon of cognitive exhaustion is potentially dysfunctional, it may have a deeply rooted adaptive value. The LH effect (presumably underlain by mental exhaustion) has been demonstrated not only for human subjects, but, even more convincingly, for infrahuman species like dogs, rats, or pigeons (see, e.g., Maier & Jackson, 1979; Maier & Seligman, 1976). These comparative findings strongly suggest that the phenomenon under consideration belongs to a repertoire of old, adaptive psychological devices, products of biological evolution.

Let us speculate a bit about its function. According to the present assumptions, mental exhaustion springs from long-term investment of cognitive effort without cognitive gain (i.e., without progress in mental structuring of the problem and getting to its successful solution). It seems plausible that organisms save not only physical, but also mental energy.[9] Therefore, prolonged engagement in unsolvable problems might activate an inhibitory mechanism preventing unreasonable usage of mental energy for an unproductive purpose. (This may permit, after a rest period, reinvestment of effort in pursuing different, controllable goals). The operation of such a hypothetical stop mechanism could manifest, among other things, in decreased access to general-purpose cognitive resources.

Prolonged loss of control may then act as a prime for this sort of mental inhibition.

Regardless of the validity of these evolutionary speculations, we hope that the present approach—the theory of mental exhaustion—will open interesting avenues for future research on helplessness and depression. Our approach springs from a broader perspective on uncontrollability as a source of psychological demobilization. However, when approaching real-life processes (such as the natural development of a depressive response), we combined this perspective with the contrastive view framing loss of control as a challenge. In particular, we relied on some assumptions and findings from the control motivation framework. It seems that simultaneous use of these apparently diverse perspectives might appear very fruitful, particularly when we attempt to understand the human psychological response to control threatening situations in its entire complexity.

NOTES

1. Uncertainty is understood here in communication theory terms as entropy of the hypothesis set (the larger the set of hypotheses and the closer they approach equiprobability, the higher the entropy, see N. Abramson, 1963; see also Kofta & Sedek, 1997).
2. As will be shown later (see the procedure of the first experiment here reported) this new method for induction of uncontrollability (Sedek & Kofta, 1990) totally eliminates social feedback from the experimenter ("correct/incorrect") to the subject's consecutive responses during an unsolvable discrimination. Of considerable interest, such a purely cognitive procedure appeared more effective in triggering subsequent helplessness symptoms than the traditional, evaluation-laden procedure (see Sedek & Kofta 1990, Experiment 1).
3. Poor modeling may also impair comprehension and adequate usage of memory-search strategies, keeping the person from discovering less salient (causal) relationships between events, from drawing correct inferences during inductive or deductive reasoning, from generating explanations, etc., because all these psychological processes are cued by mental models—working theories of a situation. These aspects of cognitive impairment, albeit important, will not be further discussed as they go beyond the scope of this chapter.
4. The task is a modified version of the DIVA task developed by Edward Necka from Jagiellonian University, Cracov. The authors are grateful to Edward for encouraging us to use this task in the present research.
5. Rationale for this within-subject manipulation will not be discussed here since it goes beyond the scope of this chapter.
6. Omega square (ω^2) statistic shows percentage of variance in the dependent measure explained by a given factor (Hays, 1973).
7. It was found for example that secretion of dopamine and other neurotransmitters is reduced in animals after LH training (cf Healey & Williams, 1988). Diminished secretion of dopamine is suggested as a neurophysiological base for an impaired effortful processing in depression by Roy-Byrne et al. (1986). See also discussion of this issue in Hartlage et al. (1993).

8. Presumably for this reason, an attributional theory of depression stemming from the original LH model (Peterson & Seligman, 1984) retreated from the assumption that the loss-of-control experience precipitates depression. In this new theory, uncontrollability was retained only as an implicit dimension of a pessimistic explanatory style influencing post hoc causal interpretations of life events. This style, a vulnerability factor for depression, means a tendency to attribute negative life events to causes that are internal, stable, and general (like lack of intellectual abilities, or shyness), that is, to causes that are extremely difficult to manipulate.
9. This assumption is now routinely accepted in the cognitive economy theorizing, behavioral decision research, and social cognition. For example, the notion of social perceiver as "cognitive miser" is commonly accepted in the latter area (e.g., Fiske & Taylor, 1989).

ACKNOWLEDGMENTS

Preparation of this chapter was supported by grant 1/H01F/079/08 from the Polish Committee for Scientific Research, and by grant BST 541/50 from the Department of Psychology, University of Warsaw.

REFERENCES

Abramson, L. Y., Alloy, L. B., & Rosoff, R. (1981). Depression and the generation of complex hypotheses in the judgement of contingency. *Behavioral Research and Therapy, 19*, 35–45.
Abramson, L. Y., Seligman, M. E. P., & Teasdale, J. (1978). Learned helplessness in humans: Critique and reformulation. *Journal of Abnormal Psychology, 87*, 49–74.
Abramson, N. (1963). *Information theory and coding*. New York: McGraw-Hill.
Ackerman, Ph. L. (1986). Individual differences in information processing: An investigation of intellectual abilities and task performance during practice. *Intelligence, 10*, 101–139.
Ackerman, Ph. L. (1987). Individual differences in skill learning: An integration of psychometric and information processing perspectives. *Psychological Bulletin, 102*, 3–27.
Alloy, L. B., & Abramson, L. Y. (1979). Judgment of contingency in depressed and nondepressed students: Sadder but wiser? *Journal of Experimental Psychology: General, 108*, 441–485.
Barber, J. G., & Winefield, A. H. (1986). Learned helplessness as a conditioned inattention to the target stimulus. *Journal of Experimental Psychology: General, 115*, 236–246.
Bargh, J. A. (1994). The four horsemen of automaticity: Awareness, intention, efficiency, and control in social cognition. In R. S. Wyer & T. K. Srull (Eds.), *Handbook of social cognition, Vol. 1. Basic processes* (pp. 1–40). Hillsdale, NJ: Erlbaum.
Bower, G. H. (1991). Mood congruity of social judgments. In J. P. Forgas (Ed.), *Emotion and social judgments* (pp. 31–53). Elmsford, NY: Pergamon Press.
Braff, D. L., & Beck, A. T. (1974). Thinking disorder in depression. *Archives of General Psychiatry, 31*, 456–459.
Brehm, J. W. (1966). *The theory of psychological reactance*. New York: Academic Press.
Brehm, J. W. (1993). Control, its loss, and psychological reactance. In G. Weary, F. Gleicher, & K. L. Marsh (Eds.), *Control motivation and social cognition* (pp. 3–30). New York: Springer.
Brewer, W. F. (1987). Schemas versus mental models in human memory. In P. Morris (Ed.), *Modelling cognition* (pp. 187–197). Chichester: Wiley.
Cole, K. D., & Zarit, S. H. (1984). Psychological deficits in depressed medical patients. *Journal of Nervous and Mental Disease, 172*, 150–155.

Davis, C. G., Wortman, C. B., Silver, R. C., & Thompson, S. C. (1995). The undoing of traumatic life events. *Personality and Social Psychology Bulletin, 21*, 109–124.
Dweck, C. S., & Wortman, C. B. (1982). Learned helplessness, anxiety, and achievement motivation: Neglected parallels in cognitive, affective, and coping responses. In H. W. Krohne & L. Laux (Eds.), *Achievement, stress, and anxiety* (pp. 93–126). Washington: Hemisphere.
Ellis, H. C. (1990). Depressive deficits in memory: Processing initiative and resource allocation. *Journal of Experimental Psychology: General, 119*, 60–62.
Ellis, H. C. (1991). Focused attention and depressive deficits in memory. *Journal of Experimental Psychology: General, 120*, 310–312.
Ellis, H. C., & Ashbrook, P. W. (1988). Resource allocation model of the effects of depressed mood states on memory. In K. Fiedler & J. Forgas (Eds.), *Affect, cognition, and social behavior* (pp. 25–43). Toronto: Hogrefe.
Fisk, A. D., & Schneider, W. (1983). Category and word search: Generalizing search principles to complex processing. *Journal of Experimental Psychology: Learning, Memory, and Cognition, 10*, 181–197.
Fiske, S. T., & Taylor, S. E. (1991). *Social cognition*. New York: McGraw-Hill.
Glass, D. C., & Singer, J. E. (1972). *Urban stress*. New York: Academic Press.
Gleicher, F., & Weary, G. (1991). The effect of depression on the quantity and quality of social inferences. *Journal of Personality and Social Psychology, 61*, 105–114.
Gopher, D. (1993). The skill of attention control: Acquisition and execution of attention strategies. In D. E. Meyer & S. Kornblum (Eds.), *Attention and performance* (Vol. XIV, pp. 300–322). Cambridge, MA: The MIT Press.
Greeno, J. G. (1968). Natures of problem-solving abilities. In W. K. Estes (Ed.), *Handbook of learning and cognitive processes. Vol. 5: Human information processing*. Hillsdale, NJ: Erlbaum.
Greeno, J. G. (1989). Situations, mental models, and generative knowledge. In D. Klahr & K. Kotovsky (Eds.), *Complex information processing* (pp. 285–318). Hillsdale, NJ: Erlbaum.
Hartlage, S., Alloy, L. B., Vazquez, C., & Dykman, D. (1993). Automatic and effortful processing in depression. *Psychological Bulletin, 113*, 247–278.
Hasher, L., & Zacks, R. T. (1979). Automatic and effortful processes in memory. *Journal of Experimental Psychology: General, 108*, 356–388.
Hays, W. L. (1973). *Statistics for the social sciences*. New York: Holt, Rinehart & Winston.
Healey, D., & Williams, J. M. G. (1988). Dysrythmia, dysphoria, and depression: The interaction of learned helplessness and circadian dysrythmia in the pathogenesis of depression. *Psychological Bulletin, 103*, 163–178.
Hertel, P. T., & Hardin, T. S. (1990). Remembering with and without awareness in a depressed mood: Evidence of deficits in initiative. *Journal of Experimental Psychology: General, 119*, 45–59.
Hertel, P. T., & Rude, S. S. (1991). Depressive deficits in memory: Focusing attention improves subsequent recall. *Journal of Experimental Psychology: General, 120*, 301–309.
Hiroto, D. S., & Seligman, M. E. P. (1975). Generality of learned helplessness in man. *Journal of Personality and Social Psychology, 31*, 311–327.
Holland, J. H., Holyoak, K. J., Nisbett, R. E., & Thagard, P. R. (1986). *Induction: Processes of inference, learning, and discovery*. Cambridge, MA: MIT Press.
Johnson-Laird, P. N. (1983). *Mental models: Toward a cognitive science of language, inference, and consciousness*. Cambridge, UK: Cambridge University Press.
Johnson-Laird, P. N. (1988). A taxonomy of thinking. In R. J. Sternberg & E. E. Smith (Eds.), *The psychology of human thought* (pp. 429–457). Cambridge, UK: Cambridge University Press.
Kahneman, D. (1973). *Attention and effort*. Englewood Cliffs, NJ: Prentice-Hall.

Kofta, M. (1993). Uncertainty, mental models, and learned helplessness: An anatomy of control loss. In G. Weary, F. Gleicher, & K. L. Marsh (Eds.), *Control motivation and social cognition* (pp. 122–153). New York: Springer.

Kofta, M., & Narkiewicz-Jodko, W. (1996). *Effects of informational helplessness training on control judgment: A preliminary report*. University of Warsaw, Department of Psychology.

Kofta, M., & Sedek, G. (1989a). Egotism versus generalization-of-uncontrollability explanations of helplessness: Reply to Snyder and Frankel. *Journal of Experimental Psychology: General, 118*, 413–416.

Kofta, M., & Sedek, G. (1989b). Learned helplessness: Affective or cognitive disturbance? In C. D. Spielberger, I. G. Sarason, & J. Strelau (Eds.), *Stress and Anxiety* (Vol. 12, pp. 81–96). Washington, DC: Hemisphere.

Kofta, M., & Sedek, G. (1989c). Repeated failure: A source of helplessness, or a factor irrelevant to its emergence? *Journal of Experimental Psychology: General, 118*, 3–12.

Kofta, M., & Sedek, G. (1997). *Uncontrollability as irreducible uncertainty*. University of Warsaw, Department of Psychology. Manuscript submitted for publication.

Lewinsohn, P. M., Hoberman, H., Teri, L., & Hautzinger, M. (1985). In S. Reiss & R. R. Bootzin (Eds.), *Theoretical issues in behavior therapy* (pp. 331–359). New York: Academic Press.

Lloyd, C. (1980). Life events and depressive disorder reviewed: Events as predisposing factors. *Archives of General Psychiatry, 37*, 529–535.

Maier, S. F., & Jackson, R. L. (1979). Learned helplessness: All of us were right (and wrong): Inescapable shock has multiple effects. *The psychology of learning and motivation* (Vol. 13, pp. 155–218). New York: Academic Press.

Maier, S. F., & Seligman, M. E. P. (1976). Learned helplessness: Theory and evidence. *Journal of Experimental Psychology: General, 105*, 3–46.

Markman, K. D., Gavanski, I., Sherman, S. J., & McMullen, M. N. (1993). The mental simulation of better and worse possible worlds. *Journal of Experimental Social Psychology, 29*, 87–109.

Marx, E. M., Williams, J. M. G., & Claridge, G. C. (1992). Depression and social problem solving. *Journal of Abnormal Psychology, 101*, 78–86.

Miller, S. M., & Seligman, M. E. P. (1982). The reformulated model of helpessness and depression: Evidence and theory. In R. J. Newfeld (Ed.), *Psychological stress and psychopathology* (pp. 149–178). New York: McGraw-Hill.

Minor, T. R., Dess, N. K., & Overmier, J. B. (1991). Inverting the traditional view of "learned helplessness." In R. M. Denny (Ed.), *Fear, avoidance, and phobias: A fundamental analysis* (pp. 87–133). Hillsdale, NJ: L.Erlbaum.

Minor, T. R., Jackson, R. L., & Maier, S. F. (1984). Effects of task-irrelevant cues and reinforcement delay on choice escape learning following inescapable shock: Evidence for a deficit in selective attention. *Journal of Experimental Psychology: Animal Behavior Processes, 10*, 543–556.

Minor, T. R., Pelleymounter, M. A., & Maier, S. F. (1988). Uncontrollable shock, forebrain norepinephrine, and stimulus selection during choice escape learning. *Psychobiology, 16*, 135–145.

Navon, D., & Gopher, D. (1979). On the economy of the human processing system. *Psychological Review, 86*, 214–255.

Niedental, P. M., Tangney, J. P., & Gavanski, I. (1994). "If only I weren't" versus "if only I hadn't": Distinguishing shame and guilt in counterfactual thinking. *Journal of Personality and Social Psychology, 67*, 585–595.

Nolen-Hoeksema, S. (1991). Responses to depression and their effects on the duration of depressive episodes. *Journal of Abnormal Psychology, 100*, 569–582.

Paykel, E. S. (Ed.) (1982). *Handbook of affective disorders*. Edinburgh, Scotland: Churchill-Livingston.

Pellegrino, J. W., & Glaser, R. (1980). Components of inductive reasoning. In R. Snow, P. A. Federico, & W. Montague (Eds.), *Aptitude, learning, and instruction: Cognitive processes analysis of aptitude* (Vol. 1). Hillsdale, NJ: Erlbaum.

Perkins, D. N. (1988). Creativity and the quest for mechanism. In R. J. Sternberg & E. E. Smith (Eds.), *The psychology of human thought* (pp. 309–336). Cambridge, UK: Cambridge University Press.

Peterson, C., & Seligman, M. E. P. (1984). Causal explanations as a risk factor for depression: Theory and evidence. *Psychological Review, 91*, 347–374.

Pittman, T. S. (1993). Control motivation and attitude change. In G. Weary, F. Gleicher, & K. L. Marsh (Eds.), *Control motivation and social cognition* (pp. 157–175). New York: Springer.

Pittman, T. S., & D'Agostino, P. R. (1985). Motivation and attribution: The effects of control deprivation on subsequent information processing. In G. Weary & J. Harvey (Eds.), *Attribution: Basic issues and applications* (pp. 117–141). New York: Academic Press.

Pittman, T. S., & D'Agostino, P. R. (1989). Motivation and cognition: Control deprivation and the nature of subsequent information processing. *Journal of Experimental Social Psychology, 25*, 465–480.

Pittman, N. L., & Pittman, T. S. (1980). Deprivation of control and the attribution process. *Journal of Personality and Social Psychology, 39*, 377–389.

Roese, N. J. (1994). The functional basis of counterfactual thinking. *Journal of Personality and Social Psychology, 66*, 805–818.

Roese, N. J., & Olson, J. M. (1993). Self-esteem and counterfactual thinking. *Journal of Personality and Social Psychology, 65*, 199–206.

Rosenbaum, M. (1988). Learned resourcefulness, stress, and self-regultion. In S. Fisher & J. Reason (Eds.), *Handbook of life stress, cognition and health* (pp. 483–496). Chichester, UK: John Wiley & Son.

Roy-Byrne, P. P., Weingartner, H., Bierer, L. M., Thompson, K., & Post, R. M. (1986). Effortful and automatic cognitive processs in depression. *Archives of General Psychiatry, 43*, 265–267.

Sedek, G., & Kofta, M. (1990). When cognitive exertion does not yield cognitive gain: Toward an informational explanation of learned helplessness. *Journal of Personality and Social Psychology, 58*, 729–743.

Sedek, G., Kofta, M., & Tyszka, T. (1993). Effects of uncontrollability on subsequent decision making: Testing the cognitive exhaustion hypothesis. *Journal of Personality and Social Psychology, 65*, 1270–1281.

Sedek, G., & McIntosh, D. (1996). Uncontrollability and dual-task processing: Results of experimental and educational studies. Manuscript in preparation.

Seligman, M. E. P. (1975). *Helplessness: On depression, development, and death*. San Francisco: Freeman.

Shiffrin, R. M. (1976). Capacity limitations in information processing, attention, and memory. In W. K. Estes (Ed.), *Handbook of learning and cognitive processes: Memory processes* (Vol. 4, pp. 177–236). Hillsdale, NJ: Erlbaum.

Shiffrin, R. M., & Schneider, W. (1977). Controlled and automatic human information processing: II. Perceptual learning, automatic attending, and a general theory. *Psychological Review, 84*, 127–190.

Simon, H. A. (1976). Identifying basic abilities underlying intelligent performance of complex tasks. In L. B. Resnick (Ed.), *The nature of intelligence*. Hillsdale, NJ: Erlbaum.

Snyder, M. L., & Frankel, A. (1989). Egotism versus learned helplessness as an explanation for the unsolvable problem effect: Comment on Kofta and Sedek (1989). *Journal of Experimental Psychology: General, 118*, 409–412.

Sosnowski, T., Krzywosz, B., Kofta, M., & Sedek, G. (1996). Uncontrollability, cognitive task performance, and heart rate: An analysis in terms of mental exhaustion and motivation decline, Unpublished manuscript.

Sternberg, R. J. (1985). *Beyond IQ: A triachic theory of human intelligence*. Cambridge: Cambridge University Press.

Taylor, S. E. (1983). Adjustment to threatening events: A theory of cognitive adaptation. *American Psychologist, 38*, 1161–1173.

Thompson, S. C. (1981). Will it hurt less if I can control it? A complex answer to a simple question. *Psychological Bulletin, 90*, 89–101.

von Hecker, U., & Sedek, G., (1996). *Uncontrollability, depression, and mental models in the social domain*. Manuscript in preparation.

Watts, F. N., & Cooper, Z. (1989). The effects of depression on structural aspects of the recall of prose. *Journal of Abnormal Psychology, 98*, 150–153.

Weary, G., Gleicher, F., & Marsh, K. L. (Eds.) (1993) *Control motivation and social cognition*. New York: Springer.

Weary, G., Marsh, K. L., Gleicher, F., & Edwards, J. A. (1993). Depression, control motivation, and the processing of information about others. In G. Weary, F. Gleicher, & K. L. Marsh (Eds.), *Control motivation and social cognition* (pp. 255–287). New York: Springer.

Weingartner, H. (1986). Automatic and effort demanding cognitive processes in depression. In L. W. Poon et al. (Eds.), *Handbook for clinical memory assessment of older adults* (pp. 218–225). Washington, DC: American Psychological Association.

Weingartner, H., Cohen, R. M., Murphy, D. M., Martello, J., & Gerdt, C. (1981). Cognitive processes in depression. *Archives of General Psychiatry, 38*, 42–47.

Wortman, C. B. (1976). Causal attributions and personal control. In J. H. Harvey, W. J. Ickes, & R. F. Kidd (Eds.), *New directions in attribution research* (Vol. 2, pp. 25–52). Hillsdale, NJ: Erlbaum.

Wright, R. A., & Brehm, J. W. (1989). Energization and goal attractiveness. In L. A. Pervin (Ed.), *Goal concepts in personality and social psychology* (pp. 169–210). Hillsdale, NJ: Erlbaum.

Yost, J. H., & Weary, G. (1996). Depression and the correspondent inference bias: Evidence for more effortful cognitive processing. *Personality and Social Psychology Bulletin, 22*, 192–200.

CHAPTER 17

INTELLECTUAL HELPLESSNESS

DOMAIN SPECIFICITY, TEACHING STYLES, AND SCHOOL ACHIEVEMENT

GRZEGORZ SEDEK AND DANIEL N. MCINTOSH

INTRODUCTION

When recalling experiences of difficulty in school, many people produce frightening tales of mathematical problems involving two trains simultaneously leaving two different stations, or continual rewrites of essays labeled 'awkward' or 'weak.' Such stories frequently end with the comment: 'I am completely stupid at that subject.'

In this chapter we suggest that the cognitive deterioration in people we refer to as "intellectually helpless" in a given domain of knowledge cannot be reduced to lower aptitude in those areas. Instead, we propose that such people might be underachievers who cease to use their normal cognitive potential to solve those tasks. Before discussing assumptions of the theoretical model and supporting research, it is worth noting several symptoms that are frequently observed among intellectually helpless students. First, such students may fail to use common sense in their reasoning. For example, a student may give without hesitation a completely absurd answer (say, a negative number) as a response to a physical prob-

GRZEGORZ SEDEK • University of Warsaw and Polish Academy of Science Faculty of Psychology, 00-183 Warsaw, Poland. E-mail sedek@sci.psych.uw.edu.pl DANIEL N. MCINTOSH • Department of Psychology, University of Denver, Denver, Colorado 80208. Email: dmcintos@du.edu.

Personal Control in Action, edited by Kofta et al., Plenum Press, New York, 1998.

lem asking for the calculation of an amount of time. This does not imply that he lacks the necessary ability to learn physics; it more clearly indicates that he no longer thinks "normally" about physics. Second, students may recurrently guess at answers. The teacher asks a question and the student immediately replies, carefully observing the teacher while doing so. If the teacher nonverbally signals that the answer is wrong, the student immediately shoots another answer in the hope that she will "hit" this time. A third common feature of intellectually helpless students is their tendency toward faithful, concrete reproduction of information and a complete lack of ability to modify or reorganize the response depending on the specific demands of the problem.

One of the most intriguing features of this intellectual helplessness is its specificity. Why should a student who is capable of demonstrating logical, analytic thinking in history classes respond quite nonsensically in chemistry? We believe that one significant cause of this domain-specific simplemindedness may be traced to some period in the student's academic career during which he or she had repeated experiences of completely ineffective intellectual effort with respect to the subject in question (i.e., the student's effort produced no progress in the comprehension of that subject).

Therefore, we here propose to explain this phenomenon within the framework of an information-processing model of helplessness developed by Kofta and Sedek (Kofta, 1993; Sedek & Kofta, 1990; Sedek, Kofta, & Tyszka, 1993). This model claims that the critical factor in the development of helplessness is long-lasting cognitive exertion without progress in problem understanding. Specifically, it is postulated that in an uncontrollable situation people engage in intensive but inefficient cognitive work. However, because of the event's uncontrollability, their cognitive efforts do not result in any reasonable task solutions. We hypothesize that after a prolonged experience of this kind, people regress to the state of cognitive exhaustion. The essential quality of this transitory state is a generalized impairment of constructive information processing (inhibition in the generation of mental models): Subjects' ability to form new ideas and generate hypotheses is diminished. When confronted with a new problem situation, they resort to relatively simple schemas of information processing and behavior control. The development of cognitive exhaustion is seen as directly responsible for the cognitive, motivational, and emotional deficits following unsolvable problems, the typical finding in learned helplessness research (Maier & Seligman, 1976; Seligman, 1975). More generally, the state of cognitive exhaustion seems especially destructive when the problem situations require nonschematic, flexible activities. In line with this approach, just after people have been exposed to uncontrollable events, they show cognitive demobilization, lack of task involvement, inhibited generation of ideas, and difficulties with attentional focus (Sedek & Kofta, 1990; Sedek at al., 1993; Sedek & McIntosh, 1996). These symptoms of cognitive exhaustion are accompanied by behavioral deficits in performance of new cognitively demanding tasks (for more detailed presentation of this theory and supporting research, see Kofta and Sedek, Chapter 16, this volume).

We believe that an understanding of the intellectual helplessness phenomenon can be gained by extending the informational model to an academic setting. In the main sections of this chapter, we describe the intellectual helplessness model in school and discuss studies testing key assumptions of this model. This includes operationalization of the construct and examination of causes and consequences of intellectual helplessness. We specifically address the cognitive (rather than motivational) bases of the phenomenon, and evaluate the extent and nature of emotional and performance sequelae to the state of intellectual helplessness. Finally, we consider and evaluate the phenomenon's context specificity throughout.

INTELLECTUAL HELPLESSNESS IN SCHOOL: ASSUMPTIONS OF THE MODEL

The model presented here was developed by applying the cognitive exhaustion view of uncontrollability to the acquisition of school knowledge. To do so, the following assumptions were adopted (for a review of the preliminary model, see Sedek & Kofta, 1992):

1. States of intellectual helplessness at school are caused by (1) faulty instruction (e.g., lack of lucidity in the presentation of new material that hinders thought about the concepts, demanding verbatim reproduction of school material); (2) dysfunctional teacher–student interaction (e.g., the teacher does not allow students to ask questions); and (3) inadequate studying strategies. In other words, we attribute intellectual helplessness primarily to environmental factors and the acquisition of inadequate behavior patterns, not to deficiencies in general aptitude.
2. The inability to understand new material in class (or when studying at home) despite prolonged mental effort is naturally conducive to states of helplessness. We call this type of experience "cognitive helplessness training."
3. This experience may lead to intellectual helplessness. Basically, intellectual helplessness consists of a blocking of the tendency toward active problem thinking (i.e., cognitive exhaustion). As in laboratory experiments, prolonged effort with no progress leads

to deterioration of the capacity to solve cognitively demanding problems involving reasoning, comparison, and generating ideas. Eventually, knowledge structures in that domain may become disorganized or dysfunctional, and thus the ability to assimilate information is inhibited and deteriorates qualitatively.

4. When repeated many times in the same educational context (e.g., during math class) transitory states of intellectual helplessness may stabilize. Due to processes such as priming or classical conditioning, cues specific to a given domain (e.g., formal symbols for math) may acquire potency for triggering this state without immediately prior helplessness training.

   We hypothesize that this state of intellectual helplessness consists of both a formal cognitive component (cognitive exhaustion, which massively reduces the ability for controlled processing of cognitively demanding problems involving reasoning, comparison, and the generation of ideas), and a content-specific component (the grossly disorganized knowledge schema in that domain). As a consequence, when one is in this state, integrated and functional representations of knowledge (e.g., effective metastructures, Gallagher, 1994; mental models, Brewer, 1987; Johnson-Laird, 1983) cannot be developed, because assimilating and reorganizing incoming information demands highly effective controlled processing and the existence of prior consistent knowledge structures.[1] More generally, when a student is in a state of intellectual helplessness it is nearly impossible for him or her to study with comprehension. At the same time mechanical or imitative learning may remain intact. Instead of learning with understanding, intellectually helpless students frequently develop survival strategies like guessing or giving any (even a mindless) answer, verbatim reproduction of written text, and the like, with the goal of obtaining some minimally passable grade. To conclude, states of intellectual helplessness contribute significantly to low academic achievement because they block the capacity to learn with comprehension.

5. By extrapolating the findings of laboratory experiments (Sedek & Kofta, 1990) to school situations and referring to recent investigations in the psychology of academic instruction it is possible to predict that states of intellectual helplessness should be accompanied by loss of intrinsic motivation (Deci, 1975; Deci & Ryan, 1985), meaning no interest in the subject in question, and absence of spontaneous readiness to study and to produce intrinsic academic goals (Ames, 1992; Elliott & Dweck, 1988; Harackiewicz & Elliott, 1993; Meece, Blumenfeld, & Hoyle, 1988).

6. Intellectual helplessness is not a personality trait. It is a state, and is specific for a given cognitive domain (e.g., a school subject). A student may be cognitively helpless at one subject and show mastery orientation at another.

ASSESSING DOMAIN-SPECIFIC INTELLECTUAL HELPLESSNESS

The first objective of the present study was to construct a scale measuring intellectual helplessness with regard to various school subjects (math, physics, Polish language) and to analyze its psychometric properties. The basic items are the same across content areas, as the psychological state is the same regardless of area. Assessment of this state can then be applied to different subjects. Great effort was taken to write a simple scale that taps familiar school experiences. The 20-item Intellectual Helplessness Scale (IHS) includes items referring to generalized cognitive difficulties in class, and to difficulties in understanding the lesson and keeping track of the teacher. Also, questions dealing with the sense of cognitive demobilization and accompanying symptoms of drowsiness and apathy were included (see Table 1).

Two samples were used to assess the reliability of the IHS. The first (N = 104) was composed of four classes of second-year high school students from several institutions. (Note: in Poland a *class* is a stable group of approximately 25 students who are taught together by different teachers for each subject. The classes used in these studies were "general profile" groups, meaning that no specific subject was of particular interest or disinterest for any of them.) In this first sample, participants completed all three intellectual helplessness scales, one for each subject (math, physics, Polish). Because completing all scales together might have inflated their internal consistency, students in the second study (N = 243, 10 classes) completed only one of the scales each.

First, it was determined that the IHS is internally consistent. Cronbach's alpha coefficients, calculated separately for each school subject, ranged from .92 to .95 across samples. Despite the mix of types of items on the scale, it appears quite reliable.

Second, the issue of domain specificity was addressed. According to theoretical assumptions, the IHS should be context specific. It should not measure a general aversion to schoolwork, for example. Does the present scale allow for such differentiation, and is it contextually related to intellectual functioning in particular school classes?

We begin with the simplest correlational analysis: If the IHS measures a general construct, correlations among the three school subjects

TABLE 1 Intellectual Helplessness Scale (IHS)

		On mathematics (or physics, or Polish language): never / rarely / sometimes / often / always
*	1.	I feel I can think clearly.
	2.	When called on to speak I forget almost everything I've learned.
*	3.	I understand perfectly what the teacher is saying when he or she lectures on a new topic.
	4.	I find I don't understand what I'm writing in my notes.
	5.	I glance at my watch to check how much time is left to the end of the lesson.
	6.	I feel helpless.
*	7.	I learn new concepts with great ease.
	8.	I feel sleepy.
	9.	It almost takes a physical effort to keep my mind on the lesson.
	10.	I feel tired.
*	11.	I know which parts of a new lesson are important and must be memorized and which are not essential.
*	12.	I can judge at once whether what I'm saying (or writing) makes sense or not.
	13.	I feel empty-headed.
*	14.	The topic of the lesson really gets me thinking.
	15.	I feel my thougths are stuck in a dead end.
	16.	It feels like it is all Greek to me.
	17.	I have difficulty keeping track of what the teacher is saying.
	18.	I have difficulty concentrating on the topic of the lesson.
	19.	I feel I couldn't care less.
*	20.	I easily follow the lesson.

Note. The asterisk before an item denotes the item was reverse scored.

should be very high. Instead, the correlation between IHS scores for math and physics was significant but low ($r = .33$), and the correlations between IHS scores for Polish and math ($r = .11$) and language and physics ($r = .15$) were nonsignificant and negligible.

Beyond relative independence of intellectual helplessness across domains is the question of discriminant prediction. Does the IHS in a given domain predict domain-specific outcomes? First, academic consequences were examined. The correlations between IHS scores for the different lessons (collected at the middle of the first semester) and grades at the end of the school year clearly suggest that it does (see Table 2). The helplessness level for particular subjects correlate negatively and significantly with the grades for that subject, whereas the correlations with the other two subjects are usually much weaker.

The positive correlation between helplessness at physics and the final grade for Polish is an interesting case and suggests a compensatory mechanism—helplessness in one cognitive domain may motivate the student to achieve high grades in another domain.[2]

TABLE 2 Correlations between Intellectual Helplessness at Midyear and Grades at the End of the Year

Intellectual helplesness in	Grades in Math	Physics	Polish
Math	−.55**	.03	.03
Physics	−.21	−.25*	.29*
Polish	.09	.11	−.29*

**$p < .01$, *$p < .05$

It is conceivable that the cognitive consequences are specific to subject, but affective reactions are more general. Difficulty in one area might stimulate a generalized sense of intellectual helplessness at school, manifesting in a tendency toward negative emotional responses to all subjects. To evaluate emotional responses, students rated the frequency with which they experienced negative emotions (anxiety, depression, hostility, and aversion toward the subject in question) during class. To determine whether emotional responses to subjects are influenced by general negative feelings toward school or, as postulated here, are context specific, we compared the two competing models using linear-structural equations.

The first model (see Figure 1A) assumes that intellectual helplessness is a general construct (a latent variable), defined by sense of helplessness (observable variables 1, 2, and 3) in different topics. In this model, this generalized helplessness affects the second latent variable (path I)—negative emotions in class—defined as negative emotions experienced with respect to three academic subjects (observable variables 4, 5, and 6). This model assumes that both intellectual helplessness and negative emotions in classes are global and form related latent variables.

According to the second, rival model (see Figure 1B), both intellectual helplessness and negative emotions experienced in different classes are specific and do not combine into one common construct. This model assumes that (1) helplessness at math correlates with helplessness at physics (line IV with the two arrows describes variable covariance), whereas there is no covariance of helplessness at Polish, on the one hand, and helplessness at physics and math, on the other (mathematical computations and symbolic formulae are involved in both math and physics; skill in composition, grammar, literary interpretation and the like as taught in language class is more independent); (2) helplessness in each given domain and negative emotions in that domain are strongly related (paths I, II, and III); (3) the relations between helplessness and negative emotions experienced during other classes are much weaker (dotted lines with arrows 1 to 6); and (4) (a very strong assumption) there are no relations what-

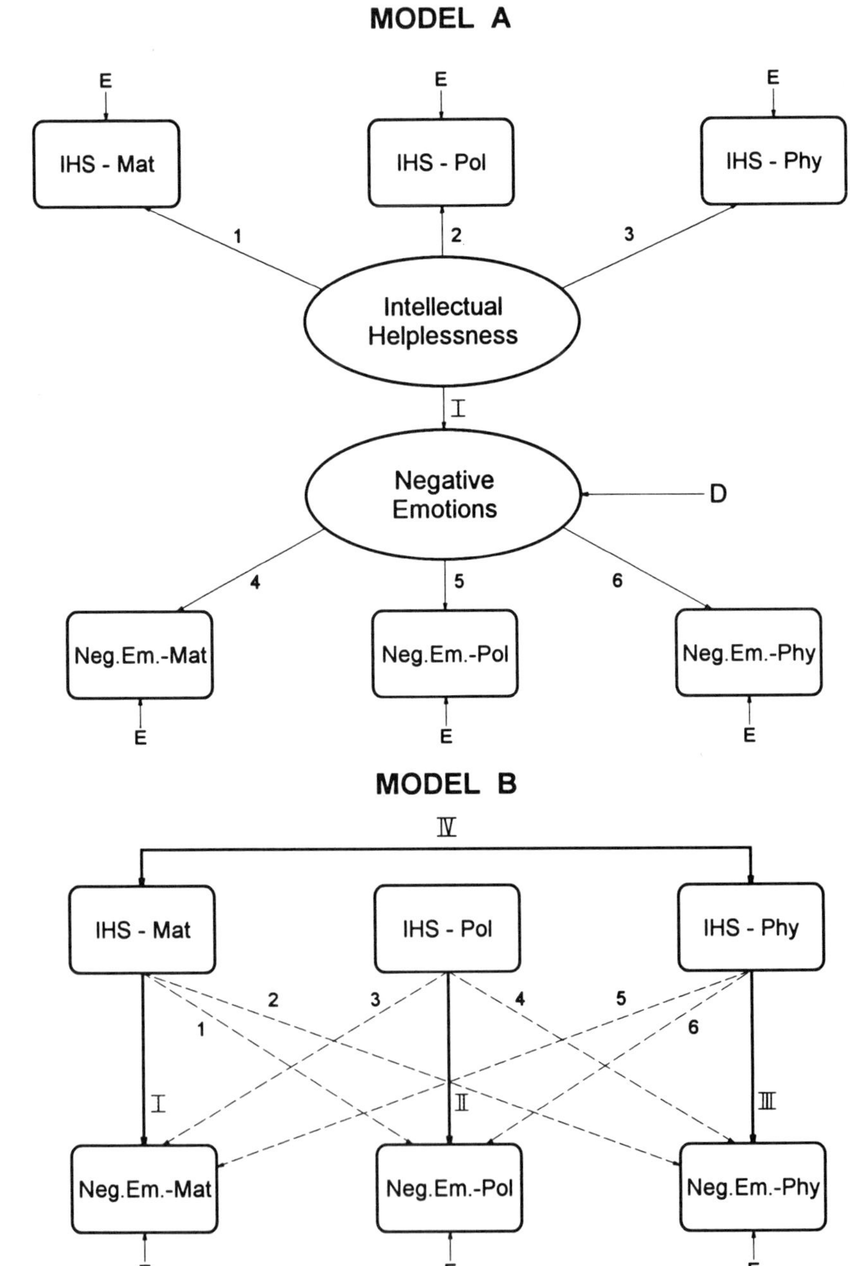

FIGURE 1 Competing models of the relation of intellectual helplessness and negative emotion: (A) generalized effect; (B) domain specific effects.

soever between the negative emotions experienced with respect to different academic subjects (as we can see in Figure 1B, there are no arrows connecting the emotions experienced at different classes).

Linear-structural analyses of the two models (EQS [Bentler, 1991], was used in these and subsequent analyses) revealed that the first model reflects the actual structure of relations between the variables very poorly and should be rejected (the Bentler-Bonett's Goodness of Fit Index, *GFI*, was very low, .18). The second model accounted for the observed relations much better (*GFI* = .99). An additional measure of the goodness of the model solution (chi square) was nonsignificant ($p < .40$), suggesting almost perfect fit between the model and the data. A closer inspection of this model reveals strong and significant ($p < .001$) interconnections between intellectual helplessness and negative emotions within each given subject (standardized alpha coefficients were .66, .61, and .63 for math, physics, and Polish respectively—see paths I, II, III in Figure 1B), and very weak relations between domains.

The findings reported to this point attest strongly that the IHS is a reliable measure of subjectively experienced intellectual helplessness relative to specific topics. Both the correlational analyses and the structural modeling confirm the hypothesis that intellectual helplessness is a domain specific phenomenon.

CAUSES AND CONSEQUENCES OF INTELLECTUAL HELPLESSNESS: A LONGITUDINAL STUDY

The objectives of this study were (1) to evaluate some potential determinants of intellectual helplessness and (2) to analyze the effects of intellectual helplessness and other psychological variables on academic achievement. In particular, the study was aimed at determining whether the state of helplessness is merely a consequence of academic difficulties or whether it contributes significantly to further academic achievements.

Overview of the Longitudinal Study

These questions were evaluated in a two-year longitudinal study. Data were collected from 15 general-interest profile classes of first-year students in Warsaw high schools. Each class was in a different school, and the three subjects of interest (math, physics, Polish) were taught by different sets of teachers in each school. First-year classes were selected on the assumption that states of intellectual helplessness are more likely to emerge at educational thresholds, when the student arrives at a new school with new teachers and is confronted with new (usually greater) cognitive demands. Indeed, research in the United States reveals the difficulties of the transition to secondary school. Adolescents making this change often experience a decrease in ability self-concepts (Marsh, 1989) and academic intrinsic motivation (Harter, 1981), as well as an increase in anxiety and depressive symptomatology (Hirsch & DuBois, 1991). Further, most students experience a decline in grades following the transition to secondary school (Blyth, Simmons, & Bush, 1978). These symptoms are reminiscent of outcomes related to cognitive exhaustion and intellectual helplessness. Thus, this population is an important one in which to study this phenomenon, and seems a likely one to provide insight into the causes of the condition.

MAIN DEPENDENT MEASURES: ACADEMIC ACHIEVEMENT AND EMOTIONAL RESPONSE

The level of academic achievement was the basic variable to be explained. The criteria of academic achievement were grades at the end of the academic year for the subject in question and the level of performance on an achievement test created for this project by outside teachers of the specific topics. These tests were used for two purposes: to assess the level of basic knowledge in a given domain and to assess the ability to use this knowledge in a relatively new, nonstandard context.

We were interested not only in the purely intellectual aspect of the students' functioning but also in their pattern of emotional response. This outcome was diagnosed with an adjective checklist measuring four factors: depression, anxiety, irritation, and positive affect. We wanted to know whether intellectual helplessness was accompanied by any characteristic pattern of emotional response to the particular school subject.

STYLE OF INSTRUCTION AND INTELLECTUAL HELPLESSNESS

ASSESSMENT OF TEACHER BEHAVIOR

The first objective of the longitudinal study was to evaluate some probable causes of intellectual helplessness. According to the first assumption of the proposed model, an inadequate style of instruction in class may contribute to helplessness in students. In the lab, cognitive exhaustion is created when an individual makes repeated efforts to solve a problem with no progress toward an answer; one determinant of such conditions in the classroom may be teacher behaviors. Thus, we attempted to determine which aspects of instructor conduct contribute to the emergence of symptoms of intellectual helplessness. This information assists in understanding the nature of intellectual helplessness, as knowing specific causes of the phenomenon suggest essential elements. Moreover, knowing which specific behaviors cause the condition has practical import for teacher training and structuring of educational environments.

Several questionnaires were constructed to test this problem. The first instrument asked students directly the extent to which the teacher promoted understanding of the topic. This Promotion of Understanding Scale describes those teacher behaviors that are conducive to learning with comprehension and independent thinking. It was directly inspired by the assumptions in the model of intellectual helplessness: Intellectual helplessness with respect to a given school subject may be caused by an inadequate style of introduction of new material in class. We wanted to know whether the teacher makes sure that students get a good grasp of the new concepts, encourages students to ask questions and signal their doubts, indicates those points where it is easy to go wrong, carefully analyzes the factors underlying incorrect answers, etc. In other words, the scale tests whether the teacher "promotes" understanding when introducing new material. According to the assumptions of the model proposed here, if the teacher does not take care to help students understand the material that is being taught, this may contribute seriously to symptoms of intellectual helplessness with respect to the subject in question.

The second was a scale with eight factors, each based to some degree on Murray's (1983) work isolating separable teaching behaviors that can be rated by students easily and without need of extensive inference. These are stimulating creativity and curiosity, maintaining discipline, "grilling" the students using a criticizing questioning style, expecting verbatim answers and rote learning, using an animated communication style with vivid expressions, stimulating individual student activity, using concrete examples and pictures or diagrams, and making evaluative statements about students' ability.

The third questionnaire simply had students indicate how many minutes are typically taken in lessons by various activities, such as lecturing, prompting students to ask questions, allowing students to voice opinions, explaining how to do homework, and discussing unrelated topics. Cognitive exhaustion is caused by repeated exposure to a particular type of situation. This measure allowed us to examine what types of situations were related to the occurrence of intellectual helplessness.

Effects of Instruction Style on Intellectual Helplessness

The data collection procedure presents a significant difficulty in testing effects of teaching style on the development of helplessness. The same students simultaneously assessed various aspects of teacher behavior in class and made self-assessments of their intellectual helplessness with regard to these subjects. One cannot trust the validity of simple correlations between these two variables: In each class those students who had trouble mastering a subject cognitively may have had a tendency to depreciate the teacher of that subject (give lower ratings of that teacher's ability to explain and transmit information interestingly, etc.).

Therefore, we applied a maximally conservative strategy that greatly reduced the amount of information but allowed us to avoid the distortion of the above-mentioned relation. Scores were averaged within classes and correlational analyses were performed on aggregated data, with the mean scores for each class being the units of analysis. The classes were rank-ordered with respect to their level of intellectual helplessness with regard to a particular subject. The teachers who taught these classes were rank-ordered with respect to their mean scores on the teaching-style measures. Because 15 classes participated in the first year of the study and 14 in the second year, this was a risky strategy; the resultant small frequencies decreased the power of the tests.

However, several of the correlations for the aggregated data proved to be quite strong, and the findings for the second year of the study replicated the findings for the first year. Note that we limit our analyses in the longitudinal study to math and Polish, as they were previously determined to be independent, and because the difficulty of the physics test created a floor effect, limiting the usefulness of analysis in this domain. Table 3 displays the significant correlations for math and Polish for both years. For math and Polish, the more the teacher was rated, on average, as promoting understanding, the lower the students' levels of intellectual helplessness. Two of the eight scales in the second questionnaire were related to intellectual helplessness for both math and Polish. The more the teachers stimulated creative thinking about the topics, and the more individual student activity they generated, the less helplessness was evident in their students. Finally, for math only, the more frequently instructors (1) asked students whether there was something they did not understand and settled their doubts, and (2) allowed students to voice their opinions in unrestricted discussion of new topics, the less intellectually helpless the students were. The results are highly consistent with the claim that certain styles of instruction play a crucial role in the development of intellectual helplessness.

An alternative view of the above findings is that it is variance in the abilities of the classes that causes the results, not variability in teaching style. For example, one class may incorporate a large group of gifted and highly motivated students, whereas another class may incorporate many low-achieving and lazy students. This suggests that classes would be di-

TABLE 3 Teaching Style Predictors of Intellectual Helplessness

	Intellectual helplessness	
Teaching style	Math	Polish
Promotion of Understanding Scale		
First year	−.75***	−.62*
Second year	−.74**	−.57*
Factors from Teacher Behavior Questionnaire		
Stimulation of creative thinking: Year 1	−.65**	−.71**
Stimulation of creative thinking: Year 2	−.76**	−.62*
Stimulating student activity: Year 1	−.68**	−.63*
Stimulating student activity: Year 2	−.80***	−.62*
Amount of time in activities		
Asking students about understanding: Year 1	−.69**	n.s.
Asking students about understanding: Year 2	−.62*	n.s.
Allowing students to voice opinions: Year 1	−.51*	n.s.
Allowing students to voice opinions: Year 2	−.56*	n.s.

*$p < .05$; ** $p < .01$; *** $p < .001$; n.s. not significant.
Note: Based on data aggregated within classes; First year n=15, Second year n=14.

visible into those that are prone to intellectual helplessness with respect to all academic subjects and those who will manifest excellent intellectual functioning in every domain. In other words, it is irrelevant which type of instructor teaches a particular subject. What is important is the structure of the class: whether the students in that class are gifted or not. If this reasoning is correct, the correlational analysis for the aggregated data should reveal a strong positive correlation between intellectual helplessness with respect to math and Polish. In fact, we find a correlation of only $r = -.07$! The level of "class" helplessness with respect to one subject is unrelated to the level of class helplessness with respect to a different subject. When combined with the results of the previous analyses this outcome shows that the teacher contributes greatly to the development of the syndrome of intellectual helplessness.

Instruction Style, Intellectual Helplessness, and Achievement

Earlier in the chapter, we showed a connection between intellectual helplessness and grades. The current finding demonstrates an influence of teaching style on intellectual helplessness. Given this pattern, a question naturally arises: Is it teaching behavior that is responsible for both helplessness and achievement, with the connection between the latter two variables being spurious? We investigated this using scores on the Promotion of Understanding Scale to predict academic achievement.

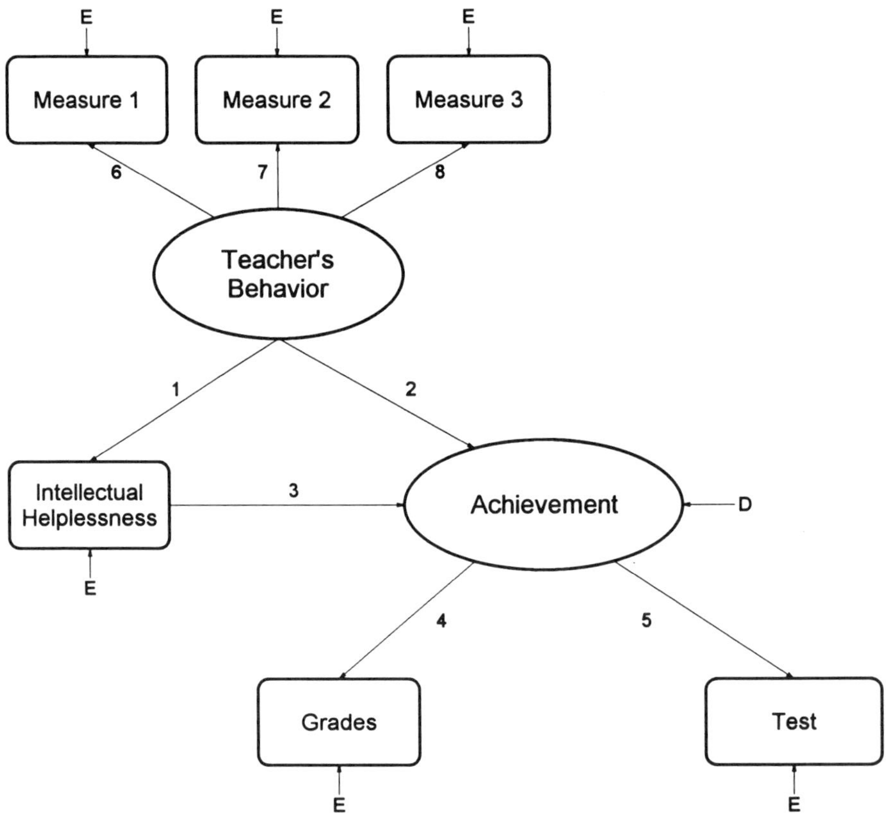

FIGURE 2 Causal model of teacher's promotion of understanding, intellectual helplessness, and achievement.

Because this is a class-level variable, and achievement and helplessness are individual-level variables, testing their interrelations required some changes in the data. Specifically, in order to generate variability in the promotion of understanding, classes were randomly split into three groups (see Marsh, 1994, for a similar procedure). The averaged scores from these three groups were used as observed measures of the underlying construct of teacher's behavior, thus providing variability, yet still having the mean differ for different teachers. Using this method, a structural equation model was used to evaluate the relations among teachers' behaviors, intellectual helplessness, and achievement. See Figure 2 for the model.

The path coefficients for this model are presented in Table 4. As can be seen, promotion of understanding influences both helplessness (path 1)

TABLE 4 Standardized Effects of Teacher`s Promotion of Understanding and Intellectual Helplessness on Achievement: Results from Structural Modeling

Path[a]	Mathematics standar. coeff.	Mathematics z test	Polish standar. coeff.	Polish z test
Direct effects				
1 Teacher—Int. Helpless.	−.25	4.06***	−.34	5.81***
2 Teacher—Achievement	.21	2.09*	.22	2.38*
3 Int. Helpless.—Achievement	−.57	5.65***	−.29	2.82**
4 Achievement—Grades	.57[f]	—	.51[f]	—
5 Achievement—Test	.29	2.93**	.68	3.45***
6 Teacher—Measure 1	.96	21.25***	.82	15.42***
7 Teacher—Measure 2	.94	20.26***	.84	16.60***
8 Teacher—Measure 3	.95	21.01***	.90	18.77***
Indirect effects				
Int. Helpless—Grades	−.32	5.65***	−.14	2.82**
Int. Helpless.—Test	−.16	3.00**	−.20	3.35***
Teacher—Grades	.20	3.30***	.16	3.34***
Teacher—Test	.10	2.31*	.22	3.35***

Note: Mathematics: Bentler-Bonett Goodness of Fit Index = .98; Polish: Bentler-Bonett Goodness of Fit Index = .94

[a]"Teacher"—Teacher's Promotion of Understanding.

[f]Fixed in order to scale the exogenous latent variable;

* $p < .05$; ** $p < .01$; *** $p < .001$.

and achievement (path 2). Meaningfully for our model, helplessness significantly alters achievement (path 3) beyond the effects caused by the mutual influence of teacher behavior on helplessness and achievement. Taken together, the indirect effects demonstrate that teaching style and intellectual helplessness influence both grades and scores on the achievement tests. This model provides a clear path from teacher behavior, through helplessness, to achievement.

Conclusions

In reviewing the types of teacher behaviors that predict later helplessness, a pattern appears to emerge. When instructors do not promote understanding, do not stimulate creative thinking about, or active engagement of, the concepts, or, for math, do not allow for discussion of new topics, then students appear prone to become intellectually helpless in that domain. Teacher behaviors that seem more motivational or affective in nature (e.g., an animated teaching style, vocally evaluating students' abilities) are unrelated to students' development of helplessness. This pattern suggests that the nature of the phenomenon is cognitively based rather than emotional or motivational. Its root appears to be lack of comprehension. Of course, as noted in the model, such difficulties in understanding likely lead to aversive emotional outcomes. The next section provides further information on cognitive versus motivational bases of intellectual helplessness.

PSYCHOLOGICAL THREAT AND INTELLECTUAL HELPLESSNESS AS PREDICTORS OF ACADEMIC ACHIEVEMENT AND STRESS

Psychological Threat

The cognitive model of intellectual helplessness presented here differs radically from some popular conceptualizations in educational psychology. The latter emphasize the role of emotional and motivational factors in academic underachievement such as test anxiety and sense of psychological threat (Covington, 1985; Meece, Wigfield, & Eccles, 1990; Sarason, 1980) or generally low academic motivation (Ainley, 1993; Ames & Ames, 1984). The above described relations of teacher behaviors to helplessness suggest, on the other hand, that the more cognitively based intellectual helplessness is responsible for difficulties. Of course, it might be that motivational or emotional factors cause both academic problems and intellectual helplessness. One goal of this longitudinal study was thus to determine whether subjective intellectual helplessness in class may be a significant predictor of later academic failure when the level of subjective threat in that class is controlled.

Extant instruments (e.g., Sarason, 1980) assessing anxiety in scholastic settings focus primarily on responses to written tests. We were interested in negative emotions in a broader range of classroom situations. So, a measure of psychological threat in class was developed for this study (eight items, with alphas ranging from .88 to .93). Many potentially threatening aspects of the student–teacher interaction were taken into consideration: the fear that the teacher might criticize the student's responses, fear of negative grades, fear of being unexpectedly called on to answer a question, feeling tense when summoned to the blackboard, and the like.

Psychological Threat, Intellectual Helplessness, and Academic Performance

In our initial causal analyses we evaluated the degree to which subjective threat or intellectual helplessness in class was responsible for later poor school achievement.

The subjective scales were administered in the middle of the first semester, whereas the level of school achievement was assessed at the end of

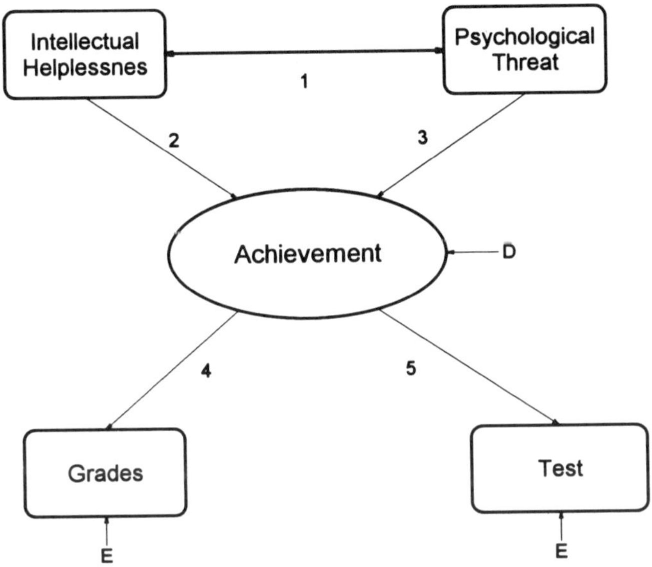

FIGURE 3 Influence of intellectual helplessness and psychological threat on achievement.

the academic year, thus allowing for a stronger causal statement to be possible.

First we tested the very simple model of causal relations presented in Figure 3. This model assumes (1) covariance (without indicating the direction of the causal relation) to some degree between scores on the Intellectual Helplessness Scale and the Psychological Threat Scale (path 1); (2) the causal effect of Intellectual Helplessness on Academic Achievement (path 2); (3) the causal effect of Psychological Threat on Academic Achievement (path 3), (4) definition of School Achievement (a latent variable) in terms of grades at the end of the academic year (path 4) and the scores on achievement tests (path 5). Comparison of the magnitude and significance of paths 2 and 3 for math and Polish allowed us to determine the relative contribution of the two theoretical constructs to low school achievement with respect to these subjects.

The goodness of fit indices were very high for both math and Polish. The standardized values of several of the most important path coefficients (the significance of these coefficients was tested using the z test) are presented in Table 5. We describe the outcome of linear-structural modeling for math first.

If we look at the various elements of the model one by one we see that (1) the Intellectual Helplessness Scale and the Psychological Threat Scale are strongly correlated ($r = .74$) and (2) intellectual helplessness is a signifi-

TABLE 5 Standardized Effects of Intellectual Helplessness and Psychological Threat on Achievement: Results from Structural Modeling

Path	Mathematics standar. coeff.	Mathematics z test	Polish standar. coeff.	Polish z test
Direct effects				
1 Int. Helpless—Threat	.74	10.13***	.64	9.27***
2 Int. Helpless—Achievement	−.47	3.87***	−.28	2.73**
3 Threat—Achievement	−.11	ns.	−.10	ns.
4 Achievement—Grades	.65[f]	—	.65[f]	—
5 Achievement—Test	.24	2.31*	.57	3.33***
Indirect effects				
Int. Helpless.—Grades	−.31	3.87***	−.18	2.73**
Int. Helpless.—Test	−.12	2.11*	−.16	2.57*
Threat—Grades	−.07	ns.	−.06	ns.
Threat—Test	−.03	ns.	−.06	ns.

Note. Mathematics: Bentler-Bonett Goodness of Fit Index = 1.00; Polish: Bentler-Bonett Goodness of Fit Index = .99.
[f]Fixed in order to scale the exogenous latent variable.
*$p < .05$; **$p < .01$; ***$p < .001$; ns., nonsignificant.

cant predictor of school achievement (path 2), even when controlling for threat, whereas psychological threat scale is completely insignificant as a predictor of academic achievement when intellectual helplessness is partialed out (path 3).

Does helplessness affect merely school grades alone or does it also influence achievement test scores? We answer this question by decomposing the effects and dividing them into direct and indirect effects. As seen in Table 5, intellectual helplessness has a very significant effect on final school grades and a significant (though weaker) effect on the level of performance on achievement tests. Psychological threat has no significant effect on either measure of academic achievement. This is important: It shows that intellectual helplessness lowers the level of academic achievement in math, as manifested in both final school grades and level of mastery of school material, as reflected in the scores of the achievement test.

With respect to Polish language, once again intellectual helplessness correlates strongly with the level of psychological threat ($r = .64$). As before, only intellectual helplessness is a significant (but not as strong as for math) predictor of school achievement. The results for indirect effects also show that the state of intellectual helplessness leads to both worse final grades in Polish language and significantly inferior performance on the achievement test for this subject.

In short, the above analyses yielded powerful confirmation of the hypothesis that emergence of a state of intellectual helplessness with regard to a given subject contributes significantly to later low academic achievement in that subject. This factor contributes considerably more strongly than subjective psychological threat to the deterioration of academic achievement (both factors are positively correlated). Note that this has been confirmed in two independent analyses, performed separately for math and Polish.

Psychological Threat, Intellectual Helplessness, and Affective States

Our proposed approach indicates that the state of intellectual helplessness in classes is the result of prolonged cognitive uncontrollability at school lessons. Since the classic studies of Lazarus and Folkman (Folkman, 1984; Lazarus & Folkman, 1984), studies of various processes of adaptation to stressful situations have put increasing emphasis on the dimension of event controllability/uncontrollability, which is viewed as a significant determinant of the type of coping response applied in a given situation (Terry, 1994; Valentiner, Holahan & Moos, 1994). When the situation is beyond control, negative emotional responses (depression, anxiety) and emotion-focused coping responses are more likely to appear. On the other hand, when the stress situation is perceived to be controllable, the more likely responses are solution-focused coping and, once a successful solution has been found, considerable goal-directed effort aimed at managing the threatening situation.

These ideas lead us to expect an interactive relation between intellectual helplessness and psychological threat in predicting negative affective states in class. When intellectual helplessness is severe (i.e., in cases of prolonged exposure to cognitive uncontrollability), psychological threat should evoke a more intense depressive emotional response than when intellectual helplessness is relatively benign. Threat will lead to depression when control is lowest. In order to test this hypothesis, hierarchical regression analyses were carried out for the different affect scales. In this model intellectual helplessness is a moderator (cf. Baron & Kenny, 1986) of the relation between psychological threat and depression at classes. As usual, the principal predictors were analyzed first and the interactions were analyzed in the next step. Psychological threat was found to be a generally more powerful predictor of depression than intellectual helplessness. However, the interaction of the two variables was also a significant predictor of depression for all the academic subjects studied.

The interactions work in the expected direction: An increase in psychological threat leads to a dramatic increase in reported depression but only in those students who are intellectually helpless at the particular classes. An increase in psychological threat does not lead to any significant increment in depression in those students who are not intellectually helpless. (We may therefore predict that if a teacher who is strict but very lucid increases his or her demands, those students who have no trouble understanding the lessons will respond with increased academic motivation, not depression).

Results for anxiety and irritation were similar to those of depression, but not as strong. The experience of positive emotions also evinced an interaction between threat and helplessness, but in a way different than those for the negative emotions. It appears that only students who were not in a state of intellectual helplessness were responsive to the degree of threat in the class. Helpless students simply experienced very few positive feelings. Nonhelpless students experienced positive feelings when threat was low, with the amount decreasing as the degree of threat increased. Only under situations of low threat, and only for nonhelpless students, did participants report a large number of positive feelings.

EXPERIMENTAL EVIDENCE OF CONTEXT SENSITIVITY AND THE COGNITIVE NATURE OF INTELLECTUAL HELPLESSNESS

The previous analyses of intellectual helplessness used questionnaire data. Based on these results, we have proposed that the underlying deficit in intellectual helplessness is cognitive, not motivational. Further, we have argued that this is a context-bound phenomenon, occurring only when cues evoke the state. We tested these ideas more directly in a recent laboratory study (Sedek & McIntosh, 1996.) First, we evaluated performance in two tasks varying on cognitive demand (using a version of the dual-task procedure developed by Necka, 1996). Generalized motivational deficits, which are central to both the classic model of learned helplessness (e.g., Maier & Seligman, 1976; Seligman, 1975) and an egotism explanation of helplessness (Frankel & Snyder, 1978), should cause decrements in performance in both the single- and dual-processing tasks, regardless of how cognitively demanding each is. Cognitive deficits, on the other hand, should occur only when more cognitive resources are needed for proper performance (i.e., during the dual-processing task; cf. Pashler, 1994). Second, we tested the hypothesis that persons who are helpless in a specific cognitive domain will manifest deteriorated controlled processing only when that domain is cued.

From the entire sample of 216 high school students who completed the Intellectual Helplessness Scale with respect to Polish and math, 40 students manifesting clearly contextual helplessness were selected: 20 students reported helplessness at math classes and quite good functioning at

Polish classes, the remaining 20 students reported just the opposite—they were only intellectually helpless at Polish lessons.

The laboratory experiment had a 2 × 2 × 2 design (person × situation paradigm): Domain of Helplessness (Polish or math), Task Context (Polish or math, invoked using a 5-min test on material recently discussed in either Polish or math classes), and Cognitive Demand (single vs. dual task). The latter was a within-subjects factor. Subjects who were helpless in either Polish or math completed the Task Context quiz, which covered topics either relevant or irrelevant to their domain of helplessness. After completion of the quiz, subjects engaged in tests of attentional resources within the dual-task paradigm. They were given two series of tasks, first single then dual (the structure of this part of the experiment was identical with the structure of Study 3 reported by Kofta and Sedek, Chapter 16, this volume). The single, primary task involves repeatedly determining whether a target lowercase letter presented on a computer screen (e.g., *a*) is the same as a previously presented capital letter (e.g., *A*); it is an easy task and requires only motivation to perform well. The dual task is more demanding, and requires not only motivation, but also greater cognitive resources. During the dual-task segment, subjects must complete not only the primary task, but must also simultaneously use computer mouse controls to keep a horizontal line, presented on the screen beside the letter field, from drifting out of a defined area (when it drifts out, an unpleasant noise is generated). Outcome is measured in accuracy (number of correct hits) for the primary task.

A significant interaction among Domain of Helplessness, Task Context, and Cognitive Demand would provide confirmation of our hypothesis. Math-helpless students should demonstrate worse performance only in the math context, and only for the dual task. Polish-helpless students should show poorer performance only in the Polish context and only for the dual task. No cross-domain effects should occur (e.g., math-helpless students should have no trouble solving the dual—cognitively demanding—task when that task is preceded by a Polish language test).

This interaction was found. Performance on the main task showed a clear-cut 2 × 2 × 2 interaction: Task Context × Domain of Helplessness × Cognitive Demands, $F(1, 36) = 5.13$, $p < .05$ (see Figure 4).

It is obvious that the predicted disturbance in attention allocation emerged only for the dual tasks; activation of a mathematical context was followed by a clear-cut deterioration of performance in persons manifesting intellectual helplessness with respect to math and, mirroring this, activation of a Polish-language context was followed by deterioration in performance only in persons manifesting intellectual helplessness in this domain.

To summarize, this study demonstrates the power of contextual cues to evoke intellectual helplessness, and the significance of cognitive per-

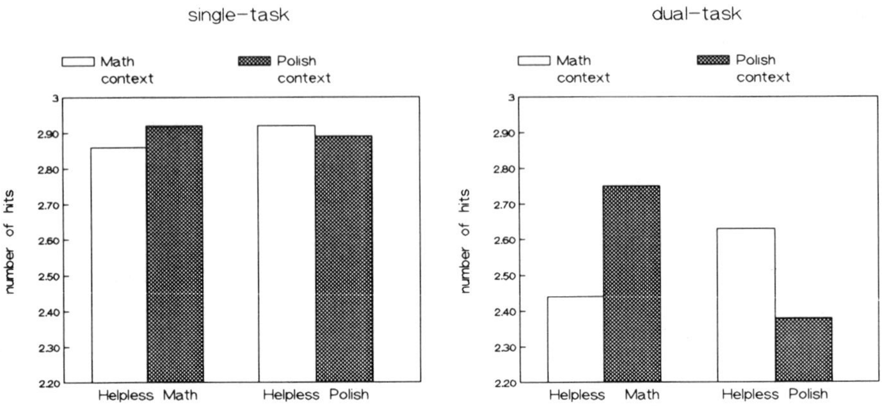

FIGURE 4 Performance of primary task (mean number of hits) in single- and dual-task conditions by domain of helplessness and task context.

formance as the primary deficit. These domain-specific findings differ from the generalized effects usually found in studies of learned helplessness (or cognitive functioning in depression): We have obtained powerful experimental confirmation of the contextual nature of the phenomenon under discussion. Performance on cognitively demanding, dual-task problems (requiring flexible allocation of cognitive attention resources) only deteriorated following previous activation of the cognitive domain for which specific intellectual helplessness had developed.

GENERAL CONCLUSIONS

The research program presented here was inspired by our previous experimental work on learned helplessness in the psychological laboratory (Kofta & Sedek, 1989; Sedek & Kofta, 1990; Sedek et. al., 1993; Sedek & McIntosh, 1996). The model of intellectual helplessness at school was based on the assumptions of the informational model and postulated that cognitive helplessness training may also take place in class, at school, when the student, despite intensive cognitive effort, is unable to understand new material.

The presented results demonstrate that intellectual helplessness is neither an "artificial laboratory entity" nor a negligible subjective experience, but that it may develop as a very significant disturbance of the educational process. If such intellectual helplessness develops in a given domain it may curtail the development of intellectual potential in that domain, leading to low achievement for specific academic subjects and later to severe consequences, blocking the realization of vital goals and plans (Cantor & Langston, 1989). This chapter provides an overview of longitudinal and experimental data showing domain specificity of the phenomenon, its cognitive basis, and causal relations between specific aspects of teaching style, intellectual helplessness, and academic achievement.

NOTES

1. Note that there are similarities between this conceptualization and Hasher and Zacks's (1988) discussion of difficulties in learning with comprehension among the elderly.
2. For a more detailed discussion of the mechanisms of intersubject compensation, see Marsh, 1990, 1992; also consider the self-esteem processes discussed by Steele, 1988.

ACKNOWLEDGMENT

Preparation of this chapter was supported by grant 1/HO1F/079/08 from the Polish Committee for Scientific Research.

REFERENCES

Ainley, M. D. (1993). Styles of engagement with learning: Multidimensional assessment of their relationship with strategy use and school achievement. *Journal of Educational Psychology, 85*, 395–405.

Ames, C. (1992). Classrooms: Goals, structures, and student motivation. *Journal of Educational Psychology, 84*, 261–271.

Ames, C., & Ames, R. E. (1984). *Research on motivation in education: Vol. 1. Student motivation.* San Diego, CA: Academic Press.

Baron, M. R., & Kenny, D. A. (1986). The moderator-mediator distinction in social psychological research: Conceptual, strategic, and statistical considerations. *Journal of Personality and Social Psychology, 51*, 1173–1182.

Bentler, P. (1991). *Theory and implementation of EQS: A structural equation program (Version 3.0).* Los Angeles: University of California.

Blyth, D. A., Simmons, R. G., & Bush, D. (1978). The transition into early adolescence: A longitudinal comparison of youth in two educational contexts. *Sociology of Education, 51*, 149–162.

Brewer, W. F. (1987). Schemas versus mental models in human memory. In P. Morris (Ed.), *Modelling cognition.* Chichester: Wiley & Sons.

Cantor, N., & Langston, C. A. (1989). "Ups and downs" of life tasks in a life transition. In L. A. Pervin (Ed.), *The goal concept in personality and social psychology* (pp. 127–167). Hillsdale, NJ: Erlbaum.

Covington, M. V. (1985). Strategic thinking and the fear of failure. In J. W. Segal, S. F. Chipman, & R. Glaser (Eds.), *Thinking and learning skills* (pp. 389–416). Hillsdale, NJ: Erlbaum.

Deci, E. L. (1975). *Intrinsic motivation*, New York: Plenum.

Deci, E. L., & Ryan, R. M. (1985). *Intrinsic motivation and self-determination in human behavior.* New York: Plenum.

Elliott, E. S., & Dweck, C. S. (1988). Goals: An approach to motivation and achievement. *Journal of Personality and Social Psychology, 54*, 5–12.

Folkman, S. (1984). Personal control and stress and coping processes: A theoretical analysis. *Journal of Personality and Social Psychology, 46*, 839–852.

Frankel, A., & Snyder, M. L. (1978). Poor performance following unsolvable problems: Learned helplessness or egotism? *Journal of Personality and Social Psychology, 36*, 1415–1424.

Gallagher, J. J. (1994). Teaching and learning: New models. *Annual Review of Psychology, 45*, 171–195.

Harackiewicz, J. M., & Elliot, A. J. (1993). Achievement goals and intrinsic motivation. *Journal of Personality and Social Psychology, 65*, 904–915.

Harter, S. (1981). A new self-report scale of intrinsic versus extrinsic orientation in the classroom: Motivational and informational components. *Developmental Psychology, 17*, 300–312.

Hasher, L., & Zacks, R. T. (1988). Working memory, comprehension, and aging: A review and a new view. In G. Bower (Ed.), *The Psychology of Learning and Motivation* (Vol. 22, pp. 193–225).

Hirsch, B. J., & DuBois, D. L. (1991). Self-esteem in early adolescence: The identification and prediction of contrasting longitudinal trajectories. *Journal of Youth and Adolescence, 20*, 53–72.

Johnson-Laird, P. N. (1983). *Mental models: Towards a cognitive science of language, inference and consciousness.* Cambridge: Cambridge University Press.

Kofta, M. (1993). Uncertainty, mental models, and learned helplessness: An anatomy of control loss. In G. Weary, F. Gleicher, & K. L. Marsh (Eds.), *Control motivation and social cognition* (pp. 122–153). New York: Springer.

Kofta, M. & Sedek, G. (1989). Learned helplessness: Affective or cognitive disturbance? In C. D. Spielberger, I. G. Sarason, & J. Strelau (Eds.), *Stress and Anxiety* (Vol. 12). Washington, DC: Hemisphere.

Lazarus, R. S., & Folkman, S. (1984). *Stress, appraisal, and coping*. New York: Springer.

Maier, S. F. & Seligman, M. E. P. (1976). Learned helplessness: Theory and evidence. *Journal of Experimental Psychology: General, 105*, 3–46.

Marsh, H. W. (1989). Age and sex effects in multiple dimensions of self-concept: Preadolescence to early adulthood. *Journal of Educational Psychology, 81*, 417–430.

Marsh, H. W. (1990). Influences of internal and external frames of reference on the formation of math and English self-concepts. *Journal of Educational Psychology, 82*, 107–116.

Marsh, H. W. (1992). Content specificity of relations between academic achievement and academic self-concept. *Journal of Educational Psychology, 84*, 35–42.

Marsh, H. W. (1994). Using the national longitudinal study of 1988 to evaluate theoretical models of self-concept: The self-description questionnaire. *Journal of Educational Psychology, 86*, 439–456.

Meece, J. L., Blumenfeld, P. C., & Hoyle, R. H. (1988). Students' goal orientations and cognitive engagement in classroom activities. *Journal of Educational Psychology, 80*, 514–523.

Meece, J. L., Wigfield, A., & Eccles, J. S. (1990). Predictors of math anxiety and its influence on young adolescents' course enrollment intentions and performance in mathematics. *Journal of Educational Psychology, 82*, 60–70.

Murray, H. G. (1983). Low-inference classroom teaching behaviors and students ratings of college teaching effectiveness. *Journal of Educational Psychology, 75*, 138–149.

Necka, E. (1996). Attentive mind: Intelligence in relation to selective attention, sustained attention, and dual task performance. Manuscript submitted for publication.

Pashler, H. (1994). Dual-task interference in simple tasks: Data and theory. *Psychological Review, 116*, 220–244.

Sarason, I. G. (Ed.) (1980). *Test anxiety: Theory, research and application*. Hillsdale, NJ: Erlbaum.
Seligman, M. E. P. (1975). *Helplessness: On depression, development, and death*. San Francisco: Freeman.
Sedek, G., & Kofta, M. (1990). When cognitive exertion does not yield cognitive gain: Toward an informational explanation of learned helplessness. *Journal of Personality and Social Psychology, 58*, 729–743.
Sedek, G., & Kofta, M. (1992). Cognitive helplessness in the classroom: A preliminary report. Unpublished manuscript, University of Warsaw, Department of Psychology.
Sedek, G., Kofta, M., & Tyszka, T. (1993). Effects of uncontrollability on subsequent decision making: Testing the cognitive exhaustion hypothesis. *Journal of Personality and Social Psychology, 65*, 1270–1281.
Sedek, G., & McIntosh, D. N. (1996). Uncontrollability and dual-task processing: Results of experimental and educational studies. Manuscript in preparation.
Steele, C. S. (1988). The psychology of self-affirmation: Sustaining the integrity of the self. In L. Berkowitz (Ed.), *Advances in experimental social psychology* (Vol. 21, pp. 261–302). San Diego, CA: Academic Press.
Terry, D. J. (1994). Determinants of coping: The role of stable and situational factors. *Journal of Personality and Social Psychology, 66*, 895–910.
Valentiner, D. P., Holahan, C. J., & Moos, R. H. (1994). Social support, appraisals of event controllability, and coping: An integrative model. *Journal of Personality and Social Psychology, 66*, 1094–1102.

INDEX